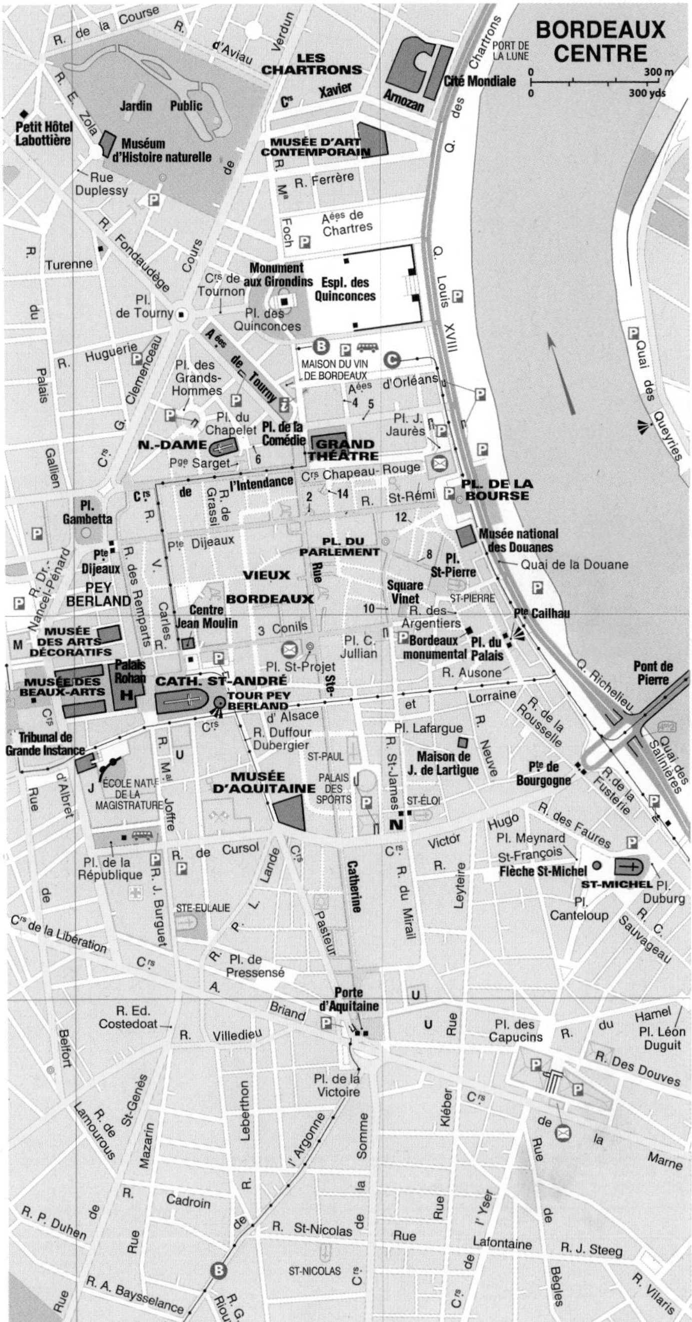

BORDEAUX CENTRE

0 — 300 m
0 — 300 yds

R. de la Course
R. d'Aviau
Verdun
LES CHARTRONS
Cité Mondiale
PORT DE LA LUNE
Q. des Chartrons
Crs Xavier Arnozan
Jardin Public
R. E. Zola
Petit Hôtel Labottière
Muséum d'Histoire naturelle
MUSÉE D'ART CONTEMPORAIN
R. Ferrère
R. Mal Foch
Aées de Chartres
Rue Duplessy
R. Fondaudège
Cours de Verdun
R. Turenne
R. du Palais Gallien
Monument aux Girondins
Espl. des Quinconces
Q. Louis XVIII
Crs de Tournon
Pl. de Tourny
Pl. des Quinconces
R. Huguerie
Cours G. Clemenceau
Aées de Tourny
MAISON DU VIN DE BORDEAUX
Aées d'Orléans
Quai des Queyries
Pl. des Grands-Hommes
Pl. du Chapelet
Pl. de la Comédie
Pl. J. Jaurès
N.-DAME
GRAND THÉATRE
Pge Sarget
Crs Chapeau-Rouge
Crs de l'Intendance
R. de Grassi
R. St-Rémi
PL. DE LA BOURSE
Pl. Gambetta
Pte Dijeaux
PL. DU PARLEMENT
Musée national des Douanes
Quai de la Douane
R. Dr. Nancel-Pénard
Pte Dijeaux
R. des Remparts
VIEUX BORDEAUX
Rue Ste-Catherine
Pl. St-Pierre
Square Vinet
ST-PIERRE
PEY BERLAND
Crs V. Carles
Centre Jean Moulin
R. des Argentiers
Pte Cailhau
MUSÉE DES ARTS DÉCORATIFS
R. des 3 Conils
Pl. C. Jullian
Bordeaux monumental
Pl. du Palais
Pl. St-Projet
Q. Richelieu
Pont de Pierre
Palais Rohan
MUSÉE DES BEAUX-ARTS
CATH. ST-ANDRÉ
TOUR PEY BERLAND
R. Ausone
Crs d'Alsace et Lorraine
R. de la Rousselle
R. Duffour Dubergier
Pl. Lafargue
Quai des Salinières
Tribunal de Grande Instance
Rue d'Albret
Maison de J. de Lartigue
R. Neuve
Pte de Bourgogne
R. de la Fusterie
ST-PAUL
MUSÉE D'AQUITAINE
ÉCOLE NATLE DE LA MAGISTRATURE
R. Mal Joffre
PALAIS DES SPORTS
R. St-James
ST-ÉLOI
R. des Faures
Crs Victor Hugo
Pl. Meynard
St-François
Flèche St-Michel
ST-MICHEL
Pl. Duburg
Pl. de la République
R. de Cursol
R. J. Burguet
Crs Pasteur
R. du Mirail
R. Leyteire
Pl. Canteloup
R. C. Sauvageau
STE-EULALIE
R. P. L. Lande
Crs de la Libération
Pl. de Pressensé
Crs A. Briand
Porte d'Aquitaine
R. Ed. Costedoat
R. Villedieu
Rue de Belfort
Pl. des Capucins
R. du Hamel
Pl. Léon Duguit
R. Des Douves
Pl. de la Victoire
R. de Lamourous
R. St-Genès
Leberthon
Crs de l'Argonne
Somme
Kléber
Crs de la Marne
Rue Mazarin
R. Cadroin
R. de l'Yser
Rue de Bègles
R. P. Duhen
R. St-Nicolas
Crs de la Somme
Rue Lafontaine
R. J. Steeg
ST-NICOLAS
R. A. Bayssélance
R. G. Rioux
R. Vilaris
Rue

THE GREEN GUIDE

French Atlantic Coast

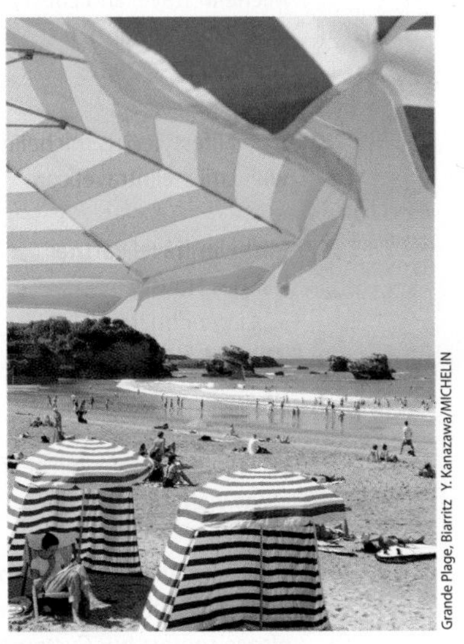

Grande Plage, Biarritz Y. Kanazawa/MICHELIN

THEGREENGUIDE **FRENCH ATLANTIC COAST**

Editor	Clive Hebard
Contributing Writers	Jane Anson, Lyn Parry
Production Manager	Natasha G. George
Cartography	John Dear
Photo Editor	Yoshimi Kanazawa
Photo Researcher	Sean Sachon
Proofreader	Karolin Thomas
Interior Design	Chris Bell
Layout	Michelin Apa Publications Ltd., Anna Gatt
Cover Design	Chris Bell, Christelle Le Déan
Cover Layout	Michelin Apa Publications Ltd.

Contact Us

Michelin Travel and Lifestyle North America
One Parkway South
Greenville, SC 29615
USA
travel.lifestyle@us.michelin.com
www.michelintravel.com

Michelin Travel Partner
Hannay House
39 Clarendon Road
Watford, Herts WD17 1JA
UK
01923 205240
travelpubsales@uk.michelin.com
www.ViaMichelin.com

Special Sales

For information regarding bulk sales, customized editions and premium sales, please contact our Customer Service Departments:

USA	1-800-432-6277
UK	01923 205240
Canada	1-800-361-8236

HOW TO USE THIS GUIDE

PLANNING YOUR TRIP

The blue-tabbed PLANNING YOUR TRIP section at the front of the guide gives you **ideas for your trip** and **practical information** to help you organize it. You'll find tours, practical information, a host of outdoor activities, a calendar of events, information on shopping, sightseeing, kids' activities and more.

INTRODUCTION

The orange-tabbed INTRODUCTION section explores the **Nature** and geology. The **History** section spans the Lower Palaeolithic period through Roman conquests to today. The **Art and Culture** section covers architecture, art, literature and music, while **French Atlantic Coast Today** delves into the region today.

DISCOVERING

The green-tabbed DISCOVERING section features Principal Sights by region, featuring the most interesting local **Sights**, **Walking Tours**, nearby **Excursions**, and detailed **Driving Tours**. Admission prices shown are normally for a single adult.

ADDRESSES

We've selected the best hotels, restaurants, cafés, shops, nightlife and entertainment to fit all budgets. See the Legend on the cover flap for an explanation of the price categories. See the back of the guide for an index of where to find hotels and restaurants.

Sidebars

Throughout the guide you will find blue, orange and green-coloured text boxes with lively anecdotes, detailed history and background information.

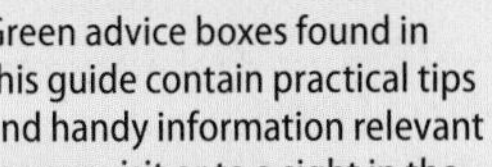

A Bit of Advice

Green advice boxes found in this guide contain practical tips and handy information relevant to your visit or to a sight in the Discovering section.

STAR RATINGS★★★

Michelin has given star ratings for more than 100 years. If you're pressed for time, we recommend you visit the ★★★, or ★★ sights first:

- ★★★ **Highly recommended**
- ★★ **Recommended**
- ★ **Interesting**

MAPS

- Country map
- Principal Sights map
- Region maps
- Maps for major cities and villages
- Local tour maps

All maps in this guide are oriented north, unless otherwise indicated by a directional arrow. The term "Local Map" refers to a map within the chapter or Tourism Region. A complete list of the maps found in the guide appears at the back of this book.

PLANNING YOUR TRIP

INTRODUCTION TO FRENCH ATLANTIC COAST

DISCOVERING FRENCH ATLANTIC COAST

DISCOVERING POITOU-CHARENTES AND LA VENDÉE

Welcome to French Atlantic Coast

The Atlantic Coast region of France stretches from the estuary of the River Loire in the north to the natural frontier of the Pyrénées mountains in the south. It is bounded on the west by the Atlantic coastline, with its fabulous beaches, and to the east by the lush countryside of Limousin, Périgord and Gascony. It encompasses the Vendée, the whole of Poitou-Charentes and the greater part of Aquitaine.

BORDEAUX AND AROUND

(pp100–141)

The largest city in the region, Bordeaux is famous for its wines and surrounding vineyards of the Médoc and St-Émilion, but deserves to be equally well regarded for its recent urban renewal, which blends 18C architecture with modern touches such as riverside jogging paths, elegant parks and a lively restaurant scene.

LES LANDES DU MÉDOC AND LE BASSIN D'ARCACHON

(pp142–159)

The Médoc peninsula stretches more than 100km/62mi to the north of Bordeaux city up to the Pointe de Grave, with the Gironde estuary to the east and the Atlantic Ocean to the west. As you approach the coastline, vines are replaced by Les Landes du Médoc, with inland lakes, wildlife reserves, surfing beaches and the Bassin d'Arcachon, the site of Europe's highest sand dune, the Dune du Pilat.

LES LANDES DE GASCOGNE

(pp160–175)

The Natural Regional Park of the Landes is located on a triangular plain running from the Gironde estuary to the River Adour. The area was originally an inland sea, which became a desolate, sand-filled depression until it was drained, cleared and reforested during the 19C. Today much of it is a protected area, with abundant wildlife.

LE PAYS DE L'ADOUR

(pp176–195)

The southern section of Les Landes, encompassing the popular spa towns of Dax, Aire sur L'Ardour and Eugénie-les-Bains, is a gentle, verdant region which mixes the cultures of Basque and Béarn.

THE BASQUE COAST AND LABOURD *(pp196–227)*

The Basque coastline lies within the Pyrénées-Atlantiques *département* at the southern end of the Atlantic Coast. The mood here is celebratory, with popular surfing beaches and lively towns including Biarritz and St-Jean-de-Luz. Head inland to French Basque Country, dotted with traditional villages.

LA BASSE-NAVARRE AND LA SOULE *(pp228–243)*

La Basse-Navarre lies within the French Pyrénées, marking the border with Spain. This is a sparsely populated area but one that is culturally distinct. Festivals are held throughout the year.

LE BÉARN *(pp244–269)*

The Béarn is crossed diagonally by the Gave de Pau and Gave d'Oléron rivers. As a dramatic backdrop, the Pic du Midi d'Ossau marks the rise of the Pyrénées mountains. The main towns include Pau, Orthez and Sauveterre-de-Béarn, all rich in culture and historical monuments.

LE LOT-ET-GARONNE *(pp270–289)*

The Lot-et-Garonne *département*, as the name suggests, is watered by the Lot and Garonne rivers, and its largest towns are found along the banks of one or other. The rivers also ensure this is a fertile region, known for its superb local produce, including the delicious Pruneaux d'Agen.

POITIERS AND LA VIENNE *(pp292–323)*

The Vienne, which gives its name to the *département*, and the Gartempe are the two main rivers of the region, which lies between the Pays de la Loire in the north and the Centre region to the east. The main city is the university town of Poitiers. Nearby is Futuroscope, a unique and fascinating theme park.

LE MARAIS POITEVIN AND LES DEUX-SÈVRES *(pp324–354)*

This region stretches over two *départements*: the Vendée and the Deux-Sèvres, which takes its name from the two River Sèvres, the Sèvre Nantaise and the Sèvre Niortaise. The important marshland areas of the Marais Poitevin lie to the west of Niort, the main town and an important financial centre.

LES COLLINES AND LE BOCAGE VENDÉENS *(pp355–376)*

The Vendée, the southernmost *département* of the Pays de la Loire, borders the Deux-Sèvres to the east. The *bocage* consists of a patchwork of fields watered by the Sèvre Nantaise, the Sèvre Niortaise, the Lay and the Vendée rivers. Generally low lying, the landscape is punctuated by rounded hills *(collines)*.

THE VENDÉE COAST *(pp377–405)*

Facing the Atlantic Ocean, the Littoral Vendée is renowned not only for its fabulous beaches, especially around St-Jean-de-Monts, les Sables-d'Olonne and Ste-Gilles-Croix-de-Vie, but also for the coastal marshland area of the Marais Breton Vendéen, and the islands of Yeu and Noirmoutier.

THE CHARENTE COAST *(pp406–455)*

The Charente Maritime, located on the Atlantic Coast, stretches south from La Rochelle, extending to the Gironde estuary, and includes the islands of Oléron and Ré. The coastline of rocks and dunes has an unusual swampy interior which has been reclaimed for crops, or mussel and oyster farming.

LE SAINTONGE *(pp456–479)*

Embracing the Roman town of Saintes with its splendid Arch of Germanicus, this small region straddling the lush Charente river valley covers most of the Charente-Maritime *département*.

ANGOULÊME AND LA CHARENTE *(pp480–505)*

The Charente abuts the Massif Central to the east and Charente Maritime to the west. At its heart, the main town is Angoulême, capital of the comic strip. A limestone plateau extends over the northern sector, while the south has more hills. In the west is the town of Cognac, where the world-famous brandy is produced.

Plage de la Madeleine, Le Petit Vieil, Île de Noirmoutier, Vendée

PLANNING YOUR TRIP

When and Where to Go

WHEN TO GO

SEASONS

In the **summer** months, the Atlantic shore is very popular with French and foreign holidaymakers, who come to enjoy the bracing atmosphere of the ocean spiced with the balsam scent of pines, a tonic for body and spirit.

Sea breezes cool the heat of the sun and the light is extraordinary: brilliant and bright at its purest, in the summertime a barely perceptible mist softens the outlines of the landscape. Across the pale blue sky trail wisps of cloudlike silk scarves in the wind.

In the **autumn** the crowds and heat subside. When waves batter the coast and rain pounds the shore, the fine weather moves inland. This is the perfect time to visit the vineyards of Bordeaux, busy with the grape harvest. The light falls obliquely from the heavens, saturating the colours of the deepening season: red vine creeping over an old stone wall, purple grapes heavy and ripe, the brown gloss of chestnuts inside their prickly husks, tender mushrooms below the forest bracken.

Winter is a splendid time of year to discover the rugged isolation of the Pyrénées. Whether glimpsed at high speed as your skis cut through fresh powder, or contemplated as you glide across the valley on a cross-country trail, the landscape is memorable.

Spring is a cool season, heralded by a profusion of flowers and flowering trees. As the equinox approaches, storms whip up cold rains which flood the river valleys. Between the dark masses of mountainous clouds, a piercing yellow light highlights the natural and architectural beauty of the land.

CLIMATE

The Atlantic Coast is exceptionally sunny, with over 2 000 hours of sunshine annually. The brightest days are between May and September; over that period the water warms up to an average 20°C/68°F as it hits the beach. Snow is rare and spring comes early. The central part of the coastal area covered in this guide is subject to 20 to 30 spectacular thunder storms a year, blown in by prevailing winds from the west.

Around Biarritz, on the Basque Coast, the mountains create a different climate with considerably more rainfall. In the winter months, frequent warm spells (up to 20°C/68°F) give the Basque "microclimate" an exotic feel. In the high mountains, snow may continue to fall well into spring.

Col d'Aubisque in the Pyrénées-Aquitaine

Climbers and campers will find late July and early September the most clement for enjoying nature in the Pyrénées. Skiers seeking fresh *néou* (as snow is called by some locals) will find slopes open from December to April.

WEATHER FORECAST

National forecast: *℘08 92 68 02* followed by the number of the *département.*

Weather information is also available online at *www.meteo.fr.*

THEMED TOURS

Travel itineraries with specific themes have been mapped out to help you discover the regional heritage. You will find brochures in tourist offices, and the routes are generally well marked and easy to follow.

For further information, contact:
La Demeure Historique,
Hôtel de Nesmond, 57 quai de la Tournelle, 75005 Paris.
℘01 55 42 60 00.
www.demeure-historique.org.

Fédération Nationale des Routes Historiques
www.routes-historiques.com.

HISTORY

Route des Abbayes et Monuments du Haut-Poitou

Roman vestiges and Romanesque churches, Gothic architecture in the Plantagenet or Angevin style, châteaux and feudal fortresses vie for the visitor's attention over this rich historical itinerary. *http://chateaux-france.com/route-hautpoitou.*

Route des Plantagenêts

Eleven itineraries in the western part of France trace this great dynasty. The brochure includes a suggested tour passing through La Sauve-Majeur, Blaye, St-Émilion, Bazas, Dax and Bayonne.
Société historique des Plantagenêts, Archives Nationales, 60 r. des Francs-Bourgeois, 75003 Paris. ℘01 40 27 60 96. www.archivesnationales.culture.gouv.fr.

Route des Trésors de Saintonge

A tour around the region of Saintes reveals a wealth of Romanesque churches in the Saintonge style, set like jewels in the beautiful green countryside.
Abbaye de Fontdouce, 17770 St-Bris-des-Bois.
℘05 46 74 77 08. http://chateaux-france.jp/route-saintonge.
℘05 46 95 60 10. www.monuments-saintonge.com.

Route Historique des Châteaux et Cités au Cœur d'Aquitaine

This tour includes the châteaux of Le Bouilh, Mongenan, Malle, Vayres, Roquetaillade and Cazeneuve as well as the medieval towns of La Réole, St-Macaire and Bazas.
Château de Roquetaillade, 33210 Mazères.
℘05 56 76 14 16.
http://chateaux-france.com/route-coeuraquitaine.

Route Historique sur les Pas de Seigneurs du Béarn et du Pays Basque

This tour visits some of the most picturesque manors, châteaux and towns of Béarn and the Basque Country, steeped in the history of Aquitaine, from the 12C to the 18C. The itinerary includes the Château d'Urtubie, Sauveterre, Navarrenx, Oloron-Ste-Marie, Orthez and St-Jean-de-Luz.
Château d'Antoine d'Abbadie, rte de la Corniche, 64700 Hendaye.
℘05 59 20 04 51.
http://chateaux-france.com/route-bearn.

La Route du Circuit Sud-Vendéen

This circuit around Fontenay-le-Comte, set in the wetlands, forests and beaches, reveals a dozen major sites recalling memories of Eleanor of Aquitaine, Richard the Lionheart and Rabelais.

M. Henri de Fontenioux – Château de Terre-Neuve, 85200 Fontenay-le-Comte. ℘02 51 69 17 75 or *Château d'Avrillé. ℘02 51 22 33 06. www.vendee-touristique.com.*

GASTRONOMY

Route du Fromage Ossau-Iraty

Traditional Pyrénéan sheep's cheese is produced in the heart of the Béarn and Basque Country. From St-Jean-de-Luz to the Col d'Aubisque (182km/113mi), some 50 stops will give you ample occasion to sample and savour this regional speciality.

Syndicat de défense de l'AOC Ossau-Iraty, Maison Baratchartenea, 64120 Ostabat Asne. ℘05 59 37 86 61. www.ossau-iraty.fr/categorie/route-du-fromage.

VINEYARDS

The Atlantic Coast region has a wealth of *caves* (wine cellars) offering *dégustations* (tastings) and tours. *See LES CÔTES DE BORDEAUX* in the *Discovering* sections of this guide to find numerous châteaux with wine cellars, stores and vineyards. While some may prefer to contact their travel agent and set off on a coach tour with an expert, others may prefer to travel the by-ways, stopping at a local wine grower's *chais* to pick up a bottle to accompany a picnic lunch. A visit to a small proprietor producing local wine – often a generations-old family affair – can be as memorable as a tour of one of the great châteaux or distilleries.

Vins de Bordeaux

- **Maison du Vin de Bordeaux**
  3 cours du XXX-Juillet, 33075 Bordeaux Cedex. ℘05 56 00 22 88. www.bordeaux.com.
- **Maison du Tourisme et du Vin de Pauillac**
  La Verrerie, 33250 Pauillac. ℘05 56 59 03 08. www.pauillac-medoc.com.
- **Maison des vins de Graves**
  61 cours du Maréchal-Foch, BP 51, 33720 Podensac. ℘05 56 27 09 25. www.vins-graves.com.
- **Maison du vin des Premières Côtes de Blaye**
  11 cours Vauban, BP 122, 33391 Blaye. ℘05 57 42 91 19. www.vin-blaye.com.
- **Maison du vin des Côtes de Bourg**
  1 pl. de l'Éperon, 33710 Bourg-sur-Gironde. ℘05 57 94 80 20. www.cotes-de-bourg.com.
- **Maison du Fleuve et du Vin de Ste-Foy-Bordeaux**
  6 r. Notre Dame, 33220 Port Ste-Foy. ℘05 53 58 37 34. www.saintefoy-bordeaux.com.
- **Maison du vin de St-Émilion**
  pl. Pierre-Meyrat, 33330 St-Émilion. ℘05 57 55 50 50. www.vins-saint-emilion.com.
- **Maison des vins des Premières Côtes de Bordeaux et Cadillac**
  la Closerie, D 10, rte de Langon, 33410 Cadillac. ℘05 57 98 19 20. www.maison-desvins-despremieres-cotes-debordeaux-etcadillac.abcsalles.com.
- **Maison du vin de Barsac**
  pl. de l'Église, 33720 Barsac. ℘05 56 27 15 44. www.maisondebarsac.fr.

A Bit of Advice

While many of the wines in the region covered in this guide are celebrated around the world, some lesser-known vintages are also worth tasting.

Vins Basques

- **Cave coopérative des vins d'Irouleguy et du Pays basque**
  rte de St-Jean Pied de Port, 64430 St-Étienne-de-Baïgorry. ℘05 59 37 41 33. www.cave-irouleguy.com.

Vins Béarnais

- **Cave des producteurs de Gan Jurançon**
  53 av. Henri-IV, 64290 Gan.

Inside an Armagnac storehouse

©S.Sauvignier/MICHELIN

℘05 59 21 57 03. www.cavedejurancon.com.

Vins Landais

- **Les Vignerons Landais Tursan-Chalosse**
  pl. de l'Hôtel de Ville, 40320 Geaune. ℘05 58 44 51 25. www.tursan.fr.

The **Guide de Vins du Sud-Ouest** is available from the Comité Interprofessionnel des Vins du Sud-Ouest, *chemin de Borde Rouge, Centre INRA, BP 92123, 31321 Castanet Tolosan. ℘05 61 73 87 06. www.france-sudouest.com.*

Vins du Lots-et-Garonne

- **Union interprofessionnelle des vins des Côtes de Duras**
  Maison du Vins, RD 668, 47120 Duras. ℘05 53 94 13 48. www.cotesdeduras.com.
- **Les Vignerons de Buzet**
  av. des Côtes de Buzet, 47160 Buzet-sur-Baïse. ℘05 53 84 74 30. www.vignerons-buzet.fr.
- **Cave de Goulens en Brulhois**
  47390 Layrac. ℘05 53 87 01 65.

Vins de Mareuil *(Vendée)*

- **Maison Mourat**
  rte de la Roche, Ferme des Ardillers, 85320 Mareuil-sur-Lay. ℘02 51 97 20 10. www.mourat.com.

Muscadet de Sèvre et Maine, Gros Plant, Muscadet *(Loire-Atlantique)*

- **Domaine La Roche Renard**
  les Laures, 44330 Vallet. ℘02 40 36 63 65.
- **Maison des Vins de Nantes**
  15 pl. du Commerce, 44000 Nantes. *℘02 40 89 75 98. www.vinsdeloire.fr.*
- **Domaine des Herbauges**
  les Herbauges, 44830 Bouaye. ℘02 40 65 44 92. www.domaine-des-herbauges.com.

APÉRITIF AND AFTER-DINNER DRINKS

Armagnac

- **Bureau National Interprofessionnel de l'Armagnac AOC**
  pl. de la Liberté, BP 3, 32800 Eauze. ℘05 62 08 11 00. www.armagnac.fr.
- **Maison du Floc de Gascogne**
  r. des Vignerons, 32800 Eauze. ℘05 62 09 85 41. www.floc-de-gascogne.fr.

Cognac *(Charente)*

Brandy producers (Camus, Hennessy, Martell, Rémy Martin, etc.) are open for tours and sales (*see COGNAC, p495*). *www.cognac.fr.*

Bise dur, La Chouanette, Rosée des Charentes, Kamok, Liqueur des Vendéens *(Vendée)*

Société H. Vrignaud, 1 pl. Richelieu, 85400 Luçon. ℘02 51 56 11 48.

Pineau des Charentes

This fortified wine is omnipresent; reds, rosés and golden white varieties are widely available throughout the region. *www.pineau.fr.*

Trouspinette *(Vendée)*

- **Maison Mourat**
  rte de la Roche, Ferme des Ardillers, 85320 Mareuil-sur-Lay. ℘02 51 97 20 10. www.mourat.com.

Trinquet Vendéen *(Vendée)*

- **Isabelle Cochain**
  11 r. Georges Clemenceau, 85160 St-Jean-de-Monts. ℘02 28 11 05 61.

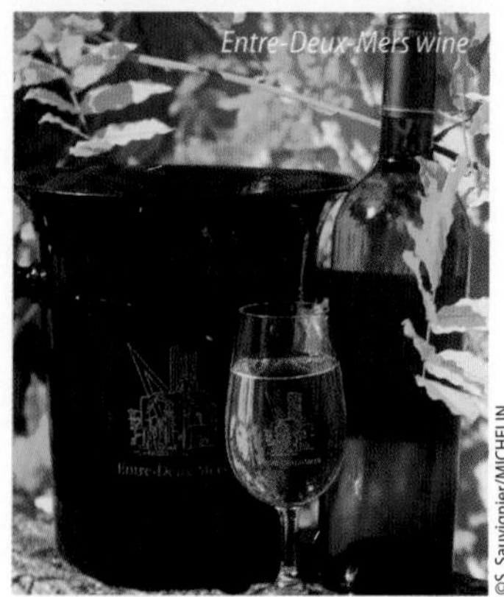

©S. Sauvignier/MICHELIN

WINE TOURS

- **Les Routes du Vin**
  Maison du Vin de Bordeaux, 3 cours du XXX-Juillet, 33075 Bordeaux Cedex. ℘05 56 00 22 88. www.bordeaux.com.
- **Route des Vins du Jurançon**
  La Commanderie du Jurançon, 64360 Lacommande. ℘05 59 82 70 30. www.vins-jurancon.fr.
- **Route des Vins et des Appellations en Entre-deux-Mers**
  Office du Tourisme, 2 r. Franklin, Monségur. ℘05 56 61 82 73.
- **Route des Vins en Bergeracois, Bordelais et Jurançon**
  Three marked itineraries. *www.tourisme-aquitaine.fr.*
- **Route des Vins de Bordeaux en Graves et Sauternes**
  Four themed itineraries using a SAT-NAV, and digital guide. *www.tourisme-gironde.fr.*
- **Route du Vignoble en Val de Loire**
  Interprofession des Vins de Loire. ℘02 47 60 55 00. www.vinsdeloire.fr.
- **Les Étapes du Cognac**
  Four marked routes with over 200 addresses, including wine producers, monuments, hotels and restaurants, provide an excellent introduction to the Cognac region. One of these, "Cognac, the stone and the estuary", traces the Gironde estuary, giving a different viewpoint of the vineyards.
  Maison des Viticulteurs, 25 r. Cagouillet, Cognac. ℘05 45 36 47 35. www.cognacetapes.com.
- **Route des vins du Haut-Poitou**, tour from cellar to cellar meeting the local winemakers.
  Mme Bureau. ℘05 49 51 21 65.
- **Route du vignoble**, in the steps of Ausone.
  Secrétariat chambre d'Agriculture. M. Barreaud. ℘05 46 48 10 79.

OENOLOGICAL COURSES

The **Office du Tourisme de Bordeaux** *(12 cours du XXX-Juillet, 33080 Bordeaux; ℘05 56 00 66 00; www.bordeaux-tourisme.com)* offers wine-tasting programmes (*courses are run early Jul–late Sept Fri–Wed 3–5pm; 24€).*

Join in the initiation to wine-tasting at the **Maison du Vin de St-Émilion** (*℘05 57 55 50 55)* daily from 11am to noon, mid-July to mid-September; or by appointment at the **Château Lynch-Bages in Pauillac** (*℘05 56 73 19 31; www.lynchbages.com).*

The **Vinoscope du Médoc** (Château Maucaillou, *33480 Moulis-en-Médoc; ℘05 56 58 01 23; www.chateau-maucaillou.eu*) teaches tasting techniques in a one-, two- or three-day course. The château also conducts vineyard discovery tours.

EQUESTRIAN TOURS

Savour the countryside at a gentle pace aboard a **horse-drawn caravan**. Obtain a brochure from the **Maison Poitou-Charentes** *(Comité Régional du Tourisme, 8 r. Riffault, BP 56, Poitiers; ℘05 49 50 10 50; www.poitou-charentes-vacances.com)* for information on hiring a caravan with bunk beds and kitchen facilities for two to seven days.

The **Comité Nationale de Tourisme Équestre** *(parc Équestre Fédéral, 41600 Lamotte-Beuvron; ℘02 54 94 46 80; www.tourisme-equestre.fr)* will supply information as well as addresses of local organisations.

The regional associations *(Comité Départemental de Tourisme Équestre)* are as follows:

- **Loire Atlantique**
  Le Moulin Roty, 44390 Saffre.
  ℘02 40 77 24 10.
- **Vendée**
  La Bironniere, 85220 Coex.
  ℘02 51 34 06 49.
- **Deux Sèvres**
  La Petit Drauniere, 79310 Mazières-en-Gatine. ℘06 10 55 72 70.
  http://cdte79.free.fr.
- **Vienne**
  Maison du Tourisme, 33 pl. de Gaulle, 86007 Poitiers.
  ℘05 49 37 48 48.
  http://cdte86.free.fr.
- **Charente-Maritime**
  13 cours Paul Doumer, 17100 Saintes. ℘05 46 93 92 24.
  www.cdte17.fr.
- **Charente**
  58 r. de l'Arsenal, 1600 Angoulême.
  ℘05 45 25 32 48.
- **Gironde**
  1 Mairie, 33420 St-Aubin-de-Branne.
  ℘05 56 00 99 28.
- **Lot-et-Garonne**
  997 r. Docteur Jean Bru, 47000 Agen.
  ℘05 53 48 02 28.
- **Landes**
  Cite Galliane, BP 279, 40005 Mont-de-Marsan.
  ℘06 37 78 60 81.
  www.cdte40.ffe.com.
- **Pyrénées-Atlantiques**
  Ferme Urkodea, Quartier Zelai, 64240 Hasparren. ℘05 59 29 15 76.
  www.cheval64.org.

HOUSEBOATS

For two to twelve people, the houseboats provide a different perspective of the region. Various packages exist: rentals by the day, for the weekend or the week.

Le Boat, *quai François-Mitterrand, 16200 Jarnac.*
℘05 45 36 59 98 or 04 68 94 42 40.
www.leboat.fr.

Base de Sireuil, *Pont de Sireuil, 16440 Sireuil.*
02 45 90 58 18. www.intercroisieres.com.

Nicols, *rte du Puy-St-Bonnet, 49300 Cholet.*
℘02 41 56 46 56 or 08 10 58 58 30.
www.nicols.com.

Rive de France, *Île de la Grenouillette, 17350 St-Savinien-sur-Charente. ℘05 46 90 35 49.*

You will find useful information about boating holidays from the Comités Départementaux du Tourisme. You can obtain nautical charts and maps from the following publishers:

Éditions Grafocarte-Navicarte, *℘01 41 09 19 00. www.navicarte.fr.*

Vagnon Les éditions du plaisancier, *℘04 72 01 58 68 . www.codes-vagnon.fr.*

Horseback riding, Conche des Baleines, the Charente coast

What to See and Do

OUTDOOR FUN

HIKING

The **Fédération Française de la Randonnée Pédestre** publishes *topo-guides* available from its information centre *(64 r. du Dessous des Berges, 75013 Paris; ☎01 44 89 93 93; www.ffrandonnee.fr)*. Some English-language editions are available. The regional guides describe long-distance trails (**GR** for *Grande Randonnée* and **GRP** for *Grande Randonnée de Pays*) and shorter ones (**PR** – *Petite Randonnée*) in detail, distances and approximate times.

SKIING

In the western Pyrénées, there are valley resorts, with high curving slopes and plateaux and contemporary, purpose-built mountain-top resorts such as Arette-Pierre-St-Martin and Gourette.

Cross-country skiing is especially good in Iraty, Issarbe and Somport-Candanchu.

ℹ Visit *www.lespyrenees.net* (English version available) or *www.pyrenees-online.fr* for information on conditions and accommodation in the main ski resorts.

CYCLING

Whereas the mountains draw climbers and hikers, the forests, plains, islands, riverbanks and moors of southwest France are favoured by cyclists. It is not unusual to see coastal travellers pedalling along with camping gear strapped to their backs; the relatively flat landscape makes for pleasant cycling. The **Île de Ré** is perfect for a one-day tour.

In the **Haut-Saintonge** area around Saintes, 32 mixed-use trails and 18 mountain-bike tours are marked out. Maps are available in tourist offices.

On Sunday mornings in **Bordeaux** you can hire a bike for the day and pedal around the city with a guide (details at the tourist office).

The **Marais Poitevin** is a great place for cycling, offering cool, shaded lanes, shimmering canals and glimpses of Gothic and Romanesque architecture in the calm, sunny countryside.

Other areas particularly suitable for cycling along marked-out tracks include the **Landes**, **Entre-deux-Mers** and **Médoc** regions.

ℹ Information and maps available from the **Comité Départemental du Tourisme de Gironde** and from the **Maison du Tourisme et du vin de Pauillac** *(☎05 56 59 03 08; www.pauillac-medoc.com)*.

Organising Your Trip

Some **SNCF** train stations (Châtellerault, Niort, La Rochelle, Royan, Les Sables-d'Olonne, Valence-d'Agen, Verdon) also rent touring and mountain bikes (in French, *VTT* for *vélo tout terrain*). Tourist offices will provide a list of private rental agencies – in summer it is a good idea to reserve.

ℹ *For more general information concerning cycling in France, contact:*

- **Fédération Française de Cyclotourisme**
  12 r. Louis Bertrand,
  94200 Ivry-sur-Seine.
  ☎01 56 20 88 87.
  www.ffct.org.

Mountain-bike enthusiasts, contact the following organisation and request the *Guide des centres VTT:*

- **Fédération Française de Cyclotourisme**
  12 r. Louis Bertrand,
  94207 Ivry-sur-Seine Cedex.
  ☎01 56 20 88 88.
  www.ffct.org.

There are many travel agencies offering **package biking tours**: look for advertisements in travel magazines, search the internet or contact your travel agent to find the offer that suits you best.

Mountain Sports

Safety first is the rule for beginners and old hands when it comes to exploring the mountains as a climber, skier or hiker. The risk associated with avalanches, mud slides, falling rocks, bad weather, fog, icy waters from glaciers, the dangers of becoming lost or miscalculating distances, should never be underestimated.

Avalanches occur naturally when the upper layer of snow is unstable, in particular after heavy snowfalls, and may be set off by the passage of numerous skiers or hikers over a precise spot. A scale of risk, from 1 to 5, has been developed and is posted daily at resorts and the base of hiking trails.

It is important to consult this Bulletin neige et avalanches (BNA) before setting off on any expeditions cross-country or hors-piste. You can also call Meteo France for a recorded update on ℘32504 (in French) or log onto www.meteo.fr.

Lightning storms are often preceded by sudden gusts of wind, and put climbers and hikers in danger.

In the event of lightning, avoid high ground, and do not move along a ridge top; do not seek shelter under overhanging rocks, isolated trees in otherwise open areas, at the entrance to caves or other openings in the rocks, or in the proximity of metal fences or gates. A car is a good refuge.

GOLF

It was at Pau that golf first appeared in France in 1856. Since this date, it has become a popular sport in Aquitaine, and today there are around 50 golf courses in a variable landscape (from sea to the mountains).

All the information on the Aquitaine golf courses can be found in the Golf du Comité Régional du Tourisme booklet.

Southwest France has many 9- and 18-hole golf courses, marked on a map entitled *Golf, les parcours français*, based on the Michelin map of France 989.

For general information, contact:

- **Fédération Française de Golf** *68 r. Anatole-France, 92300 Levallois-Perret Cedex. ℘01 41 49 77 00. and 08 92 69 18 18. www.ffgolf.org.*

WATER SPORTS

Diving

The entire region, including the Île d'Yeu, provides the ideal conditions for diving. In the ocean around Sables-d'Olonne and Noirmoutier, you will discover submerged shipwrecks.

- **Fédération française d'études et de sports sous-marins,** *24 quai de Rive-Neuve, 13284 Marseille Cedex 07. ℘04 91 33 99 31. www.ffessm.fr.*

Swimming

Along the Atlantic Ocean, it is best to swim at one of the many supervised beaches, where flags (**red** = *beach closed,* **orange** = *some danger,* **green** = *safe to swim*) advise bathers. Along the open coast, where the surf is often high, lifeguards are mobile and attentive, moving the flags marking out the area under their surveillance as rising and falling tides change the danger zones created by depressions in the sea bed and strong undertow. Sheltered beaches (Bassin d'Arcachon, Les Sables-d'Olonne, Capbreton) are more appropriate for small children, who will also enjoy the calm, relatively shallow waters of the inland lakes such as the Lac de Lacanau or the Étang de Léon.

Surfing and Windsurfing

One swimmer's breaker is another surfer's swell. The same deep underwater chasm *(le gouf)* which makes Capbreton one of the safest swimming beaches on the coast makes **Hossegor** the uncontested capital of surf in France. International competitions

Surfing in Hossegor

©E. Larribere/MICHELIN

are held in **Hossegor**, **Biarritz** and **Lacanau** every August. Novice windsurfers may want to test the waters inland on the calmer waters of a lake before hitting the ocean beach. These sports are restricted to certain areas and subject to regulations for the protection of swimmers.

Surfing the Sands

Sand-yachting and its variant, **speed sailing**, are ideally suited to the vast beaches of the Vendée Coast and Côte d'Argent, where large flat areas of sand are left uncovered at low tide. You will find centres in Notre-Dame-de-Monts, Chéray (Oléron), La Faute-sur-Mer, St-Jean-de-Monts, St-Georges-de-Didonne, St-Gilles-Croix-de-Vie, Arcachon, La Teste-de-Buch and Hendaye, among others.

General information from:

- **Fédération Française de Surf**
  Plage Nord BP 28, 40150 Hossegor. ✆05 58 43 55 88. www.surfingfrance.com.
- **Fédération Française de Voile**
  17 r. Henri Bocquillon, 75015 Paris. ✆01 40 60 37 00. www.ffvoile.fr.
- **Fédération Française de Char à Voile**
  17 r. Henri Bocquillon, 75015 Paris. ✆01 45 58 75 75. www.ffcv.org.

Canoeing – Kayaking – Rafting

The region's numerous rivers, canals and lakes offer ample opportunity to enjoy these sports.

Sea-kayaks are popular at the Bassin d'Arcachon as well as Fouras. The **Courant d'Huchet** and the **Courant de Contis** are beautiful sights for an introduction to the activity.

In the mountains, rapid water sports are practised on the rivers Garonne, Eyre and Adour. Local tourist offices can provide details.

Canyoning is a technique for body-surfing down narrow gorges and over waterfalls, as though on a giant water slide, whereas **hydrospeed** involves swimming down rapids with a kickboard and flippers; wear a wet suit and a helmet.

For further information on white-water sports in general, contact:

- **Fédération Française de Canoë-Kayak**
  87 quai de la Marne, BP 58, 94344 Joinville-le-Pont. ✆01 45 11 08 50. www. ffcanoe.asso.fr.

Other Water Sports

For **water-skiing** and **motor boating**, enquire at the tourist offices of the larger seaside resorts. The use of jet-skis is restricted in France; see *www. rya.org.uk* for more information.

Diving clubs *(clubs de plongée)* are active in St-Gilles-Croix-de-Vie, St-Hilaire-de-Riez, Royan and Les Sables-d'Olonne.

Fishing

Freshwater fishing enthusiasts will revel in the abundance of rivers, streams, marshland canals and lakes.

Fishing regulations are enforced and anglers must be affiliated with an association, thus obtaining a *carte de pêche* (permit). Apply to the **Conseil Supérieur de la Pêche** *(134 av. de Malakoff, 75016 Paris; ✆01 45 02 20 20)*, which also supplies a map, *Pêche en France (Fishing in France)*. Permits are easily obtained locally, often sold in cafés where you are likely to pick up a few tips from the regulars.

The extensive coastline, the bays, straits and the wide **ocean** itself offer almost limitless fishing options, the only restrictions being to adhere to local and national regulations and not to interfere with the business of professional fishermen. For fishing trips out to sea on fully equipped boats, ask at tourist offices, or have a walk around the marina and try to strike up conversation with a local. You can reserve a spot on a fishing boat (equipment provided).

For general information, apply to:

- **Fédération Française des pêcheurs en mer** *Résidence Alliance, Centre Jorlis, 64600 Anglet. ✆05 59 31 00 73. www.ffpm-national.com.*

Pêche à Pied

On the beaches at low tide, the bucket-and-spade brigades engage in the popular French pastime known as *pêche à pied*, digging for shellfish or scooping up shrimp. There are no administrative formalities for this activity, although quantities per fisherman may be limited, and some beaches may be posted off limits. Underwater fishing is subject to strict regulation. The *Gîtes de France* (*see WHERE TO STAY AND EAT*) has created a special category, *Gîtes de Pêche*, which identifies accommodation most suitable for anglers who are really hooked.

SPECTATOR SPORTS

Certain sports are part of the traditional lifestyle in southwest France, and their heroes are local legends. In addition to major national and international events, there are many local games going on, which will give you a feel for the people and their ways.

Rugby is big in the southwest. An early form of the game was practised in France and Great Britain in the Middle Ages, and rugby as we know it has been played since 1900. Rugby has its own periodical in France *(Midi*

Running Races

Marathon des châteaux du Médoc – It has taken place in early September for more than 20 years. The competitors, in disguise, pass through the villages and châteaux, refuelling kilometre after kilometre from the wine-tastings along the way. Registration form available by post from November from the AMCM: Maison du Vin, 33250 Pauillac. ✆05 56 59 17 20. www.marathondumedoc.com.

Course pédestre des grands vignobles – 16km/9.9mi long, it takes place on the last Sunday of October and crosses the famous St-Émilion vineyards, classed as an UNESCO World Heritage Site. Inscriptions from mid-September with M. Frustier: Secrétariat ASPTT, Cedex 203, 33500 Libourne. ✆05 57 51 12 70.

Course des Crêtes du Pays basque – Covers distances from 7km to 27 km/4.3mi–16.8mi. The competitors start from Espelette, as they have done each year for nearly 25 years. The day finishes with a dinner. Allow about 15€ to participate, sport certificate required, or failing that a medical certificate stating that you are fit to take part in the race.

Olympique; www.rugbyrama.fr); bookshops in the region can track down over 100 titles; there is a shrine known as Notre-Dame-du-Rugby in Larrivières. There is an ongoing debate between those who favour rugby union (15-a-side) and those who prefer rugby league (13-a-side, as in Carcassonne, Lézignan, Limoux). Women's teams mostly play touch rugby, without tackling each other to the ground (Les Lionnes in Auch).

More information is available from

- **Fédération Française de rugby** *3–5 r. Jean de Montaigu, 91463 Marcoussis Cedex. 01 69 63 64 65. www.ffr.fr.*

Local Sports

An unusual event known as **courses landaises** calls on courageous combatants to step into the arena with very large black cows with very long horns. More acrobatic than a Spanish-style bullfight, these events are also more humane, as the animals are not killed. Evolved from the old practices of running the bulls through the streets, the event became especially popular around 1850 with the introduction of the *écarteur*, the equivalent of a *toreador.*

Pelote Basque (a variety of which is called *jai alai* in Mexico, Havana and Miami, where it is also very popular) is a must-see for visitors to the Basque Country. The most appreciated form is the **grand chistera**, the name of the distinctive curved basket players wear on one hand. Two teams of three players hurl the *pelote* (ball, *pilota* in Basque) against the *fronton* (wall). There are many variations on this game, and an unexpected highlight is listening to the *chacharia* (announcer) sing out the score. The standard rules are similar to handball, but the court is much larger: 53.7m/176ft long. The *pelote*, a hard, round rubber ball covered by linen thread and two layers of goatskin, is 5cm/2in in diameter and can travel at 240kph/150mph.

SIGHTSEEING

RIVER CRUISING

Rivers, estuaries, canals and channels offer numerous opportunities to enjoy pleasant **boat trips** (sometimes aboard old-fashioned craft), thus slowing down the pace and alleviating the stress of a busy touring holiday.

- **Bâteau-promenade L'Escapade** *Boat trips along the Canal des Deux-Mers. Canal en Gironde, 6 allée des Ormeaux, 33210 Langon. 05 56 63 06 30. http://monsite.wanadoo.fr/canalengironde.*
- **Union des Bateliers arcachonnais** Boat trips on the Arcachon lagoon. *See Bassin d'ARCACHON.*
- **Bâteau-Croisière Aliénor** Boat trips along the Gironde estuary. *See BORDEAUX.*

Alternatively, **house-boats**, which can be hired for a day, a weekend or a week, offer a peaceful glide along rivers (Charente, Sèvre Niortaise, Lot, Baïse) and canals (Canal latéral à la Garonne).

- **Crown Blue Line** *44 L'Ecluse, 47430 Le mas d'Agenais. 05 53 89 50 80. www.crownblueline.com.*
- **Aquitaine Navigation** *Port de Buzet, Val d'Albret, 47160 Buzet-sur-Baïse. 05 53 84 72 50. www.aquitaine-navigation.com.*
- **Locaboat Plaisance,** *Port au bois, 89303 Joigny. 03 86 91 72 72. www.locaboat.com.*

TOURIST TRAINS

Several picturesque railways welcome tourists for pleasant rides through fields, woods and marshlands, including a few pulled by steam locomotives. For detailed information, see the following:

Bassin d'ARCACHON: Cap Ferret (Tourist train to Plage de l'Océan)

Les HERBIERS (Chemin de fer de la Vendée)

- Île d'OLÉRON: St Trojan-les-Bains (Pointe de Gatseau tourist train)
- Parc naturel régional des LANDES DE GASCOGNE: Marquèze (Train de l'Écomusée de la Grande Lande)
- Le MARAIS POITEVIN: Coulon (Le Pibalou)
- Haut-OSSAU (Scenic train from La Sagette to Lac d'Artouste)
- ST-ÉMILION (Train des Grands Vignobles)
- ST-JEAN-DE-LUZ: Le Labourd (Chemin de fer de la Rhune)

RAIL-BIKING

It is possible to go for a 10km/6mi ride around St-Gilles-Croix-de-Vie and along the coast. Each small truck can take up to four persons *(℘02 51 54 79 99; www.cc-atlancia.fr).*

BIRDWATCHING

There are guided tours around the **Réserve naturelle des Marais de Müllembourg**, *Fort-Larron, Normoutier-en-l'Île. ℘02 51 35 81 16. http://vendee.lpo.fr.*

NATURE AND THE ENVIRONMENT

Parc Interrégional du Marais Poitevin: *Information centre at 2 r. de l'Église, 79510 Coulon. ℘05 49 35 15 20. www.parc-marais-poitevin.fr.*
Centres Permanents d'Initiatives pour l'Environnement: These centres organise weekends and longer stays (known as *sépia*) to encourage people to become aware of nature and the environment.

Information is available from the **Union Nationale des Centres Permanents d'Initiatives pour l'Environnement** *(26 r. Beaubourg, 75003 Paris; ℘01 44 61 75 35; www.cpie.fr).*

SPAS

Hot springs, mineral waters, mud and algae packs have been used to treat afflictions and relieve stress since Roman times. The various therapeutic properties of the different spas are used in the treatment of respiratory ailments, rheumatism and dermatoses. *Thermalisme* usually refers to medically prescribed, 21-day cures, while *thalassothérapie* seawater facilities serve a more general public for leisure and fitness purposes. In addition to the medical care provided to the numerous *curistes*, many establishments offer short-term packages aimed at improving the general well-being of guests. You can even sign up for a special stay to give up smoking, lose weight or increase your stamina. Most spa towns have good sports facilities, such as tennis courts and golf courses, and many have their own casinos. Do check the details ahead of time, as some spas require a medical check-up before you can have treatments, and accommodation may be scarce at certain times of year. **The Michelin Guide France** gives more information.

For general information, contact:

- **Union Nationale des établissements thermaux**
  1 r. Cels, 75014 Paris.
  ℘01 53 91 05 75.
  www.cneth.org.
- **France Thalasso**
  ℘05 59 151 35 03.
  www.france-thalasso.com.
- **Chaîne Thermale du Soleil/Maison du Thermalisme**
  32 av. de l'Opéra, 75002 Paris.
  ℘08 00 05 05 32.
  www.sante-eau.com.

Here is a description of just three of the many spas in the region:

- **Dax** is France's leading thermal resort – and one of the largest – specialising in the treatment of rheumatism and arthritis of all types. Therapy is based on the application of warm mud packs. To obtain brochures on special 6-, 9- and 12-day packages offered by the many different establishments in town, as well as information on sports and entertainment in this busy resort, contact the **Office de Tourisme et du Ther-**

malisme, *11 cours Foch, BP 177, 40104 Dax. ☎05 58 56 86 86. www.dax-tourisme.com.*

- **La Roche Posay** is hidden deep in quiet countryside, surrounded by gentle valleys and pretty rivers and streams, far from the madding crowd. The spa treats all types of skin problems, using relaxing mineral baths, jet sprays and high-pressure showers. The Mélusine centre *(open May–mid-Oct)* offers short cures, relaxation and skin care. The town provides a service for organising business seminars. Contact the local tourist office *(14 bd Victor Hugo, 86270 La Roche-Posay; ☎05 49 19 13 00; www.larocheposay.com)* or **Société Hydrominérale de la Roche-Posay** *(☎05 49 19 48 00; www.spa-larocheposay.fr).*
- In Hendaye, the **Complexe de Thalassothérapie Serge Blanco** *(125 bd de la Mer, 64700 Hendaye; ☎08 25 00 00 15; www.thalassoblanco.com)* is well known to sports enthusiasts who appreciate the whirlpools, massages and algae packs, as well as the giant jacuzzi, sauna, weight machines and squash courts. The chic establishment, open year-round in a beautiful setting, offers personalised programmes designed to help you slim down and improve your sports performance.

Contact the spa towns' tourist offices for further information.

Vinotherapy

Les Sources de Caudalie

Chemin de Smith-Haut-Lafitte, 33650 Bordeaux-Martillac. ☎05 57 83 83 83. www.sources-caudalie.com.

We can now have body and facial treatments all based around the grape. Mineral water, rich in iron and fluorine, combined with grape extracts, grape seed oil, wine yeasts, extracts of red wine, and even tannins possess moisturising and toning properties.

ACTIVITIES FOR KIDS

Southwest France has a lot to offer children from the sands of sunny Côte d'Argent to cycling through the Landes Forest, having fun in amusement parks, or visiting zoos, safari parks, aquariums and museums of special interest. In this guide, sights of particular interest to children are indicated by a KIDS symbol () and a child entry fee is given.

SHOPPING

OPENING HOURS

Most of the larger shops are open Mondays to Saturdays from 9am to 7 or 7.30pm.

Smaller, individual shops may close for an hour or more at lunch. Food shops – grocers, wine merchants and bakeries – are generally open from 7am to 7 or 7.30pm; some open on Sunday mornings. Many food shops close between noon and 2pm and on Mondays. Bakery and pastry shops sometimes close on Wednesdays. Hypermarkets usually stay open non-stop from 9am until 8pm or later. People travelling to the US cannot import plant products or fresh food, including fruit, cheeses and nuts. It is acceptable to carry tinned products or preserves.

Souvenirs

Light and easy to carry. Fleur de Sel from Ré and Île de Noirmoutier, or dried sea asparagus (Marais Breton-Vendée), mojette beans and angelica (Marais Poitevin in Niort).

For sweetness, add the *tourteau fromager* (Poitou-Charentes, Niort), the Broyé cake, nougatines (Poitou, Poitiers), macaroons (Poitiers, St-Émilion, St-jean-de-Luz), the Vendée brioche, the *fouasse* (La Mothe-St-Héray), chocolate sardines (Royan), chocolates from Angoulême and Bayonne, prunes from Agen, *cannelé* cakes (Bordeaux), Basque tart, *coucougnette* sweets (Pau), black cherry jam (Itxassou) and honey from the mountains.

Fragile and perishable. Marennes-Oléron and Arcachon oysters, and Gironde caviar. Beef from Bressuire, **duck** and **chicken** from Challans, foie gras and confit from the southwest, Bayonne ham and Basque cured meats. **Potatoes** from Noirmoutier and l'Île de Ré, and Haut-Poitou **melons**. Finally, dairy products: **chabichou** goat's cheese (Civray), and ewe's cheese (Ossau-Iraty), not forgetting Surgères and Échiré **butter**.

Wines and Spirits

Cognac and armagnac, along with **Pineau des Charentes**, Floc de Gascogne, and **bière blanche** from Ré, also curious local apéritifs and liqueurs. Lastly, wines: the fine wines of Bordeaux, and other quality wines from **Muscadet, Haut-Poitou,** Jurançon, Tursan and Buzet.

Other Items

Fine **porcelain** from Chauvigny, and **pottery** from La Chapelle-des-Pots (La Rochelle) and Pornic. Superb enamels made at Abbaye de Ligugé. Books from one of the shops at la Cité du livre at Montmorillon, and **comic books** from Angoulême.
Authentic **charentaises** slippers (La Rochefoucauld), embroidered cloth from Angles-sur-l'Anglin, and rare **mother of pearl** objects made on the Île d'Aix. The traditional umbrella **parapluie de berger** (Pau). The famous **espadrille** and pretty linen from Pays Basque. Wool from the Pyrénées, and the authentic **béret** from a manufacturer at Oloron-Ste-Marie, Nay or Bayonne.

MARKETS

Marchés au Gras

Traditional markets, known as *marchés au gras*, were previously held in winter months only for the sale of ducks and geese and prepared and raw livers. The most picturesque of these markets are held in the following towns:

Agen (Lot-et-Garonne) – Wed, Sat and Sun 7.30am–noon.
Aire-sur-l'Adour (Landes) – Tue, Nov–Feb.
Dax (Landes) – Sat 7am–1pm.
Langoiran (Gironde) – First Sun in Dec.
Montségur (Gironde) – Second Sun in Dec and Feb.
Orthez (Pyrénées-Atlantiques) – Tue 7.30am–10am, Nov–Mar.
Villeneuve-de-Marsan (Landes) – Wed morning, Oct–Apr.
Villeneuve-sur-Lot (Lot-et-Garonne) – Tue and Sat, Nov–Mar, in the market hall.

VALUE ADDED TAX

Value Added Tax in France *(TVA)* is 19.6% on almost every purchase (some foods and books are subject to a lower rate). Non-European visitors who spend more than 175€ (figure subject to change) in any one participating store can get the Value Added Tax amount refunded. Usually, you fill out a form at the store, showing your passport. Upon leaving the country you submit all forms to customs for approval.
The refund is usually paid directly into your bank or credit card account, or it can be sent by mail. Big department stores that cater to tourists provide special services to help you (no refund is possible for tax on services). If you are visiting two or more countries within the European Union, you submit the forms only on departure from the last EU country.

BOOKS

ELEANOR OF AQUITAINE

Eleanor of Aquitaine, Queen of France and England, a 12C divorcee, patroness of poets, source of inspiration for chivalry and Courtly Love, ruler of a kingdom that spanned from Scotland to the Pyrénées, mother of 10 children (including Richard the Lionheart), lived her 82 years as few women in history before or since.
The story of her life is a good introduction to regional history, and a fascinating tale:

Eleanor of Aquitaine: A Life, Alison Weir, Ballantine Books, 2001.
Eleanor of Aquitaine: A Biography, Marion Meade, Penguin Paperbacks, 2002.
Eleanor of Aquitaine: The Mother Queen, Desmond Seward, Barnes & Noble, 1995.
Eleanor of Aquitaine and the Four Kings, Amy Kelly, Harvard University Press, Paperback edition 1973.
Beloved Enemy: The Passions of Eleanor of Aquitaine: A Novel, Ellen Jones, Simon & Schuster, 1994.

For Young Readers

A Proud Taste for Scarlet and Miniver, E L Konigsburg, Aladdin, 2001.
Queen Eleanor: Independent Spirit of the Medieval World, Polly Schoyer Brooks, Houghton Mifflin, 2001.

BOOKS ON WINE

French Wines: The Essential Guide to the Wines and Wine Growing Regions of France, Robert Joseph, DK Publishing, 2006.
This is a very useful book, in a travel-friendly paperback format, for anyone wanting to buy or taste all sorts of wine, whether during a trip to France (includes maps) or to the corner wine shop.
Bordeaux: The Wines, the Vineyards, the Winemakers, Oz Clarke, Pavilion, 2008.
This historic wine region is brought to life by Oz Clarke. It highlights the most famous wines of this fine wine region, the best vintages, and also recommends more affordable bottles.
Traveller's Wine Guide to France, Christopher Fielden, The Armchair Traveller at the bookHaus, 2003.
Well-researched book that guides you through the towns, villages and vineyards, with lots of background information.
The Winemasters, Nicholas Faith, Hamish and Hamilton, 1978.
History and people – two centuries of winemaking in Bordeaux.
The Wines of France, Alexis Lichine, Knopf, 1969.
A classic that ages well.
The Wine Regions of France, Michelin Travel Publications, 2009.
A comprehensive guide to the wine-producing regions in France.

FICTION

The Three Musketeers, Alexandre Dumas, Grosset and Dunlap Junior Library edition 1953, illustrated.
A perfect choice that is sure to fire the imaginations of young readers.
By the River Piedra I Sat Down and Wept, Paulo Coelho, HarperCollins, 2006.
A romantic adventure and search for spiritual sustenance on a journey through the French Pyrénées.

HISTORY AND PERSONAL EXPERIENCE

The Basque History of the World, Mark Kurlansky, Vintage, 2000.
This rare book in English on the political, economic, social, and even culinary history of the Basque people is an excellent introduction to this rather mysterious culture.
The Land of My Fathers: A Son's Return to the Basque Country, Robert Laxalt, Joyce Laxalt (Photographer), University of Nevada Press, 1999.
The author, who has written several novels set in the Basque Country, here gives a record of the years he spent with his family in the 1960s in a village in the French Basque Country. His descriptions of the isolated, beautiful mountain world where the Basques have lived for uncounted centuries complement his wife's photographs.
The Fronde: A French Revolution, Orest A Ranum, Norton & Co, 1994.
Unrest and turbulence in 1648 ended up in a showdown between the monarchy and insurgents in Bordeaux.
The Lost Uplands: Stories of Southwest France, W S Merwin, Counterpoint LLC, 2005. Three narrative portraits of small-town life in the

region, from the pen of an award-winning poet.

A House in the Sunflowers: Summer in Aquitaine, Ruth Silvestre, Thorndike Press, 1996. A British family's search for and discovery of the perfect French holiday home.

Jasmin's Witch, Emmanuel Ladurie, George Braziller, 1987. Popular tradition and legend, magic, witchcraft and sorcery in the Agen region; the story of a beautiful dancing girl and the poet who recounted her downfall.

FILMS

FILMS SET IN THE FRENCH ATLANTIC COAST REGION

La Foire aux Femmes (1956). Set in the Vendée, this film is the story of an orphan girl who falls in love with Jean-Pierre but is closely guarded by her jealous employer. However, tradition has it that at the Fair of Women the young men choose the girl they fancy: Jean-Pierre picks out the orphan girl. The film is set in La Rochelle and Le Vanneau.

La Ferme du Pendu (1945). The tragic story of siblings who promise their dying father they will not marry so that his farm will not be split up. Inevitably there are tragic consequences. Filmed and set in Pouzages and the Marais Poitevin.

Les Demoiselles de Rochefort (1967). The story of twin sisters and their café owning mother. The former are seeking love and life outside Rochefort but things are not always that simple. The result is an entertaining musical comedy. The film is set in Rochefort.

César et Rosalie (1972). The film, starring Yves Montard, tells the story of a happy divorcee devoted to her young daughter and her lover César. All is well until an old flame turns up and battle commences between the two men to claim the woman they both love. Set and filmed on the Île de Noirmoutier.

La Revolte des Enfants (1992). Set in 1847 during the Industrial Revolution, the film tells the story of rebellion against their cruel and repressive gaoler by the child inmates of a prison for young offenders. Filmed on the Île d'Yeu.

THE FRENCH ATLANTIC COAST CONNECTION

The Three Musketeers (1921, 1939, 1948, 1973, 1993, 2011). Alexandre Dumas' novel has probably spawned more films than any other book. The three musketeers and D'Artagnan all come from Gascony but seek adventure in Paris serving the King. Some versions have scenes set in Gascogny.

Cinq Tulipes Rouges (1949). A thriller in which a journalist and a police inspector race against time to find the killer of five riders in the Tour de France. Set and filmed, among other locations, in Bordeaux and Biarritz.

Le Promeneur du Champ de Mars (2005). A story about a journalist helping the French President, François Mitterrand, to compile his memoirs.

ON LOCATION IN THE FRENCH ATLANTIC COAST REGION

The Sun Also Rises (1957) – Hemingway's story of expatriates in Europe between the wars. Locations in Bayonne.

The Sign of Zorro (1958) – Parts of the the earlier version were shot in Biarritz and St-Jean-de-Luz.

The Longest Day (1962) – This epic about the Normandy D-Day Landings uses locations around La Rochelle and the Île de Ré for Normandy.

Raiders of the Lost Ark (1981) – The bantu wind & Nazi submarine scenes were shot in La Rochelle.

Tomorrow Never Dies (1997) – Part of the arms bazaar sequence was shot in Bayonne.

Calendar of Events

Many regional tourist offices publish brochures listing local fêtes, fairs and festivals. Most places hold festivities for France's National Day (14 July) and many organise events on 15 August, also a public holiday.

FAIRS AND HISTORICAL PAGEANTS

1 MAY

Mimizan-Plage – *Fête de la Mer.* Sea festival. *www.mimizan-tourisme.com.*

JUNE–SEPTEMBER

Le Puy du Fou – *Cinéscénie.* Historical pageant, sound and light show. (Fri and Sat 10pm, mid-June–July, 10.30pm Aug–early Sept). *www.puydufou.com.*

Bougon – *Pierres de Lune*, Musée des Tumulus (Aug). *www.deux-sevres.com/musee-bougon.*

St-Jean-de-Luz – *Fête de la St-Jean.* Midsummer festival: High Mass, concerts, *chistera*, traditional games, bonfires, ball, *toro de fuego*, etc. *www.saint-jean-de-luz.com.*

JULY

La Pierre St-Martin – *Junte de Roncal* (13 Jul). Ceremony to mark the treaty between the Roncal Valley (Spain) and the Barétous Valley (France).

SUNDAY AROUND 14 JULY

St-Étienne-de-Baïgorry – *Force Basque* traditional games championship. *www.terre-basque.com.*

LATE JULY–EARLY AUGUST

Castillon-la-Bataille – Sound and light show re-enacting the battle of Castillon, which marked the end of the Hundred Year Wars' (evenings mid-Jul–mid-Aug). *www.batailledecastillon.com.*

Clisson – Night-time pageant at the château. *www.valleedeclisson.fr.*

St-Sever – Historical pageant sound and light show. *www.saint-sever.fr.*

1ST SUNDAY IN AUGUST

Moncrabeau – This international lying contest crowns the *King of Liars*, in a Gascon tradition perpetuated by the Academy of Liars (founded 18C). *www.albret-tourisme.com.*

Hagetmau – *Les 5 jours d'Hagetmau.* Bullfights, *courses landaises*, fireworks, music. *www.tourisme-hagetmau.com.*

1ST WEEK IN AUGUST

Bayonne – *Courses de vaches landaises*, bullfights, water games, parades with floats, concerts, balls, *toro de fuego. www.bayonne-tourisme.com.*

MID-AUGUST

Arcachon – *Fêtes de la Mer.* Sea festival. *www.arcachon.com.*

Biarritz – *Nuit féerique.* Fireworks. *www.biarritz.fr.*

Dax – *Feria.* Bullfights, *concours landais*, folk dancing and music, balls, fireworks. *www.dax.fr.*

FESTIVALS

LATE JANUARY

Angoulême – International Comic Strip show. *www.bdangouleme.com.*

2ND WEEK IN FEBRUARY

Thouars – *Terri Thouars Blues.* Music festival. *www.blues-n-co.org.*

APRIL

Landes – *Printemps des Landes.* A week of activities and spectacles. *http://printemps-des-landes.com.*

2ND WEEK IN APRIL

Bayonne – *Foire au Jambon.* Ham festival. *www.bayonne.fr.*

WEEKEND OF WHITSUNDAY

Hastingues – International ceramics festival at Arthous Abbey. *www.arthous.landes.org.*

Cinéscénie, Le Puy du Fou

MAY

Pauillac – *Fête de l'Agneau.* Festival for the local lamb. *www.pauillac-medoc.com.*

Cambo-les-Bains – *Festival d'Otxote.* Traditional song festival. *www.cambolesbains.com.*

MAY–JUNE

Angoulême – *Festival Musiques métisses.* World Music Festival. *www.musiques-metisses.com.*

Melle – St-Savinien. Classical music festival (2nd half of May, early Jun). *www.ville-melle.fr.*

St-Gilles-Croix-de-Vie – International Jazz Festival (late May). *www.saint-jazz-sur-vie.com.*

JUNE

Niort – *Le Très Grand Conseil Mondial des Clowns.* Clown festival. *www.festival-mondial-clown.com.*

St-Jean-de-Luz – *Udaberria Dantzan.* Festival of traditional dance. *www.saint-jean-de-luz.com.*

Itxassou – Cherry festival. *www.itxassou.fr.*

Bordeaux – *Fête du Fleuve.* Festival on the quays, every two years. *www.bordeaux-fete-le-fleuve.com.*

Bordeaux – *Fête du Vin.* Festival on the quays, and the place des Quinconces, every two years. *www.bordeaux-fete-le-vin.com.*

St-Émilion – *Jurade de Printemps.* Wine festival. *www.saint-emilion-tourisme.com.*

Montmorillon – *Salon du livre.* Book fair, every two years. *www.montmorillon.fr.*

Villebois-Lavalette – *Le Printemps de la Danse.* Dance festival. *www.printempsdanse.org.*

JUNE–JULY

La Rochelle – International Film Festival. *www.festival-larochelle.org.*

Pau – *Festival de Pau.* Theatre, music, dance. *www.pau-pyrenees.com.*

1ST HALF OF JULY

Parthenay – International Festival of Games. *www.cc-parthenay.fr/flip/portail.*

Saintes – *Les Académies musicales de l'Abbaye aux Dames.* *www.abbayeauxdames.org.*

Cognac – *La Fête du Cognac.* Music performances and gastronomic festival. *www.lafeteducognac.fr.*

Cognac – *Blues Passions* festival (27 Jul–1 Aug). *www.bluespassions.com.*

Parthenay and area – *De bouche à Oreille* music festival (3rd week of the month). *www.metive.org.*

Fêtes de Bayonne
©E. Larribère/MICHELIN

Mont-de-Marsan – Flamenco Festival. *http://arteflamenco.landes.org.*

La Rochelle – *Les Francofolies.* French song festival (10–14 Jul). ☎05 46 28 28 28. *www.francofolies.fr.*

2ND HALF OF JULY

Lanton – *Fête de l'Huître et Folklore Maritme.* Folklore and oyster festival (from 14 Jul for three evenings). *www.tourisme-coeurdubassin.com.*

Saintes – International folklore festival. *www.ot-saintes.fr.*

Andernos-les-Bains – Jazz Festival. *www.andernoslesbains.fr.*

Etsaut – Cheese festival. *http://fetedufromage-aspe.com.*

LATE JULY–MID-AUGUST

Marciac – *Jazz in Marciac* festival. *www.jazzinmarciac.com.*

EARLY AUGUST

Oloron-Ste-Marie – *Festival international des Pyrénées.* Folklore, traditional art and popular traditions. *www.oloron-ste-marie.com.*

2ND WEEK IN AUGUST

Confolens – International folk festival. *www.festivaldeconfolens.com.*

Lusseray – *Marionnettes en campagne.* Puppet theatre. *www.grosbonhomme.com.*

3RD WEEK IN AUGUST

Uzeste – *Hestejada de las arts d'Uzeste Musical.* Pop music, theatre, poetry, art exhibits, dance, cinema, etc. *www.uzeste.org.*

1ST SUNDAY AFTER 15 AUGUST

St-Palais – *Force basque* traditional games. *www.saintpalais-tourisme.com.*

LATE AUGUST–EARLY SEPTEMBER

Anglet, **Ascain**, **Bayonne**, **Biarritz**, **Ciboure**, **St-Jean-de-Luz**, **Urrugne** – *Musique en Côte Basque.* Classical music festival. *www.musiquecotebasque.fr.*

SEPTEMBER

Agen – *Grand pruneau show d'Agen.* Prune festival. *www.grandpruneaushow.fr.*

Arette – *Fête des bergers.* Sheep dog trials. *www.valleedebaretous.com.*

OCTOBER

Poitiers – *Les Expressifs.* Open-air theatre performances. *wwwlesexpressifs.com.*

Ménigoute – *Festival International de Film Ornithologique.* International festival of ornithological film. *www.menigoute-festival.org.*

Neuville-de-Poitou– *Modelexpo.* European model fair. *www.modelexpo.net.*

Espelette– *Fête du Piment.* Espelette pepper festival. *www.espelette.fr.*

OCTOBER–NOVEMBER

Angoulême – *Piano en Valois. www.piano-en-valois.fr.* Ten days of piano recitals by French and international musicians in various locations around the town.

NOVEMBER

Cognac – *Salon de la Littérature européenne.* International book fair. *www.litterature-europeenne.com.*

Angoulême – *Gastronomades.* Local produce fair. *www.gastronomades.fr.*

Biarritz – *Festival de Cirque.* Circus festival. *www.biarritz.fr.*

SPORTS EVENTS

APRIL

Châtaillon – *Festival de Cerfs-Volants.* Kite flying festival on the beach. *www.chatelaillon-plage-tourisme.fr.*

WEEKEND OF WHITSUNDAY

Pau – *Grand Prix automobile, Formula 3000. www.grandprix-pau.fr.*

MAY

Arcachon – *Jumping des Sables.* Show jumping competition on Pereire beach. *www.arcachon.com.*

JUNE

La Rochelle – International Sailing Week. *www.larochelle-tourisme.com.*

Beauvoir-sur-Mer – *Les Foulées du Gois.* Running race against the tide. *www.lesfouleesdugois.com.*

JULY

Arcachon – *18 heures Arcachon Sud-Ouest.* Sailing race. *www.arcachon.com.*

Biarritz – Biarritz Golf Cup. *www.biarritz-cup.com.*

AUGUST

Biarritz – *Cesta Punta.* Golden Gloves championships. *www.cestapunta.com.*

St-Jean-de-Luz – World Championship *Cesta Punta* tournament. *www.cestapunta.com.*

Soustons – *Pelote Basque Grand Chistera* and Landais folk festival. *www.soustons.fr.*

Noirmoutier – Historic ships regatta. *www.ile-noirmoutier.com.*

Ascain – *Course à la Rhune.* Race up and down the mountain on foot. *www.terreetcotebasques.com.*

Mirebeau – *Fête de l'âne et du baudet du Poitous.* Donkey festival.

Lacanau – *Lacanau Pro.* Surfboard competition. *www.surflacanau.com.*

SEPTEMBER

Angoulême – Vintage car rally around the ramparts (2nd week in Sept). *www.angouleme-tourisme.com.*

La Rochelle – *Le Grand Pavois.* Boat show. *www.grand-pavois.com.*

LATE SEPTEMBER–EARLY OCTOBER

Biarritz – *Quicksilver Pro Junior.* international surfing competition. *www.landes.surfingaquitaine.com.*

OCTOBER

Pau – *Concours complet international d'equitation.* Horse riding competition. *www.event-pau.fr.*

NOVEMBER

Les Sables-d'Olonne – *Vendée Globe.* Departure of the solo sailing race, held every four years since 1988. *www.vendeeglobe.org.*

Know Before You Go

USEFUL WEBSITES

www.ambafrance-uk.org
www.ambafrance-us.org
The French Embassies in the UK and US have a website providing basic information, a news digest, and business-related information. They also offer pages for children and pages devoted to culture, language study and travel.

www.franceguide.com
The French Government Tourist Office/ Maison de la France site is packed with practical information and tips for those travelling to France. Links to specific guidance (for American or Canadian travellers, for example), and to the FGTO's London pages.

www.francekeys.com
This site has plenty of practical information for visiting France. It covers all the regions, with links to tourist offices and related sites. Very useful for planning the details of your tour in France.

www.bernezac.com
Information on all the main towns and coastal resorts along the Atlantic Coast. Useful listings of where to stay, where to eat and what to do with the kids. Covers local events too.

www.art-roman.net
Documents descriptions and photographs of the Romanesque architecture in the Poitou and Vendée.

www.alienor.org
The Conseil des Musées de Poitou-Charentes site has extensive up-to-date information on the museums of the region, including detailed information on their collections.

www.lespyrenees.net
www.pyrenees-online.fr
These two sites provide useful information on places to discover in the Pyrénées, as well as indispensable information on the ski resorts.

www.tourisme-landes.com
Comprehensive guide to the Landes, incorporating information on heritage, accommodation, restaurants, campsites, golf courses and places to visit.

TOURIST OFFICES

FRENCH TOURIST OFFICES ABROAD

For information, brochures, maps and assistance in planning a trip to France travellers should apply to the official French Tourist Office or Maison de France in their own country:

Australia – New Zealand

- **Sydney** – Level 13, 25 Bligh St, Sydney, New South Wales, Australia. ✆61 (0)2 9231 5244. Fax 61 (0)2 9221 8682. http://au.franceguide.com.

Canada

- **Montreal** – 1800 Ave McGill College, Suite 1010, Montreal, Quebec H3A 3J6. ✆(514) 288-2026. Fax (514) 845-4868. http://ca-en.franceguide.com.

South Africa

- **Johannesburg** – ATOUT FRANCE, 3rd Floor Village Walk Office Tower cnr Maude and Rivonia, Sandton. ✆00 27 (0) 11 523 82 92. Fax 00 27 (0) 11 523 82 99. http://za.franceguide.com.

United Kingdom

- **London** – Lincoln House, 300 High Holborn, London WC1V 7JH. ✆09068 244 123. http://uk.franceguide.com.

United States

Three offices are available, but the quickest way to get a response to any question or request is by phone. ✆514 288 1904. http://us.franceguide.com.

- **East Coast**
  825 Third Ave., 29th Floor, New York, NY 10022.
- **Mid West**
  205 N. Michigan Ave, Suite 3770, Chicago 60601, IL.
- **West Coast**
  9454 Wilshire Blvd, Suite 210, Beverly Hills 90212, CA.

LOCAL TOURIST OFFICES

Visitors may also contact local tourist offices for more precise information and to receive brochures and maps. In the *Discovering Aquitaine* and *Discovering Poitou-Charentes and La Vendée* sections of this guide, the addresses and telephone numbers of tourist offices, indicated by the symbol, are given in the coloured Orient panels next to the sight's name.

The following are addresses of local tourist offices of the major *départements* and *régions* covered in this guide; address enquiries to the Comité Régional de Tourisme (C.R.T.):

Aquitaine: Bureaux de la Cité mondiale, 23 parvis des Chartrons, 33074 Bordeaux Cedex. 05 56 01 70 00. www.tourisme-aquitaine.fr.

Poitou-Charentes: 8 r. Riffault, 86002 Poitiers Cedex. 05 49 50 10 50. Fax 05 49 41 37 28. www.poitou-charentes-vacances.com.

Vendée: 45 bd des États-Unis, 85006 La Roche sur Yon Cedex. 02 51 47 88 20. www.vendee-tourisme.com.

For each *département* within the region, address enquiries to the Comité Départemental de Tourisme (C.D.T.), unless otherwise stated:

Charente: 21 r. d'Iéna, 16021 Angoulême. 05 45 69 79 09. www.lacharente.com.

Charente-Maritime: Maison de la Charente-Maritime, 85 bd de la République, 17076 La Rochelle Cedex 9. 05 46 31 71 71. www.charente-maritime.com.

Deux-Sèvres: 15 r. Thiers, 79025 Niort Cedex 9. 05 49 77 87 79. www.tourisme-deux-sevres.com.

Gironde: 21 cours de l'Intendance, 33000 Bordeaux. 05 56 52 61 40. www.tourisme-gironde.fr.

Landes: 4 av. Aristide-Briand, BP 407, 40012 Mont-de-Marsan Cedex. 05 58 06 89 89. www.tourismelandes.com.

Loire-Atlantique: 11 r. du Château-de-l'Eraudière CS 40698, 44306 Nantes Cedex 3. 02 51 72 95 30. www.loireatlantique.fr.

Lot-et-Garonne: 271 r. de Péchabout, BP 30158, 47005 Agen Cedex. 05 53 66 14 14. www.tourisme-lotetgaronne.com.

Pyrénées-Atlantiques (Béarn-Pays Basque): Petite Caserne, 2 allée des Platanes, 64100 Bayonne. 05 59 46 52 52; Délégation Béarn, 22 Ter, rue J J de Monaix, 64000 Pau. 05 59 30 01 30. www.tourisme64.com.

Vienne: 33 pl. Charles-de-Gaulle, 86007 Poitiers Cedex. 05 49 37 48 48. www.tourisme-vienne.com.

In France, 137 towns and areas have been labelled **Villes et Pays d'Art et d'Histoire** by the Ministry of Culture. They are particularly active in promoting their architectural and cultural heritage and offer guided tours by highly qualified guides as well as activities for 6- to 12-year-olds.

More information is available from local tourist offices and from www.vpah.culture.fr.

INTERNATIONAL VISITORS

DOCUMENTS

Passport

Nationals of countries within the European Union entering France need only a national identity card (a passport for UK nationals). Nationals of other countries must be in possession of a valid national passport. In case of loss or theft, report to your embassy or consulate and the local police.

EMBASSIES AND CONSULATES IN FRANCE		
Australia	Embassy	4 rue Jean-Rey, 75015 Paris ℘01 40 59 33 00. www.france.embassy.gov.au
Canada	Embassy	35 avenue Montaigne, 75008 Paris ℘01 44 43 29 00. www.canadainternational.gc.ca/france
Eire	Embassy	4 rue Rude, 75016 Paris ℘01 44 17 67 00. www.embassyofireland.fr
New Zealand	Embassy	7 rue Léonard-de-Vinci, 75016 Paris ℘01 45 00 24 11. www.nzembassy.com/france
South Africa	Embassy	59 quai d'Orsay, 75007 Paris ℘01 53 59 23 23. www.afriquesud.net
UK	Embassy	35 rue du Faubourg St-Honoré, 75008 Paris ℘01 44 51 31 00. http://ukinfrance.fco.gov.uk/fr
	Consulate	16 bis rue d'Anjou, 75008 Paris ℘01 44 51 31 00
	Consulate	353 boulevard du Président Wilson, 33073 Bordeaux ℘05 57 22 21 10
USA	Embassy	2 avenue Gabriel, 75008 Paris ℘01 43 12 22 22. http://france.usembassy.gov
	Consulate	2 rue St-Florentin, 75001 Paris ℘01 43 12 22 22

Visa

No entry visa is required for Canadian, US or Australian citizens travelling as tourists and staying for up to 90 days, except for students planning to study in France. If you think you may need a visa, apply to your local French Consulate.

US citizens are advised to consult *www.travel.state.gov* for entry requirements, security and other information including contact numbers of US embassies and consulates. In an emergency call the **Overseas Citizens Services** *℘1-888-407-4747 (℘1-202-501-4444 from overseas).*

CUSTOMS

In the UK, **HM Revenue & Customs** *(www.hmrc.gov.uk)* publishes *A Guide for Travellers* on customs regulations and duty-free allowances. **US citizens** should view *Tips for Traveling Abroad* online *(http://travel.state.gov/travel/tips_1232.html)* for general information on visa requirements, customs regulations, medical care, etc.

There are no customs formalities for holidaymakers bringing their caravans into France for a stay of less than six months. No customs document is necessary for pleasure boats and outboard motors for a stay of less than six months but the registration certificate should be kept on board.

Americans can bring home, tax-free, up to US$ 800 worth of goods (limited quantities of alcohol and tobacco products); Canadians up to CND$ 750; Australians up to AUS$ 900; and New Zealanders up to NZ$ 700.

Persons living in a member state of the European Union are not restricted with regard to purchasing goods for private use, but the recommended allowances for alcoholic beverages and tobacco are listed in the table entitled "Duty-Free Allowances" *(see opposite)*.

HEALTH

First aid, medical advice and chemists' night service are provided by chemists/drugstores *(pharmacies)* identified by the green cross sign.

DUTY-FREE ALLOWANCES	
Spirits (whisky, gin, vodka, etc.)	10l/2.4gal
Fortified wines (vermouth, port, etc.)	20l/4.4gal
Wine (not more than 60l/13.2gal sparkling)	90l/19.8gal
Beer	110l/24.2gal
Cigarettes	800
Cigarillos	400
Cigars	200
Smoking tobacco	1kg/2.2lb

Since the recipient of medical treatment in French hospitals or clinics must pay the bill, it is advisable to take out comprehensive insurance coverage. Nationals of non-EU countries should check with their insurance companies about policy limitations. Reimbursement can then be negotiated with the insurance company according to the policy held. All prescription drugs should be clearly labelled; it is recommended that you carry a copy of the prescription.

British and Irish citizens, if they are not already in possession of an **EHIC** (European Health Insurance Card), should apply for one before travelling. The card entitles UK residents to reduced-cost medical treatment. Apply at UK post offices, call ✆*0845 605 0707*, or visit *www.ehic.org.uk*. You pay upfront but can reclaim most of the money *(see website for details)*.

Americans concerned about travel and health can contact the International Association for Medical Assistance to Travelers, which can also provide details of English-speaking doctors in different parts of France: ✆*(716) 754-4883. www.iamat.org*.

The American Hospital of Paris is open 24 hours for emergencies as well as consultations, with English-speaking staff *(63 bd Victor Hugo, 92200 Neuilly sur Seine; ✆01 46 41 25 25; www.american-hospital.org)*. The hospital is accredited by major insurance companies.

The British Hospital is just outside Paris in Levallois-Perret *(3 r. Barbès; ✆01 46 39 22 22; www.british-hospital.org)*. This facility is registered as a charity in the UK and provides English-speaking medical staff to the British community in France.

ACCESSIBILITY

The sights described in this guide that are easily accessible to people of reduced mobility are indicated by the symbol ♿. Many of France's historic buildings, including museums and hotels, have limited or no wheelchair access. Older hotels tend to lack lifts (elevators).

Tourism for All UK *(✆0845 124 9971; www.tourismforall.org.uk)* publishes some handy information about accessibility in various accommodation types and places. Information about accessibility is available from French disability organisations such as **Association des Paralysés de France** *(17 bd Auguste Blanqui, 75013 Paris; ✆01 40 78 69 00; www.apf.asso.fr)*.

Useful information on transport, holidaymaking, and sports associations for the disabled is available from French-language website *www.handicap.fr*. In the UK, *www.radar.org.uk* is a good source of information and support and US website *www.access-able.com* provides information on travel for mature travellers or those with special needs, including lists of experienced travel agents and useful internet links. The **Michelin Guide France** and **Michelin Camping & Caravanning France** both indicate hotels and campsites with facilities suitable for physically handicapped people.

Getting There and Getting Around

BY PLANE

It is easy to arrange air travel to one of Paris' two airports (Roissy/Charles-de-Gaulle to the north; Orly to the south). Contact airline companies and travel agents for details of package tour flights with a rail or coach link as well as Fly-Drive schemes. For example, some packages include a link from Roissy airport to the high-speed TGV train, which serves the region, stopping in Poitiers, La Rochelle, Bordeaux, Biarritz, Hendaye and Tarbes. Alternatively, there are daily connecting flights from Paris to the regional capital Bordeaux, direct regular flights from London and flights from a number of destinations outside France, including Montreal, Toronto and Shannon (in Ireland). Information is available from the French Tourist Office in your country as well as from travel agents and airlines.

The following **airlines** operate flights from the UK to the Atlantic Coast region:

- **Jet4you** – *www.jet4you.com* (flights to Bordeaux and Nantes)
- **British Airways** – *www.ba.com* (flights to Bordeaux)
- **Jet2.com** – *www.jet2.com* (flights to La Rochelle)
- **CityJet** – *www.cityjet.com* (flights to Nantes)
- **Air France** – *www.airfrance.com* (flights to Bordeaux and Pau)
- **easyJet** – *www.easyjet.com* (flights to Biarritz, Bordeaux and Nantes)
- **Flybe** – *www.flybe.com* (flights to Bordeaux and La Rochelle)
- **Ryanair** – *www.ryanair.com* (flights to Poitiers, Nantes, Biarritz and La Rochelle)

Visitors arriving in **Paris** who wish to reach the city centre or a train station may use public transport or reserve space on the **Airport Shuttle** *(from Charles-de-Gaulle; ℘01 30 11 13 00; www.paris-blue-airport-shuttle.fr).* Air France operates a coach service into town with frequent departures *(http://videocdn.airfrance.com/cars-airfrance).* The cost and duration of a taxi ride from the airport to the centre of town varies with traffic conditions. From Charles-de-Gaulle: about 45min, 50€; from Orly about 30min, 35€. There is an extra charge (posted in the cab) for baggage; the extra charge for airport pick-up is on the meter; drivers are usually given a tip of 10–15%.

For further information, log on to www.aeroportsdeparis.fr.

The main regional airports are:

- **Aéroport Nantes-Atlantique** – *(SW of Nantes)* CCI, 44346 Bouguenais Cedex. ℘02 40 84 80 00. www.nantes.aeroport.fr.
- **Aéroport de Poitiers-Biard** – *(5km/3mi W of Poitiers)* 86580 Biard. ℘05 49 30 04 40. www.poitiers.aeroport.fr.
- **Aéroport Angoulême-Cognac** – *(10km/6.2mi N of Angoulême city centre)* 16430 Champniers. ℘05 45 69 88 09. www.aeroport-angouleme-cognac.com.
- **Aéroport de La Rochelle – Île de Ré** – *(N of La Rochelle)* rue du Jura, 17000 La Rochelle. ℘05 46 42 30 26. www.larochelle.aeroport.fr.
- **Aéroport d'Agen** – 47520 Le Passage d'Agen. ℘05 53 77 00 88. www.aeroport-agen.com.
- **Aéroport de Biarritz-Anglet-Bayonne** – esplanade de l'Europe, 64600 Anglet. ℘05 59 43 83 83. www.biarritz.aeroport.fr.
- **Aéroport de Bordeaux-Mérignac** – Cedex 40, 33700 Mérignac. ℘05 56 34 50 50. www.bordeaux.aeroport.fr.
- **Aéroport Pau-Pyrénées** – 64230 Uzein. ℘05 59 33 33 00. www.pau.aeroport.fr.

BY FERRY

There are numerous **cross-Channel services** from the United Kingdom and Ireland. To choose the most

P&O Ferries	In the UK: 08716 645 645 In France: 08 25 12 01 56 www.poferries.com
Norfolkline	In the UK: 0871 574 7235 In France: 03 28 59 01 01 www.norfolkline.com
Brittany Ferries	In the UK: 0871 244 0744 In France: 08 25 82 88 28 In Ireland: 021 427 7801 www.brittany-ferries.com
Irish Ferries	In the UK: 08717 300 400 In Ireland: 0818 300 400 In France: 02 33 23 44 44 In the US: (772) 563 2856 www.irishferries.com

suitable route between your port of arrival and your destination use the **Michelin Tourist and Motoring Atlas France, Michelin map 726** (which gives travel times and mileages) or **Michelin Local maps** from the 1:200 000 series.

BY TRAIN

Le Shuttle-Eurotunnel runs a service for cars from **Ashford** (Kent) to **Calais** (*08443 35 35 35; www.eurotunnel.com*).

Eurostar (*08432 186 186; www.eurostar.com*) operates a 2hr15min daily service via the Channel Tunnel from **London** (St Pancras) and Ebbsfleet International in Kent to **Paris** (Gare du Nord). In Paris, it links to the high-speed rail network (TGV). TGV departures for the Atlantic Coast are from the Gare Montparnasse.

Eurailpass, Flexipass, Eurailpass Youth, EurailDrive Pass and **Saverpass** are five of the travel passes that may be purchased by residents of countries outside the EU. In the US, contact your travel agent. If you are a European resident, you can buy a country pass, provided you are not a resident of the country where you plan to use it. In the UK, call **Rail Europe** (*08448 484 064; www.raileurope.co.uk*).

Information on schedules can be obtained on websites for these agencies and the SNCF respectively: *www.eurail.com, www.raileurope.co.uk or www.sncf.fr.*

At the SNCF site, you can book ahead, pay with a credit card, and receive your ticket in the mail at home.

DISCOUNTS

There are numerous **discounts** available when you purchase your tickets in France, at 25–50% below the regular rate. These include discounts for using senior cards and youth cards (the nominative cards with a photograph must be purchased beforehand), and lower rates for 2–9 people travelling together (no card required, advance purchase necessary). There is a limited number of discount seats available during peak travel times, but the best discounts are available during off-peak periods. *Tickets must be validated (composter) by using the orange automatic date-stamping machines at the platform entrance (failure to do so may result in a fine).*

The French railway company **SNCF** operates a telephone information, reservation and prepayment service in English from 7am to 10pm (French time). In France call *36 35.*

BY COACH/BUS

- **Eurolines (London)** 4 Cardiff Road, Luton, Bedfordshire LU1 1PP. 08717 818 181. www.eurolines.co.uk.
- **Eurolines (Paris)** 08 92 89 90 91. www.eurolines.fr.

- **www.eurolines.com**
  The international website with information about travelling all over Europe by coach (bus).

BY CAR

PLANNING YOUR ROUTE

The area covered in this guide is easily reached by main motorways and national routes. **Michelin map 726** indicates the main itineraries as well as alternative routes for avoiding heavy traffic during busy holiday periods, and gives estimated travel times. **Michelin map 723** is a detailed atlas of French motorways, indicating tolls, rest areas and services along the route; it includes a table for calculating distances and times. The latest Michelin route-planning service is available on the internet at **www.ViaMichelin.com**. Travellers can calculate a precise route using such options as shortest route, route avoiding toll roads, Michelin recommended routes and gain access to tourist information (hotels, restaurants, attractions).
The roads are very busy during holiday periods (particularly weekends in July and August), so to avoid traffic congestion it is advisable to follow the recommended secondary routes (signposted as *Bison Futé – itinéraires bis*). The motorway network includes rest areas *(aires)* and petrol stations, usually with restaurant and shopping complexes attached, about every 40km/25mi, so that long-distance drivers have no excuse not to stop for a rest every now and then.

DOCUMENTS

Driving Licence

Travellers from other European Union countries and North America can drive in France with a valid national or home-state **driving licence**. An **international driving licence** is useful because the information on it appears in nine languages (keep in mind that traffic officers are empowered to fine motorists). A permit is available (US $15) from the **National Automobile Club** *(1151 East Hillsdale Blvd, Foster City, CA 94404; ☏650-294-7000; www.nationalautoclub.com)*; or contact your local branch of the **American Automobile Association** *(www.aaa.com)*.

Registration Papers

For the vehicle, it is necessary to have the registration papers (logbook) and a nationality plate of the approved size.

INSURANCE

Many motoring organisations offer accident insurance and breakdown service schemes for members. Check with your current insurance company regarding cover while abroad. If you plan to hire a car using your credit card, check with the company, which may provide liability insurance automatically (and thus save you having to pay the cost for optimum coverage).

ROAD REGULATIONS

The minimum driving age is 18. Traffic drives on the right. All passengers must wear **seat belts**. Children under the age of 10 must ride in the back seat. Headlights must be switched on in poor visibility and at night; use side-lights only when the vehicle is stationary. In the case of a **breakdown**, a red warning triangle and a reflective safety jacket are obligatory. In the absence of stop signs at intersections, cars must **yield to the right**. Traffic on main roads outside built-up areas (priority indicated by a yellow diamond sign) and on round-abouts has right of way. Vehicles must stop when the lights turn red at road junctions and may filter to the right only when indicated by an amber arrow.
The regulations on **drinking and driving** (limited to 0.50g/l) and **speeding** are strictly enforced, usually by an on-the-spot fine and/or confiscation of the vehicle. From Spring 2012, all cars must carry a compulsory portable alcohol breathalyzer kit.

Speed Limits

Although liable to modification, these are as follows:

- Toll motorways *(autoroutes)* 130kph/80mph (110kph/68mph when raining);
- Dual carriageways and motorways without tolls 110kph/68mph (100kph/62mph when raining);
- Other roads 90kph/56mph (80kph/50mph when raining) and in towns 50kph/31mph;
- Outside lane on motorways during daylight, on level ground and with good visibility – minimum speed limit of 80kph/50mph.

Parking Regulations

In town there are zones where parking is either restricted or subject to a fee; tickets should be obtained from the ticket machines (*horodateurs* – small change necessary) and displayed inside the windscreen on the driver's side; failure to display may result in a fine, or towing and impoundment. Other parking areas in town may require you to take a ticket when passing through a barrier. To exit, you must pay the parking fee (usually there is a machine located by the exit – *sortie*) and insert the paid-up card in another machine which will lift the exit gate.

Tolls

In France, most motorway sections are subject to a toll *(péage)*. You can pay in cash or with a credit card (Visa, MasterCard).

CAR RENTAL

There are car rental agencies at airports, railway stations and in all large towns throughout France. European cars have manual transmission; automatic cars are available in larger cities only if an advance reservation is made. Drivers must be over 21; at the ages 21–25, drivers are required to pay an extra daily fee; some companies allow drivers under 23 only if the reservation has been made through a travel agent.
It is relatively expensive to hire a car in France; Americans in particular will notice the difference and should make arrangements before leaving; take advantage of **Fly-Drive offers** when you buy your ticket, or seek advice from a travel agent, specifying requirements. There are many online services, such as **Nova** (*www.novacarhire.com; 0800 018 6682* (UK); *1866 NOVACAR* (US and Canada); *1800 200 115* (Ireland)) that will look for the best prices on car rental around the globe. *See the table "Rental Cars" for assistance in booking cars.*
A Baron's Limousine *01 45 30 21 21* provides cars and drivers (English-speaking drivers available).

MOTORHOME RENTAL

- **Worldwide Motorhome Rentals**
  Offers fully equipped camper vans for hire. You can view them on the company's webpages.
  888- 519-8969 *US toll-free*
  530-389-8316 *outside the US*
  www.mhrww.com

PETROL/GASOLINE

French service stations dispense:

- *sans plomb 98* (super unleaded 98)
- *sans plomb 95* (super unleaded 95)
- *diesel/gazole* (diesel)
- *GPL* (LPG).

For US citizens: gasoline is more expensive in France than in the US. Prices are listed on signboards on the motorways; it is usually cheaper to fill up after leaving the motorway; check hypermarkets on the outskirts of town. You can pay at the pump using credit/debit cards.

RENTAL CARS – CENTRAL RESERVATION IN FRANCE	
Avis:	08 21 23 07 60 www.avis.fr
Budget France:	08 25 00 35 64 www.budget.fr
Europcar:	08 25 35 23 52 www.europcar.com
Hertz France:	08 25 86 18 61 www.hertz.fr
SIXT-Eurorent	08 20 00 74 98 www.sixt.fr

Where to Stay and Eat

WHERE TO STAY

FINDING A HOTEL

Turn to the **Addresses** within individual sight listings in the *Discovering* sections for descriptions and prices of typical places to stay **(Stay)** with local flair. The key on the cover flap explains the symbols and abbreviations used in these sections. To enhance your stay, hotel selections have been chosen for their location, comfort, value for money and, in many cases, their charm. Prices indicate the cost of a standard room for two people in peak season. For an even greater selection, use the red-cover **Michelin Guide France**, with its well-known star-rating system and hundreds of establishments throughout France. The **Michelin Charming Places to Stay** guide contains a selection of 1 000 hotels and guesthouses at reasonable prices. Book ahead to ensure that you get the accommodation you want, not only in tourist season, but year-round, as many towns fill up during trade fairs, arts festivals, etc. Some places require an advance deposit or a reconfirmation. Reconfirming is especially important if you plan to arrive after 6pm.

For further assistance, **Le Réseau National des Destinations Départementales** is a booking service that has offices in some French *départements* – contact tourist offices for further information or visit *www.loisirs-accueil.fr.* A guide to good-value, family-run hotels, **Logis et Auberges de France** *(www.logishotels.com)*, is available from the French Tourist Office, as are lists of other kinds of accommodation, such as hotel-châteaux, bed and breakfasts, etc. **Relais et châteaux** provides information on booking in luxury hotels with character: ✆08 25 82 51 80; www.relaischateaux.com.

ECONOMY CHAIN HOTELS

If you need a place to stop en route, these can be useful, as they are inexpensive (around 45€ for a double room) and generally located near the main road. While breakfast is available, there may not be a restaurant; rooms are small, with a television and bathroom. Central reservation numbers:

- **Accor Hotels** ✆08 25 01 20 11. www.accorhotels.com/fr.
- **Akena** ✆01 69 84 85 17. www.hotels-akena.com.
- **B&B** ✆08 92 78 29 29. www.hotel-bb.com.
- **Etap Hotel** ✆08 92 68 89 00. www.etaphotel.com.

Hikers on the way to Saint-Jacques, Saint-Jean-Pied-de-Port

- **Hotel Formula 1** ℘08 92 68 56 85. www.hotelformule1.com.
- **Première Classe Hôtel** www.premiereclasse.fr.

The chain hotels listed below are slightly more expensive (from 58€), and offer a few more amenities and services. Central reservation numbers:

- **Campanile** ℘01 64 62 59 70. www.campanile.fr.
- **Etap** ℘08 92 68 89 00. www.etaphotel.com.
- **Ibis** ℘08 92 68 66 86. www.ibishotel.com.

RURAL ACCOMMODATION

The **Maison des Gîtes de France et du Tourisme Vert** is an information service on self-catering accommodation in France. *Gîtes* usually take the form of a cottage or apartment decorated in the local style where visitors can make themselves at home, or bed-and-breakfast accommodation *(chambres d'hôtes)*, which consists of a room and breakfast at a reasonable price.
Contact the **Gîtes de France** office *(56 r. St-Lazare, 75439 Paris Cedex 09; ℘01 49 70 75 75; www.gites-de-france.fr)* or their representative in the UK, **Brittany Ferries** *(Millbay Docks, Plymouth, Devon PL1 3EW; ℘0871 244 1401; www.brittany-ferries.com).*
The Gîtes de France website has a good English version. From the site, you can order catalogues for different regions illustrated with photographs of the properties, as well as specialised catalogues (bed and breakfasts, chalets in ski areas, farm stays, etc.).
You can also contact the local tourist offices, which may have lists of available properties and local bed-and-breakfast establishments.
The **Fédération Française des Stations Vertes de Vacances et des Villages de Neige** *(6 r. Ranfer-de-Bretenières, BP 71698, 21016 Dijon Cedex; ℘03 80 54 10 50; www.stationsvertes.com)* is able to provide details of accommodation, leisure facilities and natural attractions in rural locations selected for their tranquillity.
The **Centre permanent d'initiation à l'environnement** (CPIE, Environment awareness centre, *26 r. Beauborg, 75003 Paris; ℘01 44 61 75 35; www.cpie.fr)* has many regional centres dotted around the country and offers nature walks and help with local accommodation to explore national parks and conservation areas around France.

FARM HOLIDAYS

The guide *Bienvenue à la Ferme* is published by and available from the **Assemblée Permanente des Chambres d'Agriculture** (Service "Agriculture et Tourisme", *9 av. George V, 75008 Paris; ℘01 53 57 11 50; www.bienvenue-a-la-ferme.com*). It includes the addresses of farmers providing guest facilities who have signed a charter drawn up by the Chambers of Agriculture. *Bienvenue à la Ferme* farms, vetted for quality and meeting official standards, can be identified by the yellow flower which serves as their logo.

HIKERS

Hikers can consult the guide entitled *Gîtes d'étapes et Refuges* by **A and S Mouraret** *(Rando-Éditions, La Cadole, 74 r. A Perdreaux, 78140 Vélizy; ℘01 34 65 11 89; www.gites-refuges.com).*
The guide and the website are intended mainly for those who enjoy hiking, cycling, climbing, skiing and canoeing-kayaking holidays.

HOSTELS, CAMPING

To obtain an **International Youth Hostel Federation card** (there is no age requirement, and there is a senior card available too), you should contact the IYHF in your own country for information and membership applications (US *℘1 301 495 1240*; UK *℘01629 592 700*; Australia *℘61 2 9283 7195*).
There is a booking service online *(www.hihostels.com)*, which you may use to reserve rooms as far as six months in advance.

There are two main youth hostel *(auberges de jeunesse)* associations in France, the **Ligue Française pour les Auberges de Jeunesse** *(67 r. Vergniaud, 75013 Paris; ☎01 44 16 78 78; www.auberges-de-jeunesse.com)* and the **Fédération Unie des Auberges de Jeunesse** *(27 r. Pajol, 75018 Paris; ☎01 44 89 87 27; www.fuaj.org)*. The Fédération has an informative website providing online booking.

There are numerous officially graded **campsites** with varying standards of facilities along the Atlantic Coast and inland, especially round the lakes in the Landes Forest. The **Michelin Camping & Caravanning France** guide lists a selection of campsites. The area is popular with campers in the summer months, so it is wise to book in advance.

WHERE TO EAT

Turn to the **Addresses** within individual sight listings in the *Discovering* sections for descriptions and prices of typical places to eat **(Eat)** with local flair. The Legend on the cover flap explains the symbols and abbreviations used in these Addresses sections. Coin symbols correspond to the average cost of a meal and are given as guidelines only.

Cannelés - speciality from Bordeaux

S. Sauvignier/MICHELIN

Use the **Michelin Guide France**, with its famously reliable star-rating system and hundreds of establishments all over France, for an even greater choice. If you would like to experience a meal in a highly rated restaurant from the **Michelin Guide**, be sure to book ahead. In the countryside, restaurants usually serve lunch between noon and 2pm and the evening meal between 7.30 and 10pm. It is not always easy to find something in between those two meal times, as the "non-stop" restaurant is still a rarity in provincial towns. However, a traveller can usually get a sandwich in a café, and hot dishes may be available in a brasserie. Typical places to enjoy local specialities are the **bars à vin** (wine bars) of the Bordeaux region and the **cabanes à huîtres** (oyster huts) around Arcachon. Near the Spanish border, many bars offer **tapas** to eat with a glass of wine. In the Gers and Lot-et-Garonne departments, foie gras and confits are on almost every restaurant *menu* (fixed-price meal) or *carte* (as in *à la carte*). In French restaurants and cafés, a service charge is included. Tipping is not necessary, but French people often leave the small change from their bills on their table, or about 5% for the waiter in a good restaurant.

For information on local specialities, see FOOD AND DRINK in the Introduction.

Sites Remarquables du Goût

French authorities have created a quality label for "remarkable gastronomic sites", places where the unique quality of local produce deserves special mention. In Poitou-Vendée-Charentes these places include: the town of Cognac, and St-Gilles-Croix-de-Vie. In Aquitaine and the Basque Country: St-Émilion for its wines, Arcachon for oysters and eels, Labastide d'Armagnac for the eponymous spirits, the prune fair in St-Aubin, and the mountain village of Espelette for its red hot peppers *(www.sitesremarquablesdugout.com)*.

Useful Words and Phrases

Sights

	Translation
Abbaye	Abbey
Beffroi	Belfry
Chapelle	Chapel
Château	Castle
Cimetière	Cemetery
Cloître	Cloisters
Cour	Courtyard
Couvent	Convent
Écluse	Lock (canal)
Église	Church
Fontaine	Fountain
Halle	Covered market
Jardin	Garden
Mairie	Town hall
Maison	House
Marché	Market
Monastère	Monastery
Moulin	Windmill
Musée	Museum
Parc	Park
Place	Square
Pont	Bridge
Port	Port/harbour
Porte	Gate/gateway
Quai	Quay
Remparts	Ramparts
Rue	Street
Tour	Tower

Natural Sites

	Translation
Abîme	Chasm
Aven	Swallow-hole
Barrage	Dam
Belvédère	Viewpoint
Cascade	Waterfall
Col	Pass
Corniche	Ledge
Côte	Coast, hillside
Forêt	Forest
Grotte	Cave
Lac	Lake
Plage	Beach
Rivière	River
Ruisseau	Stream
Signal	Beacon
Source	Spring
Vallée	Valley

On the Road

	Translation
Car Park	Parking
Driving licence	Permis de conduire
East	Est
Garage (for repairs)	Garage
Left	Gauche
Motorway/highway	Autoroute
North	Nord
Parking meter	Horodateur
Petrol/gas	Essence
Petrol/gas station	Station d'essence
Right	Droite
South	Sud
Toll	Péage
Traffic lights	Feu tricolore
Tyre	Pneu
West	Ouest
Wheel clamp	Sabot
Zebra crossing	Passage clouté

Time

	Translation
Today	Aujourd'hui
Tomorrow	Demain
Yesterday	Hier
Winter	Hiver
Spring	Printemps
Summer	Été
Autumn/fall	Automne
Week	Semaine
Monday	Lundi
Tuesday	Mardi
Wednesday	Mercredi
Thursday	Jeudi
Friday	Vendredi
Saturday	Samedi
Sunday	Dimanche

Shopping

	Translation
Bakery	Boulangerie
Bank	Banque
Big	Grand
Butcher's	Boucherie
Chemist's	Pharmacie
Closed	Fermé
Cough mixture	Sirop pour la toux
Cough sweets	Cachets pour la gorge
Entrance	Entrée
Exit	Sortie
Fishmonger's	Poissonnerie
Grocer's	Épicerie

Newsagent, Bookshop	Librairie
Open	Ouvert
Post office	Poste
Pull	Tirer
Push	Pousser
Shop	Magasin
Small	Petit
Stamps	Timbres

Travel

	Translation
Airport	Aéroport
Credit card	Carte de crédit
Customs	Douane
Passport	Passeport
Platform	Voie
Railway station	Gare
Shuttle	Navette
Suitcase	Valise
Train/plane ticket	Billet de train/d'avion

Clothing

	Translation
Coat	Manteau
Jumper	Pull
Raincoat	Imperméable
Shirt	Chemise
Shoes	Chaussures
Socks	Chaussettes
Suit	Costume
Tights	Collant
Trousers	Pantalon

USEFUL PHRASES

Goodbye Au revoir
Hello/good morning Bonjour
How Comment
Excuse me Excusez-moi
Thank you Merci
Yes/no Oui/non
I am sorry Pardon
Why Pourquoi
When Quand
Please S'il vous plaît
Do you speak English? Parlez-vous anglais?
I don't understand Je ne comprends pas
Talk slowly, please Parlez lentement, s'il vous plaît
Where's...? Où est...?
When does the... leave? À quelle heure part...?
When does the... arrive? À quelle heure arrive...?
When does the museum open? À quelle heure ouvre le musée?
When is the show? À quelle heure est la représentation?
When is breakfast served? À quelle heure sert-on le petit-déjeuner?
What does it cost? Combien cela coûte?
Where can I buy a newspaper in English? Où puis-je acheter un journal en anglais?

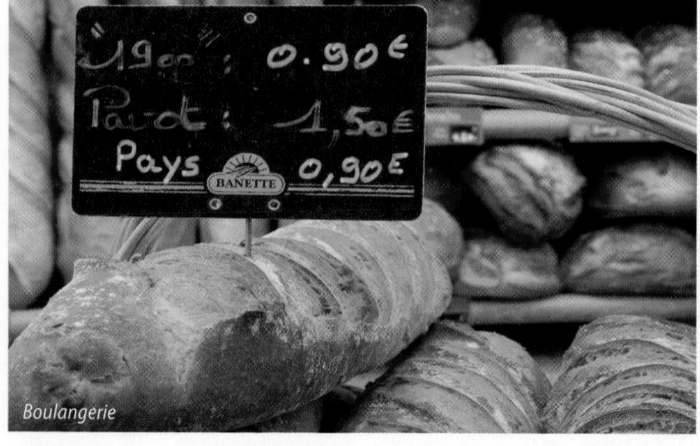

Boulangerie

Where is the nearest petrol/ gas station? Où se trouve la station d'essence la plus proche?
Where can I change traveller's cheques? Où puis-je échanger des cheques de vacances?
Where are the toilets? Où sont les toilettes?
Do you accept credit cards? Acceptez-vous les cartes de crédit?
I have an allergy to nuts/dairy products J'ai une allergie aux fruits à coque et à l'arachide/aux produits laitières

MENU READER

agneau	lamb
alose	shad
anguilles	eels
bière	beer
bœuf	beef
boudin blanc	chicken sausage
boudin noir	blood sausage
brioche	sweet egg-and-butter bread
canard	duck
cèpes	wild mushrooms
chapon	capon
charcuterie	pork meats
chipirones/seiches	squid
choux	cabbage
confit (canard)	(duck) cooked and preserved in fat
crevettes	shrimp/prawns
crudités	raw vegetable salad
éclade	mussels cooked over pine needles
escargots	snails
esturgeon	sturgeon
fèves	broad beans
foie	liver
fromage de brebis	sheep's milk cheese
fruits de mer	seafood
garbure	hearty vegetable and meat soup
glace	ice cream
haricots	beans
homard	lobster
huître	oyster
jambon	ham
langouste/ langoustines	spiny lobster
lapin	rabbit
loukinos	garlic sausage
magret	duck fillet
marrons	chestnuts
mojettes	white beans
moules	mussels
mouton	mutton
noix	walnuts
oie	goose
pain	bread
palombe	wood pigeon
pastis	flaky pastry flavoured with rum or orange blossom
pêche	peach
pétit-déjeuner	breakfast
pibales	young eels
poisson	fish
poule/poulet	chicken
poule au pot	chicken stew with vegetables
prune	plum
pruneau	prune
ravigote	seasoned white sauce
salade	lettuce salad
salmis	stew of roast fowl and game
tournedos	fillet steak
tourteau fromager	sweet cake made with cheese
tourtière	flaky pastry with prune filling
tripotcha	mutton sausage
ttoro	Basque fish stew

well done, medium, rare, raw = *bien cuit, à point, saignant, cru*

Basic Information

BUSINESS HOURS

Banks: Banks are usually open from 9am to noon and 2–5pm and are closed on either Mondays or Saturdays. Banks close early on the day before a bank holiday.
Museums: Many national museums and art galleries are closed on Tuesdays; municipal museums are generally closed on Mondays.
Post offices: see *MAIL/POST.*
Shopping: see *SHOPPING.*

DISCOUNTS

Significant discounts are available for senior citizens, students, youth under age 25, teachers, and groups for public transportation, museums and monuments and for some leisure activities such as movies. Bring student or senior cards with you, and bring along some extra passport-size photos for discount travel cards.
The **International Student Travel Confederation** *(www.isic.org)*, is an association of student travel organisations around the world. The non-profit association sells international ID cards for students, youth under age 25 and teachers. The corporate headquarters address is:

- Herengracht 479, 1017 BS Amsterdam, The Netherlands. +31 20 421 28 00. Fax +31 20 421 28 10.

For other discounts on transportation, see *GETTING THERE: BY TRAIN.*

ELECTRICITY

The electric current is 220 volts/50Hz. Circular two-pin plugs are the rule. Adapters and converters (for hairdryers, for example) are best bought before you leave home. If you have a rechargeable device, read the instructions carefully. Sometimes these items only require a plug adapter: in other cases you must use a voltage converter.

EMERGENCIES

EMERGENCY NUMBERS	
All Emergency Services	112
Police:	17
SAMU (Paramedics):	15
Fire (Pompiers):	18

INTERNET

You'll find internet access in most hotels, cyber-cafés, libraries and tourist offices. Websites such as *www.cybercafe.com* and *cybercafe.fr* are good sources of information for finding such places in France.

PUBLIC HOLIDAYS

There are 11 public holidays in France. In addition, there are other religious and national festivals days, and local saints' days, etc. On all these days, museums and monuments may vary their hours of admission.
In addition to the usual school holidays at Christmas and in the spring

1 January	New Year's Day *(Jour de l'An)*
	Easter Day and Easter Monday *(Pâques)*
1 May	May Day *(Fête du Travail)*
8 May	VE Day *(Fête de la Libération)*
Thu 40 days after Easter	Ascension Day *(Ascension)*
7th Sun–Mon after Easter	Whit Sunday and Monday *(Pentecôte)*
14 July	France's National Day *(Fête de la Bastille)*
15 August	Assumption *(Assomption)*
1 November	All Saints' Day *(Toussaint)*
11 November	Armistice Day *(Fête de la Victoire)*
25 December	Christmas Day *(Noël)*

and summer, there are long mid-term breaks (ten days to two weeks) in February and early November.

MAIL/POST

Main post offices *(www.laposte.com)* open Monday to Friday 9am–noon and 2–7pm, Saturday 9am–noon. Smaller branch post offices generally close at lunchtime between noon and 2pm and at 4pm.

Postage via airmail:

- UK: letter (20g) 0.77€
- North America: letter (20g) 0.89€
- Australia, NZ: letter (20g) 0.89€

Stamps are also available from newsagents and *bureaux de tabac*. Stamp collectors should ask for *timbres de collection* in any post office.

MONEY

CURRENCY

There are no restrictions on the amount of currency visitors can take into France. Visitors carrying a lot of cash are advised to complete a currency declaration form on arrival, because there are restrictions on currency export: if you are leaving the country with more than 7 600€, you must declare the amount to customs.

Notes and Coins

The European currency unit, the **euro**, went into circulation as of 1 January 2002, and since 17 February 2002, euros have been the only currency accepted as a means of payment in France. Coins in francs were accepted by the Banque de France until 2005; notes until February 2012.

For more information, go to www.banque-france.fr.

BANKS

For bank opening times, see BUSINESS HOURS.

A passport is necessary as identification when cashing traveller's cheques in banks. Commission charges vary and hotels usually charge more than banks for cashing cheques.

One of the most economical ways to use your money in France is by using cash dispensers **(ATMs)** to get cash directly from your bank account (with a debit card) or to use your credit card to get a cash advance. Be sure to remember your PIN number; you will need it to use ATMs and to pay with your card in shops, restaurants, etc. Code pads are numeric; use a telephone pad to translate a letter code into numbers. PIN numbers have four digits in France; enquire with the issuing company or bank if the code you usually use is longer. Visa is the most widely accepted credit card, followed by MasterCard; other cards, credit and debit (Plus, Cirrus, Maestro, etc.) are also accepted in some cash machines; check with your card issuer. American Express is more often accepted in premium establishments. Most places post signs indicating which card(s) they accept; if you don't see such a sign and want to pay with a card, ask before ordering or making a selection. Cards are widely accepted in shops, hypermarkets, hotels and restaurants, at tollbooths and in petrol stations.

Before you leave home, check with the bank that issued your card for emergency replacement procedures. Carry your card number and emergency phone numbers separate from your wallet and handbag; leave a copy of this information with someone you can reach easily. If your card is lost or stolen while you are in France, call one of the 24hr hotlines (*see box below*) These numbers are subject to change, but you can also check at ATMs, where they are usually listed.

You must **report any loss or theft** of credit cards or traveller's cheques to the local police, who will issue you with a

American Express 01 47 77 74 84

American Express (traveller's cheques) 08 00 83 28 20

Visa 08 00 90 11 79

MasterCard/Eurocard 08 00 90 13 87

certificate (useful proof to show the issuing company).

SMOKING

In February 2007, France banned smoking in public places such as offices, universities and railway stations. The law became effective for restaurants, cafés, bars, nightclubs and casinos in January 2008.

TELEPHONES

Most public phones in France use prepaid phone cards *(télécartes)*, rather than coins. Some telephone booths accept credit cards (Visa, MasterCard/Eurocard). *Télécartes* (50 or 120 units) can be bought in post offices, branches of France Télécom, *bureaux de tabac* (cafés that sell cigarettes) and newsagents and can be used to make calls in France and abroad. Calls can be received at phone boxes where the blue bell sign is shown; the phone will not ring, so keep your eye on the small digital screen.

NATIONAL CALLS

French telephone numbers have 10 digits. Paris and Paris region numbers begin with 01; 02 in northwest France; 03 in northeast France; 04 in southeast France and Corsica; 05 in southwest France.

INTERNATIONAL CALLS

To call France from abroad, dial the country code (33) + 9-digit number (omit the initial 0). When calling abroad from France, dial 00, then dial the country code followed by the area code and number of your correspondent.
International information:
US/Canada: 00 33 12 11

INTERNATIONAL DIALLING CODES *(00 + code)*			
Australia	✆ 61	**New Zealand**	✆ 64
Canada	✆ 1	**United Kingdom**	✆ 44
Eire	✆ 353	**United States**	✆ 1

International operator:
00 33 12 + country code
Local directory assistance: 12

MOBILE PHONES

In France these have numbers that begin with 06 and 07. Two-watt (lighter, shorter reach) and eight-watt models are on the market, using the Orange, Bouygtel or SFR networks. *Mobicartes* are prepaid phone cards that fit into mobile units. Mobile phone rentals (delivery or airport pickup provided):
World Cellular Rentals:
www.worldcr.com

TIME

WHEN IT IS NOON IN FRANCE, **IT IS**	
3am	in Los Angeles
6am	in New York
11am	in Dublin
11am	in London
7pm	in Perth
9pm	in Sydney
11pm	in Auckland

TIPPING

Since a service charge is automatically included in the price of meals and accommodation in France, any additional tipping is up to the visitor, generally small change, and usually not more than 5%. Taxi drivers and hairdressers are usually tipped 10–15%. As a rule, prices are significantly less expensive in the French regions than in Paris.
Restaurants usually charge for meals in two ways: a *menu*, that is a fixed-price menu with two or three courses, sometimes a small pitcher of wine, all for a stated price, or *à la carte* with each course ordered separately.
Cafés have different prices, depending on location. The price of a drink or a coffee is cheaper if you stand at the counter *(comptoir)* than if you sit down *(salle)* and it is even more expensive if you sit outdoors *(terrasse)*.

CONVERSION TABLES

Weights and Measures

1 kilogram (kg)	**2.2 pounds (lb)**	**2.2 pounds**	*To convert kilograms to pounds, multiply by 2.2*
6.35 kilograms	14 pounds	1 stone (st)	
0.45 kilograms	16 ounces (oz)	16 ounces	
1 metric ton (tn)	**1.1 tons**	**1.1 tons**	
1 litre (l)	**2.11 pints (pt)**	**1.76 pints**	*To convert litres to gallons, multiply by 0.26 (US) or 0.22 (UK)*
3.79 litres	1 gallon (gal)	0.83 gallon	
4.55 litres	1.20 gallon	1 gallon	
1 hectare (ha)	**2.47 acres**	**2.47 acres**	*To convert hectares to acres, multiply by 2.4*
1 sq kilometre (km²)	**0.38 sq. miles (sq mi)**	**0.38 sq. miles**	
1 centimetre (cm)	**0.39 inches (in)**	**0.39 inches**	*To convert metres to feet, multiply by 3.28; for kilometres to miles, multiply by 0.6*
1 metre (m)	3.28 feet (ft) or 39.37 inches or 1.09 yards (yd)		
1 kilometre (km)	**0.62 miles (mi)**	**0.62 miles**	

Clothing

Women	EU	US	UK
Shoes	35	4	2½
	36	5	3½
	37	6	4½
	38	7	5½
	39	8	6½
	40	9	7½
	41	10	8½
Dresses & suits	36	6	8
	38	8	10
	40	10	12
	42	12	14
	44	14	16
	46	16	18
Blouses & sweaters	36	6	30
	38	8	32
	40	10	34
	42	12	36
	44	14	38
	46	16	40

Men	EU	US	UK
Shoes	40	7½	7
	41	8½	8
	42	9½	9
	43	10½	10
	44	11½	11
	45	12½	12
	46	13½	13
Suits	46	36	36
	48	38	38
	50	40	40
	52	42	42
	54	44	44
	56	46	48
Shirts	37	14½	14½
	38	15	15
	39	15½	15½
	40	15¾	15¾
	41	16	16
	42	16½	16½

Sizes often vary depending on the designer. These equivalents are given for guidance only.

Speed

KPH	10	30	50	70	80	90	100	110	120	130
MPH	6	19	31	43	50	56	62	68	75	81

Temperature

Celsius (°C)	0°	5°	10°	15°	20°	25°	30°	40°	60°	80°	100°
Fahrenheit (°F)	32°	41°	50°	59°	68°	77°	86°	104°	140°	176°	212°

To convert Celsius into Fahrenheit, multiply °C by 9, divide by 5, and add 32.
To convert Fahrenheit into Celsius, subtract 32 from °F, multiply by 5, and divide by 9.

NB: Conversion factors on this page are approximate.

Vieux Port, La Rochelle

INTRODUCTION TO FRENCH ATLANTIC COAST

French Atlantic Coast Today

The French Atlantic Coast encompasses an area stretching from the Spanish border to Brittany, and contains myriad cultures. Several local languages are spoken, including Saintongeais and Poitevin to the north, Gascon (a dialect of Occitan) in its core and Basque to the very south, each with a fiercely proud identity which creates a dynamic and exuberant holiday destination.

21C

The French Atlantic Coast has become world renowned for its winemaking and agricultural industries. The locals are also blessed with a number of resorts and offshore islands, which attract a large amount of tourism during the summer months. This is also true of the Vendée and the Charente areas, where tourism businesses now account for an important source of employment.

POPULATION

The area covered in this guide has an estimated population of around seven million, of which almost one million live in the conurbation of Bordeaux, the most notable metropolitan area in the region. The area has enjoyed a steady rise in population mainly due to migration from other regions of France resulting from the array of different industries, such as agriculture, aeronautics and tourism.

LIFESTYLE

As is true of elsewhere in France, every town and village has its own weekly market, where the colours and fragrance of the local farm produce overwhelm the senses. Connoisseurs can travel to experience the gastronomic delights of, among others, the famed wines of Bordeaux or the oysters of Marennes. These sensory delights are complemented by the annual festivals and fêtes held in most villages, usually to celebrate the locally venerated saint or national holidays, such as Bastille Day. In the cities, art lovers can enjoy the cultural sights and museums of Bordeaux and Angoulême.

RELIGION

France is steeped in the belief of *laïcité* (meaning "freedom of conscience"), entailing the separation of Church and State and ensuring the free practice of religious worship. This idea of secularism means that there is no state religion, even though Roman Catholicism remains prevalent throughout the region along with other significant faiths including Protestantism, Islam and Judaism.

SPORT

A popular local nickname for the region is "l'Ovalie", or Land of the Oval Ball. Rugby union is the dominant spectator sport with teams such as Aviron Bayonnais and Biarritz Olympique competing at the highest level of competition. Other popular sports include Basque *pilota* (*pelote* in French) to the south, and the *course landaise*, a bloodless form of bullfighting, especially prevalent in Gascony. World-class surfing and yachting competitions take place along the Aquitaine Coast throughout the summer months.

MEDIA

Daily newspapers in the region include the *Sud Ouest Group*, with 21 editions across 8 *départements*, along with local newspapers such as *Le Journal du Pays Basque*. *France Bleu* broadcasts syndicated radio and *TV7 Bordeaux* is a notable local television channel.

ECONOMY

FISHING INDUSTRY

Since the western part of the region enjoys a favoured situation beside the sea, fishing is naturally one of its principal commercial assets.

Deep-Sea Fishing

Modern trawlers are ideally suited to fishing on the high seas – a branch of

Oysters

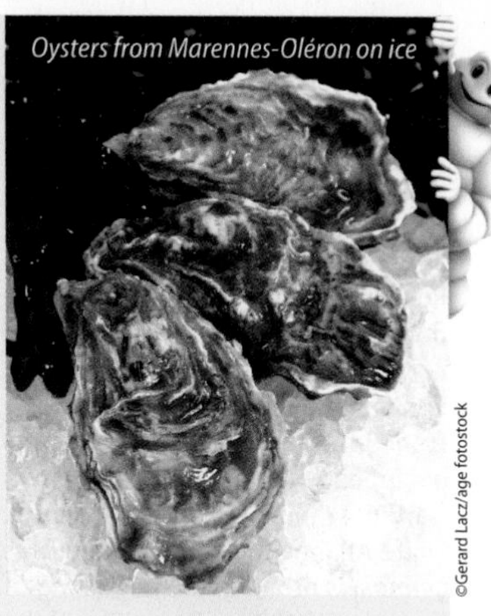
Oysters from Marennes-Oléron on ice

©Gerard Lacz/age fotostock

The Marennes-Oléron basin, which extends from the River Charente to the mouth of the Gironde, is among the most important oyster farming regions in France: the Charente-Maritime *département* alone supplies almost half the national market; Brittany is France's other major oyster-producing area.

History and Biology

The two main varieties, the flat oyster *(plates)* and the concave or deep-shelled oyster *(creuses)*, live in their natural state, respectively, on sandbanks or in beds attached to undersea rocks. The **flat oyster** is hermaphrodite and viviparous (the young are produced live and do not have to be hatched). This variety has been found in the region since Gallo-Roman times, and has been gathered or dredged since then; it was a delicacy on the table of Louis XIV, who was a great oyster lover. In 1920, however, the species was almost entirely destroyed by a disease, and flat oysters can only be found now, in very small quantities, in the region of Marennes. The fleshier, richer **deep-shelled oyster**, with a taste that is less delicate and very different, is unisexual and oviparous (the young are hatched from eggs) as well as being less sensitive to changes in the weather. The variety was introduced into the area accidentally in 1868 when a ship sheltering from a storm stayed too long in the Gironde on its way from Portugal to England with a cargo of these oysters; the cargo was in danger of going bad and the oysters had to be thrown into the sea. The surviving oysters then imposed themselves on the majority of local farms. When disease struck again in 1971, these *portugaises* were in turn supplanted by *japonaises (Crassostrea gigas)* – oysters bred in the Pacific and imported from Japan or Canada (British Columbia).

Exploitation

Ostreiculture (oyster breeding) in France remains very much a cottage industry, frequently a family affair, and still a fairly uncertain business: apart from the risk of disease, oyster farms can be destroyed by pollution, silting up, excess salinity, storms, an unusually cold spell or degeneration of the oysters – which can also be attacked by crabs, starfish or even winkles. The **nassain** (young seed oysters or spats), drifting this way and that with the currents, become attached in summer to **collectors** – lime-washed tiles, slates, wooden stakes or stones, according to the region; these are then transported to the first oyster park. After a year or two the oysters are prised off the collectors – a technique known as **détroquage** – and placed in a second park. They remain a further year or two here, usually in special **pochons** (containers) placed on tables. In the Marennes-Oléron basin the oysters receive a final treatment to mature and refine them, giving them their characteristic pale greenish-blue hue, in fattening pools known as **claires** full of microscopic blue algae. Oysters sold as **spéciales** have spent longer in the *claires* and are less densely distributed in them, than the ordinary **fines de claires**.

the industry which supplies most of Europe's fresh fish and which concentrates its activities at the limit of the continental shelf, where the depth is often 500m/1 640ft or deeper. Sole, bream and hake landed by these trawlers play an important part in the economy of La Rochelle, Les Sables-d'Olonne, the Île d'Yeu, St-Gilles and other ports in the northern coastal section.

Fishing for huge **tuna fish** takes place from June to October, from boats equipped with dragnets and live bait (sardines, anchovies, etc.). The great white Atlantic tuna, known locally as *germon*, is fished at the beginning of the season between Portugal and the Azores, and the fleets then follow its migration north from the Bay of Biscay as far as the southwest of Ireland. Tuna is the main catch brought back to St-Jean-de-Luz.

Coastal Fishing

Though coastal fishing is more limited in its scope than deep-sea fishing, it nevertheless supplies a particular demand – for varieties of fish and seafood which are especially prized when they are absolutely fresh. Small trawlers, motor-boats and local fishing smacks bring in sole, whiting, mullet, mackerel, skate, etc., according to the season and the locality.

To fish **sardines**, fishermen use "turning" nets – seines from 200m/656ft to 300m/984ft long. The catch is landed daily and sold immediately at quayside auctions. The increasing rarity of sardine banks off the Vendée Coast has, however, driven the fleets farther towards the coast of Morocco, where ships with deep-freeze compartments have to be used.

Recreational fishing uses lines, cords, fixed nets, seine nets from the beach, or regionally typical **carrelets** (suspended nets manoeuvred via pulleys from a landing stage). Carrelets remain popular, particularly in the Gironde estuary, although a certain picturesque quality may weigh more in their favour than any particular effectiveness. In the spring, when fish swarm upriver to spawn, the catches of shad and lamprey in the Gironde are at their most plentiful. The eels return at the same time; their tiny **pibales** (elvers) are fished from the shore, thousands at a time, with fine-meshed shrimping nets.

Crustaceans

Lobsters, crabs and crayfish are caught – in wicker pots or hoop nets – mainly in the cold waters off the rocky coasts of the Vendée and the Île d'Yeu. Langoustines (crayfish) are fished farther out by the trawlers. Fishermen from Royan and La Cotinière seek out shrimps and prawns on the banks of the Gironde estuary.

Mussels

The mussel is a bivalve with a blue-black shell, and in the wild lives in colonies on rocks pounded by the sea. It has been farmed since the 13C and is reared commercially along the coast of the province of Aunis – separated (except in the Baie de l'Aiguillon) from the oysters, since the two shellfish are biologically incompatible. The centres of mussel production today are the coast near Brouage, the Île d'Oléron (Baie de Boyardville) and the Anse de Fouras to the south of the province; the Baie de l'Aiguillon to the north of it.

Mytiliculture

This is the French term for mussel breeding, including their fattening and beautifying for the market. The mussels attach themselves to **bouchots** (stakes) driven into the mud or silt in long lines or arranged in grids, where they fatten and grow. The arrangement of the *bouchots* varies from district to district and is subject to strict control. In the Breton Straits the *bouchots à nassain* for the very young mussels, are well offshore, and those where the shellfish grow to commercial size much nearer the coast. The *boucholeurs* visit their mussel beds in small, flat-bottomed boats or, if the tide is low, on their *accons* – flat wooden crates which they slide across the mud with a hefty kick!

Mussels serve as the base for the preparation of a regional delicacy known as *mouclade*.

Salt Marshes

From the 11C to the 18C the marshes, bordering almost the entire Poitou Coast, were one of the principal economic assets of that area, especially in the Aunis and Saintonge regions. The salt trade played an important part in both sea and river traffic. Merchants sailing to northern Europe carried salt as far as the Hanseatic ports, where it was used to preserve fish. Then the receding sea withdrew farther still; the marshes silted up and transformed themselves into *gâts* (fever swamps). Today the only salt pans still worked are on the Île de Noirmoutier and the Île de Ré, with a few more among the Breton-Vendée marshes. The rest have been turned into pastureland, market gardens, nature reserves or *claires* (basins) for fattening oysters.

The working of salt flats is a delicate operation. The marsh is divided into a grid, squared off with small *bossis* (banks) of earth bearing a large proportion of clay. Seawater, brought by the rising tide, is carried into the grid via narrow canals or *étiers*, allowed to settle, and then concentrated in a series of reservoirs that become shallower and shallower. The water in the final pans, known as *œillets*, is no more than 5cm/2in deep. It is here, once the liquid evaporates, that the salt crystallises.

From May to September the *paludier* (salt-worker) "draws" with the help of a large rake (known as a *las* or *rabale*) the grey salt deposit from the bottom of the pan after skimming the white salt off the surface with a flat shovel. The harvest is then assembled in *mulons* (small heaps) at the side of the pan – today often protected against bad weather by plastic sheeting – to be stocked later in the local *salorges* (special salt stores, usually built of wood).

AGRICULTURE

Poitou, the Charentes and the region around Bordeaux all rely heavily on agriculture, with crops on the limestone plains and vines on valley slopes. In the Landes, the forest overshadows everything.

Mixed Farming

Mixed agriculture is still the norm in these areas; tenant farming (with a generous percentage of the crop being given to the landlord), although rapidly disappearing, still exists and the average property rarely exceeds 50ha/125 acres.

Cereals (wheat, maize, oats) in the small farms grow side by side with meadows of clover, alfalfa and other **fodder plants**. A number of slightly less common crops are also grown: in the coastal regions, for example, with their humid atmosphere warmed by the ocean, **early fruit and vegetables** flourish; on the islands (with the exception of the Île d'Yeu) and in the rich alluvial soil of the marshlands, it is easy to grow new potatoes, artichokes, carrots and peas. The melons known as Charentais also grow in this same area, and in recent years these have been so successful that they have spread as far as the Rhône Valley, where they have threatened to supplant the cantaloupe melon. **Market gardens** abound in the lower parts of the Vienne, Thouet and Garonne valleys and those of their tributaries. The Garonne basin, in addition, specialises in tomatoes, various fruits and even tobacco. **Tobacco**, largely a family business, is grown in small fields in the region around Bazas and on the alluvial soil flooring the valleys of the Dordogne, the Lot and the Garonne, where the principal centres are Marmande and Tonneins.

The Pines of the Landes

The huge forest covering the Landes consists mainly of maritime pines, although parasol varieties occur here and there. The maritime pine, with its tall bole ringed by tufts of needles, is not a beautiful tree though it does have a certain elegance – and it grows quickly; it has also brought prosperity to what was once a poor and desolate region.

Resin harvesting in the Landes forest
©A. Thuillier/MICHELIN

Since ancient times it has also been the base of the traditional activity of **gemmage** (resin harvesting). Formerly, the *gemmeur* (gum collector) periodically tapped the tree with the aid of a tool known as a *hapchot*. From the wound made, resin would then bleed into small earthenware cups (called *cramponnés* because they were clamped to the trees). Every few weeks the resin was collected, packed into barrels and sent to distilling plants. Today this practice has largely been superseded by the use of sulphuric acid, which activates the process and has the advantage of being less damaging to the tree. Today the region serves as a processing centre for turpentine, pitch, transparent wrapping material and other solids.

Even when they are very old, the pines remain useful; after they have been "bled dry" of their resin, they are felled and sent to factories which transform them into parquet flooring, crates and wood-fibre boards (especially compressed woodchip sheeting). Large factories producing paper, wood pulp and pine cellulose exist across the region, in particular at Facturen, which is responsible for half of the country's cellulose production.

LIVESTOCK

Cattle

Cattle are reared throughout the region, for both their meat and their milk. Fattening, particularly of the distinctive white Charolais breed, takes place in the fields of the Pays de Retz, the Gâtine de Parthenay, the *bocage* of the Vendée, and on the polders of marshland.

Bressuire and Parthenay, important cattle markets, handle thousands of tawny Parthenay cattle and an increasing number of Charolais. To the east, towards the Massif Central, the Charolais and the chestnut-coated Limousin breeds dominate. In the Gironde, the Blonde d'Aquitaine and Bazas cattle produce the most prized meat.

French breeds (Black-and-Whites and Normans) are bred between Poitiers and La Rochelle and between the Vendée and the Charentes, providing milk to numerous cooperatives. These areas produce cheese, long-life milk and the famous *beurre des Charentes*, a rich, creamy butter.

Sheep, Goats and Horses

Sheep, which originally appeared indigenously on the heaths and pastureland of the region, are increasingly important in these otherwise poor farming areas, in particular the eastern reaches of the Poitou, in the Berry, and in the Gâtine de Parthenay (renowned for its tender Charmoise lamb).

Goat rearing has considerably increased in the southern parts of the Deux-Sèvres and Vienne, based around dairy cooperatives that produce 50% of the country's goat's milk products. **Chabichou**, the celebrated goat's cheese, is a traditional speciality of the region.

Horse rearing has been in steady decline for decades; breeding racehorses, however, remains a thriving business, especially in the Vendée. The Poitou **baudet** (donkey) and the Mellois mule, on the other hand, have become rare to the point where measures have been taken to preserve them from extinction.

Poultry

Poultry is of great economic importance from Clisson to Mont-de-Marsan, with the emphasis on Poitou geese, Bressuire and Barbezieux hens, and white ducks from

Challans. Specialised poultry production is particularly important in the north of the Deux-Sèvres and in the Vendée.
In the east and south of the Landes forests, crops (mainly maize) and poultry farming (yellow, corn-fed chickens; geese; ducks; turkeys) are the mainstays of local agriculture alongside a flourishing foie gras industry.

WINES AND SPIRITS

The areas to the north and the south of the Gironde are known throughout the world for their fine wines, fortified wines, Cognacs and Armagnacs, which have long been exported and play a major role in the local economy.

Wines of Bordeaux

The world-famous Bordeaux vineyards, 105km/65mi from north to south and 130km/81mi from west to east, cover an area of approximately 105 000ha/405sq mi. The region, widely considered the best in the world for fine wines, contains over 8 000 wine-producing *châteaux* (which can mean an estate or simply a property, and not necessarily something resembling a castle), which between them produce wines within 54 different controlled *appellations* under 6 main "family" headings. Added to these are the Crémant de Bordeaux, a sparkling wine, and the local **digestif** spirit called Fine de Bordeaux.
Red wine accounts for approximately 89% of production and white wine for 11%, with an output of around 600 million bottles per year; 40% of the wine is exported to the United Kingdom, China, Hong Kong, Belgium, Germany and the Netherlands.

Red Wines

According to a local saying, "all the edges are rounded off in the bottle" – and red wines do indeed have a remarkable ability to improve with age. The wines of the region include the elegant wines of the Médoc, the delicate, slightly spicy and vigorous Graves, and the wines of St-Émilion, with their richly fruited character.
The Pomerol district is renowned for its warm, deep red wines, while the lesser-known Fronsacare characterised by their full flavour and body. Farther afield, the vineyards of Bourg and the Côtes de Bordeaux are known for their *grands ordinaires* – admirable wines both white and red. The two regional appellations of Bordeaux and Bordeaux Supérieur produce over 50% of the red wines of Bordeaux, also marketed as *grands ordinaires*.

White Wines

The range of white wine available is equally impressive. Pride of place must go to the great wines of Sauternes and of neighbouring Barsac, which produce arguably the best sweet white wines in the world, pressed from grapes benefiting from the effects of the famous noble rot. Less well known but also of note are the whites of Ste-Croix-du-Mont and Loupiac, on the other side of the Garonne.
The dry white Graves are wines of distinction, which, for many, typify the whites of Bordeaux: fresh on the palate, slightly fruity and well structured. An easy-drinking white wine, full of fruit and for drinking young, can be found in the Entre-deux-Mers region (meaning "Between Two Seas": as both the Garonne and the Dordogne rivers which border the region, are tidal).
The finely fragranced Cérons wines, ranging from quite dry to syrupy, are

Seasonal Progress of the Vines

Vines are pruned in the middle of winter. Leaves appear on the vine in April and small clusters of flowers follow a month later, which then turn into the grapes. By July the grapes are beginning to change colour and are left to ripen quietly for another month. The grapes are usually harvested in mid-September, after which time they are taken inside for the wine making process.

a cross between the best wines of the Graves district and Sauternes.

The town of Cadillac, in the Côtes de Bordeaux *appellation*, produces mellow, velvety white wines that are agreeably light.

Appellations

The term **"appellation d'origine contrôlée"** (AOC), which translates as "controlled term of origin", on a wine label, is an assurance of a wine's origins, carrying with it an implication – though not necessarily a guarantee – of quality. AOC products are produced in a traditional manner.

The Médoc, thanks to the variety of its *terroirs* (soils), is classified into eight *appellation contrôlée* zones: Médoc and Haut-Médoc, and more specifically St-Estèphe, Pauillac, St-Julien, Moulis, Listrac and Margaux.

Serving Bordeaux Wines

The red wines of Bordeaux should not be drunk too young (although an exception to this would be Bordeaux and Bordeaux Supérieur); the whites, on the other hand – especially the dry whites – are at their best relatively soon after bottling.

Wines of Gascogne

The region, situated northeast of the Landes and extending south to the Gers and the Pyrénées, produces palatable red wines such as the spicy, tannic Madiran and dry or sweet white wines such as the Pacherenc.

Wines of Agenais

Buzet is a light red wine good for easy-drinking. The Côtes de Duras wines, produced in the north of the Lot-et-Garonne *département* include light, fruity reds and refreshing whites. North of Marmande, the Côtes du Marmandais region is known mainly for its full-bodied fruity red wines.

Wines of Béarn

The Béarn region (*see Le BÉARN, p244*) produces several wines of note, including the famous Jurançon, a heady wine grown on the left bank of the Gave de Pau, and the Rosé du Béarn, once exported to northern Europe, as far as Hamburg.

Wines of the Basque Country

The best known Basque Country wines are the Irouléguy *appellation* red and white wines. The region also produces a yellow or green liqueur distilled from mountain plants, known as Izzara.

Muscadet

This well-known dry white wine which forms, with the Gros Plant and Côteaux d'Ancenis, part of the **Vins de Nantes** group, was accorded *appellation d'origine contrôlée* status in 1936. The vineyards producing the wines of this group extend south of the Loire.

Muscadet is made from the Melon de Bourgogne grape, which came originally from Burgundy. The vines were imported and planted in the Nantes area after the terrible winter of 1709 because of their resistance to frost.

There are three *appellations*, corresponding to three different regions: the Muscadet de Sèvre-et-Maine, which accounts for the major part of the production, the Muscadet des Côteaux de la Loire (which comes from around Ancenis) and plain Muscadet (from the neighbourhood of St-Philbert-de-Grand-Lieu). All of them yield wines that are light and dry, sometimes gently sparkling, with an alcoholic content limited to 12%. Served cold, Muscadet is the perfect accompaniment to fish and seafood.

The **Gros Plant du Pays Nantais** has been classed as a VDQS (*vin délimité de qualité supérieure* – a superior wine) since 1954, but as of the 2011 vintage it has also become an AOC. It is made from the Folle-Blanche grapes grown in the Charentes since the 16C. This light wine (11%) complements seafood in general and shellfish in particular.

Cognac

Cognac, famous for centuries throughout the world, is a distillation of white wines produced in the region of the Cognac *appellation* (essentially the Charente *département*).

A good Cognac should taste like the very essence of fresh grapes, strong and heady. More than 95% of the production is exported to 157 countries worldwide; the US alone accounts for 48% of those sales, with Singapore taking over 25%.

HISTORY

The distillation of wine to make spirits, practised in the region since the 16C, became generalised in the early 17C. The local vintners at first distilled just the wines that did not travel well but later realised that the process could help turnover, reduce excise duties and facilitate storage (between seven and ten barrels of wine are used to make one barrel of Cognac). The taste for the resulting *eau-de-vie* (spirit) spread and it began to be exported, like the wines before it, to northern Europe as an adjunct to the salt trade.

Much of the wine trade at that time was in the hands of the Dutch – who, learning that the people of Charentes burned their wine, dubbed the result *brandewijn* (burned wine). From this the English coined the word "brandy", which has been used in the Anglo-Saxon world ever since. In France the spirit took the name of the town where it was first commercialised, Cognac.

From Cognac the barges and tenders laden with barrels sailed down the River Charente to Tonnay-Charente and La Rochelle, where the cargo was transferred to full-rigged merchantmen bound either for northern Europe or for the colonies. In the late 17C and early 18C, brandy became increasingly popular in London society and as the Dutch lost commercial supremacy of the Cognac market, English merchants and traders began to play a stronger role in the promotion of the drink; the names of several famous Cognac brands still have an Anglo-Saxon ring about them.

Ruined by the devastating outbreak of phylloxera (American aphids) in the 19C, the Cognac vineyards were replanted by the burghers of Cognac, who had themselves escaped ruin because of the huge stocks they held.

THE VINEYARDS

Almost 90 000ha/222 400 acres are planted with vines, most of which are the Ugni Blanc variety (incorrectly termed St-Émilion des Charentes in the region). The vineyards are planted in an area of temperate climate – wet in winter, sunny in summer – and chalky soil similar to that found in the Champagne region, east of Paris.

The finest Cognac, known as Grande Champagne, is produced from vines planted in the centre of this region, where the chalkiest soil is found; the other five classified *crus* or growths – producing more full-bodied and highly flavoured brandies – radiate outwards from this area.

DEVELOPMENT OF COGNAC

Distilling is simply a means of concentrating the strength and flavour of any alcoholic drink by removing most of the water content. The technique stems from the fact that alcohol in chemical terms is more volatile than water: it boils at a lower temperature.

All the alcohol and most of the aromatic elements in a heated wine will therefore evaporate long before the water boils. If this vapour is collected and condensed, the resulting liquid will contain virtually all the alcohol, certain other volatile elements – known as the congenerics – and very little water.

The system of distilling first came west with the Arabs in the 14C (the Arabic term *al embic* is the root of the French *al ambic* – a still – and *al kohol* is the root of alcohol). The Cognac distillation process consists of two stages. During the first distillation, which lasts about eight hours, the wine is heated in a copper Charentais still to produce a liquid containing 25–35% alcohol, known as the **brouillis**. This liquid is then passed back into the still for a period of about 12 hours to produce a clear liquid, which has a maximum alcohol content of 72%. During the distillation process vapours compressed in the still head pass through the swan's neck into a condensing coil, which cools the vapours to produce the liquid.

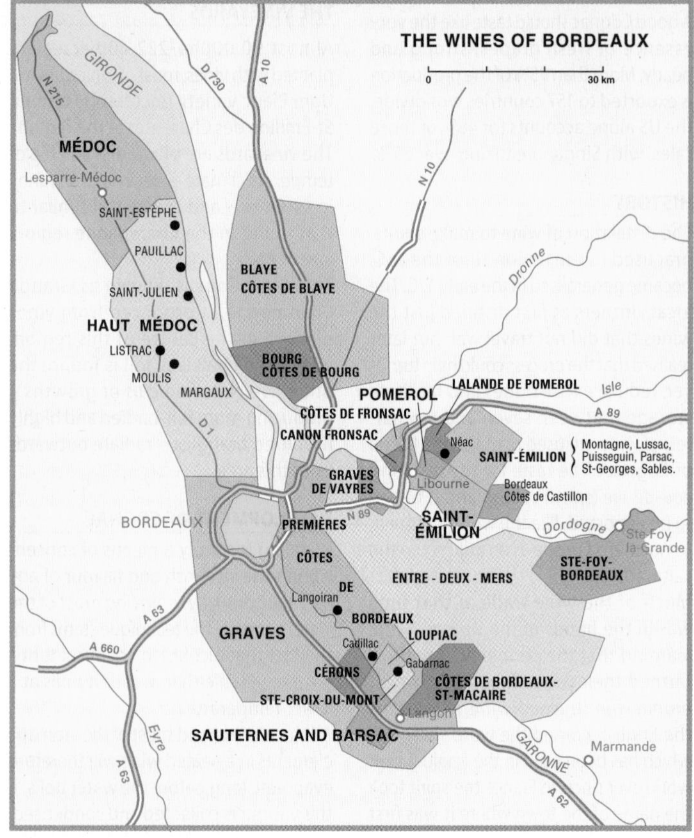

The brandy, fiery but colourless when it leaves the still, is only faintly flavoured; all its character is derived from the maturing process, which takes place in barrels left in the darkness of the producer's well-aired *chais* (stores). Here the pale oak of these barrels, brought from the hills of the Limousin, stimulates the oxidisation of the spirit, adds tannin and the characteristic amber colour of the brandy. The incredible amount of evaporation from the barrels is equivalent to the loss of 12 million bottles of spirit every year, referred to as the "angels' share".

Finally, the spirit is diluted with distilled water to the accepted legal strength for the market. It is cut and blended with brandies of different ages, from different *crus*, and sugar and caramel are added to obtain the required colour, until a consistent quality is arrived at with characteristics recognisable as typical of a particular brand.

There are several different categories of Cognac, classified according to the length of time they have spent maturing in the oak casks.

The three-star label signifies a brandy of normal quality, between five and nine years of age. The acronyms VO (Very Old) and VSOP (Very Special Old Pale) apply to Cognacs aged on average between 12 and 20 years. The terms Vieille Réserve, Grande Réserve, Royal, Vieux, XO, Napoleon, Extra, etc. are used to distinguish Cognacs that are 20 to 40 years old or even older. The words Fine Champagne on the label identify a Cognac that is a blend of the Grande and Petite Champagne growths.

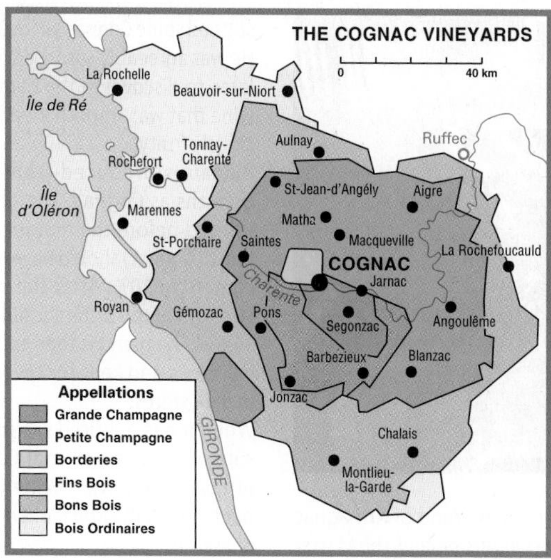

Armagnac

Armagnac is very different from Cognac both in style and in the technique used to make it. This spirit should be velvety smooth, dry and with a pungent smell; it is considered to have less finesse than Cognac.

The region legally permitted to sell its products under the name "Armagnac" extends over an area of 35 000ha/ 135sq mi, which is roughly triangular in shape. This area is divided into three sections: **Haut-Armagnac** (Upper Armagnac, the hilly region of Auch) in the east; **Ténarèze** (around Condom) in the centre; and **Bas-Armagnac** (Lower Armagnac, the Eauze region) in the west. Armagnac from Ténarèze is full and rich in flavour, whereas the brandy made in Bas-Armagnac has a more fruity character. Only white wines made from 10 approved varieties of vine may be distilled to make Armagnac, and their common characteristic is a strong, fixed level of acidity. The most popular of these grapes are the Ugni Blanc and the Folle-Blanche varieties (known as Gros Plant in the Nantes area).

Armagnac is distilled in a sort of double boiler, at a much lower temperature than Cognac. This results in a stronger flavour and aroma which, combined with the effect of the sappy black oak casks in which it is stored, adds character; it also matures faster than Cognac.

Organic Wines

Officially recognised around 15 years ago, organic winemaking has become increasingly prevalent in the region. The Organic Wine Growers Union of Aquitaine (Syndicat des vignerons bio d'Aquitaine) represents producers who follow the principles set out by this low-impact form of winemaking, which prohibits the use of chemical fertilisers, pesticides and other products. Bordeaux is among the largest organic producers in France, with over 1 300 hectares/3 200 acres of organic vines and 100 organic producers. The majority of the wines are exported to northern Europe, with Germany the largest importer. At the end of 2005, the European Commission included winemaking within its rules governing organic production, and a research programme was undertaken (2006–09) to determine which oenological practices were permitted during its elaboration.

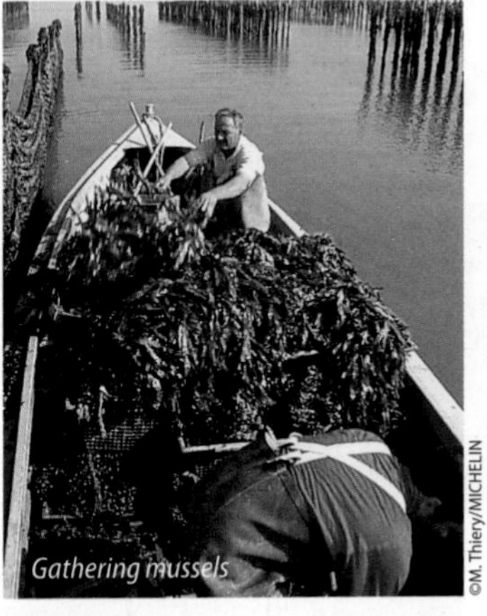
Gathering mussels

©M. Thiery/MICHELIN

Like Cognac, each brand of Armagnac has its expert *maître de chai*, the Master Blender who creates the finished product with its particular identity.

FORTIFIED WINES AND APÉRITIFS

Floc

Floc is the old Gascon word for flower. Floc de Gascogne – a fortified wine between 16% and 18%, about the strength of port or sherry – is either red or white and is drunk chilled as an apéritif. It is made from selected wines grown in the region of the Armagnac *appellation* and is a blend of the must from these wines with Armagnac of more than 52%, aged in oak barrels.

Pousse-Rapière

Also drunk as an apéritif, Pousse-rapière was invented in the 16C at Château Monluc, near the town of Condom, by Marshall Blaise de Monluc, an army commander and man of letters. It is made from Armagnac mixed with fruit. Add it to dry sparkling wine for a cocktail.

Pineau des Charentes

This is a fortified apéritif wine, classified *appellation d'origine contrôlée* and produced in the same area as Cognac; it is made in both red and rosé forms, and it should be served chilled.

The apéritif was created by accident in the 16C, when a vine-grower accidently poured grape juice into a barrel which still had some Cognac left in the bottom. He was agreeably surprised, some years later, to discover in the barrel a strong wine that was smooth, heady and deliciously fruity.

Pineau is produced from the same growths as Cognac. The grape juices utilised before the *mutage* (the addition of Cognac) should have an alcoholic content of 10%. After the *mutage* the strength of the drink should be at least 16.5%. The blend is then transferred to oak casks and kept for several months in dark stores.

When it has matured sufficiently, it is submitted to an official Commission of Tasters who will decide whether or not it merits the *appellation* Pineau des Charentes.

Pineau sells very well in France and is exported primarily to Belgium, Canada and northern Europe.

FOOD AND DRINK

Visitors to the Atlantic Coast region of France have a rich variety of fine local products to enjoy.

All along the coast itself good, fresh seafood is available whereas inland, in Poitou and the Charentes, the "simple, honest and direct, even rustic" cuisine, according to the great chef Curnonsky (1872–1956), is based on fine, fresh ingredients and careful preparation. In the Bordeaux region the accent is naturally on wines and wine sauces.

HORS-D'ŒUVRES

For lovers of seafood the obvious starter must be oysters from Arcachon or Marennes, or perhaps mussels from Aiguillon; *pibales* (elvers) from the Gironde, either grilled or *à la ravigote* (with a highly seasoned white sauce), are a delicious alternative.

Those who prefer *charcuterie* might like to try the famous Bayonne ham or the ham from Poitou, or such Basque specialities as **loukinkos** (miniature garlic sausages) and **tripotcha**, a mutton boudin or blood sausage not unlike a small black pudding. Gourmets will also delight in the rich foie gras (prepared goose and duck livers) of Gers and the Landes.

A glass of chilled Pineau des Charentes may be taken as an apéritif or savoured with foie gras, whereas a chilled white wine such as a Graves or an Entre-Deux-Mers served at 8–10°C/46.4–50°F is a delightful accompaniment to oysters, fish, crustaceans and other shellfish.

FISH DISHES

This area favoured with an abundance of water – both fresh and salt – offers the choice of sole or turbot from the *pertuis* (straits), fresh sardines from Royan or Les Sables-d'Olonne, stuffed carp in the Poitou fashion or **chipirones** – tiny cuttlefish, stuffed or cooked in a casserole. Near Bordeaux a wide range of fish is caught in the Gironde estuary, including shad, smelt, salmon, sturgeon, eels and lamprey.

MEAT, POULTRY AND VEGETABLES

The quality of meat in the region, whether it be a *chevreau* (young goat), Charmoise mutton or Pauillac lamb, is invariably excellent. Many dishes around Bordeaux are served with a wine sauce; tender steaks accompanied by this sauce will be described on the menu as *à la Bordelaise*.

The superb quality of vegetables grown in Charentes help form the base for the delicious *pot-au-feu* (beef stew) known locally as **le farci**; the local broad beans, haricots, peas and Chinese cabbage can equally well be cooked *à la crème* (with cream) or with *beurre de Surgères* (a butter sauce).

Poultry specialities include *poule-au-pot* (chicken stew), Poitou goose with chestnuts, Challans duck and green peas, Barbezieux capon or chicken, and wood-pigeon *salmi* (casserole or ragout). Duck, if it is not conserved in its own fat (the delicious *confit de canard*), may be roasted or served as a *magret* (slices of breast).

Red wines from Médoc or Graves, served cool (cellar temperature), are an ideal complement to poultry, white meat and light dishes, while those from St-Émilion, Pomerol or Fronsac, served at room temperature, are wonderful accompaniments to game, red meat, mushrooms and cheese.

CHEESE

In the Poitou, Vendée and Charentes regions it is normal to start off the dessert course with cheeses, for the local varieties are essentially unsalted cottage cheeses made from curdled milk or cream which can be taken with sugar if desired. These include **Caillebote d'Aunis**, a crustless sheep's cheese (sometimes made with goat's or cow's milk), and **Jonchée niortaise**, a goat's cheese served on a rush platter. Equally delicious is the Poitou **Chabichou**, another strongly flavoured goat's cheese. The sheep's cheeses of the Basque Country and Béarn remain characteristic local products. A traditional way to finish a meal in the Basque Country is with a slice of cheese topped with cherry preserves from Itxassou.

FRUIT AND DESSERT

Delicious Charentais melon is served in the summer months as a dessert, as are peaches and plums from the valley of the Garonne, or succulent prunes steeped in Armagnac. Baked desserts include Poitou cheesecake *(tourteau fromager)*, macaroons from St-Émilion, Charentais gâteau, and *clafoutis* (dark cherries baked in a sweet batter). Sweetmeats include Poitiers *nougâtines*, chocolate *marguerites* and *duchesses* from Angoulême, and angelica-based sweets from Niort.

Prunes of Agen

The exquisite dessert wines of Sauternes, Barsac, Ste-Croix-du-Mont and Loupiac, served very cold (5°C/41°F), are the perfect accompaniment to sweet dishes or simple sliced peaches; a fine Cognac makes an excellent digestif.

THE BASQUE COUNTRY

MYSTERIOUS ORIGINS

The origins of the Basque people and their common tongue has always been an enigma. All that is known for certain is that they were driven out of the Ebro Valley in Spain by the Visigoths and founded the kingdom of Vasconia in the western Pyrénées.

The Vascons of the plain then intermarried with the local peoples of Aquitaine and became Gascons. Those who remained in the mountains fiercely safeguarded their own traditions and their language, Euskara, which binds the race together.

TOPOGRAPHY

The landscape of the Basque Country (Pays Basque) presents a dramatic contrast with that of Bordeaux and the moors to the north. Suddenly there are mountains all around and the cliffs and rugged rocks along the coast are a complete contrast to the long, level beaches of the Landes. The Basque hinterland consists of green valleys dotted with traditional white houses. The Basque Country is one of the most distinctive regions in France.

The geology of the Basque region seems somewhat chaotic, marked by the last collapse of the folds of the Pyrénées. The valleys are full of winding roads making communications between them difficult. One 17C chronicler described it as "very bumpy country". This partly explains the former division of the country into small states, each with its separate identity. The seven Basque provinces nevertheless share a unique linguistic and cultural heritage, on both the French and Spanish sides of the Pyrénées. Their common motto, in the Basque language, is *Zazpiak-bat* – "Seven-in-One".

This guide covers the three provinces on the northern side of the border, those in the French sector of the Basque Country, including **Le Labourd**, La Basse-Navarre (Lower Navarre) and **La Soule**.

Spanish or French name and its Basque equivalent

Bayonne/Baiona
Biarritz/Miarritze
Bilbao/Bilbo
Hasparren/Hazparne
Mauléon/Maule
Pamplona/Iruña
St-Jean-de-Luz/Donibane-Lohizun
St-Étienne-de-Baïgorry/Baigorri
St-Jean-Pied-de-Port/Donibane-Garazi
St-Palais/Donapaleu
San Sebastián-Donostia
Tardets-Sorholus/Atharratze-Sorholüze
Ustaritz/Uztaritze

BASQUE AUTONOMY AND NATIONALISM

In the 9C **Íñigo Arista** founded the Basque dynasty and became King of Pamplona. Two centuries later, Sancha the Great ascended to the throne of Pamplona and reunited the Basques on either side of the Pyrénées. This is where the history of the Basque Country begins, intimately linked to that of both Spain and France. Before the French Revolution, the French Basque provinces held on to their political autonomy. Leaders from each village met to discuss territorial matters, after which each province would hold an assembly. Royal emissaries regularly consulted these assemblies before making political decisions.

The French Revolution in 1789 brought an end to these special rights and the three French Basque provinces joined with Béarn to form the Basses-Pyrénées *département*.

At the end of the 19C, the Spanish Basques were quick to join the great nationalist movement spreading through Europe. In 1895 **Sabino Arana Goiri** (1865–1903) founded the **Euzko Alderdi Jeltzalea** (Basque Nationalist Party) in Bilbao. His

Playing pilota

Pelote Basque

The traditional game of *pelote basque*, played against a high, orange-coloured wall or *fronton*, is very popular among the men and boys all over the region. One version, known as *le grand chistera* (the name of the long wicker scoop strapped to one arm), is the most frequently played in official competitions and tourist exhibitions. The ball is flung against the *fronton* wall and caught up immediately or after a single rebound, and flung back. In professional games, it is not uncommon for the hard ball, covered with goatskin, to travel at speeds of 240kph/150mph!

A more recent variation, *la cesta punta,* has gained fans. This is the *jai alai* (*jai alai* comes from the Basque for merry festival) played in Latin America, against three walls (front, left and back). Points are marked by hitting the ball between vertical lines marked on the left wall. Spectators sit on the open side, with the front wall to their right, the left wall in front of them, and the back wall on their left.

There are also older, subtler variations, which some traditionalists prefer, including *yokogarbi* (with a small glove) and barehanded *pilota* (*pelote* in French). Different games are played by teams of three or two, or one-on-one. In the *pasaka* game, players face each other across a net, as in tennis, and wear gloves. And in all the small villages in the Basque Country, wherever you see a *fronton*, there will always be boys with their *palas* (wooden rackets) practising the sport.

aim was to reunite the seven Basque provinces in France and Spain and form one confederate state, which he first called Euskeria, changing it in 1896 to **Euskadi**, the name still used today by the Basque Separatist Movement. In 1894, Arana designed the **Ikurrina** – a red flag with two green-and-white crosses. Autonomy was granted to the three Spanish Basque provinces on 11 October 1936, in exchange for Republican support against Franco's followers during the Spanish Civil War. In 1937, however, the new Basque government was suppressed in Guernica, and Franco's regime set out to repress and persecute Basque culture. This was the beginning of **ETA** (Euskadi Ta Askatasuna, meaning "Basque Homeland and Liberty"), the underground armed separatist movement. After Franco's death, the Spanish Basque Country gained greater autonomy and in 1978 became Euskadi.

EMIGRATION

Not entitled to a share in their father's estate, younger children often left to seek their fortune elsewhere, emigrating in particular to Argentina, Uruguay, Paraguay, then Chile, Colombia and Mexico. During the 19C, 90 000 French Basques travelled across the Atlantic where they raised animals, exported wool, cut wood and traded in timber, just as they had done in their homeland.

From the turn of the 20C until 1960, the Basques emigrated to the United States, and more especially, California. Most of them were shepherds from Basse-Navarre. With the help of an immigration agency, they went to tend sheep in the Rocky Mountains, where they had to endure far harsher weather conditions than they had known in the Basque Country. Some remained, totalling 57 793 in 2000. Although they are now a part of American society, they have been careful to keep up their old traditions.

BASQUE ARCHITECTURE

The town hall, the church and the *pilota* (*pelote* in French) court are the three focal points of Basque community life. They are all centred around the main village square. The **Basque church** plays a fundamental role, and the village is symbolically constructed around it. Many worshippers attend daily church services, usually celebrated in the Basque language.

The traditional houses in Labourd, perhaps the most attractive in the Basque Country, have inspired the design of many suburban villas and holiday homes. The exposed wooden framework, usually painted a reddish-brown, contrasts with the original walls of cob (compressed loam, clay or chalk reinforced with straw) coated with whitewashed rough cast. Houses are east-facing and are sheltered from rain, brought by the westerly winds from the Atlantic, by a huge overhanging tiled roof.

The houses in Basse-(Lower)-Navarre have a stone framework and semicircular balconies. The darker, slate roofs found in La Soule are an indication of the region's proximity to the Béarn region. Basque houses all share the characteristic white finish, and many proudly carry over their front doors the date of their construction or their owner's name. Nowhere else in France is the family so closely connected with the home.

Jean Baptiste Darroquy and his son Maurice Darroquy from the French Basque were perhaps the best-known architects of the 20C. Both were born in St-Jean-de-Luz, and their work can be seen in several local buildings, including the 1930s mansion of the Hotel de Chantaco and the St-Jean-de-Luz *hôtel de ville*. Jean Baptiste Darroquy also worked on the modernist exterior of the Campos Elíseos Theatre in Bilbao.

Before the French Revolution, furniture, the right to use common land, burial and church rights (the place occupied in church determined one's social status) were attached to the house, which was an economic and social entity passed down generations. The master of the household, the **etcheko jaun**, had ultimate authority and his main concern was to safeguard the family inheritance. The house was left to the son or daughter designated as the eldest child.

Basque Festivities

Basque dance in traditional attire

Jean-Daniel Sudres/hemis.fr

The Basque people are proud of their heritage, and cultural celebrations are common throughout the year, with festivals celebrating everything from the Espelette pepper to the *sagardotegi* cider houses. A rich tradition of dancing, singing and communal activities continues today, with young men – most of the traditional dances do not include female partners – travelling from village to village. Combinations of black, red and white clothing are worn. The distinctive Basque beret, made of black felt, is still widely worn by the men.

Dancing

The dances are numerous and complex. They are generally accompanied by a *tchirulä* (three-holed ocarina or flute) and a *ttun-ttun* (small drum) or a stringed tambourine, though an accordion, cornet or clarinet is sometimes used. The famous Basque leaps (danced by men only) have many different steps. The striking contrast between the stillness of the torso accompanied by an expressionless face, and the incredibly agile leg movements, is common to all of them. The **Fandango**, a dance described as "both chaste and passionate", refers to man's eternal pursuit of his female ideal. The movements of the woman's arms and the upper part of her body harmonise with alternating rhythms representing invitation and flight. For the celebrated "Wineglass Dance", the fleet-footed men from La Soule wear dazzling costumes. The *zamalzain* (a dancer who appears, in a wicker frame, as both a horse and its rider) and the other dancers perform complicated steps around a glass of wine placed on the ground. Each of the dancers stands on the glass for a fraction of a second, without breaking it or spilling a drop of its contents.

Singing

Basque songs are haunting melodies with lyrics inspired by everyday life (in much the same way as the American Blues). French Basques sometimes sing *Gernikako Arbola* ("The Tree of Guernica"), the sacred song of the Spanish Basques which has practically become their national anthem. In it, the Oak of Guernica – the Basque village devastated by Fascist air raids during the Spanish Civil War and immortalised by Picasso – symbolises *fueros*, or local freedom.

La Force Basque

If you attend a local fair, you may witness competitions between the men of neighbouring villages. There are eight established tests of strength, performed by teams of twelve; each team member has his own special prowess. The feats they perform include spinning a 350kg/770lb wagon around with one hand, chopping or sawing tree trunks at top speed, running a race with a sack weighing 80kg/176lb slung across the shoulders – all concluding with a great game of tug-of-war between the teams.

History

PREHISTORY

The Quaternary Era began about two million years ago. It was during this period that glaciers developed (the Günz, Mindel, Riss and Würm glacial stages), spreading over the highest mountains. However, the most significant event of the period was the appearance of the first humans in Europe, and more particularly in the Pyrénées. Archaeology and scientific methods of dating have made it possible to classify various phases of evolution – Palaeolithic (Old Stone Age), Mesolithic (Middle Stone Age), Neolithic (New Stone Age) – which can themselves be subdivided into different periods.

LOWER PALAEOLITHIC

The Lower Palaeolithic period is represented in the Pyrénées by Tautavel man, who came to light when the remains of a human skull were discovered in a layer of ancient sediment in the **Caune de l'Arago** in 1971 and 1979.

Tautavel man belongs to the *Homo erectus* genus, which inhabited Roussillon 450 000 years ago. He was between 20 and 25 years old and was able to stand upright, about 1.65m/5ft 4in tall. He had a flat, receding forehead, prominent cheekbones, and rectangular eye sockets beneath a thick projecting brow. Since no trace of any hearth has been found, it is assumed that this intrepid hunter, who had not mastered the use of fire, ate his meat raw.

The first hunters who came to live in the Caune de l'Arago used it for several purposes: as a look-out to keep track of the movements of animals which had come to drink from the Verdouble; as a temporary place to set up camp and dismember their prey; and as a workshop for manufacturing tools.

Palynology (the analysis of fossilised pollen grains) has helped to determine the specific characteristics of flora and fauna from different prehistoric periods. Although the alternation of climates produced changes (from grassy steppes to deciduous forests), Mediterranean plant species (such as pines, oaks, walnut trees, plane trees and wild vines) have always been present. There was much game in the area: large herbivores included various types of deer and mountain goats, prairie rhinoceros, bison, musk ox and an ancient species of wild sheep. Carnivores (bears, wolves, dogs, polar foxes, cave lions, wild cats) were hunted for their fur. Small game comprised rodents (hares, voles, beavers, field mice) and birds still to be found today (golden eagles, lammergeier vultures, pigeons, rock partridges, red-billed choughs).

The tools found are in general quite small (scrapers, notched tools). The largest tools found are pebbles, measuring on average 6cm–10cm/2in–4in, made into choppers, or flat two or poly-sided implements of varying degrees of sharpness. These early humans used material they found nearby such as quartz or schist, and more rarely limestone, flint and jasper.

MIDDLE PALAEOLITHIC

The presence of numerous Mousterian deposits is evidence that **Neanderthal man** was present in the Pyrénées. Taller than *Homo erectus*, he had a well-developed skull (1 700cu cm/104cu in). He was forced to adapt to the climatic conditions of the Würm glacial period.

Neanderthal man produced more sophisticated, specialised tools. He fashioned numerous double-sided implements, stone knives with curved edges, chisels, scrapers, pointed tools and all kinds of notched implements. His evolution is also evident in the construction of vast dwelling and burial places.

UPPER PALAEOLITHIC

With the advent of *Homo sapiens*, there was now a significant human presence in the Pyrénées. During the Aurignacian period, stone implements were supplemented with bone and horn.

The appearance of long thin wooden spears with metal tips *(assegais)*, awls and spatulas pointed to a technical evolution which progressed still further during the Solutrean and Magdalenian peri-

ods. Towards the end of the last Würm glacial period (Würm IV), a transformation in landscape and fauna occurred, with boar and deer predominating from now on. Humans both hunted and fished. However, the most revolutionary change was the birth of art. Sculpted human figures (the Aurignacian "Venuses") and cave paintings are of exceptional archaeological interest. The animals, painted in red or black, on the walls of **Niaux** cave look strikingly realistic.

MESOLITHIC AGE

At the end of the Ice Age, the historical landscape of the Pyrénées became established. The Mesolithic Age is, in fact, an intermediary phase during which a multitude of civilisations appeared. During the Azilian culture (named after the **Mas d'Azil** cave), which began at the end of the Upper Palaeolithic period, the harpoon became an increasingly important weapon. Art, on the other hand, was restricted to enigmatic pebbles with symbolic markings.

NEOLITHIC AGE

The Neolithic Age is characterised by polished (as opposed to chipped) stone tools and the use of earthenware. This evolution was accompanied by a decisive change in economy and lifestyle. However, in the eastern Pyrénées and the Ariège, evolution appears to have been slower, for it has been recorded that the local post-Palaeolithic population, who were joined by groups from outside the Pyrénées, remained static; they continued to live in caves and earthenware came into use only sometime later.
Farther north, valuable ethnological information was discovered in the Font-Juvénal shelter, between the River Aude and the Montagne Noire.
As early as the fourth millennium, agriculture and cattle-rearing had become a means of subsistence, with wheat and barley being cultivated. At the same time, dwellings were adapted to meet increasingly elaborate domestic requirements, a fact borne out by the discovery of flat hearths for cooking, air vents to raise the combustion temperature, supporting structures (posts and slabs) and silos for storage.

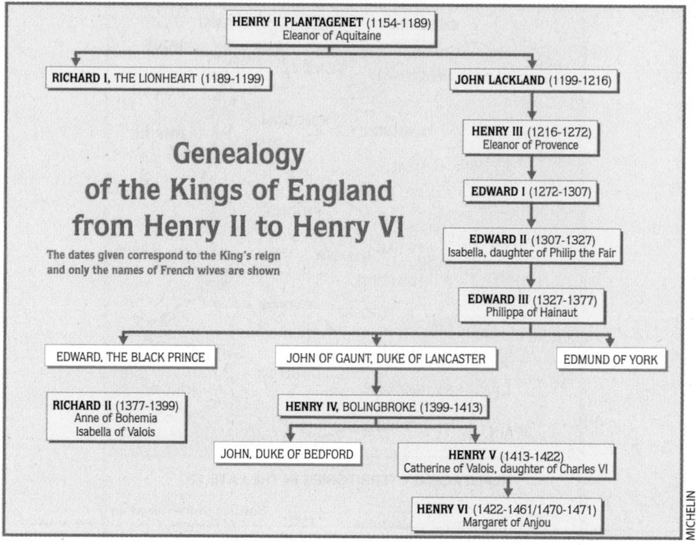

In the Narbonne region, rural communities with specialised activities, using elaborate implements, started to barter and trade with each other. Megalithic constructions (dolmens and tumili) were introduced to the Pyrénées from the western zone during the third millennium.

The middle mountain slopes were the most densely populated. Activities included stock-rearing and, increasingly, the making of weapons (arrows, axes and knives). Jewellery (necklaces and bracelets) and earthenware (bowls and vases) became more widespread. In the Catalan region, the Megalithic culture lasted until the Bronze Age.

TIME LINE

THE ROMAN CONQUEST

72 BC Foundation of Lugdunum Convenarum (St-Bertrand-de-Comminges), religious capital of the population south of the River Garonne, by Pompey.

56 BC Aquitaine conquered by Crassus, Caesar's lieutenant.

INVASIONS, THE RISE OF THE CAROLINGIAN EMPIRE AND THE HUNDRED YEARS' WAR

2C–4C AD **Introduction of Christianity** in Gaul. St Hilaire elected Bishop of Poitiers.

276 Germanic invasion.

5C **Visigoth Kingdom** in Aquitaine: continuation of the Latin culture and Roman law.

End 6C **The Vascons**, Basque mountain people from the south, driven back by the Visigoths, settle in the flat country Gascogne (Gascony).

507 Defeat of **Alaric II**, King of the Visigoths, by Clovis at Vouillé (north of Poitiers).

732 The Arab advance into Europe is halted by Charles Martel at **Moussais-la-Bataille**.

778 **Kingdom of Aquitaine** created by **Charlemagne**.

801 Barcelona taken from the Arabs by Charlemagne and Spanish Marches organised.

820 Start of the Norman incursions. Destruction of Saintes, Angoulême (c.850) and Bordeaux.

c.950 Beginning of pilgrimages to Santiago de Compostela.

1058 **Union of the duchies** of Aquitaine and Gascogne. The southwest under the hegemony of the Comtes (Comtes of Poitiers and Angoulême).

1137 Marriage of Eleanor of Aquitaine to Louis, son of the French King.

ELEANOR OF AQUITAINE (C.1122–1204) AND THE PLANTAGENET TERRITORIES

The marriage in 1137 of Eleanor, the only daughter of **William of Aquitaine**, to Louis, the French *dauphin*, brought with it a dowry which included the duchies of Guyenne, Gascogne, Périgord, Limousin, Poitou, Angoumois and Saintonge, plus suzerainty over the Auvergne and the Comté of Toulouse. Her husband was crowned Louis VII the same year. Fifteen years later, in 1152, the marriage ended in divorce; Eleanor retained her lands. Eleanor's subsequent marriage to **Henry Plantagenet** in 1154 was a political disaster for the Capetian dynasty: the combined possessions of the bride and groom, extending from the English Channel to the Pyrénées, were as vast as those of the French Crown. Henry's crowning as Henry II of England finally upset the fragile international equilibrium; the resulting Anglo-French struggle lasted on and off for 300 years.

Later, separating from her second husband, Eleanor left London for Poitiers where she held a brilliant court. From 1173 her various intrigues – she supported her son Richard the Lionheart in the fight against his father, Henry, for example – resulted in her being imprisoned in London, and she was only released on Henry's death 15 years later in 1189. She took up her plotting again, this time against her youngest son, John (Lackland), and Philippe Auguste, King of France. Eleanor spent her later life peacefully at her castle on the Isle of Oléron and finished her days at Fontevraud Abbey, where she is buried, together with her husband Henry Plantagenet.

1224 Poitou attached to the French Crown.

1345 Start of the **Hundred Years' War** in Aquitaine.

1356 The French King, **Jean le Bon**, captured by the English at the Battle of Poitiers and taken prisoner by the **Black Prince**.

1360 **Treaty of Brétigny**: the duchies of Aquitaine, Aunis, Saintonge and Angoulême become possessions of the English Crown.

1369 **Jean de Berry** installed as Governor of Poitou.

1380 Restriction of the English presence in the southwest to Bordeaux and Bayonne, thanks to the formidable **Constable du Guesclin** (who had chased the *grandes compagnies* – bands of terrorising mercenaries and brigands – into Spain).

1422 **Charles VII** proclaimed King in Poitiers.

1450–1500 Dismantling of English Gascony; re-attachment of the Comté of Armagnac and Comminges to the French Crown.

1453 Final battle of the Hundred Years' War, won by the Bureau brothers at Castillon-la-Bataille. Progressive abandonment of France by the English.

FROM THE RENAISSANCE TO THE REVOLUTION: WARS OF RELIGION

1484 **The Albrets** – Kings of Navarre – become all-powerful in the Gascon Pyrénées.

1494 Birth of **François I** in Cognac.

1515 Accession of François I. Battle of Marignano: victory for François over the Swiss and the Italians; northern Italy becomes French.

1533–34 The doctrine of the Reformation preached by

War in the Vendée (1793–96)

By early 1793 a combination of the execution of Louis XVI, years of resentment over the religious issue capped by the rounding up and persecution of priests, the imposition of arbitrary taxes and the Convention's decision to conscript 300 000 men triggered an insurrection and a wave of riots in the west of France.

In Maine, Normandy and Brittany, where the rebels were known as the *chouans* and were fairly loosely dispersed, operating in a guerrilla fashion, the authorities did regain control; in the territories south of the River Loire, however, where fewer troops were available and communications were more difficult, the government collapsed. In this area, collectively known as the **Vendée Militaire**, the rebels were able to form the Catholic and Royal Army. Their strongholds were in the Gâtine, the *bocage* and the marshes – difficult country to penetrate, criss-crossed with hedgerows and perfect for ambushes, and in the Retz district, around the Lac de Grand-Lieu.

Led at first by Royalists of peasant stock such as **Jacques Cathelineau**, a pedlar, and the game-keeper **Jean-Nicolas Stofflet**, the peasants themselves soon called upon their gentlemen (local nobles, estate stewards, priests) for help: these included **Gigost d'Elbée**, the Marquis of Bonchamps, Sapinaud, the Chevalier de **Charette**, **La Rochejaquelein** and **Lescure**, among others. They also sought help – with limited success – from the British.

These so-called brigands, armed at first only with pitchforks and scythes and later with guns taken from the Republicans, worked in cells grouped parish by parish, each wearing a cloak bearing the insignia of a Sacred Heart surmounted by a Cross; their flag was white (hence the Royalists' nickname, the **"Whites"**; Republicans were known as **"Blues"**), covered with fleurs-de-lis, and often inscribed with the motto "Long live Louis XVI". Their tactics were based on surprise: skilled marksmen, hidden in the hedgerows, would silently surround an enemy patrol and open fire, after which the ambushers would hurl themselves into the attack. If the resistance was too robust, the whole troop would melt away into the depths of the *bocage* – which was bitterly referred to by the Republican General **Kléber** as "the labyrinth".

From the spring of 1793 superior Republican troops led by generals Westermann, Kléber and Marceau were deployed in the area. Battles were won by both sides until the winter of 1794 when the Republicans got the upper hand; thousands of Whites were shot or guillotined, while the Blue **"Infernal Columns"** devastated the entire province. Following more battles and treaties the tired rebels eventually submitted to the Revolution through the diplomacy of the astute Republican General Lazare **Hoche**. Stofflet and Charette were finally captured and subsequently shot, the latter with the cry "Long live the King!" on his lips.

Calvin in Saintonge, Angoumois and Poitiers.

1539 The administration of justice reshaped by the Edict of Villers-Cotteret, which imposed French as the official language of the judiciary, instead of Latin or the Langue d'Oc.

1555 **Jeanne d'Albret** crowned Queen of Navarre (until 1572).

1562 Beginning of the **Wars of Religion**.

1569 Victory for the **Duc d'Anjou** over the Protestants in the battles of **Jarnac** and **Moncontour**. Poitiers under siege from Protestants.

1570–71 Imposition of the **Protestant faith** on Béarn by Jeanne d'Albret. Bloody rivalry between her lieutenant, Montgomery, and his Catholic adversary, Blaise de Montluc.

1579 An attempt made, with *les grands jours de Poitiers*, to end religious discord in the region.

1589 Accession of **Henri IV**, the son of Jeanne d'Albret.

1598 End of the Wars of Religion. Protestants granted freedom of worship, and 100 safe places (among them La Rochelle) in which to practise their religion, through Henri IV's promulgation of the **Edict of Nantes**.

1608 The future **Cardinal Richelieu** created Bishop of Luçon.

1627–28 **Siege of La Rochelle** and eventual submission to Richelieu.

1659–60 Treaty of the Pyrénées. Marriage of Louis XIV and the Infanta María Teresa at St-Jean-de-Luz.

1685 Revocation of the Edict of Nantes by Louis XIV. Persecution of Protestants in Béarn by the King's Dragoons *(Dragonades)*. Evacuation of many Huguenots from the country.

18C A decisive impetus to the country's economic development brought during the era of the *Intendants* (stewards or governors): the Comte de Blossac in Poitiers, Reverseaux in Saintes, Tourny in Bordeaux.

1789–99 The **French Revolution** and the end of the Ancien Régime (execution of Louis XVI in January 1793); establishment of the Convention.

1793–96 The **War in the Vendée** *(see box opposite)*; execution of Louis XVI (1793).

1794 Deportation of priests aboard the hulks of Rochefort.

FROM THE FIRST TO THE SECOND EMPIRE

1804 **Napoleon I** consecrated as Emperor of the French, and founding of the town of Napoleon-Vendée (today, La Roche-sur-Yon).

1806 The continental blockade, designed to ruin England by denying the country its economic outlets on mainland Europe, also severely reduced activity in the ports along the Atlantic Coast of France.

1815 Embarkation of the deposed Napoleon for the Isle of Aix.

1822 Plot by the **Four Sergeants of La Rochelle** to overthrow the Restoration government.

1832 Attempts by the Duchesse de Berry to provoke another Vendée uprising, this time against Louis-Philippe I.

1852–70 The **Second Empire** – a period of splendour for the Basque Coast and Country and the spas in the region.

1855 Opening of the Poitiers–La Rochelle railway link.

1857 Birth of the town of Arcachon.

1860 Opening of the Eaux-Bonnes to Bagnères-de-Bigorre Thermal Cure route.

1867 The topography of the Landes revolutionised by the extensive planting of pines.

1868 Appearance of the Portuguese oyster in the Gironde.

FROM THE THIRD REPUBLIC TO THE PRESENT DAY

1870 Installation in Tours and then in Bordeaux of a delegation from the National Defence Government, headed by Gambetta.

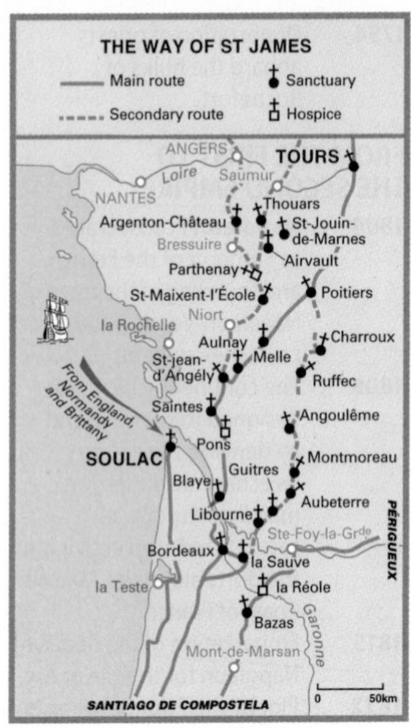

1876 **Phylloxera crisis** in the vineyards.

1905 A law separating the Church from the State pushed through by Émile Combes, Mayor of Pons, and Georges Clemenceau, a Deputy in the National Assembly.

1914 President Poincaré, the government and both chambers of the Assembly moved temporarily to Bordeaux before the first German offensive in WWI.

1929 Death of Clemenceau at St-Vincent-sur-Jard.

1939 End of the Spanish Civil War. Seizure of the Spanish gold reserves (lodged in Mont-de-Marsan) by the Fascist victors; 500 000 refugees flood into southwest France.

1940 Refuge again taken in Bordeaux by the authorities of the Third Republic after the German advance southwards following the breakthrough at Sedan during **World War II**.

1945 German forces still entrenched in the Atlantic pockets besieged by Free French soldiers and members of the Resistance.

1951 Death of Marshal Pétain on the Isle of Yeu.

1954 Inauguration of the oil wells of Parentis.

1966 Oléron becomes the first French island to be linked to the mainland via a bridge.

1987 **Parc du Futuroscope** opens near Poitiers.

1988 Completion of the bridge leading to the Isle of Ré.

1990 Opening of the high-speed Paris–Bordeaux rail link, with the **TGV**-Atlantique *(train à grande vitesse)* a journey of less than 3hrs.

1996 President **Mitterrand** is buried in his native village of Jarnac.

1997 The Cirque de Gavarnie is added to UNESCO's World Heritage Site list.

1998 The mint in Pessac begins production of **euro** coins.

1999 December – a terrible storm uproots trees and damages buildings across the southwest.

1999 Oil spill from the crude oil carrier *Erika* pollutes beaches in the Vendée and the Charentes.

1999 The Jurisdiction of St-Émilion is inscribed as a UNESCO World Heritage Site.

2002 Nicolas Sarkozy defeats Ségolène Royal, a representative for Poitou-Charentes, at the polls to become the President of France.

2007 Bordeaux, The Port of the Moon, is inscribed as a UNESCO World Heritage Site.

2013 Planned opening of the Bordeaux Wine Cultural Centre, intended to revitalise the town as a tourist destination like the Guggenheim did Bilbao.

PILGRIM ROUTES

HISTORY AND LEGEND

St James the Greater, beheaded in Jerusalem in AD 44, was the first Apostle martyred for his beliefs; according to legend, his body and head were transported to northwestern Spain in a stone boat and buried on the coast of Galicia. On the site of his tomb, miraculously rediscovered in the 9C, a church was built, and around it grew the town of Compostela. When the Moors were driven from Spain, **St James** (Santiago in Spanish) became the patron saint of Christians: in the year 844, it is said, at the height of the battle at Clavijo in Rioja, he appeared on a white charger and vanquished the enemy – a manifestation which earned him the nickname of *Matamore* ("Moor-Slayer").

THE PILGRIMAGE

As soon as the church was finished, the faithful began flocking to the site. They travelled from hostel to hostel visiting churches, abbeys and holy places along a number of well-defined routes. Throughout the Middle Ages the number of pilgrims grew to such an extent that the church in **Santiago de Compostela** became a shrine equal in importance to Jerusalem or Rome.

The first French pilgrimage was led by the Bishop of Le Puy in the year 951. Subsequently millions of **Jacquets**, Jacquots or Jacobites (*Jacques* in French means "James") set out from Paris, Tours, Le Puy, Vézelay and Arles, which developed into assembly points for pilgrims from all over Europe.

Pilgrims to Santiago wore a uniform of a heavy cape, a 2.4m/8ft stave with a gourd attached to carry water, stout sandals and a broad-brimmed felt hat, turned up at the front and marked with three or four scallop shells, the badge of the saint, which identified the pilgrim's destination. The shells, found in great banks along the Galician Coast and still called *coquilles St-Jacques* (St James' shells) in France today, were also used as a receptacle in which to collect alms. A scrip or pouch, a bowl and a metal box for papers and passes completed the equipment. The network of hostels and hospices where pilgrims could find food and shelter for a night, or receive attention if they were unwell, was organised by the Benedictine monks of Cluny, the Premonstratensians and other orders. The Knights Templar and the Hospitallers of St John with their commanderies policed the routes, marked with carved mileposts or cairns. There was even a **Pilgrim's Guide**, the first tourist guide ever written, produced in Latin in c.1135, probably by **Aymeric Picaud**, a monk from Parthenay-le-Vieux. This outlined local customs, weather conditions to be expected, spiced the more mundane information with comments on the morals and customs of the inhabitants of each region, and listed the most interesting routes, towns and sights on the way.

The main routes all converged in the Basse-Navarre district before crossing the Pyrénées. The most important junction was at Ostabat; St-Jean-Pied-de-Port was the last halt before the climb towards the frontier. The pilgrims reached Roncesvalles by a mountain route, once part of the Roman road linking Bordeaux with Astorga via the Valcarlos gap. The bell of the monastery at Ibañeta Pass would toll when it was foggy to signal the right direction to those pilgrims who might have got lost or lagged behind.

With the passage of time, however, the faith that fired people to set out on pilgrimages began to wane; false pilgrims seeking gain by trickery and robbery, and known as *coquillards*, increased; the Wars of Religion, when Christians fought among themselves, reduced the faithful even more. In the late 16C, when Sir Francis Drake attacked Corunna, the relics were removed from the cathedral to a place of safety, after which the pilgrimage was virtually abandoned. By the 18C anyone wishing to make the journey to Santiago de Compostela was obliged to provide the authorities with a letter of introduction from their parish priest and other documents certified to be true by a police official or signed by the pilgrim's local bishop.

Art and Culture

GALLO-ROMAN ERA

Despite the institutionalised vandalism of the 19C, many examples still remain of the arts which flourished in the Roman colony of Aquitaine, the capitals of which were Bordeaux, Poitiers and Saintes. The ruins of amphitheatres, theatres, temples and bathhouses, and votive arches scattered throughout these areas offer a broad view of Gallo-Roman civilisation.

ROMANESQUE PERIOD (11C–12C)

After the turbulent period of the early Middle Ages, marked by conflicts between the great feudal houses, the year AD 1000 saw a renewal of faith exemplified in the Crusades and the great pilgrimages. In the southwest of France the most important religious sanctuaries were all built along the routes leading to Santiago de Compostela in Spain (*see PILGRIM ROUTES*).

ARCHITECTURE

Church Design

In Poitou, Romanesque churches generally comprised a high, barrel-vaulted central nave, buttressed by side aisles of almost equal height.

Light entered through the window bays of these aisles. In Angoumois and Saintonge (the regions around Angoulême and Saintes) the wide, single nave was sometimes barrel-vaulted, sometimes topped by a **line of domes** showing influence from the Périgord region.

West Fronts

The façades were characterised by arcades or tiers of blind arcades. Arcading at the upper level was nevertheless typical more in Angoumois and Saintonge, whereas churches in Poitou were often distinguished by a tripartite division vertically, with large arcades separated by columnar buttresses (Notre-Dame-la-Grande in Poitiers is an exception).

The west front was usually surmounted by a triangular pediment and flanked by columns or groups of columns sometimes crowned by pierced lanterns with conical roofs. These roofs, and often those of the church belfries, would be covered by overlapping tiles. The façade itself was normally decorated with statues and low-relief sculptures, intended to deliver a message. Notre-Dame-la-Grande in Poitiers is a successful example of these façade-screens; the biblical stories depicted on the façade are easily identified and understood.

In Angoumois the west fronts are more sober, although that of St-Pierre in Angoulême is famed for its depiction, through 70 different characters, of the Ascension and the Last Judgement.

East Ends

Churches with an ambulatory at their east ends and radiating chapels buttressed

Façade of Notre-Dame-la-Grande, Poitiers

The Plantagenet Style

In the west of France the Plantagenet style, also known as Angevin, marked the transition between Romanesque and Gothic styles. This architectural style reached its peak at the beginning of the 13C and had died out by the end of the century.

Angevin Vaulting – In normal Gothic vaulting all the keys are situated at approximately the same height. Plantagenet architecture, however, is characterised by steeply recessed quadripartite vaulting – probably derived from an earlier use of the dome – in which the keystones of the diagonals are higher than the stringer or transverse keys by as much as 3m/10ft.

At the end of the 12C these Angevin vaults became lighter as the number of ribs increased and arched more gracefully, springing from slender circular columns. The early 13C saw the style at its finest, the tall, slim pillars supporting an airy tracery of lierne vaulting. Examples of the style can be seen in Vendée, Poitou (Poitiers Cathedral, Airvault, St-Jouin-de-Marnes southeast of Thouars), Saintonge and as far away as the region around the Upper Garonne.

by columns are common in Poitou: St-Hilaire, in Melle, is typical. Certain east ends in Saintonge, on the other hand, were built to a simpler design, like the church at Rioux, with a five-faced apse and columnar buttresses; the bays separating the columns have archivolts at the middle level, decorated with a row of blind arcades and miniature columns above. The whole is topped by an elegant frieze running beneath a cornice with carved, double-scroll brackets.

SCULPTURE

The use of sculpture on façades, east ends, corbels, arches, consoles and capitals was facilitated by the nature of the local limestone, which is relatively easy to work; Romanesque edifices are notable for the abundance, variety and finesse of the religious ornamentation. On these surfaces foliage, acanthus leaves in the Antique style and pre-Romanesque plaited stonework rival in complexity images of oriental monsters, biblical illustrations, legends of the saints and scenes of everyday life.

One of the most lavishly decorated west fronts in the Poitou area is that of Notre-Dame-la-Grande in Poitiers; however, it is the Saintonge that is best known for its wealth of sculpted décor. While the richness of the overall decoration can be almost overwhelming, it is also worth looking closely at the wonderful individual details.

FRESCOES AND MURAL PAINTINGS

A fresco (from the Italian word *fresco* meaning "fresh") is a wall or ceiling painting executed on a surface of freshly applied, still-damp plaster, into which the design is incorporated before the plaster dries. The number of colours that can be used is limited, since only pigments made from natural earths and iron oxides suit the technique.

The most extraordinary murals of the Poitou School are found in St-Savin, where the compositions are remarkable as much for the beauty of the colours, the harmony of the design and the perfection of the technique as for their lively content.

GOTHIC PERIOD (12C–15C)

Apart from its appearance in the Plantagenet style, which nevertheless retains many elements of the Romanesque, Gothic art raised scarcely an echo in the west and southwest of France; such examples as there are tend to be Southern Gothic, the style of the Mediterranean, characterised by a single, very wide nave and no transept. Certain English influences are evident in the square, Flamboyant towers of a few 14C and 15C

Château d'Oiron

©S. Sauvignier/MICHELIN

churches in the Saintonge (St-Eutrope in Saintes, Marennes).

RENAISSANCE PERIOD

Renaissance ideas were first introduced to France following the Italian wars at the end of the 15C.

Although this new style did not take hold overnight, the arrival of a score of Neapolitan artists brought from Italy by Charles VIII at the end of 1495 gave new life to French architecture.

Civil Architecture

The Renaissance style was brought to the west by members of the court of François I, who were natives of the Saintonge or Angoumois regions and had been influenced by the architecture of the Loire Valley. The François I Wing of the Château d'Oiron, for example, displays a characteristic series of basket-handled arches, whereas the Château de la Rochefoucauld, with its celebrated courtyard surrounded by a three-tiered gallery, is reminiscent of an Italian *palazzo.*

Extensive use of decorative arabesques and grotesques, as well as hints of Antiquity, distinguishes the châteaux of Dampierre-sur-Boutonne, Oiron and Usson: the roofs are tall, with all the slopes on each side at the same angle; the inclusion of splendid staircases accounts for the projecting façades of the central blocks.

Similar features can be found in other châteaux of the region – the old royal castle in Cognac, for instance (guardroom and gallery) – or in such Renaissance mansions as the Hôtel Fumé in Poitiers and the Hôtel St-Simon in Angoulême.

CLASSICAL PERIOD

The accession of the Bourbon dynasty in 1589, following the era of stagnation that characterised French art and architecture towards the end of the Renaissance, heralded a radical shift in direction: the period of material prosperity that coincided with the reign of Henri IV fired artists eager for change with new ideas and new interpretations of classical, antique themes. Classical art held sway in France from 1589 to 1789.

Classical Fortifications

From the 16C onwards fortifications were constructed above all to protect frontier towns, and consisted of curtain walls and bastions surmounted by platforms from which cannon could be fired. Overhanging turrets allowed the defenders to survey the surrounding ditches and keep watch over the terrain beyond.

The acknowledged master of fortifications was **Sébastien Le Prestre de Vauban** (1633–1707). Developing the ideas of his predecessors – military engineers employed by the King – he evolved a system based on the use of massive bastions complemented by ravelins or demilunes, the whole being protected by very deep defensive ditches. Vauban's designs are notable for the way he made use of natural obstacles, used only local materials and added

Religious architecture

CHAUVIGNY - Ground plan of St-Pierre (11C-12C)

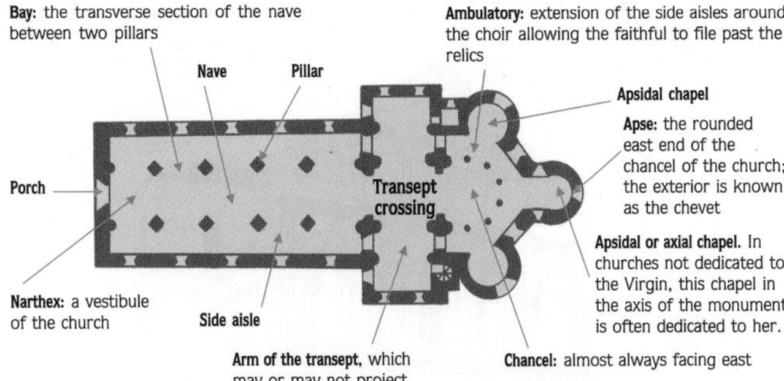

ANGOULÊME - Cross-section of the transept of the Cathédrale St-Pierre (12C)

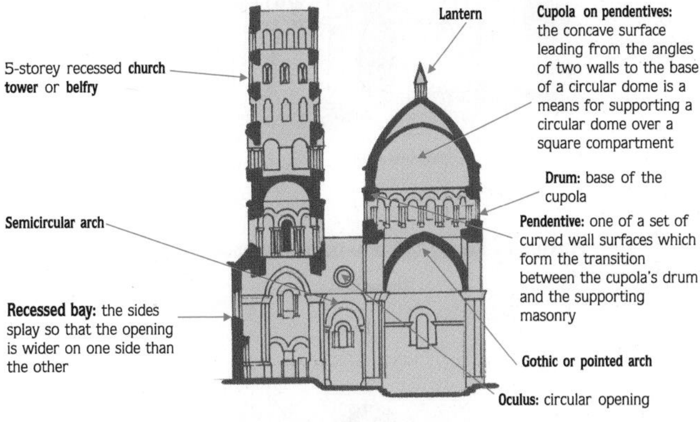

AULNAY - South portal of St-Pierre (12C)

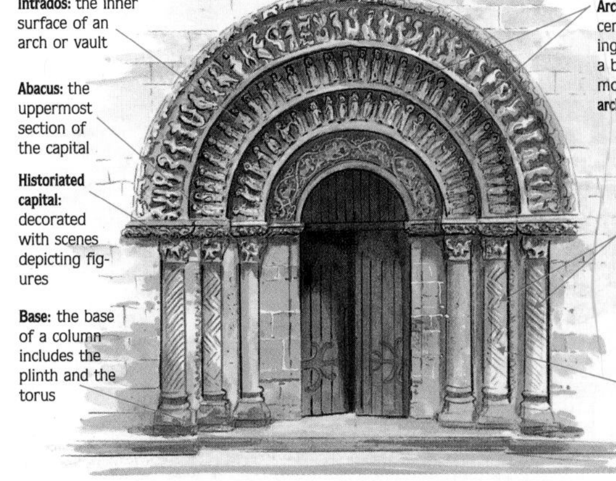

R. Corbel/MICHELIN

PETIT-PALAIS - The Église St-Pierre (end 12C)

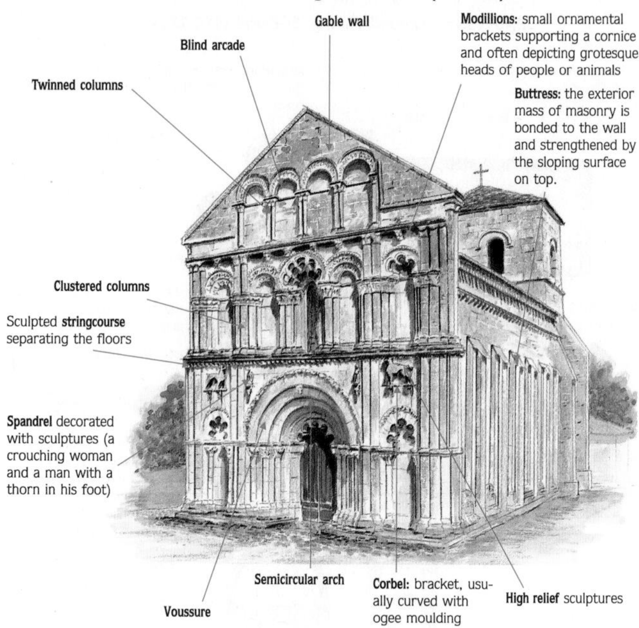

POITIERS - Façade of Notre-Dame-la-Grande (12C)

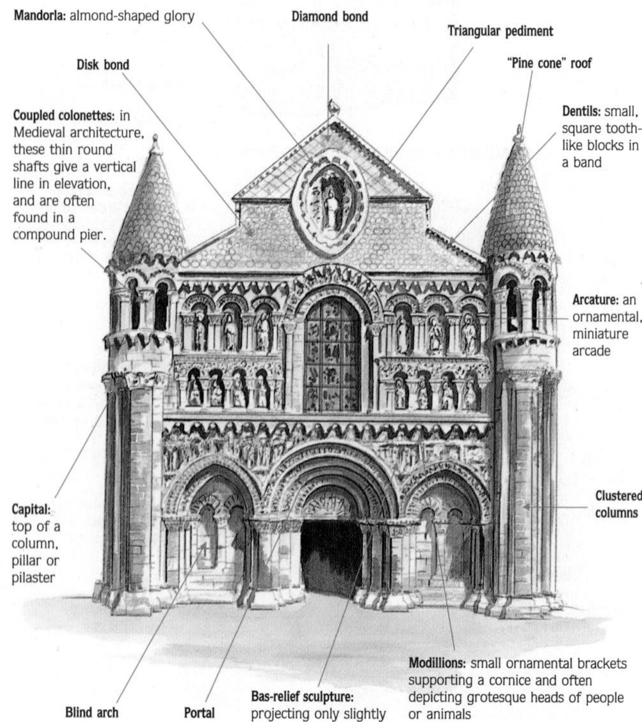

R. Corbel/MICHELIN

SAINTES - Belfry of the Église de l'Abbaye aux Dames (12C)

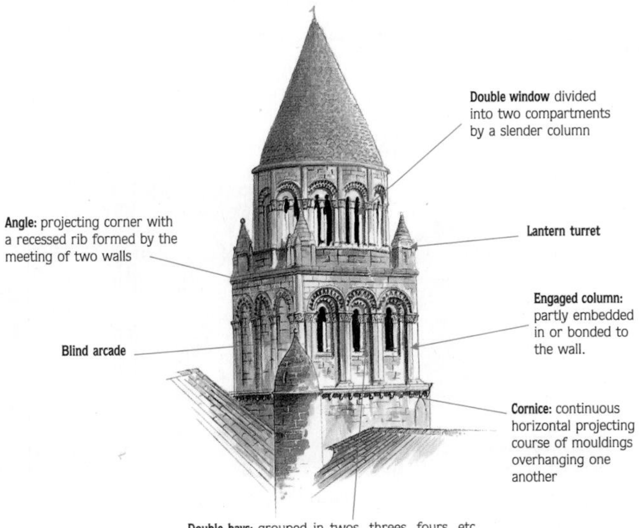

Military architecture

ROQUETAILLADE - Château neuf (14C - restored 19C)

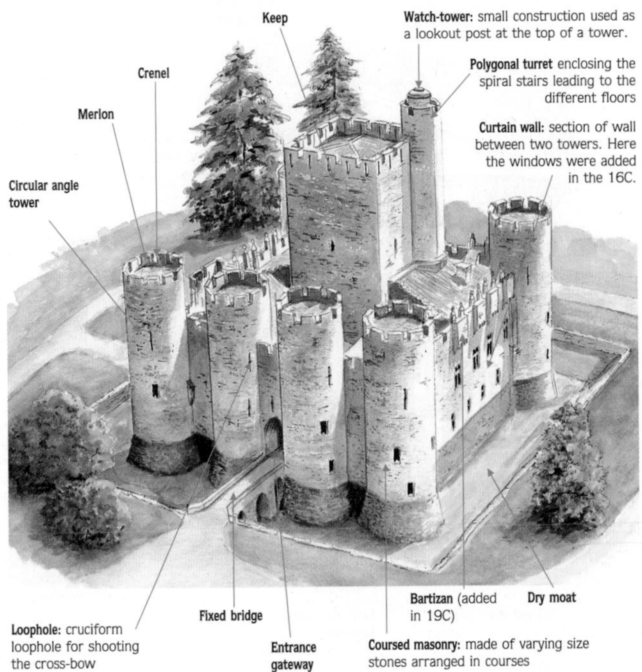

Civil architecture

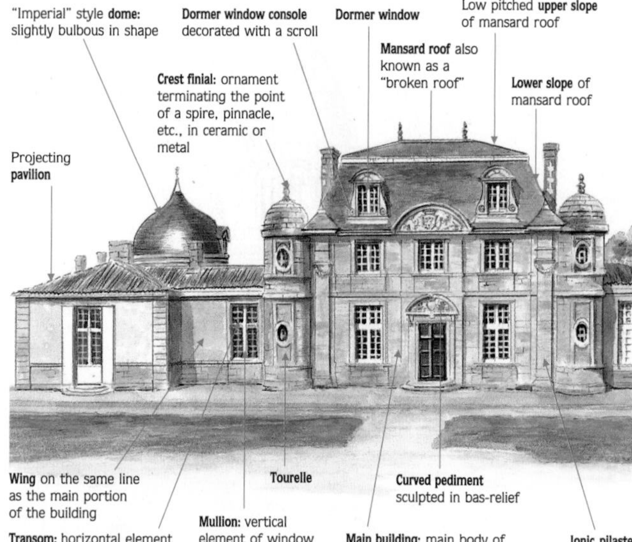

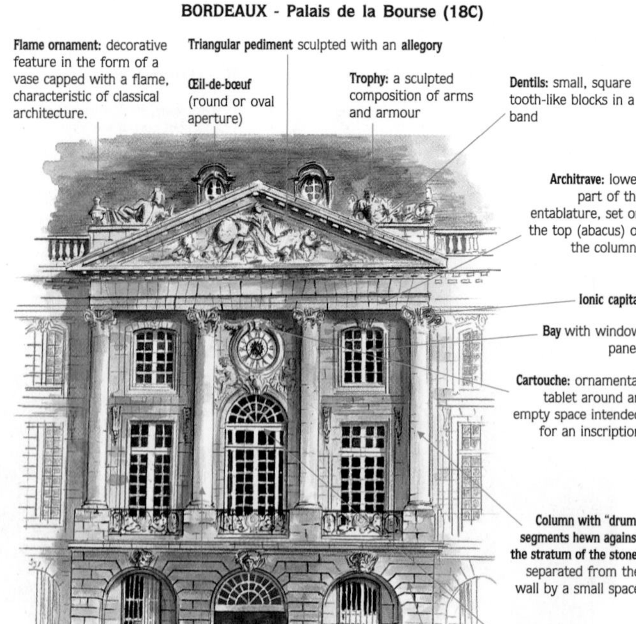

BORDEAUX - Staircase of the Grand Théâtre (end 18C)

Rose: decoration consisting of a centre or bud surrounded by leaves
Lunette: a crescent-shaped or semi-circular area on a wall or vaulted ceiling, framed by an arch or a vault
Decorative Panel
Fluted pilaster (shallow rectangular pillar attached to the face of the wall)
Caryatid: statue of female figure used as a support
Arch stone or **voussoir with crosettes:** the upper edge extends horizontally to make a strong bond with the surrounding masonry
Festoon: decorative motif in the form of a garland of stylised leaves, fruit or flowers.
Loggia
Landing
Double flight with diverging steps
Tiled landing
Sculpted banisters
Fliers: all of equal width
Central flight

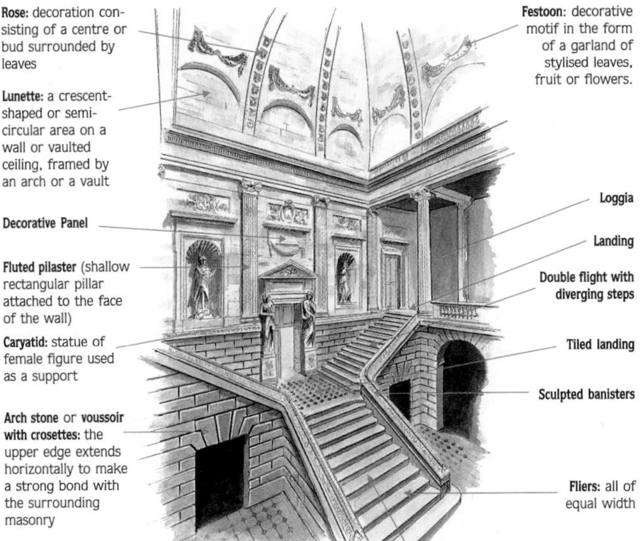

ARCACHON. Winter house - Villa Trocadéro (end 19C)

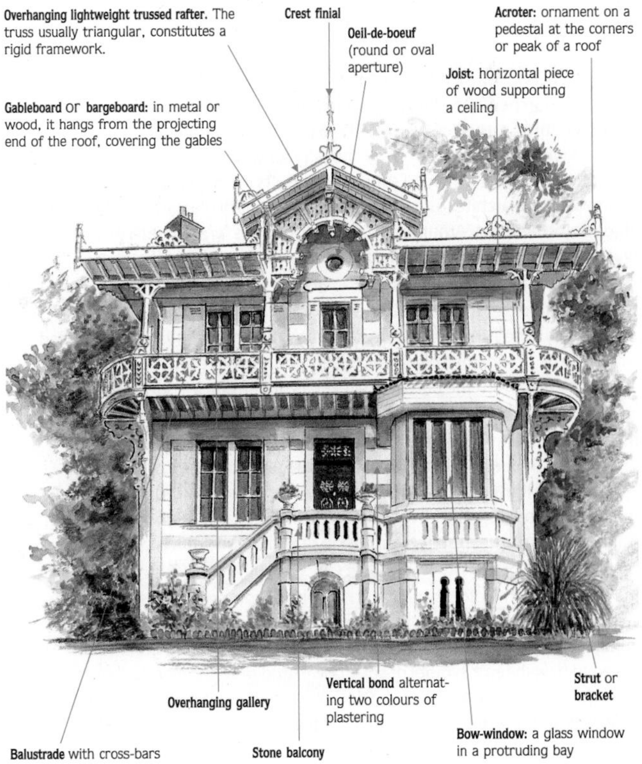
Overhanging lightweight trussed rafter. The truss usually triangular, constitutes a rigid framework.
Crest finial
Oeil-de-boeuf (round or oval aperture)
Acroter: ornament on a pedestal at the corners or peak of a roof
Joist: horizontal piece of wood supporting a ceiling
Gableboard or **bargeboard:** in metal or wood, it hangs from the projecting end of the roof, covering the gables
Overhanging gallery
Vertical bond alternating two colours of plastering
Strut or **bracket**
Balustrade with cross-bars
Stone balcony
Bow-window: a glass window in a protruding bay
R. Corbel/MICHELIN

aesthetic value to the functional works he produced, incorporating monumental stone entrance gates, often adorned with sculpture.

His talent can be admired at Blaye, where the citadel protecting the entrance to the port of Bordeaux is part of a complex defence system; further south, Bayonne and Navarrenx (south of Orthez) are also examples of the genius of this great military architect.

19C ECLECTICISM

In the 19C, European architecture was characterised by a penchant for eclecticism, bringing styles from the past (Antique, Romanesque, Gothic, Renaissance and Classical) back into fashion, and borrowing largely from foreign architectural styles, especially those of the Far East. Such buildings are found from the Gironde to the Basque Country, along the shore and in spa towns in the Pyrénées. Some of them are highly original, many are luxurious villas, lending their image to the reputation of certain resorts.

In the Bordeaux area, **Neoclassicism** is the dominant architectural style (early 19C), especially in the châteaux of local wine-growers. But some odd mixtures can be found here as well, as at the Château Lanessan, where the Spanish Renaissance meets Dutch tradition, or the original château building of Cos d'Estourel, rising pagoda-like from the vines (today contrasted with one of the most stikingly modern cellars in France).

The popular Bassin d'Arcachon inspired a building boom in the 19C, as holiday homes owned by families from Bordeaux went up in styles ranging from the Algerian villa to the Swiss chalet, the Basque house to the English cottage. These hideaways can still be seen around Cap Ferret and in the Ville d'Hiver section of town, so successfully promoted by the Péreire brothers.

Biarritz became a fashionable seaside resort thanks, in part, to Napoleon III

Basque Religious Architecture in the 17C

Most of the churches in the Basque Country were renovated during the period of the **Council of Trent** (1545–63), which generated a movement within the Catholic clergy and laity for widespread religious renewal and reform that yielded substantial results in the 17C, even affecting religious architecture. In this region, the belfry is a particularly distinguishing element. Around La Soule, a distinctive form of **belfry-calvary** is common, such as the one in Gotein. The flattened belfry rises up like a wall, with three pointed gables, each crowned with a cross.

The shape symbolises the Holy Trinity, whereas the crosses recall Jesus and the two thieves crucified. In Lower Navarre and Labourd, the belfry-wall is rounded, resembling the *fronton* of a *pilota* court. Certain churches have massive, tiered **belfry-porches**. Often the porch, whatever its dimensions, is surmounted by a room used to hold town council meetings or catechism classes.

In the northern Basque regions of Labourde and Basse-Navarre, the inner layout is characteristic: a wide nave is surrounded by two or three tiers of **galleries**, which are in theory reserved for men. The pulpit is integrated into the lower gallery. The main altar is often monumental **Baroque** in style, a profusion of gilding, sculpture, curls and wreaths typical of Catholic Baroque churches all over Europe.

In the cemeteries, the oldest and most remarkable tombstones – some dating from before the 16C – are known as **discoidal tombstones**: atop a plinth, a round, flat stone is often carved with a swastika figure, or *cruz gammata*, believed to have been a symbol of solar power and movement, possibly of Hindu origin. The exact source of the design remains a subject of speculation and debate, along with the many other unique aspects of Basque culture.

and his Neoclassical Villa Eugénie. Luxury beach houses in a range of different styles were built right up to the 1930s: the Villa de la Roche-Ronde is Medieval Revival (towers and look-outs); the Boulard château (1870–71) -Renaissance Revival; and the Françon Villa adopts the Old England look. In Hendaye, the Château d'Abbadia is influenced by Gothic architecture. Its interior is inspired by Moorish architecture, a style also in evidence at the Casino de la Plage.

ART DECO

This 20C style is most evident along the Basque Coast: the town casino, the Maritime Museum (1932–35) and the interior decoration of private homes in Biarritz; the Atrium Casino (1928) and the Splendid Hotel (1932) in Dax; the Leïhora Villa (1926–28) in Ciboure. Like the Art Nouveau movement, which preceded it, Art Deco draws from Classical motifs, but they are reduced to geometric stylisations, and the noodle, whiplash, tapeworm, and cigarette-smoke style curves of Art Nouveau give way to straight and pure lines. Architects used wrought iron, glass (creating luminous rooms within buildings) and ceramics to express these colourful designs.

During the 1920s and 30s, villas built in Hossegor, in the Landes region, were inspired by rural houses of the Basque Country and a neo-regional style developed, which combined timber-framing, typical brick bond from the Landes, overhanging roofs, projecting load bearing walls and white roughcast façades with Art Deco ornamentation.

MEDIEVAL TOWN PLANNING

MILITARY ARCHITECTURE

From the 9C to the 12C the weakness and remoteness of the central power in medieval France contributed to the establishment of powerful dukedoms and counties. When the enforced feudalism began to crumble, one of the results was a generalised increase in the scattering of new strongholds.

Fortresses proliferated in the southwest and in particular in the former Aquitaine, which had been disputed for three centuries by two different crowns. Outside the towns where, through the consolidation of existing Gallo-Roman protective enclosures, defence could usually be assured, crude new strongholds spread across the open countryside. Comprising a surrounding ditch, a palisade, and a wooden tower (later built of stone) rising on a hillock, these fortresses provided basic refuge for local inhabitants.

Keeps

Rectangular keeps built of stone made their appearance in the early 11C. They initially had a purely defensive role: the stonework was not particularly thick and there were no loopholes from which to fire at the enemy. The ground-floor level, which was dark, served as a store. The keep could only be entered at first-floor level, via either a ladder or a retractable footbridge. This design (illustrated by the keep at Bassoues), which persisted until the 14C, explains why the spiral stone staircases of so many of these structures only started at the higher level.

Before the Hundred Years' War there was a 13C–14C Gascon variant of the keep known as a **salle** – a fortified dwelling flanked by one or two rectangular towers, set along the diagonal. Again, only the upper storeys were inhabited and provided with windows.

Castles of Brick

Certain castles in the Béarn district bear the trademark of **Sicard de Lordat**, a military engineer employed by Gaston Fébus, the 14C overlord of Béarn. For reasons of economy they were built of brick rather than massive stonework. The single square tower astride a polygonal defensive perimeter served both as a keep and as a gateway. The living quarters and the barracks were built against the inside of the curtain wall.

Fortified Churches

Fortress-churches occupy a special place in the history of French military architecture, and are numerous in the southwest. Two types of machicolation were employed in their construction: the classic variety supported by corbels, and another in the form of arches curving between the buttresses (as at Beaumont-de-Lomagne). They appeared for the first time in France in the late 12C, in the Langue d'Oc country. The churches were traditionally places of asylum with their robust architecture and their belfries which could be used as watch towers; moreover, the Truce of God ordered by the Vatican Council in the 10C and 11C stipulated a "zone of inviolability", extending for 30 paces around each church, in which refugees might not be touched. The Council's orders forbade the waging of war on certain days of the week and during Advent, Lent and Easter week. Violation of the Truce was punished with excommunication.

Examples of these fortified churches still exist in the Upper Pyrénées, in the valleys once subject to cross-frontier raids from Aragon; the best known are Luz Church, enclosed within a crenellated curtain wall, and Sentein Church, which has three towers.

NEW TOWNS OF THE MIDDLE AGES

Medieval urban development in southwestern France has left only three sites still substantial enough today to be called towns: Montauban (southeast of Agen), founded by the Comte de Toulouse in 1144; the lower part of Carcassonne (1247), built on the west bank of the Aude by St Louis to shelter the homeless after the town was sacked; and Libourne (east of Bordeaux), named after Sir Roger Leyburn, Seneschal to Edward I of England (1270) (for details of Montauban and Carcassonne, *see the Michelin Green Guide Languedoc Roussillon: Tarn Gorges)*. Aquitaine, however, at first strewn with *sauvetés* and *castelnaux* (refuges and fortified towns), was above all characterised by an abundance of new towns known as *bastides* – semi-urban, semi-rural settlements which were characterised by a geometric ground plan. Many of these small country towns and villages have retained their traditional character and original layout.

Sauvetés and Castelnaux (11C and 12C)

The **Sauveté** (including Sauvetat and Sauveterre) usually arose as the result of an ecclesiastical initiative. Prelates, abbots or dignitaries of a military Order of Chivalry would found the village or hamlet; the inhabitants would clear, prepare and cultivate their lands; a host or overseer, installed perhaps in a small manor house, would supervise the work. These rural townships also provided sanctuary for fugitives.

In a similar fashion, the **castelnau** (including Châteauneuf and Castets) originated with the dependencies built by a seigneur around his château. Auvillar (southwest of Agen), Mugron and Pau were once *castelnaux*. In Gascony the name Castelnau is completed by the name of the local fief; for example, Castelnau-Magnoac, Castelnau-Barbarens.

Bastides (1220–c.1350)

The *bastide* was an entirely new concept, a purpose-built and efficiently planned town or village where people could live. By the middle of the 14C around 300 *bastides* had been created between Périgord and the Pyrénées. In Gascony and Guyenne these new towns were so numerous that it suggests that at one time they were the most important form of collective habitation in the region. Although not all of them were fully developed, and despite their relative lack of importance today – some have disappeared altogether – the *bastides* in their time were a genuine response to demographic, financial and economic needs as well as to military and political imperatives.

The construction of many *bastides* arose from a contract of *paréage*. Such contracts, frequently drawn up between the King and a local seigneur or between an abbot and a lay seigneur, could also permit two neighbouring seigneurs to detail the rights and powers of each over territories they might hold in common;

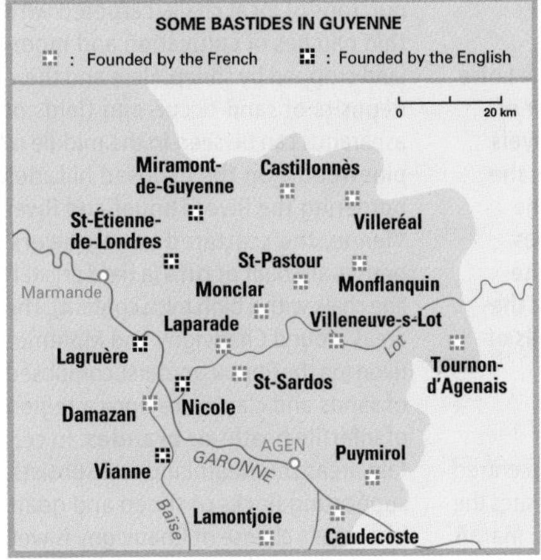

were due either to the lay of the land or to considerations of defence. The use of professional surveyors at the planning stage is evident in the rectilinear layout of the streets, always meeting each other at right-angles to form a symmetrical pattern of equal-area lots. Those moving in were allowed so much on which they could build, so much for a garden, and – outside the built-up area but not too far away – an allotment which they could cultivate.

or they could stipulate that a less powerful seigneur would enjoy the protection of his stronger neighbour in return for a fixed proportion of the former's revenues. The contracts also affected the inhabitants of the *bastide*, establishing their status, outlining the allotment of building plots and specifying the taxes to be paid. To encourage people to move into the *bastide*, new arrivals were granted – among other privileges – the right of asylum and exemption from any military service due to the seigneur. The immigrants were free to bequeath property to their inheritors and dispose of their other possessions as they wished. Penalties, on the other hand, could be imposed on those who were slow to build.

Place names of the *bastides* followed three different principles: they could evoke the settlement's status – Villefranche (Free Town); they could carry the name of the founder – Montréjeau (Mount Royal), Beaumarché, Hastingues (Hastings); or they could suggest a symbolic twinning with some famous foreign city such as Valence (after Valencia in Spain), Fleurance (Florence), Cologne or Tournay.

These settlements were fairly rigidly planned, based on the model of a right-angled grid, either square or rectangular (with the exception of Fourcès, a rare circular *bastide*). Variations on this plan

The road system was ahead of its time: the principal streets were usually 8m/26ft wide, a generous size when none of the buildings had more than two floors.

In the centre of the grid was the main (and only) square, normally closed to traffic and reserved for markets; many of the central, covered marketplaces still stand today. The square was effectively an open lot islanded among the regular ranks of buildings; the four streets framing it passed from the open air to the *couverts,* and then out again on the far side, retaining their continuity and frequently their street names. The **couverts**, most of them unfortunately now truncated or lost altogether, were covered passages surrounding the square running beneath either stone-built arcades or projecting upper storeys supported by wooden pillars.

Bastide Churches

The proliferation of *bastides* from the 13C onwards led to the construction of many new churches. They were built either close to the market square or out on the periphery of the grid, on the specified lot assigned for church and cemetery; here, therefore, the Languedoc single-nave-no-transept style was particularly suitable. Churches in Gascony share a family likeness, with their belfry-porches (Mirande, Marciac) and their wide, dark naves lit mainly through the clerestory windows of a cramped apse.

Nature

The Atlantic coastline from the Loire in the north to the vast barrier of the Pyrénées in the south, travels past the great plain of Poitou; the lush meadows of *le bocage*; the great wine growing landscapes of Charentes and Bordeaux; the lagoons and dunes of Landes; the valleys of Agenais; and the hills of Gascony.

POITOU

This large and ancient province, centred on the town of Poitiers, incorporates the Pays de Retz, Vendée and the Marais Poitevin (the Poitou marshlands).

THE PLAIN

The limestone plateau between the ancient massifs of the **Vendée** (which are the southern extremity of the Armorican peninsula on which Brittany sits) and Limousin (the region east of Angoulême) comprises a crescent stretching from Loudun to Luçon. Almost denuded of trees and cut through with deep valleys, the plain seems to roll away to infinity, its succession of fields, meadows and moors scarcely interrupted by the occasional village.

Certain subtle differences are discernable: in the north the plain is actually part of Touraine (the region around Tours); from Thouars to Châtellerault there are outcrops of local chalk, carpeted with thin patches of cultivation and moorland cropped by sheep. Here and there deposits of sand occur, and fields of asparagus can be seen in the middle of pinewoods. On the exposed hillsides bordering the River Thouet and River Vienne, the scattered winegrowers' houses are built of **tufa** (a hard crystalline chalk with a high mica content). The areas around Chauvigny and Montmorillon (on the Poitou borders), composed of sands and clay, were once a region of infertile heaths or **brandes**. In certain areas this heathland still subsists, supporting flocks of sheep and goats (the goat's cheese of Chauvigny is well known). In other places, where the heath has been cleared, Charollais or Limousin bullocks are raised. Flocks of *pirons* (a variety of goose raised for its skin and *duvet* or down) wander near the farms. West of Clain, continuing as far as Melle and St-Maixent, the Jurassic limestone, lacerated by valleys, has decomposed on the surface into what is locally called **terre de groie** (a compound soil part clay, part gravel, part lime, of proverbial fertility – especially for cereals and fodder plants such as clover and alfalfa).

LE BOCAGE

The Vendée and the **Gâtine de Parthenay**, south and west of the River Thouet, have many features in common. This is the region known as *le bocage* – an area

Marais Poitevin

©D. Mar/MICHELIN

of lush meadows bordered by hedgerows of hawthorn or broom, with sunken lanes leading to smallholdings and farms half hidden in leafy copses. The speckled brown Parthenay bullocks, bred and fattened for beef, are often seen grazing in this patchwork of small fields. The area is dotted with apple orchards and the occasional field of fodder plants grown to feed the cattle. A chain of low, rounded hills forms the backbone of this productive agricultural area, and these are known as **Les Collines Vendéennes** (the Hills of the Vendée).

MARSHLANDS AND COAST

The marsh (Marais) area extends from the schist landscapes of the **Pays de Retz** to the limestone cliffs of the **Aunis** – an ancient region centred on La Rochelle.

Between these cliffs, which mark the limit of the prehistoric Bay of Biscay (or Golfe de Gascogne as it is known in France), and the sea, salt marshes transformed into oyster farms glitter in the sun and sheep and cattle graze in the water meadows. Early fruit and vegetables ripen on the alluvial soil and wild ducks paddle the canals beneath overhanging hedgerows alive with smaller birds. The marshland, formed from debris accumulated by rivers and ancient ocean currents, lies sheltered behind the coastal dunes; rocky islets from the ancient coastline define the area's inner limit. From north to south the route passes successively through the Breton-Vendée marshland, which includes the marshes of Monts, the marshes of Olonne and of Talmont and the famous **Marais Poitevin**.

Huge beaches of fine sand lie along the foot of the dunes and on the offshore bars; between Noirmoutier and the mainland, on either side of the causeway known as the Passage du Gois, enormous stretches of mudflat are exposed at low tide. Noirmoutier itself and the more southerly Île d'Yeu (Isle of Yeu) provide yet more contrast: the one flat, peaceful and gentle; the other rocky and savage on its western coast.

CHARENTES

The region known as the Charentes comprises the two *départements* of Charente and Charente-Maritime, separated by the green and placid valley of the River Charente, which themselves embrace the ancient provinces of **Angoumois** (the Angoulême region), **Aunis** and **Saintonge** (the region around Saintes). Charente itself, abutting the foothills of the Massif Central, divides into four natural geographic areas: to the west the wine country of Cognac, at the centre the cereal-growing Angoumois, in the northeast the Confolentais with its plateaux, and to the south the Montmorélien, a hilly landscape of mixed farming. Charente-Maritime, facing the Atlantic, presents a coastline of rocks, dunes and sandy beaches, with a rural interior of forests and plains.

VINEYARDS

In the heart of the Charentes lies the town of **Cognac**, the capital of that chalky champagne area (the soil is similar to that in the Champagne region, east of Paris) bordering the south bank of the river that nourishes the grapes from which the world-famous brandy bearing the name of the town is distilled.

THE PLAIN

The limestone plateau, which extends from Angoulême to La Rochelle, provides a slightly monotonous landscape, only rarely cut by valleys (such as that of the Boutonne) dotted with small towns and an occasional whitewashed hamlet. As in Poitou, the Jurassic bedrock is cloaked with a reddish *terre de groie*, or a fertile alluvium, on which cornfields take second place to crops of clover and alfalfa or fields of sugar-beet grown as fodder.

COAST

The Charentais Coast is unusual because, especially towards its centre, alluvial deposits from the River Charente and River Seudre have combined with marine currents to form an area of marshland not unlike that in Poitou. Most of this swampy land has been either reclaimed as **polders** (low-lying lands protected by dykes) on which crops are grown, or transformed – especially near Marennes – into shallow basins in which mussels and oysters are farmed. The distance the tide goes out varies from 2km/1.2mi to 5km/3.1mi.

Not far offshore, the low-lying and sandy islands of Oléron and Ré, scattered with pretty white houses, define the outer limit of an inner sea – the **Mer de Pertuis**, so-called because the only way its waters can reach the open sea is via one or other of the straits *(pertuis)* dividing these isles from the mainland.

BORDEAUX

The region known as Le Bordelais, at the heart of the ancient province of **Guyenne** (Aquitaine), centres on the confluence of the River Garonne and River Dordogne. This transitional area between the limestone plains of Charentes to the north and the vast sandy expanse of the Landes to the south is drained by the Garonne and its tributaries towards the zone of subsidence around the estuary.

Agriculture here is dominated by the cultivation of vines.

GIRONDE ESTUARY

The Gironde is the name given to the great estuary which lies between the Garonne–Dordogne convergence and the sea. It is a modest reminder of the marine reaches which covered the Aquitaine basin long ago in the Tertiary Era.

The northern bank of the estuary is bordered by limestone hills known as the **Côtes de Bourg** and **Côtes de Blaye**. On the south bank, where the land on the whole is lower, similar limestone formations have been eroded and then covered by gravels, producing the topsoil in which the famous vines of the Médoc flourish.

Covering the limestone bedrock of the Gironde are deposits washed down by the two great rivers; these deposits, stirred by the action of the tides, have determined the formation of marshes, which are separated from the running water by an alluvial belt, the **palus**. Some of the marshland has been transformed, in the Dutch manner, into polders where meadows now lie; the rest remains the province of hunters and waterfowl. Artichokes are grown on the *palus*, and certain vines which produce a *palus* wine.

Over the centuries the movement of the water has created a number of elongated islands as well as sandbanks which are revealed at low tide.

MÉDOC

This world-famous wine-producing area is divided into three separate zones: the region of viticulture proper; a zone of coastal forest; and the *palus*, which punctuates the limestone bluffs of St-Estèphe and Pauillac. Fine red wines come from the first zone: north of St-Seurin-de-Cadourne these are produced mainly by local cooperatives and sold under the simple overall description of Médoc; to the south, from St-Seurin to Blanquefort, lies the district meriting the more distinguished Haut-Médoc appellation.

LANDES

The word *landes* (moors) still conjures up a vision of the more desolate aspect of this part of the coast, which existed prior to the 19C, when a remarkable project of reforestation transformed the area into a huge pine forest.

COAST AND DUNES

The Landes sit on an enormous plain, roughly triangular in shape, covering an area of 14 000sq km/5 400sq mi. The side of the triangle runs down the 230km/143mi of coast from the Gironde estuary to the mouth of the Adour, and turns eastwards from the two points to meet at the triangle's apex 100km/62mi inland.

This ruler-straight shoreline, known as the **Côte d'Argent** (Silver Coast), is essentially one vast beach on which the sea deposits sand at an annual rate of 15 to 18cu m per metre/20 to 24cu yd per yard of coast. The sand, especially in those reaches of the strand only reached by the highest equinoctial tides, is then dried and blown inland by the west wind, where it accumulates in dunes. Until the last century these dunes then moved away from the sea at a speed varying between 10m/33ft and 27m/89ft per year. Today, fixed in position by the plantation of shrubs, grasses and forest trees, the dunes form a continuous but static coastal belt 5km/3.1mi wide. The strip is the longest and highest series of dunes in Europe.

LAKES, LAGOONS AND THE PLAIN

Most of the watercourses in the region find themselves blocked by the dune barrier, the one exception being the Leyre (known also as the Eyre in its lower reaches), which finds its way directly to the sea via the Bassin d'Arcachon.
Elsewhere the streams have formed lakes, the surfaces of which are 15m/50ft to 18m/60ft above sea level. Most of these lakes intercommunicate; their waters force a passage through to the ocean with difficulty, via turbulent currents popular with water sports enthusiasts; the Huchet and Contis currents are typical examples.
The lakes and currents are well stocked with fish (such as trout, tench, carp and eel) but the huge areas of water involved make these coastal lakes and lagoons particularly suitable for the use of large-scale boating equipment.
Sands distributed over the inner areas of the Landes originally formed part of material gouged from the Pyrénées by Quaternary Era glaciers; they exist now as a layer of brown sandstone, no more than 50cm/20in thick, known as the **alios**. This bed inhibits the percolation of water and blocks the extension of roots, and this, combined with the poor drainage of the plains because of their negligible slopes, adds to the dampness of the region and the sterility of its soils. Until the middle of the 19C this inner zone was no more than an unhealthy stretch of moorland, transformed into a swamp when the rains came, and supporting only a scanty shepherd population which went about on stilts. Even the sheep were raised more for their manure than for their meat or wool.

The Forest Under Threat

For maritime pines the greatest danger, which in a dry climate can never be entirely eliminated, is fire, especially when allied with wind. Today the pine forest covers nearly 1 million ha/2.35 million acres in the Landes, and to preserve it a special corps of forest firefighters has been created. Numerous observation posts linked by telephone and radio ensure the rapid detection of an outbreak of fire. Air assistance can be called up. Everything possible has been done to facilitate the firefighters' access in all weathers and with the least delay. Commercial developments, access for traffic and especially camping are strictly controlled.

WAYWARD RIVER

Over the centuries the course of the **River Adour** and its outlet to the sea has been altered by the region's shifting sands. Documents reveal that in AD 907 the river left Capbreton to carve a route to the sea via Vieux-Boucau-Port-d'Albret; in 1164 it again channelled a new path, this time near Bayonne, but later returned to Capbreton. A terrible storm in the 14C blocked the river's way and so it once again flowed to Port-d'Albret. Meanwhile, the port at Bayonne was being engulfed by sand. In 1569 Charles IX insisted that the river should be given a fixed estuary, which saved the harbour at Bayonne; nine years later a channel leading through 2km/1.2mi of dunes beyond Bayonne was opened, and the port at Boucau-Neuf was created.

CONSOLIDATION OF THE DUNES

As early as the Middle Ages it was known that mobile sand dunes could be fixed by the use of maritime pines or plants with spreading roots. A number of experiments were made in the Landes but it was **Nicolas Brémontier** (1738–1809), member of the Caen Academy

Dune du Pilat, Cote d'Argent

©S. Sauvignier/MICHELIN

and an engineer from the Roads and Bridges Department, who perfected the process and started the gigantic task here in 1788.

First he constructed a dyke designed to check the movement of the sand at its starting point, then, about 70m/230ft from the high-water mark, he planted a palisade of stakes against which the sand could pile up. Adding to the height of the palisade as the accumulated sand rose higher, he progressively formed an artificial coastal dune 10m/33ft to 12m/39ft high, which acted as a barrier. He fixed the surface sand by sowing **marram grass**, a variety of grass with a thick network of rapidly spreading roots. He then turned his attention to the problem of the inland dunes.

Brémontier mixed the seeds of maritime pines with gorse and broom seeds, sowing them beneath brushwood, which temporarily held back the sand. After four years the broom had grown into bushes nearly 2.5m/8ft high. These sheltered the slower-growing pines, which eventually outgrew the bushes, and, as they died and rotted, provided fertiliser for the young trees. By 1867 the work was almost complete: 3 000ha/7 500 acres of coastal dunes were carpeted with marram grass and 80 000ha/198 000 acres of inland dunes were planted with pine trees.

CLEANING UP THE INTERIOR

At the beginning of the 19C the inner part of the Landes area was still a fever swamp unfit for cultivation; it was badly drained and resisted all attempts to establish an agricultural presence. Under the Second Empire, however, an engineer named **François Chambrelent** (1817–93) found the answer: he systematically broke up the unfertile layer of *alios* and then drew up a scheme of drainage, clearance and reforestation. The results justified the large-scale planting of maritime pines, cork oaks and ilex trees: the Landes *département* soon became one of the richest in France as the many products made from pine trees brought large returns.

AGENAIS

The Agenais is a transitional region lying between the southern section of the Périgord, Bas-Quercy (Lower Quercy, to the east) and the Landes. This fertile area is lent a certain unity by the valley of the River Garonne.

In the damp northern sector herds of dairy cows graze in the pastures covering the clays; further east, pinewoods and plantations of oak and chestnut appear. In the area around Fumel, on the River Lot, a number of small metallurgical works exploit the local sands rich in iron ore.

PAYS DES SERRES

This area stretches as far as the southern part of the Lot *département*. Unlike nearby Quercy, which has retained a variety of crops, this region of long, narrow hills tends to specialise. On the muddier plateaux of Tournon-d'Agenais wheat is the most important crop; the hillsides are used for the cultivation of vines.

LOT VALLEY

The Lot Valley is one immense orchard punctuated by nurseries and fields of tobacco. Fresh peas, green beans and the melons of Villeneuve-sur-Lot are among the renowned local products.

GARONNE RIVER VALLEY

The alluvial soils and mild climate here allow more delicate crops, most of them grown on terraces, to flourish; each town and village has its speciality. Agen, for example, is famous for its onions and its prunes: hand-picked, specially graded fresh plums, grown on grafted trees, are subsequently dried either naturally or in a slow oven to produce the **pruneaux d'Agen**. The use of grafted plum trees here dates back to the Crusades. In the 16C the monks of Clairac, near Tonneins, were the first to foresee the commercial possibilities of the plum, and 200 years later the market had grown to such an extent that it had to be government controlled. The plum variety used almost universally in the region today is the *Robe-Sergent* (Red Victoria plum). Marmande is famous for its tomatoes and pumpkins; Ste-Marie produces peaches and cherries. Since the 18C even poplar trees have been pressed into service: plantations on land subject to flooding provide wood used in carpentry and the manufacture of paper.

GASCOGNE

The Aquitaine basin is part of a series of French sedimentary beds, which resulted from the silting up of an ancient ocean depth; what distinguishes Gascogne (Gascony), the region lying between the Pyrénées and the River Garonne, is the upper covering provided by enormous masses of debris washed down by the rivers after the erosion of the mountains during the Tertiary Era.
The most common formation in Gascony is known as the **molasse** – layers of sand frequently cemented into a soft yellow sandstone penetrated by discontinuous marl and limestone beds. This geological structure has resulted in a hilly landscape of mixed topography.
From an agricultural point of view the soils here vary between **terreforts**, which are clayey and heavy to work, and **boulbènes** – lighter and slightly muddy, but less fertile and more suitable for grazing and cattle breeding.

THE HILLS OF GASCONY

The rivers, all tributaries of the Garonne, fan out northwards from the foothills of the mountains and cut through the hills of Armagnac in thin swathes. Those emerging from the major Pyrénéan valleys – the Neste d'Aure and the Gave de Pau (Aure and Pau torrents), for instance – are already discharging the deposits they carry, and this material, mixed with the detritus from ancient glacial moraines, has produced a soil that is relatively poor. As a result there is a succession of moors between the high **Plateau de Lannemezan** and Pont-Long, north of Pau, via the Ger Plateau on the western side of Tarbes.
In the hills themselves, careful watering has led to the establishment of market gardens specialising in produce such as strawberries and melons.
Vines in this region form only a part of the traditional polyculture; production of *appellation contrôlée* wines, such as the Jurançon and Madiran whites and reds, and VDQS *(vins délimités de qualité supérieure)* from Béarn and Tursan, remains limited.

PAYS D'ADOUR

The great curving sweep of the River Adour – northwards from its source, then west and finally back towards the south – creates a major demarcation line on the hydrographic chart of the region; the convergence towards Bayonne of all the rivers within this arc is evidence of a continuous sinking of the earth's crust beneath the ocean, which has persisted since the end of the Secondary Era.

Within the area encompassed by the Adour is a hilly landscape cut through by the tributaries of the river. The lower slopes of the valleys are terraced as they drop towards the cultivated alluvial strips flanking these streams.

LES PYRÉNÉES

The customary division of this mountain range into three large natural areas succeeding one another from west to east is justified by major differences in structure, climate and vegetation. The distinction is underlined by the traditions and language of the inhabitants (the Central Pyrénées and the Mediterranean section of the chain are described in the *Michelin Green Guide Languedoc Roussillon Tarn Gorges).*

FORMATION OF THE CHAIN

The remarkable view from the town of Pau of the Pyrénéan mountains rising above the hills of the Béarn district presents a seemingly endless series of finely serrated crests – a mountain barrier revealing at that distance neither individual peaks, with the exception of Pic du Midi d'Ossau, nor saddles.

The barrier itself, stretching 400km/248mi from the Atlantic to the Mediterranean, is relatively narrow (30km/19mi to 40km/25mi on the French side of the frontier) yet also massive and continuous: the average height of the Pyrénées is 1 008m/3 307ft.

HISTORY OF THE RANGE

Approximately 250 million years ago a Hercynian (Palaeozoic) mountain mass similar to the Massif Central or the Ardennes stood on the site occupied by the Pyrénées today; however, whereas the central and northern heights experienced a relatively tranquil existence, this chain between the Atlantic and the Mediterranean was sited in a particularly unstable zone. Already vigorously folded, and then partially levelled by erosion, the Hercynian block was submerged about 200 million years ago beneath a continental sea and covered by Secondary Era sedimentary deposits, before being totally resurrected – and literally shaken from top to bottom – by the Alpine folding, the earliest spasms of which occurred here. Under the enormous pressure of this mountain-building movement the most recent beds, still comparatively pliant, folded without breaking but the rigid ancient platform cracked, broke up and became dislocated. Hot springs burst through near the fractures; mineral deposits formed and metal-bearing ores appeared. During the geological eons that passed while this was occurring, the mountain mass, now tortured and misshapen, was ceaselessly worn down by erosion, and the material torn from it washed out by rivers across the plains below.

CENTRAL PYRÉNÉES

The overall structure of the Pyrénéan region is characterised by the juxtaposition of large geological masses arranged longitudinally. Starting from the Upper Garonne, the relief encompasses:

- The rises known as the Petites Pyrénées, of only medium height but remarkable for the alignment of limestone crests pleated in a fashion typical of the Jurassic period;
- The real foothills, formations of the Secondary Era (either Cretaceous or Jurassic), with folded beds more violently distorted;
- The **Axial Zone**, the true spine of the Pyrénées along which granitic extrusions, recognisable by sharply defined peaks chiselled by glacial erosion, thrust through the Primary sediments: the Balaïtous, the Néouvielle and Maladetta massifs, the Luchon Pyrénées. The summits, however, are not made up entirely of granite, since patches of extremely hard schist and limestone exist which are even more resistant to erosion;
- The southern Secondary Era sediments, under-thrust to a height of more than 3 000m/9 840ft at Monte Perdido, which are to be found largely on the Spanish side of the frontier. Two masterpieces

of mountain scenery stand out among this limestone relief: in Spain the canyon of the **Ordesa Valley** (a National Park); in France the lower part of the **Gavarnie** amphitheatre, with its gigantic platforms of horizontal strata piled one upon the other.

VALLEYS

The inner part of the chain lacks a channel, parallel to the backbone of the range, which could link up the many transversal valleys. This makes internal communications difficult, a problem exacerbated in the Central Pyrénées by the fact that most passes are impracticable in winter. Each of these valleys was therefore isolated for much of the time, and this led to a survival of socially autonomous lifestyles of the kind still to be found in such *petit pays* districts as the **Couserans**, the **Quatre Vallées** (Four Valleys) region, and the **Pays Toy**. The valleys are, nevertheless, far from being inhospitable; despite being hemmed in, they seem no more than a hilly extension of the plains of Lower Aquitaine – with the additional advantage of a sheltered climate.

GLACIERS

A thousand years ago the ancient glaciers thrust their abrasive tongues across the mountain landscape, gouging out the terrain as far as the present sites of Lourdes and Montréjeau. Since then these giant ice rivers have shrunk to negligible proportions (less than 10sq km/4sq mi for the Pyrénées, compared with 400sq km/155sq mi in just the French part of the Alps). There is only one whole glacier, complete with tongue and terminal moraine, in the entire range: **the Ossoue**, on the eastern slopes of the Vignemale.

Many of the most dramatic and appealing features to be found at the heart of the Pyrénées were formed by the old glaciers: hanging valleys, amphitheatres, canyons transformed into pastoral sweeps, jagged crests and scatters of huge boulders, lakes (over 500 in the French Pyrénées), cascades, bluffs, sudden morainic platforms and powerful waterfalls, some of which are harnessed for hydroelectric power.

SUMMITS

The frontier between France and Spain is marked by the peaks of Balaïtous (3 146m/10 321ft) and Vignemale (3 298m/10 820ft), though the greatest heights of the Pyrénées are located on the Spanish side of the border: the impressive massifs of the Maladetta (3 404m/11 168ft) and Posets (3 371m/11 059ft). The French side, nevertheless, boasts **Pic du Midi d'Ossau** (2 884m/9 462ft), which owes its majestic silhouette to the extrusion of volcanic rocks, and **Pic du Midi de Bigorre**

Pic du Midi d'Ossau

©A. Thuillier/MICHELIN

(2 865m/9 400ft), notable also for the way it towers over the plain below. The **Massif de Néouvielle** (3 192m/10 472ft at Pic Long) includes an extraordinary water tower, the contents of which are now almost totally reserved for the hydroelectric installations in the valleys of the Pau and Upper Neste torrents.

PICTURESQUE PYRÉNÉES

The **Cauterets Valley** perfectly illustrates those traditional and well-loved aspects of the Pyrénées, which have inspired so many artists: steep-sided, narrow valleys opening up in the higher reaches of their rivers into huge upland pastures, gently sculptured, jewelled with lakes and webbed with torrents both turbulent and limpid. Such attractions, added to the benefits of the hot springs, the individuality of local customs and the proximity of Spain, appeal to romantic natures. Despite the progressive abandonment of temporary dwellings (such as mountain refuges and summer sheepfolds), of upland tracks and some of the highest pastoral slopes, the Central Pyrénées retain – at least in the Axial Zone – that friendly and characteristic image of mountains that have been in some way humanised.

ATLANTIC PYRÉNÉES

This part of the range is characterised geographically by the disappearance of the Axial Zone, which has led to a confusion of the general relief, there being no longer a continuous spine or backbone to act as a "natural" frontier.

It is among the calcareous beds covering the eastern extremity of the Axial Zone that the most noticeable examples of geomorphological disturbance occur. These are the twisted contortions of the 2 504m/8 215ft **Pic d'Anie** and the savage gashes of the **Kakuetta** and **Holcarte** gorges. The subterranean levels of these fissured limestones riddled with potholes have provided an immense area of exploration and study for speleologists. The slopes of these Lower Pyrénées are abundantly wooded and relatively difficult to cross (the Forest of Iraty, for example).

Nearer the ocean a more placid topography characterises the Basque Country, typified by **La Rhune**, **Mont Ursava** (at Cambo-les-Bains) and the mountains surrounding St-Jean-Pied-de-Port. The landscape between the Adour estuary and Spain mainly comprises hills sculpted from a heterogeneous mass of marine sediments.

BASQUE PYRÉNÉES

The charm and cohesion of this region derives mainly from its oceanic climate, and the colourful language and culture of the Basque people, so closely interwoven with those in the neighbouring Spanish provinces of Guipuzcoa and Navarra. Trans-Pyrénéan traffic is largely concentrated on the coastal route but the inland passages remain very popular with tourists and locals, who have used them ever since the era of the great pilgrimages to Santiago de Compostela in Spain.

COAST

The dunes and pinewoods of the Landes region stretch beyond the mouth of the River Adour, as far as Pointe de St-Martin near Biarritz.

Farther south, however, the coastline bites into the Pyrénéan folds, and the rocks – sedimentary beds violently arched over, foliated into thin laminated layers – form the low, slanting cliffs responsible for the picturesque appearance of the Basque Corniche.

FLORA

There are three main types of vegetation in the Pyrénées, associated with the different geographic zones. To the west, the climate is affected by the Atlantic; the Central Pyrénées is a continental mountain zone; on the far eastern end of the range, the Mediterranean climate prevails. The diversity of species also depends on altitude, as in other mountainous areas. Below 800m/2 625ft, in the foothills, the forest is mostly common oak, typical of Atlantic regions. As the hills rise to 1 700m/5 580ft, the mountainsides are covered with beech on the lower slopes, and pine higher up, where the undergrowth is thick. From this level up to 2 400m/7 874ft, a robust species of hard pine (*Pinus uncinata* – it proliferates in the rocky soil around the Cirque de Gavarnie) joins birch and *Sorbus domestica*, a fruit-bearing tree resembling mountain ash. At this limit the forest grows sparse; rhododendrons and alpine meadows strewn with wild flowers predominate. From here up to 2 800m/9 186ft, few trees subsist, apart from the dwarf willow; other multicoloured vegetation hugs the ground. Beyond this altitude, the wintry landscape is one of rocks covered with the barest layer of moss and lichen, growth which resists the long months spent under snow.

There is an extraordinary wealth of native species of plants, flowers which are found nowhere else on earth. Some of them, such as *ramondia*, a small plant with deep violet blossoms and fuzzy leaves, can be traced back to the Tertiary Era, when the climate was subtropical. Countless species flourish in the mountainous, sub-alpine and alpine zones. Among the loveliest and best known are the lily of the Pyrénées, long-leafed saxifrage, blue Pyrénées thistle, campion, *sisymbrium*, Welsh poppies (blown in, no doubt, by the western wind), and wild iris (especially around the Cirque de Gavarnie). These delightful and rare plants flower in June and July, as well as in August at high altitudes.

FAUNA

A range of mountain species can be found in the different altitude zones. Among the protected species, the brown bear, now unfortunately a very rare sight, lives in the mountainous zone (wild brown bears were reintroduced to the area in 2006, and their population is slowly improving). In the beech and pine woods, the last of the lynx roam (it is uncertain how many of them survive in the wild). The *isards* (a local name for the indigenous chamois) prefer the grassy meadows and rocky outcroppings of the alpine altitudes. Beyond 1 500m/4 921ft, the riverbanks provide shelter for muskrat; the local species is known as *desman*, and these rodents grow to about 25cm/10in. The lakes and streams of the Pyrénées had been fished out, but recent efforts to reintroduce species have been successful, and trout and salmon again swim the waters. An amphibian of the *urodela* order, resembling a newt with a yellow underside and flattened tail, known as the Pyrénéan euprocte, likes to hide under flat stones in rivers and ponds (10cm–20cm/4in–8in). The area is also home to many birds of prey, including the royal eagle, the griffon vulture, and the rare bearded vulture *(Gypaetus barbatus)*, the largest bird of prey in Europe, also known as a *lammergeier*. The wood grouse is found in the underbrush, where it feeds on grains, berries and pine buds. During mating season, its courtship routine is a particularly noisy affair. Marmots come out in the early morning to start their daily routine of eating, napping, playing and keeping watch for predators.

DISCOVERING AQUITAINE

Bordeaux vineyards in autumn

The Gironde *département* takes its name from the Gironde estuary, which stretches from the Pointe de la Grave at the mouth of the Atlantic Ocean, down to the Bec d'Ambès just above the city of Bordeaux. It is formed by the convergence of the Dordogne and Garonne rivers, and is the largest estuary in western Europe. The capital city of the Gironde is Bordeaux, the second-largest city in southwest France after Toulouse, and the seventh biggest in the country. Recent years have seen large-scale investments in the city, and an annual population growth of 1% per year since 1999. The biggest group of new arrivals (40%) are aged between 24 and 40, attracted not only by the wine industry, but also by the growing aeronautics, biotechnology and tourism industries, as well as several large universities. Since 2007, the city centre of Bordeaux has been inscribed as a UNESCO World Heritage Site.

Highlights

1. Bordeaux's graceful **place de la Bourse** (p104)
2. Imposing Gothic edifice **Cathédral St-André** (p110)
3. Stroll the **Jardin Public** (p116)
4. Drive around the vineyards of **St-Émilion** (p132)
5. UNESCO-listed **Citadelle de Blaye** (p135)

Culture of Wine

Bordeaux for centuries has been the centre of the region's wine trade, and today boasts 10 000 wine producers, more than 117 000ha/289 000 acres of vines and brings in an annual 14.5€ billion of revenue to the region. It was the English who held sway here for three hundred years from the 12C to the 15C and who christened the red wine, much beloved of the Plantagenets, "claret" – a name which has come down the centuries. Today, the **Vignoble de Bordeaux** encircles the city, stretching across the entire Gironde region. The area bordering the Left Bank of the Gironde estuary produces world-famous wines such as Médoc, Haut-Médoc, Pauillac, Margaux, St-Estèphe and St-Julien. On the Right Bank of the Garonne, lying between the Garonne and the Dordogne rivers, lie the vineyards of Entre-deux-Mers, famous for its crisp white wine. Farther east on the Right Bank, clustered around the Dordogne River, are St-Émilion, Pomerol, Fronsac and the Côtes vineyards of Bourg, Blaye and Castillon. To the south of the city of Bordeaux are the dessert wine producing areas of Sauternes and Barsac, and the dry red and white areas of Pessac-Léognan and Graves.

Dune du Pilat

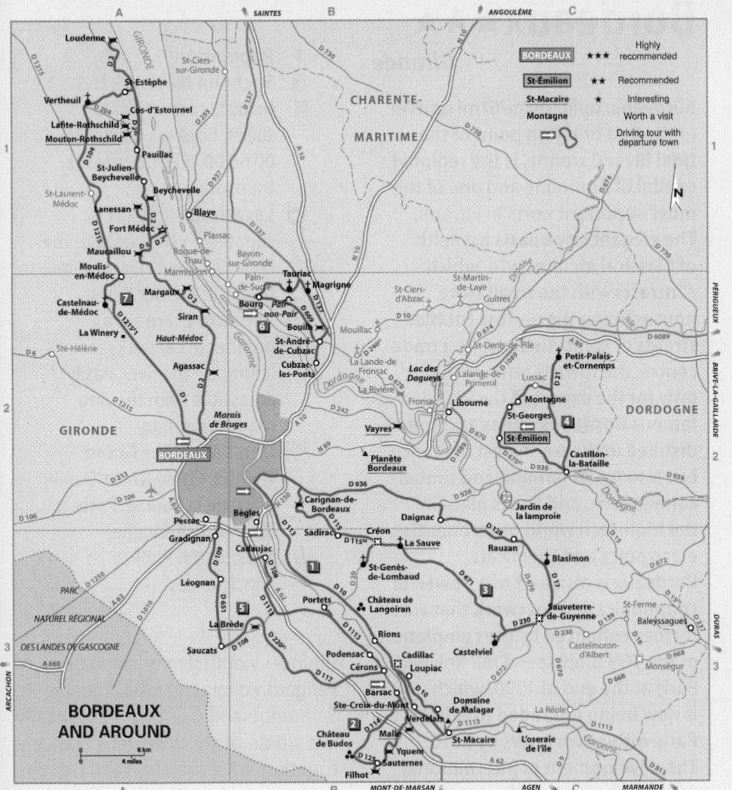

Tourism

Beyond the vineyards, Bordeaux has a wealth of attractions for visitors. The 100km/62mi of estuary has six working ports, and both cruise ships and smaller pleasure boats are able to moor right in the centre of Bordeaux. The coastal strip of the Gironde is part of the **Côte d'Argent**, and contains the highest sand dune in Europe, the Dune du Pilat, which is an astonishing natural phenomenon standing at 107m/350ft above sea level. Just to the north is the Bassin d'Arcachon, a 155sq km/60sq mi lagoon dotted with tourist resorts. For details of these areas, *see page 153*.

Farther inland, the city centre of Bordeaux boasts over 350 classified buildings listed as historic monuments, including three religious World Heritage buildings that are part of The Way of St James. Its Port de la Lune, so-called because of the crescent shape of the Garonne river in the city centre, is the largest urban conglomeration to have received the UNESCO classification, covering over half of the city's surface area, or 1 810ha/4 472 acres.

Further afield, the main centres of tourism include the Medieval village of **St-Émilion**, set on a limestone ridge 35km/22mi to the east of Bordeaux and the 17C Citadelle de Blaye, built by the military engineer Marquis de Vauban to defend the estuary.

Smaller tourist towns are dotted around the rolling hills of Entre-deux-Mers, from picturesque *bastide* towns such as Monségur and Créon, to the vestiges of former Benedictine abbeys such as La Sauve Majeure, which was founded in 1079 and although abandoned in the 16C is an important example of Romanesque architecture.

Bordeaux★★★

Gironde

Bordeaux, built 98km/61mi upriver at the first bridging point of the tidal River Garonne, is the regional capital of Aquitaine and one of the most important ports in Europe. The elegant city boasts a wealth of Classical architecture, which contrasts with the small store houses lining the narrow cobbled streets of some districts. As a trade centre, the town is renowned not only for the export of the world-famous Bordeaux wines and spirits distilled in the southwest of France, but also for its farming and timber connections, and for its place in the high-tech world of aeronautics, electronics and chemicals. Bordeaux is also part of a powerful communications network that was further enhanced by the completion of the TGV high-speed rail link with Paris at the end of 1990, which is now being upgraded to bring Paris within two hours by 2016. The development of international exhibition sites and the construction of such projects as the tramway and new sporting arenas has helped make Bordeaux an important junction between northern Europe and the Iberian peninsula.

- **Population:** 232 260
- **Michelin Map:** 335: H-5
- **Info:** 12 cours du XXX-Juillet, Bordeaux. ℘05 56 00 66 00. www.bordeaux-tourisme.com.
- **Location:** Bordeaux is situated on the banks of the River Garonne, 48km/30mi from the Atlantic Coast.
- **Parking:** There are a number of car parks alongside the river, easily accessible from the ring road (*see map*).
- **Don't Miss:** The Grand Théâtre; Église Notre-Dame; place de la Bourse; Porte de la Grosse-Cloche.
- **Kids:** Jardin Public; Cap Sciences.

A BIT OF HISTORY

Dukes of Aquitaine

Bordeaux (or Burdigala before it was colonised and developed under the Romans) was built on a choice site repeatedly attacked by Visigoths, Normans, Saracens and Moors. It was Good King Dagobert who, in the 7C, regained the town and the surrounding territory for the Frankish empire and the Merovingian dynasty, creating a Duchy of Aquitaine with Bordeaux as its capital.

Eleanor's Dowry

In 1137 Louis, son of the French King, married **Eleanor of Aquitaine**, the daughter of William X, Duke of Aquitaine. The bride's dowry comprised the Duchy of Guyenne, the regions of Périgord, Poitou, Limousin, Angoumois, Saintonge and Gascony – practically the whole of southwestern France – together with the suzerainty of the Auvergne and the Comté de Toulouse. The marriage, solemnised in Bordeaux Cathedral, was not a success. Louis, who became King Louis VII, was a religious man and an ascetic, contrary to his queen, who was frivolous and enjoyed the good things in life. After 15 years of unhappy marriage, Louis returned from the Crusades and obtained a divorce (1152) through the Council of Beaugency. The settlement gave Eleanor her freedom, and she retained the whole of her dowry. Two years later, she married **Henry Plantagenet**, Duke of Normandy, Count of Anjou, ruler of Maine and Touraine.

Henry and Eleanor's combined territories covered an area as vast as that ruled by the King of France. When, barely two months after the marriage, Henry succeeded to the throne of England and became Henry II, the resulting imbalance proved too much for the French. The conflict it provoked lasted, intermittently, for three centuries.

The Claret Connection

It was the Romans who introduced viticulture to the Bordeaux region. The red wine, christened "claret" by the English occupiers (after the local word *clairet*), was much appreciated by the Plantagenets – 1 000 casks were set aside for the coronation celebrations.

The grape at that time was a sacred fruit (the punishment for thieves was the loss of an ear) and the quality of the wines was all-important. Six sworn tasters testified to its excellence or otherwise, and no innkeeper dared broach a barrel before it had been submitted for approval. Merchants who adulterated the wine were severely punished, as were coopers whose casks proved to be defective.

Black Prince's Territory (14C)

Bordeaux was known as the capital of **Guyenne** (an old English corruption of the word Aquitaine). Under English rule the town had the right to choose its own mayor and its councillors or *jurats*, and trade flourished. Wine was exported to England, and the Bordelais (the people of Bordeaux) cheerfully sold arms to both sides. At the same time, nobles and *jurats* built themselves substantial stone houses, known as *taules* or *hostaux*, and the son of the English King, Edward III, known as the Black Prince, established his headquarters and held court here.

The Black Prince was one of the most talented military leaders of his time and one of the most savage plunderers. From his Bordeaux base, he sallied forth for one campaign after another, terrifying in turn the people of the Languedoc, Limousin, Auvergne, Berry and Poitou regions. In 1453, Guyenne was retaken by the French Royal Army after the Battle of Castillon, and the Hundred Years' War was over.

Bordeaux and the Intendants

These high-ranking provincial representatives of the French Crown first appointed by Richelieu during the reign of Louis XIV in the 17C were made an effective instrument of central government by Jean-Baptiste Colbert (1619–83), the King's Secretary of State. In the 18C the Intendants' broad vision of a spacious, well-planned city to replace the tangle of medieval streets in Bordeaux brought them into conflict with the short-sighted and penny pinching representatives of the local population, but they succeeded in their aims. The work of Claude Boucher, the Marquis of Tourny, Dupré and St Maur turned a maze of narrow, twisted and stinking lanes surrounded by swamps into one of the most beautiful towns in France. Grandiose urban concepts such as Tourny's avenues, the Bordeaux quays, the Stock Exchange complex and monuments such as the Customs House, the City Hall and the Grand Theatre date from this period. Once the new Bordeaux was established, its position on the Atlantic seaboard was exploited to the full, and it soon became the leading port in France.

Trade Boom

The Empire period (early 19C) was a bleak time for the city, as the maritime trade on which it depended was badly affected by the Continental Blockade. The Restoration, however, revived its fortunes. The great stone bridge and the Quinconces Esplanade, dating from this era, were both projects which the Intendants had no time to complete.

Under the Second Empire, the city's role as a trade centre continued to develop, largely because of improved communications and the drainage of the Landes marshes to the south.

In 1870, during the siege of Paris, in 1914 before the German offensive and again in 1940, the French government fled south to take refuge in Bordeaux – dramas which earned the town the nickname of the "Tragic Capital". After World War II, Bordeaux once again found the dynamic spirit of enterprise that its shipbuilders, financiers and merchants had enjoyed in the 18C.

OLD BORDEAUX★★

Situated between the Chartrons and St-Michel districts, the Old Town, which includes some 5 000 buildings dating from the 18C, has undergone large-scale restoration in an effort to return the city's ancient stonework to its original splendour. The façade of numerous buildings are marked by "mascarons", small carved faces or objects that are often linked to the trades of the bourgeoisie who first owned the houses. The name comes from the Italian word *maschera* meaning "mask". Often comic or grotesque, there are more than 3 000 examples across the Old Town centre.

WALKING TOURS

1 FROM LA PLACE DE LA BOURSE TO THE QUARTIER ST-MICHEL★★

Map p109. Allow one day.

This stroll leads you through a network of picturesque narrow streets between the St-Pierre and St-Michel districts.

Place de la Bourse★★

Named after the Stock Exchange (La Bourse), this magnificent square was formerly called place Royale and was the work of the father and son architects Jacques Jules (1667–1742) and Jacques-Ange (1698–1782) Gabriel. On the northern side is the Stock Exchange itself. On the southern side is the former Hôtel des Fermes (tax assessors) housing the **National Customs Museum**. Three Graces Fountain (1860) stands in the middle of the square.

Musée des Douanes

1 pl. de la Bourse. Open Tue–Sun 10am–6pm. Closed 1 Jan, 25 Dec. 3€ (1st Sun of month no charge). 05 56 48 82 82. www.musee-douanes.fr.

The Customs Museum is housed in a large hall with fine vaulting *(restored)*. On the right-hand side, the history of the customs administration is followed chronologically with the help of documents, uniforms, an old Customs Director's office, professional equipment, and prints and paintings including a portrait of St Matthew, the patron saint of customs officers.

On the opposite side, different themes are presented including the seizure of drugs and the arrest of counterfeiters. The tour ends with a display on the customs officer's latest weapon – the computer.

Continue, via r. F.-Philippart, to pl. du Parlement.

The façades and the variety of their sculpted decoration combine to form one of the best architectural examples of the Louis XV style.

The Port

Bordeaux stands strategically upriver of the Gironde estuary, just 98km/61mi from the coast, and commands the shortest land link between the Atlantic Ocean and the Mediterranean Sea, via the valley of the River Garonne and the Midi Canal (240km/149mi long), which includes Naurouze Pass. The city's importance as a port dates back to the blossoming of the wine trade during the English domination, when the exportation of claret began. This was markedly increased in the 18C by a heavy traffic in colonial products from the French West Indies. More recently, the activity of the inner-city docks has declined in favour of the new container terminal downstream at Le Verdon where the Gironde meets the ocean.

The inhabitants of Bordeaux are rediscovering the banks of the river. On the west bank, the quays (4.5km/2.8mi long and 80m/88yd wide) have been redeveloped for use by pedestrians, bikes, trams and cars as well as venues for various events and open-air cafés.

Place de la Bourse lit up at night

© Romain Cintract/hemis.fr

Place du Parlement★

Parliament Square was once a royal market. This pleasant quadrangle of Louis XV buildings is arranged around a central courtyard paved with cobblestones *(restored)*. A Second Empire fountain is set in the centre. There are many fine houses, some with ground-floor arcades, delicate fanlights and mask decorations. They are surmounted by open-work balustrades.

Take r. du Parlement-St-Pierre to pl. St-Pierre.

Place St-Pierre

Many 18C houses in the St-Pierre district have been restored. The 14C–15C church of St Peter was altered substantially in the 19C. On Thursdays the square is livened up by a market of organic produce where one can enjoy a delicious healthy meal in pleasant surroundings.

Follow r. des Argentiers.

The house at no **14**, known as **Maison de l'Angelot**, dates from c.1750. The carved ornamentation of the façade includes a haut-relief of a child, and keystones in the Louis XV rough-cast style known as *rocaille*.

At no **28** an 18C building houses the **Bordeaux monumental exhibition** *(open Mon–Sat 10am–1pm, 2–6pm, Sun and public holidays 2–6pm; no charge; 05 56 48 04 24)*, which chronicles the development of Bordeaux from Gallo-Roman town to the modern city of today.

Continue to pl. du Palais.

Place du Palace

The square owes its name to the old Palais de l'Ombrière, which was built by the dukes of Guyenne in the 10C, rebuilt in the 13C, used subsequently by the kings of England and finally, under Louis XI, became the seat of the Bordeaux Parliament in 1462. The palace was demolished in 1800 to make way for the present rue du Palais.

Porte Cailhau

pl. du Palais. Open Jun–Sept daily 2–7pm. 3€. 05 56 00 66 00.

This triumphal arch derives its name either from the Cailhau family, who were members of the Bordeaux nobility, or from the *cailloux* (pebbles) washed up around its base by the Garonne and used as ballast by ships. Built on the site of an ancient city gate, east of the old Palais de l'Ombrière, it was completed in 1495. The arch is dedicated to Charles VIII, who won the Battle of Fournoe in the same year. This might explain the juxtaposition of the decorative and defensive elements. Inside, on three different levels, an exhibit retraces the history of old Bordeaux, outlines the

important stages of urban expansion and reveals plans for the future. The top floor offers an unusual **view** across the quays to the stone bridge.

Follow r. Ausone, cross cours d'Alsace-et-Lorraine and fork right; turn right onto r. de la Rousselle.

This street is lined with the shops in which the city's wine merchants, grain and salted meat sellers once plied their trade. The buildings are characterised by tall ground floors surmounted by low-ceilinged mezzanines. No **25** was the town house of the 16C philosopher-essayist Michel Eyquem de Montaigne (1533–92).

Turn left onto r. Neuve and continue to the cul-de-sac (right).

Still preserved is a 14C wall, pierced with two windows surrounded with stone tracery. Through the porch to the right stands the city's **oldest house**, where Montesquieu's wife, **Jeanne de Lartigue** lived. On the other side of cours Victor-Hugo there is a view of **Porte des Salinières** (Salt Sellers' Gate), formerly Porte de Bourgogne (Burgundy Gate).

Take r. de la Fusterie, opposite pl. Duburg and Basilique St-Michel.

Basilique St-Michel★

pl. Canteloup et Meynard.
Open Mon–Sat 8.30am–6pm, Sun 8am–noon. 05 56 94 30 50.

The construction of St Michael's Basilica began in 1350, and lasted for two centuries, during which time the original design was much modified. The side chapels were added after 1475.

The generous dimensions of the restored basilica are impressive. Inside, the two-storey elevation is emphasised by high arcades, topped with tall clerestory windows, and wide side aisles. The lines of the flattened east end are barely affected by the three small chapels.

In the first chapel off the south aisle stands a statue of St Ursula sheltering 1 000 virgins beneath her cloak. The modern stained-glass windows, behind the high altar, are by Max Ingrand. The moulded coving of the north transept doorway frames a tympanum decorated with an allegorical scene representing Original Sin *(left)* and Adam and Eve being expelled from the Garden of Eden *(right)*. The organ loft and pulpit date from the 18C.

Flèche St Michel

pl. Canteloup. Open Jun–Sept daily 2–7pm. 3€.

The people of Bordeaux are justly proud of this late 15C hexagonal Gothic belfry, which stands apart from the basilica. At 114m/374ft tall, it is the highest tower in all of southern France (the tallest tower in the country belongs to Strasbourg Cathedral: 142m/466ft). The tower easily dwarfs the cathedral's Pey-Berland Tower, also a separate structure, a mere 50m/164ft high. Beneath the slender spire and superbly decorated façades lies a circular crypt.

Take r. Camille-Sauvageau.

Abbatiale Ste-Croix

pl. Pierre Renaudel. Organ concerts Jul–Aug Wed 6.30pm. 05 56 94 30 50.

Built in the 12C and 13C and restored during the 19C, this church has a Romanesque **west front**★ typical of the Saintonge region; the north tower is modern. The arches of the blind windows surrounding the main doorway are decorated with carvings depicting Greed and Lust.

Walk to pl. de la Victoire (a favourite haunt of students in the evening) via pl. Léon Duguit and pl. des Capucins.

Porte d'Aquitaine

pl. de la Victoire.

This imposing 18C triumphal arch is surmounted by a triangular pediment bearing the royal arms and those of the city.

Take cours Pasteur, to the right, or the tramway line B in the direction of Quinconces.

Musée d'Aquitaine★★

20 cours Pasteur. ♿ Open Tue–Sun 11am–6pm. Closed public holidays. No charge (temporary exhibitions: 5€). ℘05 56 01 51 00.

This regional museum, housed in the former Literature and Science Faculty and laid out on two levels, traces the life of Aquitaine Man from prehistoric times to the present day.

Collections in the **prehistory section** contain precious relics of arts and crafts practised by the hunters of the Stone Age. These include the famous *Venus with a Horn* (20 000 BC) from the Great Grotto in Laussel, and bison from the Cap Blanc grotto (Middle Magdalenian Age). A display of axes unearthed in the Médoc region illustrates the variety of tools fashioned by the metallurgists of the Bronze Age (4000–2700 BC). Iron Age spoils include funerary items (urns, jewellery, weapons) discovered in the Gironde burial grounds or Pyrénées tumuli, and the prestigious **Tayac Treasure** – a quantity of gold artefacts comprising coins, small ingots and a remarkable torque (necklace or collar) which dates from the 2C BC.

In the **Gallo-Roman section**, aspects of day-to-day religious and economic life in the Aquitaine provincial capital are illustrated through ceramics, glassware, mosaics, fragments of cornices and bas-relief sculptures. Of particular note are a grey Pyrénéan marble altar, an imperious **statue of Hercules** in bronze, and the **Garonne Treasure**, which comprises 4 000 bronze alloy coins bearing the effigies of emperors from Claudius to Antoninus Pius.

Early Christian times and the Middle Ages are illustrated by grey marble and limestone sarcophagi and mosaics, including a 4C representation of *The Holy Sepulchre*. Excavations and public works in the city have uncovered significant pieces, which have been added to the collections – Romanesque capitals from St Andrew's Cathedral and a Flamboyant Gothic rose window from the Carmelite monastery.

Bordeaux's golden age (18C) saw the development of grandiose urban projects and the building of splendid mansions which were luxuriously furnished. Several displays focus on country life and farming in former times. The accent is always placed on the natural resources of Aquitaine, which embraces the rural landscape of Béarn, the Landes (moors) of Gascony, the Gironde and its vineyards, and of course Arcachon and its oyster-farming. Several rooms show regional rural society and traditional activities, **19C Bordeaux** and modern, **20C Aquitaine**.

Follow the pedestrianised r. Ste-Catherine and turn right onto cours Victor-Hugo.

Porte de la Grosse-Cloche★

r. St-James.

The 15C arched gateway (Great Bell Gate), with its three round turrets and conical roofs, is another source of local pride. The clocks date from 1592 (*inside*) and 1772 (*outside*); the bell was cast in 1775. The gateway stands on the site of an older structure, porte St Éloi (St Eligius' Gateway), which was one of the entrances to the 13C walled town. When it existed, this belfry rang out the news that the grape harvest was to begin.

Follow the narrow r. St-James, which passes through the gateway, cross pl. Lafargue to r. du Pas-St-Georges and

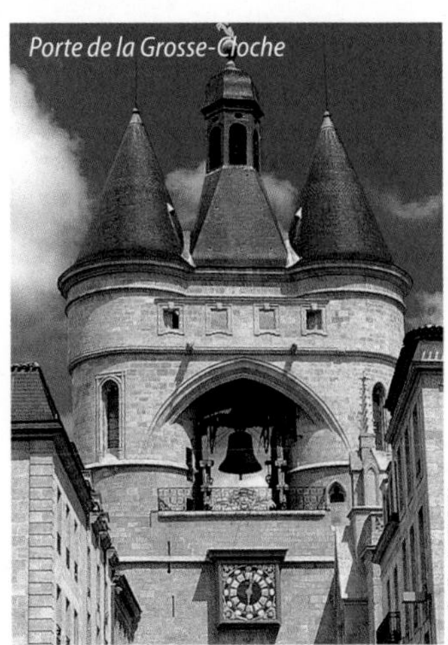
Porte de la Grosse-Cloche
©A. Thuillier/MICHELIN

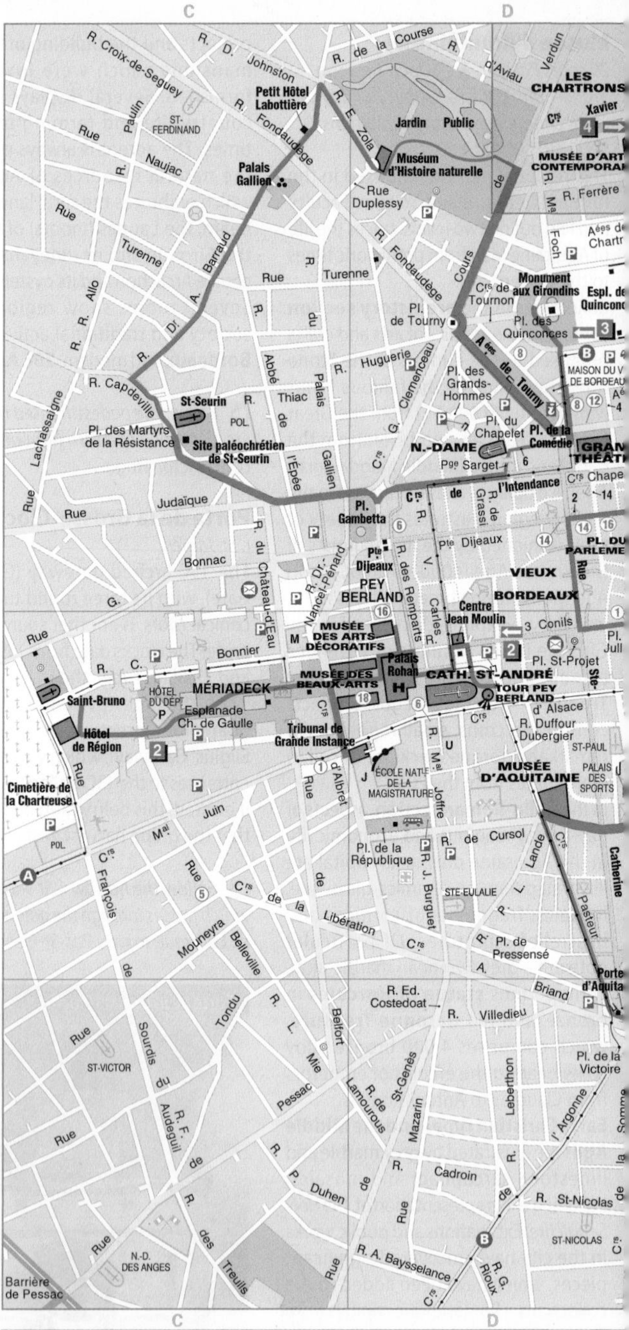

WHERE TO STAY

- Étap'Hôtel............................ 1
- Hôtel Acanthe............................ 3
- Hôtel Citéa............................ 5
- Hôtel de la Tour Intendance...... 6
- Hôtel des Quatre Sœurs........... 8
- Hôtel Opéra..................... 12
- Hôtel Presse..................... 14
- Une Chambre en Ville...... 16

WHERE TO EAT

- Le Bistro du Musée....................
- Le Café Bordelais....................
- Le Café Utopia....................
- La Petite Gironde....................
- La Tupina....................

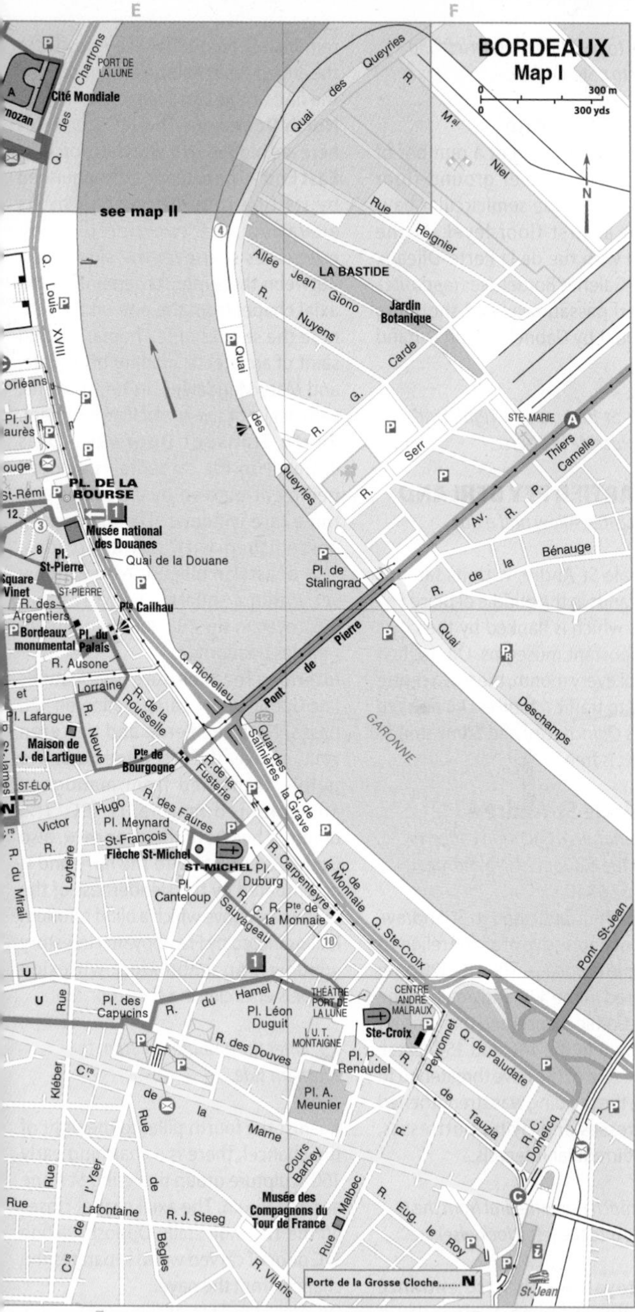

BORDEAUX
Map I

0 — 300 m
0 — 300 yds

see map II

Porte de la Grosse Cloche....... N

	INDEX OF STREET NAMES	
Lou Magret.......................... (14)	Bordelaise (Galerie).................. 2	Pas St-Georges (R. du)............10
Restaurant du Musée des Arts décoratifs............ (18)	Condé (R. de).......................... 4	Philippart (R. F.).........................12
Sarl la Cheminée Royale..... (16)	Esprit-des-Lois (R. de l')........... 5	Piliers-de-Tutelle (R. des).........14
	Mautrec (R.)............................. 6	
	Parlement St-Pierre (R. du)..... 8	

continue to pl.C.Jullian. Turn left and continue to r. Ste-Catherine.

Rue Ste-Catherine

Farther along the street a number of houses are built over ground-floor arcades, with wide semicircular bays opening at first-floor level. At the junction with rue de la Porte-Dijeaux note the Galeries Bordelaises *(opposite)*, a covered passageway and shopping arcade built by Gabriel-Joseph Durand in 1833.

The r. St-Rémi, on the right, leads back to place de la Bourse.

2 QUARTIER PEY BERLAND

Map p108. Allow half a day.

Cathédrale St-André, with its famous tower, stands in the middle of place Pey Berland, which is flanked by the city's most important museums. On the first Sunday of every month, the town centre is closed to traffic *(bikes can be hired on pl. des Quinconces)* and admission to museums is free.

Cathédrale St-André★

pl. Pey Berland. Organ concerts Jul–Aug Tue 6.30pm. No charge. 05 56 52 68 10.

This cathedral, dedicated to St Andrew, is the most impressive of all the religious buildings in Bordeaux. The 11C–12C nave was altered in the 13C and again in the 15C. The Gothic chancel and the transept were rebuilt in the 14C and 15C. Later, when the roof of the nave threatened to collapse, the building was strengthened by buttresses and flying buttresses, added at irregular intervals.

Approach the cathedral from the N and circle it to the left (clockwise).

Porte Royale★ – This 13C entrance to the right of the north doorway is renowned for its sculptures, inspired by the outstanding statuary adorning religious buildings in Île-de-France (the region surrounding Paris, where Gothic architecture originated). Most remarkable are the Twelve Apostles in the entrance bay and, on the tympanum, the fine Gothic *Last Judgement*.

North Doorway – The 14C sculptures here are hidden by a wooden porch.

East End – The exterior is distinguished by its fine proportions and by its elevation: the two-tiered flying buttresses soar over the side aisles. Between the supports separating the axial chapel from the one on the left, note the statues of St Thomas, patron saint of architects, holding his square, and Mary Magdalene, in 15C costume, with her jar of sweet-smelling ointment.

South Transept Doorway – This entrance to the cathedral is below a pediment pierced by an oculus and three rose windows. The upper part, embellished with trefoil arcades, also boasts an elegant rose window set within a square. The west front, destroyed in the 18C and then rebuilt, remains unadorned.

Interior – The impressive nave features late Gothic upper parts, resting on 12C bases. Note the lierne and tierceron vaulting over the first three bays. The pulpit, fashioned from mahogany and coloured marble, is 18C. The different height of the **chancel**★, also Gothic, contrasts with the nave and is accentuated by the slenderness of the tall arches, above which a blind triforium is illuminated by Flamboyant clerestory windows. An ambulatory with side chapels encircles the chancel.

Enter the ambulatory from the southern side.

Against the fourth pillar to the right of the chancel, there is a charming early 16C sculpture group depicting St Anne and the Virgin. The axial chapel closes off the 17C choir stalls. Opposite, a fine 17C door of carved wood separates the chancel from the nave.

On the inner face of the west front is the **Renaissance organ loft**. Below it two bas-relief sculptures trace the development of Renaissance sculpture. The group on the right shows Christ, harried by pagan deities from Hell,

descending into Limbo, whereas that on the left shows the Resurrection.

Tour Pey Berland★

pl. Pey Berland. Open Jun–Sept daily 10am–1.15pm, 2–6pm; Oct–May Tue–Sun 10am–12.30pm, 2–5.30pm. Only accessible by stairs (231 steps). Closed 1 Jan, 1 May, 25 Dec. 5€. 05 56 81 26 25. http://pey-berland.monuments-nationaux.fr.

The tower was built in the 15C on the orders of Archbishop Pey-Berland. It has always stood separate from the main body of the cathedral, beyond the east end. The steeple, shortened by a hurricane in the 18C, now supports the statue of Notre-Dame d'Aquitaine, installed in the 19C and restored in 2002. 231 steps up a narrow spiral staircase *(beware low door lintels)* take you to the top from where there is a panoramic **view**★★ of the town and its steeples.

It is worth standing back a little *(to the south)*, for an overall view of the twin spires above the north transept of the cathedral and, in the foreground, the massive, square, terraced towers flanking the south transept.

Centre Jean Moulin

48 r. Vital Carles. Open Tue–Sun 2–6pm. Closed public holidays. No charge. 05 56 79 66 00.

This museum, devoted to the Resistance and deportation under the German occupation, presents a panorama of World War II. Jean Moulin, the most famous of France's Resistance heroes, became President of the clandestine National Resistance Council after a secret visit to Général de Gaulle in Britain. Subsequently betrayed, he was caught by the Gestapo, tortured and murdered in 1943.

On the ground floor, the Centre displays Resistance pamphlets, secret communications, underground newspapers, illegal radio transmitters and other items – particularly relating to Jean Moulin – which developed as a result of the Nazi occupation. The first floor concentrates on the spread of Nazi tyranny and the deportations which followed. The displays on the second floor are devoted to the men of the Free French Forces and their exploits, and include the boat *S'ils-te-Mordent (If They Bite You)*, which, crammed with volunteers, linked the Brittany fishing port of Carantec with England. There is also a reconstruction of Jean Moulin's secret office.

Palais Rohan

pl. Pey Berland. Guided tours (1hr) Wed 2.30pm. 3€. 05 56 10 20 31. www.bordeaux.fr.

The City Hall is installed in the former bishop's palace, built in the 18C for Archbishop Ferdinand Maximilian de Meriadek, Prince of Rohan. The building marks the introduction of Neoclassicism to France.

The most notable interior features are the State staircase, the salons with their fine 18C panelling, and a banqueting hall decorated in grisailles by Lacour.

Take r. des Trois-Conils, on your left.

Musée des Arts Décoratifs★

39 r. Bouffard. Open Wed–Mon 2–6pm (temporary exhibitions open Mon and Wed–Fri 11am–6pm, Sat–Sun 2–6pm). Closed public holidays. No charge (temporary exhibitions: 5€). 05 56 10 14 00.

The Lalande mansion which houses the Museum of Decorative Arts was designed by Laclotte in 1779. It has tall slate roofs and dormer windows.

A tour of the right wing begins with the Jeanvrot Collection (items relating to the lives of the last kings of France), presented in a setting furnished in 19C fashion, and continues through rooms of elegant woodwork and fine furniture, such as the Compagnie room, containing an 18C terra-cotta statue symbolising America (on the chimney-piece), and a marble bust of Montesquieu signed by Jean Baptiste Lemoyne. In the dining room is a display of local faïence decorated with a pewter glaze, and a collection of fine 18C porcelain.

Next door, the Guestier room typifies an elegant bourgeois lifestyle, displaying

carved furniture and bronze statues by Barye. The two antechambers with their blue-and-white panelling are evocative of 18C town lifestyle in Bordeaux. The central staircase, embellished with a fine wrought-iron balustrade, leads to the first-floor rooms. The first two of these are dedicated to French and foreign ceramics. The Jonquille lounge is decorated with a magnificent Venetian glass candelabra and splendid 18C decanters and flasks. The second floor houses an exhibit of faïence from southwestern France. Ornamental ironwork, enamel inlay and pre-18C collections of the locksmith's craft are displayed on the attic floor.

Rejoin r. des Trois-Conils continuing to the left.

Musée des Beaux-Arts★★

20 cours d'Albret. Open Wed–Mon 11am–6pm. Closed public holidays. No charge (temporary exhibitions: 5€). 05 56 10 20 56.

The Fine Arts Museum bordering the gardens of City Hall displays a fine collection of 15C to 20C paintings in the north and south galleries. The **south wing** houses paintings from the Italian Renaissance (Titian's *Tarquin and Lucretia*), 17C French works, such as Vouet's *David Holding the Head of Goliath* directly inspired by Caravaggio, works from the 17C Dutch School, such as Ter Brugghen's *The Lute Player*, the captivating *Oak Struck by Lightning*, by Van Goyen, and paintings from the 17C Flemish School including the admirable *Wedding Dance*, painted in a popular rustic style by Jan I (Velvet) Brueghel. The 18C and early 19C are represented, among others, by the graceful *Portrait of Princess Louise of Orange-Nassau* by Tischenbein, Chardin's *Still Life* and four paintings by the local artist Pierre Lacour, who was the museum's first curator in 1811.

The **north wing** is given over to modern and contemporary works. The Romantic School is represented by Delacroix' famous *Greece Expiring on the Ruins of Missolonghi*, whereas *The Forest of Fontainebleau* by Diaz de la Peña (born in Bordeaux) is an illustration of work by the Barbizon School, the first school to paint in the open air. Bertrand-Jean Redon, better known as Odilon Redon (1840–1916), was born in Bordeaux. A small room in the Fine Arts Museum pays tribute to him and shows some of his works: *Char d'Apollon* (*Apollo's Chariot*, 1909), *Chevalier Mystique* (*Mystic Knight*, a charcoal and pastel work), *La Prière* (*The Prayer*), *La Lecture* (*The Reading*). The second-half of the 19C is introduced by the outrageous *Rollas* by Henri Gervex, a nude refused by the 1878 Salon, followed by Henri Martin's *Chacun sa Chimère*, a large canvas inspired by the Symbolist movement. From the 20C, there is the impressive *Église Notre-Dame à Bordeaux* by the Austrian Expressionist Kokoschka, the sinuous, tormented *Homme Bleu sur la Route* by Soutine and the extremely beautiful *Portrait of Bevilacqua* (1905), outlined in blue, by Matisse. The last room is dedicated to more contemporary works.

The **Galerie des Beaux-Arts** in nearby place du Colonel-Raynal holds temporary art exhibits.

Returning towards the Musée des Beaux-Arts, follow cours d'Albret then turn left into r. des Frères-Bonie.

Tribunal de Grande Instance de Bordeaux

Built in 1998 by architect Richard Rogers, the TGI de Bordeaux is found in the heart of the Old Town, a self-contained island for the judiciary that includes the town hall, the former Neoclassical Palais de Justice built by Joseph-Adolphe Thiac and the École nationale de la Magistrature. This parallelepiped of glass, stainless steel and wood is found beside some of the oldest vestiges of medieval Bordeaux; the remains of the fort du Hâ. The architect of the Centre Pompidou in Paris has here chosen a symbolic but entirely functional architecture: the desire for a transparent justice system is highlighted through a building where the glass walls ensure its interior function is visible from the outside. The public entrance area

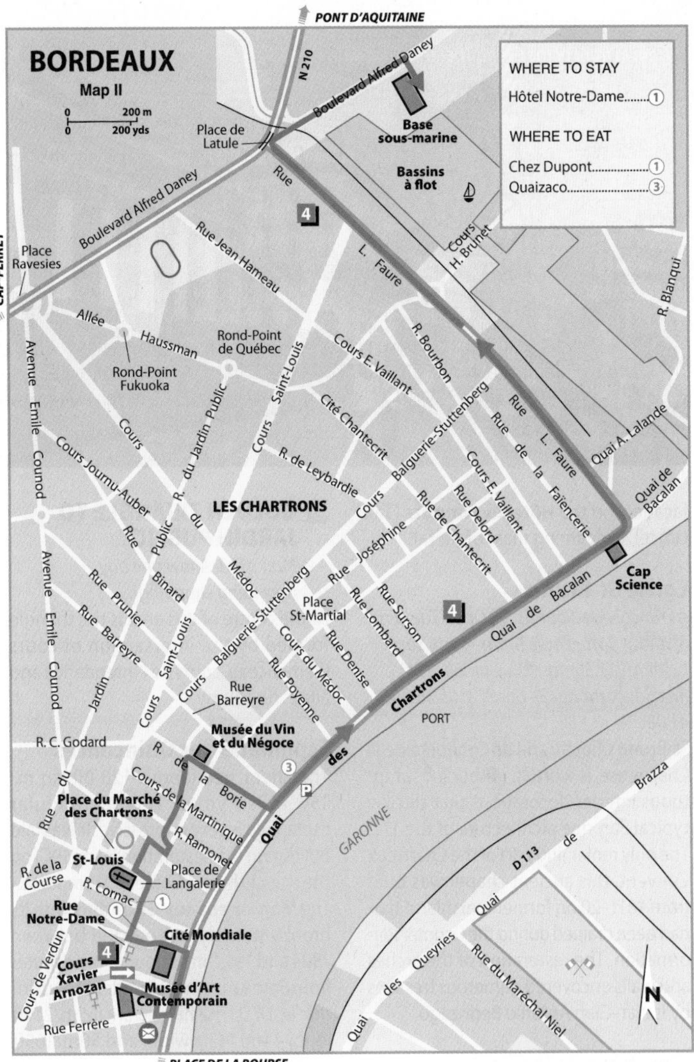

encapsualtes the idea of a justice that is open and accessible to all.

Cross back over cours d'Albret.

Mériadeck District

Named in honour of Prince Ferdinand Maximilien de Rohan, Archbishop of Bordeaux in the 18C, this ultra-modern complex is the administrative centre of the Aquitaine region.

The area includes offices, administrative buildings, apartment blocks, shopping centre, ice-skating rink and the municipal library. Esplanade Charles de Gaulle is an example of the formal gardens and ponds. Suspended footbridges lead to roads bordering the complex. Some of the cubed and rounded concrete and glass buildings are encased in metal super-structures. The most distinctive are the **Caisse d'Épargne** building with its superposed curved and rectangular forms, the mirror-walled **Bibliothèque** (Library), the **Hôtel de Région** with its harmonious, vertically lined concrete

Tram in front of the Grand Théâtre, Place de la Comédie

© Gérard Labriet/Photononstop

façade, and the **Hôtel des Impôts** (Tax Office), a gleaming mass of metal.

Église St-Bruno

r. François-de-Sourdis. Open Tue–Fri 8.30am–7pm, Sat 8.30am–6pm, Sun 8.30am–12.30pm. Guided visit first Sat of month 3–6pm. 05 56 96 41 08.

St-Bruno Church, and its Cimetière de la Chartreuse, is worth a detour for sumptuous interior decorations that display typical Baroque architecture of the 17C. The only remaining part of the Chartreux Convent, this ancient chapel was built from 1611–20 on former marshland that had been drained during the Counter Reformation. The restoration of the arches and walls uncovered numerous frescoes by Italian Gian Antonio Berinzago.

Cimetière de la Chartreuse

r. François-de-Sourdis. Open mid-Jul–Sept. Guided visits at nightfall on Sat, through tourist office.

Following the example of Père-Lachaise, the diversity of mausoleums and chapels creates a dreamy atmosphere in this cemetery. The epitaphs that moved Stendhal to describe this place as "laughter near death" speak of famous names such as Goya, Delacroix, Flora Tristan, Gauguin's mother… and many other historic figures.

3 GOLDEN TRIANGLE TO JARDIN PUBLIC

Map p108. Allow one day (including shopping).

At the centre of this area is the triangle formed by the intersection of cours Clemenceau, cours de l'Intendance and allées de Tourny.

Esplanade des Quinconces

The sheer size (about 126 000sq m/ 150 700sq yd) of this rectangular esplanade is very impressive. It was laid out during the Restoration (early 19C) on the site of the old Château Trompette.

The **Monument aux Girondins** with its bronze statuary was erected between 1894 and 1902, in honour of the *députés* from Bordeaux who fell under the guillotine in 1792. The huge work (65m/214ft long, 44m/145ft wide, and 50m/165ft high) is bursting with allegory: *Liberty Breaking Her Chains* atop the central column; various vices (Ignorance, Deceit, etc.) and virtues (Labour, Public Education, etc.) on the Republique **fountain**★ facing the Grand Théâtre; Fraternity, Abundance and Happiness on the Concorde **fountain**★ opposite.

Statues of the writers Montesquieu and Montaigne (1858) preside over the esplanade. Between the esplanade and the waterfront stand two rostral columns (ship figureheads), decorated with figures representing Commerce and Navigation.

Grand Théâtre★★

pl. de la Comédie. Guided tours Jul–Aug Mon–Tue 2.30pm. 9.50€. 05 56 00 85 95. www.opera-bordeaux.com.

The recently restored Grand Théâtre, which overlooks the **Place de la Comédie**, is among the most beautiful in France, and is a potent symbol of the richness of both French architecture and French cultural ideas at the time.

The building was designed by the architect Victor Louis (1731–1800) and erected between 1773 and 1780 on the site of a Gallo-Roman temple. From the outside, it is distinguished by its Classically inspired peristyle, surmounted by a balustrade supporting 12 statues representing Graces and Muses.

Inside the theatre, the coffered ceiling of the foyer is supported by 16 columns. Beneath the dome at the far end, a handsome staircase rises in a single flight then divides into two (an arrangement copied by Garnier when he designed the Paris Opera House; *see Introduction: Art and Culture*).

The panelled auditorium with its 12 gilded columns provides a splendid interior with perfect acoustics. From the centre of the ceiling, painted by Roganeau, hangs a chandelier glittering with 14 000 drops of Bohemian crystal.

Opposite the theatre, take r. Mautrec to pl. du Chapelet.

Église Notre-Dame★

1 r. Mably. Open daily 8.30am–12.30pm, 2.30–6.30pm. Guided tours daily Jul–Aug 3–6pm; Sept–Jun 2.30–5.30pm. 05 56 81 01 37.

This church, dedicated to the Virgin, was formerly a Dominican chapel. It was built between 1684 and 1707 by the engineer Michel Duplessy; its **façade** is in typical Baroque style.

The stonework in the **interior** is especially impressive, including barrel vaulting, pierced by the lunettes of the clerestory windows for the nave, groin vaulting in the side aisles, and an organ loft extended on each side by gracefully curving balconies. The quality and design of the wrought-iron work – in particular the gates around the chancel – provide a fitting complement to the architecture. **Cloisters** dating from the 17C adjoin the wall on the right side of the church.

Take passage Sarget on the left and turn right onto cours de l'Intendance.

Cours de l'Intendance

Cours de l'Intendance is the main street for high-fashion and luxury goods stores. From no 57, along rue Vital Carles, there is a fine view of the towers of Bordeaux Cathedral. No 57 itself, the house where the artist Goya lived and died (1828), is now a **Spanish cultural centre** *(http://burdeos.cervantes.es)*.

Place Gambetta

This square was formerly known as place Dauphine. All the houses were built in the Louis XV style (with arcades at street level and mansard roofs), giving a pleasing architectural unity. An attractive English garden has been laid out at the centre of the square which, during the Revolution, was the site of the scaffold.

Take r. Judaïque towards pl. des Martyrs de la Résistance.

Basilique St-Seurin

pl. des Martyrs-de-la-Résistance. Open Tue–Sat 8.30am–7pm, Sun 9am–12.15pm, 6–8.15pm. Guided visits possible May–mid-Sept Sat 2.30–6pm; mid-Sept–Apr Sat pm or by appointment (allow one wk). 05 56 24 24 80.

As with St-André Cathedral and the Basilique St-Michel, both of which are also on The Way of St James, the St-Seurin Basilica was declared in 1999 a UNESCO World Heritage Site.

Its 11C crypt contains Gallo-Roman capitals and columns, as well as 6C marble sarcophaguses and the 17C tomb of St Fort.

Take r. Capdeville, then turn right onto r. du Dr Albert Barraud.

Palais Gallien

r. du Docteur Albert Barraud. Open Jun–Sept daily 2–7pm. 3€.

All that remains of this Roman amphitheatre which could seat 15 000 spectators are a few rows and arcades overgrown with weeds.

Continue along r. du Dr Albert Barraud, cross r. Fondaudège and take r. St-Laurent, just in front of it.

Petit Hôtel Labottière

13 r. St-Laurent. 05 56 48 44 10.

Laclotte, an architect at the Musée des Arts Décoratifs, designed this Neoclassical private mansion (18C). It has been restored in its original style and is now a private hotel. The staircase at the right of the vestibule is worth seeing.

Jardin Public

pl. du Champ de Mars. Open daily 7am–dusk.

This 18C French-style garden was turned into an English-style park during the reign of Napoleon III. Palm trees and magnolias provide shade among colourful flower beds. It also houses the **Muséum d'Histoire naturelle**, which is closed for renovations until 2013 *(05 56 48 29 86).*

Return via cours de Verdun, pl. de Tourny then allées de Tourny.

4 LES CHARTRONS

Map p113. Allow half a day.

The Chartrons district extends to the north of Quinconces, between quai des Chartrons and cours de Verdun, Portal and St-Louis. The district was named after the 15C Chartreux Convent, and later became the centre of the wine trade. The district was at its height in the 18C, when the rich merchants built numerous sumptuous residences. During the 19C, numerous *eschoppes* were built – small workers' houses with tall, thin doors and façades that were often sculpted to resemble the wealthier merchant houses. These typical Bordeaux houses are found all over the city.

Cours Xavier Arnozan

Formerly known simply as *le pavé* (the cobbled street), this avenue reflects the wealth of the great merchant and wine-growing families of the 1770s, who had their sumptuous town houses built conveniently close to but sufficiently removed from the noisy bustle of the port. Such private projects nevertheless combined to form an architectural ensemble of remarkable unity. The three-storey Classical façades have arches at ground level. Above, squinches support magnificent **balconies★** with ornamental wrought-iron railings.

Musée d'Art Contemporain (CAPC)★

7 r. Ferrère. Open Tue and Thu–Sun 11am–6pm, Wed 11am–8pm. Closed public holidays. No charge (temporary exhibitions: 5€). 05 56 00 81 50.

The former **Lainé warehouse★★**, built in 1824 for storing goods imported from the French colonies, has been successfully remodelled into a Museum of Contemporary Art. It houses the collections of the Centre d'Arts Plastiques Contemporains de Bordeaux (CAPC), which are particularly strong on works from the 1960s and 70s.

Inside, a tall, twin-aisled central section runs the length of the building. The huge amount of space available allows even the largest exhibits to be mounted here, accommodating individual works of great dimension. The sober character of the original structure of the building was further accentuated during its conversion by the use of black metal.

The museum also functions as a cultural centre with conferences and debates, guided tours on a particular artist or aspect of contemporary art, children's workshops and film projections.

Cité Mondiale

20 quai des Chartrons.

Designed by local architect Michel Petuaud-Letang, this glass-fronted

building, overlooking the quai des Chartrons, has a harmoniously curved façade and a round tower. Inaugurated in January 1992, today it is a business and conference centre, with hotels and restaurants.

Take passage Notre-Dame behind the Cité Mondiale, then turn right.

Rue Notre-Dame

This is the backbone of Chartrons: where the wine merchants of the 19C have been replaced by antiquarians in the 21C. Perfect for window shopping, rue Notre-Dame is lined with attractive stone houses and numerous boutiques, from antique shops and interior design stores to bakeries and Italian delis.

Place du Marché des Chartrons

On the spot of the former Convent des Carmes, architect Charles Burguet built a market hall in 1869. Today restored in glass, iron and stone, the space has become an exhibition and cultural centre surrounded by pavement cafés.

Église St-Louis-des-Chartrons

r. Notre-Dame.

With two spires that are illuminated in blue at night-time, this church marks the heart of the Chartrons district. Inside is the largest organ in Aquitaine (constructed in 1881 by Wermer-Maille).

Rejoin r. Notre-Dame taking r. St-Joseph, then turn left into r. Pomme-d'Or.

Musée du Vin et du Négoce à Bordeaux

41 r. Borie. Open May–Oct Thurs 10am–10pm, Fri–Wed 10am–6pm; Nov–Apr Mon–Sat 10am–6pm, Sun 2–6pm). Visit and tasting of two wines 7€. 05 56 90 19 13. www.mvnb.fr.

This new museum is located in three vaulted cellars typical of Chartrons, and tells the history of wine merchants in Bordeaux, and the role of the port.

Follow r. Borie down towards the quai des Chartrons.

Quai des Chartrons★

Line B tramway, towards Claveau.

Lined with 18C limestone buildings, the Chartrons quays have been totally renovated, and today offer local residents a new space for recreation along the banks of the River Garonne. The former industrial hangars (H 14, 15 and H 20) have been converted into cultural spaces, restaurants and boutiques, and the locals spend much of their weekend enjoying them (whether by bike, roller blade or foot). A glass of wine and a plate of oysters at the ever-popular Sunday market has become an essential weekend ritual.

Cap Sciences

Hangar 20, quai de Bacalan. Open Tue–Fri 2–6pm, Sat–Sun 2–7pm, Mon in school holidays 2–6pm. 5.50€ (under 16 years 3.80€). 05 56 01 07 07. www.cap-sciences.net.

The region's biggest science and industry museum offers permanent exhibitions and one-off workshops.

Join cours Alfred-Daney via cours Lucien-Faure.

Bassins à Flot

Line B tramway, station "Bassins à flot".

For those willing to venture farther afield, the Bassins à flot is worth a look. At the far end of the quays from the Old Town, and for years an industrial wasteland, it is today the object of numerous renovation projects. Bars, restaurants and an art gallery (the Fonds régional d'art contemporain, or FRAC) have already opened in Hangar G2.

The **Base sous-marine**, a vast concrete submarine pen from World War II, built between 1941 and 1943 for the 12th flotilla of the German army, is one of the city's most experimental venues, offering exhibitions, music and dance evenings with a distinctly underground feel *(bd Alfred-Daney; open Tue–Sun 2–7pm; temporary exhibits; 05 56 11 11 50).*

LA BASTIDE

Via tramway line A in the direction of Dravemont or La Gardette.

From the Right Bank, particularly the Jardins de Queyries, you have a great view over the façades of limestone buildings along the quays, which hug the curve of the Garonne for more than 1km/0.6mi.

Jardin Botanique

quai des Queyries. Open daily late Mar–late Oct 8am–8pm; late Oct–late Mar 8am–6pm. No charge. 05 56 52 18 77.

This garden, designed by the landscape gardener Catherine Mosbach, is a new kind of botanical garden with the scientific aim of studying and preserving species. Ecological issues are highlighted in an "environmental gallery" and "culture fields". Besides an aquatic and an urban garden, looked after by the inhabitants of the area, a tropical greenhouse completes the landscape.

ADDITIONAL SIGHT

Musée des Compagnons du Tour de France

112 r. Malbec. Open Wed–Fri 2–5.30pm, Sat 10am–5pm. 3€ (under 12 years no charge). 05 56 92 05 17. www.compagnons.org.

This original museum celebrates various artisan skills. Set over three floors, it has gathered an important collection of carpentry, cabinet making, stone- and woodwork to explain the techniques and skills behind these trades.

EXCURSIONS

Musée de la Création Franche

S of Bordeaux (Exit 20 from the Rocade: follow Bègles-centre, then Mairie); or from Gare St-Jean, bus 2 (for Bègles-Rives d'Arcins, stop Mairie de Bègles) or 23 (for Bègles-Mussonville, stop Bibliothèque).58 av. du Maréchal-de-Lattre-de-Tassigny. Open daily 3–7pm. No charge. 05 56 85 81 73. www.musee-creationfranche.com.

An unusual visit. Created in 1989 as a place to display Art Brut, it became a *musée municipal* in 1996 which regularly displays visiting exhibitions from museums the world over, celebrating spontaneity and creativity, as well as housing 10 000 permanent works of art. At the same time, it is a beautiful place to visit; a bourgeois house surrounded by a park.

Quartiers Modernes Frugès-Le Corbusier

SE of Bordeaux, via cours du Maréchal-Gallieni, or Rocade Exit 13. Follow signs from Pessac centre.

Built in 1926 at the request of Henri Frugès, a Bordeaux industrialist who wanted to lodge his workers in a city garden, the buildings are witness to the spirit of their designer, Le Corbusier (1887–1965). The 50 pavilions have been carefully preserved.

The Maison Frugès-Le Corbusier is open to the public, and hosts temporary exhibitions on urbanism and architecture *(4 r. Le Corbusier; guided visit Thu 10am, Sun 3pm; no charge; 05 56 36 56 46).*

Marais de Bruges

N of Bordeaux, Rocade Exit 6. av. des Quatre-Ponts. Open Sat–Wed 10am–6pm, call 05 56 57 09 89 to arrange visit. 4.50€. 05 56 91 33 65. www.sepanso.org.

From the original vast marshes of Bruges remains this 280ha/692-acre nature reserve, one of the most important migratory routes in Europe.

Planète Bordeaux★

N 89 in the direction of. Libourne (Exit 5) at Beychac. Open Jun–Oct Mon–Sat 10am–7pm; rest of year Mon–Fri 9am–12pm, 2–7pm. 5€ with tasting of 3 wines or 20€ with 7 wines. 05 57 97 19 20/35. www.planete-bordeaux.net.

The headquarters of the winemakers from AOC Bordeaux and Bordeaux Supérieur. An interactive exhibition walks visitors through local winemaking techniques. Fully stocked boutique, with tastings, cookery courses and art exhibitions. Wine tours into the surrounding vineyards are also on offer. Children are catered for with games and exhibits.

ADDRESSES

STAY

Étap Hôtel – *37 cours du Maréchal-Juin. 08 92 68 05 84. www.etaphotel.com. 109 rooms. 4.70€.* Chain hotel but well located for the Old Town.

Hôtel Citéa – *1 bis r. Jean-Renaud, Dandicolle. 05 56 56 18 00. www.citea.com. 98 studios and 10 apartments. 7.50€.* A new building offering a variety of studios and doubles with an equipped kitchen, or the choice of having breakfast in the main salon. Long-stays can reduce prices.

Hôtel Notre-Dame – *36–38 r. Notre-Dame. 05 56 52 88 24. www.hotelnotredame.free.fr. 22 rooms. 7€.* An unpretentious little family hotel in an 18C house just behind the quai des Chartrons. Rooms small but well kept; reasonable prices.

Hôtel Opéra – *35 r. Esprit-de-Lois. 05 56 81 41 27. www.hotel-bordeaux-centre.com. Closed 24 Dec–2 Jan. 28 rooms. 6€.* A modest family hotel near the Grand Théâtre and the allées de Tourny. The rooms are functional with those on the street well soundproofed. Good value for money.

Chambre d'hôte Une Chambre en Ville – *35 r. Bouffard. 05 56 81 34 53. www.bandb-bx.com. 5 rooms. 9€.* In the historic Old Town, carefully decorated rooms each with individual theme. Contemporary feel.

Hôtel Acanthe – *12–14 r. St-Rémi. 05 56 81 66 58. www.acanthe-hotel-bordeaux.com. Reservations required. 20 rooms. 5.80€. Closed late Dec.* A central location and reasonable prices are the strong points of this hotel.

Hôtel des Quatre Sœurs – *6 cours du XXX-Juillet. 05 57 81 19 20. www.hotel-bordeaux-4soeurs.com. 34 rooms. 9€.* Well located and a real institution, celebrated for having housed both musician Richard Wagner and writer John Dos Passos. Recently restored.

Hôtel Presse – *6, 8 r. de la Porte Dijeaux. 05 56 48 53 88. www.hoteldelapresse.com. 27 rooms. 8€.* In the pedestrian shopping quarter of the old city, this is a nice little hotel despite the difficult access by car. Modern, functional, cosy rooms.

Hôtel de la Tour Intendance – *14–16 r. de la Vieille-Tour. 05 56 44 56 56. www.hotel-tour-intendance.com. 35 rooms. 12€.* A successful renovation has restored the traditional Bordeaux façade, and inside the rooms are comfortable, modern and air-conditioned.

EAT

Café l'Utopia – *5 pl. Camille-Jullian. 05 56 79 39 25. Open Mon–Fri 12–3pm, 7–11pm, Sat–Sun 12–11.30pm.* Former church restored as an art-house cinema with a lively café on the ground floor.

La Petite Gironde – *75 quai des Queyries. 05 57 80 33 33. www.lapetitegironde.fr. Closed Sat lunch and Sun.* On the Right Bank of the Garonne, a popular spot with relaxed atmosphere and good traditional menu.

Le Bistro du Musée – *37 pl. Pey Berland. 05 56 52 99 69. www.lebistrodumusee.com. Closed Sun and public holidays.* This bistro with a pretty green wood entrance makes a promising impression from the start. Thoughtful décor with exposed stone walls, oak parquet, moleskin seats and wine paraphernalia. Southwest cuisine and a fine Bordeaux wine menu.

Lou Magret – *62 r. St-Rémi. 05 56 44 77 94. Closed evenings (Mon–Thu), Sat lunch and Sun.* A pleasant establishment whose speciality is *canard de Chalosse,* duck served grilled or with a delicious sauce. No-frills décor and outdoor terrace.

Quaizaco – *80 quai des Chartrons. 05 57 87 67 72. quaizaco@orange.fr. Closed Sat lunch and Sun and 2 wks Aug.* Housed behind the façade of 18C warehouses, a contemporary restaurant which also houses art exhibitions

Sarl la Cheminée Royale – *56 r. St-Rémi. 05 56 52 00 52. Closed Mon lunch and Sun.* Meat is grilled under the enormous chimney in the dining room of this city-centre restaurant.

Auberge Inn – *245 r. de Turenne. 05 56 81 97 86. http://auberge-inn.cartesurtables.com. Closed Sat–Sun, 3 wks Aug and 1 wk Dec.* Exposed stone walls alternate with muted paint colours in this contemporary-style restaurant, with an attractive terrace.

Café Bellini – *15 allées de Tourny. 05 56 81 49 94.* Well located on the allées de Tourny, this was formerly called the Brasserie Bordelais, and remains a great place to eat, specialising in tapas-style, chic menus and more gourmet food. Good wine list.

Chez Dupont – *45 r. Notre-Dame. 05 56 81 49 59. Closed Sun–Mon.* A "cuisine du marché" presented with style in this charming bistro in the heart of Chartron

Les Restaurants de l'Atrium – *r. du Cardinal.-Richaud. 05 56 69 49 00. www.casino-bordeaux.com.* Two restaurants on offer in the casino. First the Atrium, with its bistro menu specialising in seafood and regional food. The restaurant La Carène is open in the evenings only, and has more gourmet food on offer.

Restaurant du Musée des Arts décoratifs – *39 r. Bouffard. 05 56 52 60 49. Closed Tue.* In the courtyard of this *hôtel particulier* which houses the Musée des Arts décoratifs, a *restaurant-salon de thé* offering an elegant place to stop.

La Tupina – *6 r. Porte-de-la-Monnaie. 05 56 91 56 37. www.latupina.com.* Relaxed atmosphere in this Bordeaux institution. Traditional southwestern food cooked over an open fire. Good wine list.

ENTERTAINMENT

La Boîte à Jouer – *50 r. Lombard. 05 56 50 37 37. www.laboiteajouer.com.* This theatre has two small rooms (60 and 45 seats) where lesser-known troupes specialising in contemporary or musical theatre perform.

L'Onyx – *11–13 r. Fernand Philippart, Quartier St-Pierre. 05 56 44 26 12. www.theatre-onyx.net.* The oldest café-theatre of the city, L'Onyx is a requisite stop for discovering local culture.

Opéra de Bordea ux-Grand Théâtre – *pl. de la Comédie. 05 56 00 85 95. www.opera-bordeaux.com.* The Grand Théâtre de Bordeaux is a showpiece of France's cultural wealth. Henri Tomasi's *Sampiero Corso* (1956), Jean-Michel Damase's *Colombe* (1961) and the French adaptation of Benjamin Britten's *Gloriana* (1967) are among the significant performances that premiered here. Symphonies, operas and ballets are performed under excellent acoustic conditions.

Théâtre du Port-de-la-Lune – *sq. Jean-Vauthier, Quartier Ste-Croix. 05 56 33 36 80. www.tnba.org.* This theatre's repertoire includes classic and contemporary drama staged by the Centre Dramatique National Bordeaux Aquitaine.

SHOPPING

Baillardran Canelés – *Galerie des Grands-Hommes. 05 56 79 05 89. www.baillardran.com.* This boutique makes delicious *canelés*, the small brown Bordelais cakes, irresistibly delicate and caramelised, that take on the shape of the ribbed *(canelé)* cake tins.

Cadiot-Badie – *26 allées de Tourny. 05 56 44 24 22. www.cadiotbadie.com.* A charming old-fashioned-style boutique founded in 1826 where incredible chocolates are made and sold.

Chocolaterie Saunion – *56 cours Georges Clemenceau. 05 56 48 05 75. www.saunion.com.* One of the illustrious chocolatiers of Bordeaux.

Conseil Interprofessionnel des Vins de Bordeaux – *3 cours du XXX-Juillet. 05 56 00 22 85. www.vins-bordeaux.fr.* Here you'll find a wine bar, workshops and tastings on Bordeaux wines and vineyards. Several different wine cellars are to be found nearby, including L'Intendant *(2 allées de Tourny)* and Bordeaux Magnum *(3 r. Gobineau)*.

Darricau Chocolatier – *7 pl. Gambetta. 05 56 44 21 49.* Since the turn of the century, this chocolatier pampers the city with the irresistible *pavé Gambetta* (praline with raisins soaked in wine), Bordeaux bottle-shaped chocolates (*confits de sauterne* or *de médoc*) and *niniches* (soft caramel with dark chocolate).

Huîtres Brunet – *7–11 r. de la Condé. 05 56 81 66 60. Open Tue–Sat 10am–12.30pm, 4–8.30pm, Sun and public holidays 9am–1pm. Closed Jul–Aug.* A daily catch is landed each morning and sold from this street-side table by the oyster cultivators who have been selling their fresh wares from the Bassin d'Arcachon for 25 years.

Passage St-Michel – *14–15 pl. Canteloup. 05 56 74 01 84. www.aupassage.fr. Open Tue–Fri 10am–6.30pm, Sat 2.30pm–6.30pm, Sun 8.30am–2pm. Closed 1 Jan and Christmas.* Flea market in a converted warehouse.

Les Côtes de Bordeaux★

Gironde

Bordeaux is synonymous with world-famous wines. The Bordeaux wine-producing region covers 117 000ha/452sq mi in the valleys of the River Garonne and River Dordogne in the Gironde *département*; it includes several distinct areas, each producing characteristic wines: Côtes de Bordeaux, Entre-deux-Mers, Sauternais, St-Émilion and Médoc.

- **Michelin Map:** 335: F-3–H-5 and I-5–K-8
- **Info:** ☎05 56 00 21 99. www.bordeaux-cotes.com.
- **Location:** Right Bank of Garonne and Dordogne rivers.
- **Kids:** Château Langoiran.
- **Timing:** Allow a full day with stops for attractions.

DRIVING TOUR

1 ROUND TRIP FROM BORDEAUX

184km/114mi. Allow one day.

Drive out of town along the D 113 and D 10, which follow the River Garonne SE of Bordeaux.

Château Langoiran

Le Pied du Château, Langoiran. Guided tours and tastings available with advanced appointment. ☎05 56 67 08 55. www.chateaulangoiran.com.

All that remains of the 13C castle is a ruined outer wall and an imposing circular keep among luxurious vegetation.

Rions

This small, fortified town is entered via the 14C Porte du Lhyan, which has kept all its original defensive features, including guardrooms on either side, grooves guiding the portcullis, and an *assommoir* (a platform from which objects could be dropped on attackers). Walking around the old houses and looking at the 18C covered market is very enjoyable. The path on the ramparts is lined with small gardens.

Cadillac

The town, originally a *bastide* founded in 1280, is situated on the north bank of the Garonne, and is known for its sweet white wines. The remains of the 14C town walls are still visible. The austere **château** (*open Jun–Sept daily 10am–6pm, Oct–May Tue–Sun 10am–12.30pm, 2–5.30pm (last admission 30min before closing); closed 1 Jan, 1 May, 25 Dec; 4.60€ (no charge first Sun of month (Oct–May)); ☎05 57 94 09 20; www.vignobles-lesgourgues.com*), built between 1589 and 1620 for the Duc d'Épernon then devastated during the Revolution and later rebuilt, stands inside its own defensive walls with bastions at the corners. Inside, there are enormous rooms with coffered ceilings and monumental, richly carved and decorated marble fireplaces. The 17C tapestries relating the history of Henri III were woven in the huge vaulted basement.

Loupiac

Loupiac, famous for its white wines, already existed in Roman times and is said to have been home to the Latin poet Ausonius (4C). The vestiges of a **Gallo-Roman villa** (*le Portail Rouge; ☎05 56 62 93 82*) are a witness to this period and remarkable mosaics can still be seen in its *thermae*.

Drive along the D 117.

The road takes you past numerous hills and valleys covered with vines. Chateaux are usually situated at the top of hills, often hidden by trees.

Rejoin the D 10 towards St-Macaire then turn left on to the D 120.

Verdelais

Park near to the Basilica and the chemin du Croix.

Notre-Dame de Verdelais was known for protecting the afflicted. Is that why Toulouse-Lautrec found repose here?

Basilique Notre-Dame *(les Allées; ℘05 56 62 02 06)* is an important place of pilgrimage. Worshippers come to venerate the 14C wooden statue of the Virgin, said to prevent drowning and heal paralytics.

Tombe de Toulouse-Lautrec – The grave of painter Henri de Toulouse-Lautrec-Monfa (1864–1901) lies to the right of the basilica, in the peaceful Cimetière de Verdelais. His simple tombstone can be found at the far end of the central alley, to the left.

Calvaire – Following a pleasant stroll along a *chemin de croix* that hugs a small copse, you will come across the imposing 19C Calvary Verdelais. This figure of Christ on the cross, with the Virgin Mary and St Jean at his feet, overlooks the Valley of the Garonne and Sauternes. You may even see the moving vanes of the Cussol windmill.

Take the D 19 towards St-Macaire.

Domaine de Malagar Centre François Mauriac

Open Jun–Sept 10am–12.30pm, 2–6pm, Oct–May Wed–Fri 2–5pm, Sat, Sun 10am–12.30pm, 2–5pm. Closed 1 wk Dec. 5.50€ (under 26 years 4€, under 12 years no charge). ℘05 57 98 17 17. http.//malagar.aquitaine.fr.

Overlooking the valley of St-Maixant and the town of Langon, this estate was for many years the summer house of François Mauriac (1883–1970). His house, a simple building that extends over two floors, enters directly onto the salon on the ground floor, "the heart of Malagar" where Mauriac wrote *Le Nœud de vipères (The Knot of Vipers)*, and where his desk still stands.

A museum to his life has been lovingly created in one of the buildings next to the house. Visitors can also take a walk through the park, stopping at the stone terrace where Mauriac used to stop to enjoy the view over his vineyards, and the Landes region beyond.

St-Macaire★

This small, medieval town of dark, narrow streets, perched on a rock above the river, has the original 12C walls, with 15C machicolations and three gates.

Église St-Sauveur

pl. de l'Église. Guided tours available by appointment. ℘05 56 63 34 52.

A huge, imposing church with an unusual trefoil-shaped Romanesque apse. Other features include the 13C murals near the chancel, the Gothic nave and polygonal belfry, and the 13C porch crowned by a Flamboyant Gothic rose window. A 13C priory and its cloisters stand nearby.

Ste-Croix-du-Mont★

The village is noted for its strange **caves**★, hollowed out from a thick fossilised oyster bed laid down by the ocean in the Tertiary Era. One of these has been turned into a **cave de dégustation** (tasting cellar; *open early Apr–mid-Oct Tue and Thu–Fri 2.30–7pm, Sat–Sun and public holidays 10.30am–1pm, 2.30–7.30pm; no charge; ℘05 56 62 01 39*), where you can appreciate the white wines which made the reputation of Ste-Croix-du-Mont. There are also splendid **views**★ from the Château de Tastes (now the town hall) stretching towards the distant Pyrénées. At the end of the hill, the church, which has undergone many changes throughout the centuries, still has its Romanesque portal.

L'église St-Martin, built in the 14C along the wall which encircles this *bastide* town, was modified in the 19C (the façade and the clock tower). **Pierre Biard** was asked to construct the funeral chapel by the Duc d'Eparnon, to house the tomb of his wife, Marguerite de Foix Candale.

The road passes along numerous limestone slopes covered with vines from AOC Côtes de Bordeaux Cadillac; making red, white and clairet wines.

Graves, Sauternes and Barsac

Gironde

On the Left Bank of the Garonne, merging in its northern tip with the *agglomération* of Bordeaux, is the Graves *appellation*. Taking its name from the gravel soils, this is the only AOC in France whose name directly reflects its geological origins. Since 1987, the northern section of the Graves, where its best *terroir* can be found, has been named AOC Pessac-Léognan. The southern part of Graves contains the sweet wine *appellations* of Barsac and Sauternes.

- **Population:** 700 in the village of Sauternes.
- **Michelin Map:** 335: H-6
- **Info:** 05 56 63 68 00. www.sauternais-graves-langon.com.
- **Location:** To the S of the city of Bordeaux, Left Bank of the Garonne river.
- **Timing:** A half-day to explore Pessac-Léognan. A full day if also driving down to Sauternes region.

DRIVING TOURS

2 GRAVES VINEYARDS

94km/58mi from Bordeaux
Allow at least half a day.

From Bordeaux, take Rocade Exit 20, then follow the D 108.

Château Malleret, Cadaujac

From the centre of Cadaujac, follow signs for port de Grimat then continue on the chemin de Malleret (*guided visit (1hr) Jul–Sept Mon–Fri am and pm, Sat–Sun by appointment, rest of year by appointment only. 5€ (under 14 years no charge); 06 85 85 88 67 or 06 07 37 30 09).*
This château (17C–19C) stands on the banks of the Garonne river, and was visited by Napoléon III. The salons are open for visits, but it is the themed gardens that are the real draw; a rose garden, a maze, with numerous lakes where peacocks strut.

Continue along the D 108,then take the D 1113.

Portets

Portets village lies right at the heart of the Graves region.

Château de Mongenan

Open mid-Feb–Apr daily and Oct–Dec Sat–Sun. Closed 31 Dec–15 Feb. Guided visits May–Sept. 6€ (under 12 years no charge), 10€(with wine tasting) ticket also allows entrance to Château Lagueloup. 05 56 67 18 11. www.chateaudemongenan.com.
Surrounded by vines and flower gardens, the pretty *chartreuse* of Mongenan (1736) has a terrace overlooking a **jardin botanique** inspired by J-J Rousseau, where visitors can find a mix of aromatic plans, flowers, unusual vegetables and fruit trees. A museum is consecrated to 18C herbs, historical documents and costumes.

Château Lagueloup

Guided visits 6€, tasting 5€. Gourmet breakfast Sat by reservation. 05 56 67 13 90. www.chateaulagueloup.com.
The owner of Château de Mongenan bought Château Lagueloup in 2000 and created a **musée de la Vigne et du Vin**. The imposing wine cellars were built at the end of the 19C by engineer **Samuel Wolff** as a factory. Various documents trace its construction, and several of its revolutionary inventions are re-created (transport of the harvest in small wagons, a steam grape press and a pump-crusher) as well as the process of making barrels (the château had its own workshop) and a collection of 18C vineyard tools.

Rejoin the D 1113.

Podensac

This village is hometown to the apéritif Lillet, a wine-based drink with added aromas of herbs and quinine. Visits possible of the Art Deco wine cellars, the processing plant and its gallery of labels dating back to the 19C (*open mid-Jun–mid-Sept 9.30am–6pm, rest of the year by appointment; no charge; 05 56 27 41 41; www.lillet.com*).

Rejoin the N 113 to Cérons.

Cérons

This little village has given its name to a tiny *appellation* of sweet wine wines that covers just 100ha/250acres. The wines are very delicate.

Follow the D 117 to Illats, then the D 109 to the N.

Château de la Brède★

In the Graves region, bordering the moors of Gironde, the austere lines of the Château de la Brède are reflected in the waters of its wide moat. There has been no change to the property since the days of **Baron Montesquieu** (1689–1755), the writer and philosopher. Château de la Brède (*brède* in the local dialect means "bush or "thorn") still belongs to his descendants today.

Visit

Allow 45min. Guided tours (45min) hourly 11–26 Apr Wed–Mon 2.30–5.30pm; 27 Apr–May and 1–25 Oct Sat–Sun and public holidays 2.30–5.30pm; Jun–Sept Wed–Mon 2.30–6pm; 26 Oct–11 Nov Sat–Sun and public holidays 2.30–4.30pm. 7€ (park 2.50€). 05 56 78 47 72. www.chateaulabrede.com.

A wide avenue, laid out by Montesquieu, skirts the moat and leads, indirectly, to the austere 12C–15C Gothic castle. The original interior courtyard was converted into a terrace during the Renaissance. Small bridges, which link two ancient fortifications, their doorways surmounted by Latin inscriptions, cross the moat and lead to the vestibule supported by six spiral columns. Montesquieu's own simple **sanctuary** remains exactly as it was when he was alive. A worn mark visible on one side of the chimney-piece was the result of Montesquieu's shoe repeatedly rubbing against it – he used to sit by the fire here and write with his papers in his lap. Note the **library**, which has panelled barrel-vaulting and used to contain 5 000 books. The estate also contains a park in which Montesquieu took a keen interest.

Take the D 108, towards Saucats.

Réserve Naturelle Géologique de Saucats-La Brède

2 walking routes (2hrs in total). Maps from Maison de la Réserve. Open Mon–Sat 3pm; May–Jun and Sept Sat 3pm, or by appointment. Guided visit (2hrs30min)Jul–Aug. 5€ (child 4€). 05 56 72 27 98. www.rngeologique-saucatslabrede. reserves-naturelles.org. Wear long-sleeved clothing and mosquito cream.

This natural reserve dates from the time, 20 million years ago, when Aquitaine was covered by the Atlantic Ocean. Seven geological sites, with explanatory boards, show examples of fossils, shark teeth, corals and tropical shells. Regular childrens workshops (by appointment).

Go to Léognan by the D 651.

Léognan

Home to numerous wine *châteaux*.

Follow the D 109.

Gradignan

Former Prieuré de Cayac – Southern exit of Gradignan, on the D 1010. In the beautiful park of Cayac, with its water features and windmill, this priory was first built in the 13C, then restored in the 17C. It was a stop on The Way of St James. Today it hosts temporary art exhibitions, and the Musée Georges de Sonneville (1889–1978), celebrating the life of the Bordelais painter famous for his depictions of the "swinging 20s" *(open Wed, Fri–Sat and 1st Sun Of month, pm; 05 56 75 34 28).*

Écomusée de la vigne et du vin – Housed in a former farm, a collection of vineyard materials from 1850 and 1950 *(288 cours du Général-de-Gaulle, at southern exit of Gradignan; guided visit (adapted for children) Wed, Fri–Sat and 2nd Sun of month 2–6pm, rest of week by appt; no charge, tasting 6.30€; 05 56 89 00 79).*

To return to Bordeaux, follows signs to Rocade or Universités, Talence.

3 VIGNOBLES OF SAUTERNES AND BARSAC

Small in size, but highly reputed for its white wines, this wine growing area is limited by the lower valley of the Ciron, near its confluence with the Garonne. The *terroir* – the land producing a given *appellation* – covers the five municipalities of Sauternes, Barsac, Preignac, Bommes and Fargues. The vines grow on the valley slopes, in walled vineyards, generally planted in rows at right angles to the river. Only three grape varieties are used – Sauvignon, Muscadelle and Sémillon. The original feature of this part of the Bordeaux region is the harvesting method used. The grapes are affected by **noble rot** or *botrytis*, a fungus peculiar to the district which increases the sugar density of the fruit. The shrivelled grapes are then picked, one by one, and transported to the press with infinite care.

Barsac

The **church** *(pl. de l'Église; open Apr–Sept daily 9am–6pm; 05 56 27 15 39; http://paroissepodensac.free.fr)*, a curious building dating from the late 16C and early 17C, has three aisles of equal height, and vaults demonstrating the survival of the Gothic style in the Classical period. The furnishings – gallery, altars, reredos and confessionals – are in the Louis XV style, and the sacristies are wood-panelled or stuccoed.

Budos

The village of Budos has preserved the **ruins** *(guided tours (1hr) Apr–Jun daily 2–5pm, Jul–Sept daily 10am–7pm, Jan–Mar and Oct–Nov with booking; 3.50€; 05 56 25 87 57; www.assoadichats.net)* of an early 14C feudal castle built by a nephew of Pope Clement.

Sauternes

This is a typical wine growers' village. A little way to the south stands the 17C **Château Filhot** *(open Mon–Fri 9am–noon, 2–6pm, Sat–Sun with booking; 05 56 76 61 09; www.filhot.com).*

Château Yquem

Estate grounds: open Mon–Sat. 05 57 98 07 07. www.yquem.fr.

Château d'Yquem stands unique as the sole *premier grand cru* (or classified first quality) of the Sauternes-Barsac region. It is home to the most prestigious Sauternes (white wine) in the world, famous since the 16C.

Château de Malle

Guided tours (30min) available Apr–Oct by appointment. 7€. 05 56 62 36 86. www.chateau-de-malle.fr.

Immediately below the Yquem Château are the fine 11 *premiers crus* and 13 *deuxièmes crus* – the Château de Malle being classed among the latter.

Entrance gates adorned with superb wrought-iron work lead into the property. The attractive château and gardens were created at the beginning of the 17C by an ancestor of the present owner. The château itself is charming, with a layout similar to that of some of the manor houses in the Gironde.

The interior of the château, resplendent with fine period furniture, boasts a collection of 17C *trompe-l'œil* silhouettes which is unique in France.

Italian-style terraced gardens are embellished with 17C carvings and statues depicting mythological themes, hunting or grape-harvest scenes.

Return to Barsac via the D 8E4 to Preignac, and the N 113 leading N.

L'Entre-Deux-Mers★

Gironde

The verdant green hills of Entre-Deux-Mers sit inbetween the Garonneand Dordogne rivers, and are carpeted with vines, copses and fields of ripening corn. AOC Entre-deux-Mers is a white-wine only appellation which makes wines largely from sauvignon blanc. These are wines for drinking young, ideally with a plate of oysters from the Bassin d'Arcachon.

- **Population:** 90 000
- **Michelin Map:** 335: I–J–K 6–7
- **Info:** 05 56 61 82 73. www.entredeuxmers.com.
- **Location:** Between the two rivers of the Garonne and the Dordogne.
- **Timing:** Allow one day for the full tour, although plenty of diversions are easily enjoyed with only half a day.

DRIVING TOUR

3 ROUND TRIP FROM BORDEAUX

105km/65mi. Allow one day.

Leave Bordeaux via the D 936 then turn right onto the D 936E5 towards Carignan-de-Bordeaux.

Maison Ginestet, Carignan-de-Bordeaux

Guided tour by request year-round Mon–Fri. No charge. 05 56 68 81 82. www.ginestet.fr.

This wine merchant company, founded in 1897, is open for visits which include barrel cellars, a boutique, and an explanation of this little-known part of the Bordeaux wine trade. The modern building may not have the charm of a château but the guide is passionate, and the tour offers a wealth of fascinating information.

Head S on the D 10E4 then take the D 115.

Sadirac

The town is an important pottery centre, where craftsmen mainly work with the local blue clay. The heyday of this traditional activity was in the 18C, and fine examples can be seen in **La Maison de la Poterie – Musée de la Céramique Sadiracaise** *(pl. Fouragnan; open Jun–Sept Tue–Sat 2–5.30pm, Oct–May Tue–Sun 2–5.30pm; 2€; 05 56 30 60 03)*. This local museum, on the site of a former workshop built in 1830 (the original furnace can be seen at the far end of the gallery), displays examples of local work (ceramics used domestically and in sugar refining) dating from the 14C to the 18C, along with models of furnaces from other periods. Production today, from the three remaining workshops, concentrates on garden pottery, building materials, and the re-creation of traditional designs.

The **Ferme-parc Oh! Légumes Oubliés** *(open Apr–10 Nov 2–6pm; 8.50€; 05 56 30 61 00; www.ohlegumesoublies.com)* is a farm devoted to preserving "forgotten" varieties of vegetables and plants, offering a tour of its orchard and kitchen gardens.

The D 115E8 and D 671 lead to Créon.

Créon

Once a *bastide* (13C arcaded square), the capital of Entre-deux-Mers is an important agricultural market. The surrounding area has many valleys.

Leave Créon to the S on the D 20.

St-Genès-de-Lombaud

The church in this village, halfway up a valley slope, is a place of pilgrimage venerating the Black Virgin. It is built on a site thought to have been occupied by

a Roman villa. The west front, with its belfry gable, is pierced by a Romanesque doorway beneath coving carved with animals and small human figures.

Return to Créon and take the D 671.

La Sauve

There are two interesting churches in this village built on the former site of a large forest cleared by monks.

The **old abbey**★ *(open Jun–Sept daily 10am–1.15pm, 2–6pm, Oct–May Tue–Sun 10.30am–1pm, 2–5.30pm; closed 1 Jan, 1 May, 25 Dec; 7€; 05 56 23 01 55; http.//.la-sauve-majeure.monuments-nationaux.fr)* was founded in 1079 by St Gérard and once had powerful dependencies stretching from Spain to England. The Romanesque and Gothic ensemble was abandoned in the 16C, though reinhabited by monks in the 17C until the time of the Revolution; the vaulting collapsed in 1809. The 12C–13C abbey church has magnificent **capitals**★ carved with scenes from the Old and the New Testaments, and 13C ruined cloisters.

The **Église St-Pierre** *(r. de l'Église; 05 57 97 02 20)* dates from the late 12C.

Église de Castelviel

Guided tours by appointment. 05 56 61 82 73.

The church is distinguished by a **Romanesque doorway**★ in the Saintonge style, with lavishly carved capitals and covings. Scenes illustrated include the combat between the Virtues and the Vices *(second cove)* and human figures linked by a rope, symbolising the community of the faithful *(third cove)*.

Return to St-Brice and take the D 671.

Sauveterre-de-Guyenne

This is a typical *bastide*, created by Edward I in 1281. It eventually became French in 1451 after changing sides 10 times. It still has four fortified gates and the central square is lively on market days, each Tuesday.

Ancienne Abbaye de Blasimon

Guided tours by appointment. 05 56 71 52 12.

Nestling in the hollow of a valley are the ruins of an old Benedictine abbey, which was once encircled by fortified walls (a tower still remains). The 12C–13C church has both Romanesque and Gothic elements (rounded and pointed arches) and a 16C open-work belfry gable.

Rauzan

r. de la Chapelle. Open Jul–Aug daily 10am–noon, 2–6pm; Sept–Jun Tue–Sun 10am–noon, 2–5pm. 3€. 05 57 84 03 88.

Rauzan features the romantic ruins of a château, built at the end of the 13C. It is a testimony to the conflict between the French and the English during the Hundred Years' War. The castle was protected by fortified walls with merlons, and has a seigniorial dwelling (14C–15C) pierced by mullion windows and a majestic circular keep, 30m/98ft high. From the top of the keep there is a fine **view** of the surrounding countryside. On the far side of the valley stands the village **church** with its three splendid 13C doorways.

Grotte Célestine – *6 r. de l'Hôpital. Visit by guided tour (45min) Jul–Aug daily 10am–noon, 2–6pm; Sept–Jun Tue–Sun 10am–noon, 2–5pm. 6.50€. 05 57 84 08 69. Reservations required.* The galleries of a subterranean river were discovered in the middle of the 19C when a well was dug in the centre of the village. Visits were organised until 1930 when the site was closed to the public, in order to preserve the caves. During World War II, the caves were used as a hiding place by two members of the French Resistance. The caves have now reopened and you can see the subterranean river.

Follow the D 128 to Daignac.

Daignac

This is a picturesque village where you find the ruins of a 13C mill.

Return to Bordeaux along the D 936.

St-Émilion★★

Gironde

The renowned wine centre of St-Émilion is a delightful town surrounded by vineyards. Ancient ramparts, monuments, a maze of narrow streets and stone stairways linking picturesque small squares, combine to form an overall picture that never fails to impress visitors. In fine weather the sun accentuates the golden tones of the old stone walls, while the ever-changing contrasts of light and shade enliven a stroll through the medieval quarters. The town is known not only for its fine wines but also for the local macaroons (crushed almond cakes).

- **Population:** 2 124
- **Michelin Map:** 335: K-5
- **Info:** pl. des Creneaux, St-Émilion. 05 57 55 28 28. www.saint-emilion-tourisme.com.
- **Location:** St-Émilion lies 10km/6.2mi E of Libourne on the slopes of a limestone plateau overlooking the Dordogne Valley.
- **Parking:** Car parks are located outside the old ramparts, at the top and at the bottom of the city.
- **Don't Miss:** The Église Monolithe; the Cloître des Cordeliers.

A BIT OF HISTORY

Centuries after the Latin poet Ausonius settled in the locality – he had property on the hillside, and his name today remains allied to one of the prestigious wine châteaux – it was a hermit named **Émilion** who found here the peace and tranquillity necessary for meditation. Émilion, originally from Brittany, was a baker by trade before embracing the monastic life at Saujon, near Royan. Withdrawing subsequently to the limestone slopes of the Dordogne Valley, he discovered a grotto watered by a natural spring in the rocky centre of what is now the town bearing his name, and lived there until his death towards the end of the 8C. Ten centuries later it was a fugitive who sought sanctuary in St-Émilion: **Marguerite-Élie Guadet** (1758–94), a native of the town and a prominent member of the Girondin Party at the beginning of the Convention. Suspected of "Moderantism" – what today would be termed deviation from the party line – Guadet became a victim of the Revolutionary leader Robespierre's hatred for the Girondins, and was obliged to flee Paris disguised as an upholsterer. He took refuge first in Normandy and later rejoined a couple of Girondin colleagues in St-Émilion. It was here, one day in 1794, that his dentity was discovered. He was arrested and taken to Bordeaux, where he was guillotined on 17 July of the same year.

WALKING TOUR

THE TOWN★★

St-Émilion faces due south, nestling within a horseshoe shape between two hillsides. At the junction of the two slopes, a tall belfry rises above a rocky spur honeycombed with caves, catacombs, a hermitage, a chapel and an extraordinary underground church. At the foot of this promontory, below the church, lies place du Marché, the main square at the heart of this busy small town. The square acts as a link between the districts sprawled over the two hills, one the site of the royal castle, the other the site of a deanery (clerical residence), reflecting the age-old rivalry between civil and religious powers.
St-Émilion is a pedestrian city. Make sure you wear comfortable shoes, as the streets are paved and steep. The picturesque network of narrow streets is ideal for a leisurely stroll.

Place du Marché

St-Émilion's main square and marketplace, in a picturesque setting at the foot of the spur, offers a fine view of the troglodyte church and its great belfry soaring heavenwards (fine view from the top).

Combined guided tours of the four sights below (1hr30min) Jun–Sept daily 11am; Oct–May Mon–Fri 2pm, Sat–Sun and public holidays 11am. 10€. Buy your ticket at the tourist office.

Ermitage St-Émilion

Enlarged to the form of a Latin cross, this grotto contains "St Émilion's Bed", his armchair carved from the limestone, and a spring, now guarded by a 17C balustrade; right at the end is an altar surmounted by a statue of the saint.

Catacombs

Near the chapel, the cliff face opens out into catacombs – rock galleries once used as an ancient burial ground, with tombs gouged from the rock. Later, the main part of this subterranean maze was used to store corpses. At the top of a central dome is an opening through which bones from a cemetery on top of the cliff were disposed of. At the base of the dome is a primitive representation depicting the resurrection of the dead: three carved figures emerging hand in hand from their sarcophagi.

GETTING AROUND

Le petit train touristique is a good alternative for those who want to tour the town but can't do it on foot. The 35min trip *(Apr–mid-Nov)* carries visitors past some prestigious wine-growing châteaux and the main monuments of the town. Departures every 45min from in front of the Collégiale church (upper town) 10.30am–6.30pm. 6€. 05 57 51 30 71. www.visite-saint-emilion.com.

Chapelle de la Trinité

Holy Trinity Chapel, a miniature sanctuary built by Benedictine monks in the 13C, includes a harmonious – and, in the southwest, rare – example of a timber-framed Gothic apse (frescoes). Inside, elegant High Gothic ribbed vaulting converges on a keystone embossed with the symbolic Lamb.

Église Monolithe★

This church is the largest monolithic sanctuary in Europe to be carved from a single solid block of rock. It was fashioned between the 8C and the 12C by enlarging pre-existing natural grottoes and caverns. The main entrance was through a tall 14C Gothic porch

Jurats and the Jurade

In the Middle Ages the famous red wines of St-Émilion (*see Driving Tour*) were qualified as "honorific" because it was the custom to offer them to royalty and persons of note. From then on it was decided that, in order to maintain the excellence and reputation of wines permitted to bear that name, they should be subject each year to evaluation by a committee of professionals. The body appointed by the town council to carry out this task was called the Jurade and its members the Jurats. The Jurade was reformed in 1948 and still operates today *(www.vins-saint-emilion.com)*.

In the spring of each year, a procession of Jurats wearing scarlet, ermine-trimmed robes and silken hoods attends a solemn Mass and then proceeds towards the cloisters of the collegiate church for ceremonial events. At the end of the afternoon, the Jurade pronounces its judgement on the new wine from the top of the King's Tower. In the autumn these same Jurats assemble at the top of the King's Tower to proclaim the official start of the grape harvest. Such solemn rites are accompanied by ritual banquets – suitably washed down with local wines – held in the Dominican Room of the local wine-growers' association.

decorated on the tympanum with a *Last Judgement* and a *Resurrection of the Dead*.
The interior of the church is impressive for the size of the aisles carved from the rock and for the perfect symmetry of its vaulting and squared pillars – only two of which support the belfry (concrete supporting posts have been added temporarily, during restoration work). At the back of the central nave, beneath the arcade of the bay, there is a bas-relief of two four-winged angels or cherubims. The majestic belfry *(198 steps)* offers a fine view of the town, its monuments and the neighbouring vineyards.

Clocher de l'Église Monolithe

Open daily early Apr–mid-Jun and mid-Sept–late Oct 9.30am–12.30pm, 1.45–6.30pm; mid-Jun–late Jul and early Sept–mid-Sept 9.30am–7pm; Jul–Aug 9.30am–8pm; Nov–Mar 9.30am–12.30pm, 1.45–6pm. 1€. 05 57 55 28 28.
You will not have climbed the 187 steps in vain: enjoy a full view of the village, its monuments and the vineyards, the whole picture being listed as a UNESCO World Heritage Site.

A ramp leads to porte de la Cadène.

Porte et Logis de la Cadène

r. de la Cadène.
This gateway stands at the end of a street off the main square, with a 15C timber-framed house beside it. The name of the arch derives from the Latin word *catena* (chain), and is a reminder of when access to the town centre was blocked by a chain across this gateway.

Turn right onto r. de la Porte-Brunet.

A covered path and a bartizan are all that remains of the **Logis de la Commanderie** (the abbot's lodgings).

Cloître des Cordeliers

2 bis r. de la Porte Brunet. Open daily summer 10am–7pm; winter 10am–noon, 2–6pm. 05 57 24 42 13. www.lescordeliers.com.
The Cordeliers – Franciscans of a strict order distinguished by a knotted cord worn around the waist – built this sanctuary in the 14C. The handsome ruins of their square **cloisters**★ include slender twinned columns supporting Romanesque arches. At the far end, on the right, a 15C Gothic archway precedes the stairway, which led to the monks' cells.
On the left, the belfry of the old church (15C) is supported by two unusual superimposed arches. Inside, the nave is separated from the apse by a triumphal arch in the Flamboyant Gothic style, which gives access down to a series of caves quarried out 20m/66ft deep in the bedrock where sparkling white and rosé wines are left to age.
There is an interesting view of St-Émilion from the esplanade nearby *(pl. du Cap-du-Pont)*.

Continue along r. de la Porte Brunet to the ramparts.

Porte Brunet

r. de la Porte Brunet.
It is one of the six gates which allowed access through the ramparts erected in the 13C and reinforced later by a machicolated watch-path. It was through this gate, one night in January 1794, that the outlawed Girondins escaped from Robespierre's men after the arrest of their companion Guadet.
From Porte Brunet, there are impressive views of the vineyards. The Tour du Roi (the King's Tower) and the spire of the church tower can be seen rising above the narrow winding streets.

Turn back and take r. de la Liberté on the left. Take the stairs on the left (after no 3), continue on the left, then turn right into r. de la Tourelle and finally right again into r. André-Loiseau.

Musée Souterrain de la Poterie

Les Hospices de la Madeleine, 21 r. André-Loiseau. Open daily 10am–7pm. Guided or night-time tours available on request. 4€ (under

12 years no charge). ☎05 57 24 60 93. www.saint-emilion-museepoterie.fr. Be aware that it can be cool and damp underground, even in summer.
In a series of underground quarries, from where much of the stone was extracted to build the Château du Roi and the town's 12C and 13C ramparts, today lies a museum containing over 6 000 pieces of pottery, from Roman to contemporary. The evolution of ceramic art in the southwest is shown to mirror the entire history of the region. Among the many fascinating objects are intricate roof finals intended to highlight the glory of their inhabitants, and a series of exhibits celebrating Michel Wohlfart, the French sculptor specialising in terracotta figures.

Château du Roi

Open Apr–Sept daily 11am–8.30pm; Oct–Dec and Feb–Mar Sat–Sun (ask at tourist office). Entrance at the top of the Tour du Roi. 1€. ☎05 57 24 61 07.
The King's Castle, founded according to some by Louis VIII and to others by Henri III Plantagenet in the 13C, was used as the town hall until 1720. From the top of the King's Tower (a rectangular keep with latrines on its outer face, standing on an isolated spur of rock) there is a fine view over the huddled rooftops of the town and across to the valleys of the Dordogne and the Isle rivers.

Follow r. de la Grande-Fontaine then the steep rlle du Tertre-des-Vaillants, which wends its way between houses dug out of the rock.

Collégiale

pl. Pioceau. ☎05 57 55 28 28.
This huge church has a Romanesque nave with a Gothic chancel. The entrance is on the north side of the chancel, via a superb 14C porch built at a time when Gaillard de Lamothe, the nephew of Pope Clement V, was dean of the resident canons. The carved tympanum represents The Last Judgement. Below, only the lower parts of the statues of the Apostles remain in their niches, the figures having been mutilated during the Wars of Religion and during the Revolution. The 15C choir stalls in the chancel are carved with an entertaining variety of characters. Inside the nave, two 12C mural paintings – *The Virgin* and *The Legend of St Catherine* – adorn the far end of the right-hand wall.

Logis de Malet de Roquefort

pl. Pioceau.
Opposite the *église collégiale*, a 15C mansion is incorporated into the ramparts; the old covered watch-path of the fortified town with its corbelled crenellations passes beneath the roof of the house.

Head to pl. des Créneaux.

Château du Roi

©Lagui/iStockphoto.com

Cloître de la Collégiale

Open same hours as the Monolithic church bell tower (see entry).
No charge. Enter via the Tourist Information Centre.

The cloisters, which lie to the south of the church, date from the 14C and are still in very good condition; they have much in common with the Cordeliers' Cloisters, particularly in the design of their twinned columns, which are extremely elegant.

Arches reinforce the corners separating the galleries – one of which houses an impressive series of covered niches formerly used as tombs.

The deanery – comprising the old refectory and the monks' dormitory – has been restored and is occupied today by the Tourist Information Centre.

Return to pl. du Marché.

DRIVING TOUR

4 ST-ÉMILION VINEYARDS

Round trip of 52km/32mi.
Allow 3hrs.

It is best to visit the wine country in autumn, when a soft golden light bathes the contours of the landscape and the bronze rows of vines are alive with the fever of the grape harvest, which is usually the second fortnight in September. The picturesque landscape of neatly planted slopes crowned by the châteaux set in groves of trees, with glimpses, here and there, of the valleys of the River Dordogne and River Isle, can nevertheless be appreciated at any time of the year.

Leave St-Émilion via the D 122 heading N.

Just before the village of **St-Georges**, its Louis XVI château can be seen on the right, crowned with a balustrade and *pots-à-feu* (classical urns from which stone flames leap).

St-Georges

This small 11C Romanesque church has a square tower wider at the top than at the base, and a curved apse with modillions carved with saucy subjects, treated in an almost Cubist style.

Montagne

The Romanesque church in this small town has three polygonal apses, topped by a square tower containing a strongroom. From the terrace, beside the church, there is a view of St-Émilion and the Dordogne Valley.

The **Écomusée du Libournais** *(le Bourg; open 1 Apr–11 Nov daily 10am–noon, 2–6pm; 6€; 05 57 74 56 89; www.ecomusee-libournais.com)* nearby

Montagne St-Émilion, surrounded by vineyards

offers visitors a trip into the rural world of the past.

There are two museums, presenting the traditional activities of local wine growers in Libourne in the late 19C and the early 20C. Temporary exhibitions explain present-day wine-growing techniques.

Continue along the D 122 – 2km/1mi beyond Lussac turn left into the D 21 and continue for 4.5km/2.8mi.

Petit-Palais-et-Cornemps★

Surrounded by its cemetery, the late 12C church in this town has a Romanesque **façade★** in the Saintonge style. The scale is perfectly proportioned and decorated with carved motifs.

The elevation presents three tiers of arches and blind arcades of different designs, some of them multi-lobed in the Arabic style. The archivolt of the central doorway is carved with a series of animals chasing one another and, in the corners, two amusing figures of a woman, and of a man pulling a thorn from his foot. The entrance is flanked by two blind doorways, which give a false impression of the interior, since in fact it only has a nave and no side aisles.

Return to the D 17 and turn S.

Castillon-la-Bataille

In 1453 Castillon was the site of the battle that put an end to English domination of Aquitaine. Led by General Talbot, the English troops were decimated by a French army under the command of the Bureau brothers (14C–15C), who modernised French artillery, which was instrumental in defeating the English here.

The town is built on a hillock overlooking the north bank of the Dordogne. The surrounding slopes produce a wine called Castillon Côtes de Bordeaux *(www.cotes-de-castillon.com).*

Return to St-Émilion via the D 130 to St-Étienne-de-Lisse and the D 245.

ADDRESSES

STAY

Château d'hôte Château Monlot – *1 r. Conte, 33330 St-Hippolyte (3km/1.8mi E of St-Émilion, towards Castillon via the D 245). 05 57 74 49 47. www.chateaumonlot.com. 6 rooms.* The foundations of this château with its chalky façade and handsome tiled roof were laid when the Capetians ruled the land. Old photographs hang in the rooms, each of which is named after a different vintage. The breakfast room is decorated in a grapevine theme. Visits to the wine storehouses and tastings available.

Chambre d'hôte La Gomerie – *La Gomerie. 05 57 24 68 85. www.ms-favard.fr. 4 rooms.* This typical Girondin building, dating from 1789, is surrounded by a working vineyard of 2ha/5 acres. The simple bedrooms are filled with pretty antique furniture. Breakfast in winter on the veranda, in summer in the garden.

Domaine de la Barbanne – *rte de Montagne. 05 57 24 75 80. www.camping-saint-emilion.com. Closed Oct–Mar. 8 rooms.* Accommodation in a chalet-motel on a fully-equipped campsite. Amenities include *épicerie*, restaurant, washroom, children's club, bike hire, swimming pool, tennis, mini golf. Bedding hire available for one night. Free minibus to village.

EAT

Le Bouchon – *3 pl. du Marché. 05 57 24 62 81. www.restaurant-st-emilion.fr. Closed Nov–Feb.* One of the best addresses on the marketplace. The recently repainted dining room has aerial photos and Botero prints on the green-and-blue walls. Traditional cuisine prepared with care and an excellent choice of wines.

L'Envers du Decor – *11 r. du Clocher. 05 57 74 48 31. www.envers-dudecor.com.* With its back to the collegiate church, this attractive wine bar has a lovely, peaceful terrace with flowers. Simply decorated dining room featuring old stonework. The cuisine focuses on fresh ingredients. Private dining terrace in summer.

Libourne

Gironde

With its stately river, limestone houses with intricate carvings, lively markets and prestigious wines that are exported world over, there is no doubt that Libourne is truly Bordeaux's little sister.

- **Population:** 21 600
- **Michelin Map:** 335: J–5
- **Info:** ℘05 57 51 15 04. www.libourne-tourisme.com.
- **Location:** On the banks of the Dordogne river, 35km/22mi E of Bordeaux.
- **Timing:** Half a day.

WALKING TOUR

PLACE ABEL-SURCHAMP

Libourne's central market square is both spacious and well laid out, bordered by houses dating from the 16C (at no 16 and no 35) up to the 19C. The 15C town hall was renovated in the early 20C in a Gothic Revival style.

Musée des Beaux-Arts

42 pl. Abel-Surchamp. Open Mon–Fri 10am–12.30pm, 2–6pm. No charge. ℘05 57 55 33 44. http://musees-aquitaine.com.

One of the centrepieces of this museum is found one the central staircase: a collection of 18C white marble works by Eugene Falconet. Several works are on display from the Flemish, French and Italian schools, covering the period from the 16C to the 20C – most notably by Jordaens, Bartolomeo, Charles Le Brun and Raoul Dufy. Local artists are represented by Lacaze, still lifes by Brieux, and an impressive collection of works by painter René Princeteau (1843–1914). Native to Libourne, René Princeteau was both teacher and friend to Toulouse-Lautrec. Despite being deaf and dumb, he enjoyed some success in Paris thanks to his mastery of pastoral and equestrian paintings.

Temporary exhibitions are held in the Carmel Chapel annex, next to the tourist office.

Quais de l'Isle and Quai des Salinières

Today a favourite walking spot, with plane trees planted along the banks of the Dordogne river, the quays were formerly the centre of activity in this once-busy port. The quai des Salinières is marked by two gates: the porte du Grand Port flanked by the Tour Richard and the Tour Barrée, remants of the old city walls that were built in 1314, after the destruction of the town by the French in 1294. Behind the tower, the rue des Chais is a remnant of the region's wine trade.

Quai Souchet

At the confluence of the Dordogne and the l'Isle, this quay is the best viewpoint for the stone bridge (1824) with its nine arches.

EXCURSION

Château de Vayres★

9.5km/6mi SE Take the D 1089 from Libourne towards Bordeaux. At Arveyres, turn right on the D 242 and, near the church at Vayres, take the small road leading up to the chateau.

Open Easter-Jun, mid-Sept–mid-Nov Sun and Wed in school holidays. Guided tours Jul–mid-Sept 3pm, 4pm, 5pm (and some evenings). Closed Dec–Easter. 9.50€ (under 15 years 7.50€). ℘ 05 57 84 96 58. www.chateaudevayres.com.

Formerly owned by the Albret family, the château was rebuilt in the 16C by Louise de Foix, the architect of the Cordouan lighthouse. Among the pieces of interest are Louis XIII and Louis XIV furniture, an Aubusson tapestry, a 14C dining room and a chapel built as a whispering gallery.

Outside, a medieval garden makes for a pleasant stroll. This is also a good spot for watching the Mascaret wave.

Blaye

Gironde

Blaye (pronounced "Bly") is known mainly for its citadel, its Côtes de Blaye wines and its port. The port is used by coastal steamers, sailing ships, and fishing boats land lampreys and shad in the spring. The Gironde estuary is also a protected reserve for sturgeon; the local caviar comes from sturgeon farms.

- **Population:** 4 687
- **Michelin Map:** 335: H-4
- **Info:** Les Allées Marines, Blaye. ℘05 57 42 12 09. www.tourisme-blaye.com.
- **Location:** Blaye is situated 43km/27mi NW of Bordeaux.
- **Parking:** There are car parks just outside the citadel and along the banks of the estuary.
- **Don't Miss:** The citadel.

CITADEL★

Guided tours (1hr) Jul–Aug Fri–Wed 2pm, 3.30pm, 5pm (departing from the tourist office; reservations required). 5€. ℘05 57 42 12 09.

Access is either on foot via porte Dauphine to the south, or by car through Porte Royale to the east. Both gateways are decorated with shields carrying fleur-de-lis, both protected by ravelins in the curtain wall.

The citadel, built by Vauban in 1689, is still inhabited and very lively in season thanks to the local craftsmen as well as music and theatre festivals. The landward side, which is 45m/148ft above the river, is defended by bastions protected by a dyke.

Château des Rudel

This medieval castle is triangular in shape, and has a romantic history. It was the birthplace of a 12C troubadour, **Jaufre Rudel**, who fell poetically in love with "a distant princess", Hodierna of Tripoli, without ever seeing her. According to legend, he sailed across the sea to join her, fell ill on the voyage, and died on arrival in the arms of his beloved.

Only two towers of the castle still stand. However, the bridge, which led to the entrance, and the foundations of the walls are also visible. In the middle of the courtyard, the coping around the ancient well can be seen, grooved by the constant rubbing of the chain or rope which lowered the bucket. From the top of the tower, Tour des Rondes, there is a good **view** of the town, the Gironde estuary and the surrounding countryside.

Tour de l'Éguillette

From the side of the tower, which rises at the northwestern end of the citadel, there is a fine **view**★ of the estuary, studded with islets as far as the open sea.

Take the pathway on the western side of the citadel.

Place d'Armes

From the esplanade on the edge of the cliff overlooking the Gironde there is another view of the estuary and the islands. Nearby there stands a former monastery belonging to the mendicant order of Minims (17C), complete with its chapel and cloisters. Temporary exhibitions are regularly hosted here.

La Manutention

This square building, erected in 1667 to house the jail of both the citadel and the city, was then used as a bakery, a warehouse and a storehouse. It houses interesting exhibitions: **Estuaire vivant** (with model ships and the maritime history of Blaye; *open Apr–Oct, please call for specific hours; 2.80€; ℘05 57 42 80 96; www.estuairegironde.net*), a bakery museum, and an archaeological museum (*open daily 28 Mar–Oct 1–7pm; Nov–27 Mar 1.30–5.30pm. 3€; ℘06 82 34 72 66*).

Bourg

Gironde

Built on a rocky outcrop and surrounded by medieval walls, this pretty village with its soft limestone buildings is a peaceful spot. The local market is liveliest on Sunday mornings, reaching its most popular the first Sunday of September where a medieval market takes place. The local wine is AOC Côtes-de-Bourg.

Population: 2 300
Michelin Map: 335: H–4
Info: ℘05 57 68 31 76. www.bourg-en-gironde.fr.
Location: At the confluence of the Garonne and Dordogne rivers, on the Right Bank of Bordeaux.
Kids: Grottes de Pair-non-Pair.
Timing: Allow half a day.

THE TOWN

The Tourist Office hires audioguides (in French) helping you to explore: **Terrasse du District**, a shady spot with an orientation point over the surroundings; the lower town with its old public wash house; the 18C **château de la Citadelle** and its horseracing museum.

DRIVING TOUR

5 CÔTES DE BOURG

35km/22mi. Allow 2hrs.

Leave Bourg on the D 23, then turn right onto the D 133.

Église de Tauriac
Roman church dominates the village.

Continue until you reach the D 137, then turn right to St-André-de-Cubzac.

St-André-de-Cubzac
9 allée du Champ-de-Foire, Square François-Mitterrand. Open Mon 2–6pm, Tue–Fri 9am–noon, 2–6pm, Sat 9am–1noon. ℘05 57 43 64 80. www.pays-hautegironde.fr.
A dolphin on a roundabout at the entrance to the village signifies that Jacques-Yves **Cousteau** was born here. Other points of interest include a Roman church, cloisters and an attractive park. To the north, the **coteau de Montalon** marks the highest point of the region and the exact crossing of the 45th parallel.

Return to St-André-de-Cubzac and take the D 669 to Bourg.

Grottes de Pair-non-Pair
Guided visit Tue–Sun mid-June–mid-Sept 10am–5.30pm; rest of year 10am–4pm. 7€ (under 18 years no charge). ℘05 57 68 33 40. http://pair-non-pair.monuments-nationaux.fr.
The Pair-non-Pair grotto was discovered by chance in 1881, when a grazing cow got its leg caught in an opening its owner later found to be a cave. These prehistoric caves have wall-paintings dating from 40,000 years ago. They may not be as impressive as those at Lascaux (although they are slightly older) but are still worth a visit, with images of mammoths, bison and horses. During excavations, other artefacts were found, including an ivory pendant from a mammoth's tusk.

The D 669 returns to Bourg.

Église de Magrigne
Roman church built by the Knights Templar, containing medieval paintings.

Château du Bouilh
Guided visits mid-Jun–mid-Sept Thu and Sat–Sun 2.3–6pm; Apr–May and Oct by appointment only. Visit of park possible Easter–mid-Oct 10am–6pm. Closed Nov–Mar. ℘05 57 43 06 59.
Surrounded by its vineyards, this château was built from plans drawn up by Victor Louis (architect of the Grand Théâtre in Bordeaux) for the Marquis de la Tour du Pin (who was hoping to entertain Louis XVI).

Haut-Médoc★

Gironde

The Upper Médoc district, with its exceptional natural conditions and fine-wine tradition dating back to the time of Louis XIV, is true château country and the origin of many wines classed as *grands crus*, which are kept carefully in wine stores and cellars. The Médoc is particularly attractive during the autumn.

- **Population:** 87 000 (entire Médoc peninsula)
- **Michelin Map:** 335: F3q3r
- **Info:** 05 57 75 18 92. www.pays-medoc.com.
- **Location:** Narrow peninsula stretching for 100km/62mi N of Bordeaux, with Garonne river to the E and the Atlantic Ocean to the W.
- **Kids:** Château d'Agassac.
- **Timing:** One day.

DRIVING TOUR

7 MÉDOC PENINSULA

145km/90mi from Bordeaux. Allow one full day.

Leave Bordeaux to the NW via the N 215. In Eysines turn right on the D 2. If leaving from the Parc des Expostions at Bordeaux Lac, follow the D209.

Château d'Agassac, Ludon-Médoc

Open Jun and Sept Tue–Sat 10.30am–6.30pm; Jul–Aug daly 10.30am–6.30pm; Oct–May Mon–Fri by appointment. Guided tour and tasting 7€ (children no charge), self-guided tour with iPod and tasting 5€ (children 2€). 05 57 88 15 47. www.agassac.com.

This château has launched an interactive tour where visitors use iPods and videos to discover the history of the estate since the 13C. One of the first estates you reach when leaving Bordeaux, the property has fairy-tale towers and a beautiful wooded park of 20ha/50 acres. Visitors to Agassac can choose to picnic in its grounds, near the carefully restored *pigeonnier* (dovecote). And once you have freed the princess, you can enjoy the wines.

Château Siran

Labarde. Guided tours (30min) available by appointment. No charge. 05 57 88 34 04. www.chateausiran.com.

You will see objects related to cooperage, a collection of antique bottles, *jacquot* jars and labels of the château, which have been illustrated each year by a different artist since 1980. After visiting the wine store, you will discover a few rooms fitted out in the outbuildings of the château. The latter, a manor house (17C Directoire) surrounded by a wood carpeted with cyclamens in the autumn, used to belong to the comtes de Toulouse-Lautrec, the ancestors of the 19C painter. In the corridors, note the engravings signed by Rubens, Velázquez, Boucher and Daumier. A painting in the style of Caravaggio, *The Young Bacchus*, hangs above the staircase leading to the first floor. The dining hall, named the Décaris Room, after the artist who depicted wine-related subjects in his paintings, displays interesting glazed earthenware decorated with twining vine motifs. On the first floor, in the reception room, do not miss the collection of richly decorated Vieillard dessert plates (hunting and wedding scenes, etc.). This room also holds interesting 19C furniture.

Château Margaux

4.5km/2.8mi NW of Siran via the D 2. Guided tours (1hr30min) Sept–Jul by appointment two wks in advance from Château Margaux, Bureau des Visites, 33460 Margaux. Closed during the grape harvest. No charge. 05 57 88 34 04. www.chateau-margaux.com.

The wine from this estate is one of the five wines of Bordeaux classed as a premier *grand cru classé*, the aristocrats of the Médoc. The **vineyards** which produce it cover an area of 85ha/210 acres including rows of gnarled and twisted vines. Visitors are shown the **wine stores**, various winemaking installations and an interesting collection of old wine bottles.

The château was constructed in 1802 by an architect named Combes. The informal appearance of the English-style gardens contrasts with the formal lines of the building.

Beyond Margaux, route D 2 follows the contour of the hillside rising above the **palus** *(the alluvial soil near to the riverside).*

At Arcins, turn left to Grand-Poujeaux. From here, turn right on the D 5 towards Lamarque.

Château Maucaillou

Open daily summer 10am–5pm; winter 10am–11am, 2–4pm. Closed 1 Jan. 6.90€ (museum and tasting). 05 56 58 01 23. www.chateau-maucaillou.com.

This estate offers a visit to the stores followed by a tour of the **Musée des Arts et Métiers de la Vigne et du Vin**, a museum which illustrates winemaking methods on this estate.

Rejoin the D 2 and continue N. At Cussac-le-Vieux turn right.

Fort Médoc

r. Vieux Cussac, Cussac-Fort-Médoc. Open daily Apr and Oct 10am–6.30pm; Nov–Mar 10am–5pm, May–Sept 9am–7pm. 2.20€. 05 56 58 98 40. http://amis-fort-medoc.fr.

This fort, designed by Vauban in 1689 to prevent the English fleet from penetrating the Gironde and approaching Bordeaux, could pepper the estuary with cannon fire, adding to the defences of Fort Pâté and the citadel of Blaye on the far side. Beyond a gateway, porte Royale with its pediment carved with a sun (the emblem of Louis XIV, the Sun King), lies the courtyard and the main features of the fort – guardroom, powder magazine and gun emplacements, etc. Beyond the courtyard, a bastion offers interesting views of the Gironde and over to Blaye and beyond, the vine-covered slopes.

Continuing N along the D 2, a lane on the left leads to Château Lanessan.

Château Lanessan

Guided tours (1hr) with booking daily 9am–noon, 2–6pm. Closed 1 Jan, 25 Dec. 8€ (museum and tasting 15€). 05 56 58 94 80. www.lanessan.com.

Wine-Growing in Médoc

Although the gravel deposited in the past by the Gironde estuary has not produced very fertile soil, at least it has the advantage of storing heat during the day and releasing it slowly at night, thus minimising spring frosts. Médoc vines are pruned down very close to the ground to take advantage of this.

Also, the steep-sided valleys, known as *jailles*, at right angles to the Gironde estuary, facilitate the run-off of excess water, offering growers a variety of exposures. The climate also helps – while the water mass in the estuary tends to keep the temperature mild, the pine forest of the Landes acts as a screen, sheltering the Médoc from Atlantic breezes.

The Médoc supplies 8% of the *appellation* wines of Bordeaux. They are exclusively red and made principally from the Cabernet grape producing a wine which is light, has a nice bouquet, is elegant, even a little astringent, and a delight to a discerning palate. The most highly rated are Château Lafite Rothschild, Château Margaux, Château Latour and Château Mouton Rothschild.

The château stands on a ridge in the middle of a 400ha/988-acre estate. It was built in 1878 by Abel Duphot, styled with a mixture of Spanish Renaissance and traditional Dutch, with stepped gables and tall stone chimneys. The outbuildings house the **Musée du Cheval**, which includes an interesting collection of horse-drawn vehicles dating from 1900, including a 15-seat stage coach. A collection of saddles, harnesses, bits and stirrups is on view in the tack room. The feeding troughs in the stables are made of marble. The wine stores (1887) can also be visited; the visit ends with a wine-tasting session.

Château Beychevelle

Guided tours (1hr) daily with booking May–Sept Mon–Sat; Oct–Apr Mon–Fri (please call for times). No charge. 05 56 73 20 70. www.beychevelle.com.

This is a delightful white manor house, rebuilt in 1757, extended in the 19C and recently restored. The wine store may be visited upon reservation. The name of Beychevelle (allegedly derived from *baisse-voile* meaning "lower sail") is a reminder of a ship's salute; customary in the 17C when vessels passed the property. It belonged then to the Duc d'Éperon, Grand Amiral de France, who exacted a toll from masters navigating the Gironde.

St-Julien-Beychevelle

This is one of the better-known names of the Médoc. The region includes such famous châteaux as Lagrange, Léoville, Beaucaillou, Talbot – after the English general who lost at Castillon-la-Bataille – and Gruaud-Larose (its proprietor, it is said, used to hoist upon the château tower a different coloured flag to signal the quality of each year's vintage).

Pauillac

Halfway between Bordeaux and "la pointe de Grave", Pauillac is a riverside town, a port with fine quays equipped to accommodate cruise liners. It is known above all, however, as a major centre of the wine trade, honoured by such famous vineyards as Château Lafite Rothschild, Château Latour and Château Mouton Rothschild. There is also a wine cooperative, La Rose Pauillac, the oldest in the Médoc.

Château Mouton Rothschild★

Guided tours (1hr) with booking Mon–Fri 9.30am–11am, 2–4pm. 6€. 05 56 73 21 29. www.bpdr.com.

At the heart of the vineyards above Pauillac rises Château Mouton Rothschild, one of the most exalted names of the Médoc. Its wine was classed *premier cru* in 1973. The **wine stores** are open to the public. The superbly furnished reception hall of the château is embellished with paintings and sculptures on the theme of wine and vineyards. The banqueting hall beyond is hung with a magnificent 16C tapestry illustrating the grape harvest. Also on view is an interesting collection of wine labels commissioned from Braque, Dalí, Masson, Carzou, Villon and other modern artists. The tour finishes at the main wine store, where the barrels containing the most recent vintage are stored, and the cellars in which thousands upon thousands of bottles containing the precious wine are racked.

Another series of very old cellars has been converted into a **museum**★★. It contains an extraordinary selection of paintings, sculptures, tapestries, ceramics and glasswork celebrating wine and its production. It includes precious stones and a dazzling collection of 16C and 17C gold plate. Among the contemporary pieces, note the fine work by the American sculptor Lippold.

Château Lafite Rothschild

Guided tours (45min) with booking 15 days before visit Nov–Jul Mon–Fri 2–3.30pm. Closed public holidays. No charge. 05 56 59 26 83. www.lafite.com.

This is perhaps the most famous of the premier *grands crus* of the Médoc. Among the treasured bottles of wine stored in the château's impregnable cellars are some known as *Comète* vintage, commemorating a celestial phenomenon of 1811. The name Lafite corresponds to the Gascon term *la hite* (originally derived from the Latin *petra ficta* meaning "carved stone"), and was used initially because the château was built on a small rise. The terrace on which it stands is planted with fine cedar trees and bordered by an elegant Louis XIV balustrade. It has belonged to the Rothschild family since the Second Empire (1868).

Beyond Château Lafite Rothschild, on the right-hand side of the D 2, the silhouette of **Château Cos d'Estournel** (*guided tours Mon–Fri 9am–12.30pm, 2–5.30pm; 05 56 73 15 50; www.cosestournel.com*) appears, reminiscent of 19C Indian-style pagodas. In fact, the founder of the château exported his wine as far as India and had this exotic mansion constructed as a reminder of his far-off business dealings. A modern winery has been recently completed.

Turn right (D 2) to St-Estèphe.

St-Estèphe

This little town, clustered around its church, rises like an island in a sea of vines. From the small port on the Gironde, east of the town, the view includes the slopes around Blaye, formerly the banks of the estuary.

About 2km/1.2mi before St-Izans-de-Médoc, take a lane on the right.

Château Loudenne

Guided tours Apr–Oct by appointment daily 11am, 2.30pm, 4pm, 5.30pm. 5€. 05 56 73 17 97. www.lafragette.com.

This lovely 17C pink manor house belonged to two Britons for 125 years until it was purchased back by the Lafragette family in 2000. The terrace opens onto **English gardens** (including a rose garden), which lead down to the estuary where the small port of the property is located. The Victorian wine stores house a **museum** explaining the history of winemaking (with antique tools and objects) and vineyards (interesting fresco representing the four seasons).

Return to St-Seurin and turn right towards Pez.

Vertheuil

The 11C **Romanesque church** (*open 15 Jun–30 Aug daily 11am–6pm; 05 56 73 30 10*), modified in the 15C, is a former abbey church whose importance can be seen in its two belfries, three aisles, and a chancel with an ambulatory and radiating chapels. On the north wall are the remains of a handsome Romanesque doorway with covings, decorated with figures.

The interior, with its 15C ribbed vaulting and aisles almost as tall as the nave, is reminiscent of the Poitou style. In the chancel, where the vaulting is reinforced by radiating ribs, are stalls carved with scenes from monastic life, and a suspended gallery. The unusual ambulatory is roofed with a series of transverse barrel-vaults. In the nave stands a 15C font, carved from a single stone block.

Impressive 18C buildings remain in the grounds of the old abbey, along with traces of its Gothic cloisters. The village is overlooked by the *(restored)* 12C keep of a ruined castle.

Turn S along the D 104.

Moulis-en-Médoc

The **Romanesque church** here was slightly altered during the Gothic period, the south apsidal chapel being replaced by a round turret enclosing a spiral stairway that led to a belfry with a strongroom. Peasants pruning vines are visible on the Romanesque portal. At the angles of the transept crossing, the columns supporting the church tower had to be reinforced at one time, thereby reducing the width of the supporting arches.

The remarkable apse has carved modillions and blind arcades on the outside, and blind arcades in the interior, their capitals naïvely carved with historiated cats and birds. The fourth on the left (Tobias carrying the fish whose venom will cure his father's blindness) is especially noteworthy. The *bénitier* (stoup) outside the church, built into the façade, was reserved – according to local history – for lepers. Notice the frescoes of the 12C–15C. Recent archaeological digs have unearthed the foundations of a 4C–5C place of worship and several Merovingian sarcophagi.

The Grand-Poujeaux vineyards have made wines from Moulis famous.

Castelnau-de-Médoc

Three features of particular interest distinguish the **church** in Castelnau: a stained-glass Renaissance window portraying the Crucifixion, a woodcarving dating from 1736 representing Pentecost, and a 14C alabaster bas-relief of the Holy Trinity, which hangs above the font.

Take the D 1215E1 towards Bordeaux.

La Winery

Rond-Point des Vendangeurs, 33460 Arsac. Open Tue–Sun 10am–7pm. 05 56 39 04 90. www.lawinery.fr.

A restaurant, a wine shop, a cultural centre, a park and an art gallery are all gathered together in this new wine centre, intended to introduce a new kind of wine tourism to France, linking wine more clearly with other art forms. Here, wine is seen as a conptemporary pleasure, and is housed in a modern architectural structure that offers 1 001 labels in the wine boutique, and the chance to discover your "wine star sign" and to match food and wine according to the results.

Return to Bordeaux via the D 1.

ADDRESSES

STAY

Chambre d'hôte Château Cap Léon Veyrin – *33480 Listrac-Médoc, 4km/2.5mi from Listrac via the D 5E2. 05 56 58 07 28. contact@vignobles-meyre.com. Closed 2 wks Dec. 5 rooms.* Set at the heart of a 20ha/50-acre wine estate, this offers simple but well-appointed bedrooms. The breakfast room overlooks the cellars. Wine-tasting available. .

Chambre d'hôte Domaine de Carrat – *rte de Ste-Hélène, 33480 Castelnau-de-Médoc (1km/0.6mi SW of Castelnau-de-Médoc). 05 56 58 24 80. Closed Christmas and New Year. 4 rooms.* Surrounded by a pine and deciduous forest, this majestic, red-shuttered house used to accommodate the stables of the neighbouring château. Considerate reception and very cosy rooms. You'll enter via the splendid paved porchway that horse-drawn carriages used to pass through.

Chambre d'hôte Château le Foulon – *2 rte de St-Raphael, 33480 Castelnau-de-Médoc. 05 56 58 20 18. 4 rooms.* This château dating from 1840 is the perfect starting point for your discovery tour of the great vintages of the Médoc. The rooms, furnished with antiques, have preserved their spacious feel. All overlook the park and the swans gliding on its waterway.

EAT

Café Lavinal – *pl. Desquet, Bages, 33250 Pauillac. 05 57 75 00 09. Closed Sun evening, and 24 Dec–mid Feb.* Attractive bistro in the small village of Bages, just outside Pauillac. The Argentinian chef serves regional food with a twist. Good wine list, including those of the owners, the Cazes family of Lynch Bages.

Le Lion d'Or – *11 rte de Pauillac, 33460 Arcins (6km/3.7mi NW of Margaux via the D 2). 05 56 58 96 79. Closed Sun–Mon 23 Dec–1 Jan, Reservations required.* Bistro ambience in this restaurant, with wall seats and big mirrors reflecting the Châteaux de Bordelais wine racks. Generous and well-prepared fare is quite popular, especially because prices are so reasonable.

Auberge de Savoie – *1 pl. Trémoille, 33460 Margaux. 05 57 88 31 76. www.lesavoie.net.* A very friendly reception awaits you in this handsome 19C stone house. Two colourful, pleasant dining rooms and agreeable terrace in the back. Well-prepared cuisine at affordable prices.

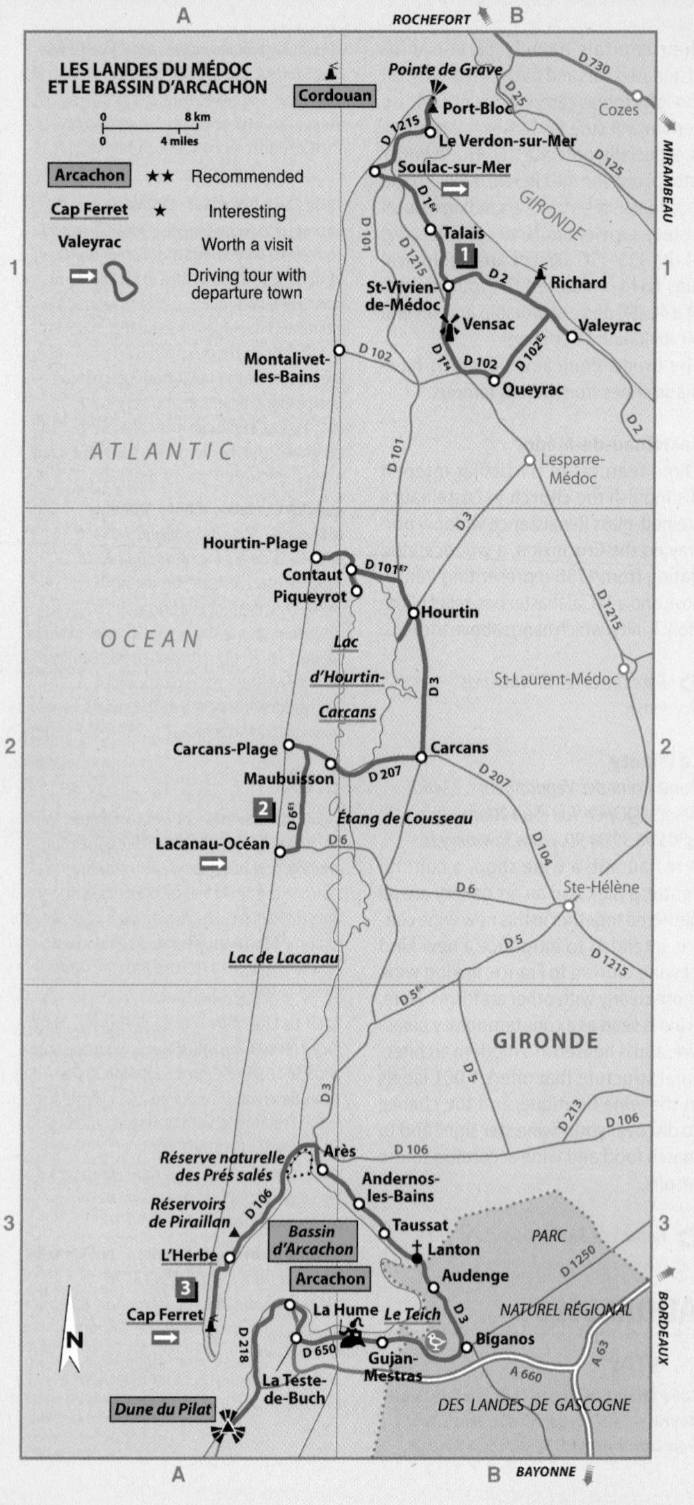
LES LANDES DU MÉDOC
ET LE BASSIN D'ARCACHON
0 8 km
0 4 miles
Arcachon ★★ Recommended
Cap Ferret ★ Interesting
Valeyrac Worth a visit
Driving tour with departure town
ROCHEFORT
Cordouan
Pointe de Grave
Port-Bloc
Le Verdon-sur-Mer
Soulac-sur-Mer
Talais
St-Vivien-de-Médoc
Richard
Vensac
Valeyrac
Queyrac
Montalivet-les-Bains
Cozes
MIRAMBEAU
GIRONDE
ATLANTIC
OCEAN
Lesparre-Médoc
Hourtin-Plage
Contaut
Piqueyrot
Hourtin
Lac d'Hourtin-Carcans
St-Laurent-Médoc
Carcans-Plage
Maubuisson
Carcans
Étang de Cousseau
Lacanau-Océan
Ste-Hélène
Lac de Lacanau
GIRONDE
Réserve naturelle des Prés salés
Arès
Andernos-les-Bains
Réservoirs de Piraillan
Taussat
Bassin d'Arcachon
Lanton
L'Herbe
Arcachon
Audenge
PARC
NATUREL RÉGIONAL
DES LANDES DE GASCOGNE
Cap Ferret
La Hume
Le Teich
Biganos
Gujan-Mestras
La Teste-de-Buch
Dune du Pilat
BORDEAUX
BAYONNE
N
D 730
D 25
D 125
D 1215
D 101
D 2
D 102
D 102E2
D 101E7
D 3
D 207
D 104
D 6
D 6E1
D 5
D 5E4
D 213
D 106
D 1250
D 218
D 650
A 660
A 63

BASSIN D'ARCACHON

The expanse of Atlantic Coast that runs from the Pointe de Grave, 100km/62mi to the north of Bordeaux, down to the wealthy holiday enclave of Arcachon Bay is marked by stretches of vast empty beaches, tracts of pine forest, nature reserves and imposing sand dunes – most notably the Dune du Pilat (locally often spelled "Dune de Pyla"), which rises 107m/350ft above sea level, is half a kilometre wide and around three kilometres in length (0.3 x 1.8mi). This section of the Côte d'Argent is less well known than the more southern stretch closer to Biarritz, but offers equally good sailing and surfing opportunities at Soulac, Lacanau and Montalivet. Set back from the coastline are a series of freshwater and seawater lakes, known locally as the Étangs du Médoc Bleu. Set in between the beaches and the vines of the Médoc, lakes such as Lacanau Lac and Hourtin-Carcans offer excellent water sports activities.

Green Tourism

This is one of the eco-tourism centres of Aquitaine, with more than 140km/88mi of bicycle trails which stretch all along the Médoc Coast, and are relatively flat. Cycling is a particularly popular form of local tourism, and all main towns will have bike hire shops.

Nature reserves, from the **Parc Ornithologique du Teich** with its thousands of migratory birds, to the water fowl at the **Banc d'Arguin Nature Reserve**, highlight the importance of conservation in an area which is always feeling the pressure of erosion to its seaboard. Pollution from increased tourism, plus increasingly violent storms and rising sea levels, has seen increased displacement of sand and rocks in recent years. There are several measures employed in the region to combat the threat.

In Soulac-sur-Mer, the local town redistributes sand back on to the main beaches, while in the Arcachon Bay, all property owners must join an association called Syndicat Intercommunal du Bassin d'Arcachon (SIBA), which manages and protects the bay – again mainly by redistributing sand to guard against erosion.

Highlights

1. Majestic Renaissance **Cordouan Lighthouse** (p145)
2. The boat harbour at massive **Hourtin** freshwater lake (p147)
3. **Arcachon**'s refined Winter Resort, at any time of year (p149)
4. Farming for delectable oysters off **Cap Ferret** (p154)
5. The **Dune du Pilat**, the biggest sand formation in Europe (p159)

Arcachon Bay

Soulac-sur-Mer★

Gironde

This seaside resort is sheltered by pine-covered dunes on one side, and from the surging surf on the other, by a high sand bank, once the site of the ancient city of Noviomagus, which was swallowed up by the sea in the 6C. Until the 16C, Soulac had a large natural harbour giving on to the Gironde estuary, where pilgrims would come ashore on their way to Santiago de Compostela. It was overrun by marshes in the 17C. From the waterfront there is a fine view of the Phare de Cordouan. Bathing is supervised along the resort's four beaches and there are possibilities for water sports, hikes and cycling.

- **Population:** 2 690
- **Michelin Map:** 335: E-1
- **Info:** 68 r. de la Plage, Soulac-sur-Mer. ℘05 56 09 86 61. www.soulac.com.
- **Location:** Soulac-sur-Mer lies on the Atlantic Coast near the Gironde estuary.
- **Kids:** The resort's sandy beaches.

SIGHTS

The central rue de la Plage, which runs between the basilica and the seafront, is the main thoroughfare: it is pedestrianised, and is where you will find the main shops, the covered market and the tourist office. A little farther out from the town centre you will find architecturally-interesting 19C **villas**, constructed of both red-brick and wood, and alongside them more recent 1920s chalets. Heading west of the seafront is the **Musée d'Art et d'Archéologie** *(near the casino)* and to the east *(near the swimming pool)* the memorial to the Forteresse Nord-Médoc, a collection of World War bunkers.

Although Soulac is relatively sheltered by its high sand dunes, lifeguards are present at its four beaches. As along the entire Atlantic Coast, numerous water sports are on offer. From the Amélie district, there is a cycle path (3.5km/2.2mi) direct to the central beach. And when it's too hot outside, the pine trees offer welcome shade. The forest contains numerous walking and cycle routes.

The discovery trail 1km/0.6mi south of Soulac is accessible along the D 101E1. The **Dune d'Amélie** is a protected site.

Basilique Notre-Dame-de-la-Fin-des-Terres

rte de Bordeaux. Guided tours available from the tourist office.

At the end of the 18C, this Benedictine abbey-church was almost entirely covered by sand. It was uncovered and restored in the 19C.

The church includes elements of 12C Romanesque architecture and has a 14C belfry which replaced the original one which stood over the transept crossing. The Poitou style of building is apparent in the windowless nave, and dimly lit by tall bays in the side aisles, which are almost as high as the nave itself.

Three remaining capitals show the tomb and shrine of St Veronica *(left pier before the chancel)*, who evangelised the Médoc region and died in Soulac; one portrays St Peter in prison *(at the entrance to the chancel, left)*, and another depicts Daniel in the Lions' Den *(inside the chancel)*. A polychrome wood statue of Our Lady of Land's End, to whom the church is dedicated, stands in the south transept.

Musée d'Art et d'Archéologie

av. El Burgo de Osma. Open Thu–Tue Easter–Jun and Sept 3–6pm; Jul–Aug 3–7pm. 2.50€. ℘05 56 73 29 37.

The town boasts an **archaeological museum** displaying flint axes, chisels, decorated pottery, arrow heads from the Neolithic and Bronze Ages, and military ensigns, money, ceramics and glassware from the Gallo-Roman period. The museum also houses the **Salon des Beaux-Arts**. On view, inside, are paintings and sculptures by contemporary local artists.

Mémorial de la Forteresse du Nord Médoc

Open Jul–Aug Tue and Fri–Sat 10am–noon, 5–7pm, rest of year by appointment. Museum 3€ (children 1€), historic sites 6€, museum and sites 7€ (children 3€). 05 56 73 63 60. http://vincent.mari.perso.sfr.fr.

This memorial museum is dedicataed to the liberation of the Médoc in August 1944. Visitors can visit the bunkers followed by a guided tour of the museum *(allow 3hrs)*.

EXCURSIONS

Montalivet-les-Bains

18km/11.2mi S.

This small seaside resort is best known as a centre of naturism, due to the presence of a large resort nearby, and for its lively daily market in the summer. There are 12km/7.4mi of beach, two hiking trails in the marshes and cycle paths in the forest.

DRIVING TOUR

1 BETWEEN OCEAN AND ESTUARY

85km/53mi. Allow 4hrs.

Leave Soulac to the N on the D 1E4 then follow the N 215.

Pointe de Grave

Park the car by the monument.

Pointe de Grave is the tip of a headland at the northernmost limit of the Landes, which curves across to narrow the mouth of the Gironde. It lies directly across the water from the beach resort of Royan.

The current monument replaces a 75m/246ft pyramid erected to commemorate the landing of American troops in 1917 and demolished by the Germans in 1942. The point was a strategic coastal defensive position and was occupied by German forces until being retaken by Allied forces in April 1945, only weeks before the armistice. The old blockhouse on top of the dune offers a vast panoramic **view**★ of the Cordouan Lighthouse 9km/5.6mi out to sea, the peninsula and lighthouse of La Coubre, the Gironde and the harbour at Le Verdon, the coves around Royan and the Atlantic Ocean.

Another lighthouse, on the point itself, houses the **Musée du Phare de Cordouan** *(r. François Le Breton; open (access is by 120 stairs) May–Jun Sun and public holidays 3–6pm, Jul–Aug 10am–noon, 2.30–6.30pm; 2.50€; 05 56 09 61 78; www.littoral33.com/cordouan)*. This museum highlights the exceptional architecture of the offshore Phare de Cordouan *(see below)* and gives some idea of the daily life of the keepers. Children's drawings on the theme of lighthouses, and an aquarium with exotic marine species complete the exhibition.

As well as providing access to the lighthouse, Pointe de Grave is the departure point for various boat trips. There is also a scenic railway.

Phare de Cordouan★★

Open Apr–Sept depending on the tide and weather conditions; wear boots or an old pair of shoes, as there is a chance of getting your feet wet. 4hr round trip. 33€ (boat crossing and entrance to the lighthouse). Reservations required. 05 46 05 30 93. www.pharedecordouan.com.

Cordouan Lighthouse watches over the approaches to the Gironde estuary, which are frequently at the mercy of dangerous currents. Once a part of the Pointe de Grave but reduced to an islet during the 16C–17C, today, the ancient land link is revealed only at low tide.

The Renaissance architecture of the lower storeys, separated from the upper Classical portion by a balustrade, makes the 67.5m/221ft-high lighthouse a majestic presence.

A postern leads into the circular bastion, which protects the building from the fury of the seas and contains the

lighthouse-keepers' quarters. On the ground floor, a monumental doorway provides access to the vestibule from which 311 steps lead up to the modern lantern. On the first floor, surrounded by an outside gallery, is the King's Apartment.

From the jetty at Port-Bloc, take the D 1215 towards Soulac.

Le Verdon-sur-Mer

Le Verdon is a large container terminal at the mouth of the estuary, protected from the ocean by Pointe de Grave. It has a deep-water port unrestricted by locks or tides, and offers direct access up the Gironde. Huge container ships and oil tankers dock here before sailing for Central America, South America, West Africa and the Indian Ocean.

The road takes you past **Talais**, a former oyster port.

St-Vivien-de-Médoc

pl. Brigade-Carnot, 33590 St-Vivien-de-Médoc, 05 56 09 58 50. Open Mon–Fri 8.30am–12.30pm, 2–5pm, Sat 8.30am–12.30pm.

Try to coincide your visit with the bustling Wednesday morning market, one of the most popular in the Médoc. Afterwards, explore the small fishing port, and the aquatic farm Eau Médoc, where prawns are raised in old salt marshes *(Mar–Jun Fri pm, Sat am, Jul–Nov am and pm; guided visits available with 3 days' notice; no charge for visit, but tasting 5€; 05 56 09 58 32).*

Take the direction to Port-de-St-Vivien then take the first right (D 2). On the right, follow signs to phare de Richard. The road passes a sea wall constructed during the 17C drainage of the Médoc marshes.

Phare de Richard

Open Jul–Aug 11am–7pm; Mar–June Wed–Mon 2–6pm; rest of year by appointment. 1.25€ (under 10 years no charge). 05 56 09 52 39. www.phare-richard.com.

Left empty since 1953, this lighthouse was reopened as a museum by the young residents of Jau-Dignac-Loirac (the closest village to the site), in a bid to preserve the memory of their ancestors. Climbing the 63 steps gives visitors an impressive view over the estuary, the alignment of the sea wall and the polders (low-lying land protected from the sea by the dykes or wall) of the Médoc.

The road goes past Port-de-Richard and Port-de-Goulée, a former oyster port.

Valeyrac

The village contains a church built by Paul Abadie, architect of Sacré-Cœur in Montmartre.

Return to Port-de-Richard and turn left on the D 102E2 to Queyrac (worth a stop if you have time). Then head N on the D 102, across the D 1215 to the D 1E4.

Moulin de Vensac

From Soulac take the D 101E6 left and follow the orange signposting to the mill. Guided tour (30min) Apr–May and Oct Sun 2.30–6.30pm, public holidays 10am–12.30pm, 2.30–6.30pm; Jul–Aug daily 10am–12.30pm, 2.30–6.30pm; Jun and Sept Sat–Sun 10am–12.30pm, 2.30–6.30pm. 3€. 05 56 09 45 00. www.moulindevensac.fr.

This traditional 18C windmill, consisting of a stone tower with a conical roof, was moved to its present location in 1858. Visitors can follow the different stages of flour-making.

ADDRESSES

STAY

Camping Les Lacs – *126 rte des Lacs, 33780 Soulac-sur-Mer (3km/2mi S of Soulac via the D 101). 05 56 09 76 63. www.camping-les-lacs.com. Reservations recommended. 228 pitches. Closed mid-Nov–early Apr.* The facilities at this friendly campsite include two pools (one covered and one outdoors), a games room, a bar, a pizzeria and a shop.

Lacanau-Océan

Gironde

Built along the ocean front, where huge rollers come crashing on the shore, Lacanau is a picturesque resort lying at the foot of a large expanse of sand dunes, carpeted with sea pines; these have long been exploited for timber and resin. The geometrically arranged plantations, rising and falling over sandy valleys, offer a pleasant contrast to the wide sandy beaches, which stretch for 20km/12.4mi. It is the ideal place for cycling and surfing enthusiasts. In recent years it has become an important tourism centre, with the opening of several thermal spas, golf courses and larger hotels. There is even a touch of nightlife.

- **Population:** 4 105
- **Michelin Map:** 335: D-4
- **Info:** pl. de l'Europe, Lacanau-Océan. ✆05 56 03 21 01. www.lacanau.com.
- **Location:** Lacanau lies 55km/34mi NW of Bordeaux along the D 6. Take care driving along the roads between Bordeaux and the Atlantic Coast, which are narrow and busy with locals.
- **Don't Miss:** The nature reserves of the Étang de Cousseau and the Lac d'Hourtin.

SIGHT

Lac de Lacanau★

This lake, a popular spot for family holidays, covers an area of 2 000ha/5 000 acres. Its 8km/5mi length teems with freshwater fish, including eels, pike and perch. It offers every imaginable water sport – swimming, sailing, windsurfing, water-skiing, canoeing and kayaking (*boats available for hire; ✆06 66 10 09 12)*. The lake can also be toured on foot or by bicycle.

DRIVING TOUR

2 BETWEEN LAKES AND OCEAN

51km/32mi . Allow 4hrs.

Étang de Cousseau

Guided tours: ✆05 56 91 33 65. Allow half a day; bring drinking water and mosquito repellent.

Access to the lake, a natural reserve, is via a footpath through Lacanau Forest or along paved bicycle paths (leave your bike in the areas indicated at the entrance to the park, as they are not allowed in the park itself).

From the D 6E1, take the coastal route to the right, along the D 207.

Carcans-Maubuisson

Two beaches with lifeguards, and good surfing possibilities for children *(www.stationskid.com)*. At Maubuisson village, the **Musée des Arts et Traditions popuaires de la Lande médocaine** recounts the history of the Landes forest *(open mid-Jun–mid-Sept Tue--hur 10am–noon, 4.30-6.30pm; 2€ (under 17 years no charge); ✆05 56 03 41 96)*.

Lac d'Hourtin-Carcans★

This vast, secluded and unspoiled lake, 19km/11.8mi long and about 3.5km/2.2mi wide, covers an area of more than 6 000ha/14 800 acres. It is like an inland sea set in a landscape of moors and forests, fringed by marshes in the north and in some parts of the east, most of which is covered in sand. It is often called Carcans-Plage (Carcans beach). Dunes, sometimes up to 60m/197ft high, line the west bank. Hourtin village is a popular departure point for travels through the network of lakes, lagoons and canals and is also a base for pleasure boats, following the development of a lakeside marina.

Arcachon★★

Gironde

The seaside resort of Arcachon is built on a lagoon and is reputed for its oyster farms. For decades the town's Winter Resort was the favourite haunt of celebrities from Alexandre Dumas to Jean Cocteau and Marilyn Monroe. Today, several festivals bring the town to life including the Arcachon Festival in late March; the Sables Show-Jumping event on Pereire beach in early June; Les 18 heures d'Arcachon (sailing competition) in July; Fêtes de la Mer (blessing of boats, music in the evening) in mid-August and the Cadences dance festival in late September.

- **Population:** 12 153
- **Michelin Map:** 335: D-7
- **Info:** esp. Georges Pompidou. ✆05 57 52 97 97 www.arcachon.com.
- **Location:** The most direct routes to Arcachon from Bordeaux (60km/37mi away) are the N 250 or the A 63. The town sits on the Bassin d'Arcachon and is divided into four separate districts, the most popular of which is the summer resort facing the sea.
- **Parking:** There is a car park near the railway station, as well as near cours Lamarque de Plaisance in the town centre *(see map)*.
- **Don't Miss:** The promenade along the seafront; the view from the jetty; the Winter Resort; the bd de la Mer; watching the fishing boats unload their catch.
- **Kids:** The local aquarium and maritime museum; the region's sandy beaches.

A BIT OF HISTORY

Birth of Arcachon

In 1841 a new branch line extended the railway from Bordeaux to La Teste, a favourite bathing place for holidaymakers from the famous wine capital. In 1845 a deep-water landing-stage was constructed 5km/3mi north of La Teste and the two towns were linked by a road across the salt marshes. Villas were subsequently built along the road, and Arcachon was born.

In 1852 the **Pereire brothers**, Émile and Isaac, founded a railway company, Compagnie des Chemins de Fer du Midi, and took over the Bordeaux–La Teste line, which they extended to Arcachon. At the beginning of the 1860s, they purchased forest land from the State. To make the line and land profitable, they started building facilities to attract clients – a station, a Chinese-style dining room, a luxury hotel, a Moorish casino and several mansions. The plans for the first buildings were mainly the work of Paul Régnault assisted by the young Gustave Eiffel. Already a summer resort popular for sea bathing, the town also became a winter resort in 1866, attracting tuberculosis patients. It was not until after 1935 that Arcachon became a popular seaside and tourist resort as well as a health resort.

THE SEAFRONT AND SUMMER RESORT★

The **Summer Resort** (Villé d'eté) stretches along the seafront between Jetée de la Chapelle and Jetée d'Eyrac, attracting tourists to its terrace cafés, casino and nautical events (sailing regattas, speedboat races).

The pleasant promenade along the tamarisk-shaded boulevard Gounouilhou and boulevard Veyrier-Montagnères, by Jetée Thiers, overlooks Arcachon's fine, sandy beaches. To the east can be seen the white façade of the **Palatium** conference centre, part of the Renaissance Revival Château Deganne, which also houses the casino. The jetty offers a general **view**★ of the resort and the lagoon.

Fishing in Arcachon

Arcachon is considered to be a pioneer port in the history of sea fishing. It was here that the *Turbot*, the first steam-operated trawler in the world (with a paddle wheel), put to sea in 1837. In 1865 Arcachon saw the first French steamers with propellers and iron hulls. At the turn of the last century, it was the second-largest fishing port in France after Boulogne-sur-Mer. In the same spirit of innovation, the first motorised trawler in France, the **Victoria**, was commissioned in 1927. Commercial fishing in Arcachon declined in the 1950s, as the trawlers left for the more profitable Breton ports, and fishing in Arcachon returned to traditional methods.

Every year, 2 000t of fine-quality fish – sole, bass, hake, mullet, turbot and squid – fetching high market prices, are unloaded onto the Arcachon jetties (do not miss the unloading of the catch, which often takes place around 6.45am). The fleet, which fishes in the **Bay of Biscay**, is made up of traditional fishing smacks and catamarans with nets. In the lagoon itself, apart from holidaymakers and locals who gather clams, cockles and winkles at low tide, traditional methods are still employed. Methods include the use of the *jagude* – three increasingly smaller-gauged nets one inside the other; the *loup* – a horn-shaped net for fishing sea bass; the *palet* – similar to the *loup* but with a spiral base; the *balai* – bunches of broom used to trap prawns; *esquirey* – a term in local patois meaning "landing net"; the *trahine* – a seine-net, one end of which is drawn along the beach and the other out to sea; and the *foëne* – a two-pronged fishing spear for catching eels.

Aquarium and Museum

2 r. Professeur Jolyet. Open daily Jul–Aug 9.45am–12.15pm, 1.45–7pm; Sept–Jun 9.45am–12.15pm, 1.45–6.30pm. 4.70€ (children 3€). 05 56 83 33 32.

30 glass tanks display marine life found in the lagoon and in the ocean beyond. Upstairs the museum boasts a special section devoted to oyster farming, and collections of birds, fish, reptiles and invertebrates native to the region. Another section displays finds from local archaeological digs.

Jetée Thiers

From the Thiers jetty is a **viewpoint★** over the entire Bassin. The stars of the sea are here: Tabarly, Florence Arthaud, Yves Parlier and others have set their footprints in the bronze. To see them, follow the **chaussée des Pieds marins**. Wall along the seafront, the take the boulevard de la Plage. The **croix des Marins** stands at the La Chapelle jetty. At the top of the road is the 19C **Basilique Notre-Dame**. Inside, **Chapelle des Marins**, adorned with numerous thanksgiving offerings, houses the revered statue of Our Lady of Arcachon.

Rejoin the **boulevard de la Mer★**. This charming seaside walk, bordered by pine trees growing in the sandy ground, skirts Pereire Park and offers fine views of the Cap Ferret peninsula.

An attractive shaded walking path skirts alongside the **plage Pereire** (3km/1.8mi). You can follow it as far as Moulleau, to see the surprising sight of a church perched on top of a hill.

THE WINTER RESORT★

2hrs. From pl. du 8-Mai, take the lift up to the edge of the grounds of the Moorish Casino, which overlooks the Summer Resort below. Guided tours (1hr30min) May–Jun and Sept Fri 3–4.30pm; Jul–Aug Sat 10.30am–noon. 4€. 05 57 52 97 97.

Farther inland and more sheltered from the sea breezes, this picturesque neighbourhood (Ville d'hiver) is a quiet, pine-shaded area filled with the fragrance of balsam, once considered beneficial for tuberculosis patients.

As a result of a real estate project inaugurated by the Pereire brothers in 1860, the Winter Resort is a sort of city park, criss-crossed with winding

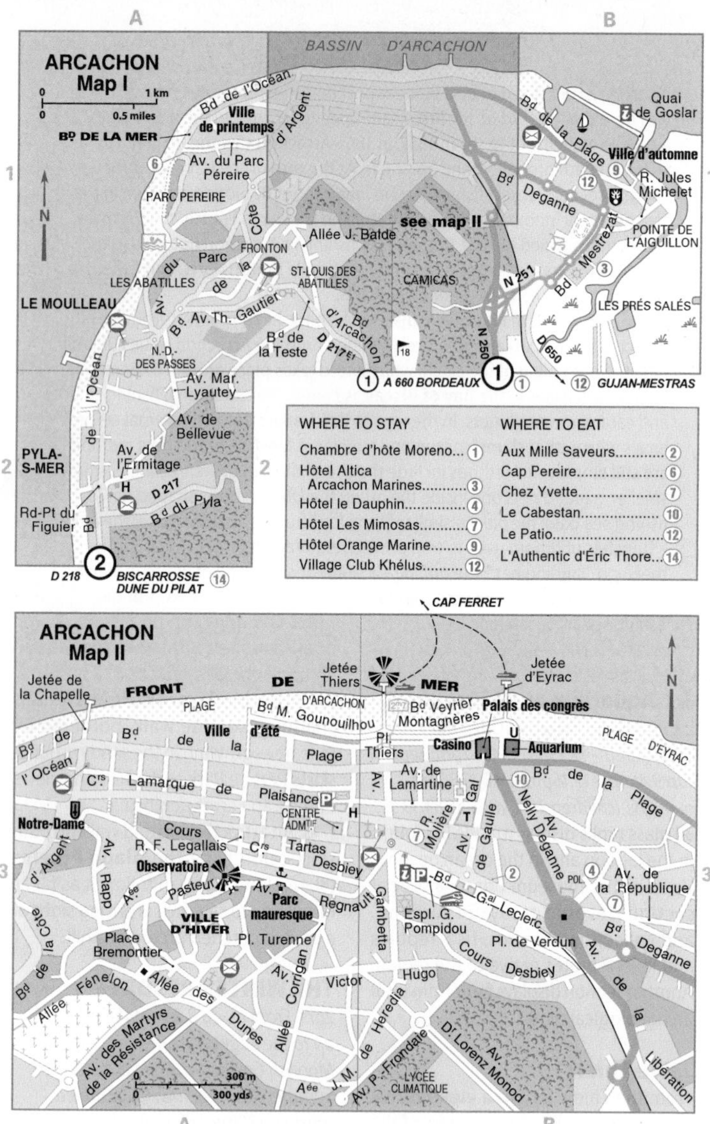

avenues skirting the dunes that protect it from the sea winds.

In 1863 the Emperor Napoleon III visited the Winter Resort, and for decades, it remained a meeting place for famous politicians, authors and artists of the time such as Toulouse-Lautrec. The broad avenues are lined with handsome late 19C and early 20C villas and today there is a strong movement towards consolidating and renovating this highly original and charmingly outdated architectural heritage, characterised by the sculpted wood of its gables, balconies and external staircases.

Below are some suggestions for places to visit on foot.

Parc Mauresque

av. Victor Hugo.

Featuring numerous exotic species, the 8ha/20-acre park offers an excellent

view of the town and the Arcachon lagoon. Many of the original buildings, including the Moorish Casino, destroyed by fire in 1977, and inspired by the Alhambra in Granada and the mosque in Córdoba, have now disappeared. A model that reconstructs its original design is on display.

Observatoire Ste-Cécile

allée Pasteur. Open daily Apr–1 Nov 7am–10pm; 2 Nov–Dec 8am–7.30pm; Jan–Mar 8am–7.30pm. No charge. 05 57 52 97 97.

This metal-framed observatory by Gustave Eiffel can be reached by a footbridge over allée Pasteur. The platform affords a **view** of the Winter Resort, Arcachon and the lagoon *(to be avoided if you suffer from vertigo)*.

Villas

Even though there is a variety of styles (Swiss and Basque chalets, English cottages, Moorish villas, Gothic Revival manors and colonial-style houses), villas usually follow the same basic design. A raised first floor above a semi-basement service floor contains the reception rooms and veranda-lined living room. The bedrooms are on the next floor.

The opulent villa roofs emerge from the vegetation, mainly tall Atlantic pines, interspersed with oaks, maples, black locust (robinia), Japanese ornamental cherry trees, nettle trees, plane and lime trees. When in bloom, mimosas, catalpas and magnolias offer a vibrant display of colour amid the dark green foliage of the pines.

Allée Rebsomen
Villa Theresa (no **4**, now Hôtel Sémiramis).

Allée Corrigan
Villa Walkyrie (no **12**), **Hôtel de la Forêt**, **Villa Vincenette** (bow window with beautiful leaded glass).

Allée Dr-F.-Lalesque
Villas l'Oasis, Carmen and **Navarra**.

On the corner of rue Velpeau and allée Marie-Christine, **Villa Maraquita** (no **8**).

Allée du Moulin-Rouge
Villa Toledo (no **7**, carved staircase).

Allée Faust
Villas Athéna, Fragonard, Coulaine, **Graigcrostan** (no **6**), Faust and Siebel.

Allée Brémontier
Villas Brémontier (no **1**, turret and balcony), Glenstrae (no **4**) and Sylvabelle (no **9**).

Allée du Dr-Festal
Villas **Trocadéro** (no **6**, finely carved balcony – *see illustration in the Introduction: ARCHITECTURE*) and **Monaco**.

Allée Pasteur
Villas Montesquieu and Myriam.
On the corner of allée Pasteur and allée Alexandre-Dumas – Villa A.-Dumas (no **7**).

THE AUTUMN RESORT

The Autumn Resort (Ville d'automne) is the maritime quarter with its large marina and busy fishing port animated by a regular stream of trawlers. Today this is the second-busiest port along the Atlantic Coast, after La Rochelle, and has space for 2 600 boats.

THE SPRING RESORT

To the west, Pereire Park with its large sports complex (bowling, swimming pool, tennis courts, golf course and riding centre) and avenues lined with wealthy mansions forms the Spring Resort (Ville de printemps). Mineral water from the **Abatilles** spring, which once supplied a local spa, is now bottled for sale, and will be on the menu in most local restaurants. Pereire beach is lined by a shaded pedestrianised alleyway. The southern end, known as Les Arbousiers, is the surfing enthusiasts' favourite spot.

ADDRESSES

STAY

Hôtel Le s Mimosas – *77 bis av. de la République. 05 56 83 45 86. www.mimosas-hotel.com. Closed 16 Nov–14 Feb. 21 rooms. 6.50€.*the outside, this villa looks like an old bourgeois residence. Albeit rather modest, the small rooms are cool and clean.

Hôtel Le Dauphin – *7 av. Gounod. 05 56 83 02 89. www.dauphin-arcachon.com. 50 rooms. 9.50€.* Housed in an attractive 19C mansion, this hotel enjoys an excellent location 300m/330yds from the sea in one of Arcachon's quiet districts.

Hôtel Orange Marine – *35 bd Chanzy. 05 57 52 00 80. www.hotelorange marine@wanadoo.com. 21 rooms. 7€. Restaurant.* Here, a stone's throw from the fishing docks, an address where you needn't spend a fortune. The rooms are simple and impeccably maintained. Ask for a seaside room.

EAT

Aux Mille Saveurs – *25 bd Général-Leclerc. 05 56 83 40 28. www.auxmille saveurs.com. Open daily Jul–Aug; closed Tue evening and Wed rest of year.* Dozens of flavour combinations on display here, often subtly spiced. A large dining room has been recently redecorated, and a larger veranda opened up.

Cap Pereire – *1 av. du Parc Pereire. 05 56 83 24 01. www.cappereire.fr. Closed JSun evening, Mon and Jan–mid-Feb.* Far from the crowds, with a view of the sea, this attractive colonial-style restaurant is situated next to the tranquil Parc Pereire. The restaurant specialises in fish and seafood.

Chez Yvette – *59 bd Général-Leclerc. 05 56 83 05 11. restaurant.yvette@orange.fr.* An institution, owned by the same family of oyster farmers for the past 30 years.

Le Cabestan – *6 bis av. du Général-de-Gaulle. 05 56 83 18 62. www.everyoneweb.coin/restaurantlecabestan.* . The chef here learned his trade at several renowned establishments, and continues to make his mark here. The refined cuisine is displayed to perfection in this simple interior. Warm welcome, quick and efficient service.

Le Patio – *10 bd de la Plage. 05 56 83 02 72. www.lepatio-thierryrenou.com. Closed Sun evening and Wed.* Contemporary décor, with pretty terrace. Specialises in seafood.

NIGHTLIFE

Café de la Plage – *1 bd Veyrier-Montagneres. 05 56 83 31 94. www.cafedelaplage.com.* This century-old bar lies in an ideal location on the Arcachon beach, near the casino and Palais des Congrès. Jazz concerts every fortnight; excellent musical ambience in the evening.

Casino de la Plage – *163 bd de la Plage. 05 56 83 41 44. www.partouche-casino-arcachon.fr.* This casino has a traditional games room, 100 slot machines, a restaurant, bars and a discotheque.

SHOPPING

Marché – *pl. du Marché.* Open daily 6am–1pm. This covered market is open every morning and stocks a wide array of foodstuffs from all over southwest France. In summer, the surrounding roads offer further stalls.

SPORT AND LEISURE

Dingo Vélos – *1 r. Grenier, Point France. 05 56 83 44 09. www.dingo-velo.com.* In addition to traditional bicycles (touring and mountain bikes), this rental shop offers a range of unusual bikes, including tandems and bikes with three or even five seats. Go-karts, family quadri-cycles and electric scooters also available.

TRANSPORT

Eho – *Mon–Sat, no charge.* These electric minibuses drive around the city centre (following the blue line on the ground). Line A : town centre, La Chapelle, Pereire, Le Moulleau; line B: town centre, Winter Resort, Abatilles; line C: town centre, Aiguillon, St-Ferdinand.

Cycle tracks – You could see Arachon's by bike in any season and follow the seafront promenade from the Eyrac to the Moulleau jetty..

Bassin d'Arcachon★★

The Bassin d'Arcachon (Arcachon lagoon) is the only major indentation along the Côte d'Argent (Silver Coast). It is almost cut off from the sea by the narrow promontory of Cap Ferret, which leaves an exit channel barely 3km/1.8mi wide. The region's prosperity is based on oyster farming, pine plantations (sawmills and paper mills), and fishing and tourism; note the many weekend cottages, holiday homes and campsites. With an annual production of 18 000t, the Arcachon lagoon is one of the major European centres for oyster production, covering almost 1 800ha/4 448 acres of the lagoon's surface. The lagoon is the main regional breeding centre and supplies seed oysters or spats to other oyster beds in Brittany, Normandy, Languedoc and the Netherlands.

- **Michelin Map:** 335: D–E–6
- **Info:** 16 allée Corrigan, Arcachon. ℘05 57 52 74 94. www.bassin-arcachon.com.
- **Don't Miss:** The Dune du Pilat; Parc Ornithologique du Teich; boat trips on the lagoon; oyster tasting.
- **Kids:** Parc de Loisirs de la Hume; les jardins du Bassin.

BOAT TRIPS

Tours of the lagoon, or fishing trips and oyster-bed tours, are available at several locations *(℘08 25 16 33 16; www.bateliers-arcachon.asso.fr)*.

Several small rivers flow into the bay, the most important being the Eyre, which irrigates the **Parc naturel régional des Landes de Gascogne** *(see pp162)*. At low tide *crassats* appear (silty sand-banks full of underwater vegetation) surrounded by secondary channels called *esteys*.

Île aux Oiseaux

This small flat island covered with dwarf vegetation used to be a birds' paradise until oyster breeders took possession of the surrounding mudflats. Do not miss the two *cabanes tchanquées* (*tchanque* meaning "stilt" in the Gascon language).

The Banc d'Arguin Nature Reserve

Fédération SEPANSO Gironde, 1 r. Tauzia, Bordeaux. Guided tours. ℘05 56 91 33 65. www.sepanso.org.

Banc d'Arguin is a small, sandy island at the mouth of the channels, constantly changing shape as the Atlantic changes mood. It was made a nature reserve in 1972 and is visited from March to August by a large colony of Cabot's sterns (4 500 mating couples) and oyster catchers. In winter, the curlew, bar-tailed godwit, red-backed sandpiper, grey plover, seagull and black-headed gull live here in great numbers.

DRIVING TOUR

3 CAP FERRET TO DUNE DU PILAT

80km/50mi. Allow one day.

Although the roads cited in the itinerary below offer few glimpses of the water, you are never far from a stretch of shore or a small jetty giving at least a partial view of the lagoon.

Cap Ferret★

The long thin promontory of Cap Ferret runs north–south at the entrance to Arcachon lagoon, sheltering narrow straits leading into the basin. The area is a popular oyster-farming centre. A **tourist train** runs to Plage de l'Océan.

Oyster Country

The famous oysters from Arcachon lagoon have long been a delicacy. The Roman poets Ausonius and Apollinaris Sindonius, and later, Rabelais, praised their excellent gastronomic qualities. Overexploitation of their natural beds, however, exhausted the supply, until the naturalist Victor Coste stepped in and started developing oyster farming or *ostréiculteur* in 1859. Until 1920, the flat oyster from Arcachon, or *gravette (ostrea edulis)*, was the most intensely cultivated in the lagoon, followed by the Portuguese deep-shelled oyster *(Crassostrea angulata)*. In the same year, a disease struck the flat oyster beds, but left the Portuguese oysters untouched. The latter were then closely observed and became the predominant species until 1970, when disease struck again and they were replaced by a Japanese variety *(Crassostrea gigas)*.

The oyster cycle lasts for about four years. It starts in July when the oyster spats are gathered in collectors consisting of sand and lime-washed semicircular tiles which are then put in wooden cages or baskets, and placed along the canal. The following spring, the oysters are prised off the collectors and placed in beds sealed off with wire netting which protects them from their predator, the crab. After 18 months, the oysters are detached from the cultch to be fattened for another year in pools of water rich in plankton. During this period, they are repeatedly turned, to give them a uniform shape. Having reached maturity, the oysters are left in degorging tanks to rid them of impurities. They are washed for a last time, packed up in small wooden crates and delivered.

The Pinasse – The brightly coloured streamlined fishing smack called the *pinasse* is the symbol of the Arcachon lagoon. It was originally made of pinewood (hence its name) and pegged together. Nowadays, it is made of iroko (African wood), locust or walnut and assembled with rivets. Formerly used for coastal fishing, the *pinasse* was adopted by the lagoon's oyster farmers in the 19C. Since it is flat bottomed, it can be easily pulled aground and pass through even very shallow channels. It is generally motor driven and 9m–10m/30ft–33ft long; the *pinasotte*, a smaller version, is 6m–7m/20ft–23ft long with either sails or oars. Because of their similarity to Venetian gondolas and Mediterranean caiques, they are highly prized and looked after with great care. The old smacks are refurbished, cosseted and raced in the lagoon during regattas.

Oyster fishermen in Bay of Arcachon

Lighthouse

pl. Souchet Valmont Cap Ferre. Open Apr–Jun and Sept daily 10am–12.30pm, 2–6.30pm; Jun–Aug daily 10am–7.30pm; Oct–Mar Wed–Sun 2–5pm. 4.50€. 05 57 70 33 30.

This landmark (rebuilt in 1947) is 52m/171ft high, with a revolving lantern which can be seen 50km/31mi out to sea. An audiovisual show and a screen gallery inform visitors about the peninsula and the lighthouse. From the platform *(258 steps)* there is a fine **panorama**★ embracing the whole of the peninsula, the lagoon, the straits, the open sea and Pilat Dune.

Centre Equestre Lège-Cap Ferret

rte du Truc Vert, Les Jacquets, Piquey. Open daily Jul–Aug 9am–noon, 3.30–8.30pm; Sept–Jun please call for exact times. 05 56 60 82 85.

A horse riding school that offers lessons and horse rides by the ocean.

Plage de l'Océan

Le petit train du Cap Ferret. Departs Bélisaire daily Apr–May 2.45–4.45pm (every 30min); 1–11 Jun and 19–30 Sept 2.45–5.15pm (every 30min); 12 Jun–7 Jul and 29 Aug–18 Sept 11.15am, 2.45–5.45pm (every 30min); 8 Jul–28 Aug 11.15am, 11.50am, 12.30pm, 2.10–6.10pm (every 20min). 5€ (return journey). 05 56 60 62 57.

A narrow-gauge railway service operates between Bélisaire landing-stage *(eastern side)* and this splendid beach on the ocean side of the promontory.

After 4km/2.5mi, at the roundabout in l'Herbe, follow the sign to bd de la Plage where there is a car park.

L'Herbe★

In the 1860s Léon Lesca, architect of the port of Algiers, chose this site to construct a large villa in the Moorish style which was demolished in 1965; it offers a good view of the lagoon and Bird Island. The oriental influence remains in a chapel, built about 150 years ago, looking out across the sea. From here, take the semi-pedestrianised road to the oyster village, where the oyster cabins are painted in a series of ice-cream colours.

The oyster villages of Cap Ferret, l'Herbe, Le Canon, Le Piraillan, Le Piquey and Les Jacquets are protected classified sites and as such are both well preserved and well visited.

Return to the D 106.

Réservoirs de Piraillan

At the exit of the village.

These former fish reservoirs, 40ha/100 acres in the middle of the forest, have become a haven for birds (particularly grey herons). Binoculars recommended. An enjoyable stroll to take either with or without a guide *(see information at the start of the chapter).*

Follow the D 106. After Claouey, at Jane-de-Boy, there is a car park.

Réserve naturelle des Prés-Salés d'Arès et de Lège

Rejoin Arès (12km/7.5mi round trip). Before leaving, ensure you have checked the high and low tides: www.reserve-naturelle-pres-sales.org. Visits with a specialised guide on request with the tourist office.

The coastal path winds its way through 200ha/495 acres of protected landscape to Arès (the largest saltwater marshes in Aquitaine). The landscape is bound up with the tides, and provides nutrition and shelter for numerous species of birds and wildlife. The resin-tappers' cabins, once lived in by men who tapped the pine trees for their precious sap, today hold an exhibition on the local flora and fauna. Regular events and guided tours are also arranged.

The D 106 wends its way between the edge of the forest and the shore of the lagoon.

Arès

Arès was originally an oyster port; it now also harbours pleasure boats and is a seaside resort. A Romanesque church stands on the town's central

square. Inside, the carved capitals of the columns are illuminated by modern stained-glass windows. The round tower *(restored)* on the waterfront was once part of a windmill.

From Arès to Biganos, the road passes through a landscape of endless pine forests, linking the towns and villages along the lagoon's eastern shore.

Andernos-les-Bains

This sheltered site at the far end of the lagoon has been inhabited by man since prehistoric times. Today, the town is one of the major local resorts, very popular in summer, with beaches stretching for over 4km/2.5mi and a casino.

Opposite the beach and next to the small church of St-Éloi, with its 11C apse, lie traces of a 4C Gallo-Roman basilica. The jetty offers extensive views over the lagoon, the town's oyster port, the beaches and the marina.

Two short walking circuits pass through the villas from the train station *(information available from the tourist office)*.

Follow the D 3.

Lanton

This commune encompasses the beach and oyster port at Taussat and the oyster huts of Cassy.

On the outskirts of Lanton stands a pretty 12C Romanesque church with an elevated apse. The central walkway is lined with columns, topped by ornate capitals of herons, pine cones and stylised leaves.

Audenge

The town, an oyster-farming centre, is also known for its fish reservoirs (a system of locks which encloses the catch at low tide).

Beyond Biganos take the D 3E12 to join the D 650. Opposite the junction

Parc ornithologique du Teich

Bird Sanctuary

A traditional stopover in the spring and autumn for tens of thousands of migratory birds (such as the spoonbill, greylag goose and black-headed gull), the meadows and dykes along the Eyre and around the old fish tanks also shelter numerous birds in the winter including teal, dunlin and cormorant. There are also nesting species such as a colony of herons consisting of more than 1 000 couples of common heron, little egret and cattle egret. In summer, the rare bluethroat rewards patient visitors with his pure song and vibrant colours.

The rich, varied vegetation will delight botany enthusiasts: wild berries (arbutus, brambles) highly appreciated by the frugivorous species; water irises, rushes and oaks planted to consolidate the dykes, as well as tamarisk and alders used by ducks and moorhens to build their nests.

is the impressive smoking bulk of the Cellulose du Pin paper mill, visible for miles around.

Biganos

The pretty oyster port of Biganos is surrounded by forest, and forms part of the Parc naturel régional des Landes de Gascogne (with picnic spots under the trees).

Turn right onto the D 650 by the D 3E12.

The route crosses the inner end of the marshy Eyre delta *(bridge over the river)* and follows the lagoon's southern shore, which remains pleasantly leafy all the way to the outskirts of Le Teich.

5km/3.1mi. The coastal path crosses the Eyre delta here, protected by sea walls on either side. It lies between the two main axes of the river, and protects an abundance of birds.

Parc Ornithologique du Teich★

Open daily 15 Apr–30 Jun and 1–15 Sept 10am–7pm; Jul–Aug 10am–8pm; 16 Sept–14 Apr 10am–6pm. 7€. 05 56 22 80 93. www.parc-ornithologique-du-teich.com.

The **nature reserve** covers a surface area of 120ha/297 acres in the Eyre delta, including 80ha/198 acres of water used in the past for fish breeding and now linked to Arcachon lagoon via a system of locks. The reserve promotes the preservation of species of wild fowl threatened with extinction, and encourages the public to discover European bird species. The reserve is divided into four parks: Les Artigues, La Moulette, Causseyre and Claude Quancard.

Visitors are given a choice of tours on foot, all well marked and equipped with look outs: the short tour (2.4km/1.5mi), the long tour (3.6km/2.2mi) and the complete tour (6km/3.7mi).

Low-Tide Fishing

At low tide, the Archachon lagoon offers the possibility of fishing for shellfish and other seafood.

Cockles and **clams** can be gathered by just scraping the surface of the sand to a depth of 4cm/1.5in. Clams are easier to locate as two small holes in the sand indicate their presence. They can be found in large numbers near the Arquin sandbank and on the mudflats uncovered at low tide. It is advisable to leave them to sweat in saltwater for a few hours before eating them. **Winkles** can be gathered by hand on the mudflats. In order to eat them as an appetiser before a meal, it is necessary to plunge them for a few minutes in boiling water. Wild **mussels**, found near the oyster beds, can be dislodged with a knife.

Green crabs also abound on the beaches at low tide; they can be caught with a net and cooked in seasoned boiling water. Fishing for **shrimps** is done with the help of a net. Gathering **razor-shells** can be an enjoyable activity. They can be detected by the key-shaped mark they leave on the sand; place two or three grains of coarse salt on this mark to trick them into coming up to the surface as they believe the high tide is returning. Razor-shells are not a refined kind of seafood but they make an excellent bait for line fishing. Gathering oysters, even wild ones, is strictly forbidden. Fishing for cockles and clams is on the other hand allowed but restricted to 2kg/4.4lb per person at every tide. Shell-gathering is sometimes forbidden for health reasons. Be careful when walking on mudflats as there is always a risk of getting bogged down.

We recommend that you hire binoculars.

Gujan-Mestras

This busy town with its six oyster farms is the oyster capital of the Arcachon area. It is extremely picturesque with tile-roofed cabins, canals crowded with fishing smacks, oyster-purging tanks and waterfront kiosks where oysters can be sampled, ordered and dispatched to family or friends.

In the port of Larros, at the **Maison de l'Huître** *(open Jun–Aug daily 10am–12.30pm, 2.30–6pm; Sept–May Mon–Sat 10am–12.30pm, 2.30–6pm; 4.50€; 05 56 66 23 71; www.maisondelhuitre.fr)*, an exhibition and film explain the different stages of oyster farming, from preparation of the collectors to consumption.

A *pinasses* yard (local fishing smacks) and oyster-packaging unit are visible. You can then sample and compare oysters in fishermen's huts in the heart of the port of Larros.

Parc de Loisirs de la Hume

This park, at the intersection of the N 250 and the D 652, offers a range of leisure facilities including a **medieval miniature golf**; **Aqualand** *(rte des lacs, Gujan-Mestras; open daily 20 Jun–5 Jul and 31 Aug–6 Sept 10am–6pm, 6 Jul–30 Aug 10am–7pm; 24.50€ (children 18€); 05 56 66 39 39; www.aqualand.fr)*, a water park; and **La Coccinelle** *(open 11 Apr–27 Jun and 2 Sept–4 Nov, please call for times, 28 Jun–31 Aug daily 10.30am–7pm; 10.50€ (children 9.50€); 05 56 66 30 41; www.la-coccinelle.fr)*, a menagerie for younger visitors, where they can feed lambs, kids and calves themselves, plus a small park with family attractions from trampolines to tourist trains.

La Teste-de-Buch

La Teste was once the capital of the former kingdom of the Buch family and is now part of one of the biggest municipalities (18 000ha/44 477 acres) in France. Settled by the Boli or Boians before the Roman colonisation, it was later developed by the English and subsequently became an important oyster port. Today the municipality includes the ancient forest of La Teste, Cazaux and its lake *(south)*, and the resorts of Pyla-sur-Mer and Pilat-Plage with its famous dune *(southwest)*. Note, near the tourist office in place Jean-Hameau, the façade of the 18C **Maison Lalanne** *(guided tours (1hr) Sat–Sun 3.30pm, 5pm; ✆05 57 73 69 20)*, adorned with representations of an anchor, rigging and the heads of the owner's children.

Arcachon★★

See ARCACHON.

The road passes through the neighbouring resort of Moulleau and then Pyla-sur-Mer and Pilat-Plage, where hotels and villas are scattered beneath the pines, before climbing in a series of hairpin bends towards the famous dune.

Dune du Pilat★★

This sand dune, at 107m/350ft the highest in Europe, is 2.7km/over 1.5mi long and 500m/550yds wide. The west face slopes gently towards the Atlantic rollers, whereas the hollowed landward side to the east drops to the pines below. To reach the summit, either scale the flank of the dune *(a fairly difficult ascent)* or climb the 154-step staircase *(in summer only)*. From the top, the **panorama★★** over the ocean and the forests of the Landes – the finest of all views over the Silver Coast – is breathtaking, especially at sunset.

ADDRESSES

 STAY

Camping Village Club Khélus – *rte de la Hume, near Aqualand, 44370 La Hume. ✆05 56 66 88 88. www.kalisea.fr. 120 chalets and maisonettes.* Located in a 20ha/50-acre park, the maisonettes and wooden chalets are well equipped and available for hire from one week, although some shorter stays may be available on request.

Hôtel Altica Arcachon Marines – *75 av. de Général Leclerc, 33120 La Teste-de-Buch. ✆05 57 52 06 50. www.altica.fr. 46 rooms.* Modern building close to the stadium that works for a short stay. Basic rooms, but with their own private bathroom, and well priced.

Chambre d'hôte Moreno – *33 chemin de la Peguilleyre, 33120 La Teste-de-Buch. ✆05 56 66 57 54. www.peguilleyre33.com.* Large villa located in a quiet residential area. Two bedrooms and a suite, well appointed and all with a small balcony. Breakfast is served on a terrace. Pool.

EAT

L'Étoile – *13 pl. de l'Étoile, 33510 Andernos-les-Bains. ✆05 56 82 00 29.* Popular restaurant located just 100m/100yds from the beach; expect good servings of traditional food, served in a family atmosphere.

L'Authentic d'Éric Thore – *35 bd de l'Océan, 33115 Pyla-sur-Mer. ✆05 56 54 07 94.- Open Thur–Mon; daily in school holidays.* Recently renovated restaurant with a summery feel, re-creating the feeling of an oyster cabin. Outside terrace with pergola perfect for warm days. Creative cooking.

Pinasse Café – *2 bis av. de l'Océan, Cap Ferret. ✆05 56 03 77 87. www.pinassecafe.com. Closed 12 Nov–1 Mar.* An original, laid-back bistro. The wood-panelled walls are decorated with paintings of boats and drawings of fish – not surprising, considering it overlooks the Bassin.

SHOPPING

Cash Vin – *r. Lagrua, 33260 La Teste-de-Buch. ✆05 56 22 22 50. www.cash-vin.com. 5€ (children 4€).* Well-stocked wine shop representing over 300 *appellations* around France and further afield. Frequent tastings.

SPORT AND LEISURE

Les jardins du Bassin – *rte des Lacs, La Hume, Gujan-Mestras. ✆05 56 66 00 71. Open mid-May–Sept Mon–Sat 10am–12.30pm, 2.30–7pm. 5€ (children 4€).* Adults and children alike will enjoy a visit to these botanical gardens, with their fruit trees, vines, cacti, exotic plants and vegetable plots.

Centre permanente de Kayak de mer – *Pont de Bredouille, 33950 Lege-Cap-Ferret. ✆05 57 70 45 55.* Sea kayak centre offering canoe trips on the sea, and wave-skiing.

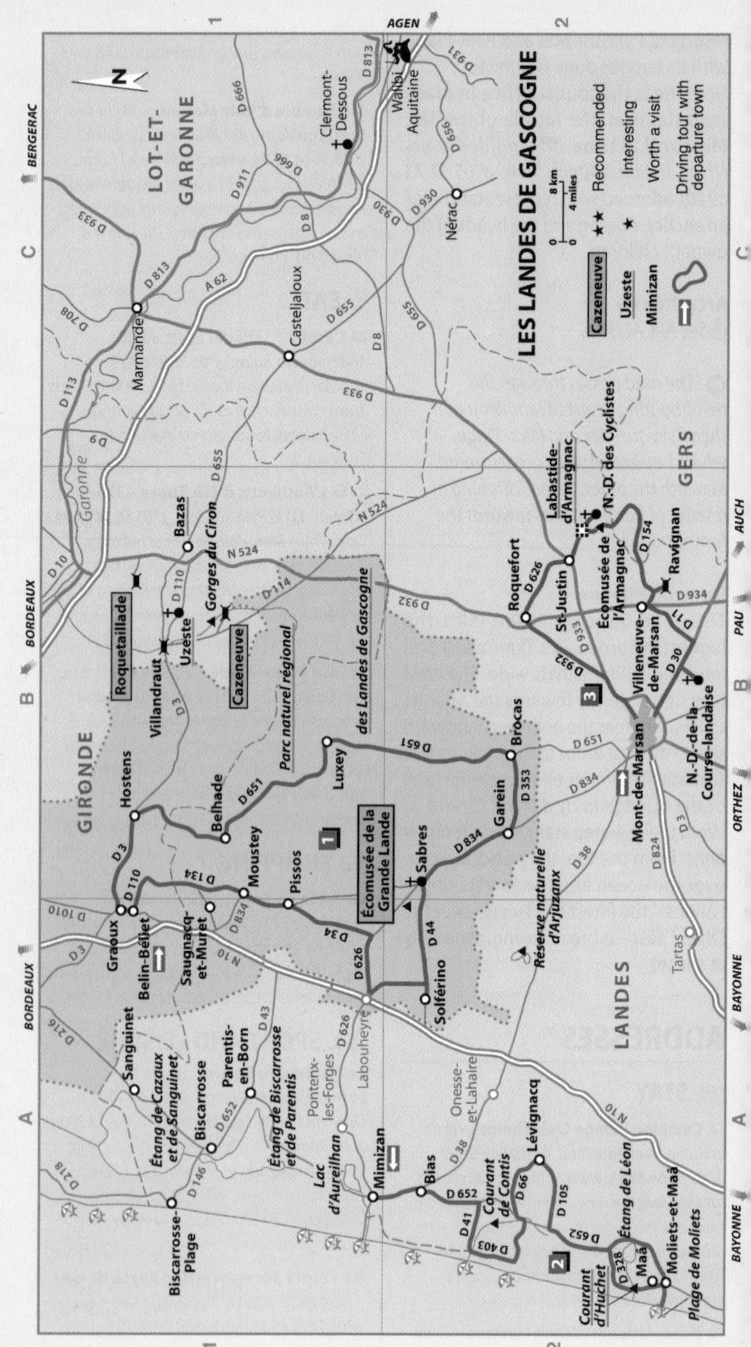

LES LANDES DE GASCOGNE
Cazeneuve ★★ Recommended
Uzeste ★ Interesting
Mimizan Worth a visit
Driving tour with departure town
0 8 km
0 4 miles
BERGERAC
AGEN
BORDEAUX
BAYONNE
ORTHEZ
PAU
AUCH
LOT-ET-GARONNE
GIRONDE
LANDES
GERS
Marmande
Casteljaloux
Clermont-Dessous
Walibi Aquitaine
Nérac
Bazas
Gorges du Ciron
Roquetaillade
Villandraut
Uzeste
Cazeneuve
Parc naturel régional des Landes de Gascogne
Hostens
Belhade
Luxey
Moustey
Pissos
Écomusée de la Grande Lande
Sabres
Garein
Brocas
Solférino
Labouheyre
Graoux
Belin-Béliet
Saugnacq-et-Muret
Sanguinet
Étang de Cazaux et de Sanguinet
Biscarrosse
Parentis-en-Born
Étang de Biscarrosse et de Parentis
Biscarrosse-Plage
Lac d'Aureilhan
Pontenx-les-Forges
Mimizan
Bias
Onesse-et-Laharie
Lévignacq
Courant de Contis
Courant d'Huchet
Étang de Léon
Maâ
Moliets-et-Maâ
Plage de Moliets
Réserve naturelle d'Arjuzanx
Tartas
Mont-de-Marsan
N.-D.-de-la-Course-landaise
Villeneuve-de-Marsan
Écomusée de l'Armagnac
St-Justin
Roquefort
Labastide-d'Armagnac
N.-D. des Cyclistes
Ravignan
Garonne
N 524
N 10
A 62

The word *landes* (moors) still suggests a vision of the more desolate aspect of this part of the coast, which existed until the 19C, when a remarkable project of reforestation transformed the area into a huge pine forest. The Landes sit on an enormous plain, roughly triangular in shape, covering an area of 14 000sq km/5 400sq mi. The side of the triangle runs down the 230km/143mi of coast from the Gironde estuary to the mouth of the Adour, and turns eastwards from the two points to meet at the triangle's apex 100km/62mi inland. The area was once a marine depression, subsequently filled with distinctive fine sands during the Quaternary Era. The vast tract is poorly drained and below the surface is a hard impermeable layer, further reducing its fertility.

During the 18C Nicolas Brémontier managed to stabilise the dunes on the Atlantic Coast by constructing dykes and sowing marram grass. However, the interior remained a fever-swamp, unfit for cultivation, until under the Second Empire when the engineer Chambrelent drew up a scheme of drainage, clearance and reforestation. Development of the region since then has concentrated on the extension of the forest, with pine and deciduous forests planted thickly between the Gironde Landes and the River Adour.

Part of this territory has now been given special protection as the Parc naturel régional des Landes de Gascogne. The park was designed for the protection of wildlife and its environment: permission was given for the restoration of several churches along The Way of St James, the creation of the Écomusée de la Grande Lande (an open-air museum including the sites of Marquèze, Luxey, Moustey), the Parc Ornithologique du Teich, as well as reserves and study centres.

Highlights

1. **Écomusée de la Grande Lande**, sustainable, educational and enjoyable tourism at its best (p162)
2. Bird watching at the **Réserve naturelle d'Arjuzanx** (p165)
3. Magnificent feudal castle and vineyard of **Roquetaillade** (p168)
4. Huge sandy beaches and rolling surf of **Mimizan-Plage** (p170)
5. Sculpture at **Musée Despiau-Wlérick** in pretty Mont-de-Marsan (p172)

The Way of St James passes through the Landes at several points, and there are some excellent opportunities for walking and hiking. For culture, head to regional capital **Mont-de-Marsan**, with its museums, art galleries and restaurants.

Way of St James, Les Landes

Parc Naturel Régional des Landes de Gascogne★

Les Landes is a region where nature rules above all else. The pine forest – and the surrounding fields which act as a fire-break – can seem monotonous at first glance, but hide countless surprises. Visitors to the region will happen across idyllic refuges for wildlife, tiny villages and picnic spots, and memories of France's rural heritage at every turn. This is a rich and varied part of Aquitaine, perfect for discovering on horseback, on foot, on bike, by canoe or by boat.

- **Michelin Map:** 335: E-6–H-10
- **Info:** 33 rte Bayonne, Belin-Béliet. ℘05 57 71 99 99. www.parc-landes-de-gascogne.fr.
- **Location:** The regional park comprises 40 municipalities of the Landes and Gironde *départements* and covers 301 500ha/745 037 acres. It stretches from the east of the Arcachon basin to the Val de l'Eyre, including the valleys of the Grande and Petite Leyre rivers and the wooded areas of the Grande Leyre.
- **Don't Miss:** Walking or cycling through the park; the Écomusée de la Grande Lande.
- **Kids:** Écomusée de Marquèze; leisure activities such as swimming, cycling and horse-drawn carriage rides through the park.
- **Timing:** You can drive through the park in a day, but if you want to spend time walking, swimming and visiting the area, there is plenty to keep you occupied for two to three days.

DRIVING TOUR

1 HEART OF THE PARK TOUR

127km/79mi. Allow one day

This route goes through the great Landes Forest, crossed by the Grande and Petite Leyre rivers, with its areas of regeneration, its glades, its hunting grounds and typical low houses.

The **Écomusée de la Grande Lande**★★, comprising three separate sites near the villages of Sabres, Luxey and Moustey in the heart of the Parc naturel régional des Landes de Gascogne, evokes the daily life and traditional activities of the region in the 18C and 19C.

The whole region is ideal for outdoor tourism; a bicycle path goes from Hostens to Mios.

Belin-Béliet

Eleanor of Aquitaine was born in this village in 1123. A bas-relief in her memory stands on the site of the castle built by the dukes of Aquitaine *(access via r. Ste-Quitterie; follow signpost to Hôtel Aliénor)*. To the north of town is the **Centre d'Animation du Graoux** *(31 rte du Graoux; ℘05 57 71 99 29)*, which offers courses about the environment and outdoor sports activities.

Leave Belin-Béliat eastwards via the D 110. At Joué, turn right along the D 110ES to Moustey via Peyrin and Biganon.

Moustey

Two churches made of ferrous rock known locally as **garluche** stand side by side on the town's main square.

A walled-up doorway in the south wall was originally used by *cagots* (outcasts). Église Notre-Dame, to the south, houses the **Musée du Patrimoine Religieux**

et des Croyances Populaires (*open Jun and Sept Sat–Sun and public holidays 2–6pm; Jul–Aug daily 10am–noon, 2–7pm, 4€; 05 58 08 01 39*) devoted to local religious heritage and popular beliefs.

Take the N 134 S to Pissos.

Pissos

The church, just outside the village, has a belfry with a shingle roof. Route de Sore, which runs through an old Landes inn, leads to the **Airial artisanal** (*05 58 08 90 66*) in which contemporary art, regional gourmet specialities and crafts are exhibited (ceramics, wood and copper crafts, fabrics and jewellery). Opposite the centre, an old shepherd's fold has been transformed into a **glass-blowers' workshop** (*05 58 08 97 42*).

Take the D 34 S. At Commensacq, the D 626 right leads to Labouheyre. As you enter the town there is a former stopping place on The Way of St James pilgrimage. A road to the left, by the church (follow the signs for the gendarmerie), leads to Solférino. It crosses the Parc de Peyre (forest cabins and a riding centre).

Solférino

In 1857 Napoleon III bought some 7 000ha/17 300 acres of marshland. Named after the Battle of Solferino (1859) that he won in present-day Italy, he set up an experimental area with model farms. A village was created in 1863.

Houses and Huts of the Landes Region

An integral part of the landscape are the whitewashed roughcast houses typical of the Landes region. They are usually built in glades, inherited from the former *airial*, or forest clearing. They are built on one level and only have an attic with a skylight in the tiled roof. A wide canopy, supported by wooden pillars, the *estantade*, protects the front of the house. Small huts once used by resin tappers to store their tools can still be seen along the forest roads. These low, rectangular, rather basic huts are made of Landes pine (planks assembled horizontally) and covered with a gently sloping tiled roof. Two huts are often joined together.

Take the D44 E to Sabres

Sabres Station – Écomusée de Marquèze

rte de Solférino, 40630 Sabres. Open Apr–May and mid-Sept–Oct Mon–Sat 2–6pm, Sun and holidays 10am–6pm; Jun–mid-Sept 10am–6pm. 13€

Ecomusée de Marquèze

Throughout the Year

The **Écomusée de la Grande Lande** organises several events aiming at reviving 19C traditions from the Landes region.
La Maillade, which takes place on 1 May, is the festival of spring: Maypoles decorated with flowers are planted in order to honour a young lady or a friend.Mid-May is the time for **shearing sheep**. **Haymaking** takes place during the first half of June: hay is cut in the fields and saved to feed cattle in winter. The biggest **laundry** of the year, known as the *bugade*, takes place in the middle of June. Ash replaces washing powder. The washing is rinsed in the river. 24 June is the **feast of St John** and midsummer's night. Large wooden crosses are burned in the hope of securing good crops.
Finally, throughout the spring/summer season (from the end of March to October), it is possible to watch craftsmen at work: tapping of pine trees, kneading and cooking bread, grinding rye, ploughing with oxen, and other tasks.

(children 9€). ℘05 58 08 31 31. www.parc-landes-de-gascogne.fr.
On the approach road to Sabres, you can find a railway station, where a tourist train sets off for Marquèze *(every 40min from Sabres; departures 1 Jun–16 Sept daily 10.10am–5.20pm; 28 Mar–31 May and 17 Sept–8 Nov Mon–Sat 2–4.40pm, Sun and public holidays 10.10am–4.40pm)*. This is also where you buy tickets for the Écomusée.
The train takes you through wooded countryside for 5km/3.1mi to the main site. While waiting for the train, visit the exhibition highlighting efforts undertaken in Les Landes starting with Napoleon III and continuing today that have transformed both the landscape and its uses for a variety of local industries from agriculture to tourism. The interactive aspect (Gascon dialects, animal and insect sounds) makes it suitable for children, and there are activities and trails aimed specifically at a younger audience *(open Apr–Jun and Sept–Oct 10am–12.30pm, 2–6pm, Jul–Aug 10am–7pm; 6€ (children 4€))*.
You can also walk to Sabres to visit its Roman church.

Marquèze★★

Access only by train from Sabres. A visitor guide is included in the price of a ticket. Certain trains (consult timetable) also offer a 1hr guided tour. This is worth following before spending time enjoying the demonstrations of local craft-making and bread-making.
This sector of the Écomusée covers almost 70ha/173 acres in the protected region of the Vallées de l'Eyre and comprises a delightful collection of traditional buildings – some original, others reconstructions on their former site – from the 30 or so structures which stood here when the clearing was occupied by three families.
The **airial** is a sort of huge esplanade, mainly planted with oak trees, where the houses and farm buildings were grouped. It is here that the master's house *(marquèze)*, dating from 1824, stands. It combines stout beams, cob walls and a three-pitched roof, and, like the other buildings, has no foundations, relying on sound timber construction for its stability.
Nearby, the more modest house with less massive beams was where the servants **(brassiers)** were lodged. Beyond is the tenant farmer's house with its barns, pigsties, beehives and chicken runs.
A path beneath the trees leads to the miller's house (1834) and the **mill** itself, with its two separate millstones for grinding the smaller and the larger varieties of grain.
The woodland walk ends at the **charbonnières** (charcoal burners), where old trees were burned very slowly to produce charcoal, before returning to

the *airial* where an information centre presents a selection of documents, maps, models and an illustrated commentary *(in French)* on the museum and the agricultural and pastoral life of the region. A nearby sheepfold contains a flock of grazing sheep; they were once used to clear the moorland for agricultural use and enrich it with their droppings. A second big house, Le Mineur, has an exhibition explaining the pastoral farming system. In the **model orchard** over 1 600 species of fruit trees native to the Grande Lande are tended; they include varieties of apple, plum, cherry, medlar and quince.

Leave Sabres to the SE on the N 134.

Graine de Forêt, Garein

Open Apr–Jun and Sept–Oct, Sun 1–6pm, school holidays 2–6pm, Jul–Aug 9.30am–12.30pm, 2-6pm; 5€ (children 3.50€). 05 58 08 31 31 or 06 88 81 30 08.

This "geographical museum" centres on the local timber industry. Forestry remains the largest industry in the region, and an interactive scale model shows the different stages of the process, from the work of the loggers to the process of transforming the wood into paper, toys and other goods. Outside, there is a 2.6km/1.6mi wooded walking path, where you can plant a pine tree.

Head E from Garein on the D 353.

Forges de Brocas

Open mid-Jun–mid-Sept Tue–Sun 3–7pm. 3.10€ (under 12 years no charge). 05 58 51 48 46.

This verdant spot, with its abandoned smithy and workers' houses, is all that remains of a former 19C blast furnace and metal workshop. To learn more, visit the Musée des Forges, located in a former flour mill.

Take the D 651 N from Brocas.

Luxey

The **Jacques and Louis Vidal Resinous Products Workshop** (*open Jun–15 Sept daily 10am–noon, 2–7pm; 5€; 05 58 08 01 39)* illustrates the traditional local industry based on resin products which dates from the beginning of the Industrial Revolution; the workshop operated commercially from 1859 to 1954. Visitors may follow every stage from the arrival of the tapped pine-tree sap to the final storage of refined turpentine.

The D 651 leads to Belhade via Sore and Argelouse.

Belhade

In the Gascon dialect, this town's name means "Beautiful Fairy". It has a church with a belfry wall and attractive sculpted columns. To the west, there is a view of the Château de Belhade.

Hostens

Between 1933 and 1963, lignite was excavated out of open quarries. The quarries were then flooded by the rising water table, forming the lakes of Lamothe and Bousquey. The **Domaine départemental d'Hostens** (*05 56 88 70 29; www.hostens.fr)*, a leisure park covering 500ha/1 235 acres, has been developed on the site. A nature trail guides visitors through the park.

Return to Belin-Béliet on the D 3 and N 10.

EXCURSION
Réserve Naturelle d'Arjuzanx

Access to the lake from Arjuzanx village, on the D38 towards Morcenx.

Guided visits and birdwatching offered. 05 58 08 11 52. www.reserve-arjuzanx.fr.

This huge nature reserve stands on a former industrial site, used by power firm EDF until 1990. It's hard to imagine that now, as the area is now France's largest hibernation spot for cranes – providing shelter to more than 20 000 birds. Parts of the site are accessible to visitors; including walking routes, horse riding and cycle paths.

ADDRESSES

STAY

Chambre d'hôte Chez M. et Mme Clément – *1 r. du Stade, 33830 Belin-Béliet. 05 56 88 13 17. maison.clem@wanadoo.fr. 5 rooms.* A handsome 19C bourgeois house in a park. The refined décor features oak woodwork, waxed parquet floors and marble fireplaces; the rooms are bright and most have direct access to the garden. One self-catering cottage.

Chambre d'hôte La Maranne – *Le Muret, 40410 Saugnacq-et-Muret (15km/9.3mi N of Pissos). 05 58 09 61 71. la-maranne@wanadoo.fr. Closed mid-Nov–mid-Apr. 5 rooms.* 19C building, surrounded by century-old trees, offering comfortable rooms. Pool, sauna, bicycles.

Chambre d'hôte Le Poutic – *rte de Cazaubon, 40240 Créon-d'Armagnac. 05 58 44 66 97. www.lepoutic.com. 3 rooms. Restaurant.* Worth a visit for the excellent regional food, cosily served in a restaurant with exposed stone walls and wooden beams. The bedrooms are equally well presented. Cookery courses on offer in winter months (duck-centric).

Chambre d'hôte Les Arbousiers – *Le Gaille, 40630 Sabres (7.5km/4.7mi W of Sabres). 05 58 07 52 52. www.chambres-landes.com. Reservations required. 6 rooms. Meals.* This typical Landaise house with its handsome wooden frame is simple and elegant. Set in a clearing of the pine forest, it has plain, cosy rooms and a friendly owner with a passion for birds.

Hôtel Au P'tit Creux – *3 r. Brémontier, 40160 Ychoux. 05 58 82 38 38. www.auptitcreux.com. 30 rooms. 7€. Restaurant.* On the village outskirts, a modern building offering clean, functional rooms. Locally sourced food.

EAT

La Bonne Auberge – *1 r. Champs-de-Seuze, 33830 Lugos. 05 57 71 95 28. Open Tues–Sun lunch; daily in summer. 5 rooms. 7€.* A welcoming inn with a pleasant garden and shaded terrace. Traditional food.

Auberge des Pins – *rte de la Piscine, 40630 Sabres. 05 58 08 30 00. www.aubergedespins.fr. Closed Jan.* Beautiful traditional Landaise house, surrounded by pine trees. Good-quality regional cuisine, and elegant bedrooms.

Le Café de Pissos – *42 r. du Pont Battant, 40410 Pissos. 05 58 08 90 16. Closed Tue and Sun evenings, Wed and 11 Nov–8 Dec, Wed.* Century-old plane trees shelter the terrace of this family ***auberge*** in the middle of town. Simple regional cuisine. A few modest rooms.

Bazas★ Gironde

Surrounded by ruined Gothic ramparts, Bazas is situated in a region of fertile hills and since the 15C has been the seat of a bishopric (the title of which, since 1937, has belonged to the Archbishop of Bordeaux). The 4C Latin poet Ausonius, born in Burdigala (Bordeaux), stayed here several times. Recent excavations have uncovered foundations of the ancient *oppidum* (settlement). Bazas is also famous for its beef – the city hosts an annual festival in honour of the prized delicacy. The city's restaurants often serve steak cooked over *sarments*, topped with shallots in a red wine sauce.

- **Population:** 4 585
- **Michelin Map:** 335: J-8
- **Info:** 1 pl. de la Cathédrale, Bazas. 05 56 25 25 84. www.ville-bazas.fr.
- **Location:** Bazas stands on a narrow promontory above the Beuve Valley, 60km/37mi SE of Bordeaux and 40km/25mi SW of Marmande.
- **Parking:** Park on pl. de la Cathédrale in the centre of town.
- **Don't Miss:** Excursions to Château de Roquetaillade and Château de Cazeneuve.

VISIT

Place de la Cathédrale

This lovely square is lined with 16C and 17C houses. No 3 called **maison de l'Astrologue** is decorated with astrological symbols (serious looking faces of the moon and the sun, oriental astrologer wearing a pointed hat).

Cathédrale St-Jean★

pl. de la Cathédrale. Guided tours available. Contact the tourist office for further information. ℘05 56 25 25 84.
The cathedral dates from the 13C–14C and was built on the model of the great Gothic sanctuaries of northern France. The blood of John the Baptist was venerated here. The west front is of an attractive and harmonious design, despite the differences in style between the three storeys. The first dates from the 13C, the second from the 16C, and the top storey from the 18C.
Doorways – Their tympana and coving still have fine 13C sculptures which the locals saved from Protestant vandals by paying the sum of 10 000 écus. The central doorway shows the Last Judgement and the story of John the Baptist, and the side doors, the Virgin and St Peter.
Interior – The long, narrow nave, with no transept, gives a striking impression of grandeur.
In the chancel, the Louis XV-style high altar in different coloured marbles is somewhat fussy. The axial chapel contains paintings by François Lemoyne from the 18C.

Jardin du Chapitre

Located to the right of the cathedral.
This garden is a haven of peace located over the ramparts, on the right side of the cathedral. It looks like a medieval garden with a few relics (from the Iron Age to the 15C). There is a fine view of the Beuve Valley.

Return to the cathedral and turn left (before the town hall) onto r. Théophile-Servière then walk along the Maurice-Lapierre ramp.

Promenade de la Brèche

Before enjoying the walk under the lime trees, beneath the old ramparts covered with moss and ivy, take some time to visit the rose garden in the **Jardin du Sultan**.

EXCURSIONS

Collégiale d'Uzeste★

8km/5mi W by the D 110.
Open Sat–Sun and public holidays 3–6pm. ℘05 56 65 22 47.
The collegiate church in the village of Uzeste is somewhat of a rival to Bazas Cathedral. **Pope Clement V** played a major part in building the church. He raised it to a collegiate church in 1312, and named it in his will as the site for his tomb.
Outside, note the arrangement of the east end and the belfry, the latter completed only in the 16C.
Enter the church by the south door, with its tympanum decorated with a fine Coronation of the Virgin. Behind the altar, holding a crucifix, thought to date from the 15C, lies the white marble figure of Clement V, which was damaged by the Protestants. In the axial chapel is a 13C figure of the Virgin which was venerated by Pope Clement (born Bertrand de Got, in Villandrault) in his youth and, in the neighbouring chapel, a 14C funerary effigy.

Château de Villandraut

13km/8mi W on the D 110 then the D 3. Open May–Jun daily 2–6pm; Jul–Sept daily 10am–7pm; Oct–Apr Sat–Sun 2–6pm. 3.50€. ℘05 56 25 87 57.
This striking example of Gothic castle architecture was built for Pope Clement V, who often stayed here. A fairly large area was for residential use, which was characteristic of medieval castles in Italy and the Middle East. The south side is more spectacular due to the alignment of its four large towers, the one on the right having been levelled in 1592 on the orders of the Parliament of Bordeaux.

Château de Roquetaillade★★

8km/5mi NW by the D 1 and D 223. *Open all year round; call or see website to confirm hours.* *6.50€.* *05 56 76 14 16. http://chateauroquetaillade.free.fr.*

See Introduction: ARCHITECTURE, p81.

This imposing feudal château was built in 1306 by Cardinal Gaillard de la Mothe, nephew of Pope Clement V. The building itself comprises two fortresses within the same high walls, dating from the 12C and 14C. All that remains of the first château are ruins, and an 11C dungeon. In the courtyard stands a powerful square keep and its turret. There are also vast vaulted rooms, monumental chimneys and gardens with a chapel.

Château de Cazeneuve★★

10km/6.2mi SW by the D 9. *Guided visit available Jun–Sept 2–6pm; Easter–May and Oct Sat–Sun 2–6pm.* *8€ (under 12 years 5€).* *05 56 25 48 16. www.chateaudecazeneuve.com.*

This 13C château was the former residence of Henri III de Navarre, future King Henri IV of France. He stayed here in 1572 with his wife Marguerite de Valois, known as La Reigne Margot, and returned in 1620. The Seigneurs of the estate – who would have prepared the sumptuous royal quarters – were the Albret family. Their descendants, the Sabran-Pontevès family, still live here. Remains of the 11C walls still exist, but the main building dates from the 17C. The imposing southern façade features two square towers, linked by a stone balustrade, and overlooks a dry moat. Inside, note Queen's Margot's salon, entirely decorated with Louis XV furniture, and adjoining the bedroom of Louis XVI. The same floor contains a 17C chapel and a round tower by which the local villagers accessed the chapel. The sleeping quarters of both Queen Margot and Henri IV are also here. The dining room and kitchens offer displays of silverware and porcelain. Outside, a large park contains troglodyte caves, a lake, a waterfall, and huge Douglas pine trees.

Gorges du Ciron

Access from the Pont de la Trave or Pont de Cazeneuve.

The Ciron, a tributory of the Garonne, flows through a narrow valley, dense with vegetation, which runs from the Pont de Cazeneuve up to the Pont de la Trave. No roadway crosses the valley floor, and the key sites are accessible only by driving in and driving back the way you came. The best way to explore the gorge is by canoe-kayak (*see Addresses below*).

From the Pont de la Trave, there is a viewpoint of the river, a reservoir, a power station, and the ruins of a 14C château.

ADDRESSES

STAY/ EAT

Auberge de la Crémaillère – *33730 Villandraut.* *05 56 25 30 67. 10 rooms.* *7.50€. Closed Fri, Sun night and 3 wks Christmas.* At the foot of the château, this renovated inn offers a warm atmosphere and refined cooking. Pleasant bedrooms.

Café-Restaurant Indigo – *25 r. Fondespan.* *05 56 25 25 52 or 06 08 65 94 91. Closed Sun–Mon.* Part brasserie, part restaurant depending on how you are feeling. A popular spot, so book ahead. Good mix of regional cuisine (this is where to order the Bazas beef) alongside some more exotic foods, and well-priced set menus.

Ferme-auberge Aux Repas Fermiers de Haoun Barrade – *33430 Cudos (5km/3.1mi S of Bazas via the N 524 towards Mont-de-Marsan).* *05 56 25 06 69 or 05 56 25 44 55. Open Sat–Sun, bank holidays (lunch only) and summer.* Country-style atmosphere, serving local farm produce. Expect plenty of duck, foie gras and other poultry… washed down with good local wine.

SPORT AND LEISURE

Club de Canoe-Kayak – *33430 Bernos-Beaulac.* *05 56 25 47 44. Take direction Captieux from Beaulac. Mid-Jun–Sept. Trips range from 1hr to 7hrs (from 10€).* The safest way to explore the Gorges du Ciron.

Biscarrosse

Landes

Once famous for its high-flying aviation pioneers and now the paradise of surfers, Biscarrosse is located on the coast, just south of the Bassin d'Arcachon. Its name refers to the dunes that abound in the area. 3 000ha/7 413 acres of coastal dunes were covered with marram grass and another 8 000ha/19 768 acres of inland dunes have been planted with maritime pines as part of a vast project to prevent them from shifting.

- **Population:** 12 031
- **Michelin Map:** 335: E-8
- **Info:** 55 pl. G. Dufau, Biscarrosse. 05 58 78 20 96. www.biscarrosse.co.uk.
- **Location:** Biscarrosse lies 81km/50mi SW of Bordeaux via the A 63.
- **Kids:** Étang de Biscarrosse.

SIGHTS

Biscarrosse-Plage

Ideal for those who enjoy exciting surfing possibilities. Fishing is a less strenuous alternative.

Musée des Traditions

216 r. Louis-Breguet. Open Jun and Sept Tue–Sat 9am–noon, 2–6pm; Jul–Aug daily except Sun am 9.30am–7pm; school holidays 2–6pm; rest of year by appointment. 4€ (child 3€). 05 58 78 77 37. http://musee traditions.com.

The history of Biscarrosse is told through its landscape of marshes, inland waterways and forests, and the industries such as resin-tapping that grew up as a result. Visits possible by barge, where the guide will explain the formation of dunes and lakes, the local flora and fauna, and its population of migratory birds.

Étang de Biscarrosse et de Parentis

This magnificent stretch of water, also known as the Southern Lake, covers an area of 3 600ha/8 895 acres. There is one beach with a marina, and **games** for children.

Étang de Cazaux–Sanguinet

This body of water, also known as the Northern Lake, is linked with its neighbour by a canal. It offers sailing and various water sports *(05 58 78 10 51)*. From Biscarrosse to Navarrosse the road runs through a pine forest, ideal for hiking, cycling and horse riding.

Musée de l'Hydraviation

332 av. Louis-Breguet, Biscarrosse-Ville. Open Jul–Aug daily 10am–7pm; Sept–Jun Wed–Mon 2–6pm. Closed public holidays. 4.30€. 05 58 78 00 65. www.asso-hydraviation.com.

The Seaplane and Flying Boat Museum tells of their evolution between the wars, when concrete runways did not exist and landing gear was unable to support the weight of ever-larger aircraft. Highlights include a cockpit reconstruction and an 18-minute film *(pms only, French)* on the giant flying boats' hour of glory.

EXCURSIONS

Sanguinet

13km/8mi NE (E of Étang de Cazaux).

The **Archaeological Museum** *(pl. de la Mairie; open Jul–Aug daily 10am–12.30pm, 2.30–7pm; 3.50€; 05 58 82 11 82; www.musee-de-sanguinet.com)* displays finds from excavations around the lake. The Iron Age dugout canoes made out of a single piece of pine are well worth seeing.

Parentis-en-Born

9km/5.6mi from Biscarrosse, SE of the Étang de Biscarrosse. pl. du Général.-de-Gaulle, 40160 Parentis-en-Born. 05 58 78 43 60. www.parentis.com.

The small village is located next to a lake which offers numerous water sport activities.

Mimizan

Landes

Ségosa-la-Mimizan, which dates back to Gallo-Roman times, was buried by sand in the 6C. The township of Mimizan was built at the end of the 10C, at the foot of a Benedictine abbey, when it became a stop on The Way of St James pilgrimage route. Buried again by the remorseless advance of the sand hills in the 18C *(on the road to Mimizan-Plage),* the ruins were saved by a local man called Teixores, who was the first to use couch-grass and rushes to consolidate the shifting dunes. The town then became a seaside resort thanks to a railway connection. The belfry of the old abbey church, built in the 13C, is still standing. Richly sculpted, it is surmounted by a *Christ in Glory* surrounded by statues of the saints, including St John, which is the oldest of its kind in the Aquitaine region

- **Population:** 6 707
- **Michelin Map:** 335: D-9
- **Info:** 38 av. Maurice Martin, Mimizan-Plage. 05 58 09 11 20. www.mimizan-tourism.com.
- **Location:** Mimizan is located 33km/20mi SW of Biscarrosse. The town comprises two different resorts: Mimizan-Ville and Mimizan-Plage, which lie about 6km/3.7mi away from each other.
- **Kids:** The beach.
- **Timing:** It's worth spending a whole afternoon at the Étang de Léon. Explore the area either on foot or by a boat trip along the Courant d'Huchet.

THE RESORT

Mimizan-Plage

At the end of the street, on the left, a short flight of steps leads to a monument commemorating the landing of the aviators Lefèvre, Assolant and Lotti on 16 June 1929, after their epic North Atlantic flight. The view in all directions from the top of the dunes is superb. Mimizan-Plage has four beaches along the ocean with supervised bathing and one along the Mimizan channel. Cycle tracks link the ocean and Lac d'Aureilhan as well as Mimizan-Plage and Contis. A footpath runs along the Mimizan channel.

Mimizan has been granted since 2000 the "Station KID" label, awarded to resorts which are especially adapted to children: activities, sports, games, adventure playgrounds have been organised for them *(www.stationskid.com).*

Lac d'Aureilhan-Mimizan

There are pleasant perspectives on this lake from the roadway.

DRIVING TOUR

2 BETWEEN TWO WATERWAYS

117km/73mi. Allow 3hrs.

Leave Mimizan S on the D 652.

Maison de l'airial, Bias

Near to the church. Open last 2 wks June and 1st 2 wks Sept Mon–Tues 3–6pm; Jul–Aug Tue–Sat 10.30am–1pm, 3–7pm, Sun 10.30am–1pm. Guided visits available through Mimizan tourist office 2.80€ (under 15 years no charge). 05 58 09 37 73. www.mediaforest.net.

An interactive display reveals all aspects of wood and forestry.

Follow the D 652. Before St-Julien-en-Born, turn right onto the D 41. The Courant de Contis will be on the left-hand side of the road.

Courant de Contis

The Contis channel takes the waters of several local streams down to the ocean through areas of vegetation as dense as

they are varied. It winds slowly through the marshes and on through the dunes, beneath a cool canopy of leaves or between high natural hedges.

At St-Julien-en-Born take the D 41 to Lesperon.

Lévignacq

This charming village boasts an ancient church and low, timber-framed houses with tiled roofs. The church, fortified in the 14C, is unusual with its porch and doorway in the Louis XIII style and its belfry tower. The **wooden vaulting★** inside was decorated in the 18C with paintings. In the chancel is an altarpiece surrounded by cabled columns, whereas in front of the altar itself there is a gilt wood representation of Jesus in the Garden of Olives.

Return via the D 105 to the D 652, turning left at Miquéou. At Vielle a little road leads to the Étang de Léon.

Étang de Léon

The cool, clear water in a peaceful countryside setting attracts tourists and water sports enthusiasts *(05 58 72 85 76).*

Return to Vielle and follow the D 328 to Moliets-et-Maa.

The road circling the lake goes through rough terrain, alternating between pine forests and marshes, and revealing typical Landes houses with their diagonal brick facing.
Just before the hamlet of Pichelèbe, a bridge crosses the River Huchet.
A small path provides a delightful walk through peaceful surroundings (30min there and back).

Courant d'Huchet★

This capricious coastal river, popular with eel fishermen, runs through lush, exotic-looking vegetation and makes for lively **boat trips** (*departures Apr–Sept 10am for Île aux Chênes (2hr; 12€); 2.30pm for Pichlèbe Bridge (3hr; 15€) and Plage d'Huchet (4hr; 20€); reservations required (3 days in advance); 05 58 48 75 39; www.bateliers-courant-huchet.fr*), especially enjoyable on hot summer mornings.

ADDRESSES

STAY

Camping Club Marina-Landes – *Plage Sud. 05 58 09 12 66. contact@clubmarina.com. Open late Apr–mid-Sept. 583 pitches. Restaurant.* Attractive pitches for tents, as well as hire of cottages, chalets and bungalows. Good amenities.

Camping municipal de la Plage – *bd de l'Atlantique. 05 58 09 00 32. contact@mimizan-camping.com. Open Apr–Sept. 680 pitches.* The pine trees destroyed by the great storms of 1999 have been replaced by a series of leafy trees which are returning shade to this well-located site. Chalets and mobile homes available for hire outside of July and August.

Camping municipal du Lac – *av. de Woolsack (2km/1.2mi N of Mimizan at Lac d'Aureilhan). 05 58 09 01 21. www.mimizan-camping.com. Open Apr–Sept. 466 pitches.* Pitches for tents and caravans. Recently restored facilities.

Hôtel Atlantique – *38 av. de la Côte-d'Argent, Mimizan-Plage. 05 58 09 09 42. www.hotelatlantique-landes.com. 30 rooms. Restaurant.* This early 20C Landaise house is near the beach yet far from the tourist crowds; pricier rooms have a balcony.

Hôtel L'Airial – *6 r. de la Papeterie, Mimizan-Plage. 05 58 09 46 54. www.hotel-airial.com. Closed Nov–Apr. 16 rooms.* A small family hotel built in the 1970s in a quiet residential neighbourhood. Friendly reception, simple, well-kept rooms.

EAT

L'Émeraude des Bois – *66–68 av. du Courant, 40200 Mimizan-Plage (5km/3.1mi W of Mimizan off the D 626). 05 58 09 05 28. www.emeraudedesbois.com. Closed 17 Sept–27 Apr.* Surrounded by the forest and overlooking the water, this hotel has a dining room with a shaded terrace, preparing delicious traditional cuisine.

Mont-de-Marsan

Landes

This is the capital of the Marsan region in the southeast of the Landes. The town lies at the confluence of the rivers Douze and Midou, which join to form the River Midouze. It enjoys a climate that is hot in summer and mild in winter. Palm trees, magnolias and oleanders flourish in the open air, spiced with the tang of pines. Mont-de-Marsan is an important administrative centre, with a curious collection of public buildings in the style known as Empire-Restauration. Some sculptures, formerly in the Despiau-Wlérick Museum, can be seen in the streets.

- **Population:** 30 230
- **Michelin Map:** 335: H-11
- **Info:** 6 pl. du Général Leclerc, Mont-de-Marsan. 05 58 05 87 37. www.tourisme-montdemarsan.fr.
- **Location:** Mont-de-Marsan is situated 130km/81mi S of Bordeaux via the A 63 and the N 134, and 60km/37mi E of Dax along the N 124.
- **Parking:** There is a free car park at the Préfecture, on bd Lattre-de-Tassigny.
- **Don't Miss:** Musée Despiau-Wlérick and the **market** held at pl. St-Roch every Tuesday and Saturday (6am–2pm), one of the most picturesque in France.
- **Timing:** Allow half a day for a leisurely stroll through the town and a visit to the Musée Despiau-Wlérick, and a full day for exploring the surrounding area.

SIGHTS

Musée Despiau-Wlérick★

6 pl. Marguerite de Navarre.
Open Jun–Sept Thu 10am–6pm, Fri–Wed 10am–noon, 2–6pm; Oct–Dec Wed and Fri–Mon 10am–noon, 2–6pm, Thu 10am–6pm. Closed public holidays. No charge. 05 58 75 00 45.

The two sections of this museum in the heart of the Old Town are housed in a pair of beautifully restored 14C buildings (a Romanesque house, a chapel and a keep *(donjon Lacataye)*, linked by a gallery where temporary exhibits are held). The monumental sculptures in the garden are by Charles Despiau (1874–1946), a native of Mont-de-Marsan who was among the artists promoting the revival of interest in sculpture at the beginning of the 20C.

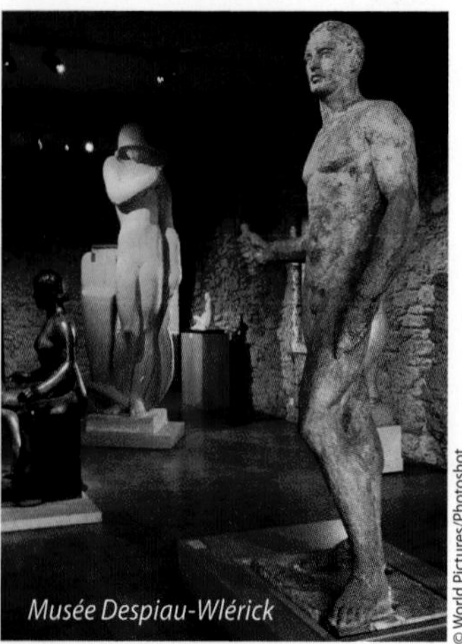
Musée Despiau-Wlérick
© World Pictures/Photoshot

The Musée Despiau-Wlérick, located in the old keep, is devoted to modern figurative sculpture. Over 700 works by 100 different artists are on display, most of them dating from the 1930s.

The sculptors include Orloff *(Pregnant Woman)*, Bourdelle, Bouchard, Zadkine *(Seated Melancholy)*, Manolo and Gargallo *(Urano)*. The upper floors are reserved for local artists. The stairway linking them is adorned with fine examples of glazed earthenware from Samadet.

Works by **Charles Despiau** occupy one whole floor: they include several female busts, among them *Paulette*, a marble which was admired by Rodin, and a

Mont-de-Marsan, River Midouze

© David Osborne/Alamy

strikingly naturalistic *Liseuse (Woman Reading)*.
On another floor *The Child in Clogs* is an early work by **Robert Wlérik** (1882–1944), the Mont-de-Marsan sculptor responsible for the statue of Marshal Foch in place du Trocadéro, Paris.

From r. des Musées, turn left onto r. Victor-Hugo.

The small rue Maubec winds between l'Hôtel Planté (The Conseil Régional administration building) and La Préfecture Empire: note the Romanesque-style house (12C) constructed from rock containing fossilised shells. On the right, avenue Victor-Duruy runs in front of the former stables for police horses (19C) before crossing the River Douze.

Continue to pl. Francis-Planté for the entrance to Jean-Rameau Park.

Parc Jean-Rameau

Named after a poet and novelist from the Landes (1858–1942), this former local government garden runs along the banks of the Douze. A green lung in the city, the garden contains various sculptures by Despiau, and is also well planted with flowers and mature trees (plane trees, magnolias). Near to the footbridge, a small Japanese garden lends a romantically faraway feel to the park.

Continue, either by the peaceful r. Corcos, or r. de la Pépinière and the equally charming r. des Landes.

The St-Jean-d'Août bridge crosses the Douze at a verdant spot, and leads onto rue Armand-Dulamond with its abundance of 18C *hôtels particuliers*.
On your right, rue de Gourgues takes you to place Charles-de-Gaulle where, just before the bridge, you will find *La Minoterie*: a 10C watermill on the banks of the Midou (just before it flows into the River Douze). Today, this mill houses the **Galerie municipale d'expositions**. Take the Abreuvoir slipway to the Pont des Droits-de-l'Homme. From the bridge, there is a pleasant view, upstream, of the old houses beside the riverbanks, and the quaysides where the grain would have been formerly loaded onto boats.
From here you can also walk down the banks of the Midouze for a longer walk along the **chemin de halage** *(to the left)*.

Centre d'Art Contemporain Raymond-Farbos

3 r. St-Vincent-de-Paul. Open during exhibitions Mon–Fri am and pm, Sat pm. 05 58 75 55 84.
Housed in a former grain warehouse, this attractive space is now a contemporary art museum which hosts several important temporary exhibitions of

sculpture and painting. The first floor and the mezzanine level display the permanent collection.

DRIVING TOUR

3 AROUND MONT-DE-MARSAN

80km/50mi. Allow one day.

Leave Mont-de-Marsan SE via the D 30, for 13km/8mi, then turn right towards Artassenx, on to the D 406 (signposted).

Chapelle Notre-Dame-de-la-Course-Landaise à Bascons

Open Wed–Fri and 1st Sat–Sun of month, pm only. Closed bank holidays. 4€ (under 12 years 2€).

Near to this 13C chapel, the Musée de la Course Landaise has an exhibition explaining the history and rules of this traditional form of bloodless bull-fighting (re-creations, videos and historical documents).

Return to the D 30, towards Le Houga, then after 6km/3.7mi turn left on to the D 11.

Villeneuve-de-Marsan

17km/10.6mi E via the D 1.

Villeneuve-de-Marsan, a former 13C *bastide*, still has its original church and ancient tower. The imposing brick church of **St-Hippolyte** *(pl. St-Hippolyte; 05 58 45 80 90)* is flanked by buttresses and surmounted by a beautiful square fortified tower. Inside, a 1529 fresco recounts the life of St Catherine of Alexandria. The top of the crenellated tower looks out over the vineyards which produce Grand Bas Armagnac (brandy).

Drive SE along the D 1 towards Eauze for 2km/1.2mi then turn right to Perquié.

Château de Ravignan

Guided tour (1hr) Jul and 15 Aug–Sept Sat–Sun and public holidays 3pm–6pm; 1–14 Aug daily 5pm; Apr–Jun and Oct by appointment. 6€. 05 58 45 28 39. www.armagnac-ravignan.com.

This castle, built on a Classical plan, is surrounded by a French garden. The interior is richly furnished and decorated with family portraits and engravings of Henri IV, and a beautiful collection of costumes from the court of Louis XVI.

Take the D 354 towards Labastide-d'Armagnac. At Arthez-d'Armagnac, follow signs to Mauléon-d'Armagnac (D 101 then D 154). 1.5km/0.9mi after Mauléon, at the crossroads, turn left onto the D 209.

Écomusée de l'Armagnac – Château Garreau

Open Apr–Oct 9am–noon, 2–6pm, Sat–Sun and bank holidays 2–6pm; Nov–Mar Mon–Fri 9am–noon, 2–6pm. 5€. 05 58 44 84 35. www.chateau-garreau.fr.

Gascony's *eau-de-vie*, otherwise known as Armagnac, has attracted gourmets since the 15C. Its production area covers Les Landes, the Lot-et-Garonne and the Gers, and is divided into three *appellations*, the best known of which is Bas-Armagnac. This museum contains a collection of old winemaking equipment, numerous alembics used in the distillation process and a collection of antique bottles.

A nature trail, with three routes, winds through the 80ha/198 acres of parkland, across vines, mushroom-filled woods and small lakes *(allow 45min–2hrs)*.

Continue along the D 209, then turn right on the D 626 towards Barbotan-les-Thermes.

Chapelle Notre-Dame-des-Cyclistes

In Aquitaine, Notre-Dame is patron saint of cyclists. This chapel has been the starting point of the 8th stage of the Tour de France since 1989. It also contains artefacts, bicycles and other souvenirs from some of the great names of the Tour.

Return to Labastide-d'Armagnac via the D 626.

Labastide-d'Armagnac★

This *bastide*, with its houses built around the main square, was founded in 1291. There is an impressive 15C bell tower. A market is held on the square in the high season *(May–Sept Sun am).*

The D 626 continues to St-Justin.

St-Justin

A map is available at the tourist office (pl. des Tilleuils; ℘05 58 44 86 06; www.saint-justin.eu).

This is the oldest *bastide* in the Landes (1280). In its heyday, such notables as Gaston Fébus and Henri IV stayed here. The hamlet's charm is still intact.

Take the D 626 through the forest

Roquefort

The home of the Vicomtes de Marsan in the 10C, Roquefort with its 12C and 14C ramparts and towers was once a fortified town. Founded by the Benedictines of St-Sever in the 11C, the **church** *(pl. du Soleil d'Or; ℘05 58 45 50 46)* later housed an order of Antonites, a hospitaller order who cared for people suffering from St Anthony's Fire (i.e. poisoning). The building is mainly Gothic, with fortifications and a square tower used as a keep. On the south side, a Flamboyant Gothic portal leading into the church is decorated with the Roquefort arms (three rocks and three stars). Nearby stands the former priory with its Flamboyant Gothic doors and windows.

Return to Mont-de-Marsan by the D 932.

ADDRESSES

STAY

Camping Le Pin – *rte de Roquefort, 40240 St-Justin (2.3km/1.4mi N on the D 626 rte de Roquefort). ℘05 58 44 88 91. camping.lepin@wanadoo.fr. Open mid-Apr–late Dec. 70 pitches. Restaurant.* The site is based around a former farm which has been converted today into the welcome centre. Pool, bar, pleasant shady pitches.

Le Domaine de Paguy – *40240 Betbezer-d'Armagnac (5km/3.1mi NE of Labastide-d'Armagnac via the D 11 and D 35). ℘05 58 44 81 57. www.domainedepaguy.com. 4 rooms.* This 16C manor house stands in the centre of a vast wine-growing estate overlooking the Douze Valley. Spacious, attractive rooms, partly renovated, open onto the landscaped park and the vineyards.

Hôtel Le Logis de St-Vincent – *76 r. Laubaner, 40120 Roquefort. ℘05 58 45 75 36. www.logis-saint-vincent.com. Restaurant closed Mon–Tue, out of season. 7 rooms. 11€.* In the heart of the village, this 19C ***hôtel particulier*** has been converted into a spacious and comfortable place to stay. Exposed stone, wooden floors and antique furniture add to the charm.

EAT

MONT-DE-MARSAN

Le Don Quijote – *7 r. St-Vincent. ℘05 58 06 22 04. Closed Sun lunch and Mon.* Tapas, *charcuteries*, ***parilladas***, paellas, *brochettes* and meat cooked *à la plancha* are all on offer at this Spanish-influenced restaurant.

Le Bistrot de Marcel – *1 r. du Pont-de-Commerce. ℘05 58 75 09 71. www.lesensdugout.com. Closed Sun lunch and Mon.* Uninspiring from the outside, but a lovely interior, with exposed stone and wood, and two terraces overlooking the river. Regional food.

BARS

La Cidrerie – *7 r. du 4-Septembre. ℘05 58 46 07 08. Closed Mon lunch and Sun.* Housed in an old stable, this *auberge* carries on the Basque cider tradition. Large wooden tables, friendly atmosphere.

ENTERTAINMENT

Arènes de Plumaçon – *pl. des Arènes. ℘05 58 75 06 09. www.fetesmadeleine.fr. Closed Sat–Sun.* Mont-de-Marsan bullring hosts a range of shows, including bloodless bullfights, ***vaches landaises*** competitions, concerts and the ***Fêtes de la Madeleine*** in late July. Guided tours daily.

LE PAYS DE L'ADOUR

The southern section of Les Landes, encompassing the spa towns of Dax, Aire-sur-l'Adour and Eugénie-les-Bains, is known officially as the Pays de l'Ardour Chalosse Tursan. A verdant, rural spot, it stretches over 2 000sq km/770sq mi, and is home to around 80 000 people. The name comes from the Adour river, which flows through many of its towns. Known for its gentle climate and the health-benefits of its local waters, this is a region for rest, relaxation and outdoor pursuits.

Highlights

1 Rare plant species and unique architecture at Dax's **Parc du Sarrat** (p180)

2 Surfing in **Hossegor** (p182)

3 Up close with macaques at **La Pinède des Singes** (p183)

4 Touring and tasting at the **Maison du jambon de Bayonne** (p194)

5 The refined spas of **Eugénie-les-Bains** (p195)

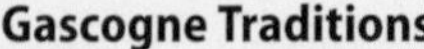

Gascogne Traditions

The Adour river flows from the Pyrénées near the Col du Tourmalet, into the Atlantic Ocean at the Bay of Biscay, near Bayonne. It is at its widest and most stately in this final section, passing through the gentle southern tip of Les Landes, and shows influences of both its source and its destination – meaning the Pays de l'Adour is rich in local traditions, part Pays Basque, part Landais.

You will find markets, festivals and open days at local farms throughout the year – celebrating everything from locally-produced *eaux-de-vie*, wines and Armagnacs, to wild honey, farm-reared ducks and chickens, roasted chestnuts, and an endless selection of local fruit and vegetables. This is truly what makes the local economy go round; over half of all agricultural businesses in Les Landes are found in the Pays de l'Adour region. All of this local food translates into an increasingly dynamic food scene – from restaurants specialising in the air-dried and salted **Jambon de Bayonne** to the prized (and delicious), free-range corn-fed chicken which has been designated *volailles fermières labellisées* since 1965. And if all this good living gets too much, spas and mineral water cures are on hand at every turn, as well as surfing for the most active visitors. Along the coast, the Gouf de Capbreton, an undersea canyon 3 000m/9 842ft deep and over 60km/37mi long, creates waves that makes **Hossegor** a playground for surfing enthusiasts.

View over Capbreton

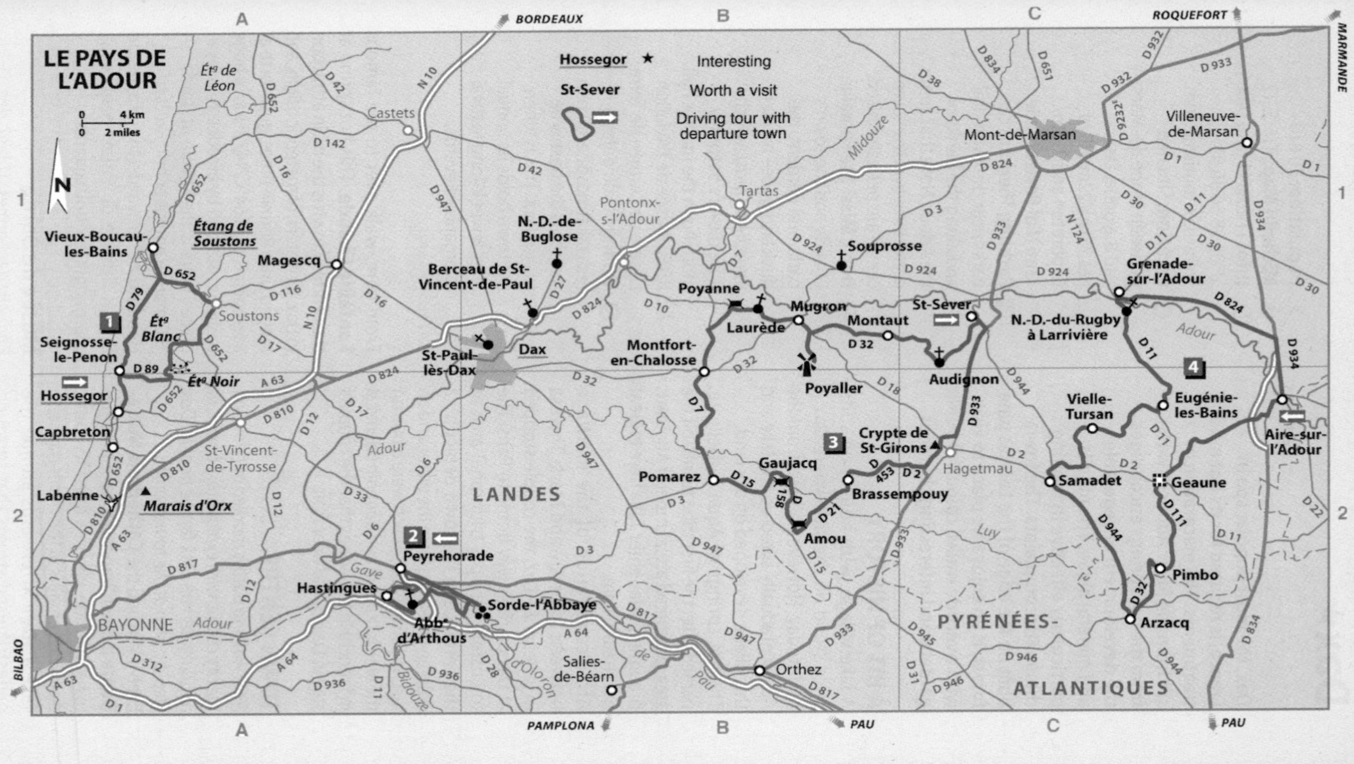
LE PAYS DE L'ADOUR
0 4 km
0 2 miles
N
Hossegor ★ Interesting
St-Sever Worth a visit
Driving tour with departure town
BORDEAUX
ROQUEFORT
MARMANDE
BILBAO
PAMPLONA
PAU
PAU
Vieux-Boucau-les-Bains
Étang de Soustons
Magescq
Soustons
Seignosse-le-Penon
Hossegor
Capbreton
Labenne
Marais d'Orx
St-Vincent-de-Tyrosse
Castets
N.-D.-de-Buglose
Berceau de St-Vincent-de-Paul
St-Paul-lès-Dax
Dax
Pontonx-s-l'Adour
Tartas
Souprosse
Poyanne
Laurède
Mugron
Montaut
St-Sever
Audignon
Poyaller
Montfort-en-Chalosse
Pomarez
Gaujacq
Amou
Brassempouy
Crypte de St-Girons
Hagetmau
Mont-de-Marsan
Villeneuve-de-Marsan
Grenade-sur-l'Adour
N.-D.-du-Rugby à Larrivière
Eugénie-les-Bains
Aire-sur-l'Adour
Vielle-Tursan
Samadet
Geaune
Pimbo
Arzacq
LANDES
PYRÉNÉES-ATLANTIQUES
Peyrehorade
Hastingues
Sorde-l'Abbaye
Abbᵉ d'Arthous
Salies-de-Béarn
Orthez
BAYONNE

Dax★

Landes

Dax, the most popular spa in France, is reputed for its hot mud treatments. The maceration of silt from the River Adour in water from the hot springs encourages the development of vegetable and mineral algae. The mud is particularly effective in treating rheumatic complaints. The town, built on the edge of the Landes pine forest, is an enjoyable place to visit with riverside walks, colourful public gardens and interesting churches.

- **Population:** 20 810
- **Michelin Map:** 335: E-12
- **Info:** 11 cours Foch, Dax. 05 58 56 86 86. www.dax-tourisme.com.
- **Location:** Situated between Mont-de-Marsan and Bayonne, Dax lies 35km/22mi NE of Capbreton and 21km/13mi N of Peyrehorade.
- **Parking:** There are car parks near the cathedral and along the banks of the Adour. Note that some of the streets in the town centre are pedestrianised.
- **Don't Miss:** The Fontaine Chaude and the town's parks and gardens; the duck and goose market *(marché au gras)*, which is held every Saturday morning in the market hall.
- **Kids:** Musée de l'Aviation Légère de l'Armée de Terre.
- **Timing:** If you enjoy a festival atmosphere, then August is the best time to visit Dax. This is when the town holds its annual *féria*, a week-long festival of organised events.

A BIT OF HISTORY

A lake village, with houses on stilts, once stood on the site where Dax is built today. However, alluvia from the Adour gradually silted up the lake and the village developed on dry land.

The hot springs of Aqua Tarbellicae, named after the first tribe to inhabit the area, prospered after Emperor Augustus brought his daughter Julia here to treat her rheumatism.

After celebration of the marriage between Louis XIV and Maria Theresa in St-Jean-de-Luz, the couple stopped at Dax on their way home to Paris. The townsfolk set up a triumphal arch at the entrance to the town depicting a dolphin emerging from the water, and an inscription in Latin, which were a pun on the words dolphin and *dauphin* (identical in French) in the hopes that the couple's stay in Dax would bear fruit.

TOWN CENTRE

A walking path is marked out through the city centre, with explanatory boards at regular intervals. Ask for the booklet Dax Step-by-Step at the tourist office.

Even if you find the **Cathédrale Notre-Dame** a touch imposing, take the time to head inside, where a fine 13C Gothic doorway remains in the north transept. Take a stroll afterwards around the pedestrianised streets that surround it (rues Neuve, des Carmes, St-Vincent, etc.), with their small boutiques, delicatessens and *salons de thé*.

From here, walk over to the famous **Fontaine Chaude**. This hot spring at the centre of town is the main attraction in Dax. Its waters, of meteoric origin, and tapped since Roman times, gush forth at a temperature of 64°C/147°F into a huge basin surrounded by arcades. Nearby in place Thiers is the statue of Borda, an 18C marine engineer born in Dax.

Heading off towards the Musée de Borda, the rue du Palais contains a charmingly tranquil square.

Musée de Borda

Chapelle des Carmes, 11 bis r. des Carmes. Open Tue–Sun 2–6pm. Guided tours of the Crypte archéologique Tue–Sun 4pm.

Closed public holidays. 2.50€ (1st Sun of month no charge). 05 58 74 12 91.

The museum is housed in the Chapelle des Carmes, which was moved inside the town walls in the 16C. It contains collections of Gallo-Roman and medieval archaeology (statuettes and 1C bronzes discovered in Dax), 18C–20C paintings of the world of bullfighting and Dutch landscapes, memorabilia belonging to the scholar Jean-Charles de Borda and the Minister of the French Colonies, Milliès-Lacroix. One room is devoted to regional folklore, another to breeds of cattle from the Landes region. A guided tour of the nearby Crypte archéologique is available.

Hot spring of the Fontaine Chaude

©S. Sauvignier/MICHELIN

Crypte Archéologique

Open Tue–Sun 2–6pm. Closed bank holidays. 2.50€ (includes entry to Musée de Borda; under 18 years and 1st Sun of month no charge). 05 58 74 12 91. www.dax.fr.

Dax is the site of one the most important archaeological remains in Les Landes: the podium of a 2C Gallo-Roman temple which has been fully exposed through careful excavation work. Accompanying the remains is an interactive exhibition which traces several centuries of local history through both Gallo-Roman and medieval remains (bronzes, ceramics, coins...). Other treasures include a bronze and silver Gallo-Roman statue of Esculape (the god of healing and medicine), and another of Mercury (god of trade, wealth and travellers), as well as animal statues of an ibex and a cockerel.

Musée Georgette-Dupouy

r. du Présidial (enter via 12 r. du Mirail). Open daily 2–6pm. Closed 1 Jan, 25 Dec. 2.50€ (under 25 years, Sun and bank holidays no charge). 05 58 56 04 34. http://ass.gdupouy.free.fr.

Privately owned museum celebrating the life of Georgette Dupouy, a self-taught painter (1901–92) who moved to Dax in 1935 on her marriage, and was forced to abandon her art despite having held a successful exhibition in Paris in 1930. Despite family hostility, she began painting again in 1942, and met Maurice Utrillo in 1943, who persuaded her to fully pursue her passion. Little known by the wider public (she refused to work with galleries), she nonetheless travelled widely. The museum contains over 100 works, from still lifes and landscapes to portraits.

A Great Seaman

Jean-Charles de Borda was born in Dax in 1733. He was a marine engineer, mathematician, surveyor and all-round seaman, worthy of being the namesake of ships serving in the navy school until the beginning of the 20C.

Borda made great progress in nautical calculation and observations. He was part of a mission directed by the Constituent Assembly, which included Méchain and Delambre, charged with establishing the metric system and measuring the meridian arch between Dunkirk and Barcelona. The museum is named after him and his statue stands in place Thiers.

Art Deco Architecture

Rejoin cours de Verdun via rue des Carmes, where you will see examples of the city's fine Art Deco architecture; the Hôtel Splendid built in 1929 by André Granet and Roger Expert. L'Atrium, located on cours Foch, offers a second example of Art Deco styling. Between the two, architect Jean Nouvel strikes a contemporary note with his Hôtel des Thermes with its slatted wooden façade.

ADDITIONAL SIGHTS

Parc du Sarrat

r. du Sel Gemme. Guided tours (1hr30min) Mar–Nov Tue, Thu and Sat 3.30pm. 3.50€. 05 58 56 85 03.

The park contains a house with a façade consisting entirely of plate glass, designed by the American architect Frank Lloyd Wright. The park is arranged in a series of theme gardens with a wide variety of vegetation, interspersed with winding canals – such as a French garden and a Japanese garden.

Musée de l'Aviation Légère de l'Armée de Terre (ALAT)

Dax Aerodrome, 58 av. de l'aérodrome (take the D 6 SW towards Peyrehorade, then the D 106 and turn right). Open Mar–Jun and Sept–Nov Tue–Sat 2–5.45pm; Jul–Aug Mon 2–5.45pm. 5€ (children 3.40€). 05 58 74 66 19. www.museehelico-alat.com.

Created in 1954, ALAT is a descendent of the balloon corps which first appeared in the French Army in 1794 and the captive balloon units used in World War I. ALAT had a high profile in Algeria during air operations, reconnaissance and rescue missions. In 1977 this air force subdivision was restructured into helicopter combat regiments. The museum houses a historical gallery with collections of documents, memorabilia, uniforms, etc.

A hangar contains more than 30 well-preserved aeroplanes and helicopters, including a Hiller UH 12 A, which is of particular interest as it was flown to Indochina by Valérie André, the first woman to reach the rank of General in the French Army in 1976.

EXCURSIONS

St-Paul-lès-Dax

Take the Bayonne road, then follow signs.

The church has attractive 11C relief carvings depicting mythical animals, the Holy Trinity, saints, the Crucifixion, dragons and Judas' kiss.

Berceau de St Vincent de Paul

4km/2.5mi northeast along the N 124, then left onto the D 27.

This site commemorates the birthplace of Vincent de Paul in 1581. Surrounding the Byzantine Revival church are buildings and chapels which recount his life, and his acts of kindness, education and relief towards the poor. A foundation created in 1865 continues his work today. The Cradle receives up to 30 000 visitors per year.

Notre-Dame-de-Buglose

9km/5.6mi NE along the N 124, then left onto the D 27.

An important pilgrimage site, this Roman Revival basilica contains, above the altar, a statue of the Virgin Mary with child which dates from 1620.

Conservatoire Avicole du Puyobrau à Magescq

11km/6.8mi to the NW along the D 16. 2695 rte de Dax. Open Mar–Sept 10am–12.30pm, 2–7pm daily; Oct–Feb Wed–Mon 10am–12.30pm, 2–7pm. Guided visits available 6€ (under 12 years 3€). 05 58 47 71 83.

What came first, the chicken or the egg? This is clearly a question that gets asked frequently at this interesting and unusual attraction, which is home to over 120 species of chickens, cockerels, ducks, turkeys, guinea fowls, and hens from the world over. Many of the birds are allowed to roam free, while others are protected species, here for breeding and preservation. Activities for young children.

ADDRESSES

STAY

Book well ahead if you want to stay in Dax during festival season (mid-Aug): the entire city is packed out for six days, and it can be impossible to find a bed at the last minute.

Étap'Hôtel – *av. de la Résistance, 40990 St-Paul-lès-Dax. 05 58 91 90 17. www.etap hotel.com. 74 rooms. 4.70€.* Chain hotel near to Casino César Palace and Lac de Christus with air-conditioned rooms. Good value for families (room price remains the same for two or three people), even in high season.

Chambre d'hôte Capcazal de Pachiou – *606 rte de Pachiou, 40350 Mimbaste (12km/7.4mi SE of Dax. Take the D 947 and C 16). 05 58 55 30 54. www. capcazaldepachiou.com. Reservations required. 5 rooms. Restaurant.* You won't want to leave this 17C house with its sculpted wooden fireplaces, antique furniture and canopied beds in the bedrooms. The friendly hosts and the real family cooking are an extra bonus.

Chambres d'hôtes L'Aiguade – *1301 rte de la Bretonnière, 40990 St-Paul-lès-Dax. 05 58 91 37 10. www.laiguade.com. Closed Nov–Mar. 3 rooms.* Antique furniture and rooms overlooking the park. Breakfast possible on the terrace overlooking the pool.

Hôtel La Néhé – *18 r. de la Fontaine-Chaude. 05 58 90 16 46. www.hotel-nehe-dax.com. Closed Jan.20 rooms. 7€.* Close to the Fontaine Chaude, recently renovated hotel with spacious, if functional, rooms.

Hôtel Calicéo – *335 r. du Centre-Aéré, 40990 St-Paul-lès-Dax. 05 58 90 66 00. www.hotelcaliceo.com. 47 rooms. 9.50€. Restaurant.* Modern hotel facing the Lac de Christus. Aquatic fitness facilities open to the public feature round pools with currents and fountains, a cardiovascular-training room, hammams and saunas.

Grand Hôtel Mercure Splendid – *cours de Verdun. 05 58 56 70 70. www. mercure.com. Closed Jan–Feb. 100 rooms. Restaurant.* This resort hotel near the River Adour has a Belle Époque atmosphere. Built in 1930, the spacious rooms have been fitted with comfortable modern facilities. Garden with pool under the trees.

EAT

Au Fin Gourmet – *3 r. des Pénitents. 05 58 74 04 26. Closed mid-Dec–mid-Jan.* Close to the Fontaine Chaude, good regional food.

Lou Balubé – *63 av. St-Vincent-de-Paul. 05 58 56 97 92. Closed Thur evening, Wed and Sun.* Changing menus depending on what the chef finds in the daily market.

L'Amphitryon – *38 cours Galliéni. 05 58 74 58 05. Closed Sat lunch, Sun evening, Mon, 2 wks Aug and Jan.* Immaculate façade and cheerful nautical atmosphere in the dining room. Regional cooking.

Ferme-auberge de Thoumiou – *chemin de Thoumiou, 40180 St-Pandelon (4km/2.5mi S of Dax via the D 29). 05 58 98 73 41. Open Jul–Aug daily lunch; Mar–Jun and Sept–mid-Dec Sat–Sun. Closed mid-Dec–1 Mar.* Enjoy delicious, traditional cuisine in this *ferme-auberge*, whose dining room is housed in its spacious old stables. Access for travellers with special needs.

Le Moulin de Poustagnacq – *chemin de Poustagnacq, 40990 St-Paul-lès-Dax (6km/3.7mi E of Dax via the D 459). 05 58 91 31 03. www.moulinde poustagnacq.com. Closed Tue lunch, Sun evening, Mon and Nov school holidays, .* You'll be enchanted with this old mill on a lake surrounded by peaceful woods. Part of the building has been converted into a restaurant; the striking dining room décor has white stucco arches. Appetising, innovative cuisine.

ENTERTAINMENT

Casino de Dax – *8 av. Milliès-Lacroix (on the banks of the Adour in the city centre). 05 58 58 77 77. www.lucienbarriere.com.* This casino has a traditional games room with roulette, blackjack, slot machines; a bar; and a restaurant.

L'Atrium – *cours du Maréchal-Foch. 05 58 90 99 09. www.atriumdedax.abcsalles.com.* The Atrium's auditorium was built in what was left of the 1928 Dax Casino, now in ruins. The ceiling, walls and stage offer a spectacular setting for the many concerts, plays and ballets that are performed here.

Hossegor★

Landes

Hossegor is a pleasant seaside resort bordered by the Canal du Boudigau, which separates the town from neighbouring Capbreton. Thanks to the efforts of successive generations of local architects, writers and painters since the beginning of the 20C, this choice natural site wooded with pines, cork-oak and arbutus has been carefully developed into a holiday centre complete with parks, gardens, hotels, a casino and a golf course.

- **Population:** 3 586
- **Michelin Map:** 335: C-13
- **Info:** pl. des Halles, Hossegor. ☎05 58 41 79 00. www.hossegor.fr.
- **Location:** 23km/14.3mi N of Bayonne and 28km/17.4mi W of Dax.
- **Don't Miss:** The lake and surrounding pine forest.
- **Kids:** Animal attractions at Labenne: la pinède des singes and Reptilarium.
- **Timing:** Allow half a day to explore the resort and its surrounding area. The lake offers plenty of options for swimming and watersports.

GEOGRAPHICAL NOTES

The climate, influenced by the coast, the lake and the forest, is temperate, with ideal humidity, making the town an invigorating place to visit.

Some way offshore is found the famous **Gouf de Capbreton**, an undersea canyon 3 000m/9 842ft deep and over 60km/37mi long. The huge groundswell produced by this submarine phenomenon has made Hossegor a playground for surfing enthusiasts and each summer, between late September and early October, the *Quiksilver Pro France*, a World Championship for professional surfers, is held here.

THE RESORT

The Beach

Pleasant resort town which became popular in the 1920s, when parks, gardens, hotels, golf courses, a casino and several sports complexes were built among the pine trees and sand dunes.

Among the attractions is a long strip of fine sand. For swimming, head to Plage du Sud and Plage Centrale; for surfing, Plage de la Gravière is best; for naturists, Plage de la Côte Sauvage (towards Seignosse). And be careful, the Dune de la Côte Sauvage is an *Espace naturel protégé*, so be sure to follow the proscribed walking routes.

Leave from Maison Hargous, to the north of Hossegor and heading towards Seignosse, on the D 152. There are five walking routes (2km–5km/1.2mi–3.1mi) through forest paths.

Numerous coastal cycle paths cover Hossegor (maps available from the tourist office), so you can happily leave your car.

Villas★

Brochure available from tourist office. Private properties, so be discreet and don't enter the gardens.

These 1920s and 30s villas are located between the sea and the lake. Their Basque Landes architecture reflects the rural Basque details (façades in white *crépi*, overhanging roofs) and those from the Landes (timber frames, exposed brick).

Le Lac★

Where once the River Ardour flowed, there is now a long tidal saltwater lake, ringed by the pine forest and villas in the local style. The lake is linked directly to the ocean by Boudigau Canal.

Lac d'Hossegor is ideal for water sports. Its beaches, with their gently lapping waters, are perfect for small children, while Plage du Rey, on the east bank, offers a wide choice of equipment and lessons.

EXCURSIONS

Capbreton★

Separated from Hossegor by the Boudigau Canal, the town was an important **port** up until the diversion of the River Adour. Decline soon followed, but today its attractive apartment buildings, large marina and sandy beach have turned it into a prosperous **seaside resort**. The church of St Nicholas was founded in the 16C *(pl. St Nicolas; ℘05 58 72 11 81)*. The jetty, known locally as *l'estacade*, is a popular vantage point for contemplating the coast, the Pyrénées and the mouth of the canal.

Capbreton is also known for its **"gouf"** or swallow-hole – a phenomenon of underwater topography, which is invisible from the surface, but which was well known to local fishermen centuries before it was scientifically identified. It is the main geomorphologic trait of the continental shelf in the Bay of Biscay. The swallow-hole is an east–west chasm running for over 60km/37mi from the exit of the harbour. It is 3km–10km/1.8mi–6.2mi wide and up to 3 000m/9 842ft deep. Various hypotheses have been put forward to explain its existence but none has been proved conclusively – that it is the result of a complex process of underwater fluvial erosion, a fracture linked to buckling of the Pyrénées, or a canyon gouged out by the River Adour during the great glaciations of the Quaternary Age, when sea levels lowered.

Labenne

6km/3.7mi of Capbreton, along the D 652.

Cycle access through the port or along the seafront. An attractive cycle path passes through Labenne.

A variety of activities are on offer, besides swimming at Labenne-Océan, and a variety of activities suitable for families.

Parc zoologique – Large zoo with variety of species, including lemurs, kangaroos, camels, monkeys, parrots, seabirds. Young children will enjoy the petting zoo *(av. de l'Océan; open Apr–Sept daily 10am–7.30pm, Feb–Apr and Sept daily 2–6pm, Oct–mid-Nov Wed and Sat–Sun 2–6pm. 8€ (4–12 years 6€); ℘05 59 45 43 93; www.oceafaunia.com)*.

La Pinède des Singes – From Labenne head south on the N 10, then left onto the D 126, signposed "route du lac d'Irieu". In a shady site, full of mature cork oak trees, this animal sanctuary is home to Java monkeys *(rte de Bayonne; open Apr–Jun and Sept Mon–Tue and Thur–Fri 2–6pm, Wed and Sat–Sun 11am–6pm, Easter, Jul–Aug and bank holidays 11am–6pm; closed Oct–Mar; 8€ (3–12 years 5€); ℘05 59 45 43 66; www.pinede-des-singes.com)*.

Reptilarium – From Labenne, head south on the N 10. Vipers, crocodiles, pythons, boas, lizards, iguanas and anacondas are among the star reptiles on display at this educational and well-organised site. Over 150 reptiles are gathered in 1 000sq m/10 750sq ft *(16 av. du Général.-de-Gaulle; open 10am–noon, 2–6.30pm; 8€ (3–12 years 6€); ℘ 05 59 45 67 09; www.reptilarium.fr)*.

La Réserve Naturelle du Marais d'Orx★

From Labenne turn left onto the D 71. The marshland (marais) is signposted. Park your car at the Maison du Marais. Avoid peak hours, as it can get crowded. ***Maison d'accueil*** *(for exhibitions, boutique and information) open Jun–Sept Mon–Fri 10am–noon, 2–5pm, Sat–Sun 2–5pm; Oct–May Sat–Sun 2–5pm. Self-guided tours available year round. Guided visits available by appointment. 5/10€ (half-day or full day), 6–16 years 3/5€. ℘05 59 45 42 46.*

9km/5.6mi. This nature reserve has been created out of former swampland, and is today a favoured stop-off point for migratory birds. Bring your binoculors. A footpath rings the site, offering beautiful views over the pine-tree-lined coast. There is information on the fauna and flora along the path, and at the Maison du Marais.

DRIVING TOUR

1 AROUND THE LAKES

55km/34mi. Allow 2hrs.

Vieux-Boucau-les-Bains

The town was renamed Vieux-Boucau ("Old Estuary" in the local dialect) and almost abandoned in 1578, when the course of the River Adour was deviated. Today, Vieux-Boucau-les-Bains has been revived by the construction of Port d'Albret, a large tourist resort built on a 50ha/120-acre lagoon among the sand and pines. The waters of the lake are renewed each day by a dam with tide-activated locks. An **esplanade** joins Vieux-Boucau to Port-Albret, a charming spot for an evening stroll, when lights on the water sparkle and flow.

Follow the D 652 towards Soustons.

Étang de Soustons★

The figure-8 shape of this 730ha/1 800-acre lake, fringed by reeds and surrounded by dense pine woods, makes it impossible to see the whole of it at once. All parts of the lake, however, are easily accessible through the woods. *30min round trip on foot*. To reach it from Soustons, follow allée des Soupirs *(left of the church)* and then avenue du Lac as far as the landing stage, banked with flowers.

Take the **GR 8** signposted rambling path, to Pointe des Vergnes, to enjoy the view. Continue along the south bank, which goes round the urban development zone ZAC des Pêcheurs. A pine forest leads to a picnic area on the water's edge.

Rejoin the D 652 towards Tosse. After 4km/2.5mi, take the right turn towards Gaillou-de-Pountaout (signposted "étang Blanc"), which runs between Étang Hardy and Étang Blanc.

Étang Blanc

This delightful "White Pool" is bordered by fishermen's huts and circled by a narrow road looping through the charming countryside and along the inviting shore.

Réserve Naturelle de l'Étang Noir

When it's wet, the pathway can become slippy. Lack of railings at certain points, so be careful with children.

30min. This marsh is circled by a discreet raised walkway (1km/0.6mi) with two viewing platforms, which allows you to view the flora and fauna from up close. This site gives a good idea of how much of the Landes looked before the widespread adoption of draining the marshes.

Visit the Maison de la Réserve *(small exhibitions and games for children; open daily; no charge; 05 58 72 85 76)*, or take a guided visit (1hr30min) during the summer *(Jul–Aug, Mon–Fri 10.30am, 3pm, 5pm, Sun 10.30am (unless raining); 3€ (under 12 years no charge)*.

Turn right onto the D 89.

Seignosse-Le Penon

av. des Lacs. Open Mon–Sat Jul–Aug 9am–7pm; rest of year 9am–noon, 2–6pm. Guide available to two walking circuits of Seignosse. 05 58 43 32 15. www.tourisme-seignosse.com.

This small coastal resort, with five manned beaches, combines villas along the seafront and hidden retreats in the pine forest. A variety of sports and leieure activities are on offer: surf, water parks, cycling paths, golf.

Six signposed circuits (4km–9km/2.5mi–5.6mi) pass through the forest and surrounds of Seignosse. Discovery paths along the coast and in the forest (2hrs30min) are available, accompanied by guides organised through the tourist office *(open last 2 wks Jun and 1st 2 wks Sept Wed 9.30am, Jul–Aug Tue and Thur 9.30am; 5€; book through the tourist office)*.

The D 152 returns to Hossegor.

ADDRESSES

STAY

Chambre d'hôte Le Bosquet – *4 r. du Hazan, 40230 Tosse (rte de St-Vincent-de-Tyrosse, 10km/6.2mi E of Hossegor via the D 33 and D 652). ℘05 58 43 03 40. www.lebosquet-landes.com. 3 rooms.* Pine and oak trees surround this low, modern house near Hossegor, with direct access to the garden from the guest rooms. Meals here are taken in the Basque-style dining room in the winter or on the terrace with barbecue in fine weather. Calm, peaceful ambience and friendly, hospitable hosts.

Chambre d'hôte L'Océanide – *22 av. Jean-Lartigau, Capbreton. ℘05 58 72 41 40. http://mallet.micheline.free.fr. Closed Nov–Feb. 3 rooms and 1 appartment.* . Madame Mallet makes for a warm and friendly host, at this appealing house with a garden that slopes down to the river. Two rooms have a terrace, while the third is large enough to accommodate families.

Hôtel Les Fougères – *91 av. de Gaujacq. ℘05 58 43 78 00. www.hotel-les fougeres.com. Closed mid-Nov–mid-Mar.* P *27 rooms. 8.50€.* Away from the bustle of the town centre, this hotel offers simple but clean rooms, some with private kitchenettes. Pool.

Chambre d'hôte Ty-boni – *1831 rte de Capbreton, 40150 Angresse (3km/1.8mi E of Hossegor via the D 133). ℘05 58 43 98 75. www.ty-boni.com. 3 rooms.* This quiet bed and breakfast has an attractive large garden with a swimming pool and small lake. The modern house, built in traditional regional style, has pleasant, simply furnished rooms. Fully equipped kitchen at guests' disposal. Friendly welcome.

Domaine Le Dunéa – *Port d'Albret Sud, 40140 Soustons, 200m/660ft from the lake. ℘05 58 48 00 59. clubdunea@libertysurf.fr. Open Apr–mid-Oct. 20 bungalows.* The bungalows are spaced out around the park, centred around the pool. Each has a kitchenette, bathroom, separate WC. Possible to rent for the night or weekend out of season.

Hôtel Barbary Lane – *156 av. de la Côte-d'Argent. ℘05 58 43 46 00. www.barbary-lane.com. Closed mid-Nov–Feb. 18 rooms and 2 suites. Restaurant.* Traditional Landaise-style house, now renovated as a hotel. Attractively decorated, with antiques, and pottery on display. In summer, brunch and half-board available.

Les Hortensias du Lac – *1578 av. du Tour-du-Lac. ℘05 58 43 99 00. www.hortensias-du-lac.com. Closed 15 Nov–1 Apr. 20 rooms. 20€.* This attractive hotel situated on the lakeshore only 500m/550yds from the sea is the perfect place for a relaxing holiday. Its white façade and round, arched windows overlook the peaceful waters of the lake. Comfortable, elegant rooms decorated in white with light wood furnishings. A few duplexes for family holidays.

EAT

Hôtel Brasserie de l'Océan – *85 av. Georges-Pompidou, Capbreton. ℘05 58 72 10 22. www.hotelcapbreton.com. 25 rooms. 8.50€.* Attractive dining room for this seafood-based restaurant.

La Ferme de Bathurt – *rte de l'Étang-Blanc, 40140 Soustons. ℘05 58 41 53 28. Closed evenings and Wed out of season, Mar and Nov.* Kids will absolutely love this farm that has been transformed into a restaurant. Play area and good-value traditional regional cuisine.

Le Voilier – *29 av. Georges-Pompidou, Capbreton. ℘05 58 72 13 47. 26 rooms. 7€.* Shellfish and other seafood are cooked expertly at this port-side restaurant.

Restaurant Michel Batby – *63 av. Gelleben, 40140 Soustons. ℘05 58 41 18 80. Closed mid-Dec–mid-Jan.* Well located by the Étang de Soustons, there is an attractive terrace shaded by plane trees. Home-cooked food.

BARS AND CAFÉS

Marcot' – *av. du Touring-Club-de-France. ℘05 58 43 52 15.* Founded in 1927, this pastry shop-cum-tea room sells a wide selection of home-made cakes, ice creams and chocolates.

Peyrehorade

Landes

Peyrehorade is the main town in Pays d'Orthe in the Landes *département*. A particularly interesting example of architectural development in southern France, the town marks the beginning of river navigation on the converging mountain streams of Pau and Oloron, the Gaves Réunis, which flow into the Adour. Along the quays, yachts are gradually replacing the sailing barges of the past. It is best to visit the town on Wednesdays when the long central marketplace is busy with stalls. Peyrehorade is one of only four fish-auction centres dealing with *pibales* (tiny elvers), a great delicacy particularly appreciated by Spanish gourmets.

- **Population:** 3 435
- **Michelin Map:** 335: E-13
- **Info:** 147 av. des Évadés. 05 58 73 00 52. www.tourisme-paysdorthe.fr.
- **Location:** Peyrehorade is situated 35km/22mi E of Bayonne and 30km/18.6mi W of Orthez on the N 117.
- **Parking:** quai du Sablot (along the bank of the Gaves Réunis). On Wednesdays the town centre is closed to traffic.
- **Don't Miss:** The Benedictine monastery at Sorde-l'Abbaye.
- **Kids:** The museum at the Abbaye d'Arthous.
- **Timing:** Allow half a day to visit Peyrehorade. Note that the Benedictine monastery at Sorde-l'Abbaye and the Abbaye d'Arthous are closed on Monday and only open in the afternoon in low season.

SIGHTS

The **Château d'Orthe** *(open for temporary exhibitions Feb–Dec Mon–Fri 8.15am–noon, 1.30–5.30pm; www.centrecultureldupaysdorthe.com)* with its four corner towers (16C–18C) stands on the riverbank. Nearby, on the main square is the tourist office where a leaflet describing the walk to the Aspremont castle ruins (11C) is available.

DRIVING TOUR

2 LE PAYS D'ORTHE

25km/15.5mi. Allow 1hr30mins.

Take the road S from Peyrehorade. After the bridge, turn right onto the D 23, which runs along the Gaves Réunis. At Hastingues, at the highest point, take the road opposite towards the car parks near the Aire d'Hastingues (on the A 64 towards Pau-Bayonne).

Aire d'Hastingues

Its geometric layout, which includes the service station, symbolises the nearby intersection of the French roads leading to Santiago de Compostela. Pathways lined with box hedges and panels illustrating well-known sites, lead to a circular building, le Centre d'Exposition St Jacques de Compostelle *(open daily May–Sept 8am–8.30pm, Oct–Apr 9am–6pm; no charge; 05 58 73 68 66)* given over to the history of the famous pilgrimage. Inside, information panels, reproductions of artworks, slide shows and interactive terminals recount the history of St James the Apostle and the daily lives of the pilgrims.

An exhibit entitled *La Fin des Terres (World's End)*, featuring the *Tree of Jesse*, which decorates the pillar of the structure dedicated to the *Glory of St Jacques*, recounts the end of the pilgrimage.

Walk back to the village (10min).

Hastingues

This tiny *bastide* is named after the King of England's seneschal, John Hastings, who founded the town in 1289 under

the orders of King Edward I of England, the Duke of Aquitaine. All that remains of the upper town, perched on a headland overlooking the meadowland of Arthous below, is a single fortified gateway to the southwest and several 15C and 16C houses. Take time to admire the charming place de l'Église, shaded by cypresses from the old cemetery.

Return to Hastingues and take the road to the right.

Abbaye d'Arthous

Open Tue–Sun Apr–Oct 10.30am–1pm, 2–6.30pm; Nov–19 Dec and Feb–Mar 2–5pm. Guided tours daily in summer 11am, 3pm, 5pm. Closed 1 May, 1 Nov, 11 Nov. 3€ (children 2€). 05 58 73 03 89. www.arthous.landes.org.

The abbey, converted into farm buildings in the 19C, was founded in the second half of the 12C and served as a staging post for pilgrims on The Way of St James. The abbey buildings were restored in the 16C and 17C.

The church is especially noteworthy for its completely restored east end. Note the decoration in the apse and two apsidal chapels; billet-moulding is supported by modillions: figures often in pairs, geometrical designs reminiscent of a bed of reeds or a pan-pipe and interwoven patterns.

Under the half-timbered gallery of the monastic buildings are two 4C mosaics from a Gallo-Roman villa in Sarbazan.

Follow the D 19 then turn right towards Peyrehorade. Before the bridge, turn right onto the D 33. After 3km/1.8mi, turn left towards Sorde.

Sorde-l'Abbaye

This former *bastide* owes its development to Benedictine monks who possessed a vast agricultural domain along with a salmon farm and a mill. The interest of the village lies in the vestiges of its abbey, listed as a UNESCO World Heritage Site in 1998, and located on the banks of one of the finest stretches of smooth water.

Benedictine Monastery

pl. de l'Eglise. Guided tour (30min) Apr–Oct Tue–Sun 10.30am–noon, 2.30–6.30pm (last admission 30min before closing); 5 Jan–31 Mar Mon–Fri 9am–11.30am, 1.30–5pm. Closed 1 May. 2€. 05 58 73 09 62.

In the chapter house are gathered Celtic discoidal stelae from the graveyard of Peyrehorade. The only remaining element from the cloister is a pillar and from the main building façades made of stone from Bidache (the marble frames of the parlour have been plundered).

Return to Peyrehorade via the D 29.

ADDRESSES

STAY

Chambre d'hôte La Maison Bel Air – *rte de Cagnotte, 40300 Bélus (6km/3.7mi N of Peyrehorade via rte de Mahoumic). 05 58 73 24 17. www.maison-belair.com. 4 rooms. Meals.* This pretty 18C house, typical of the region, has been tastefully restored. Stone walls, exposed beams and old furniture make for a cosy ambience.

Chambre d'hôte Maison Basta – *335 chemin de Basta, Nord, 40300 Orthevielle (8km/5mi N of Peyrehorade on the D 33, rte de St-Vincent-de-Tyrosse). 05 58 73 15 01. www.gite-basta.com. Closed 2 wks over Christmas. 4 rooms. Meals.* The welcoming landlords have filled their home with souvenirs from their exotic travels. Swimming pool.

EAT

Ferme-Auberge "Cout de Ninon" – *40300 Sorde-l'Abbaye. 05 58 73 06 66. Closed Mon lunch, Tue lunch and Fri (Jul–Aug), Sun evening.* Farm animals give this working farm a charm no child can resist. Farm-fresh ingredients.

Ferme-Auberge Le Bousquet – *37 bd de l'Océan, 40300 Labatut (10km/6.2mi E of Peyrehorade). 05 58 98 11 01. Closed Mon evening, Sun evening and Wed.* A splendid 18C *maison* in a tranquil country setting, with wooden beams and rustic deçor. Modern cuisine.

St-Sever

Landes

St-Sever offers good views of the River Adour and the enormous sea of pines that covers the neighbouring Landes. The one-time "city of scholars" is a useful base for excursions through the Chalosse region and the departure point of a corniche (D 32) winding above local meadows bordering the course of the Adour.

- **Population:** 4 625
- **Michelin Map:** 335: H-12
- **Info:** pl. du Tour du Sol, St-Sever. ℘05 58 76 34 64. www.saint-sever.fr.
- **Location:** St-Sever is situated 12km/7.4mi S of Mont-de-Marsan.
- **Parking:** Follow signs to the "centre historique" and park near the church.

SIGHTS

Église

pl. du Tour du Sol. Open Mon–Sat 9am–6pm, Sun 2–6pm. No charge. ℘05 58 76 34 64. http://beatus.saint-sever.fr.

The Romanesque abbey church (partly restored in the 17C and 19C) features a chancel with six apsidal chapels of decreasing depth, and transept arms which end in galleries resting on a single column which develops, above, into a purely decorative arcade. The marble columns of the chancel and transept were taken from the old palace of the Roman governors of Morlanne; their remarkable **capitals**★ include water-leaf (11C) and lion designs, historiated capitals *(inside the west front)* showing Herod's banquet and the beheading of John the Baptist, and a mixture of figures symbolising the predominance of the New Testament over the Old. The **sacristy** leads to the cloisters, only two sides of which remain.

Outside, the **east end** is crowned with a dome and a lantern, and surrounded by the Romanesque apsidal chapels which have amusing modillions.

Rue du Général-Lamarque

This street is lined with a few 18C mansions (nos **6**, **18**, **20** and **26**); others dating from the 19C include General Lamarque's former residence at nos **8** and **11**; note the Neoclassical doorway of the edifice and the two pavilions flanking it. 16C mansion at no **21**.

The former **Jacobin convent** *(open Jun–Oct daily 2–6pm, Nov–May on request a week in advance at the tourist office; ℘05 58 76 00 02; http://jacobins.saint-sever.fr)*, which has been turned into a cultural centre, has late 17C brick-built cloisters.

Promenade de Morlanne

Access by car.

From the viewpoint, the panorama encompasses the River Adour below and the vast "sea of pine trees" offering a striking contrast with the rolling hills of the Chalosse.

EXCURSION

Église de Souprosse

18km/11.2mi to W via the D 924.

The Église St-Pierre contains several unusual structures; behind an imposing solid oak altar stands a copper and brass tabernacle richly decorated with enamel work depicting the resurrection of Christ (2.2m/7ft high) and a cross (3m/10ft high) carved from an olive tree.

DRIVING TOUR

3 CHALOSSE★

90km/56mi round trip from St-Sever. Allow one day.

Leave St-Sever S along the D 933. At the Église d'Hagetmau, follow signs for Dax. At the crossroads of Larrigade, turn right. The Crypte will be signposted on your right-hand side.

Chalosse, a hilly region nestling within the great curve of the River Adour, has yet to be discovered by the crowds. Fertile patches of "wild" sand, visible in cuts and ditches, stud the region. Despite the modest aspect of the smallholdings and villages, which are in the Landes style, the agriculture is productive. Chalosse has a long history: it is in this region that Palaeolithic man fashioned such masterpieces as the celebrated Venus of Brassempouy *(now on display at the Musée d'Archéologie Nationale, St-Germain-en-Laye, near Paris)*; later, pilgrims passed through on their way to Santiago de Compostela.

Hagetmau

Imposing public buildings (colleges, a covered market) in 1950s style testify to the post-war prosperity of Hagetmau, an agricultural trade centre and a major chair-manufacturing base. The discovery of numerous prehistoric remains indicate very ancient and very large settlements at various times. In 778 Charlemagne founded the Abbaye de St-Girons, which was destroyed in 1569 by the Protestants.

Crypte de St-Girons

From the church at Hagetmau, follow signs to Dax until you get to the crossroads at Larrigade; turn right. The crypt is signposted on the right. Open Jul–Aug Wed–Mon 3–6pm; Sept–Jun please contact the town hall. 1.60€. 05 58 05 77 77.

Capital of a column, Église de St-Sever

©JD Dallet/age fotostock

This crypt, which was a halt on The Way of St James (*see lintroduction: PILGRIM ROUTES*), is all that remains of an abbey built to house the relics of St Girons, the 4C evangelist who preached the Gospel in the Chalosse region. The ceiling of the crypt rests on four central marble columns and eight recessed columns around the walls. The tomb of the saint lay between the marble columns. Scenes carved on the 12C **capitals**★ represent his battle against the forces of evil and the dangers surrounding his missionary activities.

Other capitals in the crypt show the Deliverance of St Peter and the Parable of the Rich Man.

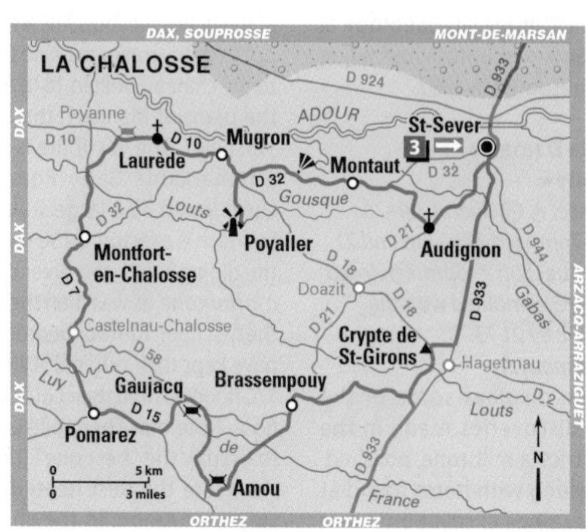

Vénus de Brassempouy (c.23 000 BC)
© The London Art Archive / Alamy

Head S, then turn right onto the D 2.

Brassempouy

This small Chalosse village, the main street of which appears to be straddled by the stone tower of the Romanesque-Gothic church, is among the world's most important prehistoric sites. It includes the earliest-known representation of a human face, carved c.23 000 years BC – the celebrated 3.6cm/1.4in ivory carving known as the **Vénus de Brassempouy** or Figurine à la Capuche (Lady with the Cowl), now exhibited in the Musée d'Archéologie Nationale in St-Germain-en-Laye. Though many important discoveries had been made over the preceding hundred years, huge archaeological tracts still remained untouched when excavations resumed in 1982.

Maison de la Dame de Brassempouy★

352 r. du Musée. Open 1 Jul–20 Sept daily 2–7pm; mid-Feb–Jun and 21 Sept–22 Nov Tue–Sun 2–6pm. Closed 1 May. 8.50€ combined with the Jardin. 05 58 89 21 73. www.brassempouy.fr.

The museum displays some of the prehistoric discoveries made in the Chalosse district (a millstone, polished axe heads) along with items found at Brassempouy since excavations were resumed (tools, bones and the remains of animals which had been eaten). Period documents recall the original 19C excavations. An exhibition of prehistoric female statuary includes reproductions of the world's most famous statuettes and copies of nine figurines discovered at Brassempouy.

Jardin de la Dame de Brassempouy

Open 1 May–5 Jul and Sept–Oct Sat–Sun, public holidays 3–6pm; 6 Jul–23 Aug Tue–Sun 2.30–7pm. 8.50€ combined with the Maison. 05 58 89 25 89.

Return to prehistoric times during a tour in a reconstructed environment (habitat, flora, fauna) with an archaeologist, and experience daily life by taking part in workshops (pottery, flint carving).

Continue S along the D 21. At Amou, follow signs to Gaujacq. Parking on the left after the cattle grid.

Château d'Amou

chemin du Ronde, Amou (16km/10mi SW of Hagetmau. Take the D 933 then the D 13. In Amou, follow signs to Gaujacq, 1st road on the right. The car park is located on the left-hand side after the grid). Guided tour (45min) May–Oct by appointment only. 3€. 05 58 89 00 08. www.chateauamou.com.

The Marquis d'Amou, ancestor of the current landlord, had this château built at the behest of Louis XIV. A fine 18C gate opens onto an alley of plane trees leading to the château built in 1678 according to the plans of Mansart, the architect of Versailles. The vestibule is paved with a remarkable Gallo-Roman mosaic surrounded by a large staircase, close to which is a restored 18C sedan chair. In the dining room, the silver cutlery is set *à la française*, as was then the custom. On the first floor, the four bedrooms in a row have kept their original style, with their 17C floor tiles and their Louis XIV wooden floor. Note that Théophile Gautier used to occupy the "best one" (the smallest, therefore the best heated!) when he stayed at Amou. In the chapel, fitted out in the 19C, a *trompe-l'œil* painting imitates wood.

The **outbuildings**, gathered around a square yard, represent an interesting example of regional architecture, alternating a dovecote from Béarn and Gascon buildings covered with special tiles. An agricultural estate used to go along with the château; a former wine press is there to remind visitors of the fact that in the past, Chalosse wine used to be exported throughout Europe.

Follow signs to Gaujacq.

Château de Gaujacq

2 rte de Brassempouy, Gaujacq. Guided tours (1hr) J Jun Thu–Tue 3–6pm; Jul–Aug daily 11am, 2–6pm; 15 Feb–May and Sept–15 Nov Thu–Tue 3–5pm; nocturnal visits 2nd and 4th Mon Jul 10pm, Aug 9.30pm. 5€. 05 58 89 01 01. http://chateau.de.gaujacq.free.fr.

The elegant château (17C) is visible behind a screen of magnolias, with the Pyrénées in the distance. The courtyard forms a cloister with a garden and a gallery.

Several rooms are open to the public. They are furnished, with wood panelling. In the guard's dining room, in which the table is set, note the cupboard with pieces of earthenware and a marble fountain. Don't miss the chest-of-drawers from the school of Boule in the green sitting room. The room called "chambre du Cardinal", in memory of François de Sourdis, Archbishop of Bordeaux, contains a *bargegno* (cabinet) from the 15C.

Plantarium – *Open Jul–Aug daily 2.30–6.30pm; Sept–Jun Thu–Tue 2.30–6.30pm. 5€. 05 58 89 24 22. www.thoby.com.* This is located at the back of the castle *(entrance on the right)* and is divided into eight colourful and fragrant flower beds and surrounded with a pergola.

Take the D 58 towards Donzacq. Take the first left, the D 339, then turn right onto the D 15.

Pomarez

Pomarez is best known for its covered arena, where the Course Landaise has been enthusiastically practised since the 1930s.

Leave the village N along the D 7.

Montfort-en-Chalosse

The nucleus of this small town is a hillock criss-crossed by narrow lanes and steep, stepped streets. The **Musée de la Chalosse** *(480 chemin de Sala; open Apr–Oct Tue–Fri 10am–noon, 2–6.30pm, Sat–Sun and public holidays 2–6.30pm; Nov–Mar Tue–Fri 2–5.30pm; 5€; 05 58 98 69 27; www.museedelachalosse.fr)* and the nearby **Médiathèque** are both devoted to country life and the economy of this pleasant rural region.

Continue along the D 7. After 4km/2.5mi turn right onto the D 420, then the D 10.

The road passes in front of the 17C château de Poyanne *(not open to visitors).*

Laurède

The village **church** *(guided tours (1hr) Fri 3pm by appointment at Mugron tourist office; 05 58 97 99 40)* boasts a striking Baroque interior. Of particular note are the monumental high altar surmounted by a baldaquin, the pulpit and lectern, and the woodwork in the sacristy.

Continue on the D 10.

Mugron

This small town is the "county town" of the region and is heavily involved in the development of agriculture in the Chalosse (wine cooperative, grain silos). At the time of the Intendants, the small port on the Adour nearby used to export the local wine as far as Holland. From the public gardens around the town hall, once the hillside home of a rich bourgeois family, there are fine **views**★ of the valley.

Follow signs to St-Aubin, to the S.

Moulin de Poyaller

Open Apr–May and Oct holidays 2–6.30pm; Jun and Sept–Oct Tue–Thu and Sun 2.30–6.30pm; Jul–Aug 12.30–7pm. Guided tour available (1hr30min) from 2.30pm (every 45min). Closed Sat (except bank holidays) and mid-Nov–mid-Mar. 5.50€ (3–11 years 3.50€, 12–16 years 4.50€). Home-made preserves on sale. 05 58 97 95 72. www.moulin-poyaller.com.

A warm welcome is offered at this pleasant rural spot. While "Madame" works the mill, and explains its history, "Monsieur" will lead you through the park, where you will find goats, deer and even kangaroos. Barge trips on the Gouanougue also available (at an extra cost).

Return to Mugron and head E along the D 32.

Between Mugron and Montaut there are frequent views of the rear of the plateau, the promontories dropping down in succession towards the Adour and the *pignada* (a local term for the forest of maritime pines).

Montaut

The main street of this old fortified village runs along the crest crowning the last fold of the Chalosse plateau; its houses look out over the plain of the Adour and the forests of the Landes. The church tower, which is also the gateway to the town, was rebuilt after the ravages perpetrated by the bands under Montgomery. The two altarpieces inside the church reveal stylistic differences: that on the right-hand *(south)* side features a strict rhythm of perpendiculars, in contrast with the sinuous lines of the Baroque reredos on the left. The former dates from the early 17C, the latter from the 18C.

Follow the D 32 towards St-Sever. After 1km/0.6mi, turn right.

Audignon

The village has a church *(pl. de Compostelle; open daily 8am–8pm; 05 58 76 29 40)* enclosed within a seemingly fortified cemetery. Note, in the chancel, the remarkable stone altarpiece with its coloured frescoes. The Romanesque east end contrasts with the belfry-porch and its octagonal Gothic spire. In the 14C the medieval keep became the church tower.

Take the northern road from Audignon along the D 21, which returns to St-Sever.Addresses

ADDRESSES

STAY

€€ **Hôtel Alios** – *129 av. de la Forêt-Mauco, 40500 Bas-Mauco (4.5km/2.8mi NE of St-Sever on rte de Mont-de-Marsan). 05 58 76 44 00. hotel.alios@club-internet.fr. Closed 3 wks Aug and 1 wk Dec. 10 rooms. 6.50€. Restaurant€€.* A practical overnight stop. Functional bedrooms and traditional dining.

€€€ **Hôtel Les Lacs d'Halco** – *3km/1.8mi SW by rte de Cazalis, 40700 Hagetmau. 05 58 79 30 79. www.hotel-des-lacs-dhalco.com. 24 rooms. 15€. Restaurant€€€.* Stainless steel, glass, wood and stone: everything is "zen", with lake and forest views.

EAT

€ **Ferme-auberge du Moulin** – *rte de Dax, 40330 Amou (11km/6.8mi S of Gaujacq by the D 158 then the D 15). 05 58 89 30 09. Closed Nov–May. 4 rooms€.* Specialising in duck in all its forms. Calm and tranquil.

€€ **Aux Tauzins** – *40380 Montfort-en-Chalosse. 05 58 98 60 22. www.auxtauzins.com. Closed Mon lunch and Jul–Aug.* Traditional building with great views from the dining room and summer terrace. Traditional local food. Almost all bedrooms have a balcony.

€€ **Restaurant Le Jambon** – *245 av. Carnot, 40700 Hagetmau. 05 58 79 32 02. www.hotellejambon.fr. Closed Sun night, Mon and Jan.* Large house in town centre with roomy bedrooms, all overlooking the courtyard pool. Generous local cooking serving Landes specialities.

Aire-sur-l'Adour

Landes

Aire-sur-l'Adour makes for an interesting visit in its own right. Known for its bullfighting, it is the capital of the Tursan area, and despite some of its unloved corners, retains a rich local culture. The banks of the Adour have been renovated into an attractive walking path, and the whole place has a gentle, welcoming feel.

- **Population:** 6 000
- **Michelin Map:** 335: J–12.
- **Info:** ℘05 58 71 64 70. www.tourisme-aire-eugenie.fr.
- **Location:** On the border of the Gers, between Mont-de-Marsan and Pau (N 124, N 134).
- **Parking:** Along the banks of the Adour (by the arenas).
- **Don't Miss:** Walking along the river.
- **Kids:** Le musée du Jambon de Bayonne.
- **Timing:** Half a day for city centre, another half a day for the surrounding area.

THE TOWN

A map offering in-depth walking routes is available from the tourist office. The lower town is perfect for wandering at your leisure, from the place du Commerce, site of the former corn exchange, to the St-Jean-Baptiste cathedral. Linger by the canal, and don't forget to explore the covered market.

Église St-Pierre-du-Mas (de Ste-Quitterie)

r. Félix-Despagnet. ℘06 77 02 43 44, 05 58 71 47 00 (town hall), or 05 58 71 64 70 (tourist office). www.aire-sur-adour.fr.

At the mid-slope of the plateau, the church has been the most sacred place in the region since the 4C. Today it is classified *Patrimoine Mondial de l'Unesco*. The imposing Gothic gateway depicts scenes of the Last Judgement. The altar was updated during the 18C, but retains two 12C Romanesque arches and delicately carved storied capitals. The **crypt** dates from the 11C, laid on the foundations of a Roman temple dedicated to Mars. The sarcophagus of Ste Quitterie★ (4C) lies within. Opposite, ensure you visit the Chapelle St-Désiré, with its whispering wall. For full effect, make sure you whisper in front of the communion table.

DRIVING TOUR

4 LE TURSAN★

90km/56mi. Allow 4hrs.

Leave Aire-sur-l'Adour S on the D 2.

Geaune

This former English *bastide* is now home to the Coopérative des vignerons du Tursan, the local wine-growers' coop. There is a lovely square with arcades along three sides.

Take the southern road from the village (D 111).

Pimbo

Welcome centre: 40320 Pimbo. Open May–Oct Mon–Fri 10am–12.30pm, 1.30–6pm. ℘05 58 44 46 57.

The oldest *bastide* town in Les Landes, where the main attraction is the collegiate church St-Barthélemy (12C.) and its botanical gardens, a stop along The Way of St James.

Follow the D 111 towards Arzacq.

Maison du Jambon de Bayonne

Open Jul–Aug daily 10am–12.45pm, 2.30–6pm; Sept–Jun Tue–Sat 10am–12.45pm, 2.30–6pm, Sun 2.30–6pm. 6€. ℘05 59 04 49 35. www.jambon-de-bayonne.com.

An interactive exhibition and museum which takes you on a journey through the entire production of Bayonne ham, ending with a tasting of this most famous of local delicacies. A film explores the history of the Jambon de Bayonne, its consumption at different times of the year, and the place it is accorded in the local society. A separate film details the importance of the geographical and climatological influence of the Adour Bassin, and why this remains the strictly defined geographical zone for the production of this air-dried salted ham. Every step is explained from the local Adour salt to the selection of the corn that is fed to the pigs. Even the pigs themselves are on display here!

Leave Arzacq N via the D 944.

Samadet

The heyday of this small town was from 1732 to 1811 when its *faïences* (glazed earthenware) were known throughout the world. The factories here were able to produce both deep and strong tones using the *grand feu* technique (high-temperature firing) and more delicate colours using the gentler *petit feu* technique. The **Musée de la Faïence** *(2378 rte de Hagetmau; open Feb–19 Dec daily 10am–12.30pm, 2–6.30pm; closed 1 May, 1 Nov, 11 Nov; 4€ (1st Sun of the month no charge); 05 58 79 13 00; www.museesamadet.org)* in the old abbot's house contains rare and beautiful collections of celebrated Samadet wares; there are items decorated with roses, carnations, butterflies, and dishes in green monochrome with grotesques and *Chinoiseries*. An 18C bourgeois interior, 18C costumes, various workshops and reconstructions of the Royal *faïencerie* are also of interest.

Musée de la Faïence

©Jean-Daniel Sudres/ hemis.fr

The Maison de la céramique contemporaine – Centre culturel du Tursan *(pl. de la Faïencerie; open May–Oct Tue–Sun 2–6pm; 05 58 79 65 45)*, adjoining the tourist office, houses a permanent exhibition of contemporary ceramics, alongside seasonal exhibitions.

Continue N along the D 2. After 5km/3.1mi, turn left onto the D 446.

Vielle-Tursan

From the terrace of the town hall, there is a pleasing view over the rolling landscape of the Tursan region. Wines from the area were exported in the 17C and have recently experienced a renewed popularity. *Courses landaises*, the sport involving deftly avoiding cows with very sharp horns, are held in local arenas.

Continue along the D 65.

Eugénie-les-Bains

The town, created in 1861, is named for the Empress Eugénie, considered the "godmother" of the town. Two springs, L'Impératrice and Christine-Marie, provide relief to visitors suffering from rheumatism, obesity, urological and intestinal problems. The spa *(www.ville-eugenie-les-bains.fr)* also offers short stays for certain treatments.

Head NE out of Eugénie; turn left onto the D 11 towards Grenade-sur-l'Adour. Before Larrivière, turn right.

Notre-Dame-du-Rugby, Larrivière

Southwest France is famous for its love of rugby. And fellow lovers of the sport will want to stop at this "church of the oval ball". Each year thousands of rugby fans travel here, many leaving mementos of their clubs – and the stained-glass windows are all rugby themed.

Courses landaises, Vielle-Tursan

©Jean-Daniel Sudres/ hemis.fr

Continue to Larrivière, then follow signs to Grenade-sur-l'Adour.

Grenade-sur-l'Adour

1 pl. des Déportés, 40270 Grenade-sur-l'Adour. Open Jul–Aug Mon–Sat 8.30am–12.30pm, 2–6pm; Sept–Jun Mon–Tue and Thurs 8.30am–noon, 1.30–6pm, Fri 8.30am–1pm. 05 58 45 45 98. www.tourismegrenadois.com. 14C English *bastide* town containing two museums: **Petit musée de l'Histoire landaise** (*open Jul–Sept Tue–Sun am, rest of year Wed–Sun am; 3€ (under 10 years no charge); 05 58 76 05 25 or 06 70 45 24 20*), covering local history during the early 20C; and **Pavillon de la Résistance et de la Déportation** (*opening hours as per Petit musée de l'Histoire landaise; 05 58 45 45 98 or 06 70 45 24 20*), which honours local villagers who were deported during World War, following Resistance action against a German convoy on 3 June, 1944.

Leave Grenade E along the N 124 back to Aire-sur-l'Adour.Addresses

ADDRESSES

STAY

Camping Les Ombrages de l'Adour – *r. des Graviers. 05 58 71 75 10. hetapsarl@yahoo.fr. Open mid-Mar–Nov. 100 pitches.* Close to the town centre and its arenas, with good shady pitches. Recently added four mobile homes (available by the night).

Hôtel Le Relais des Landes – *28 av. du 4-Septembre. 05 58 71 66 17. www.lerelaisdeslandes.com. 31 rooms. 7€.* Calm riverside location for this modern building. Practical, well-equipped bedrooms, with a pool and outside terrace overlooking the Adour.

Chambre d'hôte Le Mas – *17 r. du Château. 05 58 71 91 26. www.le-mas.net. 3 rooms and 2 suites.* A former notary's house close to the city centre. A contemporary feel, and comfortable rooms. Pool, terrace, garden, and fresh market produce at the *table d'hôte* (book ahead;).

EAT

Chez l'Ahumat – *2 r. Pierre-Mendès-France. 05 58 71 82 61. Closed 17–31 Mar and 2 wks Sept. 12 rooms. 5€.* An overnight stay at Chez l'Ahumat allows you to discover gastronomic Gascogne cooking at your leisure. Expect generous servings of regional cuisine, best sampled by choosing one of the well-priced menus. Food is served in the two rustic-looking dining rooms, with a collection of antique plates on the walls.

Les Bruyères – *1km/0.6mi N of Aire-sur-l'Adour via the N 124. 05 58 71 80 90. Closed Sun and 2 wks Oct. 8 beds. 5.50€.* Attractive old house with garden and terrace. Regional cooking on the menu. Bedrooms also, clean and quiet if a little bare.

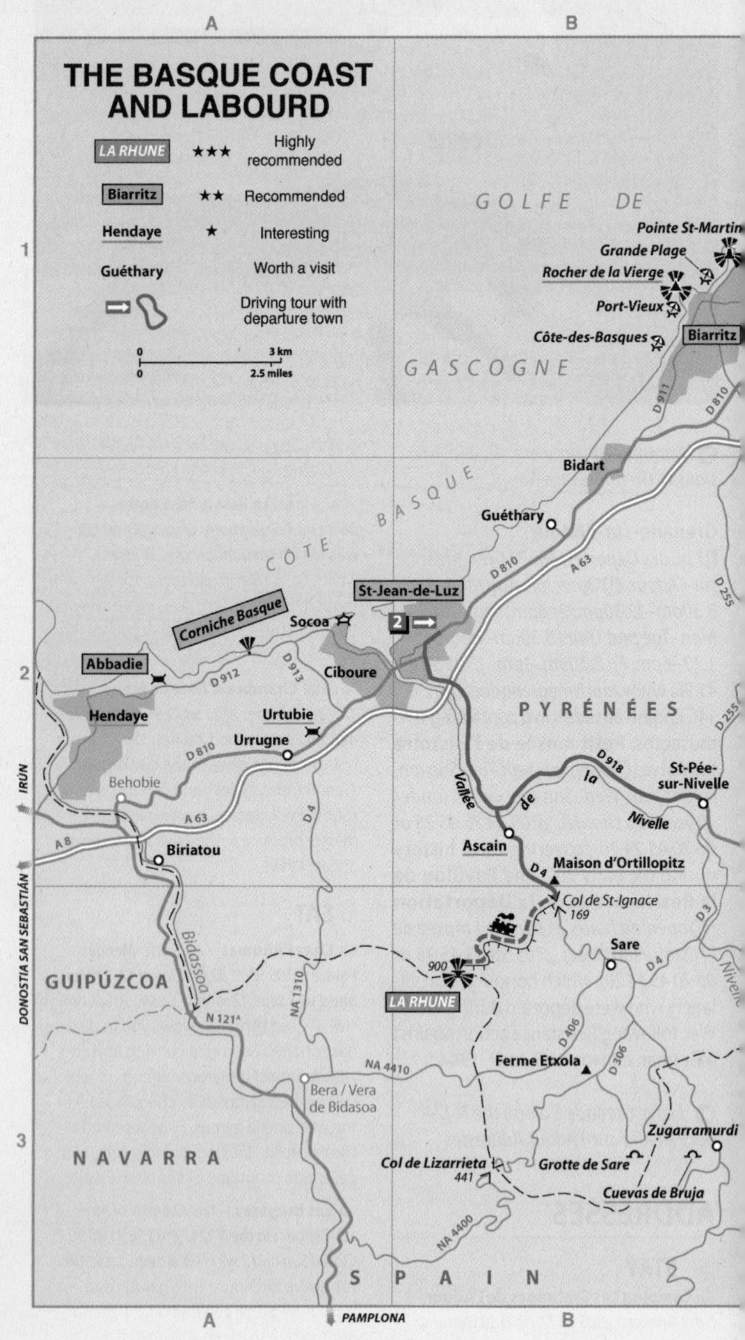
THE BASQUE COAST AND LABOURD
LA RHUNE ★★★ Highly recommended
Biarritz ★★ Recommended
Hendaye ★ Interesting
Guéthary Worth a visit
Driving tour with departure town
0 3 km
0 2.5 miles
GOLFE DE GASCOGNE
Pointe St-Martin
Grande Plage
Rocher de la Vierge
Port-Vieux
Côte-des-Basques
Biarritz
Bidart
Guéthary
CÔTE BASQUE
St-Jean-de-Luz
Socoa
Corniche Basque
Abbadie
Ciboure
Hendaye
Urtubie
Urrugne
Behobie
Biriatou
IRÚN
DONOSTIA SAN SEBASTIÁN
PYRÉNÉES
St-Pée-sur-Nivelle
Vallée de la Nivelle
Ascain
Maison d'Ortillopitz
Col de St-Ignace 169
Sare
900
LA RHUNE
GUIPÚZCOA
Bidassoa
Ferme Etxola
Bera / Vera de Bidasoa
NAVARRA
Col de Lizarrieta 441
Grotte de Sare
Zugarramurdi
Cuevas de Bruja
SPAIN
PAMPLONA
D 911
D 810
A 63
D 255
D 912
D 913
D 918
D 4
D 3
D 406
D 306
A 8
N 121A
NA 1310
NA 4410
NA 4400

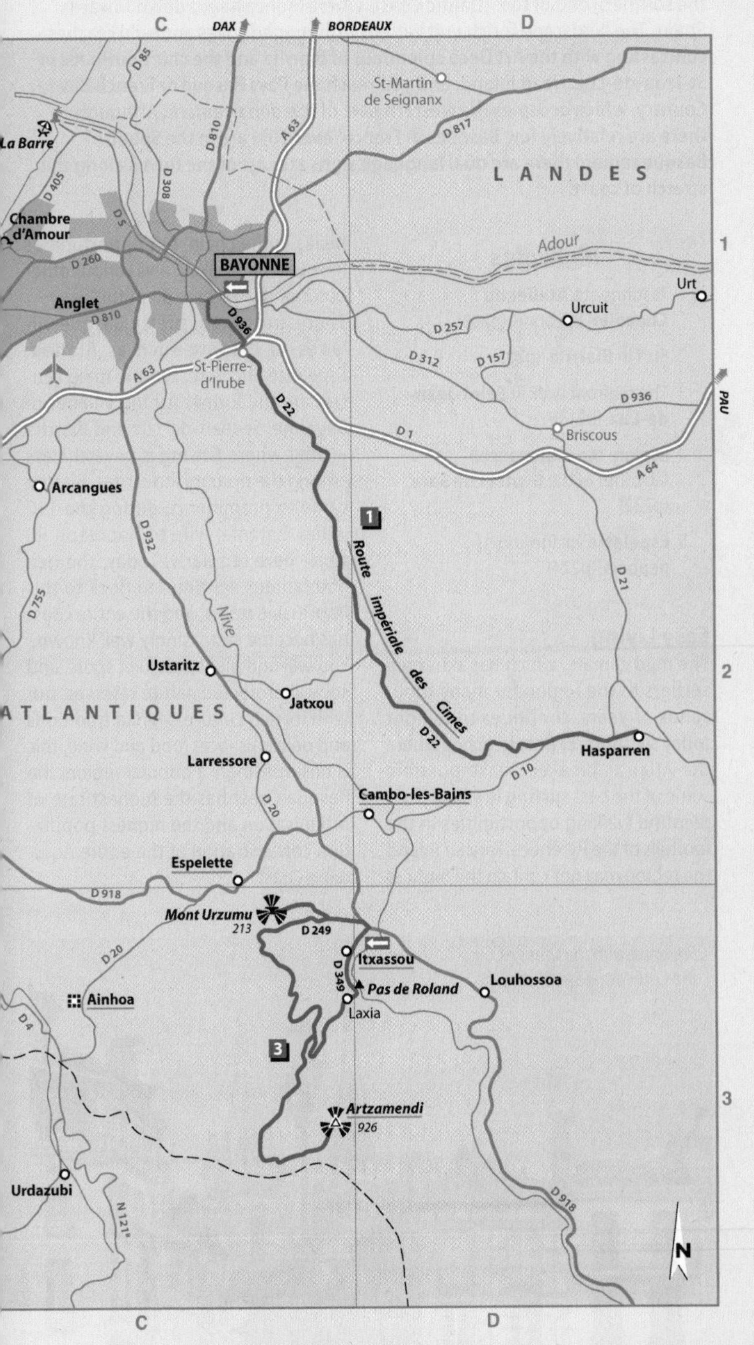

DAX
BORDEAUX
St-Martin de Seignanx
La Barre
LANDES
Chambre d'Amour
Adour
BAYONNE
Anglet
Urt
Urcuit
St-Pierre-d'Irube
PAU
Briscous
Arcangues
1
Route impériale des Cimes
Nive
Ustaritz
Jatxou
ATLANTIQUES
Hasparren
Larressore
Cambo-les-Bains
Espelette
Mont Urzumu
213
Itxassou
Pas de Roland
Louhossoa
Laxia
Ainhoa
3
Artzamendi
926
Urdazubi
N

THE BASQUE COAST AND LABOURD

The Basque coastline lies within the Pyrénées-Atlantiques *département* at the southern end of the Atlantic Coast, where France heads down towards Spain. The landscape is rich and varied, with rugged coves and wild reaches contrasting with the Art Deco splendour of Biarritz and the chic boutiques of St-Jean-de-Luz. Head inland, and you reach the Pays Basque or French Basque Country, which occupies the western part of the *département*. Although there are relatively few Basques in France (over 90% are in the Spanish Basque region) there are dual language signs at most of the towns along this stretch of coast.

Highlights

1. Tastings at **L'Atelier du Chocolat**, Bayonne (p203)
2. Surf in **Biarritz** (p205)
3. The seafront walk in **Saint-Jean-de-Luz** (p213)
4. Explore the subterranean labyrinth of the **Grottes de Sare** (p222)
5. **Espelette** village and its peppers (p224)

Easy Living

The mild climate, which has attracted settlers to the region for many thousands of years, continues to delight today's visitors. Expect beaches where the Atlantic breakers make possible some of the best **surfing** in France, and plentiful walking opportunities in the foothills of the Pyrénées. Farther inland the region may not contain the highest peaks in the chain, but opportunities for climbing, walking and various other outdoor pursuits are plentiful.

There are several pretty Basque villages to explore such as Ainhoa, Espelette and Sare, but the main centres are the former fishing villages of Bayonne, St-Jean-de-Luz and Biarritz – cities where **fishing** is nevertheless among the primary industries. Biarritz came to prominence during the 19C when Eugénie, wife of Napoleon III, came here regularly. Today, the rich and famous continue to flock to this impressive resort, and the entire coast has become increasingly well known. You will find plenty of quiet spots, and several protected nature reserves, but with its rich culture, myriad traditions and delicious local food and wine, this is unsurprisingly a popular region; the Basque Coast has the highest rate of urbanisation and the highest population concentration of the entire Aquitaine Coast.

Bayonne with the spires of the Cathédrale Ste-Marie

S. Sauvignier/MICHELIN

Bayonne★★

The heart of this lively and interesting town combines good shopping facilities with picturesque old streets, ramparts and quays on the south bank of the Adour. The main ramparts extend from the 16C Château-Vieux (Old Castle) to the Spanish Gate. Parc de Mousserolles, on the eastern side of the town known as Petit Bayonne, is a pleasant place for a stroll, with children's playgrounds and a small lake. The citadel overlooking the suburb of St-Esprit, on the northern bank of the river, was built by Vauban.

- **Population:** 44 406
- **Michelin Map:** 342: D-2
- **Info:** pl. des Basques, Bayonne. 08 20 42 64 64. www.bayonne-tourisme.com.
- **Location:** Bayonne lies near the coast on the boundary between the Landes and the Basque Country, where the River Nive joins the Adour.
- **Parking:** There are several car parks along the riverbanks, as well as in the centre of town (*see map*).
- **Don't Miss:** Cathédrale Ste-Marie; Museé Basque; Musée Bonnat; the Fêtes de Bayonne (late Jul–early Aug).
- **Timing:** Allow half a day to explore the Old Town and visit the Cathédrale Ste-Marie.

A BIT OF HISTORY

In the 12C Bayonne was part of the dowry of Eleanor of Aquitaine. When Eleanor's second husband, Henry Plantagenet, assumed the Crown of England in 1154, Bayonne became English, and remained so for three centuries.

During the Hundred Years' War, a naval force from Bayonne served with the English fleet. The port was bursting with merchandise and the town flourished. However, after the city fell to the French in 1451, the integration of Bayonne into the Kingdom of France brought heavy penalties. A war indemnity had to be paid and the English market, which had made the town prosperous, was lost.

The French kings encroached on local freedom more than their English counterparts, and laws and legal documents which they decreed, from then on, had to be written in French and not in Gascon, the local language related to Occitan and Basque. This created deep-rooted resentment among the inhabitants of Bayonne. In the 16C Charles IX decided to reopen the port, which in the meantime had silted up. The direct channel to the sea was completed in 1578 and trading began again.

Zenith

The prosperity of Bayonne reached its peak in the 18C. The Chamber of Commerce was founded in 1726. Trade with Spain, Holland and the West Indies, together with cod fishing off Newfoundland and local shipbuilding, gave the port as much business as it could handle.

Bayonne was declared a free port in 1784, and this trebled its traffic. In the same year, it was included in the famous series by the painter Claude Joseph Vernet, The Great Ports of France. The spoils of war on the high seas were considerable, and affluent citizens commissioned many privateers. The ministers of Louis XIV – Seignelay, the eldest son of Colbert, and Pontchartrain – officially decreed a system of dividing the spoils: one-tenth was to go to the Admiral of France, two-thirds to the shipowners, and what was left to the crew. A sum was also set aside for widows, orphans and ransoms to release prisoners from the Barbary pirates.

The town's Corporation of Ironworkers and Armourers is well known: their members invented the bayonet – named after Bayonne and first used by the French infantry in 1703.

WALKING TOUR

2hrs30min.

Nestling in the angle created at the joining of the Nive and the Adour rivers, **Petit Bayonne** is the town's most popular district; the narrow streets covered with graffiti are lined with small bars which come to life in the evening.

Head from the pl. de la Liberté, along the Left Bank of the Nive, above its confluence with the Adour.

Place de la Liberté

This is a busy square at the western end of Pont Mayou; the bridge crosses the River Nive at the northern end of the Old Town. The town hall, the local administrative offices and the theatre, all under the same roof, stand at one end of the square. The town's motto *nunquam polluta* ("never spoiled") is engraved on the marble paving.

From here, take r. du Port-Neuf.

Rue du Port-Neuf

This charming pedestrian precinct is lined with low arcades, beneath which famous pastry shops and confectioners tempt passers-by with mouthwatering displays of chocolates. The art of chocolate-making was brought to Bayonne in the 17C by Jews whose ancestors had been banished from Spain and Portugal.

Take r. de la Monnaie, which will lead you down towards the cathedral.

Cathédrale Ste-Marie★

r. Notre-Dame. Open Mon–Sat 7am–12.30pm, 3–7pm. No charge. 05 59 59 17 82. www.cathedrale-de-bayonne.fr.st.

St Mary's Cathedral was built between the 13C and the 16C in the characteristic style of churches built in northern France. Initially, there was only one south tower. The north tower and both steeples were added in the 19C.

A 13C sculpted knocker, known as a sanctuary ring, is fixed to the north door, leading to the transept. Any fugitive criminal who seized the knocker was assured of sanctuary within the church.

Inside, the windows in the nave incorporate fine examples of Renaissance stained glass. In the second chapel on the right (dedicated to St Jerome), a splendid window dating from 1531 depicts The Canaanite's Prayer. In the sixth chapel, a commemorative plaque (1926) recalls the Miracle of Bayonne (a celestial apparition in 1451), when English Bayonne was under siege. According to legend, a great white cross surmounted by a crown appeared in the sky, and then the crown turned into a fleur-de-lis, the emblem of France. The townsfolk interpreted this as a sign from God that He wished them to be French, and so discarded the banners and pennants bearing the red cross of St George in favour of those bearing the white cross of France. The following day, Bayonne surrendered.

The harmonious lines and beautiful proportions within the cathedral can best be appreciated from the centre of the three-tiered nave, with its ribbed vaulting, triforium and clerestory windows.

Proceed to the ambulatory where the architecture is reminiscent of the Champagne region; the ribbed vaulting of the five radiating apsidal chapels was decorated by Steinheil at the end of the 19C.

Cloisters★

pl. Louis-Pasteur. Open daily mid-May–mid-Sept 9am–12.30pm, 2–6pm; early Oct–mid-May 9am–12.30pm, 2–5pm. Closed 1 Jan, 1 May, 1 Nov, 25 Dec. No charge.

Three galleries remain from a fine 14C Gothic ensemble, with attractive twinned bays. A number of ancient

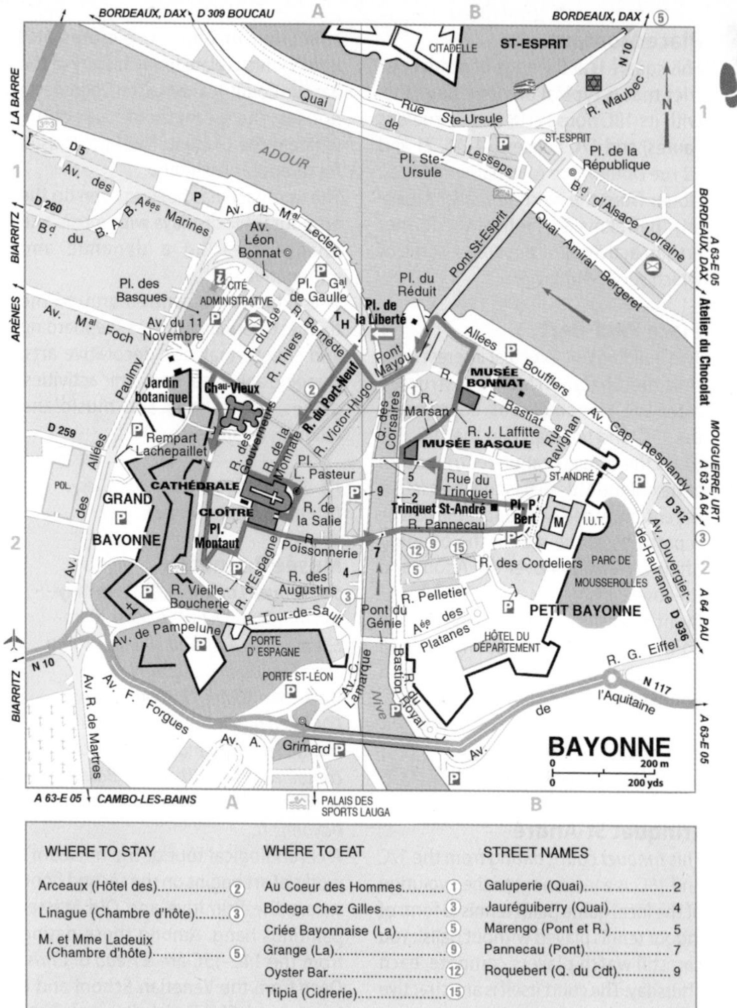

funerary stones can be seen.

From the south gallery, there is a fine view of the cathedral and its windows, celebrated for their vast dimensions and unusual design.

Return to the cathedral gates and head up r. des Gouverneurs towards Château-Vieux and its ramparts.

Château-Vieux

Built in the 12C, then reworked by Vauban in the 17C, Château-Vieux is an important example of medieval military architecture. It is not open for visitors but if the gate is open, you are able to view the interior courtyard.

Botanical Gardens

allée de Tarride. Open 15 Apr–15 Oct Tue–Sat 9.30am–noon, 2–6pm. No charge. 05 59 46 60 93.
Overlooking the ramparts is a Japanese-style garden with over 1 000 plant species.

Return to the Rampart Lachepaillet and head to r. des Faures via r. des Prébendés, ending up at pl. Montaut.

Place Montaut

This square is at the edge of a quiet district that is typical of Vieux Bayonne, with its 18C houses (18 and 51 rue des Faures) and 17C houses (14–16, 21 and 23 rue Douer). The road names (Faures, Douer from the word *tonnelier* meaning "barrel maker") reflect the former artisan activities of the area – some of which survive today.

Place Paul-Bert

Two buildings of particular interest here: first the Château-Neuf. Constructed after the French retook Bayonne in the 15C, and renovated in the 19C, it is today the administration centre, and an annex of the Musée Basque *(turn left at the entrance, and head under the porch)*. A pathway at the rear of the building offers a viewpoint over the Adour and the town.
Right next door is the Gothic Revival Église St-André, built between 1856 and 1862. Inside are paintings by Léon Bonnat and Eugène Pascau.

Continue onto r. du Trinquet, opposite the church.

Trinquet St-André

This *trinquet* court, dating from the 17C and 18C, is a testament to the evolution of the local game palm tennis (a form of indoor tennis played without balls). You can still watch players compete, each Thursday. The court itself is an attractive wooden structure.

Return to the Musée Basque via r. Pontrique and r. Marengo.

Musée Basque et de l'Histoire de Bayonne★★★

Maison Dagourette, 37 quai des Corsaires. Open Jul–Aug Wed 10am–9.30pm, Thu–Tue 10am–6.30pm; Sept–Jun Tue–Sun 10am–6.30pm. Closed public holidays. 5.50€, no charge Wed 6.30–9.30 (Jul–Aug), 1st Sun of month (Sept–Jun); , 9€ combined ticket with Musée Bonnat. 05 59 59 08 98. www.musee-basque.com.
Created in 1924, this museum has a vast collection of objects, pictures and books which relate to the history of the Basque Country. The Maison Dagourette houses the permanent collection, whereas the Château-Neuf site is used for temporary exhibits.
The approach has been to liven up the ethnographic displays with music and images creating a dynamic and informative space.
The exhibits are centred around the themes of farming (such as shepherding and cheese-making); decorative arts; shipping and other economic activities; games, sports, arts and music and religious traditions.

Take r. Marsan and r. Jacques-Laffitte to Musée Bonnat.

Musée Bonnat★★

5 r. Jacques-Laffitte. Open May–Jun and Sept–Oct Wed–Mon 10am–6.30pm; Jul–Aug Wed 10am–9.30pm, Thu–Tue 10am–6.30pm; Nov–Apr Wed–Mon 10am–12.30pm, 2–6pm. Closed public holidays. 5.50€, no charge 1st Sun of month (Sept–Jun); 9€ combined ticket with Musée Basque. 05 59 59 08 52. www.museebonnat.bayonne.fr.
A chronological tour of the museum's works of art begins on the second floor, where the Primitive and Old Master paintings hang. Among those dating from the 14C–15C are a *Head of Christ Dead* from the Venetian School and a *Virgin and Child with Pomegranate* attributed to the School of Botticelli.
The Rubens Room contains canvases showing *Apollo and Daphne* and *The Triumph of Venus*.
The 17C–18C artists represented include Vouet *(Roman Charity)* and Tiepolo (study for the royal palace in Madrid). From the Spanish and English schools from the 17C to the early 19C, there are works by Ribera *(Woman Tearing Out Her Hair)*, Murillo *(San Salvador de Horta and the Inquisitor of Aragon)*, Goya *(Portrait of Don Francisco de Borja)*, Constable *(Hampstead Heath)* and Hoppner *(Head of a Woman)*.
19C French painting is represented by

The Oath of the Horati (School of David), several works by Ingres including *The Bather, Study of a Naked Young Man* by Flandrin and, on the first floor, paintings by Delacroix, Degas and Léon Bonnat, the artist who assembled this superb collection during his lifetime (1833–1922) and left it to his native town.

ADDITIONAL SIGHT

L'Atelier du Chocolat★

7 allée de Gibéléou. ZA Ste-Croix, in St-Esprit district. Signposted from pl. de la République. Follow bd d'Alsace-Lorraine, past railway and roundabout, then first left and immediate right. Open Mon–Sat Jul–Aug 9.30am–6.30pm; Sept–Jun 9.30am–12.30pm, 2–6pm. 5.60€ (with tasting, 4–12 years 2.80€). 05 59 55 70 23. www.atelierduchocolat.fr.

The chocolatier Andrieu has created an interactive exhibit which explains the origins of chocolate, each stage of its fabrication, and its final presentation; from setting in moulds to choosing the right packaging. Clear and well presented, with explanatory boards and videos, and plenty of opportunities to smell, touch and taste. Workshops are run at regular intervals, and all visits end with a tasting.

DRIVING TOUR

1 ROUTE IMPÉRIALE DES CIMES (NAPOLEON I'S SCENIC HIGHWAY)

From Bayonne to Hasparren, 25km/15.5mi. Allow 1hr30min.

Leave Bayonne to the SE by the D 936. At the far end of St-Pierre-d'Irube turn right onto the D 22.

Napoleon I had this winding route carved out through the mountains, to link between Bayonne and St-Jean-Pied-de-Port. The **view**★ opens out on the Basque coastline and the summits of the Pyrénées nearest the sea – La Rhune, the jagged crest of Les Trois Couronnes and Le Jaizkibel, which at this distance looks like a steeply contoured island.

As the road approaches Hasparren the Basque Pyrénées of the upper Nive basin stretch from La Rhune to L'Artzamendi.

ADDRESSES

STAY

Hôtel des Arceaux – *26 r. du Port-Neuf. 05 59 59 15 53. www.hotel-arceaux.com. 11 rooms. 7€.* Small hotel on a pedestrianised road in the town centre. Some recently renovated rooms, individually decorated. Warm welcome also.

NEARBY

Relais Linague – *Chemin Linague, 64990 Urcuit. 05 59 42 97 97. www.relaislinague.com. 4 rooms.* Restful location, in the middle of a 12ha/30-acre farm that dates from the 17C. Each bedroom contains antique furniture, good-quality beds and bedding, and plenty of individual character. A *table d'hôte* also (book food in advance), often with Spanish influence.

Chambre d'hôte M. et Mme Ladeuix – *26 r. Salvador-Allende, Tarnos (5km/3.1mi N of Bayonne via the N 10). 05 59 64 13 95. www.enaquitaine.com. 4 rooms.* The perfect spot for those looking for peace and quiet. A park with chestnuts, mimosas, banana trees, pears, maples. A vast lawn with a pool, a pen where ewes graze near the rabbit hutches and chicken cages. The rooms are simple but comfortable. Self-catering cottage for four.

EAT

Au Cœur des Hommes – *64 quai des Corsaires. 05 59 59 51 17. Closed Sun.* Artisan cooking at its best. Attractive decoration. Chef Jean-Pierre and his son Jérôme serve up great bistro food, with the emphasis on local ingredients and daily market specials. Pretty terrace along the banks of the Nive.

La Criée Bayonnaise – *14 quai Augustin-Chaho. 05 59 59 56 60. Open Mon–Sat lunch and dinner.* A few tables on an outside terrace, the rest in the intimate dining room. Simple, welcoming, and great food.

Oyster Bar – Café du Midi – *24 quai Augustin-Chaho. ℘05 59 59 31 35. Closed Mon.* Pantxika offers a warm welcome at this new bar-bistro on the quayside of Bayonne. On the menu: Gillardeau oysters, Spanish ham, smoked salmon from the Pyrénées, salads, local fish… all to be eaten either at the bar, in the restaurant, or on the terrace.

Bodega Chez Gilles – *23 quai de l'Amiral-Jauréguiberry. ℘05 59 25 40 13. www.bodegachezgilles.com. Open lunch and evening.* Welcoming atmosphere with exposed stone walls and an attractive terrace. Local Bayonne specialities abound: anchovies, jambon de Bayonne, cod, beef, lamb and *piquillo* peppers.

La Grange – *26 quai Galuperie. ℘05 59 46 17 84. Closed Sun.* Set in a rustic décor of brick walls and arches, this establishment serves a regularly updated menu of Basque dishes and regional wines written on blackboards.

Cidrerie Ttipia – *27 r. des Cordeliers. ℘05 59 46 13 31. http://ttipia.364.fr. Open summer evenings only; rest of year lunch and evening Mon–Sun lunch.* A trip to the heart of Spanish Basque-style cider houses, with exposed oak beams and cider-making equipment on display. Delicious traditional food, and excellent atmosphere.

Péniche Talaia – *quai Pedros, in front of the town hall. ℘05 59 44 08 84. Open Tue–Sat.* Traditional southwest food, good views over Bayonne.

BARS AND CAFÉS

Le Petit Bayonne – Right where the Nive river meets l'Adour, le Petit Bayonne is the quarter where the city's young folk gather – the beating heart of local nightlife. As soon as the weather warms up, so does the general party atmosphere, thanks to the bars and restaurants crowding the neighbourhood. Between la rue des Cordeliers, la rue Pannecau and la rue des Tonneliers, there are a good thirty establishments. Among them, you may want to try La Txalupa *(26 r. des Cordeliers)* and the Killarney Pub *(33 r. des Cordeliers; ℘05 59 25 75 51)*.

Chai Ramina – *11 r. Poissonnerie. ℘05 59 59 33 01. Closed Sun–Mon.* Ramina, a former rugby champion, found a new calling 25 years ago when he opened this pub, a locals' bar with a lively atmosphere. A good place to sample whisky – there are 300 varieties here!

ENTERTAINMENT

Arènes de Bayonne – *r. Alfred Bouland. ℘08 92 46 64 64. www.corridas.bayonne.fr.* Tickets also available from the tourist office. From bullfighting to pop concerts, a large variety of shows are organised in the Bayonne arenas.

La Luna Negra – *7 r. des Augustins. ℘05 59 25 78 05. www.lunanegra.fr. Open Wed–Sat 7pm–2am. Closed Aug (except fêtes de Bayonne early Aug) and Sun–Tue.* This dynamic café-theatre offers a different show every evening: plays, songfests, cabarets, one-man shows, jazz, blues or rock concerts, storytelling sessions and readings of great literary works. Painting and photography exhibitions are also organised regularly.

Théâtre de Bayonne – *pl. de la Liberté. ℘05 59 59 07 27. www.snbsa.fr. Tickets also available from branches of FNAC. ℘08 92 68 36 22. www.fnac.com.* This is the national theatre of Bayonne and the Sud Aquitaine. All sorts of performances are put on here – plays, dance, opera. They hold a yearly festival called "Jazz in the Ramparts" in mid-July.

SPORT AND LEISURE

Tennis – *L'Aviron Bayonnais, 13 av. André Grimard. ℘05 59 63 33 13. www.aviron-bayonnais.asso.fr. Open Apr–Aug Mon–Tue and Thu–Fri 9am–1pm, 4–8.30pm, Wed and Sat 9am–6pm; Sept–Mar please call for booking. Closed public holidays.* The ancient fortifications of Vauban are the setting for this distinctive tennis club, founded in 1922. Two important tournaments take place at Easter and during the first fortnight of August. 12 courts.

Trinquet Moderne – *60 av. Dubrocq. ℘05 59 59 05 22. www.ffpb.net.* Many barehanded pelota matches take place between the glass walls of this covered *trinquet* (court). The French are among the finest players internationally.

CALENDAR OF EVENTS

Fêtes de Bayonne – *late Jul–early Aug. www.fetes.bayonne.fr.* The Bayonne summer festival includes bullfights, fairs, dances and concerts of traditional Basque music.

Biarritz★★

Pyrénées-Atlantiques

Biarritz, on the borders of the Basque Country, is the most fashionable and most frequented seaside resort in southwest France. The setting is magnificent, with Atlantic rollers breaking against rocks and reefs, impressive cliffs, a small port, and superb bathing beaches. The town's international status has been enhanced by nine easily accessible golf courses, two casinos and numerous sports facilities in the town itself.

- **Population:** 26 690
- **Michelin Map:** 342: C-2
- **Info:** 1 sq. d'Ixelles, Biarritz. ℘05 59 22 37 10. www.biarritz.fr.
- **Location:** The towns of Biarritz, Bayonne and Anglet form one large populated area along the Atlantic Coast, just north of St-Jean-de-Luz and the Spanish border.
- **Parking:** As parking is difficult in Biarritz, it's best to leave your car on the outskirts (such as near the lighthouse) and explore the town on foot.
- **Don't Miss:** The views from La Perspective, Pointe St-Martin and the lighthouse; Rocher de la Vierge.
- **Kids:** Musée de la Mer; Musée du Chocolat; Grande Plage, the town's sandy beach; Plage du Port-Vieux, a sheltered family-friendly beach.

BEACHES

Biarritz owes much of its charm to its hydrangea-lined garden promenades, which follow the contours of the cliffs, over the rocks and along the three main beaches, which have become an international meeting place for surfers and a focal point for local entertainment both day and night.

Grande Plage

Overlooked by the Municipal Casino, the Grande Plage is the largest and most fashionable of Biarritz's beaches. In former times, only the most daring of bathers would swim here, which led to its now forgotten nickname of *Plage des Fous* ("Madman's Beach"). To the north, it becomes Plage Miramar.

Plage du Port-Vieux

Sheltered by two overhanging cliffs, it is a small family beach and a local favourite.

Grande Plage

Y. Kanazawa/MICHELIN

VIPs in Biarritz

At the beginning of the 19C Biarritz was but a small, whale-fishing harbour. The people of Bayonne, when they started coming here to enjoy the sea, made the 5km/3.1mi journey on donkeys or mules. Then Spanish nobility from the far side of the border discovered its charms, and from 1838 onwards, the Countess of Montijo and her daughter Eugénie came each year. When Eugénie became Empress of France she persuaded her husband, Napoleon III, to accompany her on her annual visit to the Basque Coast and he too became captivated by the area. Their first trip together was in 1854. The following year, he commissioned the building of a Neoclassical villa and named it Villa Eugénie (today Hôtel du Palais). Suddenly, Biarritz was famous.

The charm of the town and its growing reputation for discreet luxury, drew the rich, famous and aristocratic from all over Europe. Villas overlooking the sea testify to the growing attractiveness of this seaside resort, whose illustrious list of visitors is hard to rival. The 1920s saw celebrities such as Rostand, Ravel, Stravinsky, Loti, Cocteau and Hemingway. After World War II, the Marquis of Cuevas gave sumptuous parties, whereas the Duke and Duchess of Windsor came here to rest and relax. It was not unusual to run into some of the great film stars of the 1950s and 60s, such as Frank Sinatra, Rita Hayworth and Gary Cooper.

In 1956, while he was filming *The Sun Also Rises*, the American script-writer Peter Viertel had a go at the Atlantic waves with a surfboard he ordered from California. The new sport became an overnight sensation!

Plage de la Côte-des-Basques

Lying at the foot of a cliff which periodically has to be shored up against landslides, this is the most exposed and best surfing beach in Biarritz, because of its long reach; it owes its name to a traditional trip to the coast held on the first Sunday after 15 August every year, which brought Basques from the inland provinces to the seaside.

SIGHTS

Château Javalquinto

sq. d'Ixelles.

An essential stop for the High Society since the Second Empire, Biarritz is filled with sumptuous villas and glittering residences like this one. Designed in a Gothic Revival style by its owner the Duke of Osuna, today it provides a glamorous base for the tourist office.

Before turning onto rue Pellot, stop by rue des Cent-Gardes to admire the Tête de Régina, created by Spanish sculptor Manolo Valdés.

Chapelle Impériale

r. Pellot. Open 15 Apr–15 Jul and 16 Sept–15 Oct Tue, Thu and Sat 3–7pm; 16 Jul–15 Sept Mon–Sat 3–7pm; 16 Oct–Dec Thu 3–5pm. 3€. 05 59 22 37 10.

Empress Eugénie ordered the chapel built in the 19C. Its style is both Romanesque-Byzantine and Hispano-Moorish.

Russian Orthodox Church

8 av. de l'Impératrice. Open Tue, Thu and Sat 4–7pm; school holidays Sat 3–6pm. No charge. 05 59 24 16 74.

Built in 1892, the year of the alliance between France and Russia, it used to be frequented by Russians who spent their holidays in Biarritz, many of whom were famous. The inside of this Byzantine church is more interesting than the outside: the icons are from St-Petersburg.

Pointe St-Martin

av. de l'Impératrice. Lighthouse is open May–Jun and Sept daily 2–7pm; Jul–Aug daily 10am–8pm; Oct–Apr Sat–Sun 2–6pm. 2€. 05 59 22 37 00.

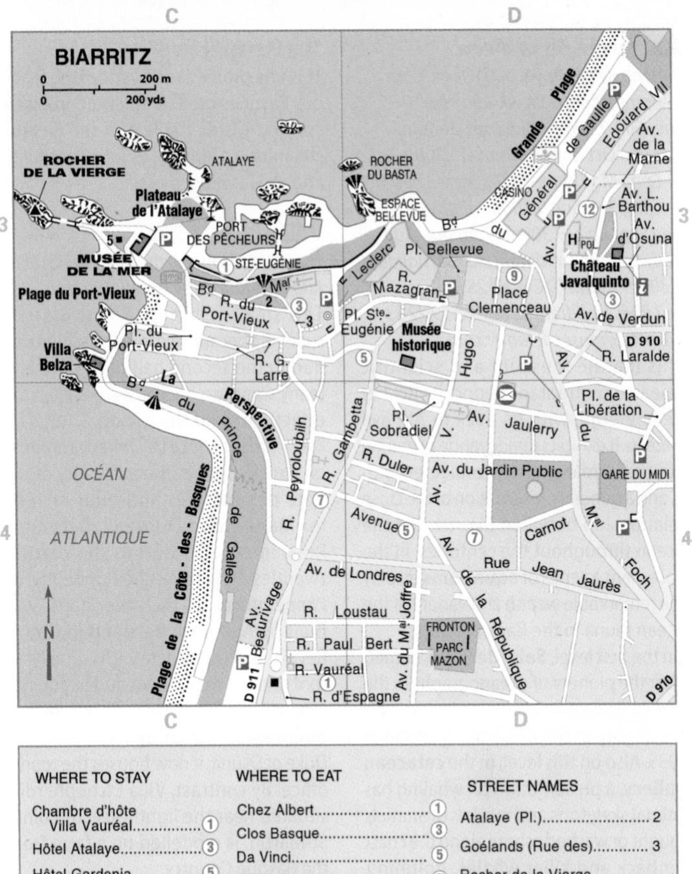

WHERE TO STAY	WHERE TO EAT	STREET NAMES
Chambre d'hôte Villa Vauréal ①	Chez Albert ①	Atalaye (Pl.) 2
Hôtel Atalaye ③	Clos Basque ③	Goélands (Rue des) 3
Hôtel Gardenia ⑤	Da Vinci ⑤	Rocher de la Vierge (Espl. du) 5
Hôtel Maïtagaria ⑦	Il Giardino ⑦	
Le Petit Hôtel ⑨	Le Cachaou ⑫	

The gardens and, in particular, the **lighthouse**, towering 73m/240ft above the sea, offer an excellent **view**★ of the town and the Basque Pyrénées. You will not regret having climbed 248 steps!

Plateau de l'Atalaye

This open stretch of ground lies between Basta Rock and the promontory bearing the town's last remaining *atalaye* or watchtower from which smoke signals were sent to fishermen when whales were sighted. Paths lead down to **Port des Pêcheurs**, a charming fishing village of whitewashed fishermen's cottages, below.

Rocher de la Vierge★

The Virgin's Rock, crowned with a statue of the Virgin Mary, is Biarritz's main landmark. It is surrounded by reefs and joined to the shore by a footbridge, made impassable in rough weather by the breaking waves. It was Napoleon III who had the idea of hollowing out the rock and linking it to the cliff by a wooden bridge. This has since been replaced by a metal one built by Gustave Eiffel.

A gently sloping footpath shaded by tamarisks leads to Rocher du Basta and Grande Plage. Throughout the year, the shoreline is illuminated from nightfall until 1am in the wintertime and 3am in the summertime.

Musée de la Mer★

Plateau de l'Atalaye. Open 1 Jan 2–6pm; 1st and last wk Jan–Mar Tue–Sun 9.30am–12.30pm, 2–6pm; Apr and Oct daily 9.30am–12.30pm, 2–6pm; May Mon–Fri 9.30am–12.30pm, 2–6pm, Sat–Sun 9.30am–6pm; Jun and Sept daily 9.30am–7pm; Jul–Aug daily 9.30am–midnight; school holidays 9.30am–6pm. Closed 25 Dec. 7.80€ (children 5€). 05 59 22 33 34. http://museedelamer.com.

This marine museum and scientific research centre stands opposite Rocher de la Vierge, with its back to Atalaye Plateau. It exhibits a wide range of marine life, the human activity connected with it, and a general presentation of the close relationship between Biarritz and the ocean throughout the centuries. In the basement a series of **aquariums** display the remarkable wealth and variety of the ocean fauna in the Bay of Biscay.

On the first level, **Salle de Folin**, named after the pioneer of oceanography in the Bay of Biscay, contains an exhibit on the history of the museum, founded in 1935. Also on this level, in the **cetacean gallery**, a presentation on whaling has animal skeletons and models of animals caught or washed ashore along the coast (finback and killer whales, dolphins, etc.). Models of boats and navigational instruments complete the section devoted to fishing methods.

The second level contains further information on the resort, including conservation of the coastline, a study of the ocean around Biarritz, and an underwater display of seals and sharks in their natural habitat.

The seals' acrobatics – especially at feeding time *(10.30am, 5pm)* – is wonderful entertainment for young children.

The terrace affords a **panoramic view** of the coast from the Landes to Cape Machichaco in Spain. The ornithological gallery at the end of the tour offers a complete display of all the sedentary and migratory species to be found along the coast and in the Pyrénées. The birdsong of 40 different species resonates in an aviary equipped with an interactive system.

"La Perspective"

This fine promenade overlooking Plage des Basques offers a splendid **view**★★ south towards the last of the Basque summits – La Rhune, Les Trois Couronnes and the Jaizkibel massif.

Villas

Guided tours of the town's villas (Jul–Aug) is organised by the tourist office.

The small fishing port of Biarritz suddenly became extremely fashionable during the second half of the 19C and many sumptuous villas were built in the eclectic style of the period. Thus, Villa Belza *(bd du Prince de Galles)*, standing on a rocky spur at the extremity of the Côte des Basques and built in 1880 for Marie-Belza Dubreuil, became a Russian cabaret during the roaring twenties. Villa La Roche Ronde *(av. de l'Impératrice)*, on the other hand, was built by Alphonse Bertrand in Gothic Revival style, complete with crenellated roof and bartizan. Château Javalquinto *(1 sq. d'Ixelles)* is another Gothic Revival building designed by its owner, the Duke of Osuna; it now houses the tourist office. By contrast, Villa Etchepherdia, situated near the lighthouse of Pointe St-Martin, is modelled on a farm from the Basque Country.

ADDITIONAL SIGHTS

Planète Musée du Chocolat

16 av. Beaurivage. Open Mon–Sat and public holidays 10am–12.30pm, 2–6.30pm; school holidays daily 10am–6.30pm. 6€ (children 4€). 05 59 23 27 72. www.planetemuseedu chocolat.com.

Let yourself be guided by the delicious aromas from this interesting museum devoted to chocolate-making. A display of sculptures, each one in chocolate, is a highlight of the visit.

Asiatica – Musée d'Art Oriental

1 r. Guy-Petit. Open school holidays Mon–Fri 10.30am–6.30pm, Sat–Sun 2–7pm; bank holidays 2–6pm; rest of year Mon–Fri 2–6.30pm, Sat–Sun 2–7pm. Guided visits available on request (2 wks advance). 7€ (children

5€). ☎05 59 22 78 78. www.museeasiatica.com.
This collection of Asian art centres around the life of the Buddha, and offers a vibrant and detailed look at life in India, China, Nepal and Tibet.

EXCURSIONS

Anglet

3.8km/2.4mi.

This coastal town links Biarritz and Bayonne and its success as a resort and tourist centre followed that of Biarritz during the Second Empire. However, geographically it is closer to the countryside of the Silver Coast north of the Adour estuary with its long straight beaches bordered by dunes, and a flat hinterland planted with pines.

Just off **Plage de la Chambre d'Amour** (the main beach), steps lead to the cave (the "Chambre d'amour") in which it is said that two lovers, caught unawares by the rising tide, were trapped and died. Each summer, in late July, Anglet hosts an annual **Beach Rugby Festival** *(www.beachrugbyfestival.com)* on the Plage des Sables d'Or. The esplanade de Quintaou hosts an open-air market every Thursday and Sunday morning, as well as an antiques fair in early August *(contact the local tourist office for further details; ☎05 59 03 77 01; www.anglet-tourisme.com)*. The area is also a haven for golf lovers, with a number of excellent-quality courses.

Surrounding Anglet are 250ha/618 acres of pine trees planted during the Second Empire. They stretch from the forests of Pignada *(to the north)* and Lazaret *(to the east)* over to Chiberta along the coast. The **Forêt du Pignada**★ takes its name from the pine cones that cover its floor at certain times of the year. It covers 220ha/543 acres and contains numerous picnic areas and walking routes. Cycle and bridle paths also pass through here, and a 2.5km/1.5mi exercise circuit opened in recent years.

Bidart

6km/3.7mi S.

The small resort of Bidart, halfway between Biarritz and St-Jean-de-Luz, is built at the highest point on the Basque coastline, on the edge of a cliff.

From Chapelle Ste-Madeleine *(accessible from r. de la Madeleine)*, the clifftop **view**★ looks over the Jaizkibel (a promontory closing off the Fontarabia natural harbour), the Trois Couronnes and La Rhune.

The charming **place centrale** (main square) is framed by the church, the pelota *(jai alai) fronton* and the town hall. Local pelota matches and competitions are always watched by enthusiastic crowds. The church is typically Basque in style with its belfry-porch, fine wooden ceiling, and enormous, brightly coloured 17C altarpiece. The mezzanine galleries were reserved for the men attending services; women sat below.

Guéthary

8.5km/5.3mi S.

Originally a traditional fishing port on a small inlet along the Basque Coast, Guéthary is now a seaside resort with well-to-do Labourd-style villas nestled in spacious grounds. The view from the terrace above the beach stretches northeast as far as Biarritz.

Beyond the N 10, on Elizalda hill, the **church** *(r. de l'Église)* houses a 17C Crucifixion, a 17C *Pietà* and a statue of Monsignor Mugabure (1850–1910), who was born and bred in the region and became the first Archbishop of Tokyo. The town is also known as a gourmet centre, with several well-regarded restaurants.

Arcangues

9.8km/6mi.

This picturesque village is particularly attractive around the church, the inn and the pelota court. Inside the church, with its carved galleries, there is a chandelier and a bas-relief representing the beheading of John the Baptist, patron saint of the parish. The Basque tombstones (a stone disc on a plinth) are set among a panoramic **view**★ of the Basque Pyrénées.

ADDRESSES

STAY

Hôtel Atalaye – *6 r. des Goëlands, Plateau de l'Atalaye. 05 59 24 06 76. www.hotelatalaye.com. Closed 15 Nov–18 Dec. 24 rooms. 6.50€.* This imposing turn-of-the century villa owes its name to the superb Atalaye Plateau overlooking the Atlantic Ocean. The rooms with a sea view are especially attractive. Free parking nearby *(Oct–mid-Jun).*

Hôtel Gardenia – *19 av. Carnot. 05 59 24 10 46. www.hotel-gardenia.com. Closed Dec–Feb. 19 rooms. 6€.* This central hotel with a pink façade has all the charm of a private home. Its quiet, attractive rooms are regularly redecorated. Prices are reasonable considering the location.

Chambre d'hôte Villa Vauréal – *114 r. Vauréal. 06 10 11 64 21. www.villa vaureal.com. Closed Jan. 8€.* Comfortable villa in a large garden full of mature trees, two minutes from the beach. Individual bedrooms. Home-made jams.

Hôtel Maïtagaria – *34 av. Carnot. 05 59 24 26 65. www.hotel-maitagaria.com. 16 rooms. 8.50€.* A warm, friendly reception in this little hotel near the garden, just 500m/550yds from the beach. The rooms, of varying sizes, are bright and functional. Small flower-filled garden in the back.

Le Petit Hôtel – *11 r. Gardères. 05 59 24 87 00. www.petithotel-biarritz.com. Closed fortnight in Nov and Feb. 12 rooms. 9€.* This appealing hotel is ideally located for exploring the town or spending time on the beach. Its soundproofed rooms have been renovated in tones of blue or yellow; all have internet access. The hotel has a seminar room above its restaurant, just 100m/110yds from the hotel.

EAT

Da Vinci – *15 r. Gambetta. 05 59 22 50 88. Closed Mon, Jan, Mon–Wed out of season.* Contrary to what the name may suggest, this restaurant concentrates on Spanish tapas/*pintxos*-style and regional Basque food. Near to the covered market, expect friendly service and a lively atmosphere.

Il Giardino – *62 r. Gambetta. 05 59 22 16 41. www.ilgiardino-biarritz.com. Open Wed–Sat lunch, Tue and Sun evening.* Brightly coloured Italian restaurant. Authentic Italian regional cuisine, with home-cooked feel and generous portions. Well-priced also. Specialities include *spinaci ripieni* (a kind of home-made spinach ravioli), risotto and *spiedini sfiziosi* (brochettes of veal cooked with raisins and pine-nuts), and the wine list is good. Finish up with a tiramisu, and you'll leave thoroughly satisfied.

Le Cachaou – *30 av. Édouard-VI. 05 59 22 59 55* - This recently opened spot from father-son team serves up traditional southwest food, with a Basque flavour in terms of spices and emphasis on local fish and meats. Well located, close to the Grand Plage, town hall and the casino. Tapas-style food also available, based around fresh seasonal produce.

Le Clos Basque – *12 r. Louis-Barthou. 05 59 24 24 96. Closed Sun evening (Sept–Jun), Mon and a fortnight in Feb and Jun.* Excellent local cuisine and a warm, friendly atmosphere mean that there's rarely a spare table in this popular restaurant. Exposed beams and *azulejos* tiles add an Iberian flavour.

Chez Albert – *r. du Port-Vieux. 05 59 24 43 84. www.chezalbert.fr. Closed Wed (Sept–Jun) and Jan.* Situated close to the church of St Eugénie, this busy fish and seafood restaurant affords fine views over the fishing port, but be warned that the terrace fills up quickly during the summer.

BARS AND CAFÉS

La Santa Maria – *esp. du Port-Vieux. 05 59 24 53 11.* The splendid view of the Rocher de la Vierge and the Port-Vieux beach is one of the attractions of this little bar perched on a rock. A terrace, a few stools and a bar counter in a cave make this a pleasant, unpretentious spot where you can sample tapas while listening to the little orchestra.

Le Caveau – *4 r. Gambetta. 05 59 24 16 17. http://lecaveau-biarritz.com.* One of the trendiest bar-discotheques in the region, Le Caveau is popular with locals and visitors, as well as the inevitable stars on holiday. *The* place to be seen in Biarritz.

L'Impérial (Hôtel du Palais) – *1 av. de l'Impératrice. 05 59 41 64 00. www.hotel-du-palais.com.* "La Villa Eugénie", the scene of Napoleon III's love affair with the Empress Eugénie, became the majestic Hôtel du Palais in 1893. Enjoy a glass of champagne and savour the atmosphere in the hotel's elegant bar, the Impérial, where a pianist makes the ambience complete from 7.30–11pm every evening.

ENTERTAINMENT

Casino Barrière de Biarritz – *1 av. Édouard-VII. ✆05 59 22 77 77. www.lucienbarriere.com.* Located on the Grande Plage, this enormous casino has a table games room (roulette, blackjack) and 180 slot machines as well as Le Café de la Plage brasserie, Le Baccara restaurant, Le Flamingo discotheque, a show room (theatre, dance) and a ballroom.

Gare du Midi – *21 bis av. du Maréchal-Foch. ✆05 59 22 44 66. www.entractes-organisations.com. Tickets available from the tourist office.* The city's main theatre, with a seating capacity of 1 400, puts on a range of plays, music concerts and ballets. It is also the home of the Biarritz ballet company.

SHOPPING

Cazaux et fils – *10 r. Broquedis. ✆05 59 22 36 03.* The Cazaux family has been involved in making ceramic pottery since the 18C. Jean-Marie Cazaux is happy to talk about his profession, describing it as "austere and solitary". The boutique also offers personalised creations – each step can be undertaken according to the customer's wishes, from extracting the clay to hand-painting the finishing touches.

Chocolats Henriet – *pl. Clemenceau. ✆05 59 24 24 15.* Established after World War II, Henriet is the local guiding light in chocolates and confectionery, featuring *calichous* (Échiré butter and fresh cream caramels) and *rochers de Biarritz* (bitter chocolate, orange rinds and almonds). Serge Couzigou, *maître chocolatier* responsible for the creation of the Musée du Chocolat *(4 av. de la Marne)*, has been running the shop for the past twenty years.

Fabrique de chistéras Gonzalez – *6 allée des Liserons, Anglet. ✆05 59 03 85 04.* Founded in 1887, the Gonzalez company produces handmade *cestas* (wicker scoops that extend from the protective pelota glove). In one hour you will learn everything about the history and manufacture of pelotas and *cestas*.

Maison Arostéguy

Jacques Sierpinski/hemis.fr

Maison Arostéguy – *5 av. Victor Hugo. ✆05 59 24 00 52. www.epicerie-fine.net.* Founded in 1875, this famous Biarritz grocery store (formerly the "Epicerie du Progrès") has kept its original walls, shelves and façade. The shop specialises in regional fare and also stocks many products difficult to find elsewhere: rare bottles of Bordeaux, prestigious Armagnacs, Basque products, flavoured teas and spices.

SPORT AND LEISURE

Euskal-Jaï Fernand Pujol – *r. Cino-del-duca. ✆05 59 23 91 09.* This pelota Basque school organises ***cesta punta*** competitions nearly every Wednesday and Saturday from June to September.

Hippodrome des Fleurs – *av. du Lac Marion. ✆05 59 41 27 34. www.hippodrome-biarritz.com.* Horse races have been held in this trotter's hippodrome on July and August evenings for over fifty years.

Piscine municipale – *bd du Général-de-Gaulle. ✆05 59 22 52 52.* Located on the shore, this municipal complex features heated seawater pools as well as a jacuzzi, hammam and sauna.

Thermes Marins – *80 r. de Madrid. ✆05 59 23 01 22. www.biarritz-thalasso.com.* This spa features a leisure pool and jacuzzi and offers various treatments, such as affusion or underwater showers, seaweed treatment booths, massages, and sea-air bath booths.

St-Jean-de-Luz★★

Pyrénées-Atlantiques

- **Population:** 13 579
- **Michelin Map:** 342: C-2
- **Info:** 20 bd Victor Hugo, St-Jean-de-Luz. ℘05 59 26 03 16. www.saint-jean-de-luz.com.
- **Location:** St-Jean-de-Luz is located on the Atlantic Coast, S of Biarritz and just 13km/8mi from the Spanish border.
- **Parking:** Park in pl. du Maréchal Foch near pl. Louis XIV and the port.
- **Don't Miss:** The port; Église St-Jean-Baptiste; Maison Louis XIV; the Corniche Basque.
- **Kids:** The railway from Col de St-Ignace to La Rhune.

As a smart summer and winter seaside resort, St-Jean-de-Luz only dates back to 1843; however, as a fishing port, the town is ancient. Today only one house survives from before the great fire of 1558, when the place was sacked by the Spanish. The seafront is determinedly modern. Ste-Barbe headland, reached on foot via promenade de la Plage and boulevard Thiers, offers a fine view southwards across the bay to Socoa fort on its rocky promontory. St-Jean-de-Luz, the most Basque of the towns north of the Spanish border, offers all the attractions and amenities of a beach resort together with the picturesque and briny delights of a busy fishing port.

PORT★

With whaling a thing of the past, local fishermen nowadays rely on hauls of sardines, anchovies and especially tuna fish for their livelihood.

The port is at the inner end of the only anchorage to break the long straight line of the Atlantic Coast between Arcachon and the Bidassoa river. The estuary, nestling between the Socoa and Ste-Barbe headlands, is further protected from westerly gales by massive dykes and the Artha breakwaters.

From the quays there are picturesque views across the busy harbour of the Old Town and inland, in the distance, the great pyramid bulk of La Rhune.

The imposing **Maison de l'Infante** *(quai de l'Infante; open 1 Jun–15 Oct and 25 Oct–5 Nov daily 10am–6pm; 2.50€; ℘05 59 26 36 82)* seems to be guarding the boats. This elegant building in the Louis XIII style, constructed of brick and stone with Italian-style galleries

Port with the Maison de l'Infante on the right

Y. Kanazawa/MICHELIN

overlooking the port, belonged to the rich Haraneder family. The Infanta stayed here with her future mother-in-law, Anne of Austria. In the large 17C room, note the immense sculpted and painted fireplace and the beams decorated with paintings from the school of Fontainebleau.

Rue Mazarin

17C shipowners used to live on the strip of land separating the roadstead from the harbour. The area has retained a few elegant houses; note in particular Maison St-Martin at no 13 rue Mazarin.

Maison Louis XIV★

pl. Louis XIV. Guided tours (30min) Wed–Mon Jun and Sept–15 Oct 11am, 3pm, 4pm, 5pm; Jul–Aug 10.30am–12.30pm, 2.30–6pm; school and public holidays 11am, 3pm, 4pm. 5€. 05 59 26 27 58. www.maison-louis-xiv.fr.

The house now named after the monarch who stayed here was built by the shipowner Lohobiague in 1643. It is an imposing building beside the port, with the façade facing the town distinguished by corbelled turrets at the corners. Inside, the "Old Basque" character of the house is evident in the sturdy, straight-flight staircase which was built by ship's carpenters: like the original floorboards in all the rooms, the treads are kept in place by large, visible, heavy-headed nails which make sanding or planing impossible. From the second-floor landing a passage leads to the apartments where Lohobiague's widow received Louis XIV in 1660; a south-facing, arcaded gallery here offers a splendid view of the Basque Pyrénées.

The huge kitchen boasts an impressive fireplace. The green-panelled dining room contains a marble Directoire table and – a gift from the royal guest to his hostess – a three-piece service in silver-gilt with inlaid enamelwork.

TOWN CENTRE

Modernised now with many pedestrian precincts (rue de la République, rue Gambetta) – the town centre has a special charm of its own. The famous "oldest house", its solid dressed-stone construction contrasting with the red-roofed, white-walled Basque buildings nearby, is at 17 rue de la République, near the harbour.

Église St-Jean-Baptiste★★

r. Gambetta. Open Mon–Sat 8.30am–noon, 2–6pm, Sun 8.30–11.30am, 3–6pm. 05 59 26 08 81.

This is the largest and most famous of all the Basque churches in France; it was founded in the 15C and was being enlarged at the time of Louis XIV's wedding. The bricked-up doorway through which the royal couple left can be seen just inside the main entrance, on the south side.

Externally the architecture is sober, even severe, with high walls and small windows. A vaulted passageway tunnels beneath the massive tower. A fine wrought-iron stairway leads to the galleries.

Interior – The sumptuous, largely 17C interior presents a striking contrast to the church's exterior. Three tiers of oak galleries (five on the end wall) surround the broad, single nave; these, traditionally, are reserved for men. The vaulted roof above the nave is lined with remarkable painted panels.

The chancel, raised high as in all Basque churches, is separated from the nave by a handsome wrought-iron screen. The dazzling gold **altarpiece**★ dates from c.1670 (restored 1987). Amid the columns and entablatures that divide it into three levels, shallow niches hold statues of the Apostles, angels and local saints.

Among other items of interest are the 17C pulpit supported by sphinxes and – in the embrasure of the walled-up doorway – a statue of **Notre-Dame des Douleurs** (Our Lady of Sorrows). Beside this is a small Virgin of the Rosary in ceremonial dress.

ADDITIONAL SIGHTS

Coastline Walk

St-Jean-de-Luz offers easy access to two sections of coastline, each totally different from the other: towards

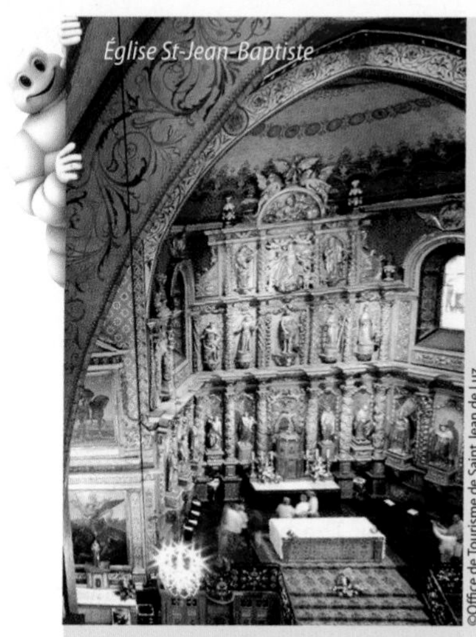

Église St-Jean-Baptiste

The Marriage of Louis XIV

The outstanding historical event connected with St-Jean-de-Luz is the marriage of Louis XIV and Maria Theresa. The wedding between the King of France and the Infanta of Spain, provided for in the Treaty of the Pyrénées, was delayed because of the monarch's passion for Marie Mancini, the niece of Cardinal Mazarin. The situation was resolved when the cardinal – successor to Richelieu and Louis XIV's chief minister – eventually sent the young girl into exile and the king yielded for "reasons of State".

Louis arrived in St-Jean-de-Luz on 8 May 1660 and was lodged, together with the royal retinue, in an imposing mansion which had been built for the shipowner Lohobiague; Maria Theresa stayed in an elegant brick and stone house nearby. On the morning of 9 June the King presented himself at the Infanta's house to claim his bride. The procession moved off towards the church between the Swiss Guards lining the route, and was led by two companies of Gentlemen-at-Arms followed by Cardinal Mazarin dressed in sumptuous robes. Behind him came Louis XIV, in black with lace trimmings, and then the Infanta, who wore a dress of spun silver and a cloak of heavy purple velvet, with a gold crown on her head. The King's brother, known in royal circles simply as "Monsieur", was a few paces behind with their mother, the imposing Anne of Austria. They were followed by the rest of the court. The marriage was solemnised by the Bishop of Bayonne and the service lasted until halfway through the afternoon. The door through which the royal couple left the church was walled up after the ceremony.

The cortège returned to the Infanta's house. From the balcony there the King himself and Mazarin threw commemorative medals to the crowd below. Later the newlyweds dined with the court in Lohobiague's mansion. Following a strict etiquette they were then led to the nuptial couch, and given the traditional blessing by the Queen Mother as she drew its curtains. Louis XIV found in Maria Theresa a gentle and worthy wife, and when she died the King remarked: "This is the first and only time she has ever made me unhappy."

Wedding Gifts

The young Queen was showered with gifts worthy of The Thousand and One Nights. From her husband she received six dazzling sets of jewellery encrusted with diamonds and other precious stones; from Monsieur, 12 jewelled dress ornaments. The present from Mazarin, who was phenomenally wealthy, outshone them all: 1 200 000 livres' worth of diamonds and pearls, a great dinner service in solid gold, and two state coaches, one drawn by six Russian horses, the other by six Indian horses, each with trappings and livery to match the colours of the carriages.

Hendaye, the walk offers views over mountains and the Basque Corniche, or cliff road (see below), but it tracks along a main road, while heading towards Bidart offers green spaces, as well as town and suburban views. For this route, leave from Jardin de la pointe de Ste-Barbe, at the far end of the Promenade des Rochers.

Écomusée de la Tradition Basque

N of St-Jean-de-Luz, along the D 810. Open Apr–Jun and Sept–Oct Mon–Sat 10–11.15am, 2.30–5.30pm; Jul–Aug daily 10am–6.30pm. 6€ includes audioguide (under 12 years 2.50€). 05 59 51 06 06. www.jean-vier.com.

An interesting exhibition told through music and film explains the history and savoir-faire of different aspects of Basque traditional arts and crafts; from the production of *izarra* liqueur, to traditional Basque fabrics (examples from the excellent Jean Vier are on sale at the boutique), berets, espadrilles and gourd drinking pouches, as well as examples of Basque sporting and dancing traditions.

EXCURSIONS

Ciboure

27 quai Maurice-Ravel, 64500 Ciboure. 05 59 47 64 56. The tourist office offers five guided visits (6.50€), three of which cover the seafront and the port.

Little sister to St-Jean-de-Luz, the charming Ciboure clings to the side of a hill, on the southside of the port.

Rue Pocalette has a mix of traditional Labourdian houses made of wooden boards (one from 1589, one the corner with rue Agorette) and imposing, noble-looking stone houses such as that at no 12, near to the church.

Église St-Vincent – 16C. The original church spire is visible from a good distance away, with its wooden construction built over two floors. The church is accessed across an attractive paved forecourt, with a stone cross dating from 1760. The interior contains an attractive blue altarpiece, and a triple gallery along the nave.

The tourist office is housed in the childhood home of **Ravel**, the composer of the famous Boléro, at 27 du quai Boléro. Walking down the quay will bring you to the harbour master's house.

On the other side of the port is the slightly rundown silhouette of the Convent des Récollets, constructed in 1610. The cloisters today house various administration centres, but retain the fountain, donated by Mazarin in 1660, and other restoration works are planned.

La Corniche Basque★★ – From the port, turn right and head up towards the lighthouse (rue du Phare), then the Sémaphore (rue du Sémaphore): for a **viewpoint★★** head southwest along the Basque coastal road, which twists from the Cap du Figuier (Cabo Higuer) in Spain right up to Biarritz. In the foreground, the cliffs plunge towards the rocks, attacked by sea spray. The entire scene is particularly enticing during rough weather out to sea.

Villa Leïhorra – *1 impasse Muskoa.* Built 1926–29 by architect **Joseph Hiriart**, this villa carries its **Art Deco** styling in both its outside architecture and its interior decoration. Everything has been meticulously restored.

Socoa

3km/1.8mi W via the D 912. Park at the port and continue (45min round trip on foot) towards the jetty.

The beginning of the dyke offers a good view of the harbour and the town.Entrance to the anchorage at St-Jean-de-Luz was formerly defended by Socoa fort, which was built under Henri IV and improved by the celebrated military architect Vauban.

Turn right, leaving the port, and climb to the lighthouse along rue du Phare, then follow rue du Sémaphore to the coastal signal station: to the southwest there is a superb **view★★** of the Basque coastline from Cape Higuer (Cabo Higuer) in Spain all the way to Biarritz.

Below, in the foreground, the foliated strata of the cliffs drop steeply down to the crashing waves of the Atlantic.

Château d'Urtubie★

3km/1.8mi SW via the D 810.
Open daily Apr–14 Jul and Sept–Oct 10.30am–12.30pm, 2–6.30pm; 15 Jul–Aug 10.30am–6.30pm. 6€. 05 59 54 31 15. www.chateaudurtubie.net.
This castle was built in the 14C with the authorisation of King Edward III of England; it has undergone many changes since and has become an elegant Classical manor house. Its two towers, which, in the 19C, used to stand on each side of the drawbridge, have now roofs *à l'impériale*. In the central tower, note a remarkable suspended corkscrew staircase from the 16C. In the chapel built in the 17C, the gilding of the choir was restored in the 19C. A bathroom was fitted out behind the sacristy in 1830.
The walls of the château are decorated with large 16C tapestries from Brussels. The château, surrounded with moats until the 18C, is now enshrined within lovely English gardens. The orangery houses an exhibition about cider.

Urrugne

5km/3.1mi SW via the D 810.
The church at the centre of the town presents an almost military aspect, with high walls and few windows. The face of the adjoining belfry-porch bears a sundial.

From the main square in Urrugne, take the hill leading up to Notre-Dame-de-Socorri.

Notre-Dame-de-Socorri

r. Notre Dame de Socorri. 05 59 54 60 80.
This pilgrimage chapel dedicated to the Virgin lies in a lovely **setting**★: the shady clearing on the site of the former cemetery offers views of the undulating countryside dominated by the great spur of La Rhune and, on the horizon, the heights of Jaizkibel and Les Trois Couronnes.

DRIVING TOUR

2 LA RHUNE AND THE VALLÉE DE LA NIVELLE

13km/8mi. Allow 2hrs.

From St-Jean-de-Luz, take the road towards Espelette (D 918). The first stop is Ascain, 6km/3.7mi away.

The Labourd coastline offers a picturesque alternation of rugged cliffs and sandy coves; away from the ocean rollers the landscape is one of gentle hills and wide moors known as *touyas*.
Mountains stand out against the clear skies but they are not high: La Rhune, the culminating peak in the range, rises to no more than 900m/2 953ft above sea level. This excursion will lead you through the traditional villages and rolling hills of this picturesque region.

Ascain★

The pretty village square, with its church, pelota court, traditional houses and welcoming hotels, has a great deal of character. The Basque church with its three-tiered galleries is preceded by a massive belfry-porch; on the right of the cemetery behind it is an interesting disc-shaped stela dating from 1657. In one of the Ascain restaurants there is a *trinquet* – a rectangular indoor court marked out for a variant of pelota, reminiscent of the English game of fives.

Take the D 4, towards Sare.

Maison d'Ortillopitz★

Open Sun–Fri 1 Apr–10 Jul and 23 Aug–25 Oct 2.15–4.45pm; 12 Jul–21 Aug 10.45am–6pm. 7€. 05 59 85 91 92. www.ortillopitz.com.
A shipowner had this large farm built (600sq m/717sq yds on three floors), hence the comfort of the place. A visit will enable you to discover the daily life of a Basque family.
The eye-catching features of the house are the nautical-style wooden stairways; the kitchen with its bread oven; the framework of the attic (built with

Le Petit Train de la Rhune

©Le Petit Train de la Rhune

600 trees!); and the cider press. 18ha/44 acres of land also belong to the estate of Ortillopitz including vineyards and an orchard.

Continue along the D 4 towards Sare until you reach the Col de St-Ignace. Free parking.

La Rhune★★★

From Col de St-Ignace (1hr10min round trip by rack-railway). Trains operate end Mar–Sept and 24 Oct–5 Nov daily 10am, 3pm; 1–23 Oct Tue–Wed and Fri–Sun 10am–3pm; trains depart every 35min in summer. 14€ return (children 8€ return). 05 59 54 20 26. www.rhune.com.

The train journey, established in 1924, is well worth it. It is possible to come back on foot (*wear suitable walking shoes*). Enquire before leaving about the visibility on the summit.

La Rhune (in Basque *larrun* means "good pastureland") is a symbol of the French Basque Country. From the summit (alt 900m/2 953ft; television transmitter) of the frontier-mountain, there is a superb **panorama**★★★ over the ocean (Bay of Biscay), the Forest of the Landes, the Basque Pyrénées and, southwards, the Bidassoa Valley.

Return to Ascain and take the D 918; St-Pée is 8km/5mi to the E.

St-Pée-sur-Nivelle

pl. du Fronton, 64310 St-Pée-sur-Nivelle. 05 59 54 11 69.

All you need is to wander through the streets of St-Pée, lined on each side with traditional houses with their painted shutters, to remember that you are truly in the heart of Basque Country here. The oldest houses surround the church, and line up along the banks of the Nivelle.

Église des Sts-Pierre-et-Paul – Of particular interest here are the cornices, with their intricate carvings which could depict either a rising sun or a seashell. These dominate the 17C framed altar-piece, painted in gold and pale blue, made in honour of St Peter, patron saint of the parish.

Château – Towards Cambo. Once belonging to the wealthy Seigneurs of St-Pée, one of the most powerful families in the region, this was the site of witch trials led by Pierre de Lancre in the 1600s. Destroyed in a fire in 1793, all that remains is one large square tower from the 15C and 17C, as well as some 18C buildings.

ADDRESSES

STAY

Camping Goyetchea – *Quartier Ibarron, 64310 St-Pée-sur-Nivelle (3.8km/2.4mi W of St-Pée-sur-Nivelle by the D 918 and D 855, rte d'Ahetze to Ibarron. 05 59 54 19 59. www.camping-goyetchea.com. Open mid-Jun–mid-Sept. 140 pitches 23.70€.* This campsite was taken over in 2002 by two dynamic sisters. The 140 pitches cover 3ha/7 acres and are well maintained. Calm and welcoming.

Camping Zélaïa – *64310 Ascain (2.5km/1.5mi W on the D 4, rte d'Urrugne (and col d'Ibardin)). 05 59 54 02 36. www.campingzelaia.com. From 40€/night–735€/wk.* Mobile homes and wooden cabins onl, for 4–6 people. Shady grounds over 2.4ha/6 acres, clean, nearly-new, facilities.

Hôtel Axafla-Baïta – *rte d'Olhette, 4310 Ascain. 05 59 54 00 30 . www.hotel-achafla-baita.com. Closed 3 wks Nov. 11 rooms.* The Inda family have owned this hotel for three generations. Undergoing a complete renovation in 2003, they now have 11 bedrooms, some with views over the mountains. Basque food served, either on the terrace on warm days, or in front of the fire when it's cold outside.

Chambre d'hôte Nun Obeki *–6 r. Élie-de-Sèze. 05 59 26 30 71. www.nunobeki.com. 5 rooms. 7€.* Large Basque house converted into an attractive *chambres d'hôtes*. Simple rooms, with a few apartments and a separate villa. Good flexibility for sleeping arrangements. Cosy decoration, close to the beach and town centre, and a lovely quiet garden.

Chambre d'hôte Olhabidea – *Maison Olhabidea, Sare (13km/8mi SE of St-Jean-de-Luz via the D 918 and D 4). 05 59 54 21 85. www.olhabidea.com. Closed Dec–Feb. 3 rooms. Restaurant. Closed Mon–Tue.* This typical 17C–18C house was restored by local craftsmen. The rooms, with their pretty Basque colours and waxed furniture, are smart and comfortable. Make sure that you book in advance in season – this is a popular B&B with a growing reputation.

Hôtel Ohartzia – *28 r. Garat. 05 59 26 00 06 . www.hotel-ohartzia.com. 17 rooms. 7€.* Central location for this attractive blue-shuttered property. Several of the rooms look out over the shady, well-planted garden, while the others have views over the road, the brasserie and its bustling terrace. The restaurant concentrates on local dishes.

EAT

Piper Beltz – *22 r. Garat. 05 59 26 14 81. Closed Tue evening and Wed. 10/25€.* Young owners who prepare an inventive, varied menu, with generous servings. It's all about the pleasure here – Basque specialities, local spices, fresh salads. Attractive terrace.

Tarterie Muscade – *20 r. Garat. 05 59 26 96 73. Closed 12 Nov–6 Feb.* Quiches, pies and tarts of all varieties are enticingly displayed in the window of this little restaurant, which has an attractive dining room decorated in pastel hues. Reasonable prices.

Chez Théo – *25 r. de l'Abbé-Onaindia. 05 59 26 81 30. Closed Sun evening, Mon and 16 Nov–31 Jan.* A family *auberge* in the Spanish Basque Country where you'll find *azulejos*, posters of *férias*, cob walls, solid wood furniture as well as a wide choice of tapas and more substantial fare served in a convivial ambience.

Au Chipiron – *4 r. Etchegaray. 05 59 26 03 41. Closed mid-Nov–Jan.* This restaurant describes itself as a "house of fish and regional specialities", the most celebrated of which is their *chipirons à l'encre* (squid in ink). The dining rooms, decorated in Basque Country colours, are cosy and attractive. Games corner for children.

Le Fronton – *Quartier Ibarron, rte de St-Jean-de-Luz, 64310 St-Pée-sur-Nivelle. 05 59 54 10 12 . jeanbaptiste.daguerre@wanadoo.fr . Closedlunch (Aug), Sun evening, Mon, Thu and 10 Feb–20 Mar.* Traditional menus, market produce, and a good choice of dishes. Comfortably decorated, with views over the garden and a terrace for warm days.

Le Brouillarta – *promenade Jacques Thibaud. 05 59 51 03 44. www.hoteldelaplage.com. Closed Sun evening and Mon.* An unbeatable view of the ocean and the hundred-year-old Artha dyke make this the perfect observation point for watching the dark and fearsome *brouillarta*, the storm that comes suddenly from the sea, to make its way towards the shore. Simple, classic décor.

BARS AND CAFÉS

Le Duke – *pl. Maurice-Ravel. ℘05 59 51 12 96.* This contemporary bar is run by Michel Chardié, a former surfing champion who named it after his idol, The Duke, a Hawaiian surfing star who rode the waves in the 1950s. Trendy music and clientele.

Maison Adam – *6 r. de la République. ℘05 59 26 03 54. www.macarons-adam.com.* Since 1660, La Maison Adam has continued to make the same macaroons that were a favourite delicacy of Louis XIV.

Maison Pariès – *9 r. Gambetta. ℘05 59 26 01 46. www.paries.fr.* Founded in 1910 by Robert Pariès, a master chocolate-maker, this shop is one of the most popular confectioneries in the town. Among the specialities, make sure you try the *mouchou basque* (macaroon made of almonds, sugar and egg whites).

SHOPPING

Maison Thurin – *32 r. Gambetta. ℘05 59 26 05 07.* This shop stocks an excellent choice of local specialities, such as Bayonne ham, sheep's cheese, bright red Espelette chilli peppers, local foie gras and poultry. There is also a selection of wines on sale, including some fine local vintages.

SPORT AND LEISURE

Association Sportive de la Nivelle – *pl. William Sharp, Ciboure. ℘05 59 47 18 99. www.golfnivelle.com. Open Fri–Wed Jul–Aug 7am–8.30pm; Sept–Jun 8am–7pm.* While the general French enthusiasm for golf is a recent phenomenon, it has always been one of the most popular sports in the Basque Country. In addition to the 18-hole golf course, this association has 3 tennis and 2 squash courts.

École de Voile Internationale – *Parking de Socoa, Ciboure (4km/2.5mi W of St-Jean-de-Luz via the N10). ℘05 59 47 06 32. www.guyonnetnautic.com. Closed Oct–Apr.* This school offers sailing and water-skiing courses and rents boats and windsurf boards.

Fronton Municipal – *1 av. André-Ithurralde. ℘05 59 51 61 53.* From July to September, you can watch *chistera* matches played on Mondays and *grand chistera* matches on Thursdays *(9.15pm)*, often accompanied by traditional singing and dancing. Open to the public except during competitions, the *fronton* is often used by local groups which run courses for adults and children alike.

Jaï-Alaï Campos Berri – *av. André-Ithurralde. ℘05 59 51 61 53. Cesta punta* is one version of the emblematic sport of the Basque Country, pelota. Like *jai alai* in Latin America, it is played against a three-wall *fronton*. From June to September, professional *cesta punta* matches take place here on Tuesdays and Fridays.

Le Spot – *16 r. Gambetta. ℘05 59 26 07 93.* This sports shop organises surf and bodyboard lessons. Two other shops in the same street, Bakea (no 37) and H2O (no 72) offer similar courses.

Sports Mer – *7 bd Thiers, Digue aux Chevaux. ℘05 59 26 96 94. www.sportsmer.fr. Closed public holidays.* Exciting activities such as para-boating (solo or tandem) and jet-skiing run by qualified instructors are organised by this company.

Trinquet Maïtena – *42 r. du Midi. ℘05 59 26 05 13. www.trinquetmaitena.fr.* The Basques practise many sports, like squash, tennis and golf, but their heart belongs to *pala*, played in a *trinquet* (small covered court). After a game, they come here to relax and sing together.

CALENDAR OF EVENTS

Cesta-Punta International – *late Jun–late Aug Tue and Fri 9pm. www.cestapunta.com.* An annual international Basque pelota competition.

Course Landaise – *throughout the summer, Arènes d'Erromardie. www.labat-france.com.* A traditional form of Tauromauchy practised in Gascony, where the bulls are left unharmed.

Festival International de Chant Choral au Pays Basque – *last wk Oct. www.chantchoralpaysbasque.net.* An intercommunal chorus festival, with the Église de St-Jean-Baptiste as the venue in the town.

International Surf Film Festival – *late May. www.surf-film.com.* An amateur film festival established in 2003.

Musique en Côte Basque– *first half Sept.* A celebration of Basque music with various performances and concerts. Please contact the tourist office for further details.

Hendaye★

Pyrénées-Atlantiques

Hendaye lies on the east bank of the River Bidassoa, which forms the Franco-Spanish border at that point.

- **Population:** 14 041
- **Michelin Map:** 342: B-2
- **Info:** 67 bd de la Mer, Hendaye. 05 59 20 00 34. www.hendaye.com.
- **Location:** Hendaye contains three separate districts: Hendaye-Gare, Hendaye-Ville and Hendaye-Plage, corresponding to the railway station, the town proper and the seafront.
- **Don't Miss:** Château d'Antoine-Abbadie.

SIGHTS

Hendaye-Plage

The resort benefits from uninterrupted views over the open sea and a climate which encourages luxuriant vegetation: magnolias, palm trees, tamarisk, oleanders, eucalyptus and mimosa line the avenues and shade the gardens everywhere. An unusual Moorish-style building houses a bustling shopping arcade with cafés and restaurants; it also marks the beginning of the GR 10 long-distance footpath. From the beach, the coastal view to the northeast is marked by the rock outcrops known as Les Deux Jumeaux (Twins), just off Pointe Ste-Anne. In the other direction Cabo Higuer (Cape Fig Tree) marks the mouth of the Bidassoa. A cycle track links the beach to the town centre via **Chingoudy Bay**. The Bidassoa estuary creates a tranquil lake at high tide; known as the Baie de Chingoudy, where you can enjoy a variety of water sports. Taxi-boats leave from the small port over to the Spanish fishing village of Fontarabie★.

Église St-Vincent

r. de l'Église. 05 59 48 82 80.

This large Basque-style church has been rearranged inside, enabling the visitor to study fragments of reredos and polychrome statues in detail. On the right is an unusual Romanesque baptismal font installed in a 17C niche with a pediment, embellished by a Basque cross. In the organ loft, the decoration of the beautiful gilded instrument portrays the Annunciation. In the Chapelle du St-Sacrement, note the 13C **crucifix**★.

Sentier du Littoral

See ST-JEAN-DE-LUZ.

The route covers 25km/15.5mi of coastline *(audioguide available for hire from the tourist office; 3€/day).*

Chemin de la Baie

From the marina to the île de la Conférence, this 15km/9.3mi walk around the Txingudi Bay offers a beautiful **view** over the towns of Irún and Fontarabie.

EXCURSIONS

Domaine d'Abbadia

Leave Hendaye by the D 912 towards St-Jean-de-Luz, the cliff road. Turn left and follow the signs "Domaine d'Abbadia".

The protected area of Domaine d'Abbadia on Ste-Anne headland has the geographical features typical of the Basque coastline; its gorse and heather-covered meadows go right up to the grey cliffs overlooking the sea. The path along the cliff edge provides an excellent view of the two famous "Jumeaux" rock formations to the west.

Return to the D 912 and turn left to enter the castle grounds.

Château d'Antoine Abbadie★★

rte de la Corniche. Guided tours (1hr) 30 May–30 Sept Mon–Fri 10am–11.30am, 2.30–6pm; 1 Feb–29 May and 1 Oct–15 Dec Tue–Sat 2–5pm. Concerts take place Jul–Aug Wed 6pm. 6.60€. 05 59 20 04 51. www.academie-sciences.fr/abbadia.htm.

The château was built in the 19C by the explorer and astronomer **Antoine d'Abbadie** (1810–97) on plans by Viollet-le-Duc. Modelled on the medieval fortress, it has crenellated towers and pepper pots which were previously used as an astronomical observatory. The park contains exotic plants and trees. The decoration and furniture, designed by Viollet-le-Duc, illustrate the life and taste of Antoine Abbadie. The polychrome ornamentation of the chapel, which is repeated throughout the castle, is reminiscent of Basque churches. The French-style ceilings are decorated with Amharic inscriptions (Abbadie studied this language in Ethiopia).

The **Grand Salon★**, housed in a round tower, is painted in deep blue as a background for the initials of Antoine and his wife Virginie. In all the rooms there are verses and mottoes in English, Basque and Amharic, illustrating Abbadie's personality (his motto was "Better to be than to seem"). From the large library which Abbadie created for the Observatory of the Science Academy, one walks down to the observatory where one can still see the telescope used by priests until 1975 to establish the position of the stars in the sky.

Biriatou

5km/3.1mi SE. Leave Hendaye via r. de Béhobie.

Beyond Béhobie the road follows the course of the Bidassoa before twisting up towards this tiny village, where it ends beside a parking area. The small square with its pelota court, adjoining inn and the church at the top of a flight of steps makes a charming ensemble. The view here embraces the wooded mountains, the frontier river below and the first few miles of Spain on the far side.

ADDRESSES

STAY

Hôtel Valencia – *29 bd de la Mer. 05 59 20 01 62. http://hotel.valencia.free.fr. Closed 20 Dec–4 Jan. 21 rooms. 7€.* Opposite the main beach, the breakfast room and four of the guest rooms have good views of the sea and Spanish coast.

Hôtel Uhainak – *3 bd de la Mer. 05 59 20 33 63. www.hotel-uhainak.com. Closed end Nov–Jan. 14 rooms. 6€.* Close to the beach, well-sized bedrooms and bathrooms. Rooms on the first floor have a balcony (ocean views are best), and all are decorated in traditional Basque-style. Simple and welcoming.

EAT

Ez Kecha Bar Lieu Dit Vin – *3 rte de Béhobie. 05 59 20 67 09. www.eguiazabal.com. Closed Sun–Mon and winter school holidays.* Located in a wine shop with over 500 wines to accompany seasonal dishes.

Château d'Antoine Abbadie

Sare★

Pyrénées-Atlantiques

This village was described, under the name of Etchezar, by Pierre Loti in his novel *Ramuntcho* (1897). The high *fronton* wall of the pelota court, the shaded streets, and the fine church with its galleries, raised chancel and Baroque altarpieces, are all typical of the Basque Country. Sare is also known as "wood pigeons' hell" due to the local method of snaring the migratory birds. The upper Sare Valley, a pastoral landscape of sheep, dairy cattle and pottock ponies between scattered hamlets with some fine dovecotes, is particularly appealing.

- **Population:** 2 271
- **Michelin Map:** 342: C-3
- **Info:** Herriko etxea, 64310 Sare. ℘05 59 54 20 14. www.sare.fr.
- **Location:** 3km/1.8mi from the Spanish border, 14km/8.7mi SE of St-Jean-de-Luz via Ascain, by the D 918 then the D 4.
- **Parking:** Parking in front of the town hall or at the entrance to the town.
- **Don't Miss:** The Grottes de Sare.
- **Kids:** The Musée du Gâteau Basque; La Ferme Etxola.
- **Timing:** Allow half a day for exploring Sare, and another half-day for the farm and caves.

SIGHTS

Église St-Martin

Built over three floors of galleries and framed altarpieces. The pulpit dates from the 18C.

Musée du Gâteau Basque

Maison Haranea, Quartier Lehenbiscay. Phone for times, charges and details of guided tours. 6€ (children 5€). ℘05 59 54 22 09. www.legateaubasque.com.

The *sukalde* ("kitchen" in Basque) is furnished with antique furniture and equipment. Visitors can choose a classic tour, where the chef *pâtissier* offers advice on creating your own *gateau basque (45min; 6€)*. The "visite plus" *(groups of more than 8 people; 1hr20min; 12€)* allows you to prepare your own cake, and take it away with you.

Grottes de Sare

Guided tours (1hr) daily Apr–Sept 10am, 2pm, 4pm, 5pm, 6pm (also 7pm Jul–Aug); Feb–Mar and Oct–Dec 2pm, 4pm, 5pm (also 10am Oct). Closed 1 Jan, 7 Jan–6 Feb, 25 Dec. 6.50€. ℘05 59 54 21 88. www.sare.fr.

The grotto or *lezea* (a Basque word meaning "cave") was gouged from the limestone at the beginning of the Quaternary Era by waters hurtling down from Pic d'Atchouria. It was occupied by humans during the Upper Perigordian period (20 000 BC).

The enormous entrance leads into a subterranean labyrinth illuminated by blue lights. The natural marvels (900m/2 953ft) are explained in an audiovisual presentation (in French).

2hrs there and back. The **sentier des contrebandiers** (smugglers' path) leads to the caves of Zugarramurdi (Navarre).

EXCURSIONS

Ferme Etxola

3km/1.8mi SW on the D 306. Just after turning for Grottes de Sare, on the left. rte des grottes de Sare and col de Lizarrieta. Open Apr–Jun 10am–6pm; Jul–Aug 10am–7pm; Sept–Oct: 10am–5pm; rest of year see website. 5€ (under 12 years 4€). ℘06 15 06 89 51. www.parc-animalier-etxola.com.

Mix of local, domestic and wild animals, delightful for children.

Col de Lizarrieta

Alt 441m/1 447ft.

The pass, with its hides and snare centres all along the crests, is a hive of activity during the pigeon-shooting season.

Ainhoa★

Pyrénées-Atlantiques

Ainhoa, a typical Basque village, grew up around a walled redoubt founded in the late 12C by monks of the Premonstratensian order as a staging post on the pilgrims' route to Santiago de Compostela. This brotherhood from northern France combined evangelism and work in their parish with a contemplative life. The D 20, which passes through the village, is one of the oldest pilgrimage and trade routes to Spain in the Nive-Nivelle region.

- **Population:** 648
- **Michelin Map:** 342: C-3
- **Info:** Maison du patrimoine, Ainhoa. 05 59 29 93 99. www.ainhoa.fr.
- **Location:** Ainhoa is 26km/16.2mi S of Bayonne, next to the Spanish border.

SIGHTS

Rue Principale★

The picturesque main street is lined with 17C and 18C houses, their overhanging roofs covered with very old tiles. The sunlit façades are freshly whitewashed each year for the Feast of St John, the shutters and half-timbering painted and the main beams sometimes embellished with inscriptions. The vast porches, known as *lorios*, decorating the front of houses, have retained the metal rings used to tie mules, when Ainhoa was a stopover for merchants en route to Spain.

Church

r. de l'Église. 05 59 54 20 28.

This traditional Basque church is notable for its two-tiered galleries, wooden ceiling and gilded woodwork in its chancel. The war memorial at the entrance to the cemetery bears the characteristic disc motif of Basque headstones.

Notre-Dame-de-l'Aubépine

Take the street to the left of the town hall and follow the red-and-white markers of the GR footpath – allow 2hrs round trip. Pilgrimage Whit Monday with Mass celebrated in the Basque language at 10.30am. 05 59 29 90 16.

This rocky path, which lies along the GR 10 footpath, leads to Notre-Dame-de-l'Aubépine, a tiny chapel perched on the side of Mont Ereby. The Virgin Mary is said to have appeared there in a hawthorn bush. Basque pilgrims flock here every year on Whit Monday. It offers a beautiful panoramic view of the harbour of St-Jean-de-Luz and Socoa and the Spanish villages in the foothills of the lofty Navarrese mountains.

EXCURSION

Zugarramurdi

7km/4.3mi SW along the D 20, then NA 4 401 after the border.

In 1600 more than 300 people were arrested here during the Spanish Inquisition. Today it is a charmingly peaceful spot, with a small museum to witchcraft (Museo de las Brujas) remembering the events. You can also visit the caves where the witchcraft suposedly took place and visit the **Cueva de las Brujas**★ *(signposed from the church; open daily 10.30am–8pm; 3.50€).*
Nearby **Urdazubi** *(also in Spain)* has more caves.

ADDRESSES

STAY/ EAT

Hôtel Restaurant Etchartenea – *Dancharia, on the Spanish border. 05 59 29 90 26. 6 rooms.* This family-run restaurant has a shady terrace overlooking the river. A short stroll over the bridge takes you across the border into Spain.

La Maison Oppoca – *Town outskirts. 05 59 29 90 72. www.oppoca.com. Closed 3 wks Jan and 3 wks Nov/Dec. 10 rooms. 9€.* .Traditional Basque building dating from 1663. Comfortable if old-fashioned bedrooms, with lovely garden for breakfast on warm days. Excellent food in the restraurant.

Espelette★

Pyrénées-Atlantiques

This village dates from medieval times, and remains a sprawling collection of Basque-style red-and-white houses lining narrow, winding streets. Espelette specialises in growing a regional variety of red chilli pepper, but there is also a brisk local trade in a breed of pony called a pottock (a Pottock Fair is held in late January: exhibitions and competitions of pottocks, market with local produce, pelota). The ponies live in herds on the slopes of the mountains along the Spanish border. Once used in the mines because of their docile nature and diminutive stature, these animals are now suited to pony trekking.

- **Population:** 1 936
- **Michelin Map:** 342: D-2
- **Info:** r. Karrika Nagusia. ✆05 59 93 95 02. www.espelette.fr.
- **Location:** 6.5km/4mi SW from Cambo-les-Bains.
- **Parking:** Park at the top of the village.
- **Don't Miss:** Market day on Wednesday morning (and Saturday morning in July and August).

SIGHTS

Église

Lower part of Espelette.

The church contains a gilt-wood reredos; in the nearby cemetery you will find 17C and 18C discoidal headstones unique to the Basque culture (perhaps a remnant of an ancient cult of sun worship).

Château des Barons d'Ezpeleta

Open Jul–Aug Mon–Fri 8.30am–12.30pm, 2–6pm, Sat 9.30am–12.30pm, 2–6pm; Sept–Jun Mon–Fri 8.30am–12.30pm, 2–6pm, Sat 9.30am–12.30pm. No charge. ✆05 59 93 95 02.

Housed in a former 11C castle, the town hall holds an exhibition on red pepper.

ADDRESSES

STAY/ EAT

Hôtel Euzkadi – *285 Karrika Neagusia. ✆05 59 93 91 88. www.hotel-restaurant-euzkadi.com. Closed Mon–Tue. 27 rooms. 7€. Restaurant.* This typical Basque establishment has a striking red façade, comfortable rooms, leisure facilities, a bar serving tapas dishes and a restaurant offering local Basque cuisine.

Pottoka – *pl. du Jeu-de-Paume. ✆05 59 93 90 92. francoiseaguerre953@orange.fr. Closed 2 wks Feb, and Mon out of season.* The striking Espelette peppers decorate the walls at this classic Basque restaurant. The cooking is based around local products, such as *axoa* (a lamb shoulder seasoned with peppers) *gâteau basque* or wild strawberry gratin. Always welcoming and great fun. In summer, there is a lovely covered terrace.

Espelette Peppers

In autumn, the façades of the houses in Espelette are draped with garlands of dark red peppers drying in the sun. The peppers were brought to the Basque Country from America and Spain in the 17C and quickly became the favourite local condiment. Baked in the oven and ground into a powder they were initially used in chocolate. They were used in local dishes such as *poulet basquaise* (chicken with ratatouille), *tripotxa* (veal sausage) and *axua* (veal cutlets). Today, Espelette peppers are an all-purpose remedy, said to cure colds and bronchitis! The Espelette Pepper Fair is held on the last Sunday in October. Festivities start with blessing of the peppers, followed by processions. At the end of the day, new Chevaliers du Piment d'Espelette (Knights of the Espelette Pepper) are elected.

Cambo-les-Bains★

Pyrénées-Atlantiques

Haut Cambo, the upper residential district of this spa, has a number of hotels and villas overlooking the River Nive, whereas Bas Cambo, the lower town, is an old Basque village nestling in a wide curve of the river. At one time Cambo was the navigable limit for barges bringing cargoes inland from Bayonne.

- **Population:** 5 671
- **Michelin Map:** 342: D-4
- **Info:** av. de la Mairie, Cambo-les-Bains. 05 59 29 70 25. www.cambolesbains.com.
- **Location:** 30km/18.6mi to the Eof St-Jean-de-Luz along the D 918.
- **Don't Miss:** Taking the thermal waters.
- **Kids:** La Foret des Lapins.
- **Timing:** Allow half a day. Cambo can also be a useful departure point for a day in the Basque mountains.

Thermes

The thermal spa was built in 1927 in Neoclassical style with Art Deco mosaics and wrought-iron work.

Église St-Laurent

Lovely church overlookin the river Nive. Richly decorated interior, with sculpted galleries, and a 17C gold-inlaid baroque altarpiece.

Villa Arnaga★★

The spacious **Villa Arnaga** *(Musée Edmond Rostand, route du Docteur Camino; open Mar Sat–Sun 2.30–6pm, Apr–Jun, Sept and 1–18 Oct daily 10am–12.30pm, 2.30–7pm, Jul–Aug daily 10am–7pm, 19 Oct–4 Nov daily 2.30–6pm; guided tours (1hr) available; 6.20€; 05 59 29 83 92; www.arnaga.com),* was built in the Labourdes Basque style under Rostand's supervision between 1903 and 1906. It stands on a promontory which the writer turned into formal gardens. The spacious house, with its great Basque roof, decorative painting and wooden balconies, contains Rostand memorabilia – furniture, documents, the original costume designs for *Chantecler*, and portraits of Rostand and Rosemonde Gérard by Pascau and Caro.

EXCURSIONS

Larressore

3.5km/2mi northwest on D 932 towards Bayonne. At roundabout, turn left on to the D 650.

From 1733 to 1906 a seminary founded here by Abbot Daguerre trained many Basque priests. Beside the pelota court is the **Atelier Ainciart-Bergara** *(open Mon–Sat 9am–noon, 2–6pm; closed public holidays; no charge; 05 59 93 03 05; www.makhila.com)*; this family-run workshop was established before the French Revolution. The workshop produces the traditional Basque staff or *makhila*, from the wood of the medlar tree. The canes are decorated with a pattern of dried sap which has oozed from incisions cut in the wood. Besides the workshop, you will find an exhibition and documentary *(30min)*.

Edmond Rostand

It is the exceptionally mild climate and a visit by the well-known poet and writer Edmond Rostand (1868–1918) that made Cambo a fashionable health resort at the turn of the last century. Arriving for the first time in the autumn of 1900, Rostand at once fell in love with Cambo and decided to live here permanently. He built a villa, the Villa Arnaga *(now open to the public)*, with beautiful gardens overlooking the Bayonne road. Rostand was inspired by his walks in the Basque countryside around Cambo to write *Chantecler*, the successor to his *Cyrano de Bergerac*.

Jatxou

6km/3.7mi NW along the D 932 towards Bayonne, then at the roundabout turn right onto the D 650.

Built in the 13C, the Église St-Sébastien was enlarged in 1782. Beautiful ceiling fresco painted onto wood.

Ustaritz

6.5km/4mi to the NW along the D 932 towards Bayonne.

After Richard the Lionheart separated Bayonne from Labourd in the late 12C, the village became capital of the province until 1790. From 1451, this was the meeting place of the *biltzar*, a Basque word for a local parliamentary body which collected taxes, looked after public property and was in charge of relations between local communities. Several attractive examples of Labourdian architecture abound in the town centre, with their striking red or green shutters. If you wander around this part of town, you will also find several late 19C villas built by the *Américains*; those Basques natives who returned here after making their fortune in America.

La Maison Labourdine

Quartier Arrauntz. Open Apr–Jun and Oct Tue–Sun 2–6pm; Jul–Sept 11am–1pm, 2–6pm. Guided visits available Sat am on request. 5€ (under 18 years 3€). 05 59 70 35 41 or 06 62 07 35 41. www.lamaisonlabourdine.com. This 17C inn contains an important collection of documents and objects recording Labourdian life in past centuries. One corner shows a typical scene from a school, another from an *épicerie* (early 19C) and another a sheep pen. The boutique offers tastings and sales of regional objects.

Itxassou★

The hamlet's cottages are set in clusters among cherry orchards, which supply the main ingredient of the famous local cherry jam. The rustic-looking **church**★ *(pl. de la Mairie, Quartier Errobi)*, standing alone near the River Nive, has three tiers of galleries adorned with statues and turned balusters, an 18C gilt wood altarpiece and a fine pulpit with decorations picked out in gold.

La Forêt des Lapins

Follow the rabbit-shaped signs, by the car workshop (on the right of the D 918 towards Louhossoa, before the road bridge). Open mid-Jun–Sept 10.15am–6pm; Oct–mid-Jun 2–5pm. 6.10€ (5–10 years 3.90€). 05 59 93 30 09. www.laforetdeslapins.com. Great care is taken over the animals here, with over 60 varieties of rabbits and 30 types of guinea pigs in runs and hutches with views across the hills. Guaranteed enjoyment for little ones, with hands-on activities throughout the year. Older visitors will enjoy the beautiful views.

Louhossoa

4km/2.5mi SE of Ixtassou via the D 918.

Founded in 1684, this Labourdian village retains a remarkable multicoloured framed altarpiece in the church of Notre-Dame-de-l'Assomption (17C). The stiking colours and the carved statues represent the Virgin Mary as she is carried by Angels.

Donostia/San Sebastián★★

25km/15.5mi SW of Hendaye. Take the A 8 towards Bilbao, or the N 10, which becomes the N 1 in Spain. San Sebastián is located in the Spanish Basque Country.

It is always a pleasure to go beyond the Spanish border to dine on tapas and seafood in the port of the old Spanish city. In the evening, stroll around the **plaza de la Constitución**, once used as an arena for races. The best way to see the site called the Concha, a scallop-shaped **bay**★★★, is to walk along the sea between beaches gardens and opulent-looking buildings.

DRIVING TOUR

3 LA ROUTE DES MONTS

20km/12.4mi. Allow 2hrs.

From the church at Itxassou, drive down to Nive passing the Hôtel du Chêne. Turn right and follow signs "Pas de Roland" on the D 349.

Pas de Roland
Park where the road widens, just beyond the parapet with a roadside crucifix. Beyond the crucifix, there is a view down to Pas de Roland.

Continue to Laxia. Leave the river and turn right;,drive up towards Artzamendi.

A narrow, windy route will take you throrugh the forest *(around 40min drive)*. Be patient, the view is worth it...

Artzamendi★
Next to the telecoms station, there is a **panorama★** extending northwards towards the lower valley of the Nive, the Nivelle basin and its upland pastures, and southwards, beyond the border, to the slopes above the Bidassoa Valley.

Return towards Laxia, and before Fagola, turn left to Itxassou.

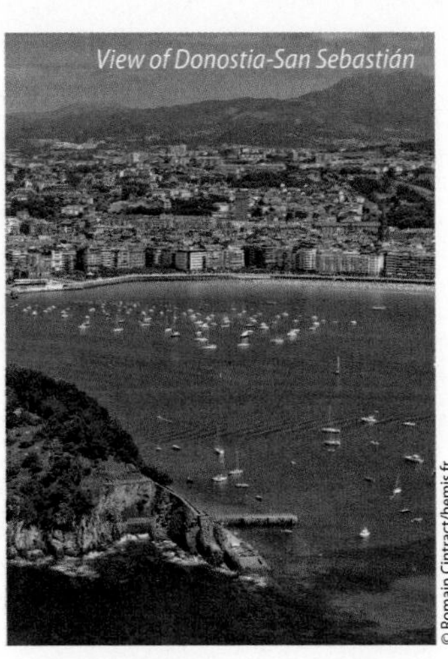
View of Donostia-San Sebastián

Mont Urzumu
From the viewing table, near a statue of the Virgin, there is a **panorama** of the Basque Pyrénées and the coast from Pointe Ste-Barbe to Bayonne.

Return to Itxassou along the same road.

ADDRESSES

STAY

Chambre d'hôte Soubeleta – *Soubeleta, Itxassou (5km/3.1mi N). ℘05 59 29 22 34. www.gites64.com/chambre-soubeleta. 5 rooms. 58/60€.* Perched above the town, this imposing 17C edifice's *tourelle* and finely sculpted granite frame are still intact. The spacious rooms are decorated with family furniture; two have marble fireplaces.

Auberge Chez Tante Ursule – *Fronton du Bas-Cambo (2km/1.2mi N). ℘05 59 29 78 23. www.auberge-tante-ursule.com. 7 rooms. 38/50€. Restaurant.* A discreet hotel across from the *fronton*, well placed for watching a game of Basque pelota. Very well-kept rooms – ask for one in the more modern annex. Traditional fare in the dining room under the wooden ceiling.

Domaine Silencenia – *64250 Louhossoa (10km/6.2mi SE, towards St-Jean-Pied-de-Port). ℘05 59 93 35 60. www.chambres-d-hotes-basques-silencenia.com. 5 rooms. 90€.* An 18C house where *art de vivre* prevails. Each room echoes one of the owner's passions – rugby, fishing, wine and good local food.

EAT

Venta Burkaitz – *Col des Veaux, Itxassou (from Itxassou, take the route to pas de Roland, then Artzmandi). ℘05 59 29 82 55. Closed evenings and Wed. 22€.* On the Spanish side of the mountain range, a *venta* with two dining rooms, one with a view of the valley from the veranda.

Domaine Xixtaberri – *4km/2.5mi E via the D 10. ℘05 59 29 22 66. www.xixtaberri.com.* Splendid view of the Basque Coast and the Pyrénées. Basque specialities to savour under the arbour or in the pleasing dining room.

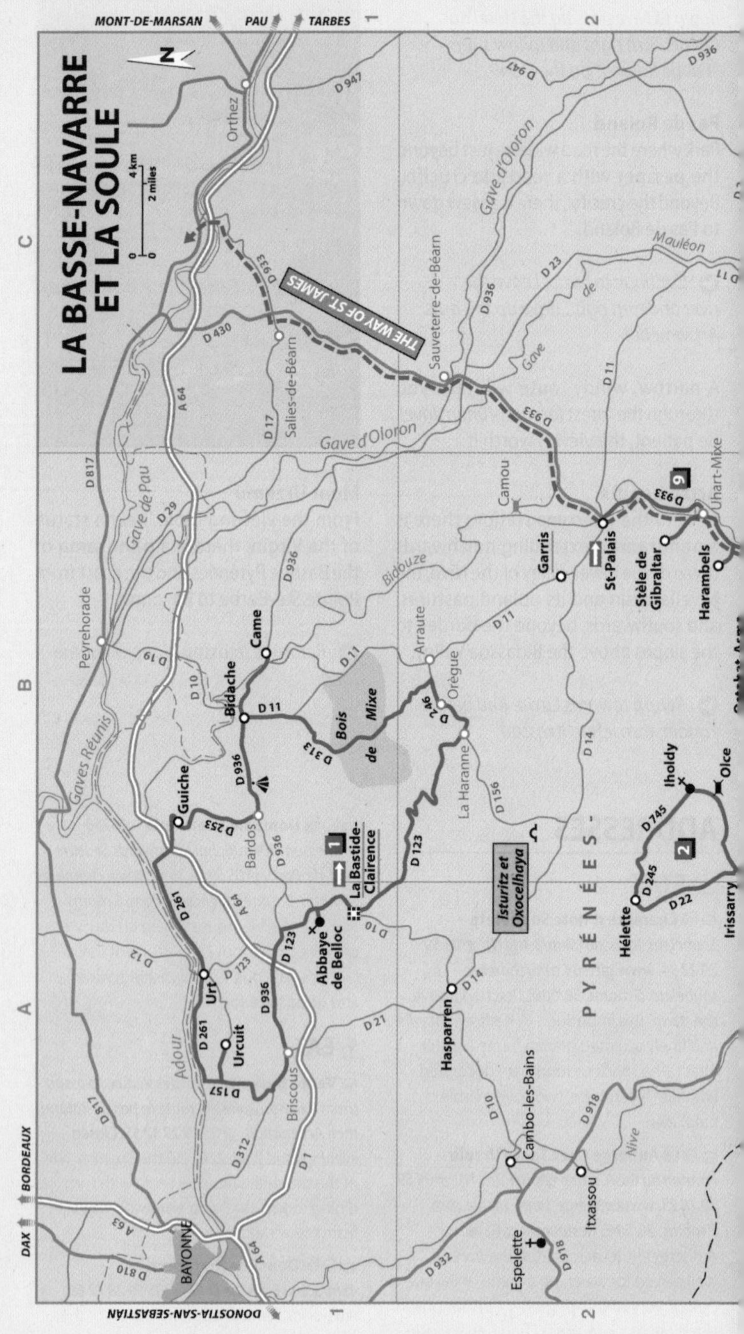
LA BASSE-NAVARRE ET LA SOULE
0 4 km
0 2 miles
MONT-DE-MARSAN
PAU
TARBES
DAX
BORDEAUX
DONOSTIA-SAN-SEBASTIÁN
THE WAY OF ST. JAMES
Orthez
Salies-de-Béarn
Sauveterre-de-Béarn
Mauléon
Gave d'Oloron
Gave de Pau
Gaves Réunis
Adour
Nive
Bidouze
Peyrehorade
Guiche
Bidache
Came
Bardos
Bois de Mixe
Arraute
Orègue
La Haranne
Camou
Garris
St-Palais
Stèle de Gibraltar
Harambels
Uhart-Mixe
Iholdy
Olce
Hélette
Irissarry
La Bastide-Clairence
Abbaye de Belloc
Isturitz et Oxocelhaya
Urt
Urcuit
Briscous
Hasparren
Cambo-les-Bains
Itxassou
Espelette
BAYONNE
PYRÉNÉES-
D 947
D 936
D 933
D 430
D 17
D 23
D 11
D 817
D 29
D 19
D 10
D 313
D 246
D 156
D 14
D 253
D 261
D 123
D 157
D 312
D 1
D 21
D 12
D 918
D 932
D 810
D 745
D 245
D 22
A 64
A 63

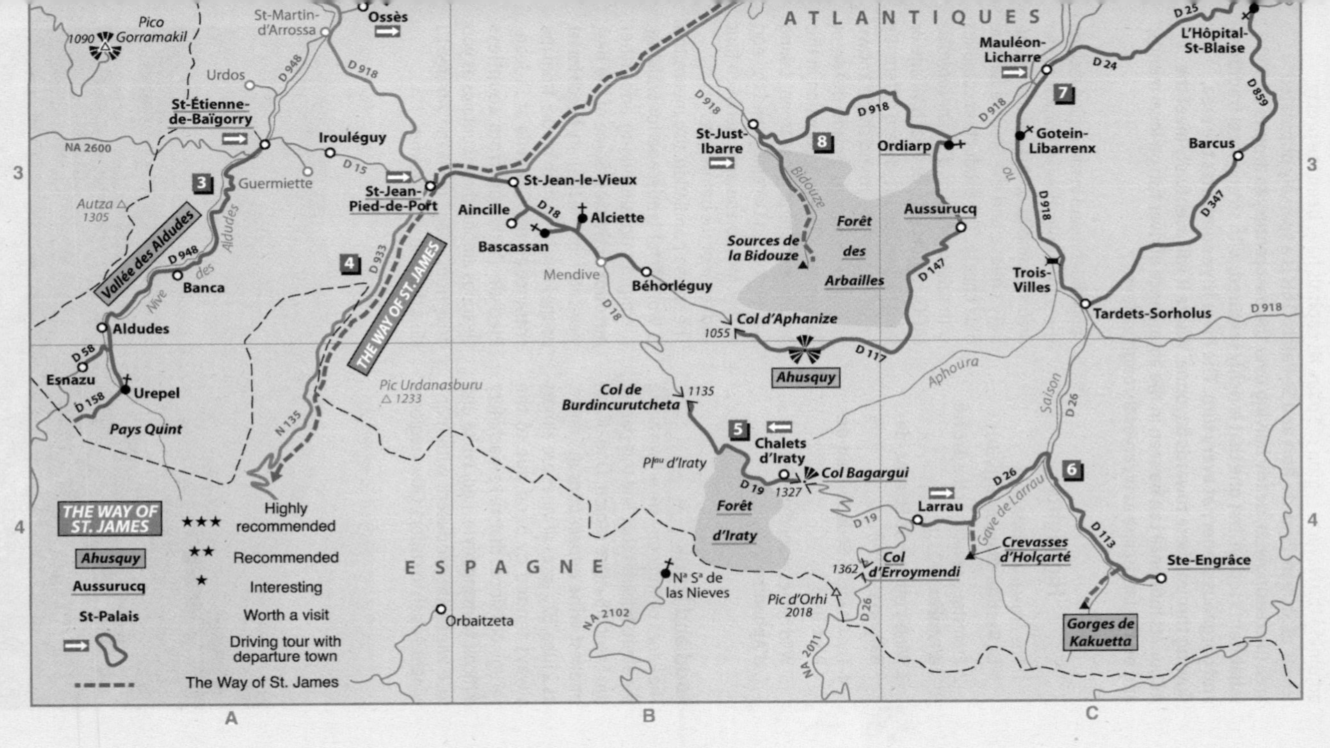

ATLANTIQUES
ESPAGNE
Pico Gorramakil
1090
St-Martin-d'Arrossa
Ossès
Urdos
D 948
D 918
St-Étienne-de-Baïgorry
NA 2600
Irouléguy
D 15
Guermiette
St-Jean-Pied-de-Port
Autza 1305
Vallée des Aldudes
Aldudes
Nive des Aldudes
D 948
Banca
D 933
THE WAY OF ST. JAMES
Esnazu
D 58
Urepel
D 158
Pays Quint
N 135
Pic Urdanasburu 1233
St-Jean-le-Vieux
Aincille
D 18
Alciette
Bascassan
Mendive
Béhorléguy
Col d'Aphanize
1055
Ahusquy
D 117
Col de Burdincurutcheta
1135
Pl^{au} d'Iraty
Chalets d'Iraty
Col Bagargui
1327
D 19
Forêt d'Iraty
Nª Sª de las Nieves
NA 2102
Orbaitzeta
Pic d'Orhi 2018
NA 2011
D 26
1362
Col d'Erroymendi
St-Just-Ibarre
D 918
Bidouze
Sources de la Bidouze
Forêt des Arbailles
Ordiarp
Aussurucq
D 147
Aphoura
Mauléon-Licharre
D 24
Gotein-Libarrenx
Trois-Villes
Tardets-Sorholus
Saison
D 26
Larrau
Gave de Larrau
Crevasses d'Holçarté
D 113
Ste-Engrâce
Gorges de Kakuetta
L'Hôpital-St-Blaise
D 25
D 859
Barcus
D 347
THE WAY OF ST. JAMES
Ahusquy
Aussurucq
St-Palais
Highly recommended
Recommended
Interesting
Worth a visit
Driving tour with departure town
The Way of St. James
3
4
A
B
C

LA BASSE-NAVARRE *and La Soule*

La Basse-Navarre, or the Lower Navarre, lies within the French Pyrénées, adjoining the Navarre region of Spain. Its capitals have been the pretty towns of St-Jean-Pied-de-Port and St-Palais. This is a sparsely populated area (increasingly so, nearly halving over the past century to around 25 000 inhabitants today), but one that is richly textured, with strong local traditions and gorgeous scenery at every turn. The River Nive dominates the area, flowing through here towards Bayonne, where it will eventually meet the Adour. Its influence can be seen in the abundance of river fish on local menus, and on the landscape as it carves through valleys.

Highlights

1 The artisan workshops of **La Bastide-Clairence** (p231)

2 Prehistoric remains at the **Grotte d'Isturitz** (p233)

3 Wine-tasting in **St-Étienne-de-Baïgorry** (p234)

4 The Citadelle, **St-Jean-Pied-de-Port** (p237)

5 Wild horses around the **Col d'Aphanize** (p243)

Food and Drink

The wines of Irouléguy are grown along the steep hillsides that line this part of the French Basque region. One of the smallest **wine** *appellations* in France, its 210ha/520 acres of vines are almost always tended by hand due to the vertiginous slopes that make machinery difficult to manoeuvre. Red, white and rosé wines are produced, with many wineries open to visitors. Other regional specialities found in this region include the ewe's milk cheese known as *pur brébis*. Examples of this include Ossau-Iraty **cheese** and the Bleu de Basque blue cheese. The production complies with strict *appellation d'origine contrôlée* (AOC) regulations, but each village or farm may shape the cheese differently (most usually in a round shape known as a cheese wheel), or add different flavourings. Cheese production in this mountainous region is seasonal, taking place between December and the end of July. Most *brébis* ages between four and ten months before sale.

The sparse population also means this is wonderful landscape for walking, hiking, mountain biking and other **outdoor activities**. Some of the best views are found in the Iraty beech forest on the French–Spanish border, from the entrance to the Citadelle at St-Jean-Pied-de-Port, and from countless clearings among the mountains as you drive from village to village. An area to slow down in, and explore.

Irouléguy vineyards

La Bastide-Clairence★

Pyrénées-Atlantiques

A visit to this spot, at the far edge of Gascony, is like stepping back in time. Filled with beautiful white-washed houses with coloured and sculpted lintels, a tiny church, an old wash-house and an arcaded central square, this *bastide* seems frozen in time. This feeling is underlined by the numerous artisan workshops dotted all over the town.
Classed as one of the *plus beaux villages de France* (most beautiful villages in France), it makes a perfect base for exploring the region.

- **Population:** 881
- **Michelin Map:** 342: E-2
- **Info:** ✆05 50 29 65 05. www.labastideclairence.com.
- **Location:** The village sits atop a hill 15km/9.3mi E of Bayonne via the A 64.
- **Don't Miss:** The artisan workshops.
- **Kids:** Bois de Mixte.
- **Timing:** Half a day is perfect for the village, then the rest of the day exploring the surrounds.

SIGHTS

The main road is criss-crossed with several roads leading onto it, the whole centred around a market square; the classic *bastide* layout. The whitewashed houses with their red beams give the place the feel of a Labourdian village, and it would be interesting to spot the difference between the Labourdian and Navarrian houses.
Around a dozen artisan workshops have been installed here, and are open for visits. Exhibitions are held regularly – from pottery to photography to cabinet-making and perfumery.

Église Notre-Dame-de-l'Assomption

Typically Basque church with galleried upper floors, it is flanked on either side by covered walkways lined with pavestones inscribed with the names of the oldest families of the *bastide*; known as a courtyard cemetery.

DRIVING TOUR

1 ALONG THE BIDOUZE AND ADOUR RIVERS★

84km/52mi. Allow 1hr30min.

Leave La Bastide-Clairence via the D 123 towards St-Palais. At Haranne, turn left on the D 246 to Orègue, then

La Bastide-Clairence

first left (D 313) towards Bidache. Continue for around 10min. Parking on the left-hand side of the road.

Bois de Mixte

Small forest covering 800ha/1 975 acres full of indigenous species (hazlenut, oak, beech) and imported trees such as the American red oak and the Virginian tulip tree. A walking route, with explanatory boards and points of interest for children, runs through the forest and crosses the Patarena stream *(1hr; path leads from the right-hand side of the picnic cabin).*

Follow the D 313 and take the D 11, on the left, to Bidache.

Bidache

This picturesque village with its single street and attractive old houses is typical of the Navarre region. From the 14C, the lords of Gramont controlled this area. which lies on the borders between Navarre, Béarn and France.

Leave Bidache on the D 936 towards Came, 3km/1.8mi away.

Came

Village laid out on both sides of the Bidouze river, where the banks have been converted to pretty walking paths. Known since the 19C for its artisinsal production of chairs, made with local woods from beech to walnut and local straw from the fields of the Adour Valley. Several workshops open to visit.

Rejoin the D 936 towards Bayonne.

After Bidache, the road heads upwards into the Basque mountains. Before reaching Bardos, there is an attractive viewpoint over the Pyrénées towards the Pic d'Anie (alt 2 504m/8 215ft), highest summit of the Cirque de Lescun.

In Bardos, take the road to Guiche via the D 253.

Guiche

Above the entrance to the cemetery is a quirky house on stilts known as Maison du Fauconnier (Falconer's House), which was once the town hall.

A little farther along, in Guiche-Bourgade, are the ruins of a castle with a square keep.

Follow the Bidouze river then the Adour on the D 261.

The road passes orchards of trellised kiwi trees.

Urt

Typical Basque village with a white church. Simple, plain interior with wooden gallery and organ. There is a walk along the banks of the Adour from the port.

Head to Urcuit on the D 261, then the D 257.

Urcuit

Like the neighbouring town of Urt, this little town has a very strong Basque character, featuring a fine Basque-style **church** *(05 59 42 90 70)* with an outer gallery. Typical discoid Basque headstones can be seen in the adjoining cemetery.

Head to Briscous, then take the D 936 and the D 123 to La Bastide-Clairence. Turn right on the D 510.

Abbaye de Belloc

Monastery dating from 1875 founded by three missionaries from Hasparre, including Jean-Léon Bastres (1832–1904). Thriving in the 19C, the community was forced to flee first in 1880, then again in 1905, taking refuge in Spain. The monks returned to fight for France in World War I, and returned to the Belloc community. Today there are 30 monks living at the site, and short retreats are possible for visitors.

Return to La Bastide-Clairence via the D 510.

Grottes d'Isturitz and Oxocelhaya★★

Pyrénées-Atlantiques

This rich archaeological site consists of two prehistoric caves hollowed out deep in the Colline de Gaztelu, containing spectacular examples of colourful stalactites and stalagmites, and drawings dating back to the Palaeolithic Era.

- **Michelin Map:** 342: E-2
- **Info:** 14 pl. Charles de Gaulle, Saint Palais. 05 59 65 71 78. www.tourisme-saintpalais.com.
- **Location:** The caves are located by the village of St-Martin-d'Arberoue *(left down rampe des Grottes).*
- **Parking:** Park near the entrance to the caves.

THE CAVES

St-Martin-d'Arberoue, Donamartiri. Guided tours (45min) daily Jun and Sept 11am–noon, 2–5pm; Jul–Aug 10am–noon, 1–6pm; 15 Mar–31 May, 1 Oct–15 Nov 2–5pm, public holidays 11am, 2–5pm. 8.30€. 05 59 29 64 72. www.grottes-isturitz.com.

The caves correspond to two different levels, each abandoned long ago, of the subterranean course of the River Arberoue. A single visit encompasses both. They witness the presence of human occupation during the Palaeolithic Age, between 80 000 and 15 000 BC.

Grotte d'Isturitz

It is through this upper cave that visitors enter the limestone stronghold of the mountain. It is mainly of scientific interest; you will see a **pillar** on which three reindeers have been carved one above the other, following the relief of the stone, as well as a horse. Traces of occupation by Palaeolithic Man from the Mousterian period to the Magdalenian have been discovered, showing an exceptional continuity. Excavations have revealed semi-rounded staffs incised with curvilinear ornamentation, and a number of carvings, examples of which are on display in the local museum.

Grotte d'Oxocelhaya

The second stage of the tour, in the lower cave, 15m/49ft below, reveals a fascinating series of chambers richly decorated with natural rock **concretions**: stalactites, stalagmites, columns, discs, translucent draperies and a glittering petrified cascade. Moreover, two reproductions illustrate the 30 **drawings** (outlines drawn with charcoal, scraped or drawn with fingers on clay) discovered on the walls, but which you will not be able to see because of the need for preservation.

EXCURSION

Hasparren

10km/6.2mi NW via the D 251, then the D 10.

The "city of oak" is a Labourdian village once renowned for its tanneries. Francis Jammes (1868–1938) moved here in 1921 spending the rest of his life in Maison Eyhartzea. He became a poet admired by Gide, Claudel, Rilke and Kafka while also a penniless father of nine *(closed for renovations; 05 59 29 60 22).*

Chapelle du Sacré-Cœur

Built in 1933, the interior contains a large fresco on the wall of the nave and a mosaic of Christ in the chancel.

Hasparren

©Daniel P Acevedo/age fotostock

St-Palais

Pyrénées-Atlantiques

One of the key points on The Way of St James, this is the former capital of the Lower Navarre. Set in attractively contoured landscape, this 13C *bastide* celebrates local traditions year-round, and your visit is almost certain to coincide with a festival.

- **Population:** 1 700
- **Michelin Map:** 342: F-3
- **Info:** 05 59 65 71 78. www.tourisme-saint palais.com.
- **Location:** 31km/19mi NE of St-Jean-Pied-de-Port along the D 933.
- **Kids:** St-Palais market.
- **Timing:** Half a day.

THE TOWN

Friday is market day on place de Foirail, one of the most lively in the region. After exploring, wander down rue de la Monnaie lined on either side with high stone walls and white-shuttered traditional houses.

EXCURSION

Garris★

3km/1.8mi NW on the D 11.

Founded along the Roman road from Bordeaux to Astorga, Garris was at its height during the Middle Ages due to its reputation as a trading centre. Today it retains an air of quiet prosperity, with well-preserved 17C and 18C houses. The oldest are located opposite the church.

DRIVING TOUR

2 THE WAY OF ST JAMES★★★

16km/10mi. Allow 1hr30min.

Leave St-Palais via the D 933 towards St-Jean-Pied-de-Port.

Stèle de Gibraltar★ – *At Uhart-Mixe, turn right on the D302.* This monument marks the intersection of three routes to Santiago de Compostela. A 10km/6.2mi path tracks the river *(3.5hrs)*.

Return to Uhart-Mixe and take the D 933 to Harambels, where the **Chapelle St-Nicolas★** contains 17C frescoes.

Take the D933 back to St-Palais via Ostabat-Asme, where a path leads to chapel.

St-Étienne-de-Baïgorry★

Pyrénées-Atlantiques

You can't help but be seduced by the easy, enjoyable approach to gourmet pleasures here, and not only because of their famous Irouléguy wines, which are made both here and in Ispoure. The whole place is picturesque and atmospheric; traditional Basque houses, a shady central square, an old Roman bridge. The town's 17 districts are divided between the two banks of the Nive des Aldudes, running along the entire valley. Once serious rivals, today they still maintain the traditions and peculiarities of a mountainous region perched in between France and Spain.

- **Population:** 1 500.
- **Michelin Map:** 342: D-3.
- **Info:** 05 59 37 47 28. www.pyrenees-basque.com.
- **Location:** 11km/6.8mi W of St-Jean-Pied-de-Port
- **Don't Miss:** St-Jean-Baptiste church.
- **Kids:** La Vallée des Aldudes; donkey treks.
- **Timing:** Half a day.

THE TOWN

Église★

Restored during the 18C from its Roman origins, this church, in the Mithelene district of the town, contains interesting galleries, and a raised chancel with three gilded altars. The church also contains a Baroque-style organ. From here, cross to the other side of the river.

The château d'Etchauz stands on the Left Bank. After the Revolution, it passed into the ownership of the Harispe family, and was then bought by the Abbadie d'Arrast family (*open daily 10am–noon, 2–5.30pm; 05 59 37 48 58).*

Pont Romain

The Roman bridge dates from 1661 but takes its name from its arch, which was inspired by Roman architecture.

DRIVING TOUR

3 VALLÉE DES ALDUDES★★

26km/16.2mi. Allow 1hr30min.

Leave St-Étienne-de-Baïgorry via the D 948 towards Banca.

Banca

This village, which hugs the side of a mountain, grew up during the 18C thanks to a foundry on the Left Bank of the river (today in ruins).

The aquaculture farm in Banca, famous for its trout production, is in a former 19C watermill *(www.truitedebanka.com).*

Aldudes

Popular centre for hunting wood pigeon. An attractive church with a vaulted wooden ceiling and original galleries stands on the small central square. The cemetery contains 19C Basque memorial plaques attached to the walls.

Walking in the Col de Lepeder★ – *4km/2.5mi (2hr)* Yellow trail markers begin from in front of the petrol station, with steps heading off on the left. A sloping stony path marks out the beginning of the walk, which then opens out onto beautiful panoramic views of this green valley which borders Spain. The circuit ends by a farm rearing the famous black pie Basque pigs.

The first right out of the village will take you to Esnazu, where a small church contains a gilded wooden altarpiece from the 17C. This altar originally stood in the ancient church of Larressore.

A 2km/1.2mi *(40min)* path around the village and its farms makes a pleasant stroll. Follow the yellow markings from the church.

Head back the way you came onto the D 948.

Urepel

A monument at the entrance to the village commemorates a local child, Fernando Aire Etxart, known as Xalbador (1920–76), a shepherd and farmer who became a famous poet and singer, known in Basque as a *bertsolari*.

Elizamendi walk★ – *2km/1.2mi (90min; follow the yellow trail markers).* From the church in Urepel, head towards Bordaluzea. The path takes you alongside the canalised river. At the first village you come to, a steep path heads off to the left. Take it: you will be rewarded by stunning **views** at the top over the valley. The path heads down through the valley, crosses a stream then heads back upwards towards the Urepel church.

Take the D 158 (6km/3.7mi round trip) from Urepel.

Pays Quint

Once evenly divided between French and Spanish valleys, today this territory is recognised as Spanish, but is inhabited and "run" by France. This has been the case since the Treaty of Bayonne in 1856, and today the post is delivered by the French while security is assured by the Spanish. Just seven families inhabit the Aldudes Valley. They are known as the Quintoars and have the rights to rents from animals grazing on the land.

Ossès

Pyrénées-Atlantiques

The village gained renown for the wrong reasons on 1 November 2004, when the Cannelle bear, the last of the Pyrénées, was killed here during a wild boar hunt. Located at the confluence of the Nive des Aldudes and the Grande Nive rivers, just a few moments from the summit of the mountains, Ossès is a gateway to the green hills of the Lower-Navarre. The village itself is notable for its traditional Basque architecture, and its surrounding fields all bathed in extraordinary light, as the mountain tops approach.

- **Population:** 800
- **Michelin Map:** A-23–B-2
- **Info:** ℘05 59 37 47 28. www.pyrenees-basque.com.
- **Location:** 14km/8.7mi NE from St-Étienne-de-Baïgorry.
- **Don't Miss:** Musée Basque du Pastoralism et du Fromage.
- **Kids:** The Village d'Artisans.
- **Timing:** Half a day.

DRIVING TOUR

2 Around Ossès

35km/22mi. Allow 1hr.

Leave Ossès via the D 8.

Irissary

The village is the site of the 12C Commanderie des chevaliers de St-Jean-de-Jérusalem, restored in the 17C by the Order of Malta. This religious group assured the security and lodging of pilgrims along The Way of St James, although the building itself was never used as a stop-off point. Rather, it was the seat of power for the local Seigneurs right up to the French Revolution. It has been fully restored, and today houses Ospitalea, an exhibition and arts centre centred around local heritage (*open Mon–Sat 10am–12.30pm, 1.30–5pm; no charge; ℘05 59 37 97 20; www.ospitalea.cg64.fr).*

Continue towards Iholdy.

Château d'Olce

Guided visits Apr–mid-Sept Thu–Tue 2–6pm. 6€ (under 16 years 3€). ℘05 59 37 51 07.

Rebuilt once by the Olce family in 1664 on the site of a 14C château belonging to the same family, and again rebuilt and restored by the current owners after years of being left to ruin. Today visitors can admire the careful restoration works to the ceilings, the stuccos dating from the reign of Louis XIV, and the ornamental fireplaces in each room. Most of the furniture dates from the 17C–18C.

Iholdy

500m/500yds farther.

Note the attractive church, with its extravagent exterior galleries.

Leave Iholdy via the D 745, towards Hélette (7.5km/4.7mi).

Hélette

Agour – Musée Basque du Pastoralisme et du Fromage

On the D 119, towards Louhossoa. Open Jul–Aug Mon–Fri 9–11am, 2–5pm; rest of year 2 visits per day at 10.30am and 3.30pm. 5€. ℘05 59 37 63 86. www.agour.com.

Charming museum recounting the production methods of this most traditional of local cheeses. The voice of shepherd Joanes explains Basque farming traditions. The visit finishes with a short film explaining all stages of production, and offers a tasting, washed down with a glass of Irouléguy wine or local cider.

Head towards Herautiz or take the D 22 back to Irissary then return to Ossès via the D 8.

St-Jean-Pied-de-Port★

Pyrénées-Atlantiques

The Old Town of St-Jean-Pied-de-Port on the north bank of the Nive is encircled by 15C ramparts dating from the time of Navarrese domination. The citadel and fortifications on the south bank, built to defend the road to Spain after the Treaty of the Pyrénées, are part of the 17C military complex designed by Vauban.

- **Population:** 1 513
- **Michelin Map:** 342: E-4
- **Info:** 14 pl. de Gaulle, St-Jean-Pied-de-Port. ℘05 59 37 03 57. www.pyrenees-basques.com.
- **Location:** The town lies in a mild, picturesque basin watered by the Nive and Petite Nive rivers, its red sandstone houses grouped around a spur crowned by the old citadel. It is situated in the foothills of the Pyrénées, not far from the Spanish border.
- **Parking:** Park near the Porte de France and follow the ramparts to the stairs that lead up to the porte St-Jacques.

A BIT OF HISTORY

The name St-Jean-Pied-de-Port is a reminder that the town lies at the foot of a port or pass: for travellers heading for Spain it was the last stop before the climb to Puerto Ibaêeta, or Port de Roncevaux as it is known on the French side (alt 1 058m/3 471ft), 25km/15.5mi away on Spanish territory.

WALKING TOUR

IN THE FOOTSTEPS OF PILGRIMS★

Allow 1hr30min.

Rue de la Citadelle

The street, sloping down towards the river, is bordered by charming 16C and 17C houses with rounded doorways and carved lintels. At no 41, the **"prison des évêques"** (bishops' jail; *open 30 Mar–4 Nov Wed–Mon 10am–12.30pm, 2–6.30pm; 3€; ℘05 59 37 03 57*) houses an exhibition evoking The Way of StJames in the Middle Ages. On the way, you will find a city map and posters in front of the Tourist Information Centre (at each door, r. d'Espagne and at the citadel).

Église Notre-Dame

r. de l'Église.

The Gothic church, dedicated to the Virgin, has handsome sandstone pillars.

Rue de l'Église

This street leads to the porte de Navarre, passing the **house of the Jassu family**, ancestors of St François-Xavier (1506–52), which is now a library.

Return to the church, pass through the vaulted passage beneath the belfry and cross the river.

Vieux Pont

From the Old Bridge there is a picturesque view of the church and the old riverside houses.

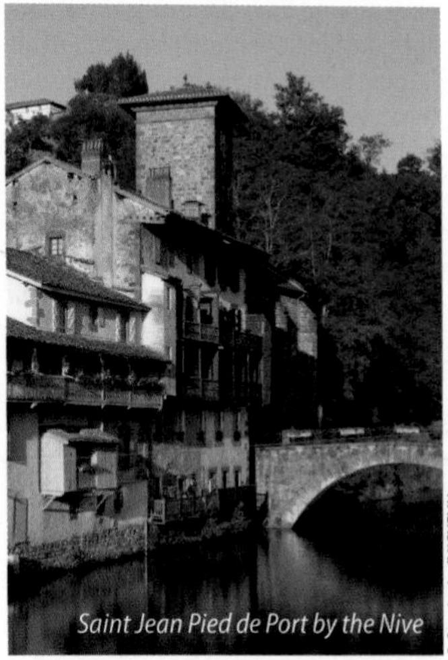

Saint Jean Pied de Port by the Nive

S. Sauvignier/MICHELIN

Rue d'Espagne

The street, which climbs uphill to porte d'Espagne, has always been a main shopping area.

Follow av. du Fronton to the left, cross the river again, walk to the back of the church and take the steps.

Citadelle

r. d'Espagne.

From the bastion facing the entrance to the citadel, the view stretches over the St-Jean basin.

Return to porte St-Jacques.

DRIVING TOUR

4 TOWARDS IRATY

25km/15.5mi. Allow 1hr30min.

Leave St-Jean-Pied-de-Port via the D 933 towards St-Palais, then head off towards the right along the D 18.

St-Jean-le-Vieux

Until the foundation of St-Jean-Pied-de-Port, this was the principal urban centre of the region, and an important stopping point for pilgrims – explaining why you find six churches and chapels here. Remains of Roman occupation exist around the village outskirts; highlights include the site of an *oppidum* (the Roman administration centre) close to the river. Artefacts found through excavation works are on display in the little Musée archéologique. Head 50m/50yds into the village when arriving from St-Jean-Pied-de-Port, then turn right *(open mid-Jun–mid-Sept Mon–Thur pm only; 2€ (under 14 years 1€); 05 59 37 91 08).*

Leave the village via the D 18 towards Mendive. After 1.5km/1.9mi, turn right and take the D 118.

Aincille

A sober exterior for the church masks an extravagant Baroque-style chancel dating from the 18C as well as a well-preserved statue of the Virgin Mary from the 14C.

Return along the D 18 and after approx 2km/1.2mi, turn right towards Bascassan.

Bascassan

Small Roman church St-André, at the highest point of the hamlet, contains frescoes in the nave which have been recently restored. Twinned with the chapel at Alciette, and many of the features are similar.

Return along the D 18 towards Mendive. Pass the intersection at Ahaxe, and take the next left (look out for the sign).

Alciette

Ask for the key to the chapel at the Ferme Bidart, in the small hamlet opposite. To find it: at the central crossroads in the hamlet, take the right-hand winding road.

Église St-Sauveur – This country chapel is delightful; touching frescoes which are in need of restoration. Note the baptistery hidden behind the wooden panels depicting the Baptism of Christ.

Return to the D 18 and drive towards Mendive. In the village turn left at the church onto the D 117.

Béhorléguy

Picturesque little village set into the hillside, with an attractive church and cemetery (notable for its Basque crosses).

You can continue farther into the Mendive: drive along the D 18, and you will reach the forest of Iraty (see opposite). By taking the D 417 to the left, you can drive first through the Forêt des Arbailles.

Forêt d'Iraty★

Pyrénées-Atlantiques

This forest of beech groves straddling the frontier supplied wood for masts for the French and Spanish navies from the 18C onwards; it is one of the largest wooded areas in Europe (in France alone 2 310ha/5 708 acres).

- **Michelin Map:** 342 E–F-4-5.
- **Info:** ℘00 34 948 890 641. www.ochagavia.com.
- **Location:** The north of the forest lies along the D 18, 32km/20mi SE of St-Jean-Pied-de-Port.
- **Parking:** Leave your car by the chalets in Iraty.

THE NORTHERN MASSIF

Chalets d'Iraty

The small resort village of Chalets d'Iraty was built in the 1960s in the heart of Iraty Forest. At an altitude of 1 200m/3 900ft to 1 500m/4 920ft, the 109km/68mi of cross-country ski runs and numerous hiking paths offer a unique view of the mountain. Once this area was populated by loggers and workers; today it is the favourite haunt of hikers and holidaymakers.

Several hiking trails start from the village but two penetrate deeper into the forest; one to the crest of Orgambideska (1420m/4658ft, 1hr, easy), and further on to the Orhy peak (5h round-trip; relatively difficult; you must be well equipped; only hike in good weather).

Col Bagargui★

On the D19 between the chalet and Larrau.

There is a **view**★ to the east of the Upper Soule mountains and the High Pyrénées in the Aspe and Ossau regions. In the foreground, on the right, is the heavy mass of Pic d'Orhi; farther away rise the elegant limestone summits of the Pic d'Anie chain, and behind them the silhouette of Pic du Midi d'Ossau. Scattered among the forest trees below are the buildings of the picturesque village of Iraty.

Col de Burdincurutcheta

9km/5.6mi to the west of Chalets d'Iraty on the St-Jean-Pied-de-Port route via the D19 and D18. Park 1km/0.6mi below the N side of the pass, where the road approaches a rocky crest. Alt 1 135m/3 724ft.

Walk to the edge of the Col de Burdincurutcheta. The view extends over the jagged foothills of the frontier massif, cut through by bleak deserted valleys; in the distance the basin of St-Jean-Pied-de-Port, centre of the Cize region, opens out.

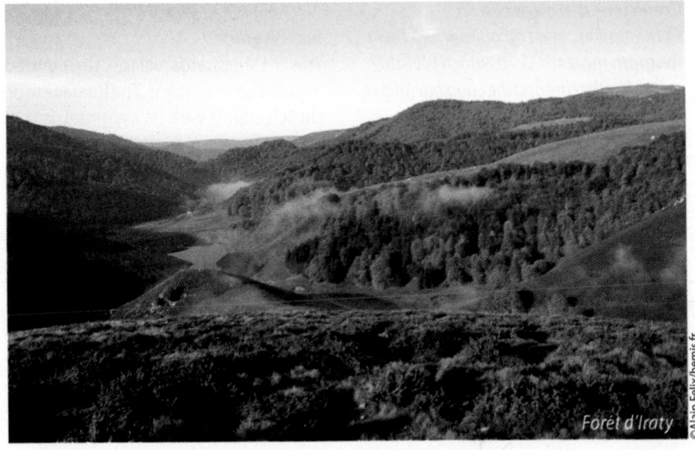

Forêt d'Iraty

Larrau

Pyrénées-Atlantiques

Former stopping point on The Way of St James, Larrau is a typical village of the Haute-Soule: steeply sloping tiled roofs, houses grouped around the church, and stunning surrounding scenery. Tucked into the foothills of the Pic d'Orhi, and opposite the black cliffs of the Massif de Mendibelza, this is a dramatic landscape, perfect for heading off walking. Particularly good access for the Gorges d'Holçarté.

- **Population:** 200
- **Michelin Map:** 342: G-4
- **Info:** ℘05 59 37 47 28. www.pyrenees-basque.com.
- **Location:** 43km/27mi SE of St-Jean-Pied-de-Port.
- **Parking:** Near to the covered *fronton*.
- **Don't Miss:** Col d'Erroymendi.

EXCURSION

Col d'Erroymendi★

Alt 1 362m/4 469ft. 7.5km/4.7mi from Larrau, by the Port de Larrau road (generally blocked by snow in Nov–Jun).

From here there is a vast mountain **panorama★** which highlights the pastoral and woodland activities in the Upper Soule region. A few yards east of the pass there is a different view: the fan of the Upper Saison valleys and, on the horizon, the rocky mass of Pic d'Anie.

DRIVING TOUR

6 LA ROUTE DES GORGES

37km/23mi. Allow 2hrs.

Leave Larrau towards Mauléon.

Crevasses d'Holçarté★

1hr30min round trip on foot, via the footpath marked GR 10, which is visible soon after the café and the Laugibar Bridge.

At Pont de la Mouline, leave the GR 10 on the left and take the right-hand alternative.

After a steep, stiff climb, the entrance to the crevasses is reached: these are narrow gorges sliced from the limestone to a depth of 200m/656ft. The path rises to the top of the Olhadubi tributary gorge, which is crossed by a dizzily impressive footbridge slung 171m/561ft above the torrent in 1920.

Gorges de Kakuetta★★

Access via the D 113, which leads to Ste Engrâce. Take the footbridge across the Uhaïtxa, climb up the opposite bank and go down into the gorge. This excursion is a demanding one, best undertaken when the water level is low (early Jun–late Oct). Stout footwear is essential. Open 15 Mar–15 Nov 8am–dusk (last admission 6pm). 4.50€. ℘05 59 28 73 44 (Bar La Cascade). www.sainte-engrace.com.

These limestone gorges are beautiful, with the beginning of the Grand Étroit (the Great Narrows), the most grandiose of all. This splendid canyon, more than 200m/656ft deep, is no more than 3m/11ft to 10m/33ft wide at the top of its sheer sides. The torrent roars through the long fissure with its dense clumps of vegetation. The path, frequently difficult, eventually arrives at the water's edge. It ends within sight of a 20m/66ft-high waterfall.

Ste-Engrâce

This is a shepherds' village, surrounded by wooded mountains. The Romanesque church stands with its asymmetric roof and its heavy masonry on a pastoral **site★**. The chancel, closed off by a robust 14C grille, has richly ornamented capitals. These include scenes involving buffoons and jesters; hunting scenes, and **Solomon and the Queen of Sheba**, the royal visitor's elephant bearing on its back a palanquin in the Indian manner.

Mauléon-Licharre

Pyrénées-Atlantiques

Mauléon is an old stronghold and the smallest capital in the seven Basque provinces. It rises on the Right Bank of the River Saison, at the foot of a hill where the ruins of the old castle stand. Mauléon is also the capital city of espadrille sandals. 70% of the French production is manufactured there.

- **Population:** 3 255
- **Michelin Map:** 342: G-3
- **Info:** 10 r. J.B. Heugas, Mauléon-Licharre. ℘05 59 28 02 37. www.valleedesoule.com.
- **Location:** Mauléon-Licharre lies 30km/18.6mi W of Oloron-Ste-Marie and 40km/25mi E of St-Jean-Pied-de-Port.
- **Don't Miss:** Exploring the Soule region to the S of the town.
- **Kids:** Aventure Parc Aramits.
- **Timing:** Half a day.

SIGHTS

Château d'Andurain de Maytie

1 r. du Jeu de Paume. Guided tour (1hr) 1 Jul–20 Sept Mon–Wed and Fri–Sat 11am–noon, 3–6pm, Sun 3–6pm. 4.50€. ℘05 59 28 04 18.

This Renaissance château was built towards the beginning of the 17C by Arnaud I de Maytie, the Bishop of Oloron. Of particular interest are the carved fireplaces and the 17C–18C furniture inside the château.

Château Fort de Mauleon

Steep ascent to the castle. Access for cars. Open spring school holidays and 15 Jun–15 Sept, daily 11am–1.30pm, 3–7pm; 1 May–14 Jun Sat–Sun 11am–1.30pm, 3–7pm. 2.50€. ℘05 59 28 02 37.

Built in the 12C on a hill overlooking the valley of the River Saison, this castle was demolished in the 17C on the orders of the King. The castle well is still visible in the courtyard. Note the three cannons dating from 1685 on the path around the battlements.

DRIVING TOUR

7 LOWER SOULE

50km/31mi. Allow 1hr30min.

The Soule province, which shares many cultural influences with Béarn – including, for instance, the types of houses – has retained the dances and folk traditions most characteristic of the region.

Leave Mauléon via the D 24, then the D 25.

L'Hôpital-St-Blaise★★

A tiny village on the Basque-Béarn border. The **church★★** *(open daily 10am–7pm; ℘05 59 66 11 12)* – a rare example of Hispano-Moorish art on the northern side of the Pyrénées – is in the form of a Greek cross, the four arms radiating from a central tower.

Leave the village towards Oloron-Ste-Marie and turn right onto the D 859.

L'Hôpital-St-Blaise

©Nicolas Thibaut/Photononstop

Barcus

The interior of this chruch is notable for the richness of its Baroque decorations, and its layout: wooden galleries, painted walls, and gilded Baroque altarpiece depicting the Ascension.

The D 347 heading towards Tardets passes through attractive hills covered with a patchwork of hedges and groves. The cows prefer to concentrate on the pastureland close to the road.

Tardets

Office de tourisme, pl. Centrale, 64470 Tardets. 05 59 28 51 28. www.valleedesoule.com.

Ancient *bastide* town with a central square lined with 17C arcaded houses. The village makes an attractive departure point for several walks and excursions (details from the tourist office).

Rejoin the road heading towards Mauléon.

Trois-Villes

The name of the village recalls the military career and the personality of Mr de Tréville, Captain of the King's Musketeers under Louis XIII. The château was built by François Mansart (1598–1666), the great Classicist architect.

The **Barétous**, a transitional region between Béarn and the Basque provinces, offers the visitor a chequerboard of maize fields and magnificent meadows punctuated by thickets of oak trees, with the limestone summits of the mountains in the background.

Continue to Mauléon-Licharre.

Gotein-Libarrenx

This Pyrénéan village has a church and belfry-calvary typical of the region.

The road continues to Mauléon.

ADDRESSES

STAY

Hostellerie du Château – *r. de la Navarre. 05 59 28 19 06. Closed 3 wks Feb. 6.50€. Restaurant.* Huge, labyrinth-style building. New owners since 2002, who have progressively restored the bedrooms and the building itself. Plentiful regional food.

Auberge du Lausset – *64130 L'Hôpital-St-Blaise (13km/8mi E of Mauléon-Licharre). 05 59 66 53 03. http://aubergedulausset.com. Closed Sun evening, Mon, a fortnight in Jan, and 3 wks in Oct.* This quiet, family-run inn opposite a delightful 12C Romanesque church serves traditional cuisine in a large, contemporary-style dining room. Eat out on the shaded terrace in summer. The *auberge* also has a few reasonably priced rooms.

EAT

Bidegain – *13 r. de Navarre. 05 59 28 16 05. bidegain-hotel@wanadoo.fr. Closed Sun evening, out of season and Mon lunch.* Housed in a former *relais de poste*, this restaurant has a delightfully old-fashioned feel. Expect beeswaxed tabletops, tapestries on the walls, open fireplaces, and a thoroughly attentive welcome. A shady terrace is particularly agreeable for summer days.

SHOPPING

Espadrille *pl. Centrale. 05 59 28 2848. www.espadrille-mauleon.fr.com. Open summer Mon–Sat 9am–1pm, 2–7pm, Sun 10am–12.30pm.* A short film shows the workshop and production of these traditional local shoes.

SPORT AND LEISURE

Aventure Parc Aramits – *Espace Forêt-Loisirs, 64570 Aramits. 05 59 34 64 79. www.aventure-parc.fr/aramits. Prices vary with activity. Closed early Nov–early Apr.* This exciting adventure park offers a range of climbing activities through the treetops (children must be at least 1.5m/4.9ft tall with arms raised), as well as bungee jumping, hiking, canyoning and potholing. The park has a dedicated area for younger children (aged 3–8), a bar-restaurant and a picnic area.

Forêt des Arbailles★

Pyrénées-Atlantiques

This is an upland forest carpeting the higher reaches of a limestone bastion standing clear of the gullies carved by the Saison, the Laurhibar and the Bidouze torrents. The forest rises to a height of 1 265m/4 150ft at Pic de Béhorléguy. The beech groves, hiding slopes strewn with boulders, riddled with hollows, give way in the south to a pastoral zone.

- **Michelin Map:** 342: G-4
- **Info:** ℘05 59 28 51 28. www.pyrenees-basque.com.
- **Location:** To the S of the road between St-Jean-Pied-de-Port and Mauléon-Licharre.
- **Don't miss:** The viewpoint from Ahusquy.
- **Timing:** You could easily pass a day here, or shorter walks lasting a few hours.

DRIVING TOUR

8 THE MASSIF DES ARBAILLES

36km/22mi. Allow 2hrs.

St-Just-Ibarre

This village on the banks on the Soule has seven districts represented by the seven sections of the fountain in front of the town hall.

Maison de St Michel Garicoïts – *From the church, head down towards the river. At the fork, head right, then left on the main road. At the village, follow signs to Ibarre. Once there, the house is signposted. No parking. No charge.* Wild grasses cover the road St Michel Garicoïts (1797–1875), sometimes known as the last saint of the Pays Basque and founder of the Pères de Bétharram.

Sources de la Bidouze

At the exit of St-Just towards Col d'Osquich and de Mauléon, take the first road which heads towards the valley and the river. The walk begins at the top of the car park *(9km/5.6mi; 3hr round trip; 350m/1 148ft of ascent)*. The path heads upwards towards the trees until it reaches the caves, and the river. Follow the yellow markers.

Return to St-Just until the D 918 then turn right towards Mauléon. After 9km/5.6mi, turn right onto the D 348 towards Ordiarp and Aussurucq.

Ordiarp★

Charming village on the banks of a river, which is spanned by a Roman bridge. One side of the river is lined with traditional houses with tiled roofs. A 12C church is the only remaining vestige of the Commanderie des Augustins de Roncevaux, who received Compostella pilgrims here *(Centre d'évocation du patrimoine souletin; open Jul–Aug Mon–Fri 10am–12.30pm, 2–6.30pm; rest of year by appointment; 3€; ℘05 59 28 07 63)*. Basque culture, mythology and art, as well as artefacts left by the Compostella pilgrims, are displayed here.

Aussurucq★

Picturesque village with several ancient farms, and the 15C Château de Ruthie.

Follow the D 147 to Ahusquy.

Ahusquy★★

There is a restored mountain inn standing on this **panoramic site★★** *(www.auberge-pays-basque.com)*, once a gathering place for shepherds.

Col d'Aphanize

Wild horses can be seen grazing on the slopes around the pass. The pastureland here is the summer home of many flocks of sheep. East of the pass the **view★★** opens out wide: from Pic des Escaliers, immediately south, to Pic de Ger on the southeastern horizon. Ossau-Iraty is a refined local cheese made from ewe's milk; gourmets like to eat it with black cherry jam.

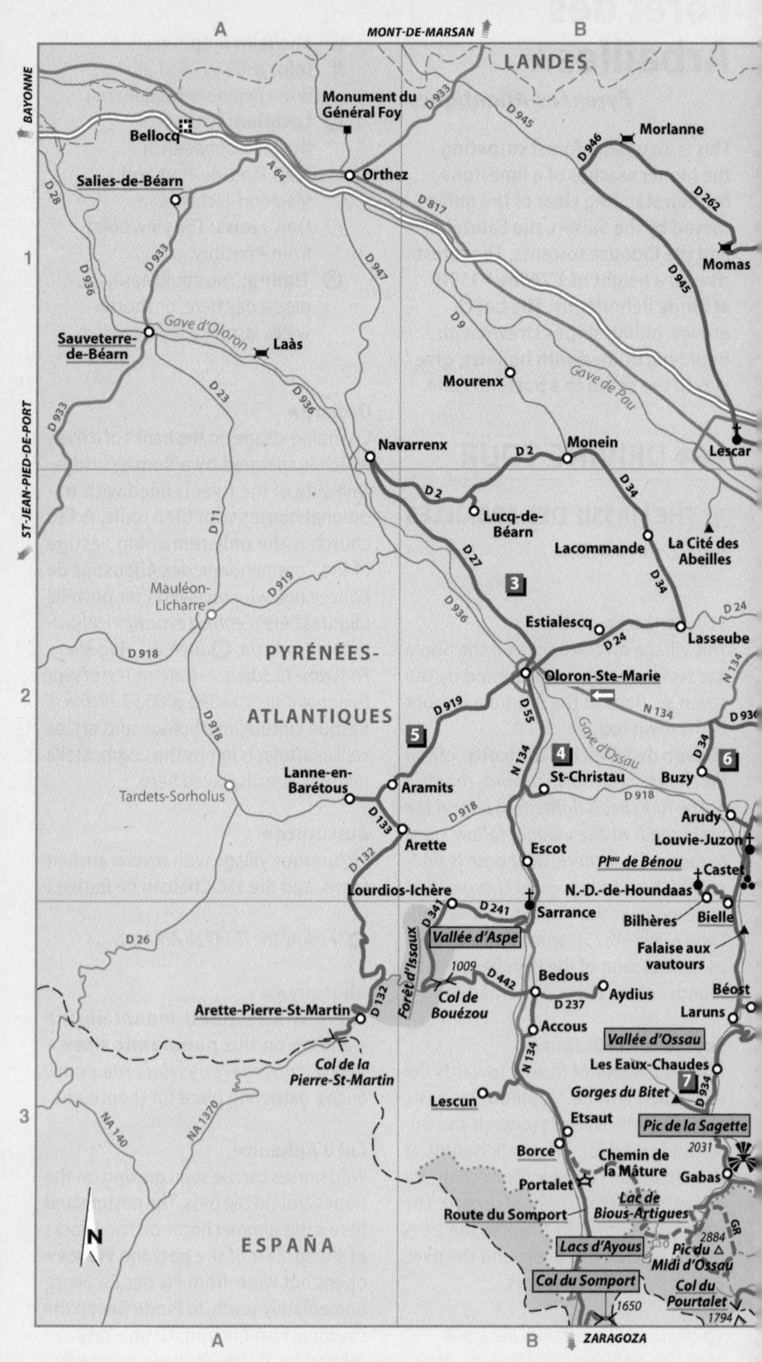
MONT-DE-MARSAN
ZARAGOZA
BAYONNE
ST-JEAN-PIED-DE-PORT
LANDES
PYRÉNÉES-ATLANTIQUES
ESPAÑA
Monument du Général Foy
Bellocq
Orthez
Salies-de-Béarn
Morlanne
Momas
Sauveterre-de-Béarn
Laàs
Gave d'Oloron
Mourenx
Gave de Pau
Navarrenx
Monein
Lescar
Lucq-de-Béarn
Lacommande
La Cité des Abeilles
Mauléon-Licharre
Estialescq
Lasseube
Oloron-Ste-Marie
Tardets-Sorholus
Lanne-en-Barétous
Aramits
St-Christau
Buzy
Gave d'Ossau
Arette
Arudy
Louvie-Juzon
Escot
Plau de Bénou
Castet
Lourdios-Ichère
N.-D.-de-Houndaas
Sarrance
Bilhères
Bielle
Vallée d'Aspe
Forêt d'Issaux
Falaise aux vautours
Col de Bouézou
1009
Bedous
Aydius
Béost
Arette-Pierre-St-Martin
Accous
Laruns
Col de la Pierre-St-Martin
Vallée d'Ossau
Les Eaux-Chaudes
Gorges du Bitet
Lescun
Etsaut
Pic de la Sagette
2031
Borce
Chemin de la Mâture
Gabas
Portalet
Lac de Bious-Artigues
Route du Somport
Lacs d'Ayous
2884
Pic du Midi d'Ossau
Col du Somport
1650
Col du Pourtalet
1794
GR
A 64
D 817
D 933
D 945
D 946
D 262
D 28
D 936
D 947
D 9
D 23
D 2
D 34
D 11
D 27
D 919
D 918
D 24
N 134
D 930
D 55
D 133
D 132
D 341
D 241
D 442
D 237
D 26
D 934
NA 140
NA 1370
A
B
1
2
3
4
5
6
7
N

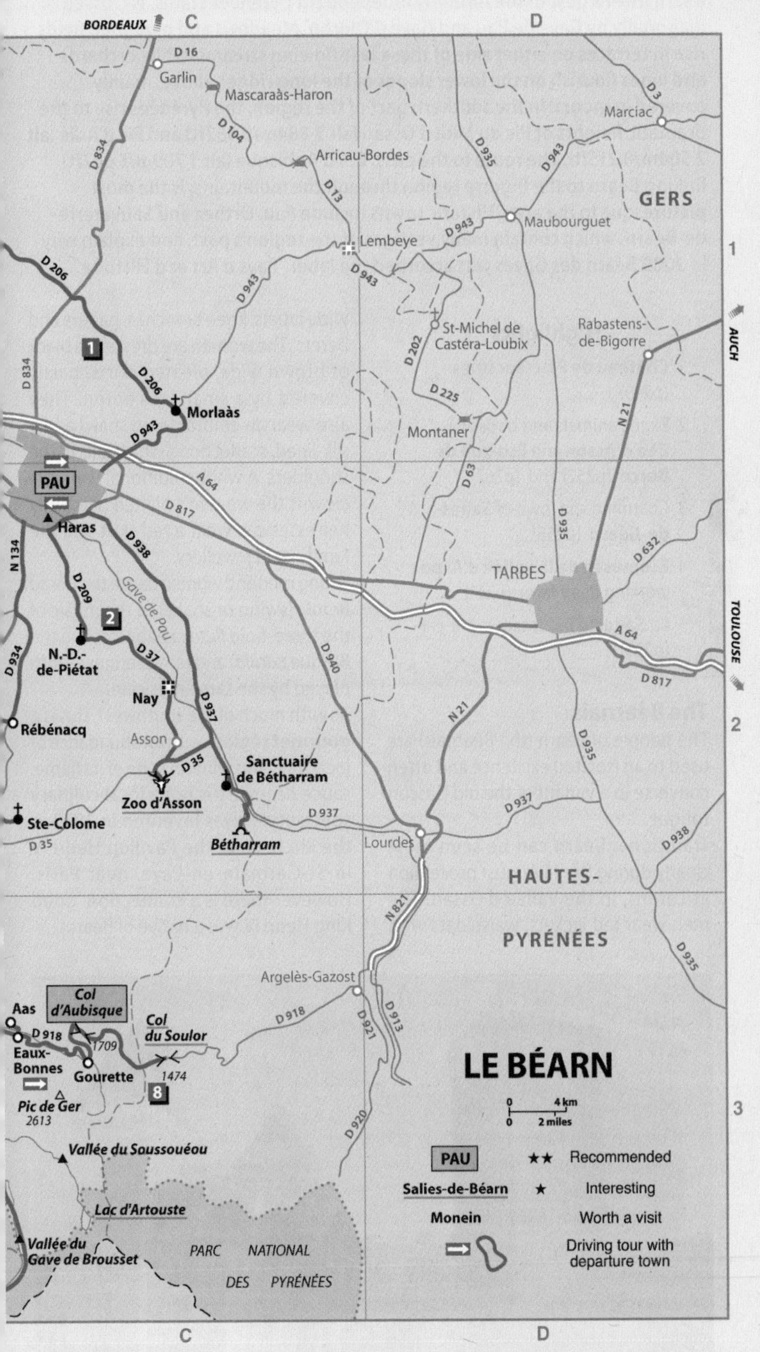

BORDEAUX
C
D
D 16
Garlin
Mascaraàs-Haron
D 834
D 104
Arricau-Bordes
D 13
D 935
D 943
D 3
Marciac
GERS
Maubourguet
D 943
Lembeye
1
D 206
D 943
St-Michel de
Castéra-Loubix
Rabastens-
de-Bigorre
AUCH
D 202
1
D 834
D 206
D 225
Morlaàs
D 943
Montaner
N 21
PAU
A 64
D 63
Haras
D 817
D 935
D 632
D 938
N 134
TARBES
D 209
Gave de Pau
2
TOULOUSE
A 64
D 817
N.-D.-
de-Piétat
D 37
D 940
D 934
Nay
D 937
N 21
2
Rébénacq
Asson
D 935
D 35
Sanctuaire
de Bétharram
Zoo d'Asson
D 937
D 937
Ste-Colome
D 938
D 35
Bétharram
Lourdes
HAUTES-
N 821
PYRÉNÉES
D 935
Argelès-Gazost
Col
d'Aubisque
Aas
D 918
D 918
Col
du Soulor
D 913
D 921
1709
Eaux-
Bonnes
Gourette
1474
LE BÉARN
8
Pic de Ger
2613
3
0 4 km
0 2 miles
D 920
Vallée du Soussouéou
PAU
★★ Recommended
Salies-de-Béarn
★ Interesting
Lac d'Artouste
Monein
Worth a visit
Driving tour with
departure town
Vallée du
Gave de Brousset
PARC NATIONAL
DES PYRÉNÉES
C
D

LE BÉARN

Béarn, the largest of the formerly independent Pyrénées states, is crossed diagonally by Gave de Pau and Gave d'Oloron. Meadows and ploughed fields rise in terraces on either side of these fast-flowing streams, while orchards and vines flourish on the lower slopes of the long ridges above, mainly covered in moors. In the southern part of the region, the Pyrénées rise to the dramatic heights of Pic du Midi d'Ossau (alt 2 884m/9 462ft) and Pic d'Anie (alt 2 504m/8 215ft). The route to the pass, Col d'Aubisque (alt 1 709m/5 607ft), linking Béarn to the Bigorre region through the mountains, is the most picturesque in the area. Historic towns include Pau, Orthez and Sauveterre-de-Béarn, which contain many vestiges of the region's past, and explain why in 2009 Béarn des Gaves was accorded the label "Pays d'Art et d'Histoire".

Highlights

1. **Château de Pau** tapestries (p249)
2. Exotic animals and birds at **Zoo d'Asson** and **Éco-zoo de Borce** (p252) and (p262)
3. Charming spa town of **Salies-de-Béarn** (p255)
4. **Écomusée de la vallée d'Aspe** working dairy farm (p261)
5. **La Sagette** mountain cable-car (p268)

The Béarnais

The people of Béarn (the Béarnais) are used to an isolated existence and often converse in a variant of the old Gascon tongue.

Traditional Béarn can be seen most clearly during the 15 August procession at Laruns, in the Vallée d'Ossau. The men wear red jackets, waistcoats with wide lapels, knee breeches, gaiters and berets. The women are dressed in black or brown wide, pleated skirts, partly covered by a small lace apron. They also wear an embroidered shawl and a silk-lined, scarlet hood which falls to the shoulders. A white traditional *bonnette* crowns the women's plaited hair. Only heiresses can wear a red skirt and the family gold jewellery.

Young men and women dance the Ossau *Branle* (swing or shake) to the music of the three-hole *fluto* (a flageolet like the Basque *txirulä*) and tambourines – both played by the same musician.

As with much of the southwest, this is a **gourmet region**, with an abundance of local food and wine. In spite of its name, sauce *béarnaise* is not a local culinary speciality; it was invented in 1830 in the kitchens of the Pavillon Henri IV in St-Germain-en-Laye, near Paris. However there is a connection: good King Henri IV was a native of Béarn!

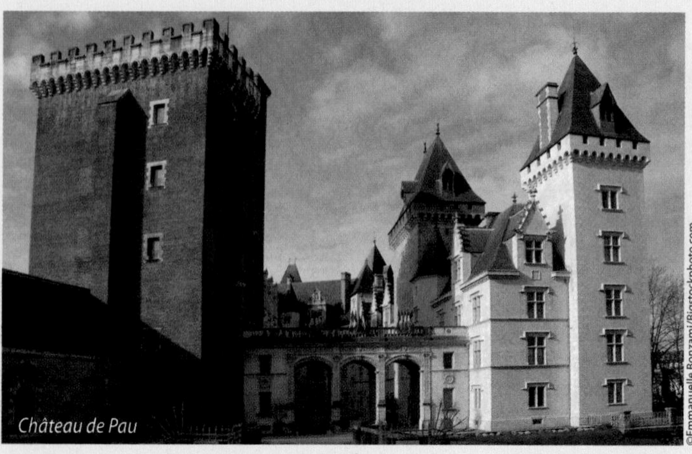
Château de Pau

Pau★★

Pyrénées-Atlantiques

Pau is the most elegant and pleasantly situated of all the towns on the fringe of the Pyrénées. It was highly prized as a tranquil winter resort by the British in the 19C, but its consistently mild climate is still appreciated today. Pau's main tourist attractions are its historical links with Henry of Navarre (Henri IV of France), its fine mountain views and excellent golf, horse racing, fox hunting and other pastimes introduced by the British. Regular events include the long-running Grand Prix de Pau *(www.grandprixautomobilepau.com)*, and the summer Festival de Pau, which has attracted tourists since 1977.

- **Population:** 83 903
- **Michelin Map:** 342: J-3
- **Info:** pl. Royale, Pau. ℘05 59 27 27 08. www.pau-Pyrénées.com.
- **Location:** Pau lies just off the A 64, which runs between Biarritz and Toulouse. It is also on the high-speed TGV line from Bordeaux to Tarbes.
- **Parking:** The main car parks can be found in pl. Clemenceau in the city centre, pl. Recaborde in the Hédas quarter (near the château) and in cours Bosquet (near the Musée des Beaux-Arts).
- **Don't Miss:** The view from the bd des Pyrénées; the château; the Romanesque church in Morlaàs; the Cathédrale Notre-Dame in Lescar.
- **Kids:** The Haras National de Gelos; the Francis Miot jam-tasting school.
- **Timing:** Spend a couple of days in Pau to explore the town.

A BIT OF HISTORY

Gaston Fébus

In the 14C he built a wall around Pau and laid the foundations of the present castle. His successors continued his work and, in 1450, the town followed Lescar, Morlaàs and Orthez as the provincial capital of Béarn.

Marguerite of Marguerites

In 1527 Henri d'Albret, King of Navarre, sovereign lord of Béarn and Comte of Foix and Bigorre, married Marguerite of Angoulême, the sister of the French King François I. The celebrated Marguerite of Marguerites transformed the castle in accordance with Renaissance taste, surrounded it with luxuriant gardens and used them for pageants and plays which she composed herself.

Henri and Marguerite's daughter **Jeanne d'Albret** married a descendant of St Louis, and her son, Henry of Navarre, later became Henri IV of France.

A British Discovery

As early as the July Monarchy of 1830 there were English residents in Pau, and they gradually grew in numbers to form a colony. Some of these expatriates were retired officers who had fought with Louis XVIII on his victorious return from Britain in 1814. It was, however, a Scot, Doctor Alexander Taylor (1802–79), who brought the town fame and fortune: in 1842 he published his theory – which was rapidly translated into most European languages – that Pau could serve as a winter resort providing cures for various ills, and many visitors came to test his claim. The local enthusiasm for sport dates from the same period the colony introduced the steeplechase in 1841 (with meetings still held at the Hippodrome de Pau; *℘05 59 13 07 00; www.hippodrome-pau.com*). Fox-hunting followed a year later and, in 1856, the first golf links on the continent were inaugurated. The year 1889, when Queen Victoria instead chose Biarritz for a one-month visit, saw the start of Pau's decline as an international winter resort.

An English Town

The English, drawn to the warm climate, settled in Pau from 1840, building sumptuous villas around the town centre. Eclectic architectural styles were adopted, similar to numerous 19C public and private buildings. Each villa has its own grounds and outbuildings: greenhouses and stables, both essential parts of the British lifestyle. Villas, usually private, can still be seen today in the area around Lawrence Park, north of the town centre, and the Trespoey district due east.

A Green City

Half of the city is covered with parks (750ha/1 853 acres). Many of them have exotic species, which adds something to the charm of the city. Just to name a few of them: the parks and the gardens of the château, the contemporary gardens in the lower city and the Johanto gardens close to the boulevard des Pyrénées.

SIGHTS

BOULEVARD DES PYRÉNÉES★★

At the initiative of Napoleon I, **place Royale** was extended to form a splendid terrace overlooking the valley and the fast-flowing waters of the Gave de Pau, which was aptly named boulevard des Pyrénées. At the end of the boulevard, the municipal casino stands in the middle of **parc Beaumont**, with its many varieties of trees, ornamental lake and **palais Beaumont**. The boulevard overlooks terraced gardens and a funicular connecting place Royale to the railway station below and offers a spectacular view of the Pyrénées described with great lyricism by many writers.

Panorama★★★ – Beyond the vine-covered slopes of the Gelos and Jurançon foothills, the sweeping view stretches from Pic du Midi de Bigorre to Pic d'Anie, with Pic du Midi d'Ossau standing out clearly in the background. In fine weather, particularly in the early morning and evening and notably in winter, the view can be quite spectacular. Plaques indicating the altitude of each peak are fixed to the railing exactly opposite each summit.

OLD QUARTER

East of the castle, a network of picturesque streets lined with antique shops and restaurants offers a pleasant stroll. Maison Sully, built in the 17C, stands opposite the castle, whereas next door stands the former building of the **Navarre Parliament**, restored in the 18C. Close to place des États, a crossroads for transhumance until the Renaissance, you can see rue du Moulin, one of the oldest in the city.

Boulevard des Pyrénées

S. Sauvignier/MICHELIN

The adjoining tower is the old belfry of **Église St-Martin**, built in the 15C. The arcaded **place Reine-Marguerite** was once the marketplace where the gallows and wheel were erected for capital punishment. Rue René Fournets, on the left, crosses the Quartier des Hédas, formerly reserved to craftspeople. Turn left and join **rue Tran** leading to **place Gramont**, which represents a renovated 19C architectural unit. Behind the fountain, the passage under the porch followed by a staircase leads to the ramparts and to the Tour de la Monnaie and to a canal (15C), which was used for the flour mill of the château.

Château★★

2 r. du Château. Guided tours (1hr15min) daily 15 Jun–15 Sept 9.30am –12.30pm, 1.30–5.45pm; 16 Sept–14 Jun 9.30am–11.45am, 2–5pm. Closed 1 Jan, 1 May, 25 Dec. 5€ (1st Sun of month no charge). 05 59 82 38 02. www.musee-chateau-pau.fr.

The castle, built by Gaston Fébus in the 14C on a spur overlooking the river, has lost its military aspect despite the square, brick keep – in typical Sicard de Lordat style – which still towers over it. Transformed into a Renaissance palace by Marguerite d'Angoulême, the building was completely restored in the 19C in the time of Louis-Philippe and Napoleon III.

Royal Apartments – This fine suite of rooms sumptuously redecorated in the 19C includes a superb collection of **tapestries**★★★ removed from the royal storehouse during the reign of Louis-Philippe (numerous Gobelins tapestries). The tour starts in the elegant 16C kitchen, where a scale model of the whole castle is on display.

The **hundred-place dining hall** – with a table large enough to accommodate that number of revellers – has a ceiling with exposed joists. Splendid Gobelins tapestries from the early 18C representing *The Hunts of Maximilian*, and part of the series of 17C tapestries showing *The Labours of the Months* – known, after its creator, as the Lucas Months Tapestries – hang on the walls.

Elsewhere, note the large and lavish first-floor reception hall, the rest of the Lucas tapestries, Sèvres porcelain vases, Gothic Revival chandeliers and 18C Japanese-style vases.

In the **royal bedroom** stands an unusual, monumental bed fashioned in the Louis XIII style.

The **Empress' Apartment** has been restored to its Second Empire style; a washstand complete with toiletries can be seen in the boudoir. Also displayed is the turtleshell from the Galapagos Islands, which is said to have been Henri IV's cradle. The historical rooms contain portraits of Henri IV (16C–17C) and stories relating to his life.

Musée Bernadotte

8 r. Tran. Open Tue–Sun 10am–noon, 2–6pm. Closed 1 Jan, 1 May, 25 Dec. 3€. 05 59 27 48 42.

The museum is in the birthplace of Jean-Baptiste Bernadotte (1763–1844), the Marshal of France who succeeded to the thrones of Sweden and Norway in 1818 under the name of Charles XIV & III John. The salons on the first floor are devoted to the display of family magnificence; on the second floor is an old Béarnais kitchen and the room where the future monarch was born. The Bernadotte family rented the second floor of this house, built in a traditional style, of beaten cob.

Musée des Beaux-Arts★

1 r. Mathieu Lalanne. Open Mon and Wed–Fri 10am–noon, 2–6pm, Sat–Sun 10am–12.30pm, 2–6pm. Closed 1 Jan, 1 May, 25 Dec. 3€. 05 59 27 33 02.

In the Fine Arts Museum old masters are exhibited next to local little-known artists in tasteful thematic displays of old and contemporary works. For instance, El Greco's *St Francis in Ecstasy* (1590), a feverish expression of mystical fervour, hangs next to an abstract work dating from 1993, *Metaphysical Reflections.*

Paintings from the French, Italian, Dutch, Flemish, Spanish and English schools from the 15C to the 20C include the works of Jordaens, Rubens, José de

Ribera, Zurbarán, Nattier, Van Loo and others.

In 1878 the Fine Arts School of Pau purchased Degas' *New Orléans Cotton Exchange*, marking the entry of Impressionism into the museum. The modern era is also represented, with paintings by Berthe Morisot, Armand Guillaumin and André Lhote. The museum also displays numerous examples of the various trends in contemporary art. Sculpture is particularly worthy of mention, with works by Jean Arp, Gillioli, Lasserre among others.

A regional tone is given by the romantic paintings of Eugène Devéria (1805–65) – mountain landscapes, *Birth of Henri IV* – and visions of fast-flowing mountain streams with the sublime ring of the Pyrénées on the horizon by his pupil Victor Galos, an exceptionally talented painter from Béarn.

Musée National des Parachutistes

Exit N of Pau via the D 834 towards Bordeaux (at the entrance to the École des Troupes Aéroportées).

Guided visit available, or self-guided (1hr to 1h30min) Mon–Fri 10am–noon, 2–5pm, Sat–Sun and bank holidays 2–5pm (am by appointment). 5€ (under 18 years no charge). 05 59 49 49 18. www.museedesparas.com. Treasure hunt for children.

This museum is dedicated to the air force, and is located at Pont Long where the first flying school was based. It covers specifically the history of French parachutists through five key periods: the early days of its development, World War II, the wars in Indochina and Algeria, and recent conflicts (through archives, videos, reconstructions, and displays of uniforms and vehicles).

EXCURSIONS

Haras National de Gelos

1 r. Maréchal-Leclerc, Gelos (leave Pau S on the road to Oloron then follow the road to Nay). Visit by guided tour (1hr30min) Mon–Fri May–Jun and Sept–Oct 2pm, 4pm; Jul–Aug 10am, 2pm, 4pm; Nov–Apr 2pm. 5€ (children 3€). 05 59 35 06 52. www.haras-nationaux.fr.

The Haras de Gelos is an equestrian breeding and rearing centre, founded in a former 18C château by Napoleon I in 1807. There are breeds ranging from pure-blood Arabs and Anglo-Arabs, breeds from Brittany, the Ardennes and Franche-Comté, pottock ponies and ponies from the Landes.

La Cité des Abeilles (City of Bees)

11km/6.8mi W. Leave Pau by the D 2 to Mourenx. At Laroin, take the D 502 hairpin road towards St-Faust-de-Bas and continue for 2km/1.2mi.

Open Apr–Jun and Sept–15 Oct Tue–Sun 2–7pm; Jul–Aug daily 2–7pm; 16 Oct–23 Dec and Feb–Mar Sat–Sun 2–7pm. 6€ (children 4€). 05 59 83 10 31. www.citedesabeilles.com.

This fascinating, open-air museum, which is undergoing continuous development, is devoted to the bee and its existence. Visitors follow a footpath climbing a slope planted with sweet-smelling, nectar-bearing flowers to discover the world of apiculture, ancient and modern: traditional old beehives from different regions of France; a covered apiary from a monastery; a glass-walled observation hive in which the workers can be studied tending their allotted honeycombs.

DRIVING TOURS

1 FORMER CAPITALS

85km/53mi. Allow half a day.

Leave Pau to the NE via the D 943. Pass the sign to Morlaàs-Berlanne, then drive through a small wooded area. Morlaàs is signposted on the left.

Morlaàs

After Lescar was destroyed in the 9C, and until Orthez replaced it, Morlaàs became the capital city of Béarn in the 9C. Nowadays, only its **Romanesque church** (*guided tours with booking*

Jul–Aug Wed 1.30pm; ℘05 59 33 46 10) indicates former glory.

Take the attractive D 206 and continue along the D 262.

Château de Momas

Open Apr–Nov Sat–Sun pm or by appointment. 5€ (under 12 years no charge). ℘05 59 77 14 71.

The ground floor of the *maison noble de la Seigneurie de Momas*, once belonging to the Viscount of Béarn, is open to the public, but the real interest are the gardens; containing numerous flowering and medicinal plants, and some rare vegetables. The owner, Madame Teillard, is happy to share her encylopedic knowledge.

The 11C church (restored in 19C) is next to the château, and also open for visits. A little farther away (3km/1.8mi SW via the D 201), the Lac d'Ayguelongue makes an agreeable visit. A walking path circles the lake (bird-watching spots, and picnic tables).

Continue along the D 262 then turn left onto the D 946.

Château de Morlanne

The small brick castle used to be one of the fortresses raised by Gaston Fébus at the end of the 14C.

Take the D 269 and join the D 945 towards Lescar.

Lescar

After the Normans had destroyed Beneharnum (c.850), a major Roman city which had given its name to Béarn and had become its capital city, a new town was constructed on the hill.

Climb up the slope and enter the old city through a fortified door.

The **Cathédrale Notre-Dame** *(r. de la Cité; ℘05 59 81 04 83; www.nd-en-bearn.fr)* was built from 1120 on, starting with the choir. The Romanesque **capitals**★ are particularly remarkable.

The **Musée Art et Culture** *(open mid-Apr–Nov 10.30am–noon, 3–7pm; no charge; ℘05 59 81 36 65)* is housed in the cellars of a former bishop's palace. Only two towers remain of the original palace on place de l'Évêché *(behind the museum)*. On display are archaeological artefacts found at the Beneharnum site and those from a 4C Gallo-Roman villa, together with contemporary art exhibitions.

Created by run-off waters from the Ousse des Bois, the little **Lac des Carolins** (signposted from the town centre) is a haven for the Cistude d'Europe freshwater turtle, and an enjoyable visit: walking path with information boards, fishing, games areas for children. Activities in summer.

2 LE GAVE DE PAU★

79km/49mi. Allow half a day.

Leave Pau to the S, towards Oloron then take the road to Nay.

Notre-Dame-de-Piétat

Opposite the 17C pilgrims' chapel, at the end of the esplanade, there is a roadside crucifix. Behind this is a viewing table providing a **panorama**★ of the Gave de Pau Valley and its many villages. Pic du Midi de Bigorre is visible in the distance *(SE)*.

Continue to the D 37 and turn right along the valley.

Between Pardies-Piétat and Nay the road passes through several pretty Béarn villages whose splendid houses have gateways decorated with piers surmounted by stone urns.

Nay

Nay (pronounced "Nigh") is a *bastide* typical of the Béarn region.

The **Musée du Béret** *(pl. St Roch; open Apr–Jul Tue–Sat 10am–noon, 2–6pm, Aug Mon–Sat 10am–noon, 3–7pm, Sun 3–7pm, Sept–Nov and Jan–Mar Tue–Sat 2–6pm, Dec daily Mon–Sat 10am–noon, 2–6pm; 4€; ℘05 59 61 91 70; www.museeduberet.com)*, situated at the entrance of the village, relates the

history of the genuine beret from Béarn and illustrates its manufacture.
In the main square is the 16C **Maison Carrée** *(pl. de la République; guided tours May–Jun, Sept–Oct and school holidays Tue–Sat 10am–noon, 2–6pm, Jul–Aug Tue–Sat 10am–noon, 3–7pm, Nov–Apr Sat, please call for hours; 3.50€; 05 59 13 99 65)*, also called Maison de Jeanne d'Albret. The inner Florentine-style courtyard shows three Classical forms of architecture, a unique example southwest France.

Leave Nay via the D 36, to the S. Access road is 3km/1.8mi after Asson (follow direction Bruges).

Zoo d'Asson★

6 chemin du Brouquet, Asson. Open daily Apr–Sept 9am–7pm; Oct–Mar 9am–6pm. 10€ (children 6€). 05 59 71 03 34. www.zoo-asson.org.
The **zoo** is planted with about a hundred palm trees and adorned with a fine Napoleon III-style greenhouse. It is home to a raucous and colourful collection of parrots, parakeets, pink Cuban flamingos, emus, panthers, lorikeets, chimpanzees and gibbons, lemurs from Madagascar, and a kangaroo park.

Return to Asson and turn right onto the D 35 then right again to the D 937.

Sites de Bétharram

The Bétharram caves and sanctuary are located near the former *bastide* of Lestelle-Bétharram, founded in 1335 by Gaston de Foix. Beautiful Renaissance and 18C houses line the streets.

Chapelle-Notre-Dame

Open daily 9am–noon, 2–6pm. 05 59 71 92 30. www.betharram.net.
The chapel has an austere Classical façade (1661) of grey marble. The interior and furnishings are Baroque in style. On the left as you go in, behind a screen, is a 14C polychrome wood statue of the Madonna Nursing Her Child; on the right, an 18C Scourging at the Pillar and, at the high altar, a plaster statue of Notre-Dame-de-Bétharram (1845).

Against the chevet *(access through a door to the left of the chancel)* the Chapelle **St-Michel-Garicoïts** (1926) contains the shrine of the priest (1797–1863) who restored the sanctuary and calvary and founded the congregation of the Sacred Heart of Jesus.
Overlooking Chapelle-Notre-Dame is a hill with 19C chapels marking the Stations of the Cross. Note the bas-relief sculptures by Alexandre Renoir (1845).

Grottes de Bétharram★

2.5km/1.5mi from the southern exit of Lestelle-Bétharram on the D 152. Guided tours (1hr20min) 25 Mar–25 Oct daily 9am–noon, 1.30–5.30pm. 12€. 05 62 41 80 04. www.betharram.com.
The caves were discovered in 1819 by local shepherds and explored the same year by naturalists from Pau. A more systematic exploration, begun in 1888 by three speleologists, took 10 years and unearthed 5 200m/over 3mi of underground galleries. In 1898 Léon Ross, a painter from St-Malo in Brittany, who had settled in Bigorre, prepared the caves for the first regular stream of tourists. After several years' excavation of the exit tunnel, it was opened to the public for the first time in 1903. First floor now accessible to people with physical disabilities.

Tour

The underground tour covers 2.8km/more than 1.5mi, and leads through five tiers of galleries, hollowed out of the limestone mountain by the river (which later flows into Gave de Pau). The upper level is the largest, comprising huge interconnected chambers. Their most interesting feature is their porous roof, which has led to the formation of beautiful stalactites in the Salle des Lustres (Chandelier Room), and a stalagmite column.
The lowest galleries are on the same level as the river, which visitors follow by boat over a short distance. A miniature train takes them through a tunnel and back into daylight.

ADDRESSES

STAY

Chambre d'Hote Maison Palu – *19 chemin Arriuthouet. ℘05 59 21 58 93. www.gites64/maison-palu.fr. 5 rooms.* Imposing farm, laid out around an inner courtyard and accessed by a narrow path through the surrounding fields. The bedrooms are simple but clean, and children will love the horses, sheep and goats. Small kitchenette available.

Hostellerie de l'Horizon – *chemin Mesplet, Gan (9km/5.6mi S of Pau via the N 134). ℘05 59 21 58 93. www.hostellerie-horizon.com. Closed Sun, Mon lunch and Tue lunch. 10 rooms. 9€. Restaurant.* This pleasant building with a blue-and-ochre façade overlooks a pretty park with many trees. The structured rooms are furnished in the style of the 1930s–40s, and the dining room has a Japanese flavour.

Hôtel Central – *15 r. Léon Daran. ℘05 59 27 72 75. www.hotelcentralpau.com. Closed 20–26 Dec. 26 rooms. 7.50€.* Guests receive a friendly welcome in this modest hotel right in the centre of Pau. The rooms, of varying comfort and sizes, are very clean and well soundproofed. Lounge with billiards table.

EAT

Au Fin Gourmet – *24 av. Gaston Lacoste. ℘05 59 27 47 71. www.restaurant-aufingourmet.com. Closed Sun evening and Mon.* Across from the train station and at the foot of the funicular, this restaurant with a big, glass-walled dining room is reminiscent of a bandstand. Brick tiles on the floor and pleasant hues make for a genteel ambience. Contemporary cuisine.

O'Gascon – *13 r. du Chateau. ℘05 59 27 64 74. www.restaurant-ogascon-pau.com. Closed Mon–Sat lunch and Tue.* Exposed stone walls, antique wooden furniture and oak-beamed ceilings all contribute to make this a welcoming, homely restaurant serving excellent regional cuisine. Expect big quantities of local classics.

BARS

Le Boucanier – *64 r. Émile-Garet, Quartier du Triangle. ℘05 59 27 38 80.* One of Pau's most attractive bars, fitted out like a ship's hold. Good choice of beer (130 different varieties) and cocktails.

ENTERTAINMENT

Casino Municipal de Pau – *Palais Beaumont, allée Alfred-de-Musset. ℘05 59 27 06 92. www.groupetranchant.com. Open Sun–Thu 10am–3am, Fri–Sat and pre-holiday evenings until 4am.* This casino boasts a hundred slot machines in addition to a traditional games room, a restaurant and a bar. Live music on Fridays.

Zénith – *bd du Cami Salié. ℘05 59 80 77 50. www.zenith-pau.fr.* This enormous, up-to-the-minute performance hall can seat as many as 6 500 spectators. Operas, classical and pop music concerts, cabarets, circuses, ice shows – they've got it all.

SHOPPING

Au Parapluie des Pyrénées – *12 r. Montpensier. ℘05 59 27 53 66. www.parapluiedeberger.com.* Since 1890, the enormous ***parapluies des Pyrénées***, or Pyrénées umbrellas, have been made here. It is the last remaining enterprise of its kind in France.

Confiseur chocolatier Verdier – *chemin de Pau, allées des Brannes. ℘05 59 72 70 30. www.chocolats-verdier.com. Closed Sun.* Monsieur Verdier wanted to be a musician, but he bowed to his father's wishes and became a pastry and confectionery chef instead, specialising in chocolate-making.

Francis Miot – *Uzos roundabout, D 37. ℘05 59 35 05 56. www.francis-miot.com. Closed Sun and public holidays.* Francis Miot has been making jam since 1985 and has collected a host of prestigious awards. A visit to his workshop includes demonstrations, tastings and a special "tasting school" for children.

Henri Burgué – *chemin des Bois, Bas de St-Faust, St-Faust (11km/6.8mi SW of Pau via the D2 and D 502). ℘05 59 83 05 91.* A producer of sweet and dry Jurançon wines, which are aged in oak barrels for three years.

Orthez

Pyrénées-Atlantiques

Orthez was the capital of Béarn before Pau; today it is a picturesque town with a fortified bridge.

- **Population:** 10 329
- **Michelin Map:** 342: H-2
- **Info:** Maison Jeanne d'Albret, r. Bourg-Vieux. 05 59 38 32 84. www.tourisme-bearn-gaves.com.
- **Location:** The town is situated 47km/29mi NW of Pau and 74km/46mi E of Bayonne.
- **Don't Miss:** The Pont Vieux.

A BIT OF HISTORY

Gaston VII Moncade, Vicomte of Béarn, was behind the town's development in the 13C. After the union of Foix and Béarn, Gaston Fébus held court here. The writer and court poet Jean Froissart (c.1337–c.1400) described in his *Chroniques* the lavish château receptions in 1388–89. Francis Jammes (1868–1938) was another poet of note associated with Orthez. He lived in the town from 1897 to 1907; his former home can be seen on the way out of town *(see Maison Chrestia, opposite)*. This literary past has led to Orthez's nickname: "City of books".

OLD TOWN

In the days of Gaston VII and Gaston Fébus the ground plan of Orthez did not lie parallel to the river, as it does now: the main axis was at right angles, clustered on each side of a line drawn from the fortified bridge to the Château Moncade. Reminders of this period remain in the old houses, some with decorated porches, which line rue Bourg-Vieux, rue de l'Horloge and rue Moncade.

Pont Vieux★

The 13C bridge is guarded by a tower pierced with an arched gateway. The tower was still in use in 1814, at the time of the struggle against Wellington.

From the bridge there is an attractive view of the Pau torrent, tumbling past huge blocks of limestone. Canoe rides offer a good way of viewing this bridge from underneath (*05 59 69 36 24*).

Château Moncade

r. Moncade. Open May and Oct Sat–Sun and public holidays 10am–12.30pm, 2.30–6.30pm; Jun–Aug daily 10am–12.30pm, 3–7pm; Sept daily 10am–12.30pm, 2.30–6.30pm. 3€. 05 59 69 36 24.

The tower is all that remains of the fortress built in the late 13C. Inside, the tower contains a model fortress and an exhibition on Gaston Fébus and his **Livre de chasse** (reproductions). There is a good view of the town from the terrace (33m/36yds high).

Église St-Pierre

r. du Général Ducournau. 05 59 69 01 41.

Once connected to the town's ramparts, this 13C church was a defensive post, as in the arrow slits in the north wall. Inside the original double nave is devoid of side aisles; along with the chancel with its ribbed vaulting (four very fine carved keystones), this is all that remains of the 13C building.

Musée Jeanne-d'Albret

37 r. Bourg-Vieux. Open Apr–Sept Mon–Sat 10am–noon, 2–6pm; Oct–1st wk Jan and Feb–Mar Tue–Sat 10am–noon, 2–6pm. Closed public holidays. 4.50€. 05 59 69 14 03. http://museejeannedalbret.com.

The elegant 16C mansion once belonged to Jeanne d'Albret, the mother of Henri IV. The building has an octagonal tower which adds to the charm of the main entrance, leading to a paved inner courtyard. The steeply sloping tiled roof is typical of the region. The carefully restored façades reveal the warm tones of the stonework. It now houses the tourist office. On the first floor, an interesting museum retraces the **history of Protestantism in Béarn**, from the Reformation to the 20C, with the help of written documents, objects, medals and small-scale models. This clear exhibition on a complex subject is worth the visit.

Maison Chrestia

7 av. Francis Jammes.
Open Mon–Fri 10am–noon, 3–5pm.
Closed public holidays. 05 59 69 11 24. www.francis-jammes.com.
Francis Jammes lived in this typical 18C house, which nowadays is home to The Francis Jammes Association, an information centre devoted to his legacy.

EXCURSIONS

Monument du Général Foy

3.5km/2.2mi N on the road to Dax.
The monument is a memorial recalling the Battle of Orthez (1814) in which Marshal Soult's 30 000 men were defeated by Wellington's army of 45 000. The monument sits in a pleasant location surrounded by fine Béarnais farms crowned by tall sloping roofs, with views of the distant Pyrénées.

Mourenx

20km/12.4mi SE of Orthez via the D 9.
In December 1951, during an exploratory mission by petroleum company Société nationale des Pétroles d'Aquitaine, the site "Lacq 3" became, at a depth of 3 550m/11 650ft, one of the most important sources of natural gas in the world. In order to house the numerous workers who serviced the site, the city built new lodgings. The tower blocks, lining up on the Béarnais hillsides, can seem a little out of place. To learn more about the history of this new section of the town, take a city walk with an audio-guide. Information from the Bibliothèque de Mourenx *(pl. Jules-Verne; 05 59 60 25 99)* or the Monein tourist office *(58 r. du Commerce; 05 59 12 30 40)* – no charge.
To the south of the town on the D 281 *(direction Navarrenx)*, a restored belvedere stands on the hillside. The car park offers good views over the industrial zone. From the other side of the car park, you have attractive views over the Béarnais hills, then the Central Pyrénées, from the Pic d'Anie to the Pic du Midi de Bigorre, and, to the south, the Vallée d'Aspe.

Salies-de-Béarn★

16km/10.2mi W of Orthez via the D 817, then the D 933.
Known since Antiquity for its salt production, the old town of Salies has carefully preserved its gorgeous 16C, 17C and 18C houses. The Saleys river is the focal point, with steeply roofed Béarnais houses lining either side of its Pont de la Lune, reflected in its waters. No visit to the region would be complete without a visit to this charming spa town, which grew to fame because of the saltwater found in its natural subterranean water sources.
Useful information boards are located outside the main sites and buildings.

La Vieille Ville

The heart of the old town is the oddly shaped place du Bayaà, location of the water source (uncovered in 1868). Opposite the town hall, water flows from a stone wild boar's head, La fontaine du Sanglier (1827), introducing a Gothic element to the scene.
The surrounding roads, with their evocative names, are filled with attractive old houses; at the far end of rue de la Fontaine-Salée, a bas-relief sculpture relates the visit of Jeanne d'Albret; at 8 rue du Pont-Mayou, the last remaining coulédé to the Salies (a stone trough in front of the house, to collect the salty water).

Musée du Sel et des Traditions Béarnaises

r. des Puits-Salants. Open Tues–Sat May and Oct 3–6pm; June–Sept 3–7pm. Closed Nov–Apr, and bank holidays. 4€ (5–12 years 1€). 05 59 38 19 25.
The Musée du Sel encompasses the former Musée des Arts et Traditions. They have been merged into one museum, located in a traditional Salisienne house. The visit will explain the reasons behind the geological presence of salt in the waters of Salies (which is 10 times saltier than seawater). The exhi-

bition also looks at the ancient civilisations that lived here, the history of the Corporation des Parts-Prenants which manages the hot springs and buildings in the town and dates back to 1587, and the extraction methods and uses of the salt over the centuries. A short film (20min) opens the visit: history of salt; geology, local crafts, and the growth of water cures. The second floor contains the Musée des Arts et Traditions. This covers in more detail 19C and early 20C life in the area, and displays a collection of furniture, clothes and other objects connected to trades such as cabinet-making and ironmongering.

Towards the hot springs, stop at the Église St-Vincent whose bell tower was part of the town's defense system.

La Ville Thermale

The tourist office is close to the Centre de Congrès. In front of the central park stands the Hôtel du Parc (1893), with a sumptuous galleried hall, a grand staircase, and a casino. It has served as a film set for numerous movies, has a recording studio and offers access to the thermal spas.

Le Pain de Sucre

1hr. The prettily named hill which overlooks Salies offers attractive views over the town, as well as a gently shaded walk to the deer park.

Bellocq

7km/4.3mi N via the D 330, from the roundabout by the casino.

Good views over valleys and vineyards along this road. Wine lovers will appreciate a visit to the wine cooperative, which has a boutique and offers tastings.

Park behind the church. This *bastide* (being renovated since 2009) is the oldest in Béarn, first fortified in the 13C by Gaston VII de Moncade. It is laid out in the typical *bastide* pattern.

On the western door of the church, you will note the first visual depictions of the beret (late 15C–early 16C).

The château, built on the banks of the river, offers, with the exception of the square entrance tower, a harmonious ensemble of four round towers intended to offer the best defence against projectiles. Restored during the 14C under the ownership of Gaston Fébus, the château was destroyed under Louis XIII for fears that it had become a refuge for Protestants. Recently, the towers have been restored, and the building is classified a Monument de France *(05 59 65 12 97 for information)*.

ADDRESSES

STAY/ EAT

Chambre d'hôte Costedoat – *64370 Hagetaubin (15km/9.3mi NE of Orthez on the D 933. Head towards Hagetmau then turn right onto the D 945). 05 59 67 51 18. www.chemindecompostelle.com/costedoat. 4 rooms.* Tempted by life on the farm? This is the spot for you. You can choose to help the owner with his daily chores, unless you prefer a game of billiards, tennis or a dip in the pool. The rooms are spacious and you are sure to fall for the delicious home-made jams served at breakfast.

Chambre d'hôtel Larroque – *114 r. Principale, 64150 Lagor (NE of Mourenx on the D 9). 05 59 71 57 02. 2 rooms.* Cheery blue blinds make this typically *béarnais* house stand out. The friendly proprietor is always willing to offer advice on local walks and sightseeing, and serves local, homemade dishes.

Hôtel au Temps de la Reine Jeanne – *44 r. Bourg Vieux. 05 59 67 00 76. www.reine-jeanne.fr. Closed 15 Oct–14 Mar. 30 rooms. 8.50€. Restaurant.* Located in the centre of the Old Town, directly opposite the House of Queen Jeanne d'Albret, this hotel provides comforts such as air-conditioned rooms, a spa, a restaurant serving regional cuisine and occasional jazz performances.

SHOPPING

Market – Orthez presents a traditional duck and goose product market *(marché au gras)* on Tuesday mornings from November to March, between la Moutète and place St-Pierre.

Oloron-Ste-Marie★

Pyrénées-Atlantiques

In the past Oloron and Ste-Marie were an important stage on the pilgrims' route to Santiago de Compostela, one of the last before the climb to Col de Somport, the pass on the Spanish border. In memory of this tradition, contemporary sculptures by artists including Guy de Rougemont, Carlos Cruz-Dies and Michael Warren have been placed at strategic points of historic interest around the town. This unusual urban initiative is part of an overall project to mark out the ancient pilgrims' road, to be continued along Vallée d'Aspe and from there into Galicia via Hecho (Spain). Other sculptures can now be seen in Agnos, Gurmençon, Sarrance and on the Sebers Bridge.

- **Population:** 10 947
- **Michelin Map:** 342: I-3
- **Info:** allée du Comte de Tréville. ℘05 59 39 98 00. www.tourisme-oloron.com.
- **Location:** The town is situated 32km/20mi SW of Pau.
- **Don't Miss:** The doorway of the Église Ste-Marie.

A BIT OF HISTORY

Oloron was once two separate towns, joined together in 1858. It is believed to have been originally an Iberian outpost and subsequently a late Roman citadel surrounded by ramparts on the present-day hillside quarter of Ste-Croix. Rebuilt into a military stronghold at the end of the 11C by the viscounts of Béarn, it served as a staging post along the route of the Reconquista – the wars against the Saracens in northern Spain. It is located at the junction of the Aspe and Ossau, which join to form the River Oloron. The river's name derives from *Iluro*, an Iberian place name and a local mountain deity.

Ste-Marie, which was both a rural and episcopal town, developed around the middle of the 11C on the terrace overlooking the west bank of the Aspe. Originally a Roman town, it became a bishopric at the beginning of the 6C before it was destroyed during the Basque incursions in the late 7C.

SIGHTS

Villa Bourdeu

allées du Comte de Tréville. Open Jul–Aug Mon–Sat 9am–7pm; 14 Jul–15 Aug Sun 10am–1pm; Sept–Jun Mon–Sat 9am–12.30pm, 2–6pm. ℘05 59 39 98 00.

Coving of the doorway depicting peasant life, Cathédrale Ste-Marie

www.tourisme-oloron.com.
This late 19C manor houses the tourist office, which is a starting point to discover the surroundings. A walkway is lined with photographs of the region (each one showing the distance from Oloron). An old-fashioned train has been turned into a cinema showing short films that create the illusion that you are riding through the landscapes.

QUARTIER STE-MARIE

Cathédrale Ste-Marie

pl. de la Cathédrale. Guided tours (1hr30min) of treasury Jul–Aug Mon–Fri 10am, 3pm. 3€. Please call tourist office for further details.
This former cathedral dates from the 12C and 13C. The belfry-porch shelters a magnificent Romanesque **doorway**★★, one of the rare examples of its period which has suffered no serious damage in spite of invasions and religious wars. The hardness of the Pyrénées marble used in its construction is responsible for the well-preserved condition: over the centuries the stone has become as smooth as polished ivory.
Among the doorway's most **impressive features** are:

- Two atlantes in chains (thought by 19C archaeologists to be Saracens – an allusion to the Moors Gaston found installed in France on his return from the Holy Land, and whom he subsequently drove out); *A Deposition; Daniel in the Lion's Den (left)* and the *Ascension of Alexander (right)*, both of which were reconstructed in the 19C.
- Coving representing Heaven: The 24 elders of the Apocalypse, carrying long-necked jars of perfume, are playing violas or rebecs – three-stringed violins used by minstrels – as they worship the divine Lamb, which carries the Cross. Evil is represented by a dragon's head. This is a literal translation into sculpture of the *Vision of St John in the Apocalypse.*
- Coving representing Earth: the craftsmen used local models to re-create the entire peasant life of the place and the period: boar hunting, salmon fishing and filleting (from 1 000 to 1 500 salmon were caught then each day at Oloron), cheese-making, preparation of hams, barrel-making, goose-plucking, etc.
- An equestrian statue of the Emperor Constantine trampling on paganism; and a monster devouring a man.

Interior

The inner chapel is dedicated to St Grat, the first bishop of the town. A lepers' stoup is inset into the first pillar supporting the organ loft on the north side (capital originally from the cloisters). At the entrance to the chancel, note the 18C gilded oak sanctuary lamp and 16C lectern carved from the trunk of a single tree.
Other features of note include the 16C pulpit, the fine organ loft (1650), the 19C organ made by Aristide Cavaillé-Coll, a 17C crib with carved wood figures *(north aisle).*

QUARTIER STE-CROIX

The Holy Cross district, surrounding the château of the Vicomtes (destroyed in 1644), is built on a projecting spur between the two torrents.

Église Ste-Croix

pl. Abbé Menjoulet. Open daily 8am–8pm. 2€. Please call tourist office for further details.
Inside, there is an unusual Spanish-Moorish dome, added in the 13C, above the 11C transept crossing. Inspired by the mosque at Córdoba, Spain, the architects of this dome mounted it above star vaulting supported by columns with historiated capitals.

Old Houses

Near the church are two fine Renaissance houses; lower down in rue Dalmais is the stately 14C **Grède tower** *(open Jul–Aug Fri–Wed 10am–noon, 3–6pm; 3€)* with its twinned bays. Beside it is a 17C building which houses the **Maison du Patrimoine** *(open Jul–21 Sept Wed–Mon 10am–noon, 3–6pm; 3€)*; departments of archaeology, ethnography and mineralogy relating to the town and the Upper Béarn region

occupy two floors of this museum, together with paintings and souvenirs of the largest wartime internment camp (*⊶ not open to the public)* in France at **Gurs** *(20km/12.4mi NW of Oloron-Ste-Marie).*
At the far end of rue Dalmais, place Mendiondou leads to the Point (currently being renovated) at the confluence of the rivers. If you do not have much time, take the left-hand bridge, stopping to admire the tile-flanked houses overlooking the Gave d'Aspe, to return to the Quartier Ste-Marie. If you have more time…

QUARTIER NOTRE-DAME

… turn right onto rue de la Justice: enjoying the view over the Gave d'Ossau, then walk to the place de la Résistance, which is lined by numberous 17C houses. This is where the rich merchants lived and worked, when the Ste-Croix district became too small for the ever-expanding markets they were holding. This district is sometimes known as "Marcadet". A lively market continues to be held on place Clemenceau on Friday mornings.

Église Notre-Dame

Roman-Byzantine-style church, dating from the 19C. Inside, wall paintings by Paul Delance (a pupil of Jean-Léon Gérôme) are worth visiting.
The crypt holds an exhibiition of religious artefacts from the 19C–20C (*open Jul–Aug Sat–Thu 10am–noon, 3–6pm; 3€ (children 1€); 05 59 39 98 00).*
Feeling in need of greenery? Or interested in viewing rare plant species? Continue along the road here as it leads upwards, where the Parc Pommé spreads out over 3ha/7 acres. This public park, once belonging to the Pommé-Jacquet family, contains 383 trees of 34 different varieties. Newly wed couples come to be photographed in this "bed of greenery". Return to the tourist office.

DRIVING TOURS

3 TRIP INTO JURANÇON

75km/47mi. Allow 3hrs.

Leave Oloron NE via the D 24.

Estialescq

2hrs. Take the D 24, 1km/06mi before the village. Slippery road when wet. The sentier des Marlères is an interesting walking route through woods which will lead you past remnants of the local lime-production trade.

Continue along the D 24.

Lasseube

The Arboretum de Payssas is the result of a passionate botanist who collected exotic species of trees during the 1930s, and planted them on his own property. Information boards explain the 26 species on display.
Return to Lasseube to visit the village itself, which has historic houses and a Gothic-style church.

Leave Lasseube to the N towards Lacommande, a halt on The Way of St James.

The Roman church of St-Blaise is worth a visit. The route des Vins du Jurançon also makes a good reason to visit here, as the Maison des Vins et du Terroir du Jurançon offers maps and information to the wine route (*open mid-June–mid-Sept Mon–Sat 10am–noon, 3–7pm, Sun and bank holidays 3–7pm; 05 59 82 70 30).*
Head off along the D 34 to drive into the heart of the vineyards.

Monein

58 r. du Commerce. 05 59 12 30 40.
Monein is rightly considered one of the best districts for winemaking in Jurançon. Judge for yourself by following the wine route here, where you will find over 60 independent producers who are open for visits.
One of the most imposing churches in the region is the Église St-Girons with

its Flamboyant Gothic architecture and 40m/130ft clock tower. The huge oak-beamed ceiling is shaped like a reversed hull, and dates from the 15C *(visit includes sound and light show; open Apr–mid-Jun and mid-Sept–Oct Tue and Thu–Fri 4pm, Wed and Sat 4pm, 6pm, mid-Jun–mid-Sept Mon–Sat 11am, 3pm, 5pm, Sun and bank holidays 5pm, Nov–Mar Wed 4pm, 6pm, Sat 3pm, 5pm; 5€ (12–16 years 2€); 05 59 12 30 40; www.coeurdebearn.com).*

Leave Monein W by the D 2. After 9km/5.6mi turn left onto the D 110.

Lucq-de-Béarn
Attractive village with well-preserved historic houses (17C–18C), the church is striking for its blend of Roman and Gothic architecture.

Return N via the D 2 then turn left.

Navarrenx
r. St-Germain-Arsenal. 05 59 38 32 85. www.tourisme-bearn-gaves.com. Guided tours of the city available.
Formerly holding an important strategic position at the crossroads of a St James route and the former main highway along the Right Bank of the Gave d'Oloron, Navarrenx is a *bastide* (founded in 1316) with fortification dating back to the early Middle Ages.

Leave from pl. des Casernes.

The porte St-Antoine, which protected the northwest tip of the Pont du Gave, is the best-preserved remnant of the former fortifications. Opposite, an exhibition covers Navarrenx through the centuries *(part of the town visit; 4. 50€; 05 59 38 32 85).*
Head past the bell tower and down towards rue St-Antoine. Turn right up towards the church (16C) then follow the path along the ramparts, which takes you back to place des Casernes.
Navarrenx offers excellent salmon and trout fishing during strictly controlled times from March to July. During salmon fishing competitions, large crowds gather around the pool of the Gave d'Oloron (look out for the salmon-measuring instrument!). Navarrenx also welcomes cigar lovers, with numerous shops in town selling products made from tobacco grown in the surrounding fields.

4 VALLÉE D'ASPE★★

120km/75mi, from Oloron to the Col du Somport – allow one day.

Leave Oloron to the SE via rue d'Aspe.

The road, following the east bank of the Aspe, crosses a rural valley planted with maize and wheat, divided occasionally by windbreaks of poplar trees. Ahead, Pic Mail-Arrouy (alt 1 251m/4 104ft) appears to block any passage south.

St-Christau
The air in this small spa is fresh and cool. The waters are rich in iron and copper and the cure centre, standing in a 60ha/148-acre park, specialises in treating ailments of the mucous membranes.

Continue S to Escot.

Escot
This was the first Aspe village, strikingly perched on a terrace at the mouth of Vallée du Barescou. In accordance with the local formalities, the Viscount of Béarn had to exchange hostages with representatives of the valley before setting foot in Escot. Louis IX, on a pilgrimage to Notre-Dame-de-Sarrance, indicated that he was leaving his own kingdom by ordering his sword-bearer to lower his blade.

Sarrance
Sarrance, a place of local pilgrimage, was visited by both King Louis XI (1461) and Marguerite d'Angoulême, Queen Consort of Navarre (1492–1549), who wrote part of her book of tales, *Heptameron*, here. The **church** *(05 59 34 54 78)*, rebuilt in 1609, has a very Baroque octagonal belfry-porch with

concave sides surmounted by a lantern. Inside are 15C wooden panels with naïve carving. The **cloisters** of the former 17C monastery have a slate roof supported by 14 small transverse gables.
At Bedous, a pronounced humpback rise affords an unexpected view of the valley's central basin and its seven villages. In the background the crests of Arapoup are visible and, to the right in the distance, the first summits of the Lescun cirque (Pic de Burcq).

The road again enters a narrow gorge. Turn right towards Lescun.

Lourdios-Ichère
The **Écomusée de la vallée d'Aspe**★ (*same opening times as the écomusée Notre-Dame-de-la-Pierre à Sarrance; 05 59 34 44 84)* is a lovely museum recounting the effect of the seasons on local life, and the pastoral traditions of the village (photo slideshows, shepherd songs, etc.).
There is a footpath through the village itself.

From here, turn left onto the D 341 (slippy in winter), which crosses the attractive Gorges d'Issaux. Turn left onto the D 441.

Forêt d'Issaux★
This road, passable only in summer, winds through forests of mature beech trees and towering pines. Largely exploited from 1772 to 1778 for the construction of French navy ships, as were most of the region's forests. The logs were taken to the port of Athas.

From the Col de Bouézou, take the D 442 through the Col de Hourarate.

At the Col de Bouézou, the countryside changes: the route hugs the slopes of the Pic de Layens (1 625m/5 331ft), and offers attractive views on the left-hand side.

Rejoin the N 134.

You will pass through the valley floor, with its seven villages.

Bedous
Busy village (good for stocking up), with the tourist office for the Aspe Valley on place de la Mairie. Exhibition of local artisan crafts (*open mid-Jul–mid-Sept am and pm; 05 59 34 59 75).*
Moulin d'Orcun – *rte d'Aydius (signposted from village exit). Open Jul–Aug. Guided visit (45min) 11am, 3pm, 4pm, 5pm, 6pm; rest of year by appointment. 4€ (6–14 years 3€). 05 59 34 74 91 or 06 08 54 45 27.* This watermill was formerly used as a forge, then a flour mill after the French Revolution, and has remained in the same family for generations. Although no longer in use, its workings are intact and the visit includes a demonstration. You might even see bread-making (workshops by appointment).
The **Chapelle d'Orcun**, in its current form dating from the 17C and 18C, has a richly decorated interior, and remains today a stop on The Way of St James (*open in the afternoons, if closed a key is available from Mme Virassamy; 05 59 34 70 67).*

Follow the D 237 to Aydius.

Aydius
The road passes, after 2km/1.2mi, a waterfall created by the porous, spongy petrification of a stream running from the Gave d'Aydius. The charming nearby village, with its historic houses and its location at the edge of a cirque, makes a pleasant stroll.

Return to Bedous.

The road takes you through a gorge before reaching Accous. You can detour via Jouers to see the Roman chapel.

Accous
The **Écomusée de la vallée d'Aspe**★ is a working dairy where you can see films and demonstrations of all aspects of cheese production, from the sheep to the shepherds to the traditional meth-

ods of creation and ageing. The visit ends with a tasting (*open Mon–Sat 10am–noon, 2.30–6pm; closed Sun except during school holidays; 05 59 34 76 06*).

3km/1.8mi after Accous, turn right towards Lescun.

Lescun★

Lescun is a favourite village with mountain lovers, owing to the surrounding cirque with its needle-like limestone peaks.

To admire the full **panorama★★**, park in the car park behind Hôtel du Pic d'Anie and walk to the viewpoint *(30min round trip on foot)*. Follow the GR 10 footpath as far as the church. Beyond a public wash-house, the footpath winds around a hillock. From here, looking back, there is a fine view of Pic d'Anie to the right and, to the left, Le Billare and Dec de Lhurs. The **route du Somport★** *(N 134)* continues to climb the valley, which is now an almost continuous succession of gorges and narrow passes. The villages, built in pairs on opposite sides of the valley, seem to be watching over one another (Eygun and Cette, Etsaut and Borce).

Etsaut

At the entrance to the village, stop at the Maison du Parc National des Pyrénées, where an exhibition is housed on the Pyrénées mountain bear (*open mid-May–mid-Sept 10am–12.30pm, 2–6.30pm; 05 59 34 88 30*).

Borce★

Follow the signposted walking path through this small medieval city. Stronghold houses, a traditional wash-house, a bread oven, a watering trough; Borce has well-preserved examples of many traditional local features.

Écomusée de la vallée d'Aspe★ – *Open Jun–Sept 10am–7pm; rest of the year, school holidays, Sat–Sun and bank holidays 10am–7pm. No charge. 05 59 34 88 99.* Armed with your pilgrim's staff, dressed in your cape, with a shell around your neck, learn all you need to know about the famous Way of St James pilgrimage at the exhibition in this former hospital.

Éco-zoo de Borce – *Open mid-Apr–mid-May and mid-Oct–mid-Nov 10am-6pm; mid-May–mid-Jun and mid-Sept–mid-Oct 1pm–6pm; mid-Jun–mid-Sept 10am–7pm . 8€ (4–12 years 5€). 05 59 34 89 33. www.eco-zoo.fr.* Above the village, this 10ha/25-acre zoo offers an ecological approach to discovering the fauna of mountains around the world. Both wild and domesticated animals of the Pyrénées (bears, the chamois goat, etc.) and farther afield, often endangered species (Rocky Mountain pumas, owls from Russia's Ural mountains), are kept in semi-liberty, or in carefully controlled enclosures which respect their natural habitats.

Chemin de la Mâture

Park at the Pont de Sebers during the summer months, and walk for around 15 minutes. You can also park directly at the starting point of the walk.

3hr round trip via the GR 10. Turn around the way you came when you reach the fields of the highest point. *Attention: the road is steep and has no guard-rail, so ensure good shoes when wet, and sun protection and water in hot weather.*

In the 18C, when logging in the Pacq woods, engineers from the Royal Marines cut a path through this section above the Gorge du Sescoué. The felled tree trunks were taken along this path, then tied together and, when the water was high enough, sent downriver towards the Bayonne naval bases. The route also passes the Fort du Portalet.

Fort du Portalet

This stronghold is perched on a sheer cliff above the river in one of the narrowest, most steep-sided sections of the valley. It was built in the early 19C, and later used for the internment of prominent anti-Nazis during the Occupation (1941–45).

From the road, the walled ramps leading to the casemates commanding the road to Urdos can be seen.

Leaving the gorge, the peaks marking the Spanish border appear as a jagged crest cut through by the Pas d'Aspe. The scene is dominated by Pico de la Garganta (2 636m/8 648ft), which is usually flecked with snow. Beyond Urdos, on the left, is Arnousse Viaduct.

Col du Somport★★

At an altitude of 1 632m/5 354ft, this pass (the only one in the Central Pyrénées accessible the whole year round) has been famous since the passage of the Roman legions. Until the 12C, it was used by pilgrims on the way to Santiago de Compostela. An important staging post at the time was St Christine's Hospice (now demolished) on the southern slopes of the range.

The high ground behind the restaurant affords an impressive view of the Aragon Pyrénées on the far side of the border.

5 VALLÉE DE BARÉTOUS

48km/30mi, from Oloron to the Col de la Pierre-St-Martin.

The smallest of the three Béarn valleys (the others being Vallée d'Aspe and Vallée d'Ossau) contains six villages. This is countryside lying between the Pays Basque and the Béarn, filled with corn fields and magnificent open expanses, dotted with oak copses, all back-dropped by limestone peaks.

Leave Oloron to the SW via the D 919.

Aramits

The former capital of Barétous was once the site of an important abbey, owned by the lay abbots of the Aramits family. All that remains today is the humpback gate. This village is the birthplace of Henri d'Aramits, equerry and lay abbot of the commune and who, becoming a musketeer in 1643, inspired Alexandre Dumas to create the character of Aramis.

Continue along the D 919 then turn right onto the D 918.

Lanne-en-Barétous

The village retains an attractive church with a double porch. The former chapel of the château was the residence of Isaac de Porthau.

Return to the intersection with the D 919 and follow it to Arette.

Arette

pl. de la Mairie, 64570 Arette. 05 59 88 95 38. www.lapierrestmartin.com or www.valleedebaretous.com.

This hamlet was completely rebuilt after the earthquake of 13 August 1967.

The tourist office is located by the new Maison du Barétous, which hosts an exhibition on the valley's history and traditions, centred around forestry and stone building materials, as well as farming traditions. One room covers speleology and seismology.

Follow the picturesque D 132 towards Arette-la-Pierre-St-Martin.

Arette-la-Pierre-St-Martin★

A small bus travels from Oloron-Ste-Marie to the ski station in school holidays and weekends during the ski season (it leaves from the train station at 8.45am).

Perched on the Spanish border, this small ski station has a pleasant Spanish feel. Perfect for a family break.

Col de la Pierre-St-Martin

Alt 1 760m/5 775ft. Location of the Junte de Roncal. Each 13 July, in recognition of a treaty allowing grazing rights in the Navarre valley of Roncal, a delegation from the local town halls formally present the official bodies in Roncal a symbolic gift of three heifers (in reality the Navarre contingent is paid in money). This six-centuries-old ceremony re-enacts a precise ritual; the joining of hands above the border marker, each mayor proclaiming *Paz Abant!* ("Peace Above All") before carrying out the exchange.

Just below here on the Spanish side is the largest cave network in Europe.

Sauveterre-de-Béarn★

Pyrénées-Atlantiques

The small town lies on a picturesque site★ above an escarpment overlooking the Oloron Torrent.

- **Population:** 1 352
- **Michelin Map:** 342: G-2
- **Info:** pl. Royale, Sauveterre. 05 59 38 32 86. www.tourisme-bearn-gaves.com.
- **Location:** Sauveterre-de-Béarn lies S of the A 64 motorway between Pau and the Atlantic Coast.
- **Don't Miss:** The view from the old bridge.

SIGHTS

Terraces by the Church and the Town Hall

From here there is a wonderful view: the old bridge, the torrent, a tree-covered island, a ruined tower, the Romanesque belfry of the church, the outline of the distant Pyrénées – a most romantic landscape.

Vieux Pont

One arch of the ancient bridge remains, surmounted by the town's 12C fortified gateway. The legend of Sancie is explained *(in French)* on a panel. From here again there is a magnificent **view★★** of the river, the fortifications, the church and the splendid Montréal Tower.

Église St-André

pl. Royale. Open daily 9am–noon, 3–6pm. 05 59 38 52 72.

The tympanum above the entrance to St Andrew's Church depicts Christ in Glory surrounded by the four Evangelists. The ribbed vaulting harmonises perfectly with the Romanesque design of the interior. A pillar on the north side of the chancel is topped by a historiated capital representing scandal-mongering and gluttony. The east end, flanked by two apsidal chapels, is surmounted with a quadrangular bell tower pierced by twinned windows.

EXCURSIONS

Chapelle de Sunarthe

1.5km/0.9mi E, follow the signs. Guided tour (1hr) mid-Apr–Jun and Sept Sat 3–6pm; Jul–Aug Tue–Sat 3–6pm. 5€. 05 59 38 57 56.

There's a *son et lumière* display on the small-scale model of the medieval city of Sauveterre-de-Béarn.

Château de Laàs

9km/5.6mi SE via the D 27. Guided tours (1hr) Wed–Mon Apr and Oct 2–7pm; May–Jun and Sept 10am–noon, 2–7pm; Jul–Aug 10am–7pm. 4€. 05 59 38 91 53.

This is an extraordinary château-museum: by collecting together **furniture★**, *objets d'art* and family paintings from three different homes, Monsieur and Madame Serbat, the last owners of this 17C manor house, created a decorative arts museum which also serves to illustrate the art of living in the Hainaut region (in the north of France) during the 18C.

Louis XVI panelling adorns the bed-chambers and salons. Mme Serbat's room is decorated with illustrations of the *Fables of La Fontaine*. Tapestries and hand-painted fabrics *(music room)* set off the fine Northern School paintings (Watteau de Lille). A first-floor bedroom recalls the aftermath of Waterloo, housing the bed Napoleon slept in at Maubert-Fontaine on 19 June 1815. In the library, there is a curious collection of 11 17C fans which have not been sewn together.

The 12ha/30-acre **park** has both a French and an English garden. On the terrace, above the Gave d'Oloron, you can see a rose garden and, below, a bamboo garden *(picnic area)*.

Vallée d'Ossau★★

Pyrénées-Atlantiques

Nature lovers will be happy here: invigoratingly beautiful landscape abounds, with mountain peaks reflected in still lakes, and waterfalls cascading down mountain faces. And to complete the picture, turn your eyes skywards to watch birds of prey swooping down on an unaware Pyrénées marmot (a type of woodchuck), or an izard goat nimbly jumping from rock to rock. Perfect for exploring by either tourist train, foot or car.

- **Michelin Map:** 342: J-3-6
- **Info:** 05 59 05 77 11. www.valleedossau-tourisme.com.
- **Location:** Southern part of Béarn region..
- **Timing:** At least one day.
- **Parking:** Park outside the villages and walk in.
- **Don't Miss:** The Lac d'Artouste, Bielle and Béost in the Lower Ossau.
- **Kids:** The Petit Train d'Artouste.

DRIVING TOURS

6 LOWER OSSAU

70km/43mi from Pau à Laruns. Allow half a day.

Leave Pau to the S along the N 134.

Rébénacq

This is the entry point for the Vallée d'Ossau. Marked walkng paths take you through the village; one through the heart of the *bastide*, and another that covers the whole place.

Leave Rébénacq to the W (D 936). After 5km/3.1mi, turn left onto the D 34.

Buzy

Farming village that makes a good starting point for walking in the Vallée de l'Escou. A megalithic tomb stands at the far side of of the village.

Follow the D 920.

Arudy

Industrially, this is the most developed town in Lower Ossau, due to the surrounding marble quarries and the various factories built on the outskirts. The **Maison d'Ossau** *(r. de l'Église; open Jul–Aug daily 10am–noon, 3–6pm, Jan–Jun, Sept and school holidays Tue–Fri 2–5pm, Sun 3–6pm; Oct–Dec Sun 3–6pm; closed 1 Jan; 2.70€; 05 59 05 61 71)*, a 17C house near the east end of the church, contains displays on prehistoric life in the Pyrénées in its basement. The former residential rooms on the ground floor include an exhibit on the flora, fauna and geology of Vallée d'Ossau. Displays on the attic floor are devoted to the history of the valley and the life of the local shepherds.

Rejoin the D 934 and take the road opposite you.

Ste-Colome

16C church along The Way of St James, and the oldest stronghold of the valley. Behind the church, a small path leads to a mound topped by three crosses offering a panoramic view (look for the ruins of a 12C château).

Return to the D 934.

Louvie-Juzon

16C church with a stone bell tower shaped like an upside-down chalice. The interior is decorated with capitals and sculpted keystones. The Pic du Midi d'Ossau can be viewed from the bridge.

Follow the D 240.

Castet

From the drinking trough, head up to the modified Roman church for a view

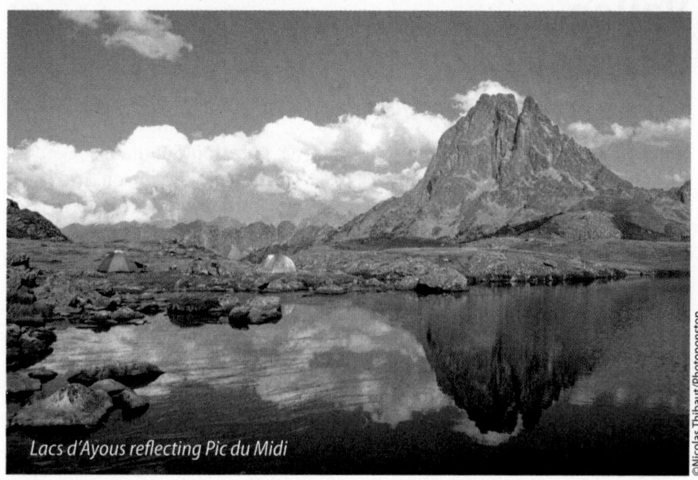
Lacs d'Ayous reflecting Pic du Midi

©Nicolas Thibaut/Photononstop

over a château keep *(not open to the public)*, the only remaining vestige of the 13C château, on the lake, and Bielle, on the facing slopes.

Return along the D 934; at the Bielle roundabout, follow the signs.

Throughout the year, the walking paths of the Espace Naturel du Castet are worth exploring. From June to September, various activities are organised.

Bielle★

This former county seat, split in two by a tributary of the Gave d'Ossau, retains a certain sleepy dignity. Several 16C town houses can be seen in the south bank district, between the main road and the church. On the north bank stands a castle built by the Marquis de Laborde (1724–94), a banker during the time of Louis XV and the Duc de Choiseul.

Follow the D 294 to Bilhères.

Bilhères

This is a scattered village containing several houses with 16C and 17C decorative elements – embellished keystones, for example, in the arched doorways.

Plateau de Bénou★

Above Bilhères the view opens out southwards as far as Pic de Ger.

The chapel of Notre-Dame-de-Houndaas *(rest stop facilities)*, shaded by two lime trees, appears in a **site**★ which is kept fresh by running water from several main springs. The road then runs into the pastureland of the Bénou basin where large flocks of sheep graze in summer.

Return to Bielle and drive upriver towards Laruns.

Aste-Béon

On the right bank of the Ossau Torrent.

On the way into Béon village is the **Falaise aux Vautours** (Vulture's Cliff) interpretation centre (*Open Apr Mon–Fri 10am–noon, 2–5pm, Sat–Sun 2–5pm, May Mon–Fri 10am–noon, 2–6pm, Sat–Sun 2–6pm, Jun–Aug daily 10.30am–12.30pm, 2–6.30pm, Sept Mon–Fri 10am–noon, 2–5.30pm, Sat–Sun 2–5.30pm, Oct, Dec, Feb school and public holidays 2–5pm; 7€ (children 5€); 05 59 82 65 49; www.falaise-aux-vautours.com)*.

At the foot of a limestone cliff are nesting grounds for a large colony of tawny vultures. The Ossau Nature Reserve was set up to protect these and other raptors' breeding habitats. These include bearded vultures, Egyptian vultures, black and royal kites, peregrine falcons and kestrels.

The exhibit, divided into 12 sections, offers an insight into the lifestyles of

these birds of prey. Of particular interest is the three-dimensional model of the cliff with a panoramic screen projecting images of the vultures' seasonal behaviour patterns, from the courting display, nest-building, hatching of the solitary egg, to the feeding and flying away of their young. There are other displays on cattle farming, tales and legends from Vallée d'Ossau and the fauna and flora of the Pyrénées.

Turn right before Laruns.

Béost★
Site of an interesting treasure hunt, where the treasures are door lintels that you interpret along a signposted route. Look out also for the attractive church gate. The adjoining château is a former secular abbey (*visits by appointment (allow one day's notice); no charge; 05 59 05 30 99).*

Laruns
Maison de la vallée d'Ossau, 64440 Laruns. 05 59 05 31 41. www.valleedossau.com. During the summer, Point Info Montagne has information on all activities and events: 05 59 05 48 94. At the service village, further information is available from the Maison de la vallée d'Ossau and the Maison du Parc national des Pyrénées (*see pxxx).*

7 LE HAUT OSSAU★★

40km/25mi from Laruns to the Col du Pourtalet. Allow one day, with walks.

Leave Laruns S via the D 934.

The road follows the Gave d'Ossau and passes through the small spa town of Eaux-Chaudes.
Just after the bridge that crosses the Bitet, a wide path through the forest heads off to the right.

Gorges du Bitet
1hr on foot round-trip by the wooded path. The path heads through shady gorges and passes various waterfalls.

Rejoin the D 934.

3km/1.8mi after the bridge across the Bitet, at Chêne de l'Ours, is a viewpoint of the Pic du Midi d'Ossau.

Gabas
This mountain village, located at the foot of large waterfalls heading down from the Pic du Midi d'Ossau, is known for its *brébis* cheese. The 12C chapel has a contemporary decoration.

Turn right onto the D 231.

The road *(open May–Oct depending on weather conditions)* climbs steeply, and opens up onto the dam of Artigue de Bious.

Lac de Bious-Artigues★
From the lake created by the dam (Left Bank), views exend over the Pics d'Ayous and the Midi d'Ossau. Particularly beautiful at sunset.
1hr to follow the footpath that circles the lake.

Pic du Midi d'Ossau
Alt 2 884m/9 462ft. With its distinctive peak shaped like a crocodile's jaws, this mountain is viewable on clear days from Pau. Its slopes provide shelter for thousands of isard goats. A tour of the Pic leaves from Bious-Artigues.

Lacs d'Ayous★★
Ascent 2hr30min, descent 1hr30min (difference in level: 560m/1 837ft). Follow the National Park placards and the red-white markers of the GR 10. From the refuge of Ayous, there is a stunning view of the Pic du Midi reflected in the waters of the lake.

Return towards Gabas and turn right along the D 934.

The road passes past the electric power stations of Fabrèges et d'Artouste, then climbs upwards towards the Artouste reservoir. The steep slopes of Pic de Soques are majestically in view.

Take the D 431 to the left, along the Right Bank of the lake until reaching Fabrèges.

Cable-Car to La Sagette
Operates May–Jun, Sept 8.30am–6pm; Jul–Aug 8.30am–8pm. 7€. 05 59 05 30 99.
The view from the upper station (alt 1 950m/6 398ft) encompasses the former glacial valley of the Gave de Brousset (partly submerged by the Lac de Fabrèges), and the silhouette of the Pic du Midi d'Ossau.
1hr round trip. Climb up til you reach the orientation map of the Pic de la Sagette.

From La Sagette to the Lac d'Artouste
OperatesJun and Sept 8.30am–2.30pm (train once an hour); Jul–Aug 8.30am–5pm (train every half-hour). 21.50€ cable-car and train round-trip (4–15 years 17€). 05 59 05 36 99. www.altiservice.com.
The small **tourist train** clings to the side of the mountain, climing over 10km/6.2mi up to an altitude of 2 000m/6 561ft. From the train, enjoy plunging views over the Vallée du Soussouéou, 500m/1 640ft below.
30min round trip. From the terminus (stop limited to 1hr30min), a walking path takes you to the Lac d'Artouste, with its backdrop of granite slopes of the cirque, whose summits reach 3 000m/9 842ft.

To return to Fabrèges, rejoin the D 934 and take the direction of the Col du Pourtalet.

The road follows the Gave de Brousset then twists and turns through the Cirque d'Anéou.

Col du Pourtalet★
The Col du Pourtalet is usually covered with snow from November to June. Alt 1 794m/5 885ft. View over the vast pastoral cirque of Anéou, and the Pic du Midi d'Ossau.

8 ROUTE DU COL D'AUBISQUE★

28km/17.4mi from Laruns to the Col du Soulor. Allow around 4hrs.

Leave Laruns to the SE via the D 918.

Eaux-Bonnes
This spa, nestling in the wooded Vallée du Valentin, offers thermal cures initially developed by the great doctor from Béarn, Théophile de Bordeu (1722–76), to treat respiratory disorders. The promenades, laid out in the 19C in the wooded foothills of the Gourzy, are witness to the refined appreciation of nature and the creature comforts of the times. The esplanade in Darralde Gardens, bordered by mansions typical of Second Empire spas, is the hub of local activity. After skiing, there is nothing better than a shower, a sauna or a bath session at the spa in Eaux-Bonnes. For further information, contact the tourist office of Eaux-Bonnes and Gourette (*05 59 05 12 17; www.gourette.com*).

Turn left to Aas.

Aas
In this village, with its steep, narrow streets, some of the locals still use the whistling language once used by shepherds to communicate with one another throughout the valley, at distances of up to 2 500m/8 200ft.
The road crosses the River Valentin (*note the waterfall*) and starts the long haul up the side of the mountain, offering splendid views of the Pic de Ger massif, especially in the early morning and at dusk.

Return to Eaux-Bonnes, but this time head E.

Gourette
Gourette is a popular winter sports resort, which owes its existence to Henri Sallanave, a native of Pau, who pioneered downhill skiing in the Pyrénées in 1903. Although international skiing championships had been held

Col d'Aubisque

© Nicolas Thibaut/Photononstop

here yearly since 1908, the resort was not opened until 1930. Apartment blocks nestle in a cirque scarred by the rugged strata of Pic de Ger (alt 2 613m/8 573ft) and the rocky jagged formation of Pène Médaa, which is an impressive **site**★.

Pène Blanque★

1hr30min round trip using the gondola lift from Gourette. 8€. 05 59 05 12 60.

The upper platform of the **gondola lift** is in the northern cirque of Pène Blanque, at the foot of Pic de Ger and not far from a group of small mountain lakes. From here, there is a fine **view**★ of Gourette and the road to Col d'Aubisque. A difficult footpath, zigzagging between Pic de Ger and Géougue d'Arre, leads to a pass *(allow an extra 2hrs round trip for this excursion)* from which there is an interesting view of the border peaks of the **Balaïtous**. Below is a lake and Vallée d'Artouste. Not far beyond Gourette, from a corner of the Crêtes Blanches (White Crests), a splendid panorama unfolds. In the distance you can see Pic du Midi de Bigorre.

Col d'Aubisque★★

As a rule, Col d'Aubisque (Aubisque Pass) is blocked by snow in Nov–Jun. The cliff road beyond Col d'Aubisque is very narrow, which makes it difficult for vehicles to pass. Consequently, traffic alternates every 2hrs.

The pass is at an altitude of 1 709m/ 5 607ft. Sports enthusiasts will recognise it from the Tour de France bicycle race. The south knoll *(TV relay – 15min on foot from the car park)* affords a striking view of the whole Gourette cirque, and an immense **panorama**★★ from Pic de Gers to Pic de Montaigu *(due E, in the distance)* with nine major peaks in between.

Beyond the pass, the road, carved into the mountainside *(D 918)*, offers views of the Vallée de Ferrières and, in the distance, the Béarn plain. After that, the **Corniche des Pyrénées** skirts Cirque du Litor at a height of almost 300m/985ft. This is one of the most impressive sections of the drive, along a road which was one of the boldest feats of 19C engineering.

Col du Soulor★

The pass lies at an altitude of 1 474m/ 4 836ft. Grass-covered peaks form the foreground to a sweeping mountain vista. Beyond the Vallée d'Azun the summits between Pic du Midi de Bigorre and, farther to the left, Pic de Montaigu, rise into view.

LE LOT-ET-GARONNE

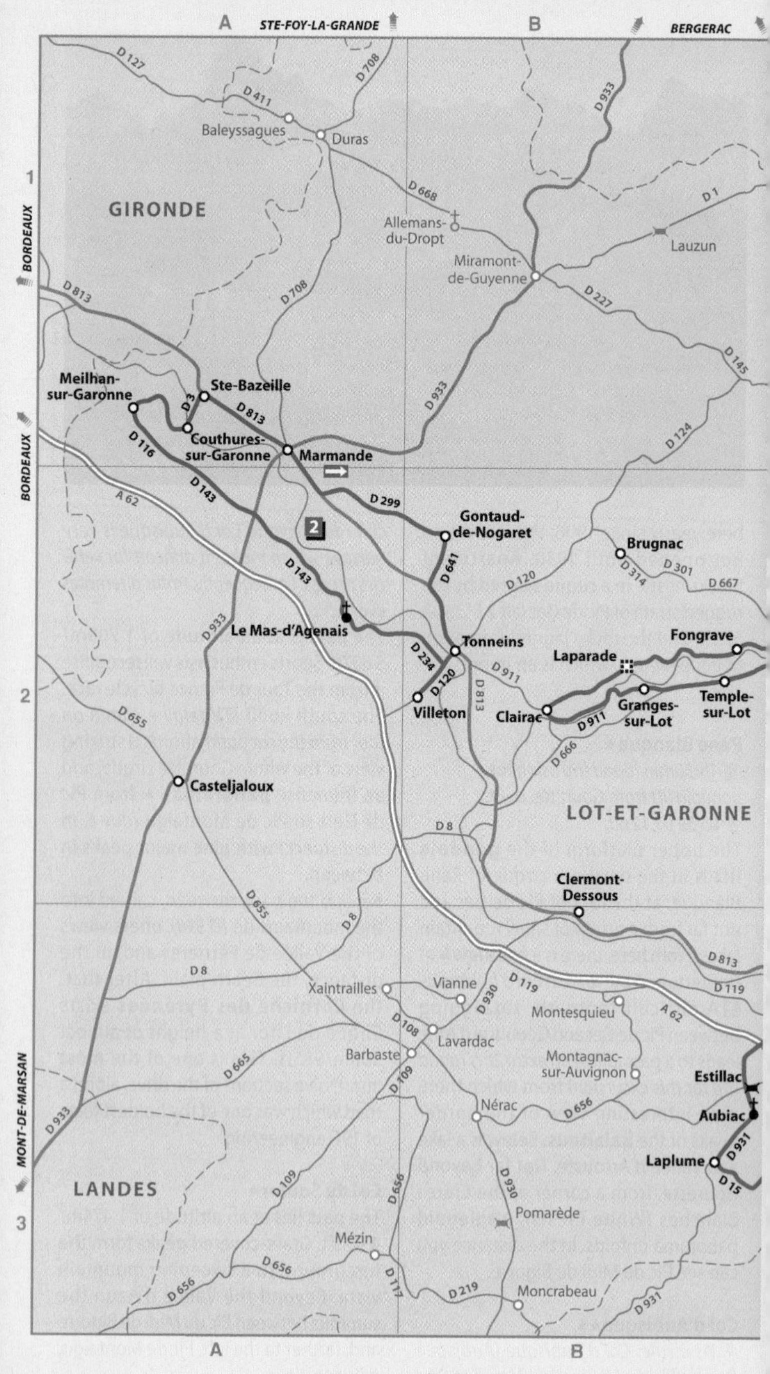

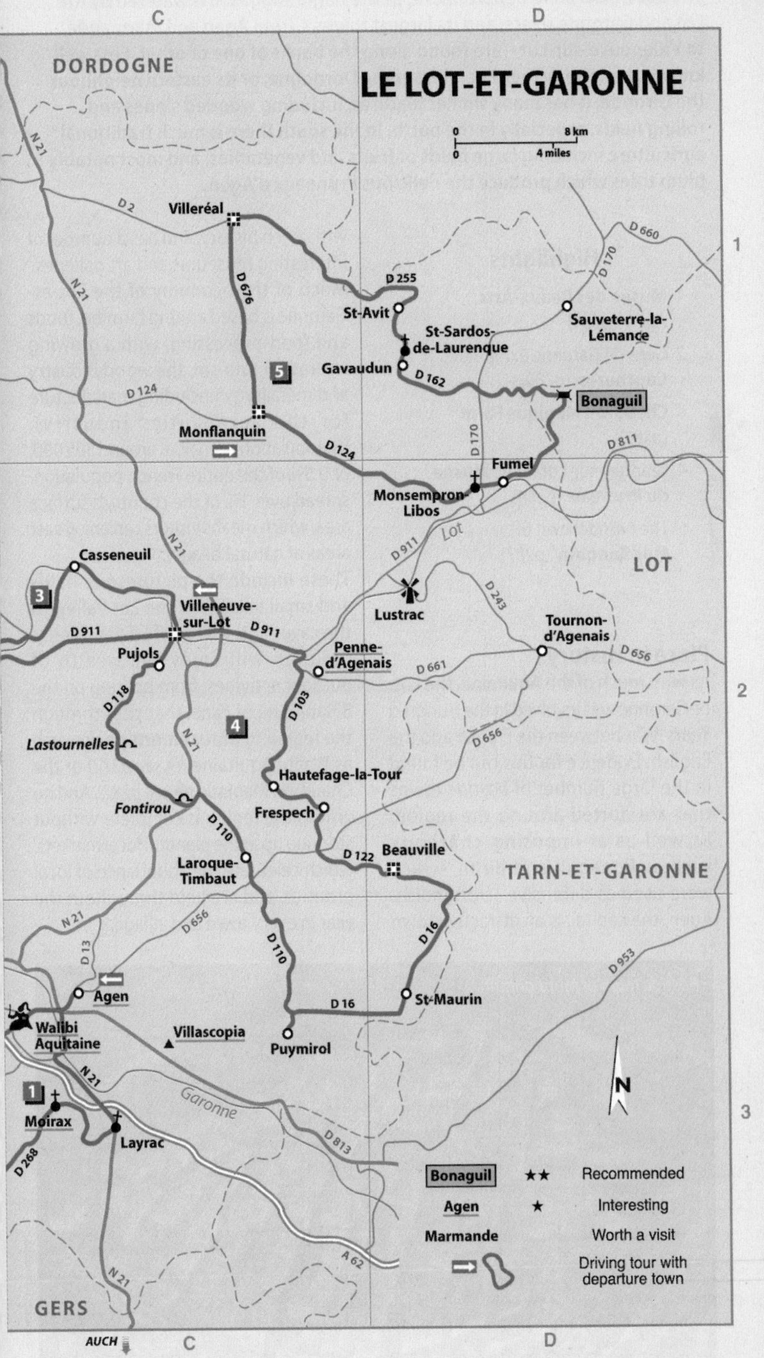
LE LOT-ET-GARONNE
C
D
1
2
3
0
8 km
0
4 miles
DORDOGNE
LOT
TARN-ET-GARONNE
GERS
Villeréal
St-Avit
St-Sardos-de-Laurenque
Gavaudun
Sauveterre-la-Lémance
Bonaguil
Monflanquin
Fumel
Monsempron-Libos
Lot
Lustrac
Casseneuil
Villeneuve-sur-Lot
Pujols
Penne-d'Agenais
Tournon-d'Agenais
Lastournelles
Fontirou
Hautefage-la-Tour
Frespech
Laroque-Timbaut
Beauville
Agen
Walibi Aquitaine
Villascopia
Puymirol
St-Maurin
Moirax
Layrac
Garonne
AUCH
N
D 2
D 676
D 255
D 162
D 124
D 170
D 660
D 811
D 911
D 243
D 656
D 661
D 103
D 118
D 110
D 122
D 16
D 13
D 953
D 813
D 268
N 21
A 62
1
3
4
5
Bonaguil ★★ Recommended
Agen ★ Interesting
Marmande Worth a visit
Driving tour with departure town

LE LOT-ET-GARONNE

The Lot-et-Garonne *département*, as the name suggests, is watered by the Lot and Garonne rivers, and its largest towns – from Agen and Marmande to Villeneuve-sur-Lot – are found along the banks of one or other. Less well known than its northern neighbour the Dordogne, or its eastern neighbour the Gironde, it has many similar features, including wooded slopes and rolling fields, especially in the north. In the south there is much traditional agriculture including large fields of fruits and vegetables, and most notably plum trees which produce the delicious Pruneaux d'Agen.

Highlights

1. **Musée des Beaux-Arts**, Agen (p234)
2. Gens de Garonne exhibition, **Couthures** (p280)
3. **Chaudron Magique Farm** (p282)
4. Granges-sur-Lot for its **Musée du Pruneau** (p284)
5. The *bastide* town of **Monflanquin** (p287)

Place in History

As with much of the Aquitaine, the Lot-et-Garonne was involved in the Hundred Years' War between the French and the English. Evidence for this can be found in the large number of *bastide* towns that are dotted around the region, as well as at imposing **châteaux** such as Bonaguil and Biron, which were used as defensive strongholds. Agen, the capital, is an attractive town with a rich history, and has a number of interesting museums and art galleries. Much of the economy of the Lot-et-Garonne is based around farming, foods and food-processing, with a growing interest in tourism, the wood industry and metallurgy (including manufacture for the aeronautics industry). Its population is small, at around 305 000, or 0.5% of the entire French population, spread over 1% of the country's surface area, which means visitors can enjoy vast areas of natural beauty.

These include the picturesque fields and small villages of the Lot Valley, to the caves and valleys of Lower Quercy. Children will enjoy the wealth of outdoor activities, from boating on the 87km/45mi of canal that pass through the region to **amusement parks** such as Walibi Aquitaine (*see p277*) or the Chaudron Magique (*see p282*). And no visit to the region is complete without stocking up at the plentiful local markets, which celebrate the abundance of local produce, and are held throughout the year in every town and village.

Bastide town of Monflanquin

©Nicolas Thibaut/Photononstop

Agen★

Lot-et-Garonne

Agen sprawls across the fertile plain between the River Garonne and the Ermitage Hills. This modern, well-planned town has wide avenues and the impressive green expanse of esplanade du Gravier. Midway between Bordeaux and Toulouse, Agen is an economic centre for the Middle Garonne region. Its practical location has made it an important market for fruit and vegetables, especially peaches, Chasselas (white) grapes and plums. Pruneaux d'Agen, the best-known prunes in France, are dried from local plums. They are often steeped in brandy.

- **Population:** 33 728
- **Michelin Map:** 336: F-4
- **Info:** 38 r. Garonne, Agen. ✆05 53 47 36 09. www.ot-agen.org.
- **Location:** Either the A 62 or the N 113 is the most direct route into the town. If you have time, follow the D roads through the attractive countryside surrounding Agen. The Canal latéral à la Garonne runs to the north of the town and the River Garonne to the west.
- **Parking:** There are several car parks on the outskirts of the town centre.
- **Don't Miss:** The Musée des Beaux-Arts; r. Beauville; Pierre Boisson confectionery for an introduction to the famous Agen prunes, including a tasting.
- **Kids:** Walibi Aquitaine amusement park; pony riding in Poney-club de Darel en Agenais; Les Vallons des Marennes farm (*see Addresses*).
- **Timing:** Allow half a day.

A BIT OF HISTORY

Artists and Scholars

Leading lights of the Renaissance were particularly prominent in Agen. **Matteo Bandello** (c.1480–c.1565), monk, diplomat and courtier, banished from Milan by papal decree after the publication of his scandalous stories in the style of Boccaccio, found peace and tranquillity as an exile on the banks of the Garonne. He later became Bishop of Agen.

Julius Caesar Scaliger (1484–1558), born in Padua but settled in Agen, brought fame to his adopted home with his sparkling personality, extensive learning and influence on many literary figures. Among other achievements, he was the first European to write a description of platinum. His tenth son, Joseph Justus Scaligero (1540–1609), born in Agen, was an eminent philologist, humanist and Protestant philosopher.

GUIDED TOURS

Contact the tourist office for times of guided tours of the town.

A. Thuillier/MICHELIN

Old-fashioned prune box

WALKING TOURS

OLD TOWN

4hrs. Start from pl. Dr-Pierre-Esquirol.

Place Docteur-Pierre-Esquirol

The square, named after a former Mayor of Agen, is surrounded by the town hall (the office of the provincial governor in the 17C), Ducourneau Theatre (✆05 53

66 26 60), built at the beginning of the 20C, and the Fine Arts Museum (*see below*).

Musée des Beaux-Arts★★

pl. Dr-Pierre-Esquirol. Open Wed–Mon May–Sept 10am–6pm; Oct–Apr 10am–12.30pm, 1.30–6pm. Closed 1 Jan, 1 May, 1 Nov, 25 Dec. 4.10€ (first Sun of month no charge). 05 53 69 47 23.

The Fine Arts Museum is made up of elegant 16C and 17C mansions – Vaurs, Vergès, Monluc and Estrades – which, though their interiors have been reorganised to make room for the exhibits, have largely retained their original façades.

Medieval Archaeology – Romanesque and Gothic capitals carved with leaves and fantastic animals adorn the walls of one of the rooms. The main exhibit is the **tomb of Étienne de Dufort** and his wife. Note also the 16C Brussels tapestry, entitled *The Month of March*, and various funerary stones.

Gallo-Roman Archaeology – Among the mosaics, amphorae and small bronzes of this section stands the museum's finest exhibit, the **Vénus de Mas**. This 1C BC Greek marble statue, discovered near Mas d'Agenais in the 19C, is noted for its elegant contours, perfect proportions and the graceful flow of its draperies.

War and Hunting – In a neighbouring room, which features an impressive Renaissance chimney-piece, are exhibits based on the themes of War and Hunting. Ancient weapons are on display. The 17C tapestry, *The Stag Hunt*, is after a cartoon by Van Orley, and the 15C profile of a woman is attributed to Mino da Fiesole. Nearby stands a large bronze Minotaur by a local artist, François-Xavier Lalanne.

Prehistoric and Mineral Collections – The cellars of Hôtel de Vaurs, once used as the local prison (note the shackles still fixed to the walls), today house the museum's prehistoric collections, ranging from the most primitive stone implements, to more sophisticated stones from the Neolithic period, as well as a collection of minerals.

Paintings and Decorative Arts – A fine spiral staircase leads to the upper floors which house a collection of 16C and 17C French and foreign canvases. Most notable among them are *The Temptation of St Anthony* by Teniers the Elder and *Portrait of a Man* by Philippe de Champaigne. Also on view are displays of porcelain and 14C–19C **ceramics**, both French and foreign, including dishes by Bernard Palissy. On the same floor is a striking series of **cameos** (porcelain cameos set in glass), on religious, historical and mythological themes, by Boudon de St-Amans (1774–1856). He was a local artist, also responsible for unique examples of earthenware designed to rival products from English porcelain factories.

The 18C paintings feature portraits by Greuze and a fine canvas, *The Dying Page*, by Tiepolo. The highlight of this section, however, is a **series of five works by Goya** which were donated to the museum by a former Spanish ambassador. Note in particular the Self-Portrait, showing a lively expression under rather heavy features.

Impressionism – Fine collection displayed on the first and second floors. French painting in the 19C is represented by Corot with his masterpiece, **L'Étang**

A Dedicated Potter

Bernard Palissy (1510–c.1590), born locally, wrote technical and philosophical treatises, though he is better known as a glassblower and potter. He worked with endless determination and at great personal sacrifice (he allegedly burned his own furniture to fuel his furnaces) and rediscovered the art of enamelling. He created a type of pottery halfway between Italian faïence and glazed earthenware. His rustic bowls, decorated with fruit, plants and animals in coloured relief, were extremely successful.

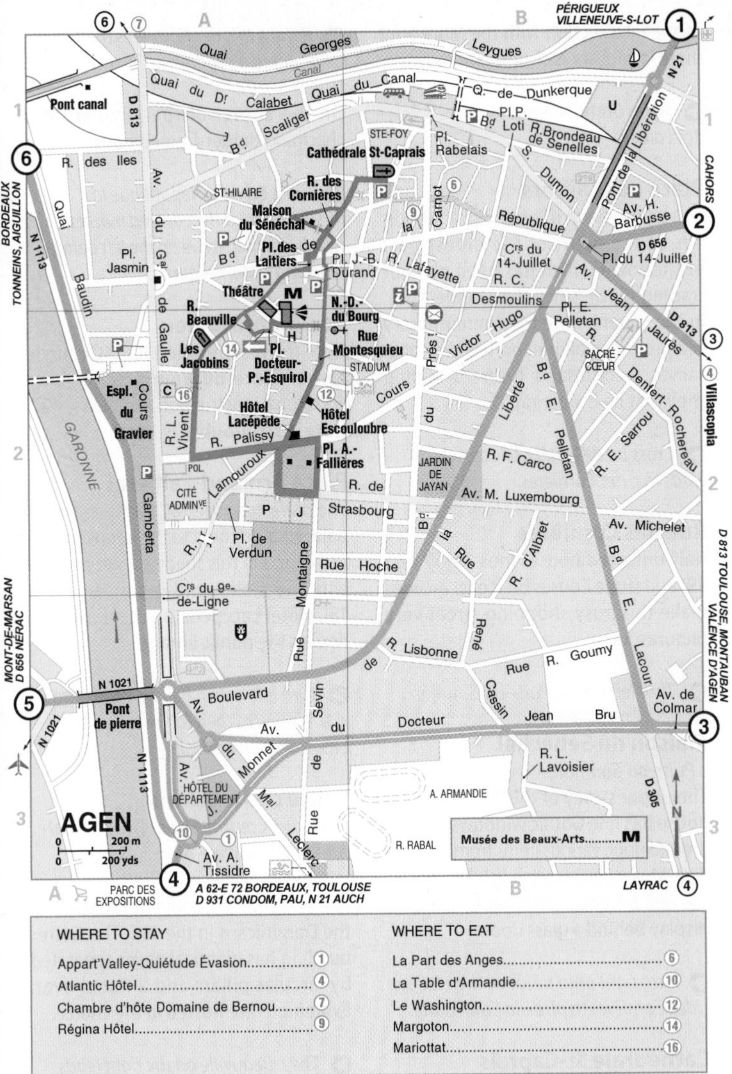

de Ville-d'Avray, Courbet and Isabey, a collection of pre-Impressionists (numerous views by Boudin) and Impressionists (Lebourg, Caillebotte, Sisley, Guillaumin and Lebasque). *Head of a Romanian Peasant Woman* was the work of the Romanian artist Grigoresco. The 20C is ushered in by a Picabia, *On the Banks of the Loing*, unusual for its Impressionist flavour.

Docteur-Esquirol Room – This room houses paintings, furniture and Asiatic figurines. The paintings include portraits by Clouet; and a fine *Head of a Child* by Greuze.

Rue Beauville

The street is lined with restored medieval houses. Note, in particular the fine timber-framed building with corbels at no **1**.

Turn right onto r. Richard-Cœur-de-Lion.

At the intersection with rue Moncorny there is another half-timbered house.

The r. Garonne leads to pl. des Laitiers.

Place des Laitiers

This square, with its arcades and shops, lies at the heart of the oldest part of the town which has been a major trading plac,e since the Middle Ages. In the square, note the contemporary sculpture of a pilgrim on The Way of St James, recognisable from the scallop shell that he is wearing.

Cross bd de la République, which leads to r. des Cornières.

Rue des Cornières

Half-timbered houses (nos **13**, **17** and **19**) and stone houses built over arcades make this busy shopping street very picturesque.

Turn left onto r. Puits-du-Saumon.

Maison du Sénéchal

r. Puits-du-Saumon.

The upper storey of this 14C steward's house has fine Gothic windows. On the ground floor, various items from the Fine Arts Museum (sarcophagi, 17C busts, the bell from the old town hall) are on display behind a glass door.

Turn right onto r. Floirac then follow r. des Cornières to pl. de la Cathédrale.

Cathédrale St-Caprais

pl. du Maréchal Foch. 05 53 66 37 27.

This former collegiate church, founded in the 11C, was granted cathedral status in 1802. Its most remarkable feature is the 12C east end, which comprises an apse flanked by three radiating chapels each pierced by semicircular arched windows with scrolled corbels in the form of carved human and animal heads.

The interior, restored in the 19C, is decorated with frescoes, which depict the patron saints of Agen. There is a view of the east end from place Raspail.

Return to r. des Cornières then take r. Banabéra on the left.

On the corner of rue Jacquard is a charming timber-framed house.

Cross bd de la République in the direction of the covered market, which you then leave on the left before reaching r. Montesquieu.

Rue Montesquieu

Note the picturesque 13C–14C church, **Notre-Dame-du-Bourg**, with its brick and stone construction and belfry-wall. **Hôtel Escouloubre** is 18C.

Place Armand-Fallières

The *préfecture*, the 18C former bishop's palace, stands next to the imposing 19C law courts in this shady square planted with magnolias and cedar trees. The 18C Hôtel Lacépède on the north side houses the public library.

Turn left onto r. Palissy, right onto r. Louis Vivent then follow r. Richard-Cœur-de-Lion opposite.

Église des Jacobins

r. Richard-Cœur-de-Lion. Open mid-Jun–late Nov Wed–Mon 2–6pm. 05 53 87 88 40.

The remains of a convent founded by the Dominicans in the 13C. The Gothic building has identical naves separated by circular pillars and a flat chevet. Exhibitions are hosted in the church.

The r. Beauville on the right leads back to pl. Dr-Pierre-Esquirol.

ALONG THE GARONNE

The banks of the River Garonne and of the canal offer relaxing walks.

Esplanade du Gravier

Plane trees and lawns on either side of a circular pond make this the most popular walk along the Garonne. The footbridge provides a good view of the river, town and bridge-canal.

On the right is the **Pont Canal**, a 500m/550yd-long bridge with 25 arches, which carries the Canal Latéral across the Garonne.

The **stone bridge** on the left was commissioned by Napoleon when he stayed in Agen.

EXCURSIONS

Villascopia à Castelculier

7.5km/4.7mi via the D 813 towards Toulouse. Open Jun and Sept Tue–Sun 10am–6pm; Jul–Aug daily 11am–8pm; Oct–Dec Wed and Sat–Sun 2–5pm; Feb–May Tue–Sun 2–5pm. 6€ (5–12 years 3€). In summer, theatrical show "Les nuits de Villascopia" (Wed 8pm). 05 53 68 08 68.

Opposite the Gallo-Roman site of Lamarque, this new *scénovision* (3D film, 30min) retells the story of every-day life in this town at the end of the 4C. It does this through two historical figures: the Latin poet Ausone, born in Aquitaine, and his grandson, Paulin de Pella. Objects recovered through excavations are on display. Guided or self-guided visits are also available of the archaeological garden created around the vestiges of the original villa (2C–4C) – the most important example of its kind in Aquitaine.

Walibi Aquitaine★

Château de Caudouin, Roquefort (4km/2.5mi SW on the D 656, rte de Neyrac. From the A 62 motorway, take Exit 7 to Agen). Open daily mid-May–Jun and Sept Sat–Sun 10am–5pm; Jul–Aug daily 10am–6pm; Oct Sat–Sun 11am–5pm. 21€ (children 21€). 05 53 96 58 32. www.walibi-aquitaine.fr.

This amusement park is perfect for a family outing, with a wide range of attractions for young and old. Younger children will enjoy the gentle carousel rides, while teenagers will want to try spinning above the ground on the Fandango chairs or rafting down the turbulent Raja river. Other popular entertainment includes a musical fountain sound and light show and a spectacular sea-lion show. For lunch, choose between a picnic or eating at the restaurant on site. Take the time to observe the 200-year-old cedar trees and the rare birds of prey which can be seen around the castle.

Clermont-Dessous

19km/11.8mi to the W via the D 813, which runs along the banks of the Garonne.

The village, which has become a popular tourist spot thanks to its location above the Garonne plains, is marked by its squat Roman church, emerging from the ruins of a château. From the car park, a signposted walk (allow 30min) offers views over the valley. In the distance, you can see Port-Ste-Marie, a former city of sailors sandwiched between the river and the steep slopes of the valley.

DRIVING TOUR

1 LE BRULHOIS

41km/25mi. Allow 3hrs.

Leave Agen to the W via the D 1021 and turn left onto the D 656.

Countryside as far as the eye can see… a landscape of gentle slopes and abrupt limestone ridges. A patchwork of vine-covered hills, cornfields and orchards. Here and there, a building perched on a hilltop, or hidden in the middle of fields.

Château d'Estillac

The Château de Monluc, with its military architecture (13C–16C), is often hidden by trees, but overlooks the Garonne plain from the last peaks of the Brulhois hills. Blaise de Monluc, famous military commander who was best known for his campaigns in Italy for the French King Francis I, lived in the Château d'Estillac around 1550. He is credited with the invention of *pousse-rapière*, a Gascon apéritif made from Armagnac liqueur and bitter oranges.

Aubiac

The Roman church seems to stand sentry over the village. The interior contains a square chancel and several friezes

painted onto the walls. The village also contains a fountain and public wash-house that is currently being restored.

Laplume

Ancient capital of Brulhois, this village is located on a crest of a well-exposed hill. In former times, numerous windmills would have been turning here.

At Laplume, turn left onto the D 15 and continue for 3km/1.8mi, then left again onto the D 268 towards Moirax.

Église de Moirax★

The church which belonged to a priory of the Cluniac order founded in the 11C, is a fine example of 12C Romanesque architecture.

The long edifice is surmounted by a conical pinnacle and a campanile over the west front. The most interesting decorative motifs are those adorning the east end and the apsidal chapels. Inside, the forward part of the chancel is no doubt the most original: square at the base, it is octagonal higher up and is topped by a cupola. The capitals are decorated with foliage and figures (note Daniel in the Lions' Den, near the crossing on the left, and the Original Sin on the right). The statue of the Virgin Mary in the chancel, the stalls and the walnut panels in the aisles were carved by Jean Tournier (late 17C).

Layrac

The terrace of place du Royal is surrounded by Notre-Dame church (12C) to the south and St-Martin church to the north, but the only vestige left of the St-Martin church is its steeple. It is worth stopping for a moment to admire the view of the River Gers running into the Garonne Valley. When Notre-Dame church was last restored and the choir regained its original height, a fragment of a Romanesque mosaic was found. It represents Samson Fighting the Lion.

Return to Agen via the D 1021.

ADDRESSES

STAY

Régina Hôtel – *139 bd du Président Carnot. ℘05 53 47 07 97. www.hotelreginagen.com. 24 rooms.* This central hotel has modern comfortable facilities. Pretty colours provide each room with a personal touch; many of them are spacious and all have double-glazed windows.

Appart' Valley – Quiétude Évasion – *1350 av. du Midi. ℘05 53 69 65 10. www.quietude-evasion.com. 8€.* This modern apartment block on the outskirts of Agen contains 77 fully equipped one-bedroomed apartments (10 of which are studios). The colours – turquoise, terra-cotta and white – are a little cold, but there is access to a pool, and they are good value.

Atlantic Hôtel – *133 av. Jean-Jaurès (E of Agen via the N 113). ℘05 53 96 16 56. www.agen-atlantic-hotel.fr. Closed 23 Dec–3 Jan. 44 rooms.* This hotel, built in the 1970s behind a petrol station, is a short distance from city centre. Don't let the surroundings daunt you – the rooms are pleasant and the more recent ones are modern and sizable. Breakfast is by the pool.

NEARBY

Chambre d'hôte Domaine de Bernou – *47340 La Croix-Blanche (14km/8.7mi N of Agen along the Villeneuve-sur-Lot road). ℘05 53 68 88 37. www.domainedebernou.com. Reservations recommended. 3 rooms. Meals.* Built in 1780, in the middle of a large estate (25ha/62 acres), this attractive mansion now houses a bed and breakfast, a riding school and a stud. The spacious guest rooms are quiet and peaceful. Good food.

EAT

La Part des Anges – *14 r. Émile-Sentini. ℘05 53 68 31 00. www.lapartdesanges.eu. Closed Sun evening, Mon, 15–31 Aug and Feb school holiday.* A pedestrian-only road, and a simple address offering good, regional food. Young owners Céline and Xavier personally ensure a warm welcome. Good-value set lunch menu.

La Table d'Armandie – *1350 av. du Midi. ℘05 53 96 15 15. latable.darmandie@orange.fr. Closed Sun–Mon and a fortnight in*

Aug. ♿ 🅿. Contemporary, clean feel, with open kitchen and big-screen TV showing key sports matches. Regional food.

⊖⊖ **Le Margoton** – *52 r. Richard-Cœur-de-Lion. ☎05 53 48 11 55. http://pagesperso-orange.fr/lemargoton. Closed Sat lunch and Sun–Mon.* Decorated with painted furniture and wooden panelling, this family-run restaurant has a warm, friendly atmosphere. Conveniently located near Agen's Old Town, the Margoton serves traditional, yet creative cuisine.

⊖⊖ **Le Washington** – *7 cours Washington. ☎05 53 48 25 50. www.le-washington.com. Closed Sat lunch, Sun and a fortnight in Aug,.* A contemporary restaurant in a house designed by French architect Charles Garnier (who also designed the Opéra de Paris and the Opéra de Monte-Carlo). Fine traditional cuisine using fresh market produce. Fine wine list.

⊖⊖⊖ **Mariottat** – *25 r. Louis Vivent. ☎05 53 77 99 77. www.restaurant-mariottat.com. Closed Wed lunch (Oct–Apr), Sat lunch, Sun evening, Mon, a wk in Apr and Nov.* This old 19C mansion, with its sculptured door pediment and slate roof, exudes character. Climb the handsome stone steps to reach the simply furnished dining rooms. Pleasant terrace.

BARS AND CAFÉS

Place Jasmin – Noisy with conversation and the clinking of glasses and cutlery, this square houses a multitude of bars and brasseries whose terraces attract crowds of locals in the summer months. Don't miss **La Bodega** *(no 7 bis; ☎05 53 48 26 83)* and its Thursday evening Latino music concerts.

Le Colonial Café – *10 av. du Général-de-Gaulle. ☎05 53 48 28 10. www.colonial-cafe.net. Closed Sun and public holidays.* A former Agen rugby player, Gérald Mayout, runs this friendly bar.

SHOPPING

Confiserie P. Boisson – *20 r. Grande-Horloge. ☎05 53 66 20 61. Closed Sun.* The Boisson family has been manufacturing delightful confectionery from the prunes for which Agen is famous since 1835. Its success dates from 1876, when a pastry cook's boy was inspired to stuff prunes with filling.

MARKETS

Farmers' markets – *Open Sat 7am–noon on the esp. du Gravier and pl. des Laitiers; Wed am and Sun am at the Halle du Pin.*

Marché au gras – *Open Nov–Mar Sat am and Sun am.* Duck and goose products.

Organic market – *Open Sat 7am–noon at pl. des Laitiers.*

Traditional markets – *Open Tue–Sun 7am–1pm, 4–7.30pm at pl. Jean Baptiste Durand; Wed and Sun 7am–noon at the Halle du Pin.*

SPORT AND LEISURE

Canoë-Kayak club de l'Agenais – *2 quai du Canal. ☎05 53 66 25 99. Closed a fortnight in Sept and Dec and public holidays.* This club rents kayaks and organises water trips. Open to all, including novices, it also offers beginners' lessons.

Les Vallons de Marennes – *47340 Laroque-Timbaut. ☎05 53 95 97 32. http://lesvallonsdemarennes.over-blog.com. Closed mid-Sept–mid-Jun.* It's worth taking a whole day to make the most of the various activities available on this farm (22ha/55 acres), with its 800 animals, and nature trails. Picnic area and snack bar on site.

Locaboat Plaisance – *port de la Gare du Pin. ☎05 53 66 00 74. www.locaboat.com. Closed Dec.* Discover the region's rivers and canals by hiring a boat or a barge at the marina.

Méca Plus – Vélo et Oxygen – *18–20 av. du Général-de-Gaulle. ☎05 53 47 76 76. Closed Sun.* This is the only place that rents bicycles in Agen – mountain bikes and children's bicycles available.

Poney-club de Darel en Agenais – *Darel, 47480 Pont-du-Casse (7.5km/4.7mi NE of Agen via the D 656). ☎05 53 96 90 33. www.poneyclubdedarel.fr. Closed Sun and public holidays.* Located on the hills outside Agen, this centre organises lessons and horse or pony rides.

Stadium Armandie – *17 cours Washington. ☎05 53 47 01 30. www.sua-rugby.com.* The municipal stadium hosts the local rugby union team, SU Agen Lot et Garonne *(season runs Sept–May).*

Marmande★

Lot-et-Garonne

Best known for its prunes, peaches, melons, tobacco and tomatoes, this is a town that has made the most of the fertile plain that surrounds it.

- **Population:** 17 100
- **Michelin Map:** 336: C-2
- **Info:** www.valdegaronne.com.
- **Location:** 70km/43mi SE of Bordeaux, 65km/40mi NW of Agen.
- **Kids:** Gens de Garonne, Couthures.
- **Timing:** One day to explore the town's surrounding areas.
- **Don't Miss:** Rembrandt's *Crucifixion* in the church of Mas d'Agenais.

ÉGLISE NOTRE-DAME

Built between the 13C and the 16C; the chancel was restored in the 17C and contains a figure of the Entombment of Christ from the same period. The first chapel to the right of the chancel contains a 17C framed altarpiece. Renaissance cloisters open onto formal French gardens.

EXCURSION

Casteljaloux

23km/14.3mi S via the D 933.

Maison du Roy. 05 53 93 00 00. www.casteljaloux.com.

Parts of this village date back to the Middle Ages. It became known as a Protestant stronghold, but was largely destroyed in 1621. There are several fine examples of its architectural past, when it was dominated from the 11C to the 16C by the Albret family – most notably the Maison du Roy.

The Lac de Clarens offers visitors a peaceful spot for swimming or walking.

DRIVING TOUR

2 LE VAL DE GARONNE

68km/42mi. Allow 4hrs.

Leave Marmande SE via the attractive D 299.

La Plaine aux Fleurs à Gontaud-de-Nogaret

Open Jun–Sept Mon–Thu am and pm, Sat–Sun pm only; Oct–May Fri–Sat pm, or by appointment. 5€ (children no charge). 05 53 83 47 90.

Small exhibition displaying fresh and dried flowers (70 varieties). From here, take the D 641 to Tonneins (note the windmill along the route). In Tonneins itself, there is an attractive walk along the quays of the Garonne.

Leave Tonneins via the D 120; turn right to Réserve de l'étang de la Mazière.

Réserve Naturelle de l'Étang de la Mazière, Villeton

Maison de la Réserve Les Mazières

– Guided visits only (2hrs) by appointment. 20€ (1–4 people, 4€/person supplement). 05 53 88 02 57. Walking boots recommended at this protected area. From here, head to Tonneins and turn left onto the D234.

Le Mas-d'Agenais

The Roman church contains an important Rembrandt painting (1631) of the **Crucifixion**★.

Leave via the D 116 to Marmande, then left onto VC1 to Couthures-sur-Garonne.

Gens de Garonne, Couthures

45min-length film; phone for times. 6€ (under 18 years 4€). 05 53 20 67 76. www.gensdegaronne.com.

The Garonne is the star of the show in this 3D film about local people's memories on how the river has affected their lives, from fishing and watering crops to flooding.

Villeneuve-sur-Lot

Lot-et-Garonne

Villeneuve was founded in 1253 on the borders between Périgord and Guyenne by Alphonse de Poitiers. It was built to serve as a "support centre" for the strongholds scattered throughout the upper Agenais region; in its day, Villeneuve was one of the largest and most powerful *bastides* in the southwest. Numerous alleys and ancient houses have been preserved from the Middle Ages, especially around place la Fayette, a typical old square. The town is today largely spread around the banks of the River Lot. The river's fertile alluvial valley produces plentiful crops of fruit and vegetables; it has turned Villeneuve into a busy trading centre and, like Agen, a regional market for plums.

- **Population:** 23 466
- **Michelin Map:** 336: G-3
- **Info:** 3 pl. de la Libération, Villeneuve-sur-Lot. 05 53 36 17 30. www.tourisme-villeneuve-sur-lot.com.
- **Location:** Villeneuve-sur-Lot is situated 33km/20.5mi N of Agen.
- **Parking:** Park in pl. La Fayette and explore the town centre on foot.
- **Kids:** The museums in Clairac in the Lot Valley.

SIGHTS

Town Gates

The two town gates – **porte de Paris** northeast of the Old Town and **porte de Pujols** southwest – are the only traces of the old ramparts. The gates are both built of brick and stone, are both crowned with crenellations and machicolations, and both covered by a roof of brown tiles. Porte de Pujols is three storeys high with mullioned windows; porte de Paris was instrumental in the fierce resistance to Mazarin's troops during the siege of 1653.

Église Ste-Catherine

r. de Penne. Open daily 9am–6pm.

This brick-built church, in Romanesque-Byzantine style, resting on a granite plinth, was consecrated in 1937. It is both stately and somewhat austere. Its north–south orientation is extremely unusual. The interior is decorated, apart from the chancel, with a series of restored stained-glass windows; those dating from the 14C and 15C – which came from the old church – have been attributed to the School of **Arnaud de Moles**, the master-enameller and painter who worked on the cathedral in Auch. Beautiful 17C and 18C gilt wood statues (of Our Lady of the Rosary, St Joseph, Mary Magdalene and St Jerome) adorn the four pillars of the nave above the doorway into the baptistery.

Pont des Cieutats (or Pont-Vieux)

This old bridge with uneven arches, which was built by the English in the 13C, offers a picturesque view over the banks of the river and over the 16C **Chapelle Notre Dame du-Bout-du-**

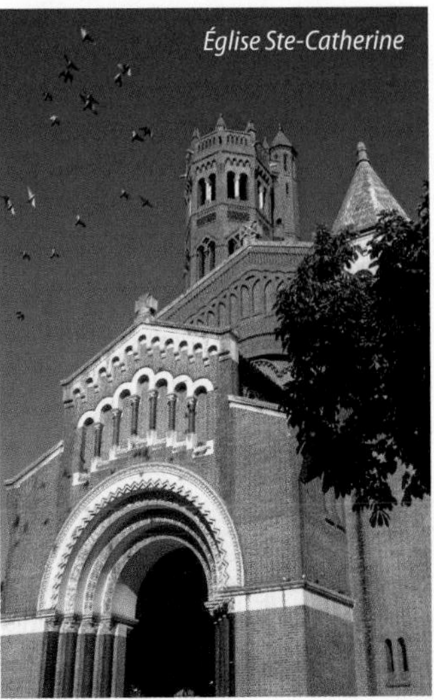

Église Ste-Catherine

Pont (Chapel at the End of the Bridge), with its east end jutting over the water. According to a legend, a sailor dived there in order to unfasten his boat, which was mysteriously blocked, and he discovered a small statue of the Virgin Mary.

Musée de Gajac

2 r. des Jardins. Open Mon and Wed–Fri 10am–noon, 2–6pm, Sat–Sun 2–6pm. Closed public holidays. 1€. 05 53 40 48 00.

The new municipal museum of Villeneuve, housed in an old windmill overlooking the Lot, contains collections of paintings from the 18C (Lebrun School), the 19C (Maurice Réalier-Dumas, Hyppolyte Flandrin, Eva Gonzalès and André Crochepierre) and the 20C (Henri Martin, Brayer). Some temporary exhibitions.

EXCURSIONS

Penne-d'Agenais★

10km/6.2mi E via the D 661.

This stronghold was once the fief of the kings of England, and so suffered during the Wars of Religion that it was nothing but ruins by the mid-20C. Greatly restored, it is now a lively summer tourist attraction.

Place Gambetta

This shady terrace is an excellent starting point for a tour of Penne. The "gateway to the town" opens onto two fine 16C houses, one of which served as a local prison for many years.

Notre-Dame-de-Peyragude

17 r. Peyragude. 05 53 41 37 80.

This modern sanctuary (in Romanesque-Byzantine style) is built on the top of a hill offering a scenic view of the valley. Very popular pilgrimages in honour of the Virgin are held here.

Viewpoint★

The orientation table overlooks the valley of the Lot, from Villeneuve to Fume: the view extends as far as the Upper Quercy in the distance.

Porte de Ferracap

The gallows used to be near this gate.

Rue de Ferracap

This, and the adjacent streets, are lined with very fine renovated houses (some with half-timbering and corbelling).

Place Paul-Froment

A remarkable brick house preceded by a house with Gothic arches contains a café and exhibit rooms.

Porte et Fontaine de Ricard

This old fortified gate and the fountain below are named after Richard the Lionheart, who was responsible for building the town's first fortifications.

Ferme du Chaudron Magique

26km/16.2mi NW of Villeneuve. 5.25€–12.50€. 05 53 88 80 77. www.chaudronmagique.fr.

Large farm which offers various types of fun and educational visits themed around cheese-making, animal-rearing and bread-making. All ages will enjoy the opportunity to feed sheep, goats and other farm animals (30 different species), as well as get hands-on with regular workshops.

Tournon-d'Agenais

16km/10mi to the E via the D 661.

Located on a hilltop close to the Vallée du Lot, this is a truly fascinating **site★**. As you enter into the village, you will discover remnants of the former ramparts (partly restored into a walking path) with houses built into them. The place has retained its *bastide* origins with straight roads crossing each other at right angles. A small public park offers a pretty **view** over the Vallée du Boudouyssou with its vines and cornfields. Note the lunar clock on the belfry.

Moulin de Lustrac

10km/6.2mi NW via the D 159 then the D 243. Turn left at Clauzade.

A dependency of the château which shares its name, this 13C fortified mill

View of the Lot Valley from Laparade

A. Cassaigne/MICHELIN

retains its working features of paddles and shafts.

DRIVING TOURS

3 LOWER LOT VALLEY

65km/40mi round trip. Allow one day.

Leave Villeneuve NW via the D 242 towards Casseneuil.

Casseneuil

The pretty brown-tiled roofs of Casseneuil, built in a bend at the junction of the Lède and the Lot, are clustered around the **church** *(05 53 41 13 33)*, which houses beautiful frescoes (13C–15C). After living off the river trade for many years, the town has now turned to preserved foods as its chief source of revenue. Many fine old houses, their loggias (15C–16C) leaning towards the Lède and surrounded by terrace gardens, are arranged throughout the village and on the roads to St-Pastour and Hauterive.

Go SW via the D 217 to Ste-Livrade and turn left along the D 667. After 1km/0.6mi, turn left to Fongrave.

Fongrave

Fongrave Priory was founded in 1130 and placed under the rule of Fontevraud, only accepting nuns of noble birth. The **church** *(open Mon–Fri 10am–6pm; 05 53 41 87 44)* has a monumental 17C carved oak **altarpiece**★ with snake-infested vines writhing around its cabled columns; an Adoration of the Magi occupies the centre.

Go W to Castelmoron-sur-Lot. Take the D 249, then the D 263 to Laparade.

Laparade

The ramparts of this *bastide* overlooking the Lot Valley offer a sweeping **view**★ from Villeneuve-sur-Lot, on the left to the junction of the Lot and Garonne, on the right *(viewpoint indicator)*. The river meanders companionably through a chequerboard of crops and orchards.

From Laparade, take the D 202 W, then the D 911.

Clairac

Picturesque, half-timbered houses with brick facings are witness to Clairac's rich past. The seat of a Benedictine abbey, it was destroyed and rebuilt many times during the Wars of Religion. The Crusaders won the town back from the Cathari (also known as Albigenses, a heretic sect seeking to achieve purity through complete ascetic renunciation), in 1224; it became a Protestant stronghold in 1560. Today it is home to three museums, which will delight children in particular.

The **Musée du Train** *(open Apr–Jun and Sept daily 10am–6pm, Jul–Aug*

daily 10am–7pm, Nov–Dec and Feb–Mar Wed, Sat–Sun, school and public holidays 10am–6pm; 8€ (children 6€), 10€/7€ combined ticket with the Forêt Magique and Abbaye des Automates; 05 53 79 34 81) presents miniature trains chugging through animated scenes.

The **Forêt Magique** *(open same hours as Musée du Train; 4.50€ (children 4€), 10€/7€ combined ticket with the Abbaye des Automates and Musée du Train; 05 53 79 34 81)*, also based on animated figures, plunges visitors into a world of elves and forest animals.

L'Abbaye des Automates – *4 pl. de l'Église. Open Apr–Sept daily 10am–6pm; Oct–Dec and Feb–Mar Wed, Sat–Sun, school and public holidays 10am–5pm. 8€ (child 5€); 10€/7€ combined ticket with Musée du Train and Forêt Magique; 05 53 79 34 81.*

This astonishing museum of automated figures explains the daily life of the abbey monks (it is said that the Clairac monks introduced prunes to the region and brought in tobacco from Brazil in 1555) and retraces the history of the town, which boasts such illustrious figures as the poet Théophile de Viau (born in Clairac in 1590) and Montesquieu, whose wife came from Clairac. Interesting to note are the French historic monuments made of matches and small-scale models of prestigious ships.

Take the D 911 E and follow the signs to Le Musée du Pruneau, just before Granges-sur-Lot.

Granges-sur-Lot

The **Musée du Pruneau**★ *(open 15 Mar–15 Oct Mon–Sat 9am–noon, 2–7pm, Sun and public holidays 3–7pm; 16 Oct–14 Mar Mon–Sat 9am–noon, 2–6.30pm, Sun and public holidays 3–6.30pm; 6.90€; 05 53 84 00 69; www.musee-du-pruneau.com)* in the Grabach estate, surrounded by plum trees whose fruit is used for prunes, shows the various tools used up until very recently to pick and prepare the dried fruit. A film explains the age-old production process and, at the end of the tour, visitors are invited to taste the estate's home-made specialities, all derived from plums and prunes, of course.

Return to Villeneuve via the D 911.

Le Temple-sur-Lot

The Jardin des Nénuphars (water lily garden) is located among the botanical gardens of **Latour-Marliac** *(Le bourg; open 15 Mar–Sept Tue–Sun 10am–6pm; 5€; 05 53 01 08 05; www.latour-marliac.com)*. Founded in 1875, this is the oldest and most prestigious aquatic tree-nursery in the world. You will see the rarest white water lilies in the ponds and on the lake. This is a nicely landscaped garden which offers a panoramic view on the site, with a pergola, an exotic greenhouse, a fountain, a Japanese bridge, and a bamboo garden. Some species of water lilies here inspired Claude Monet for his *Nymphéas*. He used to buy them here for his garden in Giverny: his signature can be seen on the order register.

4 LES SERRES DU BAS QUERCY

95km/59mi round trip. Allow one day.

Leave Villeneuve SW via the D 118.

The region of Lower Quercy consists of peaceful countryside with low elongated plateaux, cut across by chains of hills *(les Serres)* stretching between the fertile valleys.

Pujols

This very old village is perched on a hill providing an attractive **view**★ of Villeneuve-sur-Lot and the broad valley of the Lot, dotted with market gardens and fruit trees.

A passageway under the St-Nicolas bell tower leads to the old village, which is still surrounded by the remains of its 13C ramparts. The main street is lined with timber-framed houses with canopy roofs. The nave of the church of St-Nicolas has rib vaulting, while that of Ste-Foy-la-Jeune *(r. du Temple; 05 53 36 78 69)*, currently used as an exhibit hall, is decorated with 15C frescoes *(in poor condition)*. An old well, vestiges of fortifications, and Renaissance houses add to the pleasure of the tour.

Left onto D 118, then onto the D 220.

Grottes de Lastournelles
Guided tours (45min) daily Jun–Sept 10am–noon, 2–7pm; Oct–May 2–6pm by reservation. 5.50€. 05 53 40 08 09.
Bones found in the caves are displayed in glass cases at the entrance. Galleries have been hollowed out by the seepage of underground water. Small stalactites are forming on the roof. Seven chambers are open to visitors.

Join the D 212, then turn left, then left again towards St-Antoine-de-Ficalba.

Grottes de Fontirou
Guided tour (40min) Mon–Sat Easter and May–Jun 2pm, 5pm; Jul–Aug 10am–12.30pm, 2–6pm; 1–15 Sept 2pm, 5.30pm; Sun weather permitting. 6€. 05 53 40 15 29. www.grottes-fontirou.com.
The galleries and rooms hollowed out in the grey limestone of the Agenais region are decorated with reddish-ochre concretions (due to the clay content), contrasting with a number of lovely white stalagmites. Animal bones from the Tertiary Era are displayed in one of the rooms.

Go back to the N 21, turn right, then left onto the D 110.

The road goes through the Serres, limestone hills rising above the wide valleys, and through a small village which has retained a number of historic houses *(on its southern side)* and an old covered market.

Continue on the D 110.

Puymirol
Perched atop the hill that dominates the Vallée de la Séoune, this is an attractive village of white-stoned houses, topped by reddish-brown tiled roofs. The ramparts offer far-reaching views over the fertile Agen plains.

Take the D 16 to St-Maurin.

St-Maurin
The village contains the vestiges of an important Cluny abbey, and a Gothic-style church from the 17C with sculpted capitals.

Take the D 16, then the D 122.

Beauville
pl. de la Mairie. 05 53 47 63 06. www.ot-beauville.com.
Picturesque *bastide* overlooking the valley below, with arcaded central square.

Return to the D 122 then, at the crossroads with the D 656, follow signs to Frespech.

Frespech
Surrounded by 11C walls, this charming village's Romanesque church dates from the 11C, as do some stone houses. Souleille farm (3.5km/2.2mi from Frespech) houses a **Musée du Foie Gras** (*open Jul–Aug daily 10am–7pm; Sept–Nov and Feb–Jun Mon–Sat 10am–7pm, Sun and public holidays 3–7pm, Jan Mon–Sat 10am–7pm; 4€; 05 53 41 23 24; www.souleilles-foiegras.com*).

Turn right, following the signs to Hautefage-la-Tour.

Hautefage-la-Tour
Near the Gothic-style Notre-Dame-de-Hautefage, whose Flamboyant porch is surmounted by a canopy, there is a beautiful hexagonal tower used as a belfry. The upper turret is decorated with an open-work balustrade, gargoyles and pinnacles. On the square below, planted with beautiful plane trees, is an old wash-house. Against the church, also below, is a pilgrims' fountain.

Take the D103, D 223 then N 21 to return to Villeneuve-sur-Lot.

ADDRESSES

STAY

Hôtel La Résidence – *17 av. Lazare Carnot. 05 53 40 17 03. www.hotellaresidence47.com. Closed 18 Dec–3 Jan. 18 rooms.* A small family hotel with reasonably priced accommodation. The rooms in the main house are very basic; those in the building just behind are quieter and more comfortable.

NEARBY

Camping Le Pouchou – *47370 Courbiac (1.8km/1.1mi to the W via the rte de Tournon-d'Agenais. Take the road on the left). 05 53 40 72 68. www.camping-le-pouchou.com. Reservation recommended. 20 pitches.* A farm containing a small lake, which offers a dedicated camping area, and the hire of a few wooden chalets, either with or without attached bathrooms. Some are particularly well equipped, and can be hired by the night, except in July and August.

Chambre d'hôte Château de Seiglal – *47380 Monclar-d'Agenais (6km/3.7mi N of Fongrave. Take the D 238 then the D 667, kilometre post no 25). 05 53 41 81 30. www.chateau-de-la-seiglal.fr. 5 rooms. 6€.* This attractive 19C bed and breakfast surrounded by century-old trees is the perfect place for a relaxing stay. The comfortable guest rooms, named after the owner's five sisters, have fine views of the park and fields. Convivial *table d'hôte* meals served in the dining room with sculpted furniture and fireplace.

EAT

L'Amandine – *60 r. Casseneuil. 05 53 70 10 37. Open Tues–Sun. Boulangerie-pâtisserie-salon de thé*, this unassuming eatery offers small snacks and heartier fare; from sandwichs, savoury and sweet tarts, home-made chocolates and macaroons – and all at attractive prices. You can either order to take away, or eat at the several tables that are set out in the annex.

NEARBY

Lou Calel – *le Bourg, 47300 Pujols (4km/2.5mi SW of Villeneuve-sur-Lot via the D 118). 05 53 70 46 14. www.la-toque-blanche.com. Closed Sun–Mon and a wk in Jan and Nov.* A village *auberge* with two rustic dining rooms and a terrace with a panoramic view over the valley. Delicious local cuisine.

L'Air du Temps – *Mounet. 47140 Penne-d'Agenais. 05 53 41 41 34. www.restaurant-lairdutemps.fr. Closed 2 wks in Feb, 1 wk end of October, 1 wk in Nov.* Attractive brick and stone farm that offers a cosy restaurant with several secluded corners to enjoy the delicious, plentiful cuisine, plus two large terraces. It is all too easy to while away the hours here, enjoying the home-cooked food and the warm, cheerful welcome.

SHOPPING

La Boutique des Pruneaux – *11 pl. de la Libération. 05 53 70 02 75.* Many of the famous Pruneaux d'Agen are grown and processed in Villeneuve-sur-Lot and its surrounding area. This boutique, at the foot of the porte de Paris, specialises in prunes and other regional delicacies, including chocolates and vintage Armagnacs (40 to 50 years old).

Place d'Aquitaine – An organic farmers' market is held here on Wednesday mornings. Local producers from all over the Lot-et-Garonne descend, offering shoppers a variety of local products, from roasted chickens to farm honey.

Place Lafayette – Place Lafayette, also known as place des Cornières, is the hub of Villeneuve-sur-Lot. The busy streets leading from the square are full of shops, bars and cafés. It also holds a traditional market on Tuesday and Saturday mornings.

SPORT AND LEISURE

Aviron Villeneuvois – *quai d'Alsace. 05 53 49 18 27. Closed Sat–Sun.* This rowing club, situated in the heart of the city, organises boat trips up the Lot river during summer months.

Centre de Plein Air de Rogé – *La Grâce (6km/3.7mi SE via the D 661). 05 53 70 48 13. Closed Sat–Sun.* Surrounded by greenery and bordered by a loop of the River Lot, this children's outdoor centre is blessed with an idyllic setting. Kayaking, rowing, water-skiing, horseback riding, archery, trampoline and mountain biking courses are held here.

Monflanquin★

Lot-et-Garonne

The distinctive tiled roofs of this venerable *bastide*, founded in the 13C by Alphonse de Poitiers, are clustered together on a hill dominated by the slender silhouette of the church. Stendhal compared the town to "a small Tuscany".

- **Michelin Map:** 336: G-2
- **Info:** pl. des Arcades. ℘05 53 36 40 19. www.cc-monflanquinois.fr.
- **Location:** 17km/10.6mi N of Villeneuve-sur-Lot on the D 676.
- **Parking:** It can get busy in summer. A new car park has opened north of the centre.
- **Don't Miss:** Musée des Bastides.
- **Timing:** Half a day.

SIGHTS

Narrow, steeply sloping streets, sometimes spanned by covered passages *(pontets)*, climb up to the attractive **place des Arcades** covered market, where the four *cornières*, gateways to the *bastide*'s main square, are still in place. The 15C fortified façade of the Southern Gothic-style church has been restored.

A street encircling the upper town provides a pleasant walk with panoramic **views**★ of the surrounding countryside and the River Lède, tributary of the Lot. To the northeast, overlooking a crest line, the Château de Biron stands out clearly on the horizon.

Musée des Bastides

Above the tourist office, pl. des Arcades. Open daily May–Jun and Sept Mon–Sat 10am–noon, 2–6pm; Jul–Aug 10am–1pm, 2–7pm; Oct–Apr Mon–Sat 10am–noon, 2–5pm. 4€ (under 12 years no charge). ℘05 53 36 40 19. http://bastides.free.fr.

A modern, interactive museum that explains the growth of these "new towns" during the 13C and 14C in southwest France. It looks at their urban layout, their social organisation and their role in medieval society through reconstructions, documents and audiovisual material. A visit here will deepen your enjoyment not just of Monflanquin but the other *bastides* in the region.

EXCURSION

Sauveterre-la-Lémance

33km/20.5mi NE via the D 124, then the D 710.

Edward I, King of England and Duke of Aquitaine, built a fortress here at the end of the 13C to protect his lands from the French King Philip IV.

The **Musée de Préhistoire Mésolithique L.-Coulonges** displays archaeological finds from the 1920s to today in the Vallée de la Lémance, a site rich in remains of the last hunter-gatherers. An interesting exhibit explains the techniques for producing prehistoric tools *(open Apr, Sept and Oct Mon–Fri pm, Jun–Aug Tues–Fri am and pm, Sat–Sun pm only, rest of year by appointment; 3€ (under 16 years 2€); ℘05 53 40 73 03).*

DRIVING TOUR

5 A SMALL TUSCANY

80km/50mi. Allow one day.

Leave Monflanquin N via the D 676.

Villeréal

This *bastide* founded by Alfonse de Poitiers, the brother of St Louis, has kept its original right-angled grid plan, corbelled houses and overhanging roofs. In the centre of the *bastide*, the two-storied 14C markets are supported by oak pillars. Cornières (corner gateways typically found on the central square of a *bastide*) stand on the main square. The fortified 13C **church** *(pl. de la Libération; ℘05 53 36 09 65)* dominates the *bastide* with its slender silhouette, combining charm and severity. The high façade is framed by two towers crowned

Château de Bonaguil

J. Damase/MICHELIN

with pinnacle turrets connected by a crenellated watch-path; the left-hand tower is pierced with arrow slits.
A **lake** with water sports facilities lies at the foot of the village.

Continue SE along the D 255 to Lacapelle-Biron, then take the D 150.

St-Avit
Sienna-coloured stone abounds in this small hamlet, from the limestone slabs of the church to the ancient houses with their weathered roofs. Bernard Palissy (*see the Musée des Beaux-Arts in AGEN, and box p274*) is the focus of much of the interest here. The museum which bears his name offers a slideshow of his life as well as a collection of his ceramics, both early and modern works (*open May–Sept Wed–Mon afternoon, Oct–Apr Sun afternoon; closed 1 Jan, 1 May, Easter, 1 Nov, 25 Dec; 3.20€ (under 18 years 1.60€, under 12 years no charge); 05 53 40 98 22; www.ceramique.com/Palissy*). A large exhibition is held each year (from May to October).

The D 150 runs alongside the Lède river, wooded escarpments and exposed limestone rocks. A few houses appear between the trees.

Gavaudun
This is an attractive and important historicl site, found in the narrow, windy Vallée de la Lède, between the plains of the Lot and the Dordogne Valley. The impressive crenellated keep (11C and 13C) of a defensive château stronghold seems to rise from the rocks (*open Jul–Aug; guided visit (1hr) throughout the day Jun–Sept Sat–Sun only; €4; 05 53 40 04 16*).

St-Sardos-de-Laurenque
12C church with a sculpted gate, ornate capitals decorated with animals and religious figures, and a frieze decorated with fish. Impressive capitals also mark the Roman nave (*open Apr–Jun Fri–Wed pm only; Jul–Aug all day; key available from the town hall; guided visit by appointment; 05 53 40 04 16*).

Return to Gavaudun to continue along the D 150, then take the D 162 towards Fumel.

Château de Bonaguil★★
Open Apr–May and Oct daily 10.30am–12.30pm, 2–5.30pm; Jun and Sept daily 10am–12.30pm, 2–6pm; Jul–Aug daily 10am–7pm; Festival de Bonaguil (start of Aug) 10am–4pm; Nov Sat–Sun and school holidays 10.30am–12.30pm, 2–5pm; Dec–Jan school holidays 2–5pm; Feb–Mar daily 10.30am–12.30pm, 2–5pm; (last admission 30min before closing). Closed 1 Jan, 25 Dec. 6€. 05 53 71 90 33. www.boaguil.org.

This majestic fortress is one of the most perfect examples of military architecture from the late 15C and 16C. It is unique in that it appears to be a traditional defensive stronghold but its design was also a response to the development of firearms, such as the cannon and the harquebus. Bonaguil, which was built neither as a lookout post nor as a fortress but as a secure place of refuge by Bérenger de Roquefeuil, pioneered the use of firearms essentially for defensive purposes (from 1480 to 1520). His castle was never attacked and stayed intact until the eve of the French Revolution.

Tour

After passing through the outer wall, visitors come to the barbican. This was a bastion on its own with a separate garrison, powder store, armouries and escape route. The barbican formed part of the 350m/380yd-long first line of defence whose embrasures were designed for cross-firing.

The second line of defence consisted of five towers including the **Grosse Tour**, which is among the strongest round towers ever to have been built in France. It is 35m/115ft high and crowned with corbels. The upper storeys served as living quarters, whereas the lower contained weapons, such as muskets, culverins and harquebuses.

Overlooking both lines of defence, the keep **(donjon)** with its cant walls, served not only as a watchtower but also as a command post. It was shaped like a vessel, with its prow – the most vulnerable point – turned towards the north. It was the last bastion of defence. Inside, a room houses arms and objects found during excavation of the moats. Equipped with a well sunk through the rock, outbuildings (including the **baking house**) in which provisions could be stored, monumental chimneys, drainage systems, dry internal ditches and vaulted tunnels enabling the troops to move about quickly, the castle garrison of about 100 men could easily withstand a siege provided they were not betrayed or starved out.

Fumel

This is both a historic and an industrial city. You might be surprised at first sight, but try to look beyond the grey smoke and you will be charmed by the château overlooking the River Lot and by the surroundings of the city.

Monsempron-Libos

The 12C fortified village, perched on an outcrop, is worth a visit for its large, imposing Roman church. It is believed to have been built on the former site of a temple to Cybele the Earth Mother, a fact which is recalled in its architecture such as the large rounded columns.

At the foot of the medieval part of Monsempron, the modern, more industrial town of Libos lies on the banks of the River Lot and the Lémance.

Return to Monflanquin via the D 124.

ADDRESSES

STAY

Chambre d'hôte Domaine de Majoulassie – *Majoulassie, 47150 Gavaudun. 05 53 40 34 64. www.villereal-tourisme.com/majoulassie. 5 rooms. Restaurant.*
A stream, some woods, fields of green, an old water mill and a fishing lake all contribute to make this bucolic location an ideal place to stay. The bedrooms are comfortable, with small balconies and large, recently-decorated bathrooms.

EAT

Hostellerie le Vert – *46700 Mauroux (16km/10mi S). 05 65 36 51 36. www.hotellevert.com. Closed Mon–Sat lunch.*
A rustic dining room serving traditional cuisine using fresh farm produce. Cooking classes available on demand.

Église Notre-Dame-La-Grande, Poitiers

DISCOVERING POITOU-CHARENTES AND LA VENDÉE

POITIERS AND LA VIENNE

The Poitou-Charentes region lies between the Pays de la Loire in the north and Aquitaine in the south and shares a border with both the Centre and Limousin regions to the east. The Vienne, which flows into the Loire north of the region, and the Charente, which flows into the Atlantic near Rochefort, are the region's two main rivers. The region is, in the main, agricultural; cattle rearing, dairy farming, cereal growing and viticulture are the principal activities.

Highlights

1. A walk around the historic centre of **Poitiers**, stopping to admire the splendid Église Notre-Dame-la-Grande (p296)
2. Take a plunge into the virtual world at **Futuroscope** (p306)
3. The panorama from the rocky promontory towering above the charming village of **Angles-sur-l'Anglin** (p313)
4. Soak in the monastic atmosphere at **Abbaye de St-Savin**, a UNESCO-listed site (p314)
5. The drive from Chauvigny through the Gartempe Valley, known as the **Valley of Frescoes** (p318)

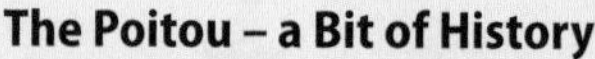

The Poitou – a Bit of History

The Poitou is an ancient region, with the town of Poitiers at its centre. It was inhabited by the Pictavi, who were subdued, like other Gallic tribes, in 56 BC by Julius Caesar and made part of the province of Aquitania. The Franks conquered the region in AD 507 which, in 732, was to play an important role in European history when the Frankish leader Charles Martel defeated a Muslim army at Poitiers, ending Islamic hopes of adding France to their possessions in Spain. From the 10C, until the marriage of Eleanor of Aquitaine and Louis, soon to be Louis VII of France, the counts of Poitou were the also the dukes of Aquitaine. With Eleanor's subsequent marriage to Henry Plantagenet, later Henry II of England, the control of the region passed into English hands until the 15C.

As the seat of the Dukes of Aquitaine, Poitiers grew in importance throughout the period and is today an important commercial centre, having the second-oldest university in France and being the capital city of both the Vienne *département* and the Poitou-Charentes region. Nearby is **Futuroscope**, a pioneering theme park, where every building is a work of art and which uses giant cinema screens and interactive displays to engage visitors.

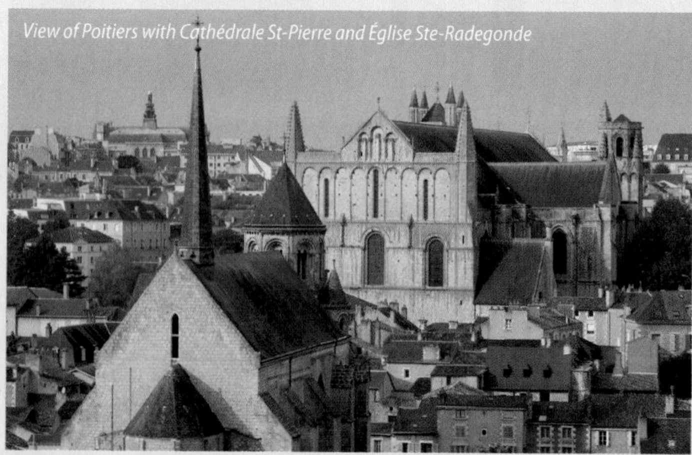

View of Poitiers with Cathédrale St-Pierre and Église Ste-Radegonde

© Brigitte Merz/Look/Photononstop

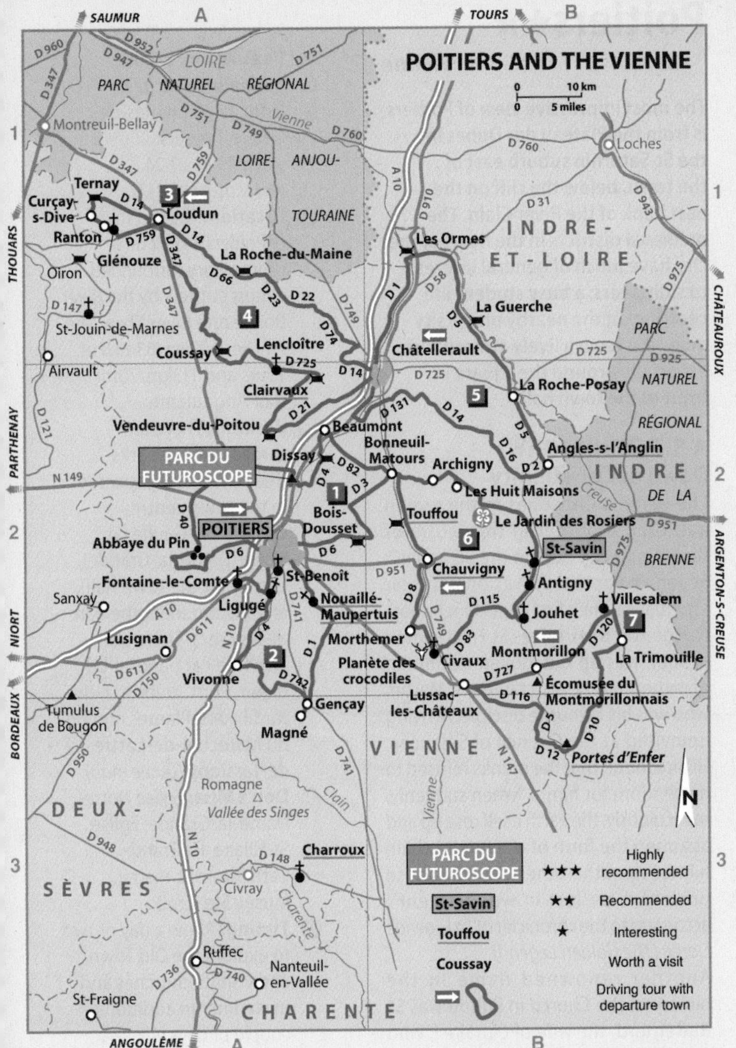

The Wines

The viticultural area, north of Poitiers, has a history of winemaking that can be traced back to Roman times; in the Middle Ages it was one of the best-known wine areas of France. Today **Haut-Poitou wines**, which were awarded the *appellation* label in November 2010, are made from vines grown on a vast plateau northwest of Poitiers on mainly clay-limestone soils covering 186ha/460 acres. Dry whites are produced from Sauvignon Blanc and Sauvignon Gris, fruity reds from Pinot Noir, Gamay, Merlot and Cabernet France, while fresh rosés are from Pinot Noir, Gamay and Cabernet France. The local cooperative, Cave du Haut Poitou, at Neuville de Poitou, produces a good selection of Haut Poitou wines.

Poitiers★★

Vienne

The most impressive view of Poitiers is from the Plâteau des Dunes in the St-Saturnin suburb east of the town, below the cliff on the east bank of the River Clain. The medieval districts in the heart of the city have much of general interest to sightseers; a busy student life centring on the nearby university gives the town a lively atmosphere, especially around the square in front of the town hall.

- **Population:** 88 776
- **Michelin Map:** 322: H–I-5
- **Info:** 45 pl. Charles-de-Gaulle, Poitiers. ☎05 49 41 21 24. www.ot-poitiers.fr.
- **Location:** The Old Town of Poitiers is built on a promontory surrounded almost entirely by the River Boivre and River Clain. The city lies 102km/63mi S of Tours and 113km/70mi N of Angoulême.
- **Parking:** There are three large car parks (fee payable) signposted in the town centre: Charles-de-Gaulle (at Notre-Dame-la-Grande), Carnot (at the town hall), and Rivaud (near the Parc de Blossac). There are also free car parks at bd Bajon, Pont Joubert, r. du Jardin-des-Plantes and bd du Maréchal-de-Lattre-de-Tassigny (*see map*).
- **Don't Miss:** Église Notre-Dame-la-Grande; Église St-Hilaire-le-Grand; Cathédrale St-Pierre; Musée Ste-Croix.
- **Timing:** Allow a day or two to explore the Old Town and visit its churches and museums; an additional couple of days will also give you time to visit Futuroscope 12km/7.4mi outside Poitiers.

A BIT OF HISTORY

Dawn of Christianity

The earliest Christians in the region gathered together in the centre of the Roman city here in the 3C and 4C: St John's Baptistery was one of their sanctuaries. Their first important bishop, the gentle **St Hilaire** (St Hilary, died c. 368), was an outspoken champion of orthodoxy; he also taught St Martin, who was his favourite disciple. Arriving uninvited at the Council of Séleucée, Hilaire found that the monks refused to make room for him – "when suddenly, miraculously, the earth itself rose up and assumed the form of a splendid chair, higher than the others, and all those present were lost in wonderment", according to the chronicler of *La Légende Dorée (The Golden Legend)*.

Another renowned name in the history of the Church in Poitou was **St Radegund**, the wife of Clotaire I, who fled to Poitiers in 559 and founded Holy Cross Monastery – where her confidant, St Fortunat, would recite poems he had written in Latin.

A Momentous Date

Of the three conflicts known as the **Battle of Poitiers**, that in which Charles Martel vanquished the army of the invading Arabs in AD 732 and saved Christianity is by far the most famous – and the most important.

Having conquered Spain, the Arabs flooded into Gaul from the south. Checked for the first time by Eudes, Duke of Aquitaine, they decimated his forces near Bordeaux and continued towards the centre of the country, sacking and pillaging everything on their way. Eudes asked for help from the Merovingian leader Charles Martel; the Arabs, who had just burned down Église St-Hilaire in Poitiers, found themselves confronted by the Frankish troops a few miles north of the town.

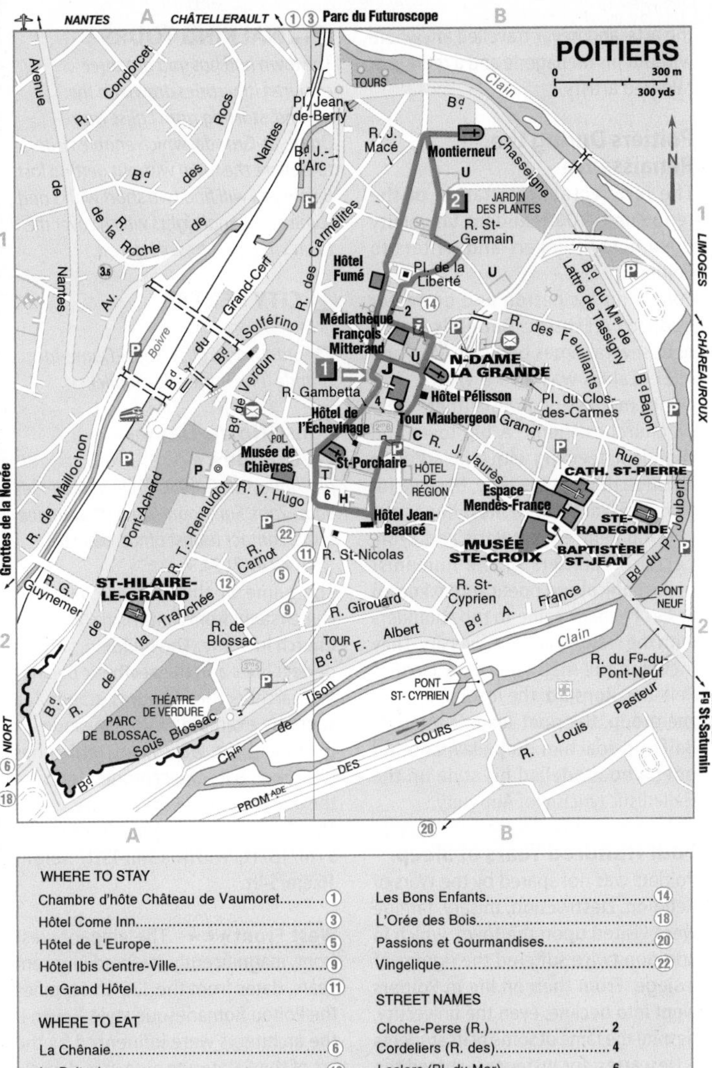

Martel's cavalry cut the Muslim army to ribbons, and little by little the invaders began to retreat from Aquitaine. The year 732 remains as an important symbol of Western Christianity's first true victory over the Muslims.

Jean de Berry's Court

The city of Poitiers, having twice fallen under English domination – in the 12C by Henry Plantagenet and Eleanor of Aquitaine, in the 14C after the second Battle of Poitiers in 1356 – was finally restored to the French Crown after General Bertrand du Guesclin (c.1320–80) had chased the English from the region. The royal representative was the brother of Charles: Jean, Comte de Poitou and holder of the Berry and Auvergne dukedoms.

De Berry's rule, which lasted from 1369 to 1416, brought fame and prosperity to Poitiers. Jean de Berry was ostentatious and sophisticated, a generous patron of the arts, and never travelled anywhere without his menagerie and a retinue of talented artists.

Poitiers During the Renaissance

The intellectual reputation of the renowned 4 000-student university drew many thinkers and writers to Poitiers.

Following his patron and protector Geoffroy d'Estissac, **Rabelais** stayed here several times between 1524 and 1527; Calvin was also a visitor. This city of monks and priests (there were 67 churches then), "A big town and confident, teeming with scholars", as it was described at the time, became for a while France's third most important cultural centre after Paris and Lyon. Certain members of the humanist philosophical and poetic group known as Les Pléiades came to rub shoulders with the learned at the university. They included the mathematician Jacques Pelletier, Ronsard, the leading light of the group, the poet Jean-Antoine de Baïf and Joachim du Bellay, another poet who modelled his style on the Hellenistic lyricism of Antiquity.

Four Hundred Years of Sleep

Poitiers was not spared by the Wars of Religion. Destruction, misery, famine were visited upon the town, which in addition twice suffered the rigours of a siege. From then on life in Poitiers went into decline; even the university, despite the fame of some of its students – Descartes, for instance – shared the same fate.

Despite the strenuous efforts of the Intendant **Comte de Blossac**, this slumber persisted until after World War II.

Since then the influence of a younger generation has injected a new dynamism into the town and has enabled it to reclaim its position as capital of the Poitou-Charentes region.

WALKING TOURS

The town hall has laid out three coloured itineraries drawn on the ground, starting from Église Notre-Dame-la-Grande, which enable visitors to explore the town without getting lost. Below you will find two short walks and some additional sights which cover the town's main centres of interest.

1 CITY CENTRE

Start from Église Notre-Dame-la-Grande (pl. Charles-de-Gaulle).

Église Notre-Dame-La-Grande★★

pl. Charles-de-Gaulle. Open Mon–Sat 9am–7pm, Sun noon–7pm. Guided tours, contact tourist office. 5.50€. 05 49 41 21 24.

The name of this former collegiate church stems from Santa Maria Maggiore Church in Rome. The building, with its perfect lines and the aesthetic balance of its architectural features, stands as a supreme example of Romanesque art in France. The west front, which has blackened over the centuries, is one of the most famous in the country.

The dimensions of the church are: length 57m/187ft, width 13m/43ft, height 16.6m/54ft.

West Front★★★ – The elegant west front, magnificently restored in recent years, dates from the 12C and typifies the Poitou Romanesque style – even if the architects were influenced by the art of the Saintonge area. It is densely carved and the lively figures are further accentuated, according to the time of day, by the play of light and shade. In the centre, at ground level, is an arched doorway with four receding lines of coving, flanked by arcades framing twinned arches within. Above these three arched elements are bas-relief sculptures of *(read from left to right and from the lower level to upper) Adam and Eve; Nebuchadnezzar on His Throne*; the *Four Prophets Moses, Jeremiah, Isaiah and Daniel*; the *Annunciation*; the *Tree of Jesse*; the *Visitation*; the *Nativity*;

the *Bathing of the Infant Christ*; the *Meditation of St Joseph*.

The central doorway is surmounted by a large, very tall arched window bay, itself flanked by a double row of blind arcades housing the Apostles and (at the extremities of the upper row) two figures said to be St Hilary and St Martin. The coving of the arcades is decorated with fine carvings representing plants and fantastic creatures.

Christ in Majesty gazes down from an oval-shaped frame in the great gable above. The figure is surrounded by the symbols of the Evangelists and crowned by a stylised Sun and Moon, metaphors for eternity in the Romanesque period. At each side of the west front a cluster of columns supports a pierced lantern with straight or arched cornices and a roof in the shape of a pine-cone, covered with scales.

North Wall – The chapels flanking this side of the church were added in the 15C *(against the chancel)* and the 16C *(along the aisle)*. Note the unusual silhouette of the square-sectioned 12C belfry with a pierced turret, again topped by a pine-cone roof.

Interior – The interior of the church, which is in the Poitou style but without a transept, was unfortunately repainted in 1851. On each side of the barrel-vaulted nave are very high rib-vaulted aisles.

A 17C copper goblin can be seen in the chancel. Behind the high altar stands a 16C statue of Notre-Dame-des-Clefs (Our Lady of the Keys), installed to replace the original, which was destroyed in 1562: the statue recalls a miracle said to have occurred in 1202, when the keys of the town were spirited away from the traitor who was going to hand them over to the besieging English. The oven vault above the chancel – painted in the 12C with a fresco depicting the *Virgin in Majesty* and *Christ in Glory* – is supported by six heavy, round columns arranged in a semicircle.

The original apsidal chapel, on the south side of the ambulatory, was replaced in 1475 by another, now dedicated to St Anne. This was founded by Yvon du Fou, the Seneschal (Steward) of the city, whose armorial bearings can be seen above the fine Flamboyant funerary niche where his tomb was lodged. In its place now is an Italian version of the *Entombment*, in polychrome stone, which dates from the 16C. The work was once in Trinity Abbey in Poitiers.

Follow r. de la Regratterie then turn left onto r. du Palais.

Palais de Justice

pl. Alphonse le Petit. Open Mon–Fri 8.45am–noon, 1.45–5.30pm. No charge. 05 49 50 22 00.

The Restoration façade of the law courts masks the Great Hall and the original keep of the ancient ducal palace, rare

Interior Palais de Justice

©Charlie Abad/Photononstop

examples of urban civic architecture dating from the Middle Ages.
The **Great Hall**★ (47m/154ft long and 17m/56ft wide) was reserved for important trials, solemn audiences and sessions of the Provincial Estates. In 1418, four years before he was proclaimed King, the fleeing Charles VII set up his court and parliament here. In March 1429 Joan of Arc was subjected to a gruelling interrogation by an ecclesiastical commission, to emerge after three weeks with an enhanced sense of her sacred mission and official recognition that the mission was religiously inspired.
Although construction of the vast hall was started under the Plantagenets, it was de Berry who commissioned the architect Dammartin to build the great gable wall with its three monumental chimneys, its balcony and Flamboyant windows. Up above, four fine statues represent *(left to right)* Jean de Berry, his nephew Charles VI, Isabeau of Bavaria, and Jean's wife Jeanne de Boulogne.
The early 12C keep, known as **Tour Maubergeon**, are visible from rue des Cordeliers. Remains of the original Gallo-Roman defensive wall can be seen in the adjacent square.

Walk from the Palais de Justice along r. Gambetta, then turn left onto r. Paul-Guillon.

Hôtel de l'Échevinage

7 r. Paul-Guillon.
No open to the public.
This 15C building with its contemporary chapel was once the town hall. It originally housed first the university's Grandes Écoles and then the local magistrate *(échevinage).*

Return to r. Gambetta.

Église St-Porchaire

r. St-Porchaire. Open daily 8am–7pm. 05 49 52 35 35.
All that remains today of the original 11C church built on this site is the belfry-porch with its four-sided pyramid roof. Three tiers of arcades and bays stand above the great Roman arch, decorated with Romanesque capitals, which serves as an entrance to the two-aisle church restored in the 16C.
Up in the belfry hangs the great bell of the university, which was cast in 1451. At one time it was used to announce the start of student classes.

Hôtel Jean-Beaucé

This Renaissance building has some original architectural elements: a tower capped by a cupola and a stair turret with slanting windows. In the left corner, the juxtaposed bays provide a view of all sides, just like a traditional watchtower.

Walk back along the r. du Puygarreau and the r. du Marché-Notre-Dame to the corner of the r. des Cordeliers.

Tour Maubergeon

This tower dates from the beginning of the 12C. It was converted into apartments for Jean de Berry. The façade, brightened up by large Gothic windows, is decorated with statues. In the adjoining square, let your gaze follow along the remains of the Gallo-Roman wall towards the apse of the Great Hall of the Palais de Justice.

Hôtel Pélisson

9 r. du Marché-Notre-Dame.
Its finely decorated façade is a good example of architecture from the Renaissance period (mid-16C).

Go up r. du Marché-Notre-Dame until you reach pl. Charles-de-Gaulle.

2 THREE QUARTIERS

Walking through this pleasant but steep district requires a certain amount of energy!

Starting from pl. Charles-de-Gaulle, follow r. de l'Université to the multimedia library.

Médiathèque

4 r. de l'Université. ♿ ⓒ Open Jun–Sept Tue 11am–7pm, Wed and Fri–Sat 11am–6pm, Thu 1–7pm; Oct–May Tue 11am–10pm, Wed and Fri–Sat 11am–6pm, Thu 1–7pm. No charge. ☎ 05 49 52 31 51. www.bm-poitiers.fr.

The multimedia library is one of the most attractive modern buildings in Poitiers. Inaugurated in 1996, it contains a fine medieval collection and works in close association with the Bibliothèque Nationale de France in Paris.

Walk down r. Cloche-Perse on the right until you reach pl. de la Liberté, then follow r. Pierre-Rat. Bear left into r. St-Germain and head up r. de la Bretonnerie. On the right you will see the Église St-Jean-de-Montierneuf. At the pl. de Montierneuf take the r. Jean-Bouchet on the left. Continue along the r. de la Chaîne, then the r. Descartes.

In the lower Romanesque part of the edifice, note the east-facing transept chapels and the radiating chapels of the apse. The Gothic upper part is flanked by graceful flying buttresses.

Hôtel Fumé

8 r. René Descartes.

Note the Flamboyant dormer windows adorning the restored façade of no **8**, a 16C building belonging to the university. There is an attractive courtyard with stair turret, **gallery** and corbelled balcony.

Return to pl. Charles-de-Gaulle via pl. Charles-VII and r. de la Regratterie.

QUARTIER ÉPISCOPAL

Cathédrale St-Pierre★

r. de la Cathédrale. ⓒ Open daily summer 8am–7pm; winter 8am–6pm. ☎ 05 49 41 21 24.

St Peter's Cathedral was begun at the end of the 12C and almost completed by the end of the 14C; it is striking for its huge dimensions.

Exterior – The wide west front, with its rose window and three 13C doorways, is flanked by two asymmetric towers. That on the left *(northern)* side retains an octagonal storey topped by a balustrade.

The tympana of the doorways are carved with fascinating sculptures, among them the *Crowning of the Virgin (to the left)*; the dead hurrying from their graves and the heavenly elect separated from the damned delivered to Leviathan *(in the centre)*; the teaching of St Thomas, patron of stone-carvers, the miraculous building of a mystical palace for the King of India *(to the right)*.

Walk around the northern flank of the cathedral as far as r. Arthur-de-la-Mauvinière.

Note on the way around the massive strength of the buttresses and the absence of flying buttresses. At the far end of the building the dizzy height (49m/161ft) of the **east end** can be appreciated.

Interior – On entering, visitors are struck by the sheer power of the architecture: the wide shell of the cathedral is divided into three aisles of almost equal height, and the impression of a perspective soaring away towards the east is accentuated by a narrowing of the aisles and a lowering of the central vault from the chancel onwards.

Twenty-four domed rib vaults – a Plantagenet influence – crown the eight spans of each of the three aisles. Despite its flat exterior, the east end is hollowed out enough to form three apsidal chapels. A cornice embellished with historiated modillions supports a narrow gallery running around the walls above a series of blind arcades.

Among the stained-glass windows at the far east end is a late-12C representation of the *Crucifixion* showing a radiant Christ flanked by the Virgin and St John. Above and below this are: the Apostles, with their faces raised towards a *Christ in Glory*, set in a mandorla; the *Crucifixion of St Peter* and the *Beheading of St Paul*.

The **choir stalls**★, dating from the 13C, are said to be the oldest in France. The

carved corner-pieces represent the Virgin and Child, angels carrying crowns and the architect at work.

The 18C organ, built by François-Henri Clicquot (1732–90), member of a celebrated dynasty of organ-makers working in Reims and Paris in the 17C and 18C, is located on the inner side of the west front, within a beautiful shell-shaped loft.

Walk along r. Ste-Radegonde, which starts behind the cathedral, then continue along r. Arthur-de-la-Mauvinière.

Église Ste-Radegonde★

1 r. Ste-Croix. Open daily 8.30am–6pm, religious festivals 8.30am–7pm. 05 49 41 21 24.

This former collegiate church was founded around AD 552 by Radegund with the idea that it would eventually become the last resting place of her nuns from Holy Cross Abbey. The church is characterised by a Romanesque apse and a belfry-porch which stand at opposite ends of a nave in the style known as Angevin Gothic.

The belfry-porch, majestic and massive in its proportions, was enhanced in the 15C with a Flamboyant portal in the niches of which today stand modern statues of the patron saints of Poitiers. At the base of the tower there remains a chamber, where ecclesiastical justice used to be dispensed.

A small garden east of the church offers a view of the **east end** and the lines of the church as a whole.

Baptistère St-Jean★

8 r. Ste-Croix. Open Apr–Jun and Sept Wed–Mon 10.30am–12.30pm, 3–6pm; Jul–Aug daily 10.30am–12.30pm, 3–6pm; Oct–Mar Wed–Mon 2.30–4.30pm. Closed Tue (except July–Aug). 1.50€ (children 0.75€) 05 49 41 21 24.

St John's Baptistery, dating from the middle of the 4C, is the oldest example of Christian architecture in France.

Originally the baptistery comprised two rectangular chambers: the baptismal hall and a narthex. The rectangular baptismal hall still exists, together with a 6C–7C quadrangular apse and two apsidal chapels, originally square but changed to a semicircular shape in the middle of the 19C. The former narthex, however, which was restored in the 10C, is now polygonal. Panels of Romanesque brickwork brace the window embrasures, which are partly blocked up and pierced with oculi. Beneath the gables are strange pilasters with capitals carved in bas-relief.

Interior – Inside, the baptistery is notable for the intricately carved capitals of its marble columns; for the colonnettes supporting the arcades; for the three tall arcades which link the narthex and the baptismal chamber. The apse and its two chapels are surmounted by oven vaults.

In the centre of the baptismal chamber is the **octagonal pool** which was used for baptism: the converts were lowered into the water to receive the ritual unction from the bishop, then dressed in a white tunic and received in the cathedral. In the 7C use of the pool was superseded by baptism by affusion (holy water poured over the head) following the installation of a cistern supplying the font; until the 12C this was the only place in Poitiers where baptisms could be consecrated.

The building now houses an interesting lapidary museum.

Romanesque Frescoes (partly over-painted in the 13C–14C) adorn the walls: an *Ascension* above the apse; *Christ in Majesty* decorating its oven vault; four horsemen, including the Emperor Constantine, in the rectangular chamber; peacocks, the symbol of immortality, on the left-hand wall.

Musée Ste-Croix★★

3 bis r. Jean Jaurès. Open Jun–Sept Tue–Fri 10am–noon,1.15–6pm, Sat–Sun 10am–noon, 2–6pm; Oct–May Tue–Fri 10am–noon, 1.15–5pm, Sat–Sun 2–6pm. 1. Closed public holidays. 4€ (1st Sun of month no charge), combined entrance ticket with Musée de Chièvres. 05 49 41 07 53. www.musees-poitiers.org.

The museum is housed in a modern building on the site of the former Holy Cross Abbey (Abbaye Ste-Croix).

Archaeology – *Basement: access down a staircase at the far end of the first hall.* The collections here concentrate on the Poitou of prehistory to medieval times. The chronology of the Palaeolithic Era is set out, with displays of flint implements, tools and other items discovered during digs (fragments of a bronze roasting spit from the 7C BC, an ingot of pure copper, objects buried c.700 BC). A number of Gallo-Roman finds are presented against a backdrop of the remains of antique walls: inscriptions, fragments of columns, bas-relief sculptures and statues, among them the head of a man and a famous **Minerva** in white marble (1C AD) unearthed in Poitiers. Fine funerary stones from Civaux, including Man as a Child, are also on show.

The rest of the collections are displayed in a number of rooms on several levels linked by stairways or steps.

Painting – The staircase at the end of the archaeology gallery leads to a fine series of paintings from Abbaye Ste-Croix by the Dutch painter Nicolas Van der Maes depicting the 17C *Mysteries of the Life of Christ*.

Other paintings include works from the **late 18C**: the local artist J A Pajou *(Oedipus Cursing Polynices)*, Géricault's circle *(Masculine Anatomy)*. The **19C** is represented by Alfred de Curzon, a local painter *(The Convent Garden)*, Octave Penguilly-l'Haridan *(The Parade of Pierrot)*, Charles Le Brun *(Portrait of Germaine Pichot)* and Léopold Burthe *(Ophelia)*. A number of works by **Orientalists** include: *Jewish Fête in Tangier* by Alfred Dehodencq, *Fantasia* by Eugène Fromentin and *A Street in Constantinople* by André Brouillet.

Sculpture – The collections include a medieval bas-relief, the *Stone-Cutter*, found near St-Hilaire-le-Grand, a Renaissance medallion embossed with the features of Christ, a marble bust of Louis XIII from the Château de Richelieu, as well as 19C exhibits: an Auguste Ottin marble, a Carrier-Belleuse terra-cotta, a plaster effigy of Mademoiselle de Montpensier by James Pradier and a marble by Jean Escoula. There is also a reconstruction of the studio of sculptor Jean-René Carrière (1888–1982).

Bronzes include small works by Rodin (*The Man with the Broken Nose* and *The Despairing Adolescent*), Maillol *(Prairie Nymphs)* and Camille Claudel. A room devoted to Camille Claudel displays *Desertion* (1888), *The Waltz* (1893), *Deep Thought* (1900) and *Fortune* (1900–04).

Ethnological Collections – The first floor houses an exhibit on trades, such as cobbler, wood turner or textile worker, and a curious carousel made by a local postman, M Bonnet.

Espace Mendès-France

1 pl. de la Cathédrale. Open Jul–Aug, Mon and Sat 2–6.30pm, Tue–Fri 9am–6.30pm; festival period Tue–Fri 9am–6.30pm, Sat–Mon 2–6.30pm; Sept–Jun Mon–Sat, please check website for exact times. Closed public holidays. 8€ (under 26 years 4€). 05 49 50 33 08. www.maison-des-sciences.org.

This modern building houses scientific, technological and industrial exhibitions. The **planetarium** *(contact for programme; closed public holidays; 6€ (children 3€); 05 49 50 33 08; www.maison-des-sciences.org)* offers a election of astronomic shows and themed exhibitions.

LE CENTRE AND LE QUARTIER ST-HILAIRE

Musée de Chièvres

9 r. Victor-Hugo. Open Jun–Sept Mon–Fri 10am–noon, 1.15–6pm, Sat–Sun 10am–noon, 2–6pm; Oct–May Tue–Fri 10am–noon, 1.15–5pm, Sat–Sun 2–6pm. Closed public holidays. 4€ (1st Sun of month and Tue no charge), combined entrance ticket with Musée Ste-Croix. 05 49 41 07 53. www.musees-poitiers.org.

The former private home of François Rupert de Chièvres is consecrated to 15C –18C paintings and decorative art: fine collection of furniture, 16C and 18C porcelain, and Limoges enamel. On the ground floor note two portraits by Jean Valade,

18C Poitevin painter, Mars defeated by Minerva by Doyen, two 3C marble busts, a superb representation of St-Sépulcre; also portraits from the Flemish and Dutch schools of the 16C and 17C.

Église St-Hilaire-le-Grand★★

r. St-Hilaire. Open Mon–Fri 9am–7pm. 05 49 41 21 24.

This ancient church is considered to be the most interesting in Poitiers. Before going inside, it is worth walking around the church to admire the group of chapels grafted onto the transept and ambulatory.

Interior – The church of St-Hilary-the-Great, which was completed in 1049, was always an important sanctuary as well as being a large one; the three aisles, covered with timber ceilings, frequently sheltered members of the earliest pilgrimages to Santiago de Compostela. Unfortunately, in the 12C the church was ravaged by fire and the gutted timbers were replaced by stone vaults. However, as the distance it was possible to span in stone was naturally less than it was with wooden beams, the architects charged with the restoration were obliged to divide each of the original side aisles longitudinally in two, adding central columns to support the ribbed vaulting above; at the same time two rows of columns were added to the nave, linked ingeniously to the original walls and bearing a whole series of small domes. The final arrangement, as it is today, has a central nave bordered by three aisles on either side – the only seven-aisle church in Europe.

Two of the northern aisles incorporate the 11C belfry, the base of which forms an impressive room with remarkable archaic capitals. Both transept and **chancel** are raised above the level of the aisles. The floor at the front of the chancel is covered with a fine mosaic. The pillars framing it have interesting capitals that represent the burial of St Hilary. The ancient frescoes on the four pillars preceding the transept represent bishops of Poitiers. In the chapels, more frescoes illustrate episodes in the lives of St Quentin and St Martin.

The chancel is separated from the ambulatory by a semicircle of eight columns, linked at the base by fine 12C wrought-iron grilles. In the ambulatory is an unusual statuary group of the *Holy Trinity*. In the **crypt** is a casket (19C) containing the relics of St Hilary.

FAUBOURG ST-SATURNIN

This district lies to the east of the city centre on the opposite bank of the River Clain. Climb boulevard Coligny to the top of the Plateau des Dunes, where the **statue of Notre-Dame-des Dunes** overlooks Poitiers: a splendid **view**★ *(viewing table; 215 steps; no charge).*

Statue de Notre-Dame-des-Dunes

A few hundred metres to the right of this statue, there is a viewing table from where there is a superb **view**★ of the Old Town.

Hypogée des Dunes

Access via r. de la Pierre-Levée, then r. de St-Saturnin (1st road on the left). Closed to the public for conservation reasons. 05 49 41 07 53.

In a garden of conifer trees stands a Gallo-Roman building. It houses one of the strangest monuments of the Middle Ages, not discovered until 1878: an underground chapel, built at the end of the 6C, in the centre of a Primitive Christian cemetery, by an abbot who installed his tomb here.

The steps are decorated with symbolic features characteristic of early Christianity. The tomb contains diverse pieces of furniture, altar, funerary stelae, bas-reliefs. On one of the columns there are two tortured figures representing the crucifixion of the two thieves.

La Pierre Levée

Access by r. de la Pierre-Levée, then r. du Dolmen (2nd road on the left).

This dolmen, broken in the 18C, was a destination for excursions, popular in the days of Rabelais.

DRIVING TOURS

1 FROM THE FORÊT DE MOULIÈRE TO THE VALLÉE DE LA BOIVRE

110 km/68.5mi. Allow about one day.

Leave Poitiers going E along the D 6, which runs past the Parc des expositions and the charming 17C manor of **Breuil-Mingot**. *Follow the D 6 to Bignoux, then turn right and take the D 139.*

Le Logis du Château du Bois-Dousset
Open Jun–Sept 9am–6pm. No charge. 05 49 44 20 26.
Elegant 16C–17C building with a listed garden. Now a *chambres d'hôtes*.

Continue along the D 139. At Lavoux, go NW on the D 20 for 5km/3.1mi.

In the Moulière Forest, at Grand Recoin is located the **Maison de la forêt** (*open mid-Jan–24 Dec Tue–Wed and Sun 2–5pm; closed holidays; no charge; 05 49 56 59 20*).

At the following crossroads, turn right onto the D 3.

There are pleasant forest trails, ideal for walking, bordering the road. **Bonneuil-Matours** has a watermill and an interesting Romanesque church.

Leave Bonneuil W along the D 82.

Réserve Naturelle du Pinail
Admire the wild flowers and thousands of ponds, left over from the former mining of millstones. Two marked itineraries go through the reserve (135ha/334 acres).

Take the D 82.

Parc de Loisirs de St-Cyr
Open Jun–Aug; 2€; rest of year no charge. 05 49 62 57 22.
A range of activities are available at this vast (85ha/210-acre) artificial lake.

Follow the D 82, crossing the D 910.

Beaumont
From the Grand-Place there is a path leading to a dismantled keep: view over the Clain and Vienne valleys.

Leave Beaumont SW. The road passes under the D 910.

Château de Dissay
Open May–Jun, Sept–Oct Sun and bank holidays 10am–noon, 2–5pm; Jul–Aug Thu–Tue 10am–noon, 3–6pm. 6€. 05 49 52 40 22.
In the courtyard there is a polygonal stair turret. The chapel has fine murals.

Leave Dissay SW on the D 4.

Château de Vayres
Charming manor, dating from the 15C and 16C with terraced gardens and a magnificent dovecote.

Leave along the D 20, pass in front of Futuroscope, take the D 62 to Vouillé, then drive through the Vouillé-St-Hilaire forest on the D 40.

Abbaye du Pin
Only the walls and the west gable remain of this abbey, founded in 1130. The 16C monastic buildings have been transformed into a château.

Follow the D 6. Go left after 4km/2.5mi.

Château de Montreuil-Bonnin
Partly ruined 13C château. The 15C seigniorial house is still in good condition. Lovely view over the Boivre Valley.

Leave Montreuil-Bonnin E. Take the D 3 for 500m/550yds, towards Poitiers, then turn left onto the D 6.

The picturesque road runs along the Left Bank of the Boivre. The **Grottes de la Norée** at Biard have interesting formations (*phone for opening times; 5.50€; 05 49 41 30 30*).

The rte de La Cassette leads back to Poitiers.

2 THE VALLEYS OF THE CLAIN

65km/40mi. Allow half a day.

Leave Poitiers via av. de la Libération and turn left to drive along the Clain.

The **Clain Valley** leads to the so-called "threshold" which separates Poitou from Angoumois, the countries of *langue d'oïl* (northern language) from those of *langue d'oc* (southern).

St-Benoît

This village sits between wooded hills.
Church – A former Benedictine abbey built in a sober Romanesque manner. The interior suggests an 11C construction, while the stalls and woodwork date from the 18C. To the right of the church are the ruins of a 12C cloister.

Leave St-Benoît SW and join the D4. When you reach Ligugé, turn right onto the D 87.

Abbaye de Fontaine-le-Comte

This ancient St Augustin abbey was built around 1126–36 by the Comte de Poitiers Guillaume VIII, father of Aliénor d'Aquitaine.

Return along the D 87 to Ligugé, then take the D 4 S.

Abbaye de Ligugé

pl. de Pannonhalma, Ligugé.
Ligugé claims the title of the Oldest Monastery in the West. After more than three centuries of interruption, monastic life here was resumed in 1853 by Benedictine monks from Solesmes.
Excavations – The digs here, which were started in 1953, have revealed an exceptional series of pre-Romanesque structures.
Église St-Martin is today the parish church of Ligugé.
Monastery – A number of ancient features are included within the monastery as a whole. In the **Galerie d'Émaux** (*open daily 9am–11am, 2.30–5.30pm; no charge; 05 49 55 21 12; www.abbaye-liguge.com*) there is an exhibition of the enamelwork that has made this monastery famous.

The visit ends with a tour of the small **museum** (*same times and charges as for the Galerie d'Émaux*) which traces the monastic history of the area.

Continue along the D 4.

Château d'Aigne

Restored Renaissance building with a view over the valley. Look for the "Rabelais" cave on the hillside.

Continue along the D 4.

Vivonne

Perched on a rocky outcrop this village dominates over the confluence of the rivers Vonne, Palais and Clain.
Church – Its architecture comprises a 12C northern transept, a Gothic nave, and a 16C southern transept and apse.

Leave Vivonne SE and take the D 742.

Château-Larcher

The remains of village's fortifications and château can still be seen. The Romanesque church has a carved portal; in the cemetery is a 12C lantern of the dead.

Leave Château-Larcher heading S on the D 144. After Marnay, turn right onto the D 742.

Gençay

The ruins of the fortress tower above this small village.

Continue S along the D 13.

Magné

This small village on the banks of the Belle focuses around a tiny Romanesque church. Château de la Roche and the Merovingian cemetery make up some of its historic past.
Parc de la Belle – Nestling in the Belle Valley, this park extends over 10ha/25 acres (*6€; 05 49 87 80 86; www.parcdelabelle.com*).
Château de la Roche – This château has a Renaissance façade, and another from the Louis XIII era (*8€; 05 49 59 31 07*).
The outbuildings house the **Musée de**

l'Ordre de Malte about the history of the Order of the Knights of Malta.

Return to Gencay and take the D 1.

St-Maurice-la-Clouère
The Poitevin Romanesque church is worth visiting.

Continue along the D 1.

Château de Chambonneau, Gizay
The original 13C fortress was part of a vast system of defence comprising seven châteaux linked together by underground passages. The present-day building dates from the 15C *(6€; 05 49 42 94 07).*

Continue along the D 1. After the church at Nieuil-l'Espoir, turn left onto the D 12.

Abbaye de Nouaillé-Maupertuis★
Partially destroyed towers, and a moat are all that remain of the fortifications *(guided tours 3.50€; 05 49 55 35 69).* In the courtyard the 15C abbey house has a lovely stair turret.

The D 12C leads directly back to the southern district of Poitiers.

ADDRESSES

STAY

Chambre d'hôte Château de Vaumoret – *r. du Breuil Mingot (10km/6.2mi NE of Poitiers; take the D 3 towards La Roche-Posay, then the D 18 to Sèvres-Anxaumont). 05 49 61 32 11. www.chateaudevaumoret.com. 5 rooms.* Housed in a delightful 17C château with attractive guest rooms furnished in traditional style.

Come Inn – *13 r. Albin Haller. 05 49 88 42 42. www.hotelcomeinn.com. Closed 24 Dec–5 Jan mid-Jul–Aug. 44 rooms. 8€. Meals.* Functional rooms in this hotel situated not far from Aquitaine motorway. Traditional cuisine.

Hôtel de l'Europe – *39 r. Carnot. 05 49 88 12 00. www.hotel-europe-poitiers.com. Closed 24 Dec–3 Jan. 88 rooms. 8€.* Near to the pedestrianised streets, this hotel has rooms decorated in diverse styles.

Hôtel Ibis Centre-ville – *15 r. du Petit-Bonneveau. 05 49 88 30 42. www.ibishotel.com. 75 rooms. 8€.* City-centre chain hotel.

Le Grand Hôtel – *28 r. Carnot. 05 49 60 90 60. www.grandhotelpoitiers.fr. 41 rooms. 12€.* Centrally located hotel with an Art Deco theme. Comfortable rooms and large terrace for summer breakfasting.

EAT

Les Bons Enfants – *11 r. Cloche-Perse. 05 49 41 49 82. Closed Sun evening and Mon.* This little restaurant with a green façade specialises in regional cuisine.

La Chênaie – *Les Hauts de Croutelle La Berlanderie, r. du Lejat. 05 49 57 11 52. www.la-chenaie.com. Closed late Jul–mid Aug, Feb, Sun evening, Mon and school holidays.* Old farmhouse serving contemporary dishes.

L'Orée des Bois – *13 r. de Naintré, St-Benoît. 05 49 57 11 44. http://oreedesbois.objectis.net. Closed Sat lunch, Sun evening, Mon, and 12–21 August.* This is a restful place serving traditional local fare.

Passions et Gourmandises – *6 r. du Square, St-Benoît (4km/2.5mi S of Poitiers via the D 88). 05 49 61 03 99. www.passionsetgourmandises.com. Closed Sun evening, Wed lunch, Mon and early Jan.* Lovely terrace for sunny days, while the dining room inside has a modern feel.

Poitevin – *76 r. Carnot. 05 49 88 35 04. Closed Sun evening (16 Apr–2 May) and Jul.* The accent is on traditional regional cuisine in this busy restaurant.

Vingelique – *37 r. Carnot. 05 49 55 07 03. Closed Sat lunch, Sun, 25 Dec–1 Jan and Aug.* Gastronomic cuisine. Lovely courtyard terrace.

Futuroscope★★★

Vienne

This modern, original complex was constructed in 1987 on the outskirts of Poitiers, between the River Clain and the A 10 motorway. Sporting a Futurist décor, designed by the French architect Denis Laming, Futuroscope offers a range of exciting shows, games and interactive attractions.

- **Michelin Map:** 322: I-4
- **Info:** Futuroscope Destination, av. du Téléport, F-86360 Chasseneuil-du-Poitou. ℘05 49 49 30 80.
- **Location:** Futuroscope lies 10km/6.2mi N of Poitiers. (see General Information).
- **Parking:** Futuroscope's car park costs 6€ per day. Keep valuables locked out of sight.
- **Don't Miss:** Try to experience at least one of the IMAX attractions.
- **Kids:** This is a child's paradise. As soon as they reach the height restriction of 1.2m/4ft, they will head for the bone-shaking, adrenalin-soaring rides.
- **Timing:** There's plenty to keep you occupied for a two-day visit here; spending a night will also allow you to watch the spectacular evening show.

LE PARC EUROPÉEN DE L'IMAGE★★

The 70ha/173-acre park introduces the public to the realities of modern technology and the changes brought about by an image-dominated society. Paths fan out from a shop-lined square to the various attractions scattered throughout the grounds. The visitor is immediately plunged into a Modernistic architectural universe of glass and steel. A play area and a footbridge spanning two man-made lakes contribute to the overall harmony.

Les Ailes du Courage

Wearing special glasses relive the adventures of the Aéropostale airmail service pilot as he battles over the Andes Mountains.

Voyageurs du Ciel et de la Mer★★

The building's anthracite tubes sparkle and shimmer in the lake below. The audience is whisked away over sea and land – a feat achieved by the double IMAX screens, one **vertical screen**, measuring 672sq m/7 221sq ft, and the other **horizontal screen**, measuring 748sq m/8 051sq ft. The latter, 25m/80ft beneath a glass floor under the spectators' feet, projects a series of fantastic images which create the illusion of flight.

Sous les Mers du Monde★

Wearing liquid-crystal glasses, spectators see an Omnivax image on a 900sq-m/1 076sq-yd screen. The illusion creates a sensation of being suspended in the water surrounded by the fauna of the sea. It is so complete that you want to reach out and touch the fish as they swim past.

Les Astromouches

IMAX technology using polarising filters, creates a dazzling 3D effect, to follow the adventure of three flies who are passengers on the famous Apollo 11 mission to the moon in 1969.

Chocs Cosmiques

Witness the dramatic cosmic crashes that shape our universe.

La Vienne Dynamique + d'Effets★★

Inside each seat is a simulator that produces realistic movement effects that match the on-screen images as you travel through the Vienne *département* in various modes of transport. A real white-knuckle ride.

Futuroscope

©Jean-Luc Audy/Parc du Futuroscope

Les Animaux du Futur
Using specially built virtual-reality binoculars, visitors are taken on an interactive safari, to imagine how animals on the planet will evolve millions of years into the future.

EcoDingo
A futuristic space rally aboard ecological flying vehicles with commentary by a wacky journalist.

Van Gogh
Opened 2010. Scenario around the life and work of the painter.

Tempête sur le Bayou
Opened 2010. Sensational trip around the marshlands of Louisiana.

Arthur, l'Aventure 4D
A mini-film in 4D (3D with added special effects such as wind, smell, etc.) where visitors accompany Arthur in his adventures. Inspired by the second film of the Minimoys trilogy by Luc Besson.

La Meilleur du Dynamique★
Several films, which alternate, where visitors experience, on hydraulic seats, eventful adventures.

Danse avec les Robots★★
Seated on the end of a 7m/23ft robotic arm you are whisked through a wild waltz to the beat of salsa, hip hop and disco. The arms move along seven axes and acceleration can reach 3Gs.

THE PARK: GENERAL INFORMATION

Location: By **car:** take Exit 28 on the A 10 motorway (Paris–Bordeaux). The park is just 2min from the main entrance. By **rail:** Futuroscope-TGV station. By **bus:** from Poitiers train station in the city centre, take bus 9 or E. **At the park:** pick up a map of the park when here to help you find your way to any of the 22 attractions, and find restaurants and toilet facilities.

Timing: Open early Feb–mid-Nov and mid-Dec–early Jan daily 10am–dusk (or to the end of the late show); mid-Nov–mid Dec Sat–Sun 10am–dusk (or to the end of the late show). Allow a whole day to get the most out of the park.

Fees: 35€ (children 25€) for 1 day; 66€ (children 45€) for 2 days. Evening show 15€ (children 10€).

Les Yeux Grandes Fermés

With a blind guide, journey through a world where eyes do not see.

Star du Futur!★

Turn up for an audition and then visit major film studios to see how special effects are created.

La Cité du Numérique★

This building, with its neo-Futuristic design – a crystal and a sphere – offers interactive challenges, karaoke and workshops. The robot dogs are a recent addition.

Cyber Avenue – This underground space covering some 800 sq m/957 sq yds has a number of video games *(charge)*.

OUTSIDE ATTRACTIONS

A gigantic wheel which looks like a film spool, **La Gyrotour**★ spirals up a 45m/148ft-high pylon. It continues to turn at the top, providing the visitor with a panoramic view of the spectacular grounds below.

Le Monde des Enfants is a playground, surrounded by pools of water, with open-air attractions (giant slides and water games).

Embark on a family trip aboard a boat armed with water pistols on **Mission: Eclabousse**. It's action-packed fun, but be prepared to get showered by jets of water!

Four *îles vertes* illustrate different views of European landscape art in **les jardins d'Europe**.

Sculptures by artist Xavier Toutain are scattered throughout the park.

ADDRESSES

STAY

Chambre d'hôte La Ferme du Château – *39 rte de Chasseneuil, Martigny, Avanton (3km/1.8mi W of Futuroscope towards Avanton). 05 49 51 04 57. www.lafermeduchateau.fr. 3 rooms.* The guest rooms in this bed and breakfast are housed in the château's stylishly renovated old outbuildings. In summer, breakfast is served in the large garden. Attractive swimming pool. A pleasant base not far from Futuroscope.

Ibis Futuroscope – *av. Thomas Edison, 86960 Futuroscope-Chasseneuil. 05 49 49 90 00. www.ibishotel.com. P 140 rooms. 8€. Meals.* Functional rooms, comfortable salon bar, conference rooms. This Ibis is frequented by both corporate clients and followers of the fourth dimension. In the restaurant, nautical décor and a buffet, focusing on seafood.

Mercure Aquatis Futuroscope – *av. Jean-Monnet, Téléport 3, 86360 Chasseneuil-du-Poitou. 05 49 49 55 00. www.mercure.com. P 140 rooms. 14€. Meals.* This sleek building has practical rooms, those in the new wing are more spacious. Vast restaurant with grand columns, arches and statues; traditional dishes.

EAT

The four Futuroscope restaurants are: Le KaDéliScope, La Crêpe Volante, Saveurs de Soleil, Le Cristal (reservations 05 49 49 59 06). http://uk.futuroscope.com/resto.php.

Le Cristal – *Parc du Futuroscope, 86960 Chasseneui-du-Poitou. 05 49 49 11 12. Open Apr–Aug, and holidays.* Discover the molecular cuisine of the future, under the leadership of gourmet chemist Hervé.

Saint-Fortunat – *4 r. Bangoura-Moridé, 86170 Neuville-de-Poitou (10km/6.2mi W of Futuroscope on the D 62). 05 49 54 56 74. Closed Sun evening and Mon.* A short drive from Futuroscope, the St-Fortunat offers two dining options: on the ground floor, a restaurant serving fine cuisine at reasonable prices, and on the first floor, a bistro-style eatery where the menu focuses on more simple fare.

ENTERTAINMENT

Construisons Demain – A wooden construct explores sustainable living as a "house of tomorrow".

Le Mystère de la Note Bleue – An evening show using special effects, lasers and water screens to create a lavish musical fairy tale.

Loudun

Vienne

Loudun's past is linked to unsolved mysteries and the intellectual heritage of Théophraste Renaudot, the father of the French press. The town has elegant 17C and 18C stone mansions, bright flower-filled streets, and wide shady avenues.

- **Population:** 7 704
- **Michelin Map:** 322: G-2
- **Info:** 2 r. des Marchands, Loudun. ℘05 49 98 15 96.
- **Location:** Loudun lies 54km/33mi N of Poitiers. Wide boulevards encircle the town, which sits on a hill.
- **Parking:** There are car parks in the town centre.
- **Don't Miss:** The Musée Théophraste Renaudot; the Château de Ternay chapel.
- **Timing:** Allow 2hrs to walk around the town, and around 2hrs for the Côte Loudunaise drive.

THE TOWN

Musée Théophaste Renaudot

Open Tue–Sun Jul–Aug 2.30–6pm; Sept–Jun 2.30–5.30pm. 3.50€ (8–18 years 1.50€). ℘05 49 98 27 33. www.museerenaudot.com.

Housed in this lovely 16C house, where Théophraste Renaudot lived, this waxwork museum traces the life of the founder of the French press.

Espace Ste-Croix

Open May–Oct 10am–noon, 2–7pm; Nov–Apr 2–6pm. Closed 2 wks Jan. no charge. ℘05 49 98 62 00.

This Romanesque church, now converted for art exhibitions and classical music concerts, housed the market until 1991. Frescoes, dating from the 13C, were discovered during its renovation.

Tour Carrée

Overlooking the town, this 31m/102ft watchtower was built in 1040 by Foulques Nerra, Count of Anjou.

DRIVING TOUR

3 LA CÔTE LOUDUNAISE★

20km/12.5mi. Allow 2hrs.

Leave Loudun heading SW on the D 759. The road weaves along the hillsides overlooking the poplar forest of the Dive Valley, passing through the orchards and vineyards.

Église de Glénouze

Small Romanesque building with a gabled bell tower.

Leave Glénouze W on the D 19.

Ranton

The entrance to the château, a 14C fortified gateway, flanked by a machicolated tower, has traces of a drawbridge. The church has a Romanesque porch.

Continue along the D 19.

Curçay-sur-Dive

In this village, stands a 14C keep, with 19C turrets and machicolations.

Leave Curçay from the N taking the D 39, then the D 19. When you reach Ternay village, turn right onto the D 14.

Château de Ternay

Guided tours Apr–Sept by appointment only. 6.50€ . ℘05 49 22 97 54. www.chateau-de-ternay.com.

A tree-lined avenue leads to this imposing 12C château. Around 1440, Bertrand de Beauveau, Seneschal of Anjou, and his wife Françoise de Brézé made significant improvements. Severely damaged by the Wars of Religion the château was rebuilt in the 17C and the 19C. Only the octagonal keep and the chapel remain from the Middle Ages.

The D 14 leads back to Loudun passing through the Bois de Fête.

Châtellerault

Vienne

Châtellerault is a pleasant town for a stroll, with wide tree-lined avenues and an attractive pedestrianised district. The city lies on the banks of the River Vienne, and owes its name to Ayraud, Vicomte de Poitou, who built a château on the site in the 10C.

- **Population:** 34 402
- **Michelin Map:** 322: J-4
- **Info:** 2 av. Adrien Treuille, Châtellerault. ℘05 49 21 05 47. www.ot-chatellerault.com.
- **Location:** Situated 35km/22mi NE of Poitiers, the most direct access to Châtelleraut is via the A 10.
- **Parking:** There are several car parks in the town centre, including along the bd de Blossac, which separates the Old Town from the modern suburbs.
- **Kids:** Musée Auto Moto Vélo.

A BIT OF HISTORY

The growth of the modest local metal-working trade from the 13C onwards led to the establishment of a cutlery industry in the city in the 18C. Later (1820), the metallurgy business expanded into arms manufacture and an arsenal. The former, which operated until 1968, played an important role in the economic success of Châtellerault.

WALKING TOUR

Allow 2hrs.

Start from the bd de Blossac and enter the pedestrianised district. Follow r. Bourbon on the right.

Maison Descartes

r. Bourbon.

The philosopher Descartes spent some of his childhood in this 16C house.

Walk along the pedestrianised r. Bourbon to a small square, then turn right to reach the church.

Église St-Jacques

The west front and the two Romanesque Revival towers of this former priory church dedicated to St James date only from the 19C, but the transept and the east end with its buttress-columns were built in the 12C–13C.

The nave has quadripartite vaulting in the Anjou Gothic style whereas the south side chapel has lierne and tierceron vaulting with historiated keystones.

A wooden 17C polychrome statue of St James dressed as a pilgrim, is a reminder that Châtellerault was one of the stages on The Way of St James. A **carillon** of 52 bells is housed in the north tower.

Go past the Musée Municipal to the Henri IV Bridge.

Pont Henri-IV

The bridge (144m/472ft long and 21m/69ft wide) was built between 1575 and 1611 by Charles Androuet du Cerceau, a member of a famous family of architects. Two slate-roofed towers, once linked by a central block, protected the west entrance; a wise precaution so soon after the Wars of Religion.

Walk across the bridge, then head upriver along an avenue, shaded by plane trees, until you reach the Manu.

La Manu

quai des Martyrs-de-la-Résistance.

This former weapons foundry, set in shady grounds on the Left Bank of the River Vienne, has been restored and encompasses a circus college, which puts on shows during high season *(℘05 49 85 81 81; www.ecoledecirque.org)*, an Automobile Museum and the Comme deux tours.

Musée Auto Moto Vélo

3 r. Clément Krebs Site de la Manu.

Open Jul–14 Sept Wed–Mon 10am–noon, 2–6pm; 15 Sept–Dec

and Feb–Jun Wed–Sun 2–6pm. 5€ (children no charge). 05 49 21 03 46.
This interactive museum, covering a surface area of 4 300sq m/46 300sq ft, retraces the very early beginnings of the motor vehicle and its subsequent popularisation through a series of gleaming motorcars. The motorbike collection is remarkable.

Comme deux tours
In 1994 the artist Jean-Luc Vilmouth added a platform and a spiral staircase to a couple of high factory chimneys, so that people could climb up and admire the town and its surroundings.

From here, it is possible to continue the walk as far as the Envigne Canal.

Canal de l'Envigne
Situated on the west bank of the River Vienne, the canal offers water sport activities *(06 68 49 71 32).*

MUSEUM
Musée Sully
14 r. de Sully. Closed for renovation; reopening date undetermined. 05 49 21 01 27. www.alienor.org.
in Hôtel Sully, a mansion built in the 17C by Androuet du Cerceau. Collections of weapons, knives, 17C–19C porcelain and earthenware are on view, together with carved wooden chair backs, sculptures, paintings and other works of art.
One room is devoted to **Rodolphe Salis** (1851–97), who was born in Châtellerault and later founded the famous Parisian cabaret, Le Chat Noir.
Local history is traced in another department, including an archaeological display of the Gallo-Roman site of Vieux-Poitiers.
Documents, photos and explanatory tableaux in a section on the Acadians follow their odyssey to the New World and back, and examine the economic and cultural role played by Acadia today (New Brunswick and Nova Scotia).
Regional headdresses, bonnets, shawls and christening robes from the 18C to the early 20C can also be seen.

DRIVING TOURS

4 LES ROUTES DE RICHELIEU★
130km/81mi. Allow 6hrs.

Leave Châtellerault W taking the D 725. Cross the motorway, then take the D 14 on the right to Thuré. At the village, go N on the D 43, then left on the D 74.

St-Gervais-les-Trois-Clochers
In the church on the left, the Crucifixion is by the School of Brueghel.

Leave St-Gervais going W on the D 22and join the D 46 going in the direction of Richelieu by taking the D 23 on the right and the D 66 on the left.

Château de la Roche-du-Maine
Built c.1520 by Charles Tiercelin, captain of the armies of Louis XII and François I in Italy, this stately home possesses defensive characteristics inherited from the Middle Ages. Talented designers have given it an Italian appearance. Above the entrance, Charles Tiercelin is represented on horseback, like Louis XII at Blois.

Follow the D 66, then the D 14.

Loudun
See LOUDUN.

Leave Loudun S on the D 347 towards Poitiers. At Angliers, turn left onto the D 64. After Guesnes, the D 64 and D 67, then the D 24 pass through the Scévolles Forest. Before arriving at Verrue, turn left onto the D 20, then right onto the D 7.

Château de Coussay
This 16C château belonged to the future Cardinal Richelieu when he was still Bishop of Luçon.
The corner tower houses the International Museum of Chess, an interesting collection of chess sets from all over the world. Look out for the chess set of Napoleon I and that of Admiral Nelson, and even a tiny set that fits into a precious Fabergé egg. Outside, there is a magnificent dovecote.

Follow the D 725 in the direction of Lencloître for1km/0.6mi, then turn left onto the D 43.

Vendeuvre-du-Poitou

The Château des Roches (1519) comprises the fortifications and a steep-roofed stately home protecting the entrance flanked by two machicolated towers. The philosopher Michel Foucault is buried in this small village.

Leave Vendeuvre going E on the D 21 in the direction of Châtellerault.

Marigny-Brizay

This winemaking village produces the red and white wines of Haut-Poitou.

Return to Châtellerault on the D 21.

5 THE VIENNE AND CREUSE VALLEYS

115 km/71.5mi. Allow half a day.

Leave Châtellerault going N on the D 1 which runs along the Left Bank of the Vienne.

Les Ormes

The château sits at the side of the main road, north of the village. At the far end of the courtyard majestic buildings extend symetrically: the main early 20C building is joined by two low galleries to two 18C pavilions. The ancient stables are found on the opposite side of the main road.

Leave Les Ormes in an easterly direction. At Lilette, turn right onto the D 5.

Château de la Guerche

Open last weekend in Jun–journée du Patrimoine in Sept Mon–Sat 10am–1pm, 2–7pm, Sun 1– pm. 6€ (under 12 years 4€). 02 47 91 02 39. www.chateaudelaguerche.com.

Amid a beautiful park rises this imposing building, built towards the end of the 15C, on the banks of the Creuse. The defensive architecture reflects the importance of its role in southern Touraine.

The south residence is noteworthy for its master bedroom featuring a painted fireplace and carved cornice; immense dining room, prison, artillery shelters and magnificent granary.

Continue along the D 5.

La Roche-Posay

The largest European spa, devoted exclusively to skin diseases, has a picturesque medieval town centre.

Leave La Roche-Posay SE on the D 5 which follows the Gartempe.

Angles-sur-l'Anglin★

See ANGLES-SUR-L'ANGLIN.

Leave Angles SW crossing the Anglin on the D 2. At St-Pierre-de-Maillé, cross over the Gartempe, then turn into the second road on the right taking the D 16 to Pleumartin. Continue along the D 14 for 14km/8.7mi towards Châtellerault, then left onto the D 133, and at Senillé, take the D 131 to Netpuis.

Vestiges du Vieux-Poitiers

Rte de Chezelles, 86530 Naintré. Open Apr–Jun and Sept Sun pms; Jul–Aug pms. Closed public holidays. 3€ (children no charge). 05 49 23 45 63.

A section of the fortifications of the ancient *théâtre*, on the slope facing the Clain, is all that remains of the Gallo-Roman city. Just 400m/400yds away are Gallo-Roman potters' furnaces. Below, on the plain, a menhir bears a Celtic inscription.

The famous Battle of Poitiers took place, in 732, between the ruins of Vieux-Poitiers and Moussais-la-Bataille (*see Poitiers p294*).

Cross over the Clain to return to the D 910, which leads back to Châtellerault.

Angles-sur-l'Anglin★

Vienne

The terraced village of Angles is sited above the River Anglin and beneath the ruins of a castle. Its names derives from Angles, a warlike tribe from Germania that invaded Britain in the 5C. Cardinal Balue, a native of Angles, born around 1421, was sentenced to prison for treason by Louis XI. Freed by the Pope 11 years later he emigrated to Rome where he was showered with honours. *Les jours d'Angles,* a highly prized form of drawn-thread embroidery, is still made in the village today. Archaeological excavations in the neighbouring rock shelters have unearthed important carvings dating from the Magdalenian (Late Palaeolithic) Era.

- **Population:** 388
- **Michelin Map:** 322: L-4
- **Info:** 2 r. du Four Banal, Angles-sur-l'Anglin. 05 49 48 86 87. www.anglessuranglin.com.
- **Location:** The town is located 17km/10.6mi N of St-Savin.

SIGHTS

Site★

There is a splendid **view**★ of the village from the southeastern end of the bluff where the castle stands, beside a roadside cross and a small Romanesque chapel. Beyond a breach in the cliff are what remains of the walls and towers of the old castle.

To the north, on another promontory, the Romanesque belfry of the upper church rises above the rooftops, and at the foot of the escarpment, the River Anglin, with its reeds and water-lilies, winds between two rows of poplars. Beyond the turning wheel of an ancient watermill, a stone bridge leads to the Ste-Croix Quarter, where the former abbey church has a fine 13C doorway.

Frise Magdalénienne du Roc aux Sorciers

Route des Certeaux, beneath the château. Open Easter–All Saints 10am–12.30pm, 1.30–6.30pm; Jul–Aug daily until 7pm; winter Mon–Tues; school holidays daily. 7€ (7–12 years 5€). 05 49 83 37 27. www.roc-aux-sorciers.com.

In 1950 Suzanne Cassou de St-Mathurin brought to light at Angles-sur-l'Anglin a carved frieze dating from the Magdalenian period. This exceptional 15 000-year-old piece of heritage, considered to be the "Lascaux of sculpture", is closed to the public for conservation reasons. But the interpretation centre presents a digital restitution of the frieze.

Castle Ruins★

Phone for opening times. 1.50€. 05 49 48 61 20.

Angles Castle, an important stronghold in the Middle Ages due to its commanding position and the strength of its defences, was abandoned in the 18C. The Revolution (1789) added to its downfall as builders were allowed to use the derelict castle as a stone quarry.

ADDRESSES

STAY

Gîte Les Terrasses – *20 r. du Four-Banal. 05 49 37 19 77. 10 people.* This large, restored house has four rooms and a terrace that overlook the château ruins. Reservations must be made with Gîtes de France.

EAT

Le Relais du Lyon d'Or – *rte de Vicq. 05 49 48 32 53. www.lyondor.com. Closed lunch, Mon evening andlate Nov–early Mar.* Copious dishes served in a rustic dining room. Also has pretty guest rooms.

Abbaye de St-Savin★★

Vienne

St-Savin is famous for its Romanesque abbey church, which is decorated with the finest and most complete series of mural paintings in France. The site is on UNESCO's World Heritage List.

- **Michelin Map:** 322: L-5
- **Info:** 20 pl. de la Libération, St-Savin-sur-Gartempe. 05 49 48 11 00. www.saintsavin.com.
- **Location:** The Abbaye de St-Savin is situated on the west bank of the River Gartempe, 42km/26mi E of Poitiers.

A BIT OF HISTORY

Part of the Legend

Towards the middle of the 5C in Macedonia, two brothers, Savin and Cyprien, were summoned to appear in front of the Proconsul Ladicius for having refused to worship certain idols. The brothers were condemned to death, and all pleas for mercy were in vain. They were imprisoned but managed to escape and left for Gaul, though their executioners caught up with them on the banks of the Gartempe: the brothers were decapitated on the spot. Savin's body was buried by priests on a height known at the time as Three Cypresses Mount, not far from where the town of St-Savin stands today.

The Building Stages

The first abbey church was erected in the 9C, near the sacred burial site, and placed under the patronage of the martyr Savin. Louis the Debonair installed 20 Benedictine monks in the abbey under the tutelage, it is said, of Benoît d'Aniane. In 878 the abbey was pillaged by the Normans, despite its being protected by a line of fortifications. Reconstruction did not begin until the 11C but was finished in a relatively short space of time. The painted decoration, which completely covered the interior of the church, was added as the building work progressed.

Decline and Rebirth

The Hundred Years' War brought to an end the period of relative prosperity enjoyed by the monks up to that time; the abbey was caught up in violent battles between soldiers loyal to the King of France and those fighting for the Black Prince. In the 16C the Wars of Religion saw the Catholics and the Huguenots in furious conflict over possession of the abbey: it was devastated in 1562 and 1568 by the Huguenots, who burned the choir stalls, the organ and the timber roof, and pillaged six years later by the Royal Army. Most of the buildings were later demolished as their upkeep was too expensive.

From 1611 to 1635 an adventurer who liked to call himself the Baron of the Francs installed himself in the church as though it were a stronghold. The arrival, in 1640, of monks from St-Maur finally brought an end to the profanities to which the abbey had been subjected for three centuries. However, though the monks saved the buildings from total ruin, the wall paintings suffered from various efforts to restore them.

In 1836 Prosper Mérimée, the writer and Inspector of Historic Monuments, had the church listed as a historic monument and organised important restoration works which continued for almost a century.

VISIT

pl. de la Libération. Open Apr–Jun and Sept–Oct Mon–Sat 10am–noon, 2–6pm, Sun 2–6pm; Jul–Aug daily 10am–7pm; Nov–Dec and Feb–Mar Mon–Sat 10am–noon, 2–5pm, Sun 2–5pm. Guided tours (1hr30min) Mon–Sat 10.30am, 2.30pm, 4pm, 5.30pm, Sun 2.30pm, 4pm, 5.30pm. Closed 11 Nov, 25 Dec, 31 Dec. 6€. 05 49 84 30 00. www.abbaye-saint-savin.fr.

1 Creation of the stars (God adds the Sun and the Moon to the firmament).
2 Creation of Woman – God presents Eve to Adam – Eve and the Serpent.
3 Eve, seated, spins.
4 The offerings of Cain and Abel (Abel, God's chosen one, is the only one haloed).
5 Abel's murder – Cain's curse.
6 Enoch, his arms raised to heaven, invokes God – God tells Noah of the forthcoming flood and invites him to build the ark.
7 Noah's ark during the flood.
8 God blesses Noah's family leaving the ark (showing the famous "Beau Dieu" representation of God).
9 Noah sacrifices a pair of birds and a lamb in thanksgiving.
10 Noah's vineyard.
Before continuing with the story of Noah on the right-hand section, note the scenes on the lower register which tell the end of Exodus and include the life of Moses.
11 Passage through the Red Sea: the waters swallow up the Egyptian cavalry and Pharaoh's chariot.
12 The Angel of God and the column of fire separate the Egyptians and the Hebrews and protect the latter who march in rows, led by Moses.
13 Moses receives the Tables of Law from God.
14 Noah drinks and dances, a goblet in hand.
15 Drunken Noah lies asleep, his robes in disarray; Ham mocks his father, while his brothers Shem and Japhet cover him with a blanket.
16 Noah curses Canaan in front of Shem and Japhet.
17 Construction of the Tower of Babel.
18 The call of Abraham.
19 Abraham and Lot's separation.
20 Announcement of the combat of the kings and call for help from Lot of Abraham.
21 The combat of the kings *(removed)*.
22 Meeting between Abraham and Melchizedeck, King of Salem and priest of Most High, who brings him bread and wine *(removed)*.
23 Death of Abraham.
24 Isaac blesses his son Jacob.
25 Joseph sold by his brothers.
26 Joseph bought by Potiphar, one of Pharaoh's officers.
27 Joseph, Potiphar and his wife (the temptation of Joseph).
28 Joseph in prison.
29 Joseph explains Pharaoh's dream.
30 Pharaoh puts his ring on Joseph's finger and makes him his administrator.
31 Joseph's triumph.

Wall Paintings★★★

Some paintings were destroyed during the devastation visited on the abbey, others were damaged by whitewash which the monks applied, still others suffered as a result of the first phases of restoration.

Unlike most frescoes painted from a preliminary sketch, the paintings here were drawn directly onto the wall, using a process halfway between the fresco technique and distemper-painting: the colours were applied to old plaster, thereby penetrating only the top level of this coating and forming a very thin layer. The few colours used include yellow-ochre, red-ochre and green, mixed with black and white.

The overall effect is one of gentle tones but avoids being insipid through the use of contrast: the different characters are portrayed with great liveliness, their feet suggesting movement, their forms revealed by the moulding of their clothes, their hands often disproportionately long, accentuating the expressive qualities. This dancing, rhythmic allure is also found in Romanesque sculpture. Faces have large, simple, bold features, with red-and-white marks describing cheeks, nostrils and chins.

In the **narthex** the various painted scenes recount episodes from the Apocalypse: Christ in Majesty in Celestial Jerusalem, Combat between the Archangel and the Beast, the New Jerusalem, the Plague of Grasshoppers. The predominantly pale tones (green, yellow-ochre, red-ochre) allow the scenes to be clearly read despite the darkness inside the porch.

The **nave**, however, is the setting for the true masterpiece, which is highlighted by the purity of the architecture. The stories told in the carefully restored paintings on the vaulting unfold at a height of over 16m/52ft and cover an area of 412sq m/4 435sq ft.

Wall paintings, Abbaye de St-Savin

©Jean-Pierre De Mann/age fotostock

The most striking thing initially is the soft tones – beige and pink – of the columns supporting the vaulting. The vaulting itself is covered with scenes from the Book of Genesis and the Book of Exodus, ranged in two rows along either side of the centre ridge, which forms a decorative band. A painting behind the main door shows the Triumph of the Virgin.

Two sections are distinguishable in the nave. The first three bays, which make up the first part of the nave, are separated by transverse ribs, while the rest of the vaulting is a continuous barrel which made painting that section of the ceiling easier; the painter nevertheless added a false rib between the fifth and sixth bays.

Stand in the south aisle to see the frescoes on the left-hand side of the nave. Then cross the transept crossing and stand at the beginning of the left-hand aisle to view the paintings on the right-hand side of the ceiling.

The scenes listed in the illustrations are recognisable.

Abbey Buildings★

These were rebuilt in the 17C in the extension of the church's transept arm; they have since been restored.

The old **refectory**, to the right of the entrance, houses exhibits of contemporary mural art organised by CIAM, the International Centre for Mural Art, which is based within the abbey.

To the left, in the **chapter house**, photographs reveal the appearance of the church crypt.

From the garden, which the river runs through, there is an attractive view over the elegant rear face of the abbey buildings, from the bishop's lodgings *(on the left)*, which are of medieval origin, although remodelled in the 17C and 19C, across to the east end of the church with its apse, apsidal chapels and belfry.

Abbey Church★★

The church, a handsome combination of harmony and sobriety, is also striking for its sheer size: 76m/249ft long with a transept 31m/102ft across and a spire rising to 77m/253ft.

Inside the church, in the nave, there are fine **capitals** carved with foliage and animals; those by the chancel are decorated with acanthus leaves and lions.

The best **view**★ of the church is from the far side of the river. On the left extend the abbey buildings and the elegant belfry-porch – overshadowing the apse, the apsidal chapels and the squat belfry; it is crowned by a crocketed spire surrounded by turrets. On the right stands **Vieux Pont** (the Old Bridge), which dates from the 13C and 14C.

Chauvigny★

Vienne

Chauvigny was an important medieval stronghold, which later developed as a trade and industrial centre specialising in the manufacture of porcelain. Traditional quarrying of local freestone – a fine-grained limestone with regular cleavage – has also remained important.

- **Population:** 6 916
- **Michelin Map:** 322: J-5
- **Info:** 5 r. St-Pierre, Chauvigny. 05 49 46 39 01. www.chauvigny.cg86.fr.
- **Location:** Chauvigny is situated 23km/14.3mi E of Poitiers.
- **Parking:** Park in the upper town.
- **Don't Miss:** The upper town; Église St-Pierre; Donjon de Gouzon.
- **Kids:** Falconry display at the château.

UPPER TOWN★

Standing on a spur, the upper town *(Ville Haute)* is surmounted in turn by the jagged ruins of forts and castles dominated by the elegant belfry of St Peter's.

Château Baronnial

r. St-Pierre. Open daily Jul–Aug 10am–12.30pm, 2–7pm; Sept–Jun 2–7pm. 05 49 46 47 48.

This 11C baronial castle, built when the bishops of Poitiers were also the lords of Chauvigny, comprises both an upper section – with an enormous keep – and a lower section surrounded by ramparts, revealing traces of the Château Neuf (New Castle) ruins.

Falconry Display – *Shows in Easter holidays daily 3pm, 5pm; May and Sept Mon–Fri 3pm, Sat–Sun and public holidays 3pm, 5pm; Jun daily 3pm, 5pm; Jul–Aug daily 11am, 3pm, 5pm. 9.50€ (children 6.50€). 05 49 46 47 48; www.geantsduciel.com.* The castle precinct lends itself perfectly to demonstrations of birds of prey in flight (eagles, falcons, vultures).

Château d'Harcourt

r. du Moulin St-Léger. Open for temporary exhibitions. 05 49 46 35 45.

The castle originally belonged to the earls of Châtellerault, who built it in the 13C–15C, on the crest of the promontory. Massive ramparts with a fortified entrance gate still exist.

Collegiale St-Pierre★

r. St-Pierre. Guided tours available from the tourist office. 4€. 05 49 45 99 10.

Capital, Collegiale St-Pierre

M. Thiery/MICHELIN

The construction of this former collegiate church, founded by the lords of Chauvigny, started in the 11C with the apse and was completed in the following century by the erection of the nave. The style is Romanesque, and the building material a fine grey stone. There are two different levels of open-work in the square belfry. The east end, richly decorated with sculptures, is notable for the pleasing proportions of the apse and chapels.

The interior of the church has unfortunately suffered from overenthusiastic 19C repainting.

The capitals of the columns, supporting the broken barrel-vaults in the nave, are decorated with palm leaf designs. The **capitals in the chancel★★** are particularly interesting, embracing a fascinating selection of biblical, evangelical and mythical scenes – the *Annunciation*, the *Adoration of the Magi*, the *Weighing of the Souls*, the *Arrival of the Shepherds*, the *Temptation* and other religious subjects alternate with an extraordinary phantasmagoria of winged monsters, sphinxes, sirens and demons subjecting resigned humans to the worst possible torments.

Église Notre Dame

This 12C church in the lower town saw damage during the Revolution, but maintains its Romanesque chancel and 14C frescoes.

Donjon de Gouzon★

pl. du Donjon.

This keep is all that remains of a castle acquired in the late 13C by the Gouzon family and subsequently (around 1335) bought by Bishop Fort of Aux. The square keep was originally supported by rectangular buttresses, which were later surmounted by rounded buttresses.

The keep is now host to the **Espace d'Archéologie Industrielle** (*open Apr–14 Jun and Sept–Oct daily 2–6pm, 15 Jul–Aug Mon–Fri 10am–12.30pm, 2.30–6.30pm, Sun 2.30–6.30pm, Nov–Mar Sat–Sun and public holidays 2–6pm; closed 1 Jan, 25 Dec; 5€; 05 49 46 91 56)*, a local archaeological exhibition set up in the keep after its restoration in 1988.

Musée des Traditions Populaires et d'Archéologie

pl. du Vieux Marché.

Open same hours as the Espace d'Archéologie Industrielle. 4€.

05 49 46 35 45.

This typical example of local traditional architecture houses a display on objects relating to life in Chauvigny in bygone days and an archaeology room.

EXCURSION

Église St-Pierre-les-Églises

2km/1.2mi S on the D 749.

This small pre-Romanesque building stands in the middle of a Merovingian cemetery, which has several sarcophagi. The church has a semi-circular apse, decorated with a series of frescoes depicting episodes from the New Testament. A recent carbon 14 dating has confirmed that this artwork was carried out between 780 and 980, which makes it one of the oldest medieval frescoes in Western Europe.

DRIVING TOUR

6 BETWEEN VIENNE AND GARTEMPE

95km/59mi. Allow half a day.

Leave Chauvigny heading NW along the Left Bank of the river Vienne.

The Gartempe Valley, known as the Valley of Frescoes, is dotted with relgious and civil buildings decorated with murals, including Abbaye de St-Savin, Eglise Notre-Dame d'Antigny, and Montmorillon *(Pays d'art et d'histoire montmorillonnais; 05 49 84 30 00).*

Château de Touffou★

6km/3.7mi NW. Open mid-Jun–mid-Sept Mon and Wed–Sat 10am–noon, 2–6pm, Sun 2–6pm. 7€. 05 49 56 08 48. www.chateaudetouffou.com.

The warm, ochre-coloured stone of this château helps to form a unified whole,

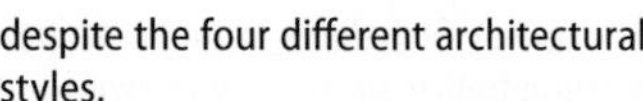

despite the four different architectural styles.

The oldest part of Touffou Castle is the massive keep, which was formed during the Renaissance. At each of the outer corners the buttresses are crowned by elegant turrets. Four huge round towers were added in the 14C.

The Renaissance wing was added c.1560. It is adorned with mullioned windows and dormers; the triangular pediments carry a series of 17 different coats of arms, representing the genealogy of the Chasteignier family.

The main features are François I's Chamber, the chapel, the guardroom and its cells, the bakery and kitchen.

Continue N until you reach the D 86. Turn right and cross the Vienne. Turn left onto the D 749, then, at the Pont de Bonneuil-Matours, right onto the D 3.

Archigny

The name of this village is inextricably linked with the story of the Acadians – early 17C emigrants from the Poitou region who settled in the eastern part of French Canada. Acadia, corresponding roughly to the present-day Nova Scotia and New Brunswick provinces, was ceded to the British in 1713. After the Treaty of Paris at the end of the Seven Years' War (1763), the British government in Canada colonised the area and, in 1773 and 1774, forcibly repatriated the 10 000 French living there to make room for English immigrants. Returning to Poitou, they settled southeast of Châtellerault.

La Ligne Acadienne, the Acadian Line, was the name given to a series of farms established on the heath between Archigny and La Puye: 58 clay and brushwood houses on rubble foundations, which the ex-colonists hoped to own. Some, impatient with delays, moved to Nantes and later to French Louisiana. Those that remained received their title deeds only in 1793.

Today, 34 of these houses are still standing. Each year on 15 August, in the hamlet of **Huit-Maisons** (Eight Houses), descendants of the Poitou Acadians organise a fête to commemorate this period in their history.

Continue along the D 3. After 3km/1.8mi, take the D 9 right.

Musée de la Ferme acadienne

Les Huit Maisons (6km/3.7mi E of Archigny, signposted). Open Apr–Sept Sat–Thu 3–7pm; Oct Sat–Sun and public holidays 3–6pm. 3€. 05 49 85 57 46.

An old Acadian farm at Huit-Maisons has been converted into a museum. Here visitors can see living quarters with furniture of the period, a cow shed containing agricultural implements, and the barn, where documents relating to the history of the Acadians and their return to Poitou are on display.

Continue on the D 9.

Le Jardin des Rosiers

3km/1.8mi S of La Puye. Open 8 May–late July Tue–Sun pms. 7€ (children 4€). 05 49 46 99 96.

In the shadow of an ancient farm, this vast garden hides a treasure: 300 old rose bushes.

Return to La Puye. At the church turn right onto the D 2, then at the exit of the village (Calvary) turn right onto the D 2A.

St-Savin★★

See Abbaye de ST-SAVIN.

Leave St-Savin going S on the D 11.

Antigny

A 12C lantern of the dead stands in front of the Romanesque Notre-Dame church. Inside there is a chapel whose barrel-vault is decorated with murals (late 15C), painted in a naïve style. Outside, the roof canopy on the south wall shelters Merovingian sarcophagi.

Continue along the D 11, then turn left onto the D 11B.

Jouhet

Funeral Chapel – Near the bridge, opposite the monument to the dead. The frescoes were painted in the 15C.

Go back to the Gartempe, then take the D 115, and after, the D 83.

Civaux

The number of archaeological treasures found around Civaux confirms the importance of this village in relation to the spread of Christianity in the Poitou region.

Nécropole Mérovingienne★

This ancient burial ground dates from Merovingian times (AD c.500–750). The origin of the burial ground remains a mystery. It is thought that the graves might have been those of warriors who fell in a battle between Clovis and Alaric, the King of the Visigoths, or perhaps they were the tombs of penitents who had expressed a wish to be buried on the site of their conversion.
A ruined chapel, dedicated to St Catherine, has been remodelled several times since the Romanesque period.

Musée Archéologique

30 pl. de Gomelange. Open Tue–Sun; Jul–15 Sept 11am–1pm, 2.30–7pm; Feb–Jun and late Oct–early Nov 3–6pm; closed Wed in Mar, May, Jun and 16 Sept–Oct; school and public holidays 3–6pm. 3€ (15–18 years 1.5€). 05 49 48 34 61. www.ville-civaux.fr.
This museum, not far from the cemetery, contains exhibits from Merovingian and Gallo-Roman times. Of special interest are the reconstructions of graves discovered in the necropolis – both with and without coffins, directly in the earth or surrounded by a drystone frame, in sarcophagi or in simple cairns.

Église St-Gervais et St-Protais

pl. de l'Église. Open daily 8–10am, 6–9pm. Guided tours by reservation. 05 49 48 34 61.
The church was built on the site of a Roman temple, the ruins of which still contain a loggia converted into a baptistery.
The apse, which dates from the 4C, has a stone belfry adorned with two tiers of blind arcades. In the nave (10C), the cylindrical columns are topped by **historiated capitals** embodying themes which reflect fears of hell and damnation. In the south wall of the apse is an engraved 4C funerary stone.

Leave Civaux heading N (D 114).

Morthemer

Fine group of 14C and 15C buildings, the château and the church testify to the past importance of the Baronnies du Poitou in the Middle Ages. All that remains of the château is the imposing pentagonal keep. Adjoining the château, the church presents a mixture of Romanesque and Gothic styles. In the crypt there are 14 and 15C frescoes.

The D 8 leads back to Chauvigny.

ADDRESSES

STAY

Hôtel Lion d'Or – *8 r. du Marché, lower town. 05 49 46 30 28. Closed 24 Dec–mid Jan. 26 rooms. 7€. Meals.* This hotel in the lower town has been tastefully renovated. Bright, individually decorated rooms, hall and lounge furnished with originality. Traditional cuisine served in a dining room with Art Nouveau chairs, wrought-iron trellises and an ivy-clad ceiling.

EAT

Les Choucas – *pl. du Donjon. 05 49 46 36 42. www.leschoucas.net. Closed Sun evening, Tue evening and Wed (Nov–Mar).* This small restaurant is housed in a medieval building. Choose between the bar-crêperie on the ground floor and the restaurant with mullion windows, fireplace and wooden beams on the first floor. Regional cuisine or medieval menu *(must be ordered in advance).*

Montmorillon

Vienne

A village renowned for its delicious macaroons. The historic Medieval centre, with picturesque streets, comes alive during the *salon du livre* (book fair), held every two years.

- **Population:** 6 584
- **Michelin Map:** 322: L-6
- **Info:** 2 pl. du Maréchal-Leclerc, Montmorillon. 05 49 91 11 96
- **Location:** Montmorillon is 25km/15.5mi SE of Chauvigny.
- **Don't Miss:** The Crypte Ste-Catherine; the Prieuré de Villesalem.
- **Kids:** La Trimouille.
- **Timing:** Allow half a day for Montmorillon, and a day for Gartempe Valley.

THE TOWN

In the Medieval district of Brouard the narrow streets abound with bookshops and craft shops.

Built in the 11C, **Église Notre-Dame** has a semicircular Romanesque apse, and a transept topped by a cupola.

Magnificent late 12C frescoes can be viewed in the **Crypte Ste-Cathérine**. An 11C **octagonal monument**★, formerly a funeral chapel, is one of the town's more unusual sights.

DRIVING TOUR

7 THE VALLÉE DE LA GARTEMPE

80km/50mi. Allow one day.

Leave Montmorillon SW on the D 727.

Lussac-les-Châteaux

Lake – The cliff bordering the lake has prehistoric caves and rock shelters. At L'Ermitage there is a strange stone building called Léproserie.

Leave Lussac-les-Châteaux heading SE on the D 116.

Saulgé

The **Écomusée du Montmorillonnais** traces the agricultural history of Montmorillon (*open 15 Apr–Jun Wed, Fri and Sun 2.30–6pm, Jul–16 Sept Tue–Thu and Sun 2.30–6.30pm, Fri 10am–6.30pm; 5.50€ (families 10€, 6–18 years 4€); 05 49 91 02 32; www.ecomusee-montmorillonnais.org*).

Take the D 5 towards Plaisance. After 1.5km/0.9mi, turn left; the road borders the Gartempe river. Rejoin the D 12, then cross the Gartempe on the D 10.

Les Portes d'Enfer★

45min there and back. Before the bridge over the Gartempe, park the car and take, the marked path, slippery and rugged, which follows the Right Bank of the river. Halfway there, the rock platforms tower above the rapids. When the trail splits, take the right path. The trail ends 100m/110yds beyond there is a rock split in three, and downstream, the rocks called Portes d'Enfer.

Continue along the D 10. At Bourg-Archambault, take the D 33, then after St-Léomer, the D 727.

La Trimouille

Around 300 specimens of crocodiles and lizards, Ophidians, chelonians and amphibians, are presented in their natural environment at **L'Île aux Serpents** (*open daily; 9€ (5–12 years 7€); 05 49 91 23 45*).

Leave La Trimouille N on the D 675.

Prieuré de Villesalem

The monastery buildings were partly destroyed during the Revolution. The church narrowly escaped destruction.

Turn back and continue on the D 120. At Journet, take the D 121, which joins the D 727, leading to Montmorillon.

Charroux★

Vienne

Charroux, which lies 50km/31mi south of Poitiers in a valley on the east bank of the Charente, grew up around a Benedictine abbey dedicated to the Holy Saviour, on the way to Santiago de Compostela. A 15C wooden market still stands in the main square.

- **Population:** 1 184
- **Michelin Map:** 322: I-8
- **Info:** 2 rte de Châtain, Charroux. ✆05 49 87 60 12. www.charroux.fr.
- **Location:** Charroux is located 28km/17.4mi NE of Ruffec, in the Charente Valley.

A BIT OF HISTORY

Holy Relics

The success of Holy Saviour Abbey was assured from the start because the original monks were under the patronage of Charlemagne himself. The abbey church was consecrated by Pope Urban II in 1096. The abbey, the guardian of priceless relics (flesh and blood of Jesus Christ, parts of the True Cross), attracted impressive numbers of wealthy pilgrims who enriched the treasury with gifts of money and magnificent works of art.

Decline

The Wars of Religion in the 16C put an end to this prosperity, and the abbey was sacked. By the beginning of the 19C, more than half the buildings had been demolished. The preservation of what remained is the work of Mérimée, Inspector-General of Historic Monuments under the Second Empire.

Polygonal tower

M. Thiery/MICHELIN

Excavations and restoration work carried out 1946–53 have exposed the ground plan of the abbey church and revealed the crypt. The cloisters have been restored. Building works in the chapter house led to the discovery of sarcophagi containing a collection of funerary items.

Abbaye St-Sauveur★

pl. St-Pierre. Open May–mid-Jul and mid-Aug–end Aug Tue–Sun 9.30am –12.30pm, 2–6.30pm; mid-Jul–mid-Aug daily 9.30am–12.30pm, 2–6.30pm; Sept–Apr Tue–Sun 10am–12.30pm, 2–5.30pm. Closed public holidays. 3.50€. ✆05 49 87 62 43. http://charroux.monuments-nationaux.fr.

Abbey Church – The ground plan here allied the traditional Latin cross outline with the circular design of the Holy Sepulchre Church in Jerusalem. The church comprises a narthex, a nave, a transept with side chapels, and an apse with radiating chapels. In the centre of the transept crossing was a circular sanctuary surrounded by three concentric aisles, positioned above a crypt. It was surmounted by a surviving tower. The building as a whole, which was 126m/413ft long, is reminiscent of certain early Middle Eastern churches.

The church was built in the Poitou Romanesque style with the exception of the west front, which was Gothic. Several elements from here are incorporated in the walls of a nearby house.

The polygonal **tower**★★ dates from the 11C and was in the exact centre of the church. It stands like a gigantic canopy above the rotunda sheltering the altar, which itself surmounts the crypt in which the sacred relics were displayed. The first two storeys of the tower were actually inside the church. The upper part was probably crowned by a spire.

Cloisters – The cloisters, extensively plundered, were reconstructed in the 15C under the direction of the Abbot Jean Chaperon, whose heraldic arms, three hoods, are reproduced on the columns in the chapter house.

Chapter House – The large, impressive building houses a number of excellent 13C **sculptures**★★, which once adorned the main doorway of the west front. These include *Christ in Judgement*, originally on the tympanum, and several prominent figures (kings, former abbots, etc.) decorating the arches, and the delightful statuettes of the *Wise and Foolish Virgins*. These works are attributed to the sculptor who worked on the doorways of Poitiers Cathedral.

The **treasury**★ houses a collection of Romanesque pastoral staffs and pieces by Gothic goldsmiths and silversmiths, discovered in the abbots' tombs excavated beneath the chapter house. Two silver-gilt reliquaries stand out among the gold and silver plate – one, dating from the 13C, is particularly remarkable: two angels hold a box which contained the relics.

Lusignan

Vienne

This small town lies along the crest of a promontory overlooking the valley of the River Vonne and a vale in which a business district has been built flanking the main road to Poitiers.

- **Population:** 2 565
- **Michelin Map:** 322: G-6
- **Info:** pl. du Bail, Lusignan. ✆05 49 43 61 21. www.ot-lusignan.fr.
- **Location:** Lusignan is located between the N 10 and A 10 motorways, SW of Poitiers.

SIGHTS

Castle Ruins

The fortress, built at the extremity of the promontory overlooking the steep-sided Vonne Valley, belonged originally to the Lusignan family, whose members, at one time, ruled over Jerusalem and Cyprus. All that remains of the castle today is a group of buildings along with subterranean chambers and the foundations of several towers which were once part of the surrounding fortifications. In the 18C the castle grounds were transformed into the Promenade de Blossac, named after the steward. An avenue of lime trees surrounded by flower gardens now leads to a terrace from which there is an attractive **view** of the Vonne Valley, spanned by a 432m/472yd viaduct.

Church

This fine example of Poitou Romanesque architecture with particularly impressive proportions was built by the Lusignan family in the 11C. The recumbent statue in the south aisle is Gothic. The high altar stands above a crypt with triple barrel-vaulting. Outside, a porch added to the southern elevation in the 15C faces an interesting house with half-timbered, projecting upper storeys, dating from the same period.

EXCURSION

Église de Jazeneuil

6km/3.7mi NW on the D 94.

This Romanesque building rears its beautiful apse with column-buttresses to the Vonne river. Outside, admire the carved semicircular porch and the modillions of the south wall. Inside: curiously reduced southern transept, pendentive dome, arches, decorated capitals.

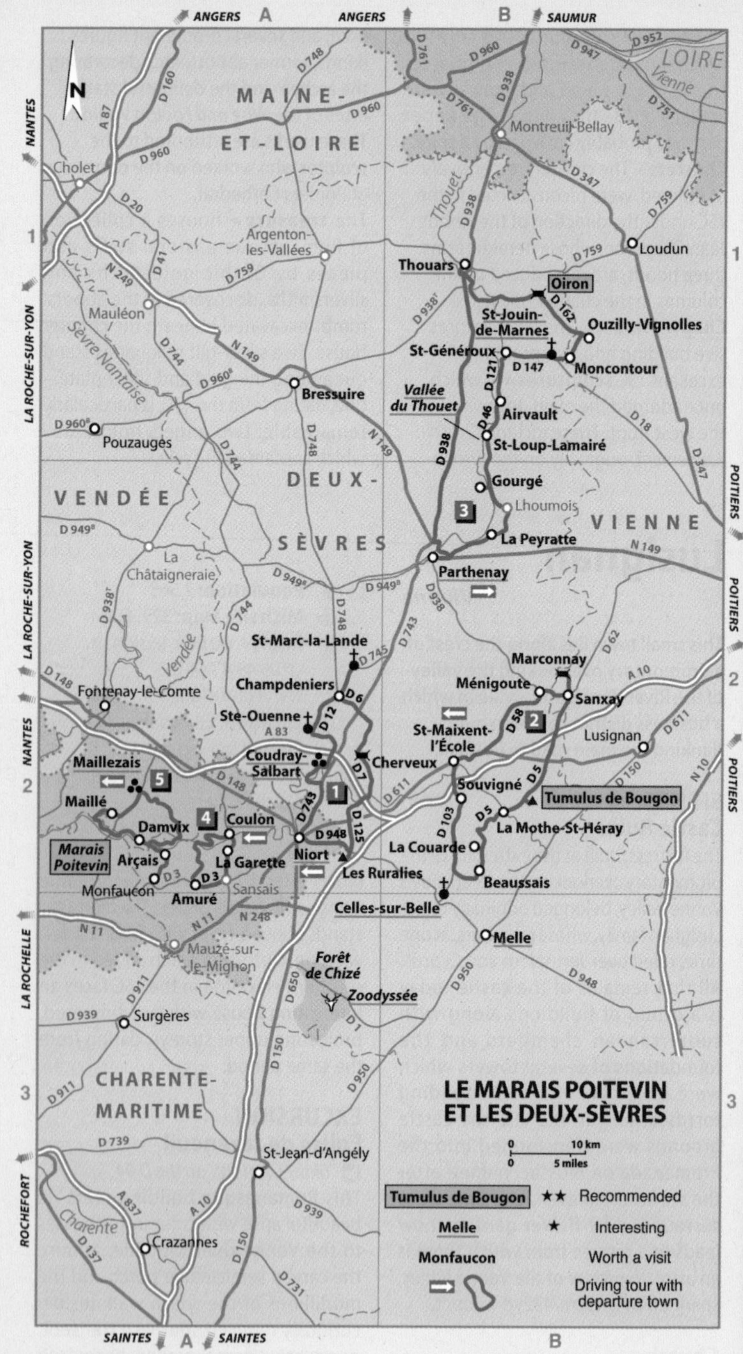
LE MARAIS POITEVIN
ET LES DEUX-SÈVRES
MAINE-
ET-LOIRE
DEUX-
SÈVRES
VENDÉE
VIENNE
CHARENTE-
MARITIME
Cholet
Argenton-les-Vallées
Mauléon
Bressuire
Pouzauges
La Châtaigneraie
Fontenay-le-Comte
Thouars
Oiron
St-Jouin-de-Marnes
Ouzilly-Vignolles
St-Généroux
Moncontour
Montreuil-Bellay
Loudun
Vallée du Thouet
Airvault
St-Loup-Lamairé
Gourgé
Lhoumois
La Peyratte
Parthenay
St-Marc-la-Lande
Champdeniers
Ste-Ouenne
Coudray-Salbart
Cherveux
Marconnay
Ménigoute
Sanxay
St-Maixent-l'École
Lusignan
Souvigné
Tumulus de Bougon
La Mothe-St-Héray
La Couarde
Beaussais
Celles-sur-Belle
Melle
Maillezais
Maillé
Damvix
Coulon
Marais Poitevin
Arçais
La Garette
Niort
Les Ruralies
Monfaucon
Amuré
Sansais
Mauzé-sur-le-Mignon
Forêt de Chizé
Zoodyssée
Surgères
St-Jean-d'Angély
Crazannes
ANGERS
SAUMUR
NANTES
LA ROCHE-SUR-YON
POITIERS
LA ROCHELLE
ROCHEFORT
SAINTES
LOIRE
Vienne
Thouet
Sèvre Nantaise
Vendée
Charente
0 10 km
0 5 miles
Tumulus de Bougon ★★ Recommended
Melle ★ Interesting
Monfaucon Worth a visit
Driving tour with departure town

Famed for its beautiful rivers and wooded valleys, the Deux-Sèvres derives its name from two river Sèvres: the Sèvre Nantaise, which joins the Loire at Nantes, and the Sèvre Niortaise, which flows into the Atlantic north of La Rochelle. A sight of strategic importance since the late Middle Ages (hence its charming historic centre), Niort today is a major financial centre of France with banking, insurance, chemistry and aeronautics the main employers. It is the ideal starting point for exploring the labyrinth of waterways of the Marais Poitevin, also known as Green Venice.

Emblem of the Marais

Found in both the Marais Poitevin and the Marais Breton-Vendéen, the European eel *(Anguilla anguilla)* remains for some 10 years in freshwater, where it acquires its characteristic silver colour, before swimming down estuaries and across the Atlantic Ocean, a journey of about 6 000km/3 730mi, in order to breed at great depths in the Sargasso Sea (near Bermuda).

The larvae then migrate back across the Atlantic and reach the coasts of Europe between seven and nine months later. Upon their arrival, the transparent young **eels** swim up estuaries and rivers between November and March. While they are growing, they are called yellow eels.

Eels are caught with wicker hoop nets or with a *vermée*, a piece of rope on which worms have been tied and which is hung from a long rod. As eels do not like light, fishing is usually done at night. Recent surveys have shown a radical decline in the number of eels, possibly due to pollution of the habitat, the diminishing wetland area, parasites and overfishing.

Local Produce

The region is still very rural, producing dairy products of high quality in large quantities. Near to Niort, the little town of Échiré is renowned for its butter, which has its own *appellation*, and St Maixent and Bourgon both produce excellent **goat's cheese**. Since the Deux- Sèvres region alone produces around 50% of all France's goat's cheese, it isn't surprising that *tourteau fromager* is one of the local specialities.

While cereal crops and vegetables are the main products grown, this is also an important area for growing angelica, which is said to have many medicinal qualities. Locals once believed that it cured the plague: it was planted around Niort in the early 16C to stem an epidemic. Mainly crystallised, it is also used to flavour a liqueur, omelettes and trout dishes.

Highlights

1. The walk through **Niort**'s historic Old Town (p326)
2. **Bougon:** Trace the evolution of man at the fascinating museum, then follow the discovery trail to the five ancient tumuli (p331)
3. Boat trip on a flat-bottomed boat in the **Marais Poitevin** (p336)
4. Picturesque villages on a drive through the **Vallée du Thouet** (p347)
5. Architectural riches of **Château d'Oiron** (p352)

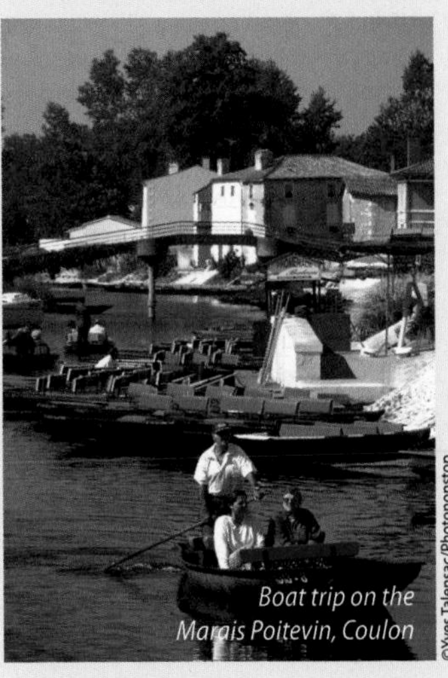

Boat trip on the Marais Poitevin, Coulon

Niort★

Deux-Sèvres

Niort rises beside the green waters of the Sèvre Niortaise, distilling a charming air of placid bourgeois prosperity, especially in season when the many flowers around the town come into bloom. Gastronomic specialities include eels and *petit-gris* (snails) from the nearby marshes, *tourteau fromager*, a cake made with fresh goat's cheese, and angelica treats made from *Angelica archangelica*, an aromatic plant whose stalks are crystallised (confectionery), cooked (jam) or distilled (angelica liqueur).
Today, while still a centre of glove-making and *chamoiserie* (tanning and oiling skins to make them supple), Niort has become headquarters to a number of French *mutuelles* (mutual insurance companies).

- **Population:** 58 066
- **Michelin Map:** 322: D-7
- **Info:** pl. de la Brèche, Niort. ✆08 20 20 00 79 www.niortmaraispoitevin.com. The tourist office organises guided tours of the town (1hr) all year (Mon–Sat). Reservations required. 6.50€.
- **Location:** Niort lies just off the A 10 motorway, SW of Poitiers, some 60km/37mi from the coastal town of La Rochelle. It makes a good base for excursions into the Poitou marshlands *(see Le MARAIS POITEVIN)*.
- **Parking:** There are several car parks in the town centre, as well as a large car park in pl. de la Brèche *(see map)*.
- **Don't Miss:** The Donjon; the Pilori; the Château du Coudray-Salbart.
- **Kids:** Zoodyssée in the Forêt de Chizé S of Niort.

A BIT OF HISTORY

Madame de Maintenon

Françoise d'Aubigné, the granddaughter of the poet Agrippa d'Aubigné, was born in Niort in 1635, in a house on rue du Pont that stood in the shadow of the castle where her father was locked up for non-payment of debts.
Sent in disgrace to an Ursuline convent at the age of 14, she escaped and eventually married the poet Scarron, 25 years her senior. After his death the young widow became part of the Court, as governess to the children of Louis XIV by his mistress Madame de Montespan, and soon caught the King's eye herself; he subsequently made her Marquise de Maintenon.
Françoise and the King were secretly and morganatically – that is, her rank remained unchanged – married in 1683, the year Madame de Montespan fell from favour. When the Sun King died in 1715, Madame de Maintenon retired to the establishment she had founded in St-Cyr in 1685: an institution for the education of impoverished daughters of the nobility. After a remarkable ascension from barnyard to palace, she died there in 1719.

WALKING TOUR

The town is built on the slopes of two facing hillsides: on one stands the castle keep and the Church of Our Lady; on the other the former town hall and the St-André district. The heart of the town, rue Victor-Hugo, crosses the site of the old medieval market in the lowest part of the valley.
At the eastern extremity of place de la Brèche, a huge square bordered by trees, the main roads leading to the town centre converge. Here ancient houses roofed with round tiles line the narrow, twisting streets climbing the slope, many of which have retained their original names: rue de l'Huilerie (Oil Mill Street), rue du Tourniquet (Turnpike Lane), rue du Rabot (Wood Plane Street), etc. Rue du Pont and rue St-Jean were once shopping streets bustling with market stalls.

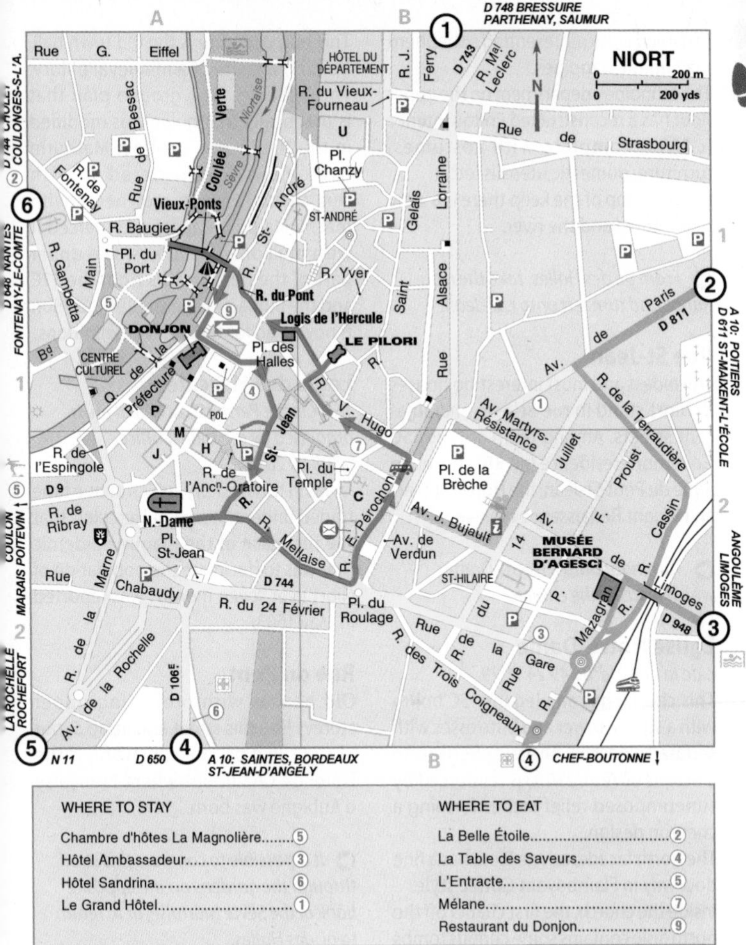

Leave the car in the car park on pl. des Halles, where the walk starts.

Donjon★

r. du Guesclin. Open Tue–Sun 10am–12.30pm, 2–6pm. 3.50€. 05 49 28 14 28.

This **keep** was the most important element in a fortress begun by Henry II Plantagenet in the 12C and completed by his son Richard the Lionheart. It was surrounded by a defensive perimeter 700m/770yds in circumference. The ensemble formed a small town within the town, which included houses, gardens and a parade ground flanked by the collegiate church of St-Gaudens, destroyed during the Wars of Religion.

Under the Bourbons the keep was used as a state prison.

Today its unusual silhouette still towers over the Sèvre. The plan and elevation are original; two tall, massive bastions, square in shape and linked by a 15C building are bordered by turrets.

Inside the keep, the **Hall of Glove-making and Chamoiserie**★ focuses on Niort's traditional trades. The lower rooms house the town's **archaeology collection**. This includes stone tools, an early Bronze Age gold necklace, ceramics discovered during excavations at Bougon, a 9C BC chariot wheel, Merovingian sarcophagi, coins from the Carolingian era found at Melle, a late Gauloise stela, and a 14C knife-handle

of carved ivory representing a shepherd playing the bagpipes.

The ethnology department on the upper floor has a reconstructed Poitou interior (c.1830) complete with costumes, furniture, domestic utensils, etc.

From the top of the keep there is a view of the town and the river.

From pl. des Halles, take the r. du Rabot and turn left onto r. St-Jean.

Rue St-Jean

The oldest and most interesting houses in Niort stand in rue St-Jean and adjacent streets. Among them are the 15C Governor's residence (no **30**) and, at no **3** rue du Petit-St-Jean, the Hôtel Estissac, an elegant Renaissance mansion.

Turn right onto r. Notre-Dame, which leads to the church.

Église Notre-Dame

r. de la Cure. 05 49 24 18 79.

This church has an elegant 15C belfry with a square tower and buttresses with serrated pinnacles. The steeple, rising to a height of 76m/250ft, is reinforced by superimposed relief arches forming a chevron design.

The north façade, on rue Bion, has a fine doorway in Flamboyant Gothic style.

Inside the church, the first chapel off the north aisle contains some curious tombs dating from 1684: Charles de Baudéan-Parabère, Governor of Niort, his wife and his son are all represented climbing out of their graves on Resurrection Day. In the third chapel hangs *St Bernard Trampling the Decree of Pope Anaclet*, an 18C painting by Lattainville. The early 16C font was used for the baptism of Françoise d'Aubigné. A Way of the Cross and the carved wood pulpit in the Gothic style date from 1877.

Follow r. Mellaise, then r. Pérochon, which leads to the tourist office. From there, walk to the pl. de la Brèche then turn left towards the Pilori.

Le Pilori★

pl. du Pilori. 05 49 78 73 82.

This odd structure is the old town hall, built on the site of a medieval pillory. The building, on a ground plan that is practically triangular, was modified in the 16C by the architect Mathurin Bertomé, who bordered it with semicircular towers, crowned it with machicolated parapets and pierced it with mullioned windows. The upper part of the belfry dates from the 17C and the pinnacle from the 19C. Le Pilori is now used for temporary exhibitions.

Logis de l'Hercule

16 r. Cloche Perse. Guided tours organised by the tourist office. 08 20 20 00 79.

It was in this hostelry, which at one time traded under the sign of Hercules, that the first case of the plague epidemic that was to decimate the population of Niort over seven months was reported in May 1603.

Rue du Pont

Old houses with projecting upper storeys line this street and at no **5**, out of sight in a private courtyard, is the Hôtel de Chaumont where Françoise d'Aubigné was born.

It is possible to continue this stroll through the gardens on the opposite bank of the Sèvre Niortaise, or to return to pl. des Halles.

Coulée Verte

This promenade comprises the renovated Cronstadt, La Regratterie and La Préfecture quays and is a pleasant place for a quiet riverside stroll. From the **Old Bridges** (Vieux Ponts) there is a splendid view of the castle keep.

ADDITIONAL SIGHT

Musée Bernard d'Agesci

28 av. de Limoges. Open Tue–Sun May–15 Sept 10am–6pm; 16 Sept–Apr 10am–5pm. 3.50€. 05 49 78 72 04.

Set up in the former Lycée Jean Macé (secondary school), the museum is named after the local painter Bernard d'Agesci, and houses some of his work. There is another room dedicated to the contemporary local sculptor, Pierre-Marie Poisson. Both the **Musée de Beaux Arts** (Fine Arts Museum) and the **Musée Histoire Naturelle** (Natural History Museum) are located here.

EXCURSIONS

Moulin de Rimbault

Guided tours organised by the Beauvoir tourist office. 05 49 05 43 62.
Built in 1682 on the northeast edge of Forêt de Chizé, the windmill was abandoned in 1928. It has been restored, complete with a revolving cap on a greased wooden rail, a *guivre*, and part of the internal machinery and sails with adjustable wooden slats.

Forêt de Chizé

20km/12.4mi S via the N 150 and D 1.
The Forêt de Chizé southeast of Niort, once part of the vast Argenson Forest which covered the whole region in the Middle Ages, contains more than 5 000ha/12 350 acres of oak and beech. This picturesque forest, crossed diagonally by the D 1, offers numerous starting points for forest walks.

Zoodyssée★

Open Apr and 1–15 Sept daily 10am–6pm; May–Aug daily 10am–7pm; Feb–Mar, 16 Sept–Nov Wed–Mon 1–6pm (last admission 1hr before closing). 11€ (13 – 18 years 8.50€, 4–12 years 6€). 05 49 77 17 17. www.zoodyssee.org.
The aim of the zoo, which occupies a former military base, is to facilitate the observation and study of European fauna including nearly 600 animals in a 25ha/62-acre forest setting. The first part of the park is devoted to predatory mammals (wild cats, marten, civet, wolves, otter, lynx, brown bears and red fox), birds, reptiles and amphibians (vivarium), all of whom live in conditions resembling their original habitat.
The rest of the zoo is inhabited by larger mammals – spotted deer, sika, roe-deer, agile ibex, chamois and moufflons (wild mountain sheep from Corsica) and a herd of rare European bison and wild boar. The park also has auroch (wild bulls) and tarpan (wild horses), two almost extinct species. A distinctly local animal is the Poitou donkey, which has successfully escaped extinction here.

DRIVING TOUR

1 L'EGRAY AND LA SÈVRE NIORTAISE VALLEYS

75km/46mi. Allow half a day.

Leave Niort heading NE on the D 743, towards Parthenay. At Échiré, turn left onto the D 107, then right after 1km/0.6mi.

Château du Coudray-Salbart★

The path up to the ruins starts near the bridge over the river. Open Apr–Jun and Sept–Oct Sat–Sun and public holidays 10am–noon, 2–6pm; Jul–Aug Wed–Mon 10am–12.30pm, 2.30–6.30pm. Guided tour (1hr30min) Jul–Aug Wed–Mon 11am, 3pm, 5pm. 5€ (guided tours 6.50€). 05 49 25 71 07. www.salbart.org.
The castle, which rises on an escarpment overlooking the Sèvre Niortaise, is a fascinating example of 13C military architecture. Its construction (1202–25) is linked to the battle between the Capetians and the Plantagenets for possession of the Guyenne region.

Continue NE on the D 748. Just after Rouvre, turn left to Breilbon.

Église de Ste-Ouenne

This Romanesque church is remarkable for its small square belfry and elegant apse, with column-buttresses. The nave has interesting capitals, especially in the choir (leaves and birds).

Leave Ste-Ouenne going N on the D 12.

Vallée de l'Egray

Hikers and climbers can stretch their legs. About 2km/1.2mi before Champdeniers you will see, on the left, steep rocky outcrops covered with pine and chestnut trees. A marked path leads to

the Rochers de la Chaize, where there is a climbing school. From here, there is a splendid panoramic view.

Champdeniers

Two storytellers, Suzanne Bontems and Yannick Jaulin, have taken up residence at Champdeniers.

Church – Situated above the Egray Valley, the church is a fine example of Poitou Romanesque architecture, even though the octagonal tower resembles an Auvergne or Limousin architectural style. The apse dates from the 15C. In the aisle on the north side of the choir, large 17C wooden statue of the Virgin, inside, note the capitals, decorated with leaves and grimacing heads. In the crypt, the double-barrelled vaults rest on Monolithic columns with 11C capitals.

Leave Champdeniers NE on the D 745. then turn right onto the D 134.

Église de St-Marc-la-Lande

This church has a remarkable Louis XII façade. Its main feature, aside from the quality of the sculpture, is the juxtaposition of the Gothic and Renaissance elements.

Return to Champdeniers and turn left onto the D 6. About 2km/1.2mi after crossing the D 743, turn right onto the D 122 going to St-Christophe-sur-Roc.

Château de Cherveux

Guided tours Apr–Oct Sat–Sun 10am–noon, 3–7pm. 5€.(children 3€). 05 49 75 06 55. www.chateau-de-cherveux.com.

This castle is a fine example of 15C military architecture with a keep and machicolated towers.

ADDRESSES

STAY

Hôtel Ambassadeur – *82 r. de la Gare, Niort. 05 49 24 00 38. www.ambassadeur-hotel.com. Closed 26 Dec–3 Jan. 32 rooms. 7€.* The rooms of this hotel, near to the train station, are practical and well maintained.

Sandrina – *43 av. St-Jean-d'Angély, Niort via the D 106E. 05 49 79 28 42. www.hotel-sandrina.com. Closed 26 Dec–4 Jan. 18 rooms. 7€.* Functional hotel in the city centre. Well maintained, gaily decorated rooms. Car park available.

Chambre d'hôtes La Magnolière – *16 impasse de l'Abbaye, 79000 St-Liguaire. 05 49 35 36 06. www.lamagnoliere.fr. Closed 22 Dec–1 Jan. . 3 rooms. .* Elegant mansion house with cosy rooms.

Le Grand Hôtel – *32 av. de Paris, Niort. 05 49 24 22 21. www.grandhotelniort.com. 39 rooms. 9€.* Centrally located hotel, the rooms overlooking the garden are quieter. Buffet breakfast; garage.

EAT

L'Entracte – *9 bd Main, Niort. 05 49 26 31 07. Closed Sun–Mon.* . Popular restaurant with lovely river view from the terrace.

La Table des Saveurs – *9 r. Thiers, Niort. 05 49 77 44 35. www.tabledessaveurs.com. Closed Sun except public holidays.* An attractive restaurant with excellent daily specials.

Restaurant du Donjon – *7 r. Brisson, Niort. 05 49 24 01 32. www.borelweb.com/ledonjon. Closed Sun, 1–15 Aug and spring and bank holidays.* The chef uses fresh local produce. Good daily specials.

Mélane – *1 pl. du Temple, Niort. 05 49 04 00 40. www.lemelane.com. Closed Sun–Mon.* Traditional dishes with a modern twist.

La Belle Étoile – *115 quai Maurice Métayer (2.5km/1.5mi W). 05 49 73 31 29. www.la-belle-etoile.fr. Closed Wed evening, Sun evening and Mon.* This pretty house overlooking the river serves regional cuisine with a contemporary flavour.

Tumulus de Bougon★★

Deux-Sèvres

This important Megalithic site, parts dating from c. 4700 BC, lies hidden in a wood near Bougon, a village known for its goat's cheese. The site comprises five tumuli or barrows (ancient burial mounds), predating the Egyptian pyramids by 2 000 years. Circular or rectangular in shape, built with stones and earth, these are one of the oldest examples of funerary architecture in the world, and were the work of Neolithic tribes living in the neighbourhood; of their dwellings, very little remains.

Michelin Map: 322: F-6

MUSEUM★

La Chapelle, Bougon. Open May–Sept Wed 1–6.30pm, Thu–Tue 10am–6,30pm; Oct–Dec and Feb–Apr Mon–Tue and Thu–Fri 10am–5.30pm, Wed and Sat–Sun 1–5.30pm. Closed Jan. Guided tours available. 4.50€ (1st Sun of month no charge); guided tours 6€. 05 49 05 12 13. www.deux-sevres.com/musee-bougon.

This elegant, ultra-modern metal and glass structure, built on limestone, encompasses the ruins of a Cistercian priory. Start here for a walk through prehistory, from the creation of the universe to the necropolis of Bougon.

The modern-style exhibition retraces human evolution. Partial, lifesize reconstructions give a realistic idea of a primitive world which is still the basis of our society, dwellings from the Çatal Hüyük village in Anatolia (one grotto is painted with huge vultures carrying off tiny men), a dwelling made with branches and rushes from Charavines in Isère, a chamber with a megalithic passage grave from Gavrinis (Morbihan) and lastly an exhibition room dedicated to the Tumuli of Bougon where offerings and skulls (one cut into three pieces) lie in a reconstructed funerary chamber. There is a 12C **chapel** on the way from the museum to the Neolithic site.

NEOLITHIC SITE★★

The site is accessed via a footpath lined with interesting reconstructions such as a sun and lunar calendar (based on Stonehenge in England), and the erection of a megalithic flagstone. There is also a botanical garden.

Tumulus A

This circular construction, the first to be discovered in modern times (1840), dates from c. 4000 BC. The funerary chamber, one of the largest known (7.8m/26ft long), is roofed with a single

Tumulus de Bougon

S. Sauvignier/MICHELIN

stone slab weighing 90t. A smaller slab, standing vertically, divides the chamber in two. As well as the 220 skeletons seen here, the tumulus also yielded a collection of funerary objects.

Tumulus B

The shape of this barrow is elongated. The interior revealed two funerary vaults at the east end and two passage graves at the west. Shards of pottery discovered here have been dated to the middle of the fifth millennium BC, which makes this the oldest monument on the site.

Tumulus C

This circular mound, 5m/16ft high, dates from 3500 BC. It shelters a small passage grave and also has a rectangular platform, which may have been used for religious ceremonies. A 35m/115ft-long wall runs between Tumulus C and Tumulus E. It appears to have been designed to separate the sanctuary into two distinct zones.

Tumulus E

The barrow contains an east-facing passage, which leads to two chambers where bones and funerary objects dating from 4000 to 3500 BC were found. These are the oldest-known passage graves in the centre-west of France.

Tumulus F

This, the longest enclosure (80m/262ft), encompasses two more barrows. F2, to the north, dates from 3500 BC and has a passage grave of the type known here as *angoumoisin* (in the Angoulême style). The passageway leads to a rectangular chamber. FO to the south dates from c.4700 BC.

Melle★

Deux-Sèvres

Melle owes its existence to the silver-bearing veins of lead in the hills of St-Hilaire, on the west bank of the Béronne; they were used in medieval times for the production of coins in a local mint. Melle is unusual for its three Romanesque churches. Two of them, originally attached to Benedictine monasteries, accommodated pilgrims on the road to Compostela. The town was won over at the time of the Reformation and enjoyed a certain prosperity after the foundation of its college in 1623. Melle was once famed for raising the local breed of donkey, the Poitou *baudet* (*see DAMPIERRE-SUR-BOUTONNE*).

- **Population:** 3 659
- **Michelin Map:** 322: F-7
- **Info:** 3 r. Emilien Traver, Melle. ℘05 49 29 15 10. www.ville-melle.fr.
- **Location:** Melle is situated 8km/5mi SE of Celles-sur-Belle. The best view of the town is from the D 950 via St-Jean-d'Angély.
- **Don't Miss:** Église St-Hilaire.
- **Kids:** The Mines d'Argent des Rois Francs.

SIGHTS

Église St-Hilaire★

r. du Pont St Hilaire.
www.culture.gouv.fr/poitou-charentes.
St Hilary's Church, built in the Poitou Romanesque style, was part of St-Jean-d'Angély Abbey. The sober east end and the west front with its coned pinnacles are particularly attractive.

Above the north doorway stands a carving of a **horseman** *(le Cavalier de Melle)*: the crowned rider has been identified as either Charlemagne, Jesus Christ Suppressing the Ancient Law, or as Emperor Constantine.

The east end includes three apsidal chapels with buttress-columns and carved modillions radiating from an ambulatory joined to the transept. Two more chapels lead off the transept; above the crossing rises a belfry-tower.

Interior – The scale of the nave, aisles and ambulatory indicates that the church was designed as a place of pilgrimage. The barrel-vaulting is supported by pillars, quadrilobed in section, with interesting carved capitals; the third on the right, entering from the west front, depicts a wild boar hunt. A doorway leading into the south aisle is decorated on its inner side: on the archivolt, Jesus and the Saints accompanying Him overcome fantasy animals representing the forces of evil.

Église St-Pierre

r. St Pierre.

This church dedicated to St Peter once belonged to a priory attached to St-Maixent Abbey. It was built in the Poitou Romanesque style, and stands on a hill overlooking the Béronne. The east end and the side entrance are remarkable for their carved ornamentation: a cornice above the south doorway is supported by historiated modillions between which are carved Signs of the Zodiac, and Christ in Glory occupies a niche above this cornice. The east end is noteworthy for the decoration of the bays, the modillions of the axial chapel, and – crowning one of the buttress-columns – a capital featuring two peacocks, symbols of immortality.

Mines d'Argent des Rois Francs (Kings' Silver Mines)★

r. du pré du Gué. Guided tour (1hr30min) 1 Apr–mid Jun and mid-Sept–4 Nov Mon–Fri 10.30am, 3pm, Sat–Sun and public holidays 10.30am, 2.30pm, 4.30pm; mid-Jun–mid-Sept daily 10.30am, 2.15pm, 3pm, 3.45pm, 4.30pm, 5.15pm. 7.50€ (children 4€). 05 49 29 19 54. www.mellecom.com/~mines/index.htm.

The porous limestone on which Melle stands harbours a quantity of geodes – pockets or cavities containing crystallised minerals, in this case lead ore with a small proportion (3%) of silver. The mine from which the ore was extracted, which had been worked since the 5C, became, under Charlemagne, the supplier of silver to a local mint designed to strike the royal coinage. In the 10C the mint was moved and the disused mine was forgotten until the 19C.

During the underground tour, primitive ventilation chimneys can be seen, along with a number of concretions, a small lake and traces of the oxidisation caused by the firing which broke up the rock.

Chemin de la Découverte

Arboretum

This footpath, which follows stretches of disused railway line, encircles nearly the whole of the Old Town within its 5km/3.1mi circuit. Vegetation native to the region alternates with zones in which 650 different species of exotic trees have been planted. Of particular interest is the **Bosquet d'Écorces** (Bark Grove), north of St Hilary's Church.

EXCURSIONS

Chef-Boutonne

16km/10mi SE on the D 948, then the D 737.

The name is derived from "Head of the Boutonne", because the Boutonne river rises nearby. Downstream at Javarzay the church dates from the 12C and the 16C.

Château de Javarzay

Information 05 49 29 86 31.

Former property of the Rochechouart family, it was built around 1515. All that remains of its fortifications, once boasting 12 towers, is an attractive gatehouse, flanked by two towers with Renaissance windows, and a round machicolated tower. Owned by the town since 1982, Javarzay now houses a museum with a superb collection of around 400 bonnets and caps, and rooms dedicated to Jean-François Cail, an important industrialist born in the town. It hosts temporary exhibitions.

Pers

20km/12.4mi E on the D 950, then the D 14 and the D 15.

In the cemetery next to the church, a lantern of the dead (13C) stands with a stone base flanked by four columns.

The capitals at the top of the columns, support a lantern crowned by a cross. Below the pyramidal roof, four semi-circular windows indicate the place where the oil lamps burned during the funeral ceremonies. East of the lantern there are five 11C and 12C sarcophagi .

Celles-sur-Belle

7.5km/4.7mi NE.

The small town of Celles grew up in the shadow of the tall, imposing belfry of an old Augustinian abbey built on a terrace above the valley of the River Belle.

The **Église Notre-Dame** (*r. des Halles; 05 49 79 83 47*) a former abbey church, is the site of a pilgrimage to the Virgin known as the Septembresche *(1st Sun of Sept)*. King Louis XI was a regular worshipper here. The church was destroyed by the Huguenots in 1568, but rebuilt a century later, in 15C style, by the architect **François Leduc**. He was known as François the Tuscan because of his taste for Tuscan architecture.

The Romanesque main **doorway**★ of the original abbey church is unusual. Its multi-lobed arching, decorated with grimacing masks, betrays an Eastern influence. Inside, the church is striking for the luminosity of the nave and aisles, and for the purity of line seen in the pillars complemented by the vaulting.

Abbaye Royale – *Access via the doorway below the church. Guided tours (1hr15min) 15 Apr–14 Jun and 16 Sept–15 Oct Tue and Fri 10.30am–12.30pm, 2.30–5.30pm; 15 Jun–15 Sept daily 10.30am–12.30pm, 2.30–6.30pm. 4.50€ (children 1.55€) 05 49 32 14 99).*

Three of the past abbots here left their mark on history – Geoffrey d'Estissac, Cardinal de La Rochefoucauld, Louis XIII's prime minister, and the famous minister Talleyrand.

The monastic buildings and their dependencies were, like the church, the work of Leduc. The main façade (85m/279ft long) features Ionic columns resting against scrolled buttresses. The right wing features a fine staircase and a cloister gallery, dating from the 17C.

Maison du Poitou Protestant

11km/6.8mi to the N

Beaussais

pl. de la Mairie. Open 29 Mar–2 Nov Sat–Sun and public holidays 2.30–6pm (1 Jul–15 Sept Tue–Sat 10.30am–noon, 2.30–7pm, Sun 2.30–7pm); school holidays Tue–Sun 2.30–6pm. 5€. 05 49 32 83 16.

This **temple**, a former 12C Catholic church, now houses a small **museum**. The collection traces the activities of Protestants in France, with special emphasis on Poitou. A film tells the history of Jean Migault, a Protestant school teacher forced into exile. Major events are highlighted: the coming of Calvin to Poitiers, the history of Reformation, Wars of Religion and the Edict of Nantes. A Huguenot footpath links Beaussais to La Couarde *(4km/2.5mi, details from museum)*.

Take the D 10 N to La Couarde.

La Couarde

This section of the **Maison du Protestantisme Poitevin** is housed in a church (1904). Open for temporary exhibitions.

ADDRESSES

STAY/ EAT

Les Glycines – *5 pl. René Groussard, Melle. 05 49 27 01 11. www.hotel-lesglycines.com. Closed Sun evening (Sept–Jun) and 2nd –3rd wk Jan.* Popular with locals and visitors alike, it specialises in traditional, regional cuisine. Also has cosy guest rooms.

Hostellerie de l'Abbaye – *1 pl. Époux-Laurant, Celles-sur-Belle. 05 49 32 93 32. www.hostellerie-de-abbaye.fr. Closed Sun evening (Sept–Jun). 20 rooms. 7.50€.* Next to the church, the hotel rooms overlooking the courtyard are more pleasant than those facing the road. Traditional dishes are served in the bright dining room, or on the terrace in summer. Good choice of menus. Simple rooms.

Le Marais Poitevin★★

Since 1975 the Poitou Marshlands have been a conservation area extending over three *départements*. Meadows are bordered by poplar and willow trees; the black boats of the marshlanders glide along innumerable watercourses. The marshes attract a multitude of birds. Various species can be observed, depending on the season: gulls and terns, wild ducks, geese, large waders such as herons, egrets, spoonbills and storks, and small wading birds such as sandpipers, plovers, redshanks, oystercatchers, stilts, avocets and lapwings.

- **Michelin Map:** 316: H–6-L9
- **Info:** r. du Docteur Daroux, Maillezais. ✆02 51 87 23 01. www.maraispoitevin-vendee.com.
- **Location:** Divided into the Dry Marsh, near the sea and the Wet Marsh, bounded on the north by the Vendée and to the south by the Aunis hills.
- **Don't Miss:** A boat trip through the marshlands.
- **Kids:** Le Pibalou train; boat trips along the Wet Marsh.

MARAIS MOUILLÉ★★

The Wet Marsh, nicknamed the "Green Venice", covers 15 000ha/37 000 acres. A profusion of alders, lofty ash trees, willows and poplars of the species known as Poitou Whites lines the banks, and overhangs the labyrinth of narrow channels parcelling the rich fields in which herds of Friesians, Normans and locally bred cattle graze. The plots under cultivation produce an abundant harvest of artichokes, onions, garlic, melons, courgettes, broad beans and the delicious haricots, usually white, known as mojettes.

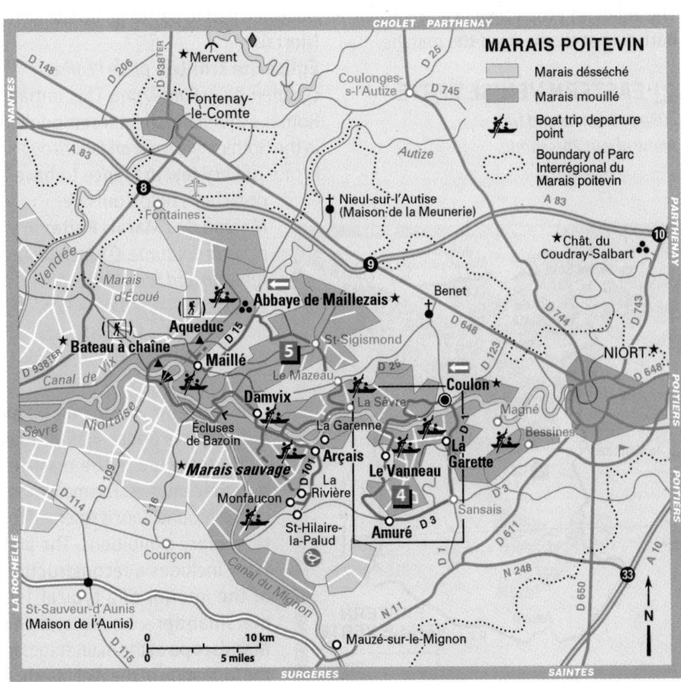

In summer, the relatively cool Wet Marsh offers charming pastoral landscapes. During the February and March floods, however, visitors can appreciate how difficult the marshlanders' life was in the past.

Proceed with care; some roads can be impassable.

Boat Trips

The best way to really experience the uniqueness of the Wet Marsh is to go by boat. The vessels glide in summer beneath a dense vault of foliage filtering the bright light through shades of grey-green to jade.

The expansion of tourism in the area has led to the creation of many landing-stages. For your first exploration of this maze of waterways, it would be better to rent a flat-bottomed boat (the traditional wooden one has unfortunately been replaced by a plastic one), steered by a guide.

DRIVING TOURS

The following trips take in a few small harbours at the heart of the marsh.

2 EASTERN VENISE VERTE

30km/18.6mi round trip.
Allow about 2hrs30min.

Coulon★

This small town is the capital of the Wet Marsh and the main departure point for **boat trips** through this attractive canal country, locally known as "Green Venice". *(contact Embarcadère La Pigouille (52 quai Louis tardy; open 10 Feb–25 Nov; 05 49 35 80 99; http://auberge-embarcadere-la-pigouille.com); Embarcadère DLMS Tourisme (6 r. de l'Église; open Apr–mid-Nov; 05 49 35 14 14; www.coulontourisme.com); Embarcadère Cardinaud (La Repentie de Magné; open all year; 05 49 35 90 47; www.marais-poitevin.com)).*

The marshlands can also be explored by **Le Pibalou** *(miniature train; 20km/12.4mi, 1hr15min)* of the Marais Poitevin) which leaves from Coulon *(DLMS Tourisme, 6 r. de l'Église; open Apr–Oct; 9€ (children 7€); 05 49 35 14 14; www.coulontourisme.com).*

Below the bridge across the River Sèvre Niortaise, the river flows peacefully between quays lined with boatmen's houses. Going back along the jetties on the Right Bank, **place de la Coutume** recalls the customs duties which boatmen had to pay to go up the Sèvre Niortaise.

Église Ste Trinité – *pl. de l'Église.* *Open daily 9am–7pm.* This initially Romanesque church later remodelled in the Gothic style *(west and south doors)*, is one of very few in France to have a preacher's pulpit outside.

Maison des Marais Poitevin – *pl. de la Coutume. Open daily Apr–Jun and Sept 10am–noon, 2–6pm; Jul–Aug 10am–7pm. 5.50€; 05 49 35 81 04. www.maisons.parc-marais-poitevin.fr.*

The museum, housed in the old customs house, has various exhibits on life in the marshes over the centuries. The main room on the ground floor is reserved for temporary exhibitions. The first floor includes a reconstruction of the interior of a typical 19C marshlander's house and the **Maraiscope** of the main stages in the formation of the Wet Marsh. A

The Marshland

Aiguillon Bay, an Atlantic inlet which is gradually silting up, is all that remains of the vast gulf which stretched in ancient times from the limestone plain in the north to the hills of the Aunis. The gulf, which penetrated inland as far as Niort, was scattered with rocky islets (now towns such as Maillezais, Marans and St-Michel-en-l'Herm). The former shoreline is apparent in the remains of cliffs, laid out along Moricq, Luçon, Velluire, Fontaines and Benet to the north, and Mauzé-sur-le-Mignon, Nuaillé-d'Aunis and Esnandes to the south.

Little by little the rivers Lay, Vendée, Autise and Sèvre Niortaise discharged their alluvium into the gulf, while at the same time sea currents were piling up a clay-like silt known locally as *bri*, and as a consequence the marine inlet was transformed into a huge salt-marsh.

Drainage work began in the 13C when monks from the neighbouring abbeys dredged out the Canal des Cinq-Abbés (Five Abbots' Canal), which drained the northern part of the swamp.

The work, interrupted by wars, was resumed under Henri IV by an engineer from Bergen-op-Zoom in Holland, leading to the progressive colonisation of the marshlands. Around Aiguillon Bay itself Dutch-style polders protected by dykes were reclaimed from the sea between the 16C and the 19C.

The Marais Today

The marshes, extending on either side of the River Sèvre Niortaise, cover an area of 80 000ha/198 000 acres. The general configuration of the Marais includes a network of embankments or dykes, known locally as *bots*, along the top of which run roads and tracks and below which are the principal channels *(contrebots)*. When the rivers draining into the marshes are in spate, excess water surges into subsidiary channels *(achenaux)*, which divert the flow again into *rigoles* and finally *conches*, marked by lines of small trees. Between these waterways the land, which is extremely fertile, is used both for crops and for grazing. The green duckweed *(lemnaoideae)* covering the canals has earned the marshes its nickname of the **Venise Verte** ("Green Venice").

Traditions

The marshlanders lived in low, whitewashed houses grouped in villages either on limestone islets or on the dykes, where there was no risk of flooding. Each householder owned some kind of cabin in an isolated spot. Most houses were flanked by a *cale* – a miniature creek in which boats could be moored. Boats were the normal means of transport, manoeuvred with either a *pigouille* (a hooked pole) or a short oar called a *pelle*. There were two types of boat: the slim, lightweight *yoles* for daily use and the larger, more heavily built *plates* taking the place of vans or trucks, delivering commercial produce.

The marshlanders delivered their milk to local cooperatives, which produced much-praised butter, returning the whey for the fattening of pigs. Fishing brought in mullet, perch, carp, crayfish and eels. Hunting for waterfowl and other game birds (duck, plover, snipe) was restricted to the winter months.

Ecological Threat

The increase in cereal growing during the last few years is gradually causing the marsh to dry up and the use of fertilisers and pesticides is threatening the entire ecosystem. Plans have been forwarded to return to traditional agriculture.

nature room illustrates the environment (fauna and flora) and the traditional activities of the marshlanders. The visit ends with a presentation of local boat building *(balai)* and objects from the Bronze Age found during local excavations.

On leaving Coulon, drive W along the D 123. At the end of the village, take r. du Port-de-Brouillac towards Grand Coin. At the end of the road, turn left and cross the canal. Immediately after the bridge, turn left again.

The Grand Coin dam offers a good example of **boat transfer** technique. The road skirts the canal lined with poplars and weeping willows providing shade for anglers. Across the bridge there is a sturdy Poitou farmhouse with remarkable stone bond.

At the end of the canal, turn right onto the D 123 towards Irleau.

Ash trees mark the beginning of the Wet Marsh; planted to consolidate the banks, they owe their appearence to the way they are trimmed every few years.
The Right Bank of the Sèvre Niortaise offers striking views of charming cabins. The course of the river is punctuated by *conches* and *rigoles* and its gradient drops at the **Sotterie lock** from 30cm per km (1ft per 0.6mi) to less than 5cm (2in); the flow of water, considerably slowed down, floods the marsh.

Beyond the Pont d'Irleau, follow the first road on the left. Turn right at the end of the road. At the crossroads, continue straight on, then turn left onto the D 102.

Le Vanneau

This boatmen's village has a well-equipped **harbour**★: the remarkable view embraces a pastoral setting. The main *conche* penetrates into the Wet Marsh beyond a screen of poplars.

The r. de Gémond (right) then r. des Vergers (left) lead to the D 102: turn left towards Sansais; 200m/220yds farther on, take a small road on the right (bike tour no 1 markings).

A change of scenery: cereal crops enclosed by hedges have replaced the woods.

At the end of the road, turn left (unsurfaced road), then right (surfaced road): 200m/220yds farther on, turn left.

Surrounded by greenery once more, visitors can cross a bridge to appreciate the beauty and charm of the site.

Turn right at the next intersection and, a little way farther on, cross a small bridge. Turn right at the crossroads.

Trees suddenly give way to cultivated fields.

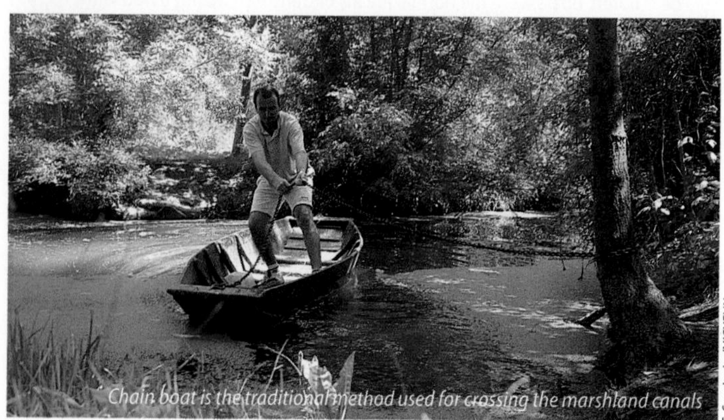

Chain boat is the traditional method used for crossing the marshland canals

S. Sauvignier/MICHELIN

At the crossroads, drive straight ahead and join the D 115. Turn left as you leave St-Georges-de-Rex, then, at the Chausse intersection, turn left again onto the D 3 towards Sansais. 400m/440yds farther on, take the V 8 on the left.

Amuré

The old cemetery (15C Hosanna cross and graves raised on piles) is 300m/330yds away from the new cemetery where two megaliths are said to have healing powers.

Continue eastwards along the D 3 to Sansais; after 2km/1.2mi, turn left onto a minor unsurfaced road (bike tour no 3 markings); 900m/0.5mi farther on, turn left onto the surfaced road.

At a place called Vollette, look for a fine example of a traditional Poitou farmhouse, turned into a *gîte rural*.

At the crossroads, follow the D 102 on the right and turn left 400m/440yds farther on; at the next intersection (700m/770yds), turn left and stop following the bike tour markings.

From Pont de la Chaume du Château, one re-enters the Wet Marsh. This section of road may be closed during flooding or when wild ducks cross the area *(morning and evening)*.

Follow the surfaced road. After 2.2km/1.4mi, the road is closed by a wooden gate; turn right, cross a small bridge and turn left 600m/660yds farther on.

La Garette

This former boatmen's hamlet is characteristic of the area, with its rows of houses built without foundation, which open onto a *conche* on one side and onto the road on the other. The high street *(closed to traffic)* extends as far as the Vieille Sèvre.

From the car park follow the street to the D 1; turn left at the crossroads.

The road goes through the eastern part of La Garette and crosses the Vieille Sèvre: from the bridge, there is a fine view of the river. The D 1 marks the border between the wet area *(on the left)* and the dry area *(on the right)*.

3 SÈVRE NIORTAISE TO AUTIZE

50km/31mi round trip. Allow 3hrs.

Maillezais★

See MAILLEZAIS.

Drive S out of Maillezais along the D 15. In Croix-de-Maillé, turn right onto the D 25 and continue to the bridge N of Maillé. Leave the car and follow the towpath on the right.

Aqueduc de Maillé

1km/0.6mi there and back.

Set in pastoral surroundings, this hydraulic complex enables the Canal de Vix (Dry Marsh) to cross that of La Jeune Autise (Wet Marsh).

Maillé

This old village is at the centre of many legends as testify the characters (acrobats, athletes carrying lions) which decorate the **Romanesque doorway** of the Église Notre-Dame *(pl. de l'Église)*. Situated along the banks of the Canal du Bourneau, the landing-stage nestles under a group of willow trees. Beyond the lock-bridge, it is possible to take a trip to the Île de la Chatte.

Take the road signposted "Dognon, Millé" opposite the church.

Agrippa d'Aubigné's keep (where *Les Tragiques* was printed in 1616, *see MAILLEZAIS*) used to stand in **Fort Dognon**. The road crosses a small bridge offering an extended view of the marsh. Strange white-plastic rafts can be seen along the *conches*: they are meant to trap the proliferating nutrias.

1.3km/0.8mi beyond the Millé farm, a footpath starts in a bend (the path

is closed off by means of a chain: no vehicles allowed).

Sentier du Bateau à Chaîne★

Take the street in front of the church, then follow "Dognon, Millé". The path is 1.5km/0.9mi away on your left, after the farm of Millé. 600m/660yds there and back. Follow the marked itinerary "Entre Sèvre et Autizes".

This unusual itinerary, running alongside a *conche*, offers the discovery of the fauna and flora of the marsh. It leads to one of the last **bateaux à chaîne** (flat-bottomed boats propelled by pulling on a chain) in the area, which can be used to cross a *conche*.

Continue along the same road. At the crossroads, turn left onto the D 25B. Cross the River Sèvre then turn left as you come off the Pont du Sablon.

The itinerary follows the Left Bank of the Sèvre Niortaise and offers fine views of the Île de la Chatte and its fishermen's cabins.

A picnic area is available near the lock of the Rabatière Canal.

At the intersection of the Croix-des-Mary Bridge, carry straight on towards Damvix. At the next crossroads, turn left and cross over the lock.

Several bridges in succession make it possible to reach the Right Bank of the Sèvre Niortaise.

Damvix

This small marshland village in a pleasant location on the Sèvre Niortaise contains a number of low cottages linked by footbridges over the narrow canals.

Cross the Sèvre Niortaise and follow the D 104 towards Arçais; 200m/220yds farther on, turn right onto a minor road (Camping des Conches) which runs across a bridge. Beware: the itinerary leading to the village of La Rivière through the Marais Sauvage follows an unsurfaced road only suitable in dry weather; in rainy weather, go to Arçais by the direct route.

Le Marais Sauvage★

A few planks of wood across a *conche* followed by *(take the left-hand road)* the dam of La Garette *(fine view)* give access to the Marais Sauvage *(turn right at the fork)*. This conservation area covering 1 600ha/3 954 acres is criss-crossed by 100km/62mi of waterways.

The village of **La Rivière** stands on the edge of the marsh. To the north, the road which joins the D 101 offers a striking contrast between the wooded marsh *(on the left)* and the vast expanse of rolling fields *(on the right)*; **Monfaucon** to the south has a fine landing-stage.

Parc Ornithologique Les Oiseaux du Marais Poitevin

Le Petit Buisson 79 210 St-Hilaire-la-Palud. Open late Mar–early Nov – contact for times. 7€ (3–12 years 4.50€). 05 49 26 04 09. www.oiseauxmaraispoitevin.com.

A stroll in the 8ha/20-acre park is a pleasant way to discover around 70 bird species.

For a different viewpoint, jump aboard a canoe or a boat and explore the waterways.

Arçais

Set up in the bend of a reach, the **Grand-Port★★** consists of a large paved dock; the landing-stage faces a typical wooden cabin. There are remarkable farmhouses along the Minet reach in the northern district of **La Garenne**.

From the Grand-Port, follow the D 102 towards Damvix. At Les Bourdettes, cross the dam then the lock and take the chemin de la Foulée on the right.

The itinerary follows the Right Bank of the Sèvre Niortaise to the Village de la Sèvre.

When you reach a footbridge, take the road on the left leading to Mazeau harbour (landing-stage after the bridge).

Maillezais★

Deux-Sèvres

A little way outside this Poitou village, on the edge of the flat marshlands which make up the Marais Poitevin, stand the imposing ruins of Maillezais Abbey.

- **Population:** 963
- **Michelin Map:** 316:L-9 – Local map, *see Le MARAIS POITEVIN.*
- **Info:** r. du Docteur Daroux, Maillezais. 02 51 87 23 01. www.maraispoitevin-vendee.com.
- **Location:** The abbey is situated 12km/7.4mi SE of Fontenay-le-Comte.

ABBAYE DE MAILLEZAIS★

Open daily Jun–Sept 10am–7pm; Oct–early Jan and Feb–May 9.30am–12.30pm, 1.30–6pm. 5€. 02 51 87 22 80. http://abbayes.vendee.fr.

Much of the fortified wall built around the monastery on Aubigné's orders is still standing. The work transformed the abbey into a true fortress: on the left of the entrance a bastion shaped like the prow of a ship faces the Marais wetlands. It was surmounted by a bartizan watchtower, and because the prow pointed due south, it also served as a giant sundial.

A Bit of History

The abbey was founded by Guillaume Fier-à-Bras, Comte de Poitou, at the end of the 10C. At that time the limestone rise on which it is built was washed by the Atlantic surf – part of the enormous Gulf of Poitou. The abbey, dedicated to St Peter, was first inhabited by monks of the Benedictine order. In the 13C it was sacked by Geoffroi la Grand-Dent, a member of the Lusignan family who claimed to be the son of Mélusine, and who was subsequently used by Rabelais as a model for the brave giant Pantagruel in his novel of the same name.

In 1317 the French Pope John XXII elevated Maillezais to the status of a bishopric but allowed the monks to remain in the abbey.

During the Wars of Religion the buildings were badly damaged and the Bishop of Luçon, Richelieu, ordered the episcopal seat to be transferred to La Rochelle.

Abbey Church

Building of the church began in the early 11C, though only the narthex and the wall of the north aisle remain from this period. The narthex was flanked by two square towers, following a Norman pattern where abbey churches were distinguished by tower strong points on either side of the west front. The façade of the church here was later incorporated into the wall built by Aubigné.

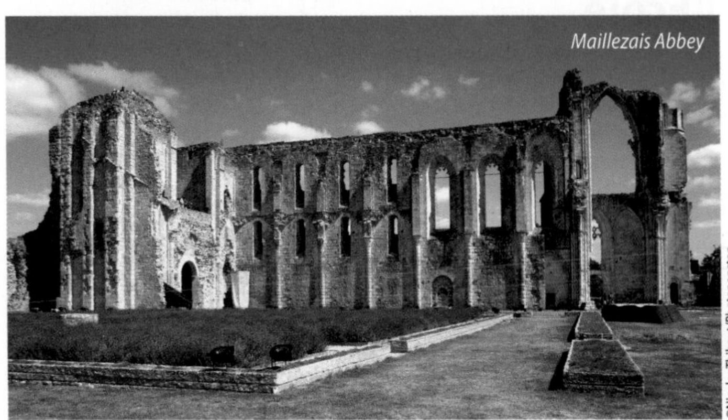

Maillezais Abbey

The three tall, crowned openings piercing the existing aisle wall reveal that the nave was altered in the 13C. The aisles were originally topped by galleries – again as in Norman abbeys.

The transept, of which only part remains, was a 14C Gothic addition. Climb to the top of one of the truncated turrets flanking its gable, for a good view of the ruins, the village and the marshes. The outlines of the chancel can still be made out.

Monastery

Most of the monastic buildings date from the 14C. The foundations of the old cloisters have been uncovered, along with sections of the paving, a 12C storeroom, a *lavabo* where the monks washed their hands before entering the refectory, a well and a number of abbots' or bishops' tombstones.

One wing of the monastery still stands and includes the salt cellar *(basement)*; the kitchen, and the refectories *(ground floor)*; the guests' dorter *(dormitory)* and infirmary.

Boat Trip

Embarcadère de l'Abbaye. Open Apr–Oct. 15€ (1hr boat trip with guide). 02 51 87 21 87. www.marais-poitevin-tourisme.com.

A ride in a typical flat-bottomed boat propelled by a long pole along the canals of **Green Venice**, as this part of the Marais Poitevin is known locally, is a complement to the tour of the abbey.

EXCURSION

Nieul-sur-l'Autise

8km/5mi NE.

This village grew around an old **abbey** *(1 allée du Cloître; open daily May–Sept 10am–7pm, Oct–early Jan and Feb–Apr 9.30am–12.30pm, 1.30–6pm; 5€; 02 51 50 43 00; http://abbayes.vendee.fr)* founded in 1068. In the 13C monks began to drain the neighbouring marshes. The abbey was secularised in 1715 and soon abandoned. The Romanesque abbey church in Poitou style was restored in the 19C and features a richly carved west front. There are good views from the original square **cloisters★**.

Maison de la Meunerie

16 r. du Moulin. Open May Sat–Sun 2–6pm; Jun and Sept Sun–Fri ; Jul–Aug daily 10.30am–7pm (last admission 40min before closing). 5€. 02 51 52 47 43. www.maisons.parc-marais-poitevin.fr.

This restored old watermill now houses a museum: the mill workings and domestic rooms are on view.

St-Maixent-l'École

Deux-Sèvres

St-Maixent is the base for the prestigious National Active Non-Commissioned Officers' School (ENSOA). This native town of politician and serviceman Denfert-Rochereau benefits from a military history, because it was initially home to the Military School of infantry, established in 1881. However, the town is named after the Benedictine abbey, where St Maixent lived in the 5C.

- **Population:** 7 643
- **Michelin Map:** 322: E-6
- **Info:** porte Chalon, St-Maixent-l'Ecole. 05 49 05 54 05. www. haut-val-de-sevre.com.
- **Location:** St-Maixent is located 24km/14.9mi NE of Niort.
- **Don't Miss:** Musée de la Coiffe, Souvigné; Gallo-Roman site at Sanxay.
- **Timing:** Allow 2hrs to explore the town, and half a day for the drive.

THE TOWN

Porte Chalon

This ancient 18C gateway to the city curiously resembles a triumphal arch. Admire the arms of St Maixent on the wrought-iron gate.

Allées Vertes

Blossac, Intendant du Poitou, had them traced out in the 18C on the site of the fortifications *(av. Gambetta)*. They form a perspective with the place Denfert. In one corner of this square, the chapel Notre-Dame-de-Grâces (15C) was built to thank Charles VII for granting freedom to the people of the town.

Hôtel Balizy

This manor house in rue du Palais an excellent example of Renaissance architecture.

Abbaye

It was founded in the 5C by the hermit Agapit and his follower Adjutor (St Maixent). In the 7C Abbot St Léger, future Bishop of Autun and martyr, lived here. Later the Benedictine abbey was badly damaged during the Wars of Religion. It was restored by the architect François Leduc, known as "Tuscany,,, who died at St-Maixent in 1698.

Church – It appears, as a whole, as a late Gothic building, but different styles can be distinguished: the side walls and the vestibule are Romanesque; the choir, Gothic, dating from the 13C, rebuilt in the 17C; the bell tower, Gothic, from the 15C; the nave, Gothic, from the 17C. Most of the furniture dates from the 17C. In the south transept, near the sacristy, look out for a beautiful recessed tomb and a 17C painting from the French school. Near the entrance there is a niche where, in 1962, a Romanesque passage was discovered leading to the ancient cloisters, destroyed during the Wars of Religion. It had been walled up for 300 years. The 6C and 7C sarcophagi (empty) of St Maixent and St Léger lie under the high altar, in the Romanesque crypt.

Monastic Buildings – Converted into barracks. A monumental gate leads to the courtyard. Take a glimpse of the stone staircase with its wrought-iron rail and the 17C cloister.

Maison Ancienne

13 r. Anatole-France. This 15C house was built for an apothecary who put up the inscription *Hic valetudo* ("Here is Health").

Musée du Sous-Officier

Quartier Marchand – Open Wed–Sun 10am–noon, 1.30–6pm. Closed late Jul–15 Aug and last 2 wks Dec. The collection is devoted to the history of the military schools established in St-Maixent since the end of the 19C. This military past is related through photographs, uniforms, weapons and medals, from the Ancien Régime to the present day.

DRIVING TOUR

4 FROM HAUT-VAL DE SÈVRE TO LA VONNE★

70km/43mi. Allow half a day.

Leave St-Maixent S towards Melle on the D 10.

Souvigné

At the heart of Huguenot Poitou, this village, where the church and the temple stand opposite one another, has numerous paths lined with chestnut trees. Along the walking trails, you will discover fountains, wash-houses and a few isolated Protestant cemeteries.

Musée de la Vie Rurale et de la Coiffe – *1 pl. du Prieuré. Open May–mid-Jul and Sept–Oct Sat–Sun and bank holidays 2.30–6.30pm; mid-Jul–Aug Wed, Sat–Sun and bank holidays 2.30–6.30pm. €4€ (under 15 years 2€). 05 49 76 23 60.*

Housed in a priory dating from the 11C and 14C, the museum traces the evolution of the regional headwear through 80 different models. Other period rooms include an early 20C classroom, and a laundry room.

Leave Souvigné S on the D 103.

Temple de Beaussais
See p334.

Leave Beaussais N on D 10.

Temple de la Couarde
See p334.

In the northeast corner of the Hermitain Forest stands the Dame de Chambrille rock *(explanation at the foot of the rock)*, which is a starting point for walks.

La Mothe-St-Héray
Moulin l'Abbé, R. Pont-L'Abbé, rte de Niort, 79800 La Mothe-St-Héray. Open Wed–Mon early Jul–mid-Sept 10:30am–12.30pm, 2.30–6.30pm, rest of year pms. Closed 25 Dec, Jan. 3.50€ (12–16 years 2€). 05 49 05 19 19. www.moulin-labbe.fr.
The town is named after its feudal castle. Rebuilt in the 16C, the château was destroyed in the 19C. All that remains is the orangery, and two pavilions, and the chapel's painted woodwork, now on display in the Bernard d'Agesci in Niort Museum *(see p328)*.
Maison de la Haute-Sèvre – *Moulin l'Abbé, in the same place as tourist office. Same opening times. 3.50€ (12–16 years 2€).* On the banks of the Sèvre, the Pont-l'Abbé mill no longer produces flour, but houses the Maison du Parc. When mechanisation arrived, the old water mill, dating from 1041, was replaced by a modern grist mill, or flour mill, in 1920.
Today there is an exhibition on milling, techniques and milling machines, a regional geology collection, and a mention of the local festival: la Fête des rosières *(1st weekend of Sept)*.

Leave La Mothe-St-Héray NE via the D 5.

Musée de Tumulus de Bougon★★
See p331.

Return to the D 5. At Sanxay, head N towards the water tower.

Château de Marconnay
Guided tours pms, by appointment. 1€. 05 49 53 53 70.
This fortified 15C building still has its original gate and drawbridge, and seigniorial residence built after 1650.

Return to Sanxay.

Sanxay
Site Gallo-Romain – *Open mid-May–mid-Sept 9.30am–12.30pm, 2–6.30pm; rest of year Sun–Fri 10am–12.30pm, 2–5.30pm. Closed 1 Jan, 1 May, 1 Nov, 11 Nov, 25 Dec. 5€ (under 26 years no charge). 05 49 53 61 48.*
This is a huge rural sanctuary, which occupied 25ha/62 acres on both sides of the Vonne. Very popular, judging by the size of the buildings that have been discovered, this major place of worship, spa and entertainment centre, built in the 2CAD, was gradually abandoned by the 4C.
On the site can be seen the remains of an amphitheatre, which could seat around 6 500 spectators. On the opposite bank stand the walls of the sanctuary.
The path leads to the ruins of a temple that once overlooked the sanctuary.

Continue on the D 3.

Ménigoute
This village has a 16C Hosanna cross, but it is best known for the International Festival of Ornithological film *(05 49 69 90 09; www.menigoute-festival.org)*.
The **Musée d'Arts et Traditions populaires Raoul-Royer** houses a collection of art and rural traditions, including the reconstruction of an early 20C classroom *(open Jul–mid-Sept daily 3–6pm; 1€ (children no charge); curator 05 49 69 00 38)*.

The D 58 and the D 121 lead back to St-Maixent-l'École.

Towards the end of the tour, look out for views overlooking the town from the coteau d'Exireuil.

Parthenay★

Deux-Sèvres

Parthenay is the capital of the Gâtine region, an agricultural area renowned for its sheep farming, dairy products, apple orchards and above all cattle-breeding. The cattle market, held every Wednesday in the Bellevue district is the second largest in France. The town is also home to a number of hi-tech industries in the Parthenay Palais des Congrès. From Pont Neuf there is a fine view★ of the oldest part of Parthenay.

- **Population:** 10 494
- **Michelin Map:** 322: E-5
- **Info:** 8 r. de la Vau-St-Jacques, Parthenay. 05 49 64 24 24. www.cc-parthenay.fr.
- **Location:** Parthenay is sited picturesquely on a rocky spur circled by the River Thouet, 43km/27mi NE of Niort.
- **Parking:** There are two car parks in the Old Town, one near the porte de la Citadelle and the other near the château.
- **Don't Miss:** The view from the Pont Neuf; Pont and porte St-Jacques; r. de la Vau-St-Jacques; Église Notre-Dame-de-la-Couldre; the Musée Municipal Georges-Turpin.
- **Kids:** Mouton Village, Vasles; Jardin des Histoires, Pougne-Hérisson.

WALKING TOUR

MEDIEVAL TOWN

1hr. The walk starts from the town hall.

Citadel

Old Town. Guided tours from tourist office Jul–Aug Mon 2.30pm, Thu 4pm. 5€. 05 49 64 24 24.

Perched high up at the extremity of the promontory, the citadel protected the castle keep, the seigneurial residence and two churches behind its massive ramparts (12C). Down below, the fortifications were strengthened by the natural barriers of the river and the Vaux-St-Jacques Valley. In the Middle Ages Parthenay had the reputation of being impregnable.

Porte de la Citadelle (or porte de l'Horloge; *1 r. de la Citadelle*) leads into the fortress. Farther on along rue de la Citadelle, on your right are the collegiate church of Ste-Croix (12C; *4 r. de la Citadelle*) then **Église Notre-Dame-de-la-Couldre** (*28 r. de la Citadelle*). The street leads to the vast esplanade where the castle used to stand.

Take the steps down and follow the narrow r. du Château.

Pont and Porte St-Jacques★

1 r. de la Vau St-Jacques.

The narrow 13C bridge across the River Thouet was, and is, the entrance to the town from the north. A drawbridge unites it with the St-Jacques gateway.

Rue de la Vau-St-Jacques★

This was once Parthenay's main shopping street and links the two town gateways, porte St-Jacques and porte de la Citadelle. The street has some ancient half-timbered houses with projecting upper storeys and wide bays at street level, marking the location of former shops and stalls.

The road continues up through place du Vau-Vert (Green Vale Square), skirting the walled citadel.

Musée Municipal Georges-Turpin

1 r. de la Vau-St-Jacques.

Open May Mon and Wed–Fri 10am–noon, 2–6pm; mid-Jun–Sept 10am–noon, 2–6pm, Sun 2.30–6.30pm; Oct–Apr Wed–Fri 10am–noon, 2–6pm. Closed public holidays. 2€ (1st Wed of month no charge). 05 49 64 53 73.

Housed in the **Maison des Cultures de Pays**, a contemporary building, the museum has a collection of animated

Pilgrims' Way

In medieval times Parthenay was one of the important stops on The Way of St James. Arriving from Thouars, the pilgrims would go first to the church hospital (a chapel still exists on the road to Thouars). Having left there those who had fallen ill on the journey, the pilgrims would cross the bridge, go through the fortified gateway and enter the town. Once they had found accommodation in the taverns of rue de la Vaux-St-Jacques they would then pay ritual visits to the local sanctuaries (there were 16), churches such as Notre-Dame-de-la-Couldre and Ste-Croix. The pilgrims were then free to disperse among the taverns in the town or to admire the graceful women of Parthenay, who were celebrated in song for their looks.

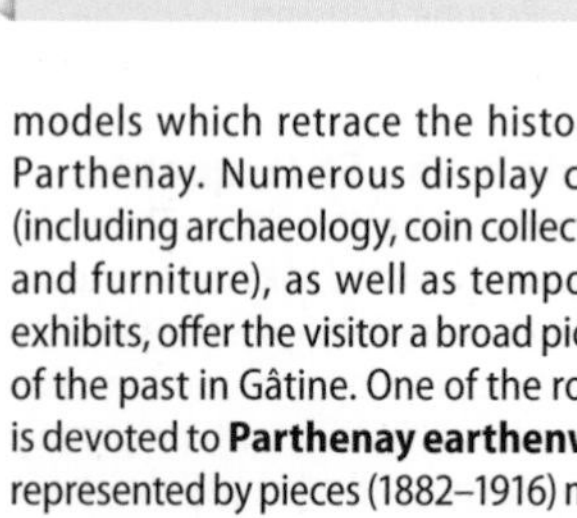

models which retrace the history of Parthenay. Numerous display cases (including archaeology, coin collections and furniture), as well as temporary exhibits, offer the visitor a broad picture of the past in Gâtine. One of the rooms is devoted to **Parthenay earthenware** represented by pieces (1882–1916) made by the Jouneau-Amirault duo, who revived this popular art.

EXCURSIONS

Parthenay-le-Vieux

1.5km/0.9mi W of Parthenay.

An octagonal tower soars up from the church of the priory of Parthenay-le-Vieux, founded by the monks of La Chaise-Dieu.

Église St-Pierre

Its Poitou Romanesque façade is outstanding for its symmetry. The portal and its two blind arcades, surrounded by three bays, have three archivolts. The uniform interior has a barrel-vaulted nave, the octagonal bell tower rises up from the intersection of the transept, and at each side of the choir there are capitals carved with lions and goats.

Pougne-Hérisson

15km/9.3mi W. Follow the Parthenay signposts marked "Le Nombril du Monde".

Situated on the ancient salt route, this village was once the most important in the Gâtine. In the 1990s the storyteller and actor Yannick Jaulin created the "Nombril du Monde"; today the village is known for its festival and themed park.

Jardin des Histoires★

Open Apr–Jun and Sept–Oct Sat–Sun and public holidays 1.30–7.30pm; Jul–Aug daily 1.30–7.30pm. 7€ (children 5€). 05 49 64 19 19. www.nombril.com.

In this imaginary universe you participate in inventing myths and stories.

Vasles

20km/12.4mi SE on the D 59.

The road crosses the Terrier St-Martin, the highest point of the *département*, from where there is a fine view of the *bocage*.

Mouton Village

r. de la Butée. Open Apr–mid May daily 11am–6pm, mid May–June, Sept–Nov Wed, Sun, public holidays and school holidays 1.30–6pm, July–Aug daily 10am-7pm. 9€ (4–16 years 6€). 05 49 69 12 12. www.moutonvillage.fr.

A woodland (6ha/15 acres), is the setting for this tourist park dedicated to sheep farming. After a short stop at the Maison du Mouton to watch the slide show, continue the visit, equipped with an audioguide, and discover the 22 different breeds of sheep that inhabit the Jardin des agneaux. The different stages of processing the sheep's wool is explained at La Place des 1 001 Laines, and ewe's cheese can be tasted at the Bergerie cheese shop.

DRIVING TOUR

5 THE VALLÉE DU THOUET★

80km/50mi. Allow half a day.

This valley is dotted with old mills and ancient bridges, brought to life by cows and sheep. Very popular with fishermen, the Thouet is brimming with fish.

Leave Parthenay heading E on the N 149 towards Poitiers. Just after the large crossroads, turn left onto a small road for La Peyratte.

La Peyratte

This village has a Hosanna cross near the 12C church. To the north, a small road leads to the Forge à Fer.

Leave La Peyratte E on the D 165. After 2km/1.2mi, turn left onto the Lhoumois road. At the exit of the village, turn left.

Gourgé

Situated on the left riverbank, Gourgé was a staging point along the Poitiers–Nantes Roman route. Crossing a Roman bridge over the Thouet, you reach a fortified church, dating from the 10C and 12C. Inside there are polychrome coats of arms. Leaving Gourgé, there are beautiful views from the road which passes along the Right Bank of the Thouet.

St-Loup-Lamairé

Château de St-Loup-sur-Thouet – *Open Easter–Journées du Patrimonie Sat–Sun and public holidays 2–7pm. Guided tour of château Jul–Aug 4pm. 9€ château and gardens, 7€ gardens (children no charge). 05 49 64 81 73.*

Due to its strategic position at the confluence of the Thouet and the Cébron rivers, from the 11C St-Loup has been important as a defensive military post. In the 14C the Black Prince imprisoned Jean II le Bon in the keep. The construction of the present-day château (1609–26) is attributed to Claude Gouffier and his son Louis (see OIRON), then Governor of Poitou. All that remains of the original feudal fortress is the square tower and keep, which has been renovated and converted into *chambres d'hôtes*.

The château has preserved the archives of its park and gardens as they existed from the Renaissance to the Revolution. In 1992 an ambitious project was initiated which aims to re-create the gardens as they looked in the 18C.

Houses, dating from the 15C and 16C, brick and timber framed, line the **Grande Rue**.

Leave the village heading N on the D 121.

Airvault

Situated at 24km/14.9mi northeast of Parthenay, Airvault overlooks the Right Bank of the Thouet. The centre comprises the rue des Halles, the place St-Pierre and the place du Minage.

Église Abbatiale St-Pierre – *Open Mon–Sat and Sun pm. Guided tours available mid-Jun–mid-Sept. 05 49 64 78 92.* This remarkable church has been built in limestone. Its architecture unites the Poitevin (12C) and Angevin (13C) styles. The façade has been designed in the Romanesque Poitevin style with column-buttresses. However, the 13C belfry is from the Angevin School.

Like many churches along The Way of St James pilgrim route, Airvault church was constructed to facilitate the circulation of pilgrims inside the building.

Abbaye-Musée des Arts et Traditions Populaires – *10 r. de la Gendarmerie. Open May–Sept pms, rest of year Wed pm. 3€ (children 1€). 05 49 70 84 07.* Restored by volunteers, these impressive monastery buildings (11C–17C) now house interesting collections relating to the everyday life of the Poitevin people from the 19C to the early 20C. Before leaving, take a look at the prison (12C), embedded in the 15C ramparts, and the abbey chapel, situated over the 11C cellars. The wine cellar houses an old loom, which is in working order, and exhibitions.

Vieux Château d'Airvault – Crowning the hill, the Vieux château has fortifications with three square towers.

Underground Fountain – Situated under the place du Minage, this former public fountain was covered over in the 19C for security reasons. A narrow staircase leads to a vaulted room, from where the St Pierre stream flows down to the wells that once supplied the town with water.
Pont de Vernay – *1km/0.6mi to the S.* The road runs along the hillside by the Thouet. This 12C bridge was built by the Augustins d'Airvault. From the bridge there is a charming **view**.

Leave Airvault N on the D 121.

St-Généroux
This village is named after a monk from St-Jouin-de-Marnes. The church, built in the 9C–10C, is a fine example of pre-Romanesque architecture, apart from the façade. Remarkable workmanship from the 13C, the Vieux Pont was built by the monks from the neighbouring abbey of St-Jouin.

Leave St-Généroux E on the D 147.

Église de St-Jouin-de-Marnes★
Exterior – This former abbey church, built from 1095 to 1130, represents Romanesque Poitevin architecture at its best. Its façade is decorated with sculptured archivolts and has a triangular gable. The portals have archivolts decorated with plants, masks, shells and small scenes referring to the months. The bays are surrounded by high reliefs. Inside, it is pure Poitevin with three naves, and blind arcades around the ambulatory and the choir.

Leave St-Jouin-de-Marnes S on the D 37, then turn left onto the D 46.

Moncontour
The village of Moncontour is famous for its massive 12C keep.

Leave Moncontour N on the D 19.

Ouzilly-Vignolles
This village, in the heart of the Dive wetlands, partially drained, has an ethnological heritage unique in Poitou-Charentes: traditional mud houses.
Logis Terra Villa – *Open mid-Jul–mid-Aug Sat–Sun, phone for times. 2.50€ (children 1.30€). 05 49 22 61 61.* The village's houses, barns and sheds were constructed by laying successive layers of cob (mixture of earth, reeds, aggregates and water), without foundation or formwork systems.

Return to the D 19. At Sauzeau, turn right on to the D 162.

Oiron★
See p352.
Leaving the village from the eastern side, the road goes through the Parc d'Oiron.

Cross the D 37, then at Maranzais, take the D 172 crossing the Thouet.

Thouars★
See opposite.

Leave Thouars heading S on the D 938, which returns to Parthenay.

ADDRESSES

STAY

Chambre d'hotes Château de Tennessus – *79350 Amailloux (9km/5.6mi NW). 05 49 95 50 60. www.tennessus.com. Closed 24–31 Dec. 3 rooms.* A 14C castle complete with moats, a draw-bridge and spiral staircases. Sleep in a four-poster bed in one of the medieval guest rooms. One self-catering cottage with a pool.

EAT

La Truffade – *14 pl. du 11-Novembre. 05 49 64 02 26. Closed Tue–Wed and 3 wks spring and autumn.* Serves copious portions of hearty Auvergne specialities.

SHOPPING

Marché de Bellevue – *Champ de Foire. Wed morning.* A cattle markethas been held here since the 12C. Come to see the local Parthenaise breed traded.

Thouars★

Deux-Sèvres

The best view of the site of this Old Town is from the southern approach (D 39), across the bridge over the River Thouet. From Pont Neuf (New Bridge) there is a view of the rocky promontory and of the roofs, a mixture of Romanesque tiles and Angevin slates, of the houses clustered below the castle walls. Celebrations in traditional costume bring the town to life in the summer.

- **Population:** 10 256
- **Michelin Map:** 322: E-3
- **Info:** 3 bd Pierre Curie, Thouars. ℘05 49 66 17 65. www.pays-thouarsais.com.
- **Location:** Thouars is located N of Parthenay and NW of Poitiers.
- **Parking:** Parking is available on the outskirts, as well as near pl. St-Médard in the town centre.
- **Don't Miss:** The façade of Église St-Médard; the houses in the Old Town.

A BIT OF HISTORY

Origins

For many years Thouars remained faithful to the Plantagenets but the town eventually fell to **Bertrand du Guesclin** (1320–80), one of the generals who chased the English from the region, after a memorable siege in 1372. Having purchased Thouars from the Amboise family, Louis XI stayed here several times, and his wife, Margaret of Scotland, expressed a wish to be buried here. Charles VIII gave the town to the House of La Trémoille, and the family remained seigneurs of Thouars until the Revolution. The Protestant faith had been embraced by the inhabitants; after the revocation of the Edict of Nantes, Thouars lost half of its population.

Thouars was the birthplace of the medieval general Louis de La Trémoille. In 1619 his heir Henri de La Trémoille married Marie de la Tour d'Auvergne, sister of Turenne. She razed the old Gothic château-fort to build the present château.

WALKING TOUR

OLD TOWN

Allow 1hr.

The walk starts from pl. St-Médard, where you can park the car.

Église St-Médard★

pl. St-Médard. Open daily 10am–6pm. ℘05 49 68 16 25.

The church, standing adjacent to a 15C square tower with overhanging cor-

View of Thouars

M. Thiery/MICHELIN

ner turrets, is a Romanesque building despite the Gothic rose window adorning its fine Poitevin **west front**★★. The extensively decorated entrance is surmounted by a Christ in Glory worshipped by angels. The archivolts – the last one breaks the ranks with a resurrected Christ Rising from the Tomb – spring from historiated capitals depicting the Punishment of the Vices. Splendid effigies of St Peter, St Paul, the Prophets and the Sibyls stand above the lateral arcades.

The Romanesque doorway with festooned arches on the north side of the church is of Moorish inspiration. Inside, the three original Romanesque naves were replaced in the 15C by a single nave with lowered vaulting.

Follow r. du Château, which prolongs r. St-Médard.

The two streets once formed the town's high street and led to the old bridge.

Old Houses★

Rue du Château boasts two brick-and-timber houses including the Hostellerie St-Médard, flanked by a vaulted passageway, and several corbelled façades beneath sharp, steep gables – notably that of the 15C Hôtel des Trois-Rois (Three Kings Mansion) at no **11**.

It was here that the future Louis XI slept when he was still *dauphin* (heir to the throne). A moulded corbel on the façade supports a bartizan where guards could mount to keep watch over the street.

Opening onto the esplanade, that was once the seigneurial courtyard, are the Chapelle Notre-Dame and the Château.

Chapelle Notre-Dame

Rond point du 19 mars 1962. Guided tours available from tourist office. 5.10€. 05 49 68 16 25.

This chapel was built above a series of crypts, one of which is still the family tomb of the La Trémoilles. The superb Flamboyant Gothic façade is surmounted by a Renaissance gallery with shell decorations.

Château (Collège Marie-de-La-Tour-d'Auvergne)

1 pl. du Château. Guided tour (2hrs) Apr–Jun and Sept Sun 3.30pm; Jul–Aug Tue, Thu and Sun 3.30pm. 5.10€. 05 49 68 06 44.

A domed pavilion housing a monumental staircase projects from the central block and there are two other pavilions at the extremities.

Walk up av. de La-Trémoille to Abbaye St-Laon.

Ancienne Abbaye St-Laon

pl. St-Laon. Guided tours Jun–Aug Wed, please contact tourist office for exact times. 5.10€. 05 49 68 16 25.

This former abbey first staffed by Benedictine monks and then by Augustinians includes a 12C–15C church with a square Romanesque belfry. Margaret of Scotland is buried here. The old (17C) monastic buildings house the town hall.

Follow r. Régnier-Desmarais, r. St-Médard and turn right towards Chapelle Jeanne-d'Arc.

Chapelle Jeanne-d'Arc

r. du Jeu de Paume. Open Tue–Sun 2–6pm. No charge. 05 49 66 66 52.

Built in 1892, the chapel now houses regular exhibitions of contemporary art.

Walk along r. du Guesclin to porte au Prévôt.

Porte au Prévôt

This is the gateway forced by Du Guesclin when he penetrated the town in 1372 to end the siege. It is framed by two ravelin towers on octagonal bases.

Follow r. du Président-Tyndo.

Tour du Prince-de-Galles

r. Felix Gellusseau. Open Jul–Aug 2.30–6.30pm. No charge. 05 49 66 66 52.

The Prince of Wales Tower is round and massive and capped with small bartizans. It has also gone under the name

of *Faux-Sauniers*, in reference to unscrupulous salt dealers who, spurred on by an unpopular salt tax, were locked up in narrow cages visible on the second floor of the tower by the "salt police".

The r. Prince-de-Galles and r. Saugé lead back to pl. St-Médard.

EXCURSIONS

Argenton-les-Vallées

20km/12.4mi to the W on the D 759. *13 r. Porte Virèche, 79150 Argenton-les-Vallées. 05 49 65 96 56. www.tourisme-pays-thouarsais.fr.*
Frescoes and Romanesque sculptures feature highly in the religious monuments of Argenton-les-Vallées. This small village is the ideal spot for walks.

Église St-Gilles
Built in granite, it has an outstanding Romanesque portal whose archivolts are sculpted with elongated figures. To the left of the archivolt, a scene depicts the parable of the feast of Dives, while on the right, two other scenes show the Damned cast into the jaws of a monster (Hell) and the chosen in the bosom of Abraham (Heaven). On the capitals imaginary animals symbolise lust. Inside, there are brick and stone arches from the 13C and 15C, and 11C bays.

Chapelle St-Georges
Situated near the ruins of the medieval château where Philippe de Commynes (1447–1511), Seneschal of Poitou and famous columnist, once lived, it has frescoes (discovered in the 20C).

Chemin de la Salette
About 100m/328ft S of the Thouars and Angers crossroads, walk along a path to the Salette oratory. 15min there and back.
This walk provides views of Argenton-les-Vallées and the Lac d'Hautibus.

Lac d'Hautibus
Nestling at the bottom of the Ouère Valley, this artificial lake was created in 1969. Various activities on offer.

Moulin des Plaines

1km/0.6mi W along the D 759. 05 49 65 70 32 only during the Journées du Patrimoine.
This 18C windmill, now in working order, has wooden sails (Berton system) that are turned to catch the wind by orientating the roof with a large pole. Admire the frescoes.

Château d'Ebaupinaye

2.5km/1.5mi NE on the D 759 (towards Thouars), then the D 31.
Ebaupinaye is a 15C château built in a pretty pink shade of granite. It has a moat and four corner towers.

Pont de Grifferus

5.5km/3.4mi E on the D 759 (towards Thouars), then the D 181.
Beautiful view down over the Argenton gushing between the schist gorge.

ADDRESSES

STAY

Hôtellerie St-Jean – *25 rte de Parthenay. 05 49 96 12 60. www.hotellerie-st-jean.fr. 18 rooms. 7€. Restaurant. Closed Sun evening and Feb.* Enjoy the view over the Old Town of Thouars. Rooms are decorated impeccably. Serves classic dishes in the smart dining room.

EAT

Le Logis de Pompois – *13 r. de la Gosselinière, Ste-Verge (5km/3.1mi NW of Thouars. Take direction Doué-la-Fontaine and Pompois). 05 49 96 27 84. www.logis-de-pompois.com. Closed Sun evening, Mon–Tue and 4–10 Jan.* Enjoy outdoor dining in summer at this old winery dating from the 18C and the 19C. In the winter, guests eat in the elegant dining room. Fine cuisine.

SHOPPING

Local speciality – **Le Duhomard** – Invented at the beginning of the 1920s, Le Duhomard is an apéritif made from wine mixed with orange zest, quinine and gentian roots.

Oiron★

Deux-Sèvres

The small village of Oiron is the home of two splendid but little-known architectural monuments: the château of the Gouffier family and a delightful Renaissance collegiate church.

- **Population:** 954
- **Michelin Map:** 322: F-3
- **Info:** 3 bis bd Pierre Curie, Thouars. 05 49 66 17 65. www.tourisme-pays-thouarsais.fr.
- **Location:** The village is located between Thouars and Loudun.

A BIT OF HISTORY

The Gouffier Family

Artus Gouffier, chamberlain to François I, accompanied his sovereign to Italy and was so overwhelmed by Italian art that in the early 16C, he began building a church in the Renaissance style. At the same time he organised the construction of a tower and a wing of the château.

Both church and château were completed under the direction of his eldest child, Claude, who also began collecting the works of art to be displayed in the residence. Master of the King's Horses and extremely wealthy, Claude Gouffier held the title of Comte de Caravas: in legend he became the Marquis de Carabas (the fictitious title given to his impoverished master by *Puss in Boots*, the hero of Charles Perrault's fairy tale of 1697).

In 1705 Mme de Montespan acquired the château; she stayed here often until her death in 1707.

Part of a project combining **contemporary art** and historical monuments, the château now houses a collection of specially commissioned works, called Curios & Mirabilia (Curiosities & Wonders, 1993). The contemporary artists drew inspiration from the 16C fashion of cabinets of curiosities – or miscellanea, assembled by scientifically minded people – and the theme of the five senses and four elements, as well as the château itself.

CHÂTEAU★★

Open daily Jun–Sept 10.30am–6pm; Oct–May 10.30am–5pm (last admission 1hr before closing). Closed 1 Jan, 1 May, 1 Nov, 11 Nov, 25 Dec. 7€. 05 49 96 51 25. www.oiron.fr.

Beyond two small pavilions stands the main body of the château, a central block flanked by two square pavilions crowned by balustrades, and two wings framing the central courtyard.

On the left, the first-floor wing, begun by Artus Gouffier in 1515, was completed by his son Claude. Of Gothic inspiration, the **Galerie des Chevaux**, with its basket-handle arcades, is surmounted by marble medallions depicting Roman emperors in profile. On the walls of the gallery, the Master of the King's Horses commissioned paintings of Henri II's best mounts. After many years all that remained was a yellowish colour where they hung on the wall, and the brands of the stud farms (still visible) where the horses were bred. In 1992 these ochre panels framed by the arcades were painted in pure, dancing lines by Georg Ettl; the horses they depict trot down the length of the gallery.

A beautiful staircase, its ramp formed by the spiral moulding of the central newel, leads to the next floor forming a majestic **gallery**★★. Here, 14 superb paintings of remarkable composition and draughtsmanship, their colours now faded, line the walls with subjects taken from the history of Troy and the Aeneid. The Louis XIII ceiling was commissioned by Louis Gouffier. Its 1 670 caisson panels depicting various subjects are like an overhead encyclopedia. The gallery leads to the Pavilion des Trophées and the former chapel of Claude Gouffier.

The **central pavilion**, begun by Louis Gouffier and completed by La Feuillade, still contains its original 16C works. The admirable Renaissance staircase, with its hollow central newel and straight flight of stairs, was inspired by that of Azay-le-Rideau. The **Salle du Roi** (also known as

Richly painted ceiling in Château d'Oiron

S. Sauvignier/MICHELIN

the Salle des Armes), has a remarkable polychrome ceiling, dizzying in its multitude of images. Rather than the usual hunting trophies, the walls here are hung with surprising works by Daniel Spoerri, 12 *Corps en Morceaux* (1993), compositions of objects reflecting the diversity of nature, chaos controlled.

The **Pavillon du Roi** houses two rooms with the decorative exuberance characteristic of the Louis XIII style. The King's Chamber has an extraordinary ceiling overloaded with heavy gilt motifs framing painted caissons.

The Salon des Ondes houses the highly original *Étuis d'Or* by Hubert Duprat (1993), gold and pearl cases, which appear to be insects in metamorphosis.

The tower's Cabinet des Monstres includes imaginary animals created by Thomas Grünfeld in 1992.

Sol Lewitt's Wall Drawings Room on the second floor is worth a detour and so are the ground floor rooms.

In the **Tour de Madame de Montespan** *(south wing)*, from the **Salles des Ouvrières de la Reine** wafts a penetrating fragrance, emanating from a wall of beeswax erected by Wolfgang Laib. Under the domed tower is the *Decentre Acentre* (1992), by Tom Shannon. The smooth aluminium forms fit perfectly into the luminous, round room: a disc is suspended from the ceiling, slicing a sphere in two (the upper half is floating on a magnetic field), creating an image reminiscent of planets and galaxies.

COLLEGIATE CHURCH★

r. de l'Église. ✆05 49 96 51 26.

The Renaissance façade includes twinned doors and a large arch surmounted by a pediment bearing the arms of the Gouffier family.

In the transept lie the family tombs, executed by sculptors from Tuscany named Juste, who had settled in Tours. The two largest date from 1537; the smaller pair, from the studio of Jean II Juste, from 1559. In the northern arm of the transept is the tomb of Philippine de Montmorency, second wife of Guillaume Gouffier, who died in 1516. Nearby is the mausoleum of her son, the Amiral de Bonnivet, killed in 1525 while fighting with François I during the French defeat after the Battle of Pavia.

The tomb of Artus Gouffier, founder of the church and brother of the admiral, is in the south transept, beside that of his son Claude; the figure of Artus is clothed in armour. A 16C painting by Raphael represents John the Baptist.

The seigneurial chapels, on either side of the chancel, are decorated in the Renaissance style. The south chapel contains a 16C portrait of St Jerome; the painting of the *Holy Family* in the north chapel dates from the 18C. The keystones in each chapel are very elaborately worked. Also noteworthy are the 16C statues of the Apostles on the high-altar reredos, the portrait of Claude Gouffier on the north wall of the chancel, and a fine *Resurrection*, in the Flemish Mannerist style of the 16C, on the south wall.

Bressuire

Deux-Sèvres

The low houses, roofed with convex tiles, cling to the hillside on the banks of the River Dolo. The capital of the Vendée *bocage* paid heavily for its Royalist alliance and still bears the scars of its turbulent past. Today, it is a major centre for cattle breeding and the food industry. It is particularly reputed for its local beef.

- **Population:** 18 225
- **Michelin Map:** 355: D-3
- **Info:** pl. de l'Hôtel de Ville, Bressuire. ℘05 49 65 10 27. www.tourisme-bocage.com.
- **Location:** Bressuire is 32km/20mi NW of Parthanay.
- **Don't Miss:** The romantic château ruins.
- **Timing:** Allow 2hrs to visit the town.

THE TOWN

Église Notre-Dame

Its architecture is similar to that of sanctuaries in the Loire Valley and the Plantagenet style of the 13C: a single nave, Romanesque portals and capitals. Similarly the late Gothic chancel displays the influence of the Angevin style. The tower (16C) unites Gothic and Renaissance styles *(top section)*.

Musée municipal

pl. de l'Hôtel-de-Ville. Open during exhibitions, contact tourist office. No charge. ℘05 49 74 46 30 or 05 49 65 10 27.

On the place de l'Hôtel-de-Ville stands a small museum dedicated to local history. Inside, the displays include a collection of regional porcelain, and mementos of the Vendée Wars.

Château

Guided tours Tue and Sat 3pm. 4€ (under 18 years 3€). Temporary exhibitions, phone for times. ℘05 49 74 46 30 or 05 49 65 10 27.

Once the headquarters of the powerful Barony of Beaumont-Bressuire, it comprises two walls punctuated by 48 semicircular towers. Following the outer wall (13C) to the left, visitors are rewarded with a view of curtain walls and crumbling towers. The inner wall dates back to the 11C. A postern leads into the main courtyard. Burned down during the Revolution, the 15C seigniorial residence, also in ruins, has been replaced by a Troubadour-style building.

EXCURSIONS

Mauléon

22km/13.7mi NW on the N 149.

The main road leads to the entrance gate of the former feudal castle; pass through here to access the esplanade.

Musée du BRHAM

Open Mon–Fri 10am–noon, 2–6pm, Sat–Sun and public holidays 2.30–6pm. 2€ (under 16 yearsno charge). ℘05 49 81 86 23.

Housed in the former Abbaye de La Trinité (17C–18C) the museum's collection, extending over two floors, is dedicated to local geology and prehistory, the Vendée Wars and regional heritage.

St-Aubin-de-Baubigné

26km/16.2mi NW on the N 149, then the D 154.

A statue, by Falguière (1895), stands in homage to Henri de La Rochejaquelein (1772–94), who is buried here, near to the remains of his cousin the Vendée chief Lescure.

Château de la Dubelière

2km/1.2mi N of St-Aubin-de-Baubigné on the D 153.

The château is mainly in ruins, after being destroyed by fire in 1793. It is here that Henri de La Rochejaquelein was born in 1772. At the head of the army, Catholic and Royal, after a stint in Brittany, he was killed by a Republican Bleu at Nuaillé, near Cholet, in 1794.

The Vendée has been the battleground for several turbulent uprisings from the Hundred Years' War (1337–1453), to the French Wars of Religion (1562–98), and the Vendée Wars (1793–96). Today these lush meadows and moors, with a backdrop of low-lying hills, form an unspoiled landscape scattered with farms, orchards and agricultural crops. A true wonder for nature lovers, the *bocage*, criss-crossed by hedgerows, hides a wealth of bird species. The only battles that take place now, are re-enactments at the spectacular Cinéscénie historical theme park, at Puy du Fou.

Heroes of the Vendée Wars

François Charette (2 May 1763–26 March 1796,) a French nobleman, soldier and politician, served in the French Navy, notably during the American War of Independence. After leaving the navy in 1789, a few years later he returned to live at his home in La Garnache. He protected King Louis XVI and Marie Antoinette from the mob in Paris during an attack on the Tuileries Palace, where the King resided. In 1793 Charette was asked by the peasants to become their leader during the Vendée Wars. He accepted and fought many battles alongside the Armée Catholique et Royale. However, he was eventually captured outside La Chabotterie and taken to Nantes for trial. He was sentenced to death and was shot by firing squad.

Jean-Nicolas Stofflet (1751–23 February 1796) was a mainstream Vendéan leader against the Republicans. The son of a miller, he first became a soldier for the Swiss Guard, and later gamekeeper for Count Colbert-Maulévrier. He joined the Vendée Army and serving under Elbée, distinguished himself in several major battles. He succeeded Henri de la Rochejaquelein as commander-in-chief in 1794. Later that same year he was taken prisoner by the Republic, sentenced to death, and shot at Angers.

Louis Lazare Hoche (24 June 1768–19 September 1797), born at Versailles, served first as a soldier for the Gardes françaises, and later became general of the Revolutionary army. In 1794 he was appointed to command the army against the Royalists in the Vendée. He successfully defeated the counterrevolutionaries, and restored some order to the region by applying the Convention's conciliatory measures. He finally died of consumption at Wetzlar in Germany.

Highlights

1. The historic extravaganza at **Le Puy du Fou** (p358)
2. A retro train trip with the family starting from **Les Herbiers** (p360)
3. Take the drive from **La Chabotterie** and retrace the retreat of the Vendée troops (p367)
4. A stroll around the splendid **Parc Floral**, near **St Cyr-en-Talmondais** (p371)
5. The haunting tour of the **Centre Minieur de Faymoreau** and its mining village (p376)

Les Secret de la Lance, Puy du Fou

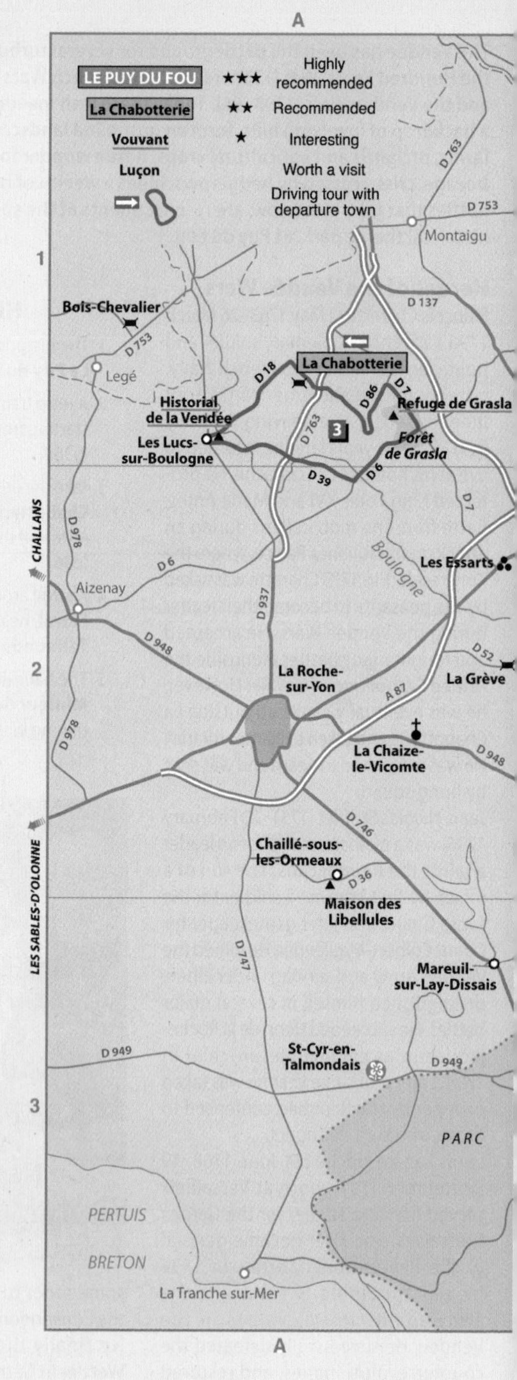
A
LE PUY DU FOU
★★★ Highly recommended
La Chabotterie
★★ Recommended
Vouvant
★ Interesting
Luçon
Worth a visit
Driving tour with departure town
1
2
3
Bois-Chevalier
Legé
D 753
D 763
Montaigu
D 137
La Chabotterie
D 18
D 86
D 7
Refuge de Grasla
Historial de la Vendée
Les Lucs-sur-Boulogne
3
Forêt de Grasla
D 39
D 6
CHALLANS
D 978
D 6
Aizenay
Boulogne
Les Essarts
D 937
D 948
La Roche-sur-Yon
D 52
La Grève
A 87
La Chaize-le-Vicomte
D 948
LES SABLES-D'OLONNE
D 746
Chaillé-sous-les-Ormeaux
D 36
Maison des Libellules
D 747
Mareuil-sur-Lay-Dissais
St-Cyr-en-Talmondais
D 949
PARC
PERTUIS
BRETON
La Tranche sur-Mer

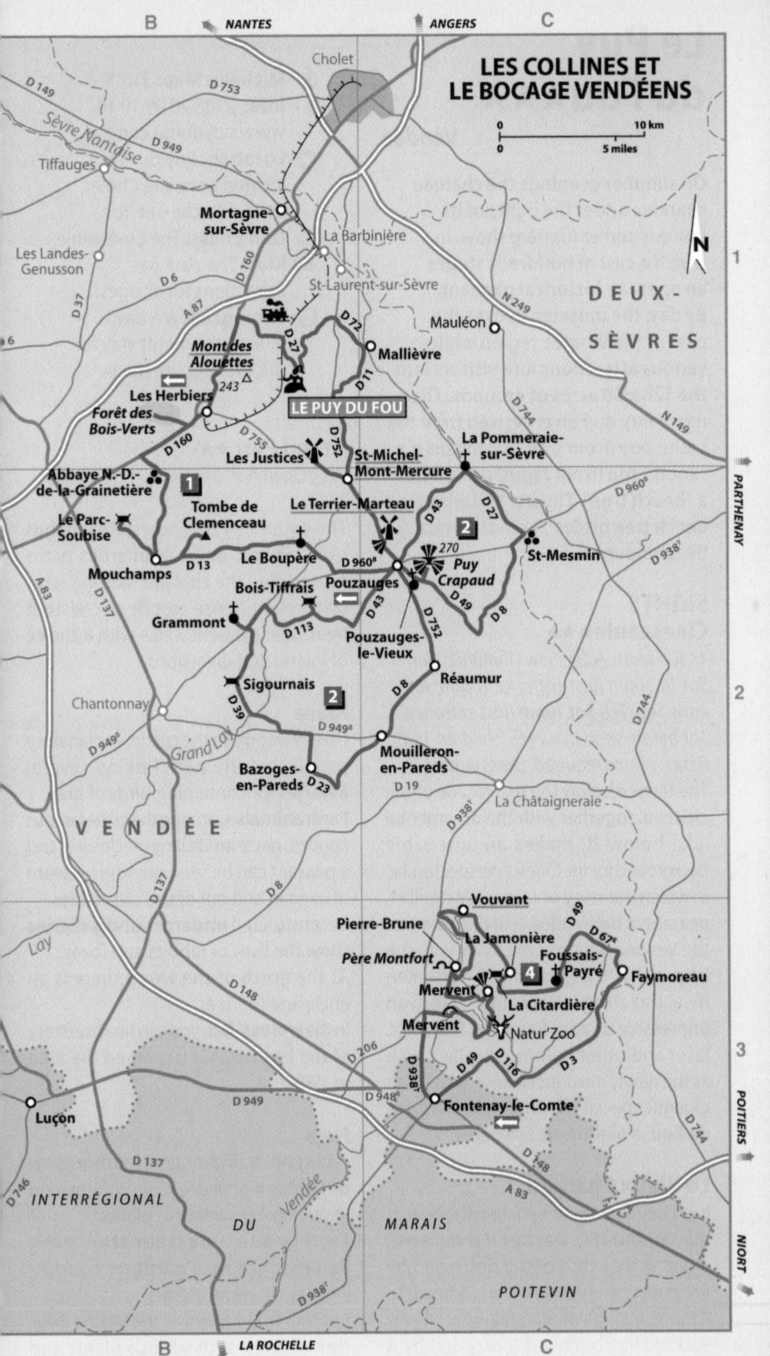
LES COLLINES ET LE BOCAGE VENDÉENS
NANTES
ANGERS
PARTHENAY
POITIERS
NIORT
LA ROCHELLE
Cholet
Tiffauges
Mortagne-sur-Sèvre
La Barbinière
Les Landes-Genusson
St-Laurent-sur-Sèvre
Mauléon
Mallièvre
Mont des Alouettes
LE PUY DU FOU
Les Herbiers
Forêt des Bois-Verts
Les Justices
St-Michel-Mont-Mercure
La Pommeraie-sur-Sèvre
Abbaye N.-D.-de-la-Grainetière
Tombe de Clemenceau
Le Parc-Soubise
Le Terrier-Marteau
Puy Crapaud
St-Mesmin
Mouchamps
Le Boupère
Pouzauges
Bois-Tiffrais
Grammont
Pouzauges-le-Vieux
Réaumur
Sigournais
Chantonnay
Grand Lay
Bazoges-en-Pareds
Mouilleron-en-Pareds
La Châtaigneraie
VENDÉE
DEUX-SÈVRES
Vouvant
Pierre-Brune
La Jamonière
Père Montfort
Foussais-Payré
Faymoreau
Mervent
La Citardière
Natur'Zoo
Fontenay-le-Comte
Luçon
Lay
Vendée
INTERRÉGIONAL DU MARAIS POITEVIN

Le Puy du Fou★★★

Vendée

On summer evenings the château sparkles under the lights of its famous *son et lumière* show, in which a cast of hundreds stages an open-air historical pageant. By day, the museum evokes the past of the Vendée region while various attractions lure visitors into the 12ha/30 acres of grounds. The name Puy du Fou is derived from the Latin: *puy* (from *podium*) means a "knoll"; *fou* (from *fagus*) designates a "beech tree". Thus, a "hill where a beech tree grows", or more lyrically, Beechmount.

- **Michelin Map:** 316: K-6
- **Info:** 08 20 09 10 10. www.puydufou.com.
- **Location:** Puy du Fou is located between Cholet and La-Roche-sur-Yon.
- **Don't Miss:** The Cinéscénie.
- **Kids:** The park has attractions for all ages.
- **Timing:** Allow a day, plus an overnight stay for the evening spectacle.

SIGHTS

Cinéscénie★★★

13 500 seats. Show (1hr40min) Jun Sat 10.30pm (last entrance 10pm); Jul–early Sept Fri–Sat 10pm (last entrance 1hr before show). 24€ (children 15€). Reservations required. Dress warmly.

The terrace below the rear façade of the château, together with the ornamental lake below it, makes an agreeable background for the Cinéscénie spectacular, in which the story of Jacques Maupillier, peasant of the Vendée, and the history of the Vendée region come to life with the help of 1 200 actors and 50 horsemen in a dazzling show, including an impressive array of fountains, fireworks, laser and other lighting displays such as the newly introduced Rêve show with gigantic special effects; and **Les Orgues de Feu**, a night-time fire ballet.

Le Vieux Château

It is likely that the original castle, built in the 15C and 16C, was never completed; it was in any case partly destroyed by fire during the Vendée Wars. A fine late Renaissance pavilion remains at the far end of the courtyard, preceded by a peristyle with recessed Ionic columns. This now serves as the entrance to the museum. The left wing of the château is built over a long gallery.

Grand Parc★★

Open Apr–Sept. 27€ (children 17€).

The entire Puy du Fou estate extends over 35ha/86 acres. Numerous paths surrounding the château, skirting lakes or crossing dense woods of chestnut trees, offer pleasant walks with a choice of interesting diversions.

Fauna

On the way up to the castle, explanatory panels line the path linking several **aviaries**★★ containing birds of prey. **Farm animals**★, among them the famous *baudets*, graze inside large enclosures and a peasant can be seen guiding his team of oxen in and out of the old stables.

Reconstructed **underground galleries** show the lives of rabbits and foxes.

At the north of the wood there is an enclosure for deer.

In the **wolves' lair**, you can hear the story of the last wolf who roamed the area in 1908.

Flora

A pleasant trail through the **Arboretum de France**★ provides useful information about a great variety of plants.

There is also a **heather trail** and a **Renaissance rose garden**★ containing 100 different species.

Another trail, known as the **Vallée fleurie**★★, lined with various plants and trees, winds round ponds and waterfalls. An artificially created mist adds a romantic touch.

Le Signe du Triomphe, a show at Puy du Fou

Remembering the Vendée Wars

This historic trail can upset young children and sensitive persons.

The underground trail is lined with dramatic scenes of massacres perpetrated during the Vendée Wars.

Music

Every 15 minutes, a **peal** of 21 bells plays ancient melodies and regional characters come alive every 30 minutes. Costumed musicians forming a **brass quintet**★ play Baroque music. It is possible for visitors to control the play of fountains from a distance.

Shows

Bataille du Donjon – *30min show; 3 500 seats.* Reconstruction of the battle which led to the first Puy du Fou castle being taken by the English in 1429. Stunts and special effects.

La Bal des Oiseaux Fantômes★★ – *30min show; 1 700 seats.* The ruins of a 13C **castle** provide the background for a display of falconry – free-flying trained birds – with running commentary by a falconer in period costume.

Les Vikings★★★ – *30min show; 3 000 seats.* Spectacular special effects (a longship emerging from the water), cavalcades and fighting illustrate the story of this monk who died in Noirmoutier in 685.

Le Magicien-Ménestrel★ – *20min show; 800 seats.* Jugglers vie for the applause of bystanders with feats of skill and virtuosity beneath the ramparts of the medieval city.

Gladiateurs★★ – In a reconstruction of a **Gallo-Roman amphitheatre**★ watch a Roman circus of gladiators in hand-to-hand combat, chariot racing and fighting wild animals.

Mousquetaire de Richelieu★– In the **Grand Carousel**★ with its 2 800sq-m/3 349sq-yd stage, the atmosphere of 17C theatres has been re-created. Here there is a show of combat, fencing, acrobatics, dancing and horsemanship from musketeers.

Théâtre d'Eau★★ – *20min show; 600 seats.* A fairy-like display of 1 500 computer-controlled fountains enhanced by spectacular light effects.

Théâtre pour Enfants – *15min show; 400 seats.* Puppet show for children.

Villages

Three villages of different periods have been reconstructed north of the site.

Inside the **Fort de l'an Mil**★★, craftsmen can be seen at work in their thatched stone houses.

A drawbridge leads to the **Cité médiévale**★★★, protected by its ramparts. Inside, craftsmen and minstrels walk about their business along the narrow lanes.

In the **18C village**★★, the work of craftsmen in period costume can be admired while musicians and jugglers demonstrate their talent.

ADDRESSES

STAY

Hôtel de France – *pl. Dr-Pichat, 85290 Mortagne-sur-Sèvre. 02 51 65 03 37. hmortagne@aol.com. Closed Sat–Sun (mid-Oct–mid-May). 7.50€.* A 17C coaching inn has guest rooms furnished with period furniture, and two restaurants. The Taverne (classic cuisine), and the Petite Auberge (good daily specials).

Chambre d'hôte Le Logis de la Devinière – *20 r. du Puy-du-Fou, 85590 Les Épesses. 02 51 57 30 46. http://logis-la-deviniere.fr. 5 rooms. . Meals.* Beautiful 18C house with a pleasant garden. Individually decorated rooms, in a modern or traditional style. Three family rooms. Heated pool, jacuzzi and hammam.

Villa Gallo-Romaine – *Parc du Puy du Fou, 85000 Épesse. 08 20 09 10 10. www.puydufou.com. Closed mid-Sept–mid Apr. 100 rooms.* It is now possible to stay at the Puy du Fou in this Roman villa-themed hotel complete with l'Atrium restaurant. The hotel has direct access to the park.

EAT

Restaurant L'Auberge – *Domaine du Puy du Fou, 85590 Les Épesses. 08 20 09 10 10. www.puydufou.com. Closed Oct–May.* At the north end of the Puy du Fou grounds, this *auberge* serves regional dishes in a convivial setting. Costumed service and an excellent fixed-price "Gourmets" menu.

Le Relais de Poste – *Domaine du Puy du Fou. 08 20 09 10 10. Closed Oct–mid-Apr. Extended opening hours during Cinéscénie evenings.* At the north end of the site, an attractive room opens onto a courtyard where diners can enjoy entertainment as they eat. The Puy du Fou intendant introduces each of the dishes served by pages.

Les Herbiers

Vendée

This little town is the ideal starting point for a drive through windmill country. The manufacture of clothes and shoes remains the traditional economic activity of Les Herbiers.

- **Population:** 14 833
- **Michelin Map:** 316: J-6
- **Info:** 2 grande rue St-Blaise, Les Herbiers. 02 51 92 92 92. www.ot-lesherbiers.fr.
- **Location:** Les Herbiers is located 19km/11.8mi NW of Pouzauges.
- **Don't Miss:** The windmill at Mont des Alouettes.
- **Kids:** Chemin de Fer de la Vendée.
- **Timing:** Allow a day to explore the Route des Moulins.

SIGHTS

Chemin de Fer de la Vendée

Leaving from av. de la Gare, Mortagne-sur-Sèvre. Open early Jun–Sept (journey time 2hrs30min). 15€ (children 10€) return journey. 02 51 63 02 01. www.vendee-vapeur.fr.

In season, this quaint train runs on an old line linking Les Herbiers and **Mortagne-sur-Sèvre**. It is an original way of peacefully exploring 22km/13.7mi of Vendée farmland, with a stop at Les Épesses station. The train also has a dining car. **Gare des Épesses**, on the Herbiers–Mortagne line, is typical of the architecture of early 20C country stations.

Musée de l'Histoire des Chemins de Fer en Vendée – 02 51 92 92 92. In this little station museum, posters, exhibits and documents trace the short but eventful history of the railways.

DRIVING TOUR

1 ROUTE DES MOULINS★

Round trip 90km/56mi. Allow a full day.

Windmill Country

In the past the Vendée hills offered both strategic and tactical advantages to armies. The Romans built a road linking the crests, and a temple crowned Mont Mercure. For centuries the heights were dotted with countless windmills which turned every time the sea winds blew, sometimes throughout the night, grinding wheat and rye from the fertile plains nearby. During the Revolution, however, local Royalist supporters used their mills as a kind of rural semaphore system, altering the position of sails and vanes to telegraph information concerning the movements of the enemy. As a result, many were burned down by Republican troops. Mechanisation in the 19C put any surviving windmills out of business but today, many are again being restored to working order.

A typical example is stone built, cylindrical in shape, and topped by a movable, conical roof or "cap" covered with shingles (this type is known as a tower mill because of its fixed, tower-like base). Four sails are fixed to the revolving roof to which a *guivre* is frequently attached (a long pole reaching to the ground), to help turn the sails to face the prevailing wind. The wooden sails are either covered with canvas (hemp in earlier times) or made of wooden slats articulated using the Berton system, invented in 1848.

Leave Les Herbiers going W via the D 160 towards La Roche-sur-Yon.

Forêt des Bois-Verts

This little wood and lake is a popular spot for picnics and walks in fine weather.

Return via the D 160 for 4km/2.5mi, then go left.

Abbaye Notre-Dame-de-la-Grainetière

La Grange. Open daily 9am–7pm. 2€. 02 51 67 21 19.

The abbey, devoted to Our Lady of the Corn Chandlers, was built in 1130 by Benedictine monks from the Monastery of Fontdouce, near Saintes. With the help of the local overlords, the monks became sufficiently powerful in the 13C to build the fortifications which enabled them to resist the English when they laid siege to the abbey in 1372. In the 15C, however, the monks' power waned, becoming even weaker during the Wars of Religion. Revolutionary uprisings and the Vendée Wars finally destroyed the abbey at the end of the 18C. Subsequently used for farming and as a quarry, it underwent restoration in 1963. In 1978 a Benedictine priory was established in the abbey.

Only the west end of cloisters remains, with an ambulatory of twinned columns. Opposite, the 12C chapter house still has its original vaults resting on granite pillars. Three apsidioles are all that remain of the abbey-church. The Tour de l'Abbaye is the only part of the fortifications still standing.

Return to the crossroads and turn right, then right again 500m/550yds farther on.

Mouchamps

This village, situated above the Petit-Lay Valley, is the birthplace of Commandant Guilbaud, who, in 1928, was lost in the Arctic aboard his seaplane, *Latham 47*, as he was attempting to rescue the airship *Italia*. Since the 17C, Mouchamps has been a Protestant enclave in a Catholic area: until recently, Catholic houses were singled out by a white cross above the door.

Leave Mouchamps towards the NW along the D 13.

Château du Parc-Soubise

Le Parc-Soubise. 06 79 12 79 51. www.chateau-du-parc-soubise.abcsalles.com.

The estate once belonged to the powerful Rohan-Soubise family; the 16C–17C castle was burned down in 1794 (during the Revolution) and 200 women, children and old people perished; the roof alone has been restored. Situated near a 28ha/69-acre lake surrounded by ancient oak trees, the edifice has retained memories of Henri IV, who stayed there in 1589 and tried to seduce his cousin, Anne de Rohan. When he asked her the way to her bedroom, she is said to have replied: "Through the chapel, your Majesty!" Today, the château hosts conferences and events.

Return to Mouchamps and continue eastwards along the D 13.

Tombe de Clemenceau

Following the Petit-Lay Valley, the road leads to the 16C manor of **Le Colombier**, which belonged to the Clemenceau family. At the end of the road, walk through the doorway opening onto an alleyway. Below, on the way down to the Petit-Lay, you can see the graves of Clemenceau and his father beside a cedar tree.

Return to the D 13, for Pouzauges.

Église du Boupère

pl. Clément V. Guided tours Jul–Aug Tue–Sun 3–7pm. 02 51 91 41 65.

This curious 13C church was fortified in the 15C. Its façade is surrounded by buttresses pierced with arrow slits and loopholes and two bartizans linked by a crenellated watchpath. The sides were defended by gatehouses.

Continue along the D 13 then turn left onto the D 960.

Pouzauges

See POUZAUGES.

Leave Pouzauges NW via the D 752 in the direction of Les Herbiers.

Moulins du Terrier-Marteau★

See POUZAUGES.

Go back along the D 752 in the direction of Les Herbiers.

The road winds back down into the small valley separating Pouzauges from St-Michel-Mont-Mercure.

St-Michel-Mont-Mercure★

This town swarms with granite houses clustered around the church dedicated to St. Michael, whose cult following has succeeded that of Mercury, protector of travellers. The church, modern (1898) and 47m/154ft high, surmounted by a gigantic copper statue (9m/29ft) of St. Michael, is visible for miles around.

Belltower - From the top (194 steps), discover the vast panorama which extends to the sea. The bocage, seen from above, looks like a dense forest. One can see to the south Folly wood, near Pouzauges, north of Mount Alouettes near Herbiers.

Leave St-Michel-Mont-Mercure NW via the D 755 towards Les Herbiers.

Moulin des Justices

Guided tours Jul–Aug Tue–Sun 2–7pm. 2€. 02 51 57 01 37.

This mill owes its name to the fact that it is perched on top of a bluff from which justice was administered in former times. The mill, which still operates, has a roof which can be rotated using a winch. The width of the sails can be varied.

Return to St-Michel and follow the D 752 on the left.

After St-Michel, the D 752 winds its way through the valley, past a hill with a windmill without sails (Moulin des Landes) to Les Épesses with its two churches standing side by side.

Mallièvre

This old weaving centre is built on a granite outcrop overlooking Vallée de la Sèvre Nantaise. The village can be toured on foot by taking the Sentier Génovette, punctuated with water fountains and information points.

Mills, Mont des Alouettes

S. Sauvignier/MICHELIN

Leave Mallièvre, going back over the River Sèvre Nantaise, then turn right on the D 72 towards St-Malo-du-Bois.

Puy du Fou★★
See Le PUY DU FOU.

Drive N along the D 27 and take the Cholet road.

Mont des Alouettes★
This 231m/758ft-high hill marks the northwestern limit of the Vendée hills. The name is derived from the bronze skylarks *(alouettes)* which decorated the helmets of Gallic warriors when they enlisted in the Roman legions based in the area. In 1793 the seven mills on these moors were among those most frequently used to send signals by the "Whites" or Royalists. One of them was started up again in 1989.
The mills are all typical of the region, with oak *guivres* or tails and shingled conical roofs. One of them is dedicated to the Vendée writer Jean Yole.
Mill – *Guided tours (20min) May Sat–Sun and public holidays 10am–12.30pm, 2–6pm; Jun and 1–16 Sept Wed–Mon 10am–12.30pm, 2–6pm; Jul–Aug daily 10am–7pm. 3€. 02 51 66 80 32.* This mill, with its canvas-covered sails, still grinds corn. The chapel in the Troubadour Gothic Revival style was begun in 1823 in honour of the Royalist Catholic Army.
The wide-reaching **view★★** encompasses Nantes and the Atlantic Ocean.

Take the N 160 to Les Herbiers.

ADDRESSES

STAY

Chambre d'hôte La Métairie du Bourg – *5km/3.1mi NE of Les Herbiers (take the D 755, D 11 and a side road). 02 51 67 23 97. 2 rooms.* This B&B on a farm has spacious bedrooms and serves substantial breakfasts.

Hôtel Chez Camille – *2 r. Mgr-Massé. 02 51 91 07 57. www.chez-camille.com.*  *13 rooms. 7.50€. Meals.* Plain, functional rooms. The restaurant serves unpretentious cuisine.

EAT

Auberge du Mont Mercure – *r. de l'Orbrie, 85700 St-Michel-Mont-Mercure. 02 51 57 20 26. www.aubergemontmercure.com. Closed Mon evening (Sept–Jun), Tue evening and Wed.* A family *auberge* with rustic décor. Children's menu.

Le Centre – *6 r. de l'Église. 02 51 67 01 75. Closed Fri evening, Sun evening, Sat, 3–14 Aug and 22 Dec–6 Jan. 9 rooms. 8€.* Small place serving creative cuisine using fresh local produce. Well-maintained rooms.

Pouzauges

Vendée

Pouzauges stands on the slope of a hill crowned by the Bois de la Folie, overlooking an attractive rural landscape of fields and hedgerows.

- **Population:** 5 326
- **Michelin Map:** 316: I-7
- **Info:** 28 pl. de l'Église, Pouzauges. 02 51 91 82 46. www.paysdepouzauges.fr.
- **Location:** Pouzauges is located 19km/11.8mi SE of Les Herbiers.
- **Don't Miss:** Le Terrier-Marteau.

SIGHTS

Old Château

Open Jul–Aug Tue–Sun 2–7pm. 2€. 02 51 57 01 37. www.pouzauges.com.

This medieval fortress comprises walls incorporating 10 ruined towers and a square keep, flanked by turrets, which protected the entrance. A cross recalls the 32 Vendée Royalists who were shot here during the Revolution.

Église St-Jacques

pl. de l'Église. 02 51 57 01 37. http://orgue.pouzauges.free.fr.

St James' Church was built of granite in the Vendée style with a square tower over the crossing; it has a short nave and a 12C transept which is in a transitional Romanesque-Gothic style. The large, Flamboyant Gothic chancel with three bays is 15C.

EXCURSIONS

Moulins du Terrier-Marteau★

1km/0.6mi along the D 752 and a minor road on the right. Guided visit Jul–Aug Tue–Sun 2–7pm. 2€. 02 51 57 01 37.

On the right-hand side are the white windmills of the region. It is pleasant just to watch the canvas sails go round. These two 19C windmills have been restored and still have their mobile roof, so that the sails can be turned using a *guivre* (long pole). Attractive **view**★ of the farmland criss-crossed with trees and hedges to the west.

Bois de la Folie

Near Le Terrier-Marteau.

This was probably a *luccus*, or sacred wood, in Roman times, after being a meeting place for the Druids who gathered mistletoe and performed ritual sacrifices.

The wood, situated on a mound of granite, has an isolated clump of trees known to the locals as *Pouzauges Bouquet*, or the Vendée Lighthouse. It affords a **view**★ of the typical farmland to the northeast.

DRIVING TOUR

2 BETWEEN SÈVRE NANTAISE AND GRAND LAY

80km/50mi. Allow 7hrs.

Leave Pouzauges heading SW on the D 43, then turn right onto the D 113.

Château du Bois-Tiffrais

Le Bois Tiffrais, 85110 Monsireigne.

The château houses a museum which traces the history of Protestantism in western France.

Musée de la France Protestante de l'Ouest – *Open 28 Jun–13 Sept Tue–Sun 2–6pm. 4€. 02 51 66 24 40. www.museeprotestant.org.*

Well-documented explanatory panels illustrate the major events, such as Calvin's sermon in Poitou (1534), which led to Protestant emigration and the practice of secret worship during the period known as The Desert, and finally, the Edict of Tolerance (1787). Various exhibits, including Bibles and copies of *méreaux* (medals to identify the clandestine faithful) and a collapsible pulpit (for assemblies held in secret), recall the days of oppression.

Continue along the D 113 then follow the Chantonnay road, turning right after 2km/1.2mi.

Prieuré de Chassay-Grammont
Open 1 Jun–18 Sept daily 10am–7pm. 3€. 02 51 66 47 18. www.pays-de-la-loire.culture.gouv.fr.
This restored monastery was founded by Richard the Lionheart in c.1196. It is a good example of the architecture of the **Order of Grammont**, a community of hermits who attached great importance to poverty.
At Chassay, all of the monastic buildings as well as the church, are built around a cloistered courtyard. The church has a single nave stripped of all embellishments. On the ground floor, there is a chapter house with Romanesque vaulting and the large refectory with 13C Anjou Gothic vaulting. The monks' dormitory is on the first floor.

Return and cross the D 960bis.

Château de Sigournais
r. du Donjon. Open 28 Jun–21 Sept daily 2.30-6.30pm. 4.50€ (12–18 years 2.50€). 02 51 40 40 71.
Built in the late 15C, five towers, some partially destroyed, of its fortifications are still standing. The beautiful keep, flanked by two towers, is well preserved; it is topped by a covered walkway. Inside, there is a heraldic collection comprising hundreds of coats of arms from Vendée, France and Europe.

From Sigournais head SE on the D 39. Turn left onto the D 949bis and, after 2km/1.2mi, turn right onto the D 23.

Donjon de Bazoges-en-Pareds
cours du château. Open Easter–late Sept 2.30–6pm. 4€ (8–18 years 1.50€). 02 51 51 23 10. www.bazoges-en-pareds.fr.
Imposing 14C keep standing in the village centre. Inside, several rooms illustrate daily life in the Middle Ages. The Hall of Justice has a beautifully arched ceiling. Admire the lord's chamber with mullioned windows, and the squire's dormitory. From the walkway there is a splendid view of the countryside.

Leaves Bazoges to the SE on the D 23; after 2km/1.2mi, turn left onto the D 8.

Mouilleron-en-Pareds
Les Sources de la Vendée, La Tardière, La Châtaignerie. 02 51 52 62 37. www.paysdelachataigneraie.org.
Two of the most outstanding men in the recent history of France, **Georges Clemenceau** and **Jean-Marie de Lattre de Tassigny**, were born in this small village typical of the Vendée *bocage*. It was also the birthplace of the celebrated 19C astronomer **Charles-Louis Largeteau** (1791–1857).
National Museums – *1 r. Plante Choux. Open daily 15 Apr–15 Oct 9.30am–noon, 2–6pm; 16 Oct–14 Apr 10am–noon, 2–5pm. Closed 1 Jan, 25 Dec. 3.50€ (1st Sun of month no charge). 02 51 00 31 49. www.musee-deuxvictoires.fr.*
The town hall, which stands not far from the **church** *(3 pl. du Maréchal de Lattre; 02 51 00 31 46)* with its 12C belfry, houses the **Musée des Deux Victoires**. This establishment reviews the career of two extraordinary men, Clemenceau and De Lattre. Among displays are a walking stick presented to Tiger Clemenceau by his *poilus* (soldiers), as well as the eagle's head once surmounting the pediment of the Reichstag, which was presented to De Lattre by the Soviet Marshal Zhukov.
In the village, plaques identify the birthplaces of Clemenceau and De Lattre, who was called *Le Roi Jean* (King John) by his troops. The birthplace of the latter is now the **Musée Jean-de-Lattre-de-Tassigny**. The De Lattre family's aristocratic lifestyle has been re-created inside; there are displays evoking the life and the career of the marshal.
Opposite the house is the cemetery where the body of De Lattre lies beside his son, who was killed in Indo-China.
Two sites are devoted to De Lattre: the **Mémorial** at La Boinière and the

Jean de Lattre de Tassigny (1889–1952)

The life of Jean de Lattre is interwoven with the history of the first half of the 20C. Scion of an aristocratic Vendée family, he was admitted to the elite St-Cyr military academy; he became a dragoon and then an infantry officer during World War I.

In 1920 he was posted to Morocco, where he distinguished himself in the Rif War. A brilliant tactician, he was promoted to colonel, and then general in 1939. After the fall of France in World War II, he was arrested by the Germans in 1942 but escaped a year later and made his way to London to join the Free French, and from there went to Algiers. In 1944 he led the French 1st Army during the invasion of Provence. He was among the Allied leaders who signed the German Act of Capitulation on 8 May 1945. In 1950 he was appointed High Commissioner of Indo-China. De Lattre died in Paris in January 1952; four days later he was posthumously elevated to the rank of Marshal of France.

Oratoire (memorial chapel) housed in a windmill situated on **Colline des Moulins** *(2km/1.2mi E)*. From this hillside there is a fine view of the *bocage*.

Leave Mouilleron-en-Pareds heading NE on the D 8.

Réaumur

Manoir des Sciences – *Open late Jun and early Sept daily 2–6pm; Jul–Aug daily 11am–7pm; mid-Sept–Oct and Feb–mid-Jun Tue–Thu 2–6pm. 5€ (8–13 years 3.50€). 02 51 57 99 46. www.manoirdessciencesde reaumur.fr.* T
he multimedia exhibition brings to life the work of this great scientist of the Age of Enlightenment, René Antoine Ferchault de Réaumur (1683–1757).

Église de Pouzauges-le-Vieux – *Guided tours available through tourist office.* The granite **church** dates from the Romanesque period, apart from the chancel, which was remodelled in the 14C. The pure lines of its architecture became a model for many other churches in the region.

Take the D 49 in the direction of Montournais.

Puy Crapaud

At an altitude of 270m/885ft, it is one of the highest points on the Vendée hills. It is crowned with the remains of a windmill, converted into a restaurant *(for access to the viewing table, steep staircase, ask at the restaurant; 02 51 91 85 00)*. From the top, there is a **panorama**★★ of the hills between Pouzauges and St-Michel-Mont-Mercure.

Continue on the D 49; at Montournais, take the D 8 N to St-Mesmin.

About 1km/0.6mi beyond St-Mesmin, on the road to Cerisay, are the medieval ruins of the picturesque **Château de St-Mesmin** *(open 1 May–7 Jun Sun and public holidays 3–7pm and 8 Jun–7 Jul and 31 Aug–20 Sept daily 10.30am–12.30pm, 2.30–6.30pm, 8 Jul–30 Aug daily 10.30am–1pm, 2.30–6.30pm; 6€; 05 49 80 17 62; www.chateau-saintmesmin.fr)*, whose machicolations of the keep are still intact.

At the crossroads, turn left on the small road which joins the D 27.

La Pommeraie-sur-Sèvre

A Gothic **church** *(free access; 02 51 92 81 80)*, with Plantagenet vaulting in the nave, and 15C frescoes. There is a Roman bridge across the Sèvre.

Leave La Pommeraie-sur-Sèvre and take the D 43 W to return to Pouzauges.

La Chabotterie ★★

Vendée

It is in the woods of La Chabotterie that the Vendée Wars ended with the capture of the Royalist leader, Charette (1796).

- **Michelin Map:** 316: H-6
- **Info:** 21 r. du Peplu, 85620 Rocheservière. ℘02 51 94 94 05. www.cc-canton-rocheserviere.fr. 6€.
- **Location:** St Sulpice-le-Verdon (27km/16.8mi N of La Roche-sur-Yon, off the D 763).
- **Kids:** The Refuge de Grasla.
- **Timing:** Open Jul–Aug daily 10am–7pm; rest of year Mon–Sat 9.30am–7pm (winter 6pm). Closed1 Jan, 25 Dec 3 wks Jan.

THE MANOR

Developed in the Vendée in 1560, the *logis clos* is a fortified courtyard enclosing the manor and its attendant outbuildings. This typical configuration was found in Vendée until the 18C. The refined atmosphere of the 18C – a mixture of country ways and gracious living typical of the rural society of the time in Bas-Poitou – has been brought to life again through careful restoration of the manor house to which Charette was brought after his capture, thus putting an end to the Vendée Wars.

The **salles historiques**★ feature authentic period pieces in a reconstructed dining room (table laid for a meal, hallmarked chairs, cut-crystal chandelier), bedroom (canopied bed made of fabric from Nantes, 1783) and study (17C and 18C Aubusson tapestries). The **salle des maquettes** contains scale models of many traditional houses of the Vendée region.

The **walled garden** is divided into flower beds where roses are tended, and a vegetable plot, where the flowers can also be spectacular.

A granite cross, the **croix de charette**, can be reached from La Chabotterie (*30min on foot there and back).* Erected in 1911 in La Chabotterie Woods, the cross marks the place where the Royalist leader was captured.

Parcours Spectacle

Children and particularly sensitive people may find the subject matter here disturbing.

In the modern building, visitors can learn about the local history, including the Vendée Wars.

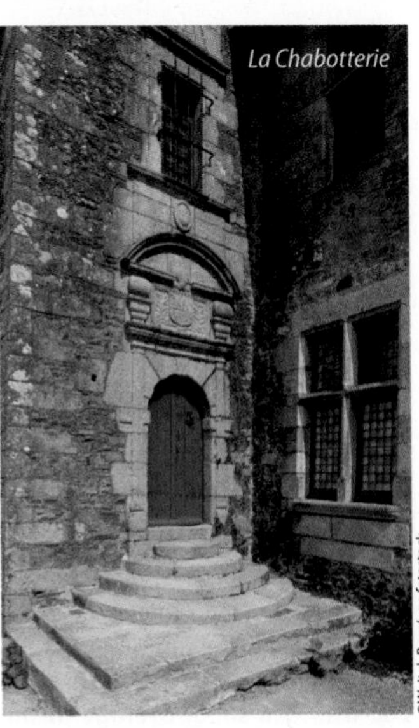

La Chabotterie

©Wojtek Buss/age fotostock

EXCURSION

Château du Bois-Chevalier

20km/12.4mi W. ℘06 09 77 61 04.

The central body of this Louis XIV château is crowned by a dome and flanked by six wings with high French roofs; the ensemble is reflected in the waters alongside. Charette stayed here during the Vendée Wars. The château now organises concerts and events.

DRIVING TOUR

3 IN THE FOOTSTEPS OF CHARETTE

45km/28mi round trip. Allow 3hrs.

From Logis de la Chabotterie, join the D 18 and turn right; cross the D 763 and continue to La Copechagnière, turn left onto the D 86 to Les Brouzils, then right onto the D 7 towards Les Essarts.

Roads D 7 then D 6 *(towards Belleville-sur-Vie)* run close to the edge of **Grasla Forest** where Charette and his troops sought refuge on 11 January 1794. A cross stands at the entrance of a village hidden in the forest.

Refuge de Grasla
Open end Apr–May Sun and public holidays 2–6pm; Jun–13 Sept daily 11am–6pm; 14–27 Sept Sun 2–6pm. 6€. 02 51 42 96 20. www.refugedegrasla.fr.
In 1793 many inhabitants of the surrounding parishes, fleeing the Blues (Republican Army, sought refuge in Grasla Forest.

Continue along the D 6. In St-Denis-la-Chevasse, turn right onto the D 39 to Les Lucs-sur-Boulogne.

Les Lucs-sur-Boulogne
On 28 February 1794 one of General Cordelier's Infernal Columns slaughtered many of the inhabitants of Grand-Luc, and, on 5 March, parishioners of Petit-Luc who had sought refuge in the church. This, however, was not the only place where the Republican Infernal Columns held sway, and the memorial inaugurated in May 1993 was erected to the memory of all their victims.
The historiated stained-glass windows of **Église St-Pierre**, built in 1902, tell of the 1794 massacres.

Historial de la Vendée★ – *At Les Lucs. Follow the signs for the Historial et le Mémorial de Vendée. OpenApr–Jun and Sept Tue–Sun 10am–7pm; Jul–Aug daily 10am–7pm; Oct–Mar Tue–Sun 10am–6pm. Closed 1 Jan, 25 Dec. 8€ (under 18 years no charge, under 26 years 5€). 02 51 47 61 61. http://historial.vendee.fr.*
The Historial incorporates the collection of the former Ecomusée de la Vendée. Blending entirely into the landscape, with its vast vegetal roof, this new museum retraces, in 3 100sq m/3 700sq yds, the history of the Vendée from prehistoric times to the present, through interactive exhibits and audiovisual shows.
There is also an area for children, where discovery workshops are held.
Le Chemin de la Mémoire des Lucs★ – *Close to the Historial. Open daily 9am–7pm. No charge. 02 51 46 51 28.*
Dedicated to the memory of the martyrs and victims of the Reign of Terror, the memorial in Les Lucs is an architectural and landscaped ensemble leading from the banks of the Boulogne to the hilltop chapel.
Many historic landmarks lie along the **Allée de l'Histoire**, recalling the major events in the Vendée Wars from March to December 1793.
Farther along stands the **Memorial de Vendée**. The corridor of memory evokes the end of the insurrection and the destruction of Vendée through reconstructed scenes and symbolic objects.
On the other side of the footbridge over the Boulogne stands a blackened wall, symbolising the mass burning of villages.
A path leads to the **Chapelle Notre-Dame-du-Petit-Luc**, built in 1867 on the remains of the former church.

Rejoin the D 18 and turn right towards St-Sulpice-le-Verdon to return to Logis de la Chabotterie.

La Roche-sur-Yon

Vendée

This unusual town is striking for its straight streets crossing each other at right angles, its large central esplanade and an impressive equestrian statue of Napoleon. Further exploration will reveal an attractive modern building housing the offices of the *département* and a renowned stud farm. Spend some time in the town between July and mid-August and you'll enjoy free musical concerts on Thursday and Friday evenings as part of the "Cafés de l'Été" festival.

- **Population:** 50 717
- **Michelin Map:** 316: H-7–8
- **Info:** r. Georges Clemenceau, La Roche-Sur-Yon. 02 51 36 00 85. www.ot-roche-sur-yon.fr.
- **Location:** La Roche-sur-Yon is situated on a plateau overlooking the River Yon and a landscape of fields and hedgerows.
- **Parking:** The main car parks in the centre are Clemenceau and des Halles.

A BIT OF HISTORY

La Roche-sur-Yon was born out of an imperial wish to install a strategic military stronghold designed to prevent further uprisings in the Vendée. In 1804 Napoleon transferred the provincial capital from Fontenay to La Roche-sur-Yon, a modest small town which was subsequently renamed "Napoléon-Vendée". Plans for a military transformation were drawn up by the engineer **Duvivier**, but the lack of stone in the region constrained him to build in cob; as a consequence, when Napoleon passed through in 1808 to have a look at the new fortifications, Duvivier was sacked, being reproached for having created "a mud-walled town".

La Roche found its definitive shape during the Restoration: a geometric, straight-line plan with a grid of streets crossing each other at right angles, the wide main arteries converging on a huge esplanade. This town took the form of an irregular pentagon from which six main routes permitted a rapid rectilinear deployment of troops.

The name of the town was nevertheless changed several more times: it became Bourbon-Vendée under the Restoration and the July Monarchy, Napoléon-Vendée at the time of the Second Empire and returned to La Roche-sur-Yon in 1870.

SIGHTS

Place Napoléon

The great esplanade, designed to accommodate 20 000 soldiers, is surrounded by Neoclassical buildings. In the centre of the square stands an equestrian statue (1854) of Napoleon I.

Hôtel du Département

r. du Maréchal Foch. 02 51 34 48 48.

This comprises an old Napoleonic hospital in which exhibitions are held and, just behind it, a modern building (1990) by Roland Castro and Jean-Luc Pellerin.

Musée de La Roche-sur-Yon

r. Jean Jaurès. Open Tue–Sat 1–6pm. No charge. 02 51 47 48 35.

As well as archaeological collections from the prehistoric, Gallo-Roman and medieval periods, the museum offers a panorama of 19C Parisian academic painting and a series of canvases by local artists of the same period – Milcendeau and Baudry, for instance.

The museum has a collection of works by contemporary artists including Beuys.

Le Haras National (Stud Farm)

21 r. Gallieni. Guided tour (1hr) with reservation Wed and Sat–Sun 2–6pm. 4.50€. 02 51 46 14 47. www.haras-nationaux.fr.

Established in 1842 during the Bourbon Restoration, this is one of the most important stud farms in France. A

Place Napoléon, La Roche sur Yon

©Alain Le Bot/Photononstop

number of thoroughbred stallions as well as French trotting horses are stabled here.

EXCURSIONS

Église de La Chaize-le-Vicomte

11km/6.8mi E on the D 948.

This granite church is built upon a rocky outcrop facing the feudal castle ruins. Admire the fortified façade of this Romanesque church and its majestic nave. Interesting capitals.

Maison des Libellules

Chaillé-sous-les-Ormeaux, 10km/6.2mi S on the D 85, then the D 36. 9 pl. de l'Église. Open Jul–Aug am and pm. Guided tours Apr–Jun and Sept–Oct Sun–Fri 2pm, 3.30pm, 5pm. 4.50€ (chlldren 3€). 02 51 06 03 15.

A small exhibition explains the history and characteristics of the dragonfly, and the influence that this elegant insect has had on literature and art. Outside, a discovery trail takes you through the gardens and orchards to a pond.

Les Essarts

20km/12.4mi NE along the D 160. 1 r. Armand-de-Rougé. 02 51 62 85 96.

This large market town is situated in a valley, in the heart of the *bocage*.

Vieux Château – *Open Jul–Aug daily 10am–6.30pm. Guided tour available. 4€ (10–16 years 2€). www.chateau-des-essarts.com.* A gateway, flanked by two round towers, provides access to the ruins of the fortress, seat of a powerful barony in the Middle Ages. To the right of the entrance stands the 11C keep, and to the left a Gallo-Roman tumulus. In the background stands the seigniorial residence, rebuilt in the 15C and burned down in 1794.

The modern château was constructed between 1854 and 1857 by Phidias Vestier (1796–1874), an architect specialising in the Gothic Troubadour style, while the park was designed in the 19C by Bühler.

Château de la Grève

8km/5mi from Essarts via St-Martin-des-Noyers. Open mid-June–mid-Sept 2–7pm; Easter holidays 2–5pm. 5€ (12–18 years 2.50€, under 12 years no charge). 02 51 07 86 36. www.asso-chateau-greve.com.

Charming 12C château built on the edge of a lake. Fortified during the Hundred Years' War, and greatly altered during the Wars of Religion, the château was converted in the 19C and 20C into a working farm. Admire the 16C living quarters and vaulted 15C cellars; the great tower, also 16C, whose wooden framework has been completely restored using traditional techniques; and a large 19C barn, built using the original stones.

Luçon

Vendée

This charming episcopal town, on the borders of the Poitou marshlands and plain, was once a seaport. Today it is an important trading and agricultural centre.

- **Population:** 9 682
- **Michelin Map:** 316: I-9
- **Info:** sq. Édouard Herriot, Luçon. 02 51 56 36 52. www.tourisme-lucon.com.
- **Location:** Luçon lies W of Fontenay-le-Comte and SE of La Roche-sur-Yon.
- **Don't Miss:** Cathédrale Notre-Dame; Jardin Dumaine.
- **Kids:** The botanical gardens at St Cyr.
- **Timing:** Allow 3hrs to visit the town.

SIGHTS

Cathédrale Notre-Dame

pl. du Général Leclerc. Guided tours Jul–Aug Thu 4pm from tourist office. 2€. 02 51 56 36 52.

This former abbey-church became a cathedral in 1317. As well as Richelieu, it counts at least one other celebrated bishop: Nicolas Colbert, the brother of the minister, who governed the bishopric from 1661 to 1671. The church is largely Gothic in style, although the northern arm of the transept is Romanesque. The west front was remodelled in the late 17C under the supervision of the architect François Leduc. The overall balance and Classical layout of this façade contrasts vividly with the slender, tapered Gothic spire, which was rebuilt in 1828 and rises to a height of 85m/279ft. The façade as a whole serves today as a belfry-porch. The well-proportioned nave and chancel date from the Gothic period; the latter is adorned with ornamental woodwork and a rich 18C canopy. Richelieu himself is said to have preached from a pulpit, delicately painted with fruit and flowers, in the north aisle. In the south transept is a 16C *Deposition (restored)* from the Florentine School. The 19C organ in the gallery is by Cavaillé-Coll.

Évêché (Episcopal Palace)

pl. du Général Leclerc. 02 51 28 53 00.

South of the cathedral is the 16C façade of the old bishops' residence. Entrance – via the **cloisters** – is through a doorway surmounted by a Gothic arch framing the armorial bearings of Louis, Cardinal de Bourbon, Bishop of Luçon (1524–27). Galleries juxtaposing both Gothic and Renaissance elements were added in the 16C. The western side is pierced by Renaissance windows.

Jardin Dumaine★

A lovely park, recalling the Napoleon III era, with tree-lined alleys, lawns and flower-filled borders, palm trees, ponds and a wrought-iron gazebo.

EXCURSIONS

Mareuil-sur-Lay-Dissais

10km/6.2mi NW on the D 746.

Mareuil, famous for its "Fiefs Vendéens", wines, is built above a loop in the Lay river. A fine view from the bridge.

St-Cyr-en-Talmondais

13km/8mi to the W on the D 949.

This village, bordering the *bocage* and drained Marais, has a splendid botanical flower garden.

Parc Floral et Tropical de la Court d'Aron★ – *Open Apr–Sept 10am–7pm. 10€ (special offers for Fête des Lotus) (5–12 years 6€). 02 51 30 86 74. www.lacourtdaron.com.* This 10ha/25-acre botanical garden is charming, with small wooden bridges leading to spectacular lotus ponds. Beautiful arches of bamboo, eucalyptus groves, a profusion of flowers and plants are waiting to be discovered in this enchanting park. Other treats include a zen garden, a tropical greenhouse, and even a reconstruction of a Vendée farm.

Fontenay-le-Comte

Vendée

Fontenay was the capital of the Vendée until 1804. This attractive town lies in a sheltered spot on the banks of the River Vendée, bordering the plain, the *bocage* (farmlands criss-crossed with hedgerows), and the Poitou marshlands. Its limestone houses, sometimes coated with roughcast, sprawl between two thoroughfares perpendicular to the river. The name of the town is derived from the Quatre-Tias fountain.

- **Population:** 14 354
- **Michelin Map:** 316: L-9
- **Info:** 8 r. de Grimouard, Fontenay-le-Comte. 02 51 69 44 99. www.tourisme-sudvendee.com.
- **Location:** Fontenay-le-Comte lies 37km/23mi NW of Niort. The pl. Viète, now the centre of the town, occupies the site of a bastion which was once part of the old curtain wall. The Old Town lies to the E, beyond r. des Loges in the areas around Église Notre-Dame and Église St-Jean. The modern part of Fontenay extends SW of the line traced by r. Clemenceau and r. de la République.
- **Parking:** There are car parks in pl. Viète and near the river in the town centre.
- **Don't Miss:** The bell tower of Église Notre-Dame; Château de Terre-Neuve.

A BIT OF HISTORY

In the Middle Ages and during the Renaissance, Fontenay was a fortified town accustomed to violent attacks. In 1372 local heroine Jeanne de Clisson defended it against Bertrand du Guesclin, one of the generals responsible for ousting the English from France. At the end of the 16C, Fontenay was disputed by the Protestants and Catholics. Two centuries later, the Republicans twice fought the Royalists in the Vendée region, beneath Fontenay's walls.

A Renaissance Centre – In the 16C, Fontenay was a centre of Renaissance exuberance. In 1520 the young **Rabelais** knocked at the gates of the Franciscans' headquarters, which stood on the site of the present town hall. He had left the Franciscans of Angers and hoped to study Greek literature under Friar Pierre Amy, a precursor of the Reformation. Amy put him in touch (by letter) with the Hellenist scholar Guillaume Budé (1467–1540), a humanist whose later *Correspondance* with Rabelais and others became an important document in the literary history of the period.

In Fontenay, Rabelais and his friends would meet at the home of **André Tiraqueau** (c.1480–1558), a learned legal writer, father of 30 children and author of a treatise on matrimonial laws for which Rabelais composed an epigraph in Greek verse. In 1523, however, Rabelais sought refuge with the Benedictines in Maillezais after his Father Superior discovered pro-Reformation books among Rabelais' belongings.

In the second half of the century, other Fontenay humanists found fame, including Barnabé Brisson, Head of the Paris Parliament, who was hanged in 1591 during the disputes concerning the Catholic League, and **François Viète** (1540–1603), the brilliant mathematician who invented algebra. The poet and strict magistrate **Nicolas Rapin** (c.1540–1608) was another major local figure. During the *Grands Jours* of Poitiers, he took part in a poetry competition. Rapin won the prize with his piece *La Puce (The Flea)*, which was followed by *L'Anti-Puce*. Later, in Paris, he was one of the chief instigators of *La Satire Ménippée* (a political pamphlet directed against the Catholic League) before retiring to his country residence, **Château de Terre-Neuve** (see p374).

THE TOWN

Église Notre-Dame

r. Gaston Guilemet. ℘02 51 69 44 99.
The church is marked by a slender, elegant 15C **belfry★** which was remodelled in 1700. The 82m/270ft tower, crowned by a spire decorated with crockets, is similar to that of Luçon Cathedral. The main doorway is Flamboyant Gothic, with a large stone filigree opening replacing the tympanum. Wise Virgins with upright lamps and Foolish Virgins with their lamps upside down are carved in the coving. A delicate 19C Madonna adorns the pier niche.

A Louis XVI pulpit is among the features worth noting inside the church. Others include the Brisson chapel and the apsidal chapels, dating from the time of François I, which are now partly concealed by the outsized 18C altarpiece.

The small 9C **crypt**, discovered by chance in the 19C, is a rare and important example of early architecture in the Lower Poitou region. Roman mortar was used for the groin vaulting. The capitals of the supporting pillars are in the Byzantine style.

Rue du Pont-aux-Chèvres

A number of interesting old houses can be seen in this street. The former Benedictine priory at no **3** has a staircase tower. At no **6**, the Villeneuve-Esclapon mansion is adorned with a monumental Louis XIII entrance surmounted by a Laocoon (an antique sculpture group representing Laocoon, the priest of Apollo, strangled with his two sons by serpents. The original is in the Vatican). The figures are flanked by statues of Hercules and Diana. No **9** boasts a fine balustraded staircase. The property belonged in the 16C and 17C to the bishops of Maillezais. No **14** is a splendid example of a Renaissance private house. It belonged once to André Rivaudeau, mayor of Fontenay in the late 16C and author of the tragedy *Aman*, which inspired Racine to compose *Esther*.

Place Belliard

The statue in the quiet square represents General Belliard (1769–1832), who saved the life of Napoleon Bonaparte at Arcole by shielding him with his own body. The general was born at no **11**.

Five interesting houses (three of them with arcades), flanking one side of the square, were built by the architect Jean Morisson during the reign of Henri IV. Morisson himself lived at no **16** – the pediment is crowned by a statue of the architect holding a pair of compasses, the emblem of his profession. His personal motto, *Peu et Paix* (roughly equivalent to "Less is More") is carved above the first-floor bay.

Fontaine des Quatre-Tias

r. de la Fontaine.
In the local dialect, the word *tias* means "pipes". The fountain, built in 1542 by the architect Lienard de Réau, bears the Latin inscription *Fontanacum Felicium Ingeniorum Fons et Scaturigo* ("The Fountain and Source of Fine Minds") – a motto bestowed on the town by François I. The King's coat of arms, complete with emblematic salamander, is engraved on the pediment.

Rue des Loges

In the 18C this street, flanked by quaintly named lanes and alleys – rue du Lamproie (Lamprey Lane), rue de la Grue (Crane Street) and rue de la Pie (Magpie Alley) – was the town's main street. Today rue des Loges is a pedestrian shopping precinct, still bordered by a number of houses with fine old façades. Among these are the house at no **26** with wrought-iron balconies and carved human faces, no **85**, with an impressive late 16C doorway of carved stone, and no **94**, a medieval building with projecting upper floors. On the corner of rue St-Nicolas stands a carefully restored early 16C half-timbered house.

ADDITIONAL SIGHTS

Musée Vendéen

pl. du 137ème. Open May–Sept Tue–Sun 2.30–6pm; Oct–Apr Wed and Sat–Sun 2.30–6pm. Closed Jan, 1 May, 25 Dec. 2.50€. 02 51 69 31 31.

The ground and first floors of this museum contain collections of archaeology, ornithology and ethnography.

The second floor is given over to the history of the town and to artists with Vendée connections, including the painters Paul Baudry, August Lepère and Charles Milcendeau. Also on view are sketches by Lepère.

A small modern art department includes works by Émile Lahner. A sculpture, by the brothers Jan and Jol **Martel**, represents *An Olonne Woman Wearing a Shawl.*

Château de Terre-Neuve

Take r. Rabelais W out of pl. Viète and turn first left onto r. Barnabé-Brisson to the château. Open May–Sept 9am–noon, 2–7pm; Oct–Apr by appointment only. 6.60€. 02 51 69 17 75. www.chateau-terreneuve.com.

The architect Jean Morisson was commissioned by his friend Nicolas Rapin to build this country retreat at the end of the 16C. It was here that Rapin wrote his well-known work, *Plaisirs du Gentilhomme Champestre*. The archaeologist and engraver Octave de Rochebrune restored the château inc.1850. The building comprises two main blocks at right angles to one another, with turreted bartizans at each corner. The façade is adorned with Italian Renaissance muses in terra-cotta, and a porch, which was originally part of another château.

The **interior**★ has a number of remarkable features – Louis XIV woodwork from Chambord Château on the Loire, a door from François I's study, fine Louis XV and Louis XVI furniture, 17C and 18C paintings and a handsome chimney-piece, designed by Philibert Delorme. The Renaissance decoration of the dining hall includes a monumental doorway, an imposing chimney-piece, and a coffered ceiling of carved stone.

DRIVING TOUR

4 FORÊT DE MERVENT-VOUVANT★

55km/34mi round tour from Fontenay-le-Comte. Allow 4hrs.

This National Forest lies at the junction of the Vendée plain and **le bocage**. It covers 5 000ha/20sq mi of a granite plateau gashed by steep-sided valleys. Three of these have been flooded to form a 130ha/320-acre reservoir enclosed within four separate dams. In the 12C the forest belonged to the house of Lusignan, and later was annexed to the royal domain in 1674, and then assigned to the Comte d'Artois in 1778. Following the French Revolution, it became the property of the State. Numerous well-marked footpaths, cycle tracks and bridle paths cross the area.

N along the D 938 for La Châtaigneraie; 1.5km/0.9mi beyond Pissotte, take a one-way road on the right.

Barrage de Mervent★

The approach to Mervent Dam is marked by a stone sculpture representing a Siren, the work of the Martel Brothers (20C). The 130m/426ft-long dam plugs the Vendée Valley and supplies water to the southern half of the département.

Natur'Zoo

Open Apr–Jun daily 11am–7pm; Jul–Aug daily 10am–7pm; Sept daily 2–6pm; Oct–Nov and Feb–Mar Sat–Sun and school holidays 2–6pm. 10.50€ (3–6 years 6.50€). 02 51 00 07 59. http://naturzoomervent.free.fr.

In the heart of the forest, lions, camels, monkeys, tigers and kangaroos roam around this 6ha/15-acre park.

Continue along the D 65, and then turn onto the D99.

Mervent

This town is perched on a rocky spur in thick woodland. From the town hall gardens there is a fine **view★** down over the reservoir with its beach.

Follow the D 99; right on the D 99A.

Grotte du Père Montfort

Louis-Marie Grignion de Montfort, a Catholic preacher, sought refuge in the forest around 1715, while converting Protestants. This cavern became a place of pilgrimage. The footpath leading to it starts behind a shrine on road D 99A. From the grotto the path descends to La Maison du Curé, where another priest retired in seclusion.

You can return to the Grotte or continue on foot (15min) to Pierre-Brune by turning right onto the path that follows the Right Bank of the Mère river.

Pierre-Brune

Near a small dam and opposite a sheer rock, there are restaurants, a hotel and an amusement park. A little train, the Tortillard, goes through the Vallée de Pierre-Brune (*operates mid-Jun–early Sept daily; 11€; 02 51 00 20 18; www.mervent-foret.com).*

Continue along the D 99A, then turn left. After 2km/1.2mi, turn left and rejoin the D 938ter (right). At the Alouette district,turn right onto the D 30.

Vouvant★

Vouvant retains an old-world atmosphere. According to legend, the Fairy Mélusine is said to have built Vouvant Château in a single night.

Church★ – The church was founded by the monks of Maillezais Abbey. The 11C nave was damaged by partisans of the Reformation in 1568 and only the walls of the first three bays remain. The original three apses were rebuilt in the 12C along with the crypt and the Romanesque doorway of the northern transept; this doorway, the main **façade★**, flanked by clustered columns and topped by a gable, form a readable page of sculpture.

The **main doorway** consists of arched doors twinned beneath a common

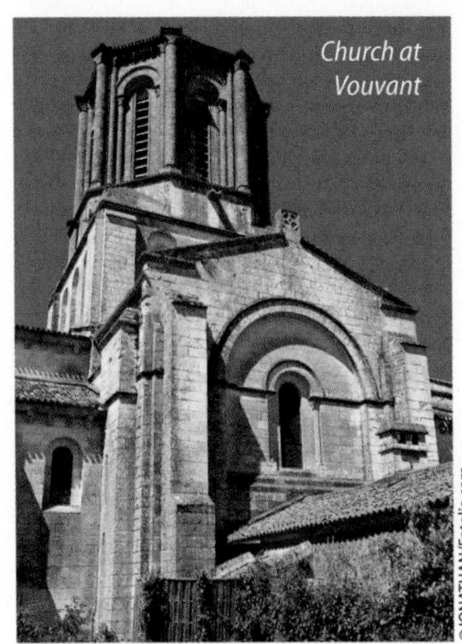
Church at Vouvant

archivolt, surmounted on the tympanum by stone carvings depicting Samson and Delilah.

The first coving of the **archivolt** features a line of supporting atlantes; the second features carved biblical and mythological characters. On the left above the arch is a *Virgin and Child*, balanced on the right by an effigy of John the Baptist. Higher still are two **friezes** on modillions: the *Last Supper (below)*; the *Apostles Witnessing the Ascension (above)*.

Château – *Open Jul–Aug Mon–Sat 10am–12.30pm, 2–6.30pm, Sun 10am–noon, 3–6pm. 02 51 00 86 80.* The old fortress of the Lusignans in medieval times barred the neck of the promontory girdled by a loop of the river. Its defensive walls demarcate place du Bail, a grassy esplanade planted with chestnut trees. From the edge there are attractive views over the River Mere.

Tour Mélusine★– *pl. du Bail. Information and tickets at tourist office or the Café du Centre. 2€. 02 51 00 86 80.* Once a keep, the tower was built in 1242. The walls, up to 3m/10ft thick, enclose two chambers, one above the other, with curious pyramid vaulting. The top of the tower can be reached by a stairway of 120 steps. From here there is a magnificent **panorama★** – encapsulating the village, the plateau in the south and the *bocage* farmland in the north.

Leave Vouvant SE along the D 31 towards Foussais-Payré; 5km/3.1mi farther on, turn right onto the D 65 towards Mervent.

La Jamonière Musée des Amis de la Forêt
127 rte de la Bironnière, Mervent. Guided tours of the forest with reservation. 02 51 00 00 87.
This museum contains information on the forest, its flora and fauna, and traditional woodland activities.

Continue SW to Quillères.

Château de la Citardière
Open Jun–Sept Thu–Tue 2–7pm. 02 51 00 27 04.
The château, partly hidden behind a belt of ancient trees, has a fine 17C façade reflected in a wide moat. A restaurant now occupies the interior.

Leave Quillères by the D 99 and continue SE.

Foussais-Payré
Fine Renaissance houses and a 17C covered market distinguish this small town renowned for its annual folklore festivals.
Church – *r. Mélusine. 02 51 51 42 88.* The entrance and west front feature religious scenes carved in the 11C by Giraud Audebert, a monk from the Abbey of St-Jean-d'Angély.

Head N from Foussais-Payré on the D 49. At Puy-de-Serre, turn right onto the D 67.

Centre Minier de Faymoreau
Open Apr–Jun and Sept Tue –Sun 2–7pm; Jul–Aug daily 10am–7pm; Oct–Dec and Feb–Mar Sat–Sun 2–6pm. Closed 25 Dec. 6€ (8–16 years 3.50€), 8.50€ combined ticket for the mine and village. 02 51 00 48 48. www.centre-minier-vendee.com.
The museum, housed in the former glass workshops, offers an interesting visit which includes the *salle des pendus* or the changing room; the lamp room; a virtual descent down a shaft; and finally, in the mine buildings, a model of the mine, a film and exhibitions.
Outside the museum, the mining village has typical 19C working-class architecture: mining cottages, offices, glassworks, hotel and the Chapelle des Mineurs. Inside the chapel, there are 19 contemporary stained-glass windows designed by Carmelo Zagari.

ADDRESSES

STAY/Y/EAT

Le Capt'ain – *35 r. du Port. 02 51 69 02 10. lecaptain.sm@wanadoo.fr. Closed 2Sun, 1 wk in Aug, 2 wks in Feb and public holidays.* The locals know this seafood restaurant well. Specialities include meat or fish skewers, and in season, over 20 different mussel dishes.

Auberge de Maître Pannetier – *8 pl. du Corps-de-Garde, 85120 Vouvant. 02 51 00 80 12. www.maitre-pannetier.com. Closed Mon (Sept–Jun) and 20 Dec–20 Jan. 7 rooms. 6.50€.* Traditional dishes served in a rustic dining room. Pretty rooms, and a family suite.

Hôtel Fontarabie et restaurant la Glycine – *57 r. de la République (Exit 8 from the A 38). 02 51 69 17 24. www.hotel-fontarabie.com. Closed Christmas holidays. 49 rooms. 8€. Meals.* This 16C coaching inn in the city centre has practical, contemporary rooms, some in a modern annex. Regional cuisine.

Le Rabelais – *19 r. Ouillette. 02 51 69 86 20. www.hotel-lerabelais.com. 54 rooms.* Most of the rooms have a view of the garden. The restaurant features a large buffet of starters and desserts.

L'Auberge de la Rivière – *r. du Port de la Fouarne, 85770 Velluire (11km/6.8mi SW of Fontenay-le-Comte via the D 938ter and D 68). 02 51 52 32 15. www.hotel-riviere-vendee.com. 11 rooms. 11€. Closed Sun evening, Mon and Jan–Feb.* Fish and seafood are the specialities of this pretty inn. Spacious, well-kept guest rooms.

The Vendée is the southernmost *département* of the Pays de Loire region, and takes its name from the Vendée river. The Vendée Maritime lies on the west side, bordering the Atlantic Ocean. The area is renowned for its fabulous beaches, especially those found along the Côte de la Lumière (Coast of Light), and the long, fine sandy beaches of the Île d'Yeu. The vast fields of sunflowers extending over this low-lying landscape are a wonderful sight in the summer.

Windmills and Sail Boats

Windmills were once scattered across the Vendée landscape. The oldest dates from the 14C, but the majority were built during the 18C and 19C, although most are in ruins today.

There remains only a handful still in working condition, some converted into homes. During the **Vendée Wars** the windmills were used as an early warning system. A code was devised, by changing the position of sails, to warn the Vendée troops of the arrival of the Republican armies.

Today, modern wind turbines have made their appearance on the scenery. At the coast, parallel to the Dain dyke you can see a line of wind turbines from the route de Bouin at Beauvoir-sur-Mer. Inland, walkers, horse riders and cyclists can follow the 8km/5mi path that starts at La Croix (2.5km/1.5mi east of La Garnache) which passes close to the giant aerodynamic turbines.

There are some ancient windmills that are still in operation today: Moulin de Rairé and the Petit Moulin de Châteauneuf can be visited. On the Île de Noirmoutier, there are around 20 windmills dispersed around the island. The last working windmill here stopped operating in the 1950s.

The **Vendée Globe** sailing race takes place every four years at Les Sables-d'Olonne. The race starts and finishes from the port here and the competitors sail around the world non-stop without assistance, covering nearly 39 976km/24 845mi in around three months.

Highlights

1 Discover the marshlander's way of life at the fascinating **Écomusée du Marais breton-Vendéen** (p382)

2 Cross the Gois causeway on **Île de Noirmoutier** (p389)

3 Unspoiled scenery of the **Île d'Yeu** (p391)

4 Drive through the forests and marshlands of **Olonne** (p397)

5 Fine views over the immense plains of the **Marais Poitevin Maritime** (p402)

Boats off Île de Noirmoutier

©Brigitte Merle/Photononstop

THE VENDÉE COAST

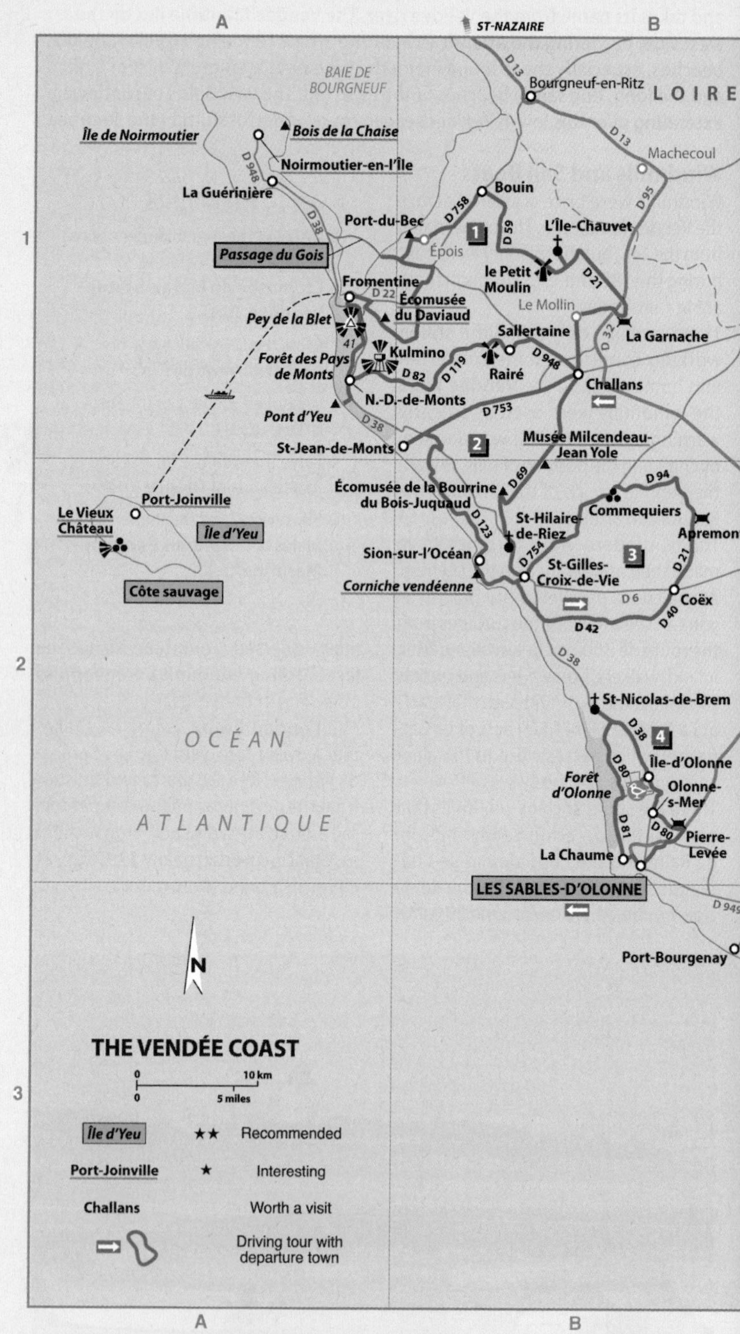

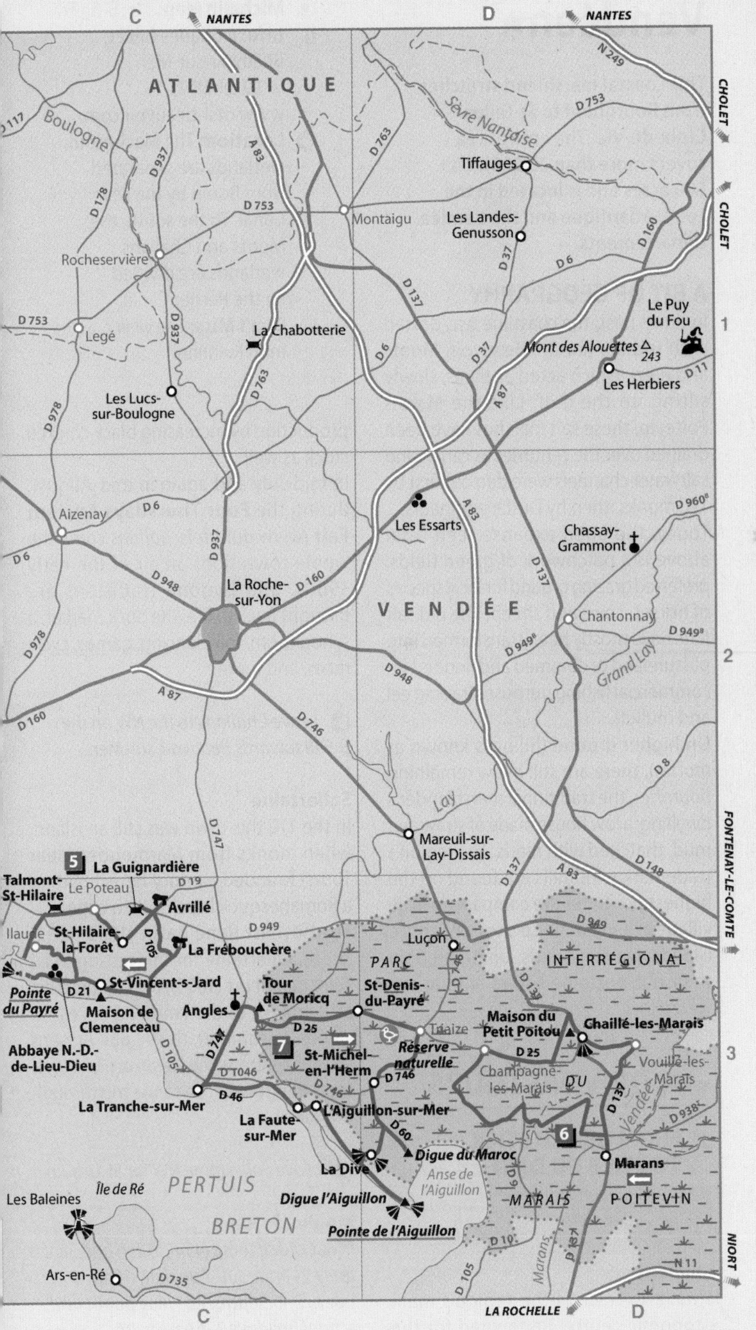
NANTES
NANTES
ATLANTIQUE
VENDÉE
CHOLET
CHOLET
FONTENAY-LE-COMTE
NIORT
LA ROCHELLE
Tiffauges
Montaigu
Les Landes-Genusson
Rocheservière
Legé
La Chabotterie
Le Puy du Fou
Mont des Alouettes
Les Herbiers
Les Lucs-sur-Boulogne
Aizenay
Les Essarts
Chassay-Grammont
La Roche-sur-Yon
Chantonnay
Mareuil-sur-Lay-Dissais
La Guignardière
Talmont-St-Hilaire
Le Poteau
Avrillé
St-Hilaire-la-Forêt
La Frébouchère
Pointe du Payré
St-Vincent-s-Jard
Maison de Clemenceau
Abbaye N.-D.-de-Lieu-Dieu
Angles
Tour de Moricq
St-Denis-du-Payré
Luçon
PARC
INTERRÉGIONAL
Maison du Petit Poitou
Chaillé-les-Marais
Réserve naturelle
St-Michel-en-l'Herm
Champagne-les-Marais
Vouillé-les-Marais
La Tranche-sur-Mer
La Faute-sur-Mer
L'Aiguillon-sur-Mer
Digue du Maroc
La Dive
Marans
Anse de l'Aiguillon
Digue l'Aiguillon
Pointe de l'Aiguillon
MARAIS
POITEVIN
Les Baleines
Île de Ré
PERTUIS
BRETON
Ars-en-Ré
Sèvre Nantaise
Boulogne
Grand Lay
Lay
Vendée
Marans
A 83
A 87
N 249
N 11
D 753
D 763
D 937
D 178
D 117
D 978
D 6
D 37
D 137
D 160
D 11
D 948
D 746
D 747
D 960
D 949
D 8
D 148
D 19
D 105
D 21
D 25
D 1046
D 46
D 60
D 938
D 10
D 735

Marais Breton-Vendéen★

This coastal marshland stretches from Bourgneuf to St-Gilles-Croix-de-Vie. The entire area covers more than 20 000ha/49 500 acres and is located in the Loire-Atlantique and the Vendée *départements*.

Michelin Map: 316: E-6 –F-7
Info: r. Charles Gallet, Beauvoir-sur-Mer. 02 51 68 71 13. www.otsi-beauvoir.com.
Location: The Machecoul wetlands are separated from Bouin by the Dain Canal. To the south, the Monts and Challans wetlands are divided by the Perrier Canal.
Don't Miss: The view from Kulmino.

A BIT OF GEOGRAPHY

In times past, the coastline was dotted with islands (Bouin, Beauvoir, Monts and Riez), which acted as dams, slowly silting up the gulf. Like the Marais Poitevin, these salt marshes have been drained over the centuries as canals and saltwater channels were dug out first by 17C monks, then by Dutch engineers.
Today, the open expanse seen from above is a patchwork of green fields, preferred grazing ground for local species of horses, cows and sheep. The old salt flats have mostly been transformed into pastureland or dammed and flooded for commercial fishing purposes (raising eel and mullet).
On higher ground (hillocks known as *mottes*), there are still a few remaining *bourrines*, the traditional marshlander's dwelling; a low house made of straw and mud, thatched with reeds. The region's trademark windmills are found on the highest points, in the company of little villages; many of these sites were once islands. On the canals, boatmen pole their flat-bottomed *yoles* among the waterfowl.

DRIVING TOURS

1 FROM GRAND ÉTIER TO ÉTIER DU DAIN★

105km/63mi round tour from Challans. Allow 6hrs.

Challans

This farm town is the region's main economic centre. Renowned for the ducks raised here, in demand by the greatest chefs, Challans has diversified production by increasing black chicken stock as well.
In mid-July and again in mid-August, during the **Four Thursdays Ancient Fair** *(www.autrefoischallans.com)*, the whole town dons an air of the early 1900s, and bygone traditions are brought back to life: the duck market, a schoolroom, folk dancing, games, cycle races, and more.

Leave Challans to the NW on the D 948 towards Beauvoir-sur-Mer.

Sallertaine

In the 11C this town was still an island, when monks from Marmoutier (near Tours) founded a priory here, building a Romanesque church with a cupola. The novelist René Bazin (1853–1932) chose Sallertaine for the setting of *La Terre qui meurt* (1899), proclaiming his attachment to the land and ancestral values. In summer, the Île aux Artisans (a crafts centre; *www.lileauxartisans.fr*) is the starting point for a canoe trip through the marsh.

Leave Sallertaine NW for St-Urbain.

Moulin de Rairé

Guided tours (45min) Jun and Sept daily 2–6pm; Jul–Aug daily 10am–noon, 2–6.30pm; Feb–May public and school holidays 2–6pm. 4€. 02 51 35 51 82. www.moulin-a-vent-de-raire.com.

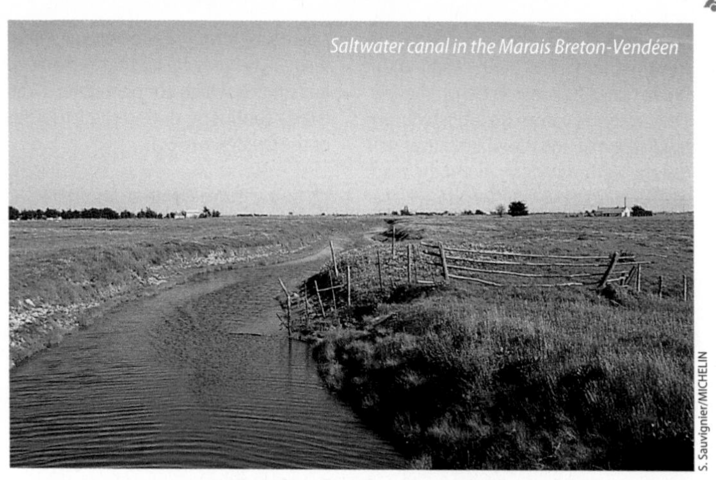

Saltwater canal in the Marais Breton-Vendéen

S. Sauvignier/MICHELIN

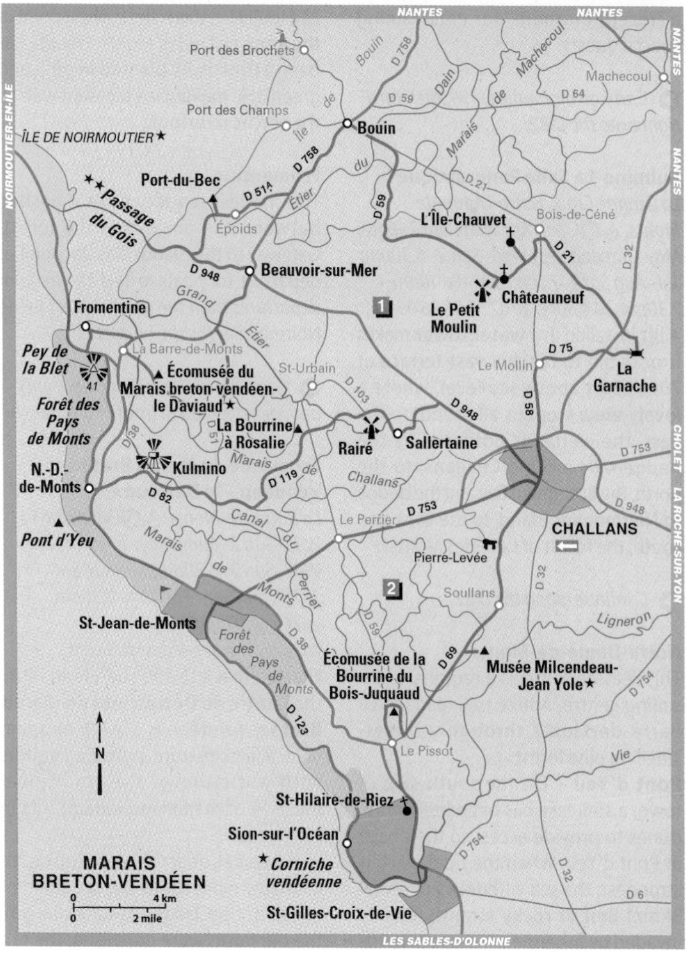
NANTES
NANTES
NANTES
NANTES
NOIRMOUTIER-EN-ÎLE
CHOLET
LA ROCHE-SUR-YON
LES SABLES-D'OLONNE
Port des Brochets
Port des Champs
Machecoul
Bouin
Marais de Machecoul
Dain
Bouin
D 758
D 59
D 64
ÎLE DE NOIRMOUTIER ★
Île de Bouin
Étier du Dain
D 21
Port-du-Bec
★★ Passage du Gois
D 51A
Époids
D 59
L'Île-Chauvet
Bois-de-Céné
D 21
D 32
D 948
Beauvoir-sur-Mer
Châteauneuf
Le Petit Moulin
1
Grand Étier
Fromentine
La Barre-de-Monts
D 75
Le Mollin
La Garnache
Pey de la Blet
41
Écomusée du Marais breton-vendéen-le Daviaud ★
St-Urbain
D 103
D 948
D 58
Forêt des Pays de Monts
La Bourrine à Rosalie
D 51
D 38
Rairé
Sallertaine
D 753
Kulmino
Marais de Challans
D 119
N.-D.-de-Monts
D 82
Canal du Perrier
Le Perrier
D 753
D 948
CHALLANS
Pont d'Yeu
Marais de Monts
Pierre-Levée
2
Soullans
D 32
St-Jean-de-Monts
Ligneron
Forêt des Pays de Monts
D 38
D 59
Écomusée de la Bourrine du Bois-Juquaud
D 69
Musée Milcendeau-Jean Yole ★
D 754
D 123
N
Le Pissot
Vie
St-Hilaire-de-Riez
Sion-sur-l'Océan
D 754
D 32
MARAIS BRETON-VENDÉEN
★ Corniche vendéenne
0 4 km
0 2 mile
D 6
St-Gilles-Croix-de-Vie

Standing tall above the marshland, this tower windmill has been catching the breeze since its construction in the 16C. The rotating cap can be adjusted from inside the mill, and the white canvas sails use the Berton system. Along the road, you soon cross over the Grand Étier (*étier* means "tide channel" or "marsh creek").

La Bourrine à Rosalie

Le Robinet, Sallertaine. Open Easter holidays, Jun and Sept daily 2.30–6pm; Jul–Aug Mon 10.30am–12.30pm, Tue–Sun 10.30am–12.30pm, 2–7pm. 1.80€. 02 51 49 43 60.

This typical marshlander's house has a reed roof, a common room with a raised bed (in case of flooding), and a "reception room" for entertaining special guests.

Carry on along the D 199, then turn right onto the D 82.

Kulmino-La Salle Panoramique

La Grande Croix, Notre-Dame-de-Monts. Open Apr Wed–Sun 2–6pm; May–Jun and Sept Wed–Sun 2–6.30pm; Jul–Aug Sat 2–7.30p,. Sun–Fri 10am–7.30pm. 4.50€. 02 51 58 86 09.

A lift installed in a **water tower** makes it possible to reach a vast terrace at 70m/230ft above sea level, where a lovely **view**★ opens all round: to the east, the wetlands bordered by the hedgerows around Challans; to the north, the Bourgneuf Bay and the bridge to Noirmoutier Island; to the west and south, the forest of Côte des Monts.

Continue along the D 82.

Notre-Dame-de-Monts

This seaside resort is a regional land-sailing centre. A bike trail leads to La Barre-de-Monts through a sweet-smelling pine forest.

Pont d'Yeu – On the south side of town, a staircase has been built in the dunes to provide access to the beach at Pont d'Yeu. When the tidal reach is strongest, the sea withdraws to reveal 3km/1.8mi of rocky strand, quickly invaded by fishermen (*as soon as the tide turns, return to the beach without delay*). This may be all that remains of an isthmus which connected Île d'Yeu to the continent, during the Ices Ages of the Quaternary Era.

Leave Notre-Dame-de-Monts to the N by a little road running parallel to the D 38.

The picturesque **Route de la Rive** traces the border between the **Pays de Monts Forest** and the first glimmerings of the marsh. Many paths lead from the forest to the ocean, through the sea oats waving atop the dunes.

Pey de la Blet

At 41m/135ft, this is the highest point of the former island of Monts. The site has been attractively planted in pine and green oak, making it a pleasant walk to the **scenic overlook**.

Fromentine

This modest seaside resort is nestled between the ocean and the forest. Gateway to the islands, it is the point of departure for boats to Île d'Yeu *(regular departures from the jetty)* and for Île de Noirmoutier *(by the bridge)*.

Go to the centre of Barre-de-Monts and take the road in front of the church.

Écomusée du Marais Breton-Vendéen – le Daviaud★

La Barre-de-Monts. Open Apr Wed–Sun 2–6pm; May–Jun and Sept Wed–Sun 2–6.30pm; Jul–Aug Sat 2–7.30pm, Sun–Fri 11am–7.30pm. 7€. 02 51 93 84 84. www.ecomusee-ledaviaud.com.

Housed in a late 19C sharehold farm, the **Centre de Découverte du Marais Breton-Vendéen** is a living museum of local architecture, providing visitors with a picture of the traditional lifestyle of marshland inhabitants in bygone days.

In a typical *bourrine* sod house, an animated model describes the different construction methods and the way the old farms were organised; the salt

store, located next to the marsh where salt was collected, displays an exhibit on that process. The Écomusée is in a whitewashed building made of clay and straw, with a reed roof, once used as a barn and stable and now featuring presentations on the local environment and wildlife (geomorphology, fauna, flora, migratory birds). A bit farther on, a reconstitution of the inside of an ordinary dwelling at the turn of the 20C gives a good idea of the austere lives led there.

You can try your hand at some of the marshlanders' special skills, by manoeuvring a *yole* down the canal, or vaulting over a stream with a long pole.

Continue until you reach the D 51, then turn left.

Beauvoir-sur-Mer

This village used to be on the shore and was the site of an 11C castle, which was laid to siege by Henri IV in 1588, then destroyed one year later. The church, **St-Philibert** *(02 51 68 71 13)*, also dates from the 11C; the bulky bell tower rises in contrast to the elegant doorway.

Take the D 948 W out of Beauvoir-sur-Mer.

Passage du Gois★★

See ÎLE DE NOIRMOUTIER.

Head back towards Beauvoir-sur-Mer, and turn left after 2km/1.2mi.

Époids

The oyster beds of **Port-du-Bec**, situated in the bay of Bourgneuf, have been contributing to the local economy since the 1950s. South of the Bouin polders, related activities have developed, including fish hatcheries, shellfish breeding and algae farms. When the tide is low and the channel known as the Étier du Dain empties out, a veritable forest of wooden piles and footbridges is revealed, an unusual landscape which gave the wharf the nickname of **port chinois**.

At Époids, take the D 51A, then turn left onto the D 758.

Bouin

Once an island encircled by the ocean and the Dain tidal channel, this town suffered repeated flooding up until 1940, when a sturdy dyke, 14km/8.7mi long, was built to protect the charming streets and oyster beds of Bouin.

Leave Bouin SE on the D 21; after 2km/1.2mi turn right onto the D 59.

Châteauneuf

The bell in the church tower was made in 1487.

Le Petit Moulin – *Guided tours daily Jul–Aug 11am–7pm; Mar–30 Jun and 1 Sept–8 Nov 2–7pm. 3.80€; 02 51 49 31 07. http://moulin.chateauneuf.free.fr.*

Since 1703, when it was erected to replace a wooden mill, this restored tower mill has been grinding grain. The cap can be turned from inside to face the sails to the wind, and the Berton system of adjustable vanes increases efficiency.

Leave Châteauneuf on the D 28 NE.

Abbaye de l'Île-Chauvet

Bois-de-Céné. Open Jul–mid-Sept Sun–Mon pms. 4.50€. 02 51 68 13 19.

The abbey was founded around 1130 by Benedictine monks beckoned by the lord of La Garnache. The site was then a deserted island. The building was damaged during the Hundred Year's War, and abandoned by the monks in 1588, in the heat of the religious wars ravaging France. In 1680 the abbey came back to life when members of the Camaldolite order moved in; they lived there until 1778. The French Revolution finally closed the book on the abbey's history.

Among the vestiges, admire the pointed arch of the doorway, its covings and decorative interlaced patterns.

Nothing is left of the Camaldolite buildings. In the Benedictine wing, the dormitory and its impressive 13C roof

beams are open to visitors. The pilgrims' hostel stands next to it.

Before arriving in Bois-de-Céné, take the D 21 straight ahead.

La Garnache

Once a fortified medieval refuge in the hands of powerful feudal lords who possessed much of the surrounding land, La Garnache stands at the north-eastern border of the Marais.

Château – *Open Jul–Aug daily 2.30–6.30pm combined ticket with museum. 3€. 02 51 93 11 08).* The once-proud edifice was long left to sleep beneath a thick cover of vines. First erected in the 12C, it was renovated in the 13C and 15C, before Louis XIII ordered it razed in 1622; the Vendée Wars finished the task. Time has left the ramparts and two hollow towers erect, and the base of the square keep still marks the ground.

Musée Passé et Traditions – *Same times and charges as the château.* This museum offers a reconstruction of a peasant dwelling. There is also a collection of headdresses and clothing, farm tools, and a dairy.

Leave Garnache on the D 75 W.

The road is bordered by pine groves.

At Mollin, the D 58 leads back to Challans.

2 FROM THE SHORE INLAND

60km/37mi round tour from Challans – allow 3hrs.

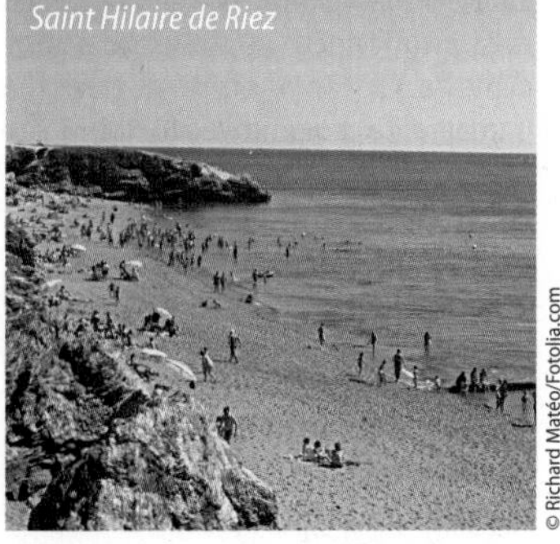

Saint Hilaire de Riez

© Richard Matéo/Fotolia.com

Challans

See Driving Tour 1.

Leave Challans on the D 753 W.

St-Jean-de-Monts

A popular seaside resort, the big sand beach at St-Jean is part of the long stretch reaching from Fromentine to Sion, 26km/16.2mi interrupted only by the rocky Pont d'Yeu tidal flat.

The town centre is sheltered by wooded dunes; the church was reconstructed in 1935, with due respect for its 14C charms, and the shingled belfry is 17C.

Leave St-Jean-de-Monts to the S and take the D 123 by the seafront.

Sion-sur-l'Océan

This seaside resort is popular with shore fishing anglers, because of the quality of the local prawns.

Corniche Vendéenne★

South of Sion, the coast road overlooks rocks sculpted by the sea into shapes reminiscent of ancient ruins; a set of five clustered together are known as **les Cinq Pineaux**. The rocky cliff-face is pierced by tidal inlets and creeks. At the far end of a promontory, a plaintive wail may be heard rising from the **Trou du Diable** (Devil's Hole).

The corniche ends at Grosse Terre Point; take the steps near the lighthouse to reach the bottom of the cliff.

The road continues along the Corniche de Boisvinet, lined with Belle Époque villas. From the scenic overlook, take in the view of Pointe de la Garenne and the entrance to the port.

St-Gilles-Croix-de-Vie

See ST-GILLES-CROIX-DE-VIE.

Leave St-Gilles-Croix-de-Vie via the D 38B north towards Perrier.

To the right, the marshlands stretch all the way to the horizon.

St-Hilaire-de-Riez

This village looks out over the Vie Valley. The **church** *(pl. de l'Église; open daily 10am–6pm; guided tours summer Tue 10.45am; 02 51 54 31 97)* was rebuilt in the 19C; note the three 17C polychrome altarpieces.

Go back to the D 38B. At Pissot, go straight on via the D 59 towards Perrier.

Écomusée de la Bourrine du Bois-Juquaud

4 chemin du Bois-Juquaud. Open Apr Tue–Sun and public holidays 2–6pm; May–Jun and Sept Mon–Sat 10am–noon, 2–6pm, Sun and public holidays 3–7pm; Jul–Aug Mon–Sat 10am–12.30pm, 2–7pm, Sun and public holidays 3–7pm; Feb–Mar Mon–Fri 2–6pm; All Saints and Christmas holidays Tue–Sun 2–6pm. Guided tours (1hr) 10.30am, 3pm. Closed 1 Jan, 1 Nov, 25 Dec. 2.80€. 02 51 49 27 37.

Tucked away in a grove, this typical marshlander's property has been faithfully restored part and parcel.

In the farmyard, or *tcheraïe*, are several small buildings: the *bourrine* with early 20C furnishings and adjacent bread oven; the barn; shelters for keeping the wheelbarrow and the firewood dry; the chicken coop; the dairy.

Continue along the country lane, then turn left onto the D 69 towards Soullans.

Passio, Musée Milcendeau-Jean Yole★

Le Bois Durand, Soullans. Open May–Jun and Sept Wed–Sun 2–6.30pm; Jul–Aug daily 11am–6.30pm; spring, All Saints and winter holidays Wed–Sun 2–6pm. 3.50€. 02 51 35 03 84. www.museemilcendeau.fr.

The museum is devoted to two artists with roots in the Marais Breton-Vendéen, the painter Charles Milcendeau (1872–1919) and the author Jean Yole. The house was purchased by Milcendeau in 1905. A student of Gustave Moreau, the young artist used sketching and pastel techniques. Inspired by the daily lives of marshlanders, the portraits and domestic scenes he painted are like an ethnological record.

From Soullans, the D 69 towards Challans runs along a wooded area.

ADDRESSES

STAY

Hôtel de l'Antiquité – *14 r. Galliéni, 85300 Challans. 02 51 68 02 84. www.hotelantiquite.com. 20 rooms.* A modern house built in the local style. Individually decorated rooms overlooking the courtyard; those in the annex are particularly attractive. Swimming pool.

Hôtel du Commerce – *1 r. Galliéni, 85300 Challans. 02 51 68 06 24. www.hotelducommercechallans.com. Closed late Dec–early Jan. 21 rooms. 6.50€.* Simple white building with practical, pastel-coloured rooms. Buffet breakfast.

Le Relais des Touristes – *rte de Gois, 85230 Beauvoir-sur-Mer. 02 51 68 70 19. www.lerelaisdestouristes.com. Closed mid-Feb–early Mar. 39 rooms. 8€.* Practical, plain guest rooms.Indoor pool.

EAT

Ferme-auberge du Jaunay "L'Île Sauvage" – *Le Jaunay, 85230 Bouin. 02 51 49 12 11. www.ferme-auberge85.fr. 5 rooms. 4.60€. Half-board available.* Welcoming *auberge* in the middle of the marsh. Home-farmed lamb or duck on the menu. Guest rooms, and camping available.

Chez Charles – *8 pl. du Champ de Foire, 85300 Challans. 02 51 93 36 65. www.restaurantchezcharles.com. Closed Sun evening, Mon and 23 Dec–24 Jan.* A family-run bistro serving classic seasonal cuisine, using regional produce. Children's menu available.

La Pitchounette – *48 r. Bonne-Brise, 85230 St-Gervais. 02 51 68 68 88. Closed Mon–Tue (Sept–Jun), 10 days in Jun and 2 wks in Sept–Oct.* . Pretty, white building with green shutters, and an original Baroque interior with chandeliers and an open fireplace. Unfortunately, the terrace is a little noisy.

Île de Noirmoutier★

Vendée

The low-lying island, blessed with a mild climate, luminous skies and numerous beauty spots, is a popular holiday retreat. Auguste Renoir, having stayed here with paintbrush and palette, wrote to a friend: "It is an admirable place, lovely as the South, but the sea is beautiful in a different way."

- **Population:** 4 855
- **Info:** rte du Pont, Barbatre. 02 51 39 12 42. www.ile-noirmoutier.com.
- **Location:** The long, thin island of Noirmoutier frames the western margin of a gulf S of the Loire estuary, separated from the mainland only by a narrow channel that recedes at low tide.
- **Don't Miss:** Passage du Gois.
- **Kids:** Aquarium-Sealand.

GEOGRAPHICAL NOTES

Noirmoutier comprises three sectors. To the south, the Barbâtre dunes stretch towards the Vendée Coast, from which they are separated by the **Fosse de Fromentine**, a gap only 800m/80yds across but scoured by violent currents. The centre of the isle is similar to the Dutch landscape, with **polders** (stretches of land reclaimed from the sea) and salt marshes below sea level, protected by dykes. The area is criss-crossed by canals, the most important of which, the **Étier de l'Arceau**, crosses the island from one side to the other.

To the north, a series of creeks indent a rocky coast carpeted with oak, pine and acacia – the flowers, commonly sold as mimosa, are exported each year by the tonne. Here again there are dunes, planted this time with maritime pines, on which several windmills stand.

A BIT OF HISTORY

This haven of peace was not spared by the Vendée Wars, since it was of strategic importance for both sides. The island changed hands several times, which led to the inevitable massacres.

Since Roman times, successive subsidence has been reducing the area of Noirmoutier so that although the island is still 20km/12.4mi long, it is now scarcely 1km/0.6mi wide at La Guérinière – where, in 1882, heavy seas almost cut the place in two.

The islanders live in houses with red-tiled roofs and whitewashed walls. Since 1959 an undersea pipeline has supplied them with mainland fresh water. A 700m/2 300ft-long pre-stressed concrete bridge on nine twin piers has spanned the Fromentine Channel since 1971.

NOIRMOUTIER-EN-L'ÎLE

Noirmoutier is the island capital, with white, sun-bleached buildings extending parallel to a canal-port drained of water at low tide. The 1km/0.6mi-long Grande-Rue (main street) ends at a former parade ground opening onto the port.

PRACTICAL INFORMATION

GETTING THERE

Pont Routier – Leave the mainland at Fromentine and cross this concrete bridge, toll free.

Passage du Gois – Leave from Beauvoir-sur-Mer to take this causeway, which is only accessible at low tide. Follow the instructions and check the times of the tides by consulting the website http://vendee.online.fr/meteo.htm.

GETTING AROUND

Even if vehicles aren't forbidden on the island, the best way to get around is by bike or, even better, on foot.

For a brochure outlining the marked footpaths, or a map of the cycle paths, contact the local tourist offices.

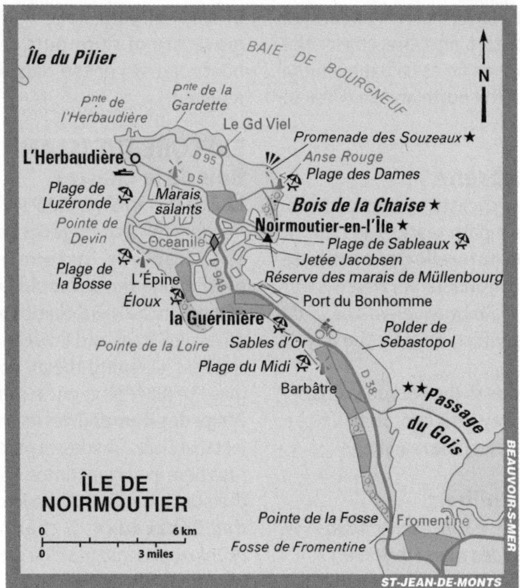

Place d'Armes

The Royalist **Général d'Elbée** was executed by a Republican firing squad on this parade ground on 6 January 1794. A little way back from the esplanade, the castle and the church stand side by side on a slight rise.

Two fine 18C buildings are nearby: on the right, facing the castle, the Lebreton des Grapillières mansion (now a hotel); on the left the Jacobsen house, named after a Dutch family who worked on the draining of the island during the 18C.

Château

pl. d'Armes. Open mid-Jun–mid-Sept daily 10am–7pm; early Feb–mid-Jun and mid-Sept–early Nov Wed–Mon 10am–12.30pm, 2.30–6pm. 4.25€. 02 51 39 10 42.

The 15C defensive perimeter, bare and austere, forms a rectangle interrupted only by two corner towers with bartizan turrets. Picturesque views of the town, the salt marshes and the sea can be seen from the covered way running around the castle's circumference. Inside the enclosure are the old governor's residence and a square 11C keep, which houses a **museum**.

Ground Floor – This floor is devoted to local history: archaeology and the Vendée Wars. The armchair in which Général d'Elbée was shot is on display; incapable of moving because he had not recovered from wounds suffered in the Battle of Cholet, the general was transported in this chair to place d'Armes, where the executioners waited. A 19C painting by Julien Le Blant illustrates the drama.

First Floor – This section contains a diverse assortment of items connected with the ocean: ships' figureheads, model boats, a pirate's axe and sabre, an early 19C cross made from seashells.

Second and Third Floors – These floors, devoted to the fine arts, contain works by artists attracted by the beauty of the island (A Baudry, F Palvadeau, O de Rochebrune).

Logis du Gouverneur – This floor houses a splendid collection of English **Staffordshire pottery**★ (18C and 19C), some of it known as **Jersey pottery** because it was there that the pieces were stored. The variety of shapes, the decorative motifs and the colours used lend this collection a particular brilliance.

From La Vigie turret there is a **panorama** of Noirmoutier and the coast: the view extends as far as La Baule on the mainland to the north and Île d'Yeu to the south.

Jetée Jacobsen★

Reserved for cyclists and pedestrians, this pleasant path marks the limit of the **Réserve naturelle des marais de Müllembourg** *(Maison de la réserve, Fort Larron, 85330 Noirmoutier-en-l'Île; ℘02 51 35 81 16)*, which borders the Bay of Bourgneuf.

The jetty leads to the Bois de la Chaise; along the way you can observe the fauna and flora of the marshes.

Église St-Philbert

r. du Cheminet. Open daily 10am–7pm. Guided tours (1hr30min) including this church. 5.50€. ℘02 51 68 68 81. http://doyenne-stjeandemonts.catho85.org.

This former Benedictine abbey-church combines the Romanesque (chancel) and Gothic (nave) styles. Beneath the chancel, flanked by sumptuous Baroque altars, a fine 11C **crypt** occupies the site of the original Merovingian chapel. The crypt houses the cenotaph of St Philbert – an empty tomb installed in the 11C, the original sarcophagus was transferred at the time of the Norman invasions.

Aquarium-Sealand

Le Vieux Port. Open daily Jul–Aug 10am–8pm; Sept–mid-Nov and early Feb–Jun 10am–12.30pm, 2–7pm. 11€ (children 9€). ℘02 51 39 08 11. www.aquariumdenoirmoutier.com.

Local and tropical sea creatures are on show here in a setting featuring underwater caverns and the hulks of sunken ships.

Musée de la Construction Navale

r. de l'écluse. Closed for renovation. ℘02 51 39 24 00. www.ville-noirmoutier.fr.

In this former shipwright's workshop, housed in the old salt storehouse, the museum presents the various stages of shipbuilding. Take a look at the graveyard of ships outside. Here lie boats too old or too damaged to be repaired.

EXPLORE THE ISLAND

Bois de la Chaise★

2km/1.2mi NE via the D 948 (follow the signs towards Plage des Dames).

This fragrant, harboured wood overlooking the sea could be a corner of the French Riviera: clumps of umbrella pines, ilex trees and flowering mimosa thickets, scenting the air combine to give the place its exotic reputation.

Plage des Dames owes its name to the fact that Gallic Druidesses practised their rites here in ancient times. The beach is the starting point of the **Promenade des Souzeaux**★, a charming walk *(45min round trip)* past the creeks of the island's northeastern coast.

Leave the beach via the footpath under the ilex trees on the left of the small landing-stage, then follow the first track climbing upwards, again on the left.

After the lighthouse, pines are again interspersed with the ilex. The rocky cliffs here overlook a sea studded with reefs and there are views of the Côte de Jade (Jade Coast), west of Pornic on the mainland. The clifftop path passes above the Anse Rouge (Red Cove), dominated by Plantier Tower, before leading to Souzeaux beach.

L'Herbaudière

5km/3.1mi NE along the D 5.

A busy traffic of brightly coloured boats animates this small fishing port where the catch is sold daily at quayside auctions. A forest of masts rises above the pleasure craft moored in a neighbouring basin.

From the jetty separating this marina from the fishing port there is a view of Île du Pilier, which was once linked to Noirmoutier by a causeway.

La Guérinière

4km/2.5mi S along the D 948.

The Port du Bonhomme with its oyster-breeders' cabins shelters on the north coast of the village, whereas the south coast is lined with beaches overlooked by the Bois des Éloux and windmills.

Musée des Traditions de l'Île

pl. de l'Église. Open daily Apr–Jun and Sept–15 Oct 3–6pm; Jul–Aug 10am–12.30pm, 3–7pm. 3.50€. 02 51 39 41 39.

This museum presents a survey of local activities and folk art in the late 19C and early 20C. The museum also houses reconstructed local interiors, collections of costumes and headdresses, and such local folk art as seascapes painted on fragments of sail canvas by *cap-horniers* (Cape-Horners) – sailors who had worked aboard the full-rigged clippers navigating the seas around Cape Horn in the cargo races of the 19C.

Maison des Écluses et Pêches Traditionnelles

10 r. du Petit Franc. Open daily 3–6pm. 1€. 02 51 35 81 65.

Housed in a World War II bunker, this small museum illustrates the history of fishing on the Atlantic Coast.

Passage du Gois★★

12km/7.4mi SE via the D 948.

This 4.5km/2.8mi submersible causeway, formed by shoals, was the only way for vehicles to reach the island until 1971, when the toll bridge was opened. Floats are provided at regular intervals along the way so that people caught by the rapidly rising waters can hoist themselves to safety. It is a busy spot for fishermen, oyster and mussel farmers (*opening hours depend on the tide level*).

ADDRESSES

STAY

Chambre d'hôte Baranger – *8 r. de la Mougendrie. 02 51 39 12 59. yvan.baranger@wanadoo.fr. Closed 15 Sept–Easter. 5 rooms.* Just two steps from the château, this house offers guests simple rooms that open onto an enclosed garden. One studio with kitchen and terrace.

Hôtel Autre Mer – *32 av. Joseph-Pineau. 02 51 39 11 77. www.autremerhotel.fr. Closed mid-Nov–late Mar. 27 rooms. 8.50€.* Freshly renovated hotel with contemporary décor in the rooms.

Hôtel Turquoise – *26 r. de la Fontaine, 85330 Noirmoutier-en-l'Île, 200m/220yds from the château. 02 28 10 68 90. www.hotel-turquoise.fr. Closed early Dec and Jan. 12 rooms. 9€.* In a quiet residential area, these typical low houses have ground-floor guest rooms, each with a private terrace.

Château du Pélavé – *9 allée de Chaillot, Bois de la Chaise. 02 51 39 01 94. chateau-du-pelave@wanadoo.fr. 18 rooms. Restaurant.* This late 19C granite villa is surrounded by a pretty park. Its sunny rooms, four with private terraces, have modern furniture.

Hôtel Fleur de Sel – *10 r. des Saulniers. 02 51 39 09 07. www.fleurdesel.fr. Closed Nov–Mar. 35 rooms. Restaurant.* Near the Sableux beach, this charming low house offers rooms decorated with yew or waxed pine furniture. Pool.

EAT

La Plage de Jules – *at the Plage des Dames (on the approach to Noirmoutier en l'Île, towards Bois de la Chaise). 02 51 39 06 87. www.laplagedejules.com. Reservations recommended. Closed Oct–early Apr.* A delightful setting to enjoy the fish and seafood specialities, accompanied by the island's famous potatoes.

L'Île d'Her – *10 pl. d'Armes. 02 51 39 11 93. Reservations recommended in high season. Closed Sun evening and Mon.* A popular address with locals, largely due to its big terrace. A varied menu, focusing on fish and seafood.

Le Grand Four – *1 r. de la Cure. 02 51 39 61 97. www.legrandfour.com. Closed Dec–Jan, Sun evening and Mon (Sept–Jun).* Quaint little restaurant behind the château. Regional flavours and seafood.

St-Gilles-Croix-de-Vie

Vendée

The fishing boats moored here supply fish merchants and factories with lobsters, crabs, tuna fish and sardines for canning or freezing. While the fishermen live in picturesque houses in the Petite-Île district, holidaymakers flock to the beaches of Croix-de-Vie (Plage de Boisvinet) and La Garenne. In the summer there are boat trips around the coast, leaving from the port.

- **Population:** 7 281
- **Michelin Map:** 316: E-7
- **Info:** bd de l'Égalité, St-Gilles-Croix-de-Vie. ℘02 51 55 03 66. www.stgillescroixdevie.com.
- **Location:** The fishing port of Croix-de-Vie and the town of St-Gilles-sur-Vie, on the south bank of the Vie estuary, NW of Les Sables-d'Olonne, combine to make the single commune of St-Gilles-Croix-de-Vie.

DRIVING TOUR

3 BETWEEN JAUNAY AND VIE

45km/28mi. Allow half a day.

Leave St-Gilles-Croix-de-Vie S on D 38, then turn left towards L'Aiguillon-sur-Vie.

Coëx – Jardin des Olfacties★ *– pl. de l'Église. Open daily 5 Apr–11 Jun and 31 Aug–27 Sept 2–7pm; 12 Jun–30 Aug 10.30am–7pm. 6.80€. ℘02 51 55 53 41. www.lejardindesolfacties.com.*

The Gué-Gorand stream runs through this pleasantly floral garden. A path takes visitors through a series of "fragrant chambers" combining different plants and scents. Flower beds encircle a pond surrounded by sculptures, cultural exhibitions and leisure facilities.

Leave Coëx heading N on the D 40.

Apremont

pl. du Château. ℘02 51 55 70 54. www.apremontpaysdepalluau.fr.

In contrast to the surrounding flat landscape this village stands on a steep cliff. Near to the dam there is a pleasant spot, at the lake's edge, offering diverse activities (swimming, pedalos).

Château – Built in the 12C, it was remodelled in the early 16C by Philippe Chabot, Amiral de France under the reign of François I (*open Apr–May 2–6pm, Jun–Aug 10.30am–7pm, 1–20 Sept 10.30am–7pm; 3.50€ (12–16 years 2.50€); ℘02 51 55 73 66).*

Château d'Eau – The tower's lift takes you up to the glass rotunda, from where there is an immense panorama over the Vendée countryside to the ocean in the west (*open Jul–Aug 10.30am–7pm; 4.50€ combined ticket with the château (12–16 years 3€); ℘02 51 55 73 66).*

Leave Apremont heading NW on D 21, towards Challans. After 5km/3.1mi, turn left.

Château de Commequiers

Built in the 15C for Louis de Beaumont, it was dismantled on Richelieu's orders in 1628. The château still has its eight towers. Take the footbridge over the moat to visit the inner fortifications.

Leave Commequiers going SW on the D 754, which leads to St-Gilles.

ADDRESSES

EAT

La Crêperie – *4 r. Gautté. ℘02 51 55 02 77. Closed 7–21 Mar and 3–16 Oct, Mon off-season except school holidays.* Pretty 17C house serving home-made pancakes. Pleasant shady terrace.

Île d'Yeu★★

Vendée

The Isle of Yeu off the Atlantic Coast has a typical island feel with its unspoiled nature, mild temperature, sunny climate and limited motor traffic. The scenery of the island's often grandiose coastline is very varied. The unspoiled "Côte sauvage" faces the open sea, its crystalline schist rock formations making the island look much like Belle-Île, off the coast of Brittany. However, the eastern and southern coasts look more like the Vendée, with pine trees, evergreen oaks, dunes and long sandy beaches.

- **Population:** 4 880
- **Michelin Map:** 316: B-7–C-7
- **Info:** pl. du Marché, Île d'Yeu. ✆02 51 58 32 58. www.ile-yeu.fr.
- **Location:** The island's geographic location and geology have earned it nicknames such as the **Corsica of the Atlantic** and the **Grain of Granite**. Standing watch over the mainland, the 10km/6.2mi-long and 4km/2.5mi-wide island is one of the furthest from the west coast of France (10 nautical miles).
- **Don't Miss:** The Côte sauvage; Port-de-la-Meule; the views of the coast from the Vieux Château.

A BIT OF HISTORY

The island has been inhabited since prehistoric times and this was possibly the island where, according to the Greek geographer Strabo, a religious "college" of Druidesses was established.

A monastery was founded on Yeu in the 6C. The future St Amand, the "Apostle of Flanders", was drawn here at the beginning of the following century. In the 8C the island was given the enigmatic name of Insula (isle) Oya. In the 16C the entire population of a village in Cornouaille, southwest Brittany, led by its priest, settled on Yeu. The prefix *ker-*, attached to certain villages, is a distortion of the Lower Poitou dialect word *querry*, meaning a "village". Île d'Yeu was ruled by various seigneurs, including Olivier de Clisson, the brilliant warrior who became Commander-in-Chief of the French Army.

Aside from tourism, the islanders' main resource is fishing. The island's fishermen hold the national record for white tuna (101t). The port of Île d'Yeu supports nearly 260 fishermen.

EXPLORE THE ISLAND

Allow one day.

Cliff paths around the coast offer visitors a succession of splendid views – especially in the south and west – as well as the opportunity to explore the attractive coves and beaches below.

Port-Joinville★

This, the largest town on the island, was originally called Port-Breton; the present name derives from Admiral de Joinville, the third son of Louis-Philippe I, who brought Napoleon's body back to France in 1840. It is one of the most important tuna fishing ports in France. Tourists arriving from Fromentine or Noirmoutier can enjoy a picturesque view of the tiny port crammed with fishing boats and small trawlers, their multicoloured pennants, dressed above a series of buoys, fluttering in the breeze. Behind the masts and rigging is a quay bordered by white houses.

With the exception of the outer harbour, the port is left dry at low tide. Beyond the waterfront there is one shopping street and a network of lanes close-packed with fishermen's cottages.

Musée de la Pêche

Aside from tourism, fishing is the main activity. Fishermen specialise in quality fish, bass, monkfish, hake and white tuna or *albacore*. Start your tour with the former seaman's shelter, created in 1898 to provide support and assistance to the sailors, and perpetuate seafaring

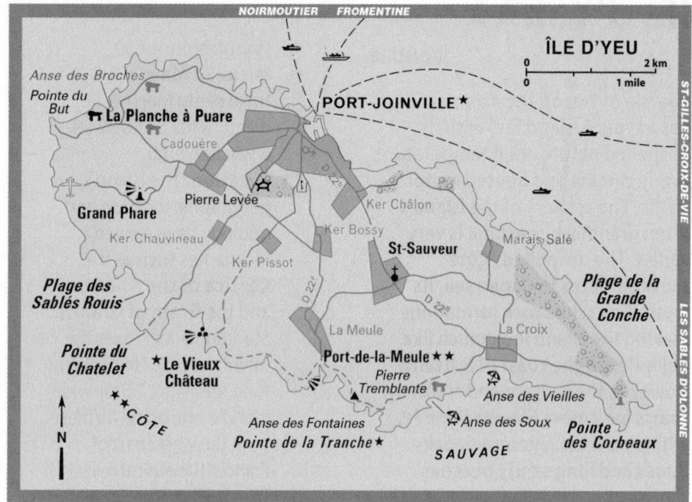

traditions. Today it houses this museum, whose collection includes model ships, marine instruments, photos and various objects, as well as an exhibition on fishing in the Amazon *(quai de la Chapelle; open Apr–Jun and Sept Fri–Sun 10am–1pm, Jul–Aug daily 10am–1pm, and in wet weather 5–7pm, check times before visiting; 4.50€ (under 15 years 3€); 02 51 59 31 00 or 02 51 58 32 58 (tourist office)).*

Cross the road to reach the lifeguard's shelter, which is also open to visitors. An exhibition is dedicated to the history of lifesaving: clothes, tools, different types of lifeboats, etc. Return to the seaman's shelter to watch a film on fishing techniques.

Grand Phare

Open Apr–Jun and 1–15 Sept Wed and Sat 11am–12.30pm, 2.30–4.30pm; Jul–Aug daily 11am–12.30pm, 2.30–6pm. 3€. 02 51 58 32 58.

The upper platform *(201 steps)* of the lighthouse is 41m/135ft above the

PRACTICAL INFORMATION

GETTING THERE

BY BOAT – On the mainland, there are three embarkation points for ferries crossing, on a regular or seasonal basis, to the Île d'Yeu (Port-Joinville). There is another crossing from the Île de Noirmoutier.

BY PLANE – The company Oya-Hélicoptères flies from the Barre-de-Monts heliport (on the mainland) to Port-Joinville (quai de la Chapelle, on the Île d'Yeu). 02 51 59 22 22. Reservation advised. Flight time 10min. 85€ (2–12 years 64€).

GETTING AROUND

As soon as you land at the port you will be approached by bike rental companies based at Port-Joinville. They all essentially hire out the same material (mountain bikes, Dutch bikes, children's seats or trailers) at the same price. Walking and cycling circuits with a map are recommended by the island's tourist office. There is also a bus service which runs to the Côte sauvage. Guided tours by coach are available April–September (departure in front of the ferry terminal). There's a small train in July and August. Another option is the **package bus + hike on the Côte sauvage** (contact tourist office for information).

Le Vieux Château, Île d'Yeu

©Hervé Gyssels/Photononstop

ground (and 56m/184ft above sea level). There is a splendid **view**★ looking out over the island to the ocean and, in clear weather, to the coast from Noirmoutier to St-Gilles-Croix-de-Vie.

Dolmen de La Planche à Puare

This megalith stands on a stretch of moorland near the **Anse des Broches** cove, at the northwestern tip of the island. It is constructed of schistose granite blocks and is unusual in that it has a central passage with lateral chambers (two each side of the passage). Ancient bones have been found here.

WALKING TOUR CÔTE SAUVAGE★★

The island is best explored along the ancient customs cliff paths, on foot or by bike.

This rugged coastline stretches from the Pointe du But to the Pointe des Corbeaux, indented in an irregular fashion. The ocean views are magnificent. Two of the best are from a cliff path linking the old castle with Port-de-la-Meule. Perched above sheer rock-faces plunging into the sea, the path leads walkers to a picturesque **view**★★ looking down over the creek.

Le Vieux Château★

Open Apr–Jun some weekdays 11am–4.30pm; Jul–Aug daily 11am–6pm; Sept some weekdays noon–5.30pm . 4.50€. 02 51 58 32 58.

This old castle occupies an imposing site at the seaward end of a moor. Its walls rise from a granite spur gashed by a narrow crevasse 17m/56ft deep; down below, the ocean waves boom like thunder.

It was built in feudal times (possibly the 11C) and remodelled in the 16C, and this wild pirates' lair now forms a

A Marshal Detained

On 16 November 1945 a naval escort vessel landed an old man of 90 on the island. He was to be incarcerated in the citadel at Pierre-Levée. The old man was the "ex-Marshal" Philippe Pétain, head of Vichy (collaborationist) France from 1940 to 1944, whose death sentence for treason had been commuted to life imprisonment. In 1951 he was struck by a double pulmonary congestion and taken to hospital. He died on 23 July. Men who had fought under him at Verdun, in World War I, carried the coffin to the cemetery at Port-Joinville, where he lies.

rough trapezoid flanked by defensive bastion towers.

A footbridge, replacing the old drawbridge, leads inside the walls. From the top of the keep *(beware: there is no parapet)* there are marvellous **views**★★ of the Côte sauvage and the sea.

Port-de-la-Meule★★

A long, narrow inlet penetrating the coast. At the inner end is the slipway of the crabbers and lobster boats which sink their pots along the rocky depths of the Côte sauvage.

From the moorland heights above, the small white Chapel of Notre-Dame-de-Bonne-Nouvelle watches over the tiny port. The local sailors take part in an annual pilgrimage here.

The cliff path continues beyond the chapel as far as **la Pierre Tremblante**, an enormous boulder perched above the sea which can be made to rock gently by pressing on a certain spot.

Pointe de la Tranche★

A number of rocky creeks surround this headland; Anse des Fontaines, named after its freshwater spring; and another two particularly calm, sheltered and suitable for bathing – the Anse des Soux, where there is a marine grotto, and the **Anse des Vieilles**, the island's prettiest beach.

Pointe des Corbeaux

This is the southeastern extremity of Île d'Yeu, from where the island's two different landscapes can best be appreciated – the rocky, storm-tossed, Breton-style coast on the west; a sandy, pine-clad shoreline on the east.

St-Sauveur

This is commonly referred to simply as "the Town" as it was once the island capital. There is a Romanesque church *(open daily 9am–6pm)* with a square tower above the transept crossing.

ADDRESSES

STAY

Atlantic Hôtel – *3 quai Carnot, Port-Joinville. 02 51 58 38 80. www.hotel-yeu.com. Closed 5 Jan–1 Feb. 18 rooms. 8€.* On the fishing docks above a fishmonger's, this hotel is one of the island's better addresses. Access is by a narrow stairway next to the shop. Its small modern rooms are simple, functional and well kept.

Chambre d'hôte M et Mme Cadou – *10 r. de Ker Guérin, St-Sauveur. 02 51 58 55 13. Closed Oct–Mar. 3 rooms.* This house is one of the few places to stay in the picturesque village of St-Sauveur. All blue and white, the décor of the spacious rooms is inspired by that of a ship's cabin.

Chambre d'hôte Villa Monaco – *Villa Monaco, Pointe des Corbeaux. 02 51 58 76 56. www.villamonaco.info. 6 rooms. Meals.* Situated on the eastern tip of the island, this blue-shuttered Vendée house has an unbeatable location. Simple rooms tastefully decorated, let by the week in the summer. Self-catering cottage available only in the winter.

Hôtel l'Escale – *14 r. de la Croix du port, Port-Joinville. 02 51 58 50 28. www.yeu-escale.fr. Closed 15 Nov–15 Dec. 29 rooms.* This hotel is a good base for exploring the island. The décor is bright and cheerful. Simple, well-maintained rooms.

EAT

Le Père Raballand – *6 pl. de la Norvège, Port-Joinville. 02 51 26 02 77. www.lepereraballand.com. Reservations recommended. Closed Dec–Feb.* A very popular address in the port. The outdoor terrace is perfect for watching the activity in the busy harbour. Off-season, meals are served in an attractive dining room decorated with marine paraphernalia. Simple cuisine.

Les Bafouettes – *8 r. Gabriel-Guist'hau, Port-Joinville. 02 51 59 38 38. Closed Sun–Mon (16 Sept–Mar).* This restaurant is one of the best addresses on the island. Several cosy dining rooms, the menu focuses on seafood prepared with creativity.

Les Sables-d'Olonne★★

Vendée

- **Population:** 15 596
- **Michelin Map:** 316: F-8–9
- **Info:** 1 promenade Maréchal Joffre, Les Sables-d'Olonne. ℘02 51 96 85 85. www.lessablesdolonne.com.
- **Location:** The resort stretches between a small port and an immense sandy beach, more than 3km/1.8mi long, at the foot of the Remblai (an embankment-promenade).
- **Parking:** There are car parks along the seafront, and in the town centre *(see map)*.
- **Don't Miss:** The Remblai promenade.
- **Kids:** The town's long sandy beach; the Parc Zoologique de Tranchet.

Les Sables-d'Olonne is an important seaside resort on the Côte de la Lumière (Coast of Light), built on the sands of what was once an offshore bar. Port Olona is the starting point for the round-the-world yacht race held every four years, known as the "Vendée Globe" – a tough challenge for single-handed sailing boats with no ports of call allowed and no help on the way *(www.vendeeglobe.org)*.

During the summer season's folklore festivals visitors will see the traditional, ancestral costume of short skirts with pleated petticoats, black stockings, sabots with heels, and tall headdresses with quivering "wings".

A BIT OF HISTORY

In the Middle Ages the site here was no more than an outer port for Olonne, a small town on the Vertonne estuary, now a little way inland. Then, little by little, the inlet silted up, finally turning into a swamp and then a salt marsh; Les Sables-d'Olonne (the Sands of Olonne) was created.

Under the patronage of Louis XI, who visited the area with the chronicler Commynes, the Seneschal (Steward) of Poitou, the port was dredged out and shipyards were built. Some of the vessels launched here took part in the great voyages of discovery. In the 17C a local sailor, **Nau the Olonnais**, distinguished himself in the West Indies during the bloody guerrilla warfare waged against the Spaniards by the buccaneers of Turtle Island and the privateer-pirate gang known as the "Brothers of the Coast". The seafarer met a gruesome fate, devoured by hostile natives.

SIGHTS

Le Remblai★

This embankment was built in the 18C to protect the town from the incursions of the sea. Today the fine promenade along its top is bordered by shops, hotels, cafés and luxury apartment blocks with splendid views of the beach and the bay. At the western extremity of Le Remblai is the municipal swimming pool and one of the casinos (Casino de la Plage, which includes a 700-seat theatre and a conference hall which can accommodate 1 000). Behind the modern blocks, the narrow streets of the Old Town beckon.

La Corniche

This southerly prolongation of Le Remblai leads to the new residential district of La Rudelière. After 3km/1.8mi the clifftop route arrives at **Le Puits d'Enfer** (Hell's Well) – a narrow and impressive cleft in the rock, where the sea foams and thrashes.

Quartier de la Rudelière

This district is near the **Lac de Tanchet**, with its lakeside sailing school. In the same area are the town's second casino, Casino des Sports, a thalassotherapy centre (Centre de Thalassothérapie), sports grounds and a zoo.

Les Sables d'Olonne

M.Thiery/MICHELIN

Parc Zoologique

rte du Tour de France. Open daily early Apr–Jun and Sept 9.30am–7pm; Jul–Aug 9.30am–7.30pm; 1–21 Oct and mid-Feb–early Apr 1.30–6.30pm. 14€ (children 9€). 02 51 95 14 10. www.zoo-des-sables.com.

In this pleasantly laid out "green belt" environment, visitors can observe a variety of wildlife including camels, llamas, kangaroos, monkeys and rare birds.

Église Notre-Dame-de-Bon-Port

51 r. du Palais. Guided tours Jul–Aug Tue 8pm. 2€. 02 51 96 95 53.

The church was built in 1646 by Richelieu. In the nave, the Gothic vaults are supported by pilasters of the Corinthian order.

Le Quartier de l'Île Penotte

Nestling in the Old Town, this is a charming district, with narrow, shady streets, hollyhocks, and façades decorated with shell mosaics, part of an urban development plan initiated by Danielle Aubin-Arnaud, then developed by the local residents with the help of children from neighbouring schools. In the middle of summer, you will welcome the cool, calm rue d'Assas.

Musée de l'Abbaye Ste-Croix

r. de Verdun. Open Tue–Sun 15 Jun–30 Sept 1–7pm; 1 Oct–14 Jun 2.30–5.30pm. Closed public holidays. 4.60€ (1st Sun of month no charge). 02 51 32 01 16.

The old Holy Cross Abbey, founded in the 17C by Benedictine monks, is now a cultural centre. The ground floor of the museum is devoted to the last works of Victor Brauner: *Mythologies et Fêtes des Mères* (1965).

On the first floor are works by Gaston Chaissac (1910–64), one of the leaders of the Art Brut movement. A second room is devoted to temporary exhibitions.

The second floor houses works by contemporary painters such as Baselitz, Beckmann, Cahn, Magnelli and Marquet. The 17C attics contain collections of **popular art and traditions**, including a marshland domestic hut interior, traditional costumes from Les Sables and the surrounding marshlands, seascapes by the local painter Paul-Emil Pajot, and a number of model boats.

Museum du Coquillage

8 r. du Maréchal-Leclerc. - Open May–Aug 9am–8pm; rest of year 9.30am–12.30pm, 2–6.30pm. Closed Sun am (Sept–Apr), 1 Jan, 25 Dec. 7€ (under 12 years 4€. 02 51 23 50 00. www.museum-du-coquillage.com.

Housed in an early 20C building, the museum has an impressive collection, covering two floors, of tropical seashells from around the world.

Around 230 display cases are crammed with barnacles, horseshoe crabs, seahorses, trigger fish, clams, spondylus,

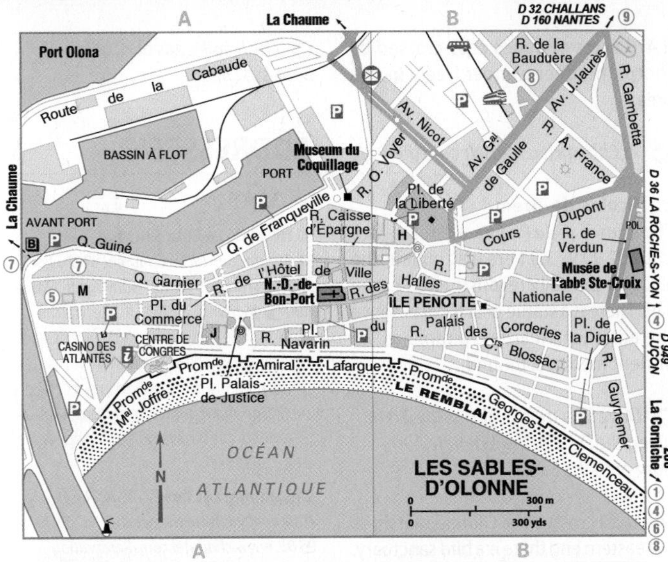

WHERE TO STAY

- Atlantic Hôtel ... ①
- Camping Les Roses ... ④
- Chambre d'hôtes Le Château de la Millière ... ⑨
- Hôtel Antoine ... ⑤
- Hôtel de La Côte Sauvage ... ⑦
- Hôtel Le Chêne Vert ... ⑧

WHERE TO EAT

- Cayola ... ④
- La Pilotine ... ⑥
- Le Clipper ... ⑦
- Le Puits d'Enfer ... ⑧

sea snails, sponges, limpets, starfish, and many more… The shop, on the ground floor, sells pretty shells at reasonable prices.

EXCURSION

Les Marais Salants

The exploitation of salt from the salt marshes, north of the town, is in decline today: there are plans to convert them to an oyster and mussel farming area. In contrast, the vegetable gardens of Chaume still produce fruit and vegetables (artichokes, strawberries, etc.).

DRIVING TOUR

4 OLONNE COUNTRY

40km/25mi round tour. Allow half a day.

Drive W out of Les Sables-d'Olonne.

La Chaume

This former fishermen's district has retained its small houses with tiled roofs in stark contrast to the Modernism of the resort. A shuttle service links La Chaume *(from quai Guiné)* to Les Sables.

Tour d'Arundel – *pl. Maraud. Open daily Apr 3–6pm; May–Sept 10am–12.30pm, 3–6pm. 5€; 02 51 90 84 10.* This tower, once the keep of a fort built in the 12C for Lord Arundel, is used today as a lighthouse. There is a fine view of the bay from the top.

Prieuré St-Nicolas – The 11C priory chapel, transformed into a fort in 1779, stands on a pleasant site offering a splendid view of the bay. The surrounding garden has a mosaic memorial (1971) to sailors lost at sea.

D 87 N from La Chaume.

On your right lies the abandoned **salt marsh zone**.

Forêt d'Olonne

This stretch of woodland standing alone between the ocean and the Vertonne marshes extends for 15km/9.3mi north of Les Sables. Oak thickets beneath clusters of tall pines carpet over 1 000ha/

2 470 acres of dunes criss-crossed by footpaths; deer wander freely in this area.

At Champclou turn left onto the D 80.

St-Nicolas-de-Brem

The church *(r. du Prieuré, Brem-sur-Mer; 02 51 90 92 33)* here was built in the 11C and partially reconstructed in the 17C. There is a statue of St Nicolas above the entrance. Nearby is a tumulus, an ancient medieval mound.

Drive SE out of St-Nicolas-de-Brem along the D 38. At Île-d'Olonne, turn right onto the D 87.

The road crosses the Olonne marsh; at the eastern end there is a bird sanctuary. The marsh was formed because of the gradual silting up, in prehistoric times, of what was the Bay of Olonne.

Observatoire d'Oiseaux de l'Île-d'Olonne

2 bis r. des Marais. Open Easter weekend, last weekends in Apr, mid–end Jun and early–mid-Sept 10am–5pm; Jul–Aug 9.30am–6pm. 2.90€. 02 51 33 12 97.

The observatory allows visitors, with the help of telescopes, to study the birds in the Chanteloup Hunting Reserve. Every summer the 38ha/94-acre reserve accommodates, among many other species, an important colony of avocets.

Return to Île-d'Olonne and continue along the D 38.

Olonne-sur-Mer

This one-time coastal port now stands a little way inland, the effect of the silting up of the bay.

Leave Olonne-sur-Mer E via theD 80.

Château de Pierre-Levée

This charming 18C folly in the Louis XVI style was built by Luc Pezot, a tax collector for Les Sables district.

The N 160 leads back to Les Sables-d'Olonne.

ADDRESSES

STAY

Hôtel de La Côte Sauvage – *3 r. Montauban, at La Chaume. 02 51 32 06 57. www.hotel-la-cote-sauvage.fr. Closed Jan. 16 rooms. 7€.* Situated in the centre of the picturesque village of Chaume, this hotel has well-maintained rooms. Some, recently redecorated, have coffee machines and fridges; the others (due to be redecorated) have an equipped kitchen area. Free Wi-Fi.

Camping Les Roses – *r. des Roses, 400m/440yds from the beach. 02 51 33 05 05. www.chadotel.com. Reservation recommended. Open early Apr–early Nov. 200 pitches.* This campsite is in the centre of the seaside resort, a few minutes' walk from the beach. There are 200 pitches and mobile homes.

Le Chêne Vert – *5 r. de la Bauduère. 02 51 32 09 47. www.lechenevert.com. Closed late Dec–mid-Jan. 33 rooms. 8€. Meals.* This 1970s hotel, opposite the railway station, is being progressively renovated. Smart, spacious rooms. The restaurant offers everyday dishes at reasonable prices.

Hôtel Antoine – *60 r. Napoléon. 02 51 95 08 36. www.antoinehotel.com. Closed Oct–mid Mar. 20 rooms.* Between the harbour and the beach in the old fishermen's quarters, this elegant hotel doubles as a family boarding house. Spick-and-span rooms of varying sizes, friendly reception.

Atlantic Hôtel – *5 promenade Georges-Godet. 02 51 95 37 71. www.atlantichotel.fr. 30 rooms. 12€. Restaurant.* This 1970s hotel is on the promenade. Its pleasant rooms are spacious. Ask for a seaside room – you'll get a balcony as well as a view. The hotel's Le Sloop restaurant specialises in seafood. Partially covered swimming pool.

Chambre d'hôte Château de la Millière – *85150 St Mathurin (9km/5.6mi NE of Les Sables via the N 160). 02 51 22 73 29. www.chateau-la-milliere. com. Closed Oct–*

Apr. 3 rooms. This elegant 19C residence is nestled in a 25ha/62-acre park. Large rooms, decorated with period furniture. The pool is set in a pretty garden. Two self-catering cottages available.

EAT

La Pilotine – *7–8 promenade Clemenceau. 02 51 22 25 25. pvp.pilotine@tele2.fr. Closed SSun, Mon and Tue (Sept–Jun.* Seafront restaurant featuring seafood and fish dishes.

Le Clipper – *19 bis quai Guiné. 02 51 32 03 61. www.leclipper.com. Closed Thu lunch, Tue, Wed (16 Sept–14 Jun), 15 Feb–3 Mar and 20 Nov–17 Dec.* Elegant restaurant with parquet floors and Louis XVI chairs. Traditional cusine, fish and seafood.

Le Puits d'Enfer – *56 bd de Lattre-de-Tassigny via the Corniche road. 02 51 21 52 77. puits.enfer@wanadoo.fr. Closed weekday evenings (Nov–Mar) and 10–31 Jan.* Facing the sea, this restaurant is decorated in a contemporary style (wood, slate, designer furniture). Regional dishes using spices and seasonal produce.

Le Cayola – *76 promenade Cayola, Anse de Cayola, 85180 Château-d'Olonne (7km/4.3mi SE of Les Sables on the coast road). 02 51 22 01 01. www.le-cayola.com. Closed Sun evening and Mon except public holidays.* Perched high up on a cliff, this handsome contemporary villa has a sea view. Its large modern dining room opens onto a teak terrace, overlooking the swimming pool and the sea in the distance. Tasty, well-prepared contemporary cuisine.

St-Vincent-sur-Jard

Vendée

St-Vincent, a seaside village on the Vendée Coast, evokes the fighting spirit of the French political leader Georges Clemenceau (1841–1929), who spent the last years of his tumultuous life here.

- **Population:** 1 146
- **Michelin Map:** 316: G-9
- **Info:** pl. de l'Église, St-Vincent-sur-Jard. 02 51 33 62 06. www.ot-stvincentsurjard.com.
- **Location:** St-Vincent-sur-Jard is situated on the Atlantic Coast, S of La Roche-sur-Yon and N of the Île de Ré.
- **Don't Miss:** Pointe du Payré nature reserve.

MAISON DE GEORGES CLEMENCEAU

bd de l'Océan. Guided tour (30min, last admission 1hr before closing) 15 May–15 Sept daily 9.30am–12.30pm, 2–6.30pm; 16 Sept–14 May Tue–Sun 9.30am–12.30pm, 2–5.30pm. Closed 1 Jan, 1 May, 1 Nov, 25 Dec. 5€. 02 51 33 40 32. http://maison-clemenceau.monuments-nationaux.fr.
The low building, typical of the Vendée, has been preserved exactly as it was when Clemenceau died. The tour includes the salon, Clemenceau's bed-room-study, a kitchen-dining room and the thatched summer-house, filled with souvenirs recalling his political life.
In the garden, which flowers with the roses Clemenceau always loved, there is a bust of the grand old man.

Georges Clemenceau

Clemenceau, the son of a bourgeois family in the Vendée, launched himself into politics in 1869 after visiting the United States. He was Mayor of Montmartre by 1870, and in 1906 became Minister for Home Affairs. Ousted by the Radicals in 1909, he was recalled in 1917 to the Presidency of the Conseil. He presided over the 1919 peace conference, resigned in 1920 and retired to his house in St-Vincent.

DRIVING TOUR

5 LE TALMONDAIS

55km/34mi round tour. Allow 3hrs.

Leave St-Vincent-sur-Jard to the W.

Abbaye Notre-Dame-de-Lieu-Dieu
rte du Payré.
The imposing mass of this ancient abbey, founded in 1190 by Richard the Lionheart, lies between the marshes of Talmont and the coastal pine woods of Jard. Sacked and pillaged during the Hundred Years' War and ruined by the Protestants in the 16C, the abbey was rebuilt by Premonstratensian monks in the 17C. By the end of that century, however, the abbey was again abandoned. Today the fine Plantagenet vaulting can still be admired in the chapter house.

Follow the road to a car park in front of a farm called St-Nicolas.

Pointe du Payré★
The best way to explore this nature reserve is on foot *(2hr30min round trip)*. A path leads through a forest of evergreen oaks, holly and ivy, among dunes and marshes. Closer to the shorelines, the sea winds and salt spray have twisted the evergreen oaks into fantastic shapes.
The view from the water's edge takes in the sandy Plage des Mines on the right and the cove of St-Nicolas on the left. On the way back through the undergrowth along the shoreline it is important to keep to the footpath in order to protect the ecosystem. The view can be admired from the rocky outcrops along the way. Pointe de Payré affords a fine view of Le Veillon cliffs.

Return via Jard-sur-Mer, then take the D 21 northwards. After 2km/1.2mi, turn left.

La Boulière marshes run along the side of the road to the left.

Turn left along the D 810.

The road leads to the **port**, which marks the beginning of a zone of oyster farms at the junction of the Île Bernard and Payré channels.

Rejoin the D 108 and continue northwards.

Talmont-St-Hilaire
This town is in the marshy alluvial zone of the Payré estuary, east of the Sables-d'Olonne. The 11C **château de Talmont** *(open Apr–Jun 10.30am–12.30pm, 2–6pm; July–Aug 10.30am–7pm 4.50€ (Jul–Aug Mon–Fri 8€), 02 51 90 27 43)*, now in ruins, rises up above the former port; the view from the top of the keep extends as far as the sea.
Tourists can also admire the 150 vehicles in the **Musée Automobile de Vendée★** *(2.5km/1.5mi NW of town on rte des Sables d'Olonne; open daily Apr–May, 1 Sept–1 Oct 9.30am–noon, 2–6.30pm; Jun–Aug 9.30am–7pm; closed 1 Jan, 25 Dec; 9€; 02 51 22 05 81; www.musee-auto-vendee.com)*. The vintage automobiles on display, made between 1885 and 1970, are restored and in working condition.

Port-Bourgenay
5.5 km/3.4mi SW on the D 4A.
This small seaside resort has grown since its creation, on Côte de la Lumière, in 1985. Nearby, separated from the sea by a pine forest, at the Village du laca, holiday homes with imaginative architecture are arranged around a golf course and a lake. Opposite stands the abbey-chapel Notre-Dame-de-l'Espérance.

Return to Talmont and drive Ealong the D 949 for 4km/2.5mi. At Poteau, turn right.

St-Hilaire-la-Forêt
This little village is the gateway to the Talmondais megalithic region. Together with Île d'Yeu (see ÎLE D'YEU) this area has the richest collection of Neolithic upright stones in the Vendée.
Centre Archéologique d'Initiation et de Recherche sur le Néolithique – *Open Apr–Jun, Sept and All Saints'*

Day Sun–Fri 2–6pm; Jul–Aug daily 11am–7pm. 5€ (Jul–Aug 7€); 02 51 33 38 38. www.cairn-prehistoire.com. This archaeological research centre focuses on the Neolithic period. Explanatory panels convey information on this ancient civilisation and there is a fine display of photographs illustrating the principal sites in western France.

A visit to the centre is completed by an interactive tour, in 3D on a giant screen, of a Neolithic village as it existed over 5 000 years ago. Outside, in season, there are **demonstrations of prehistoric techniques★**: the building of a dolmen, stone polishing, etc. Plants known to have flourished in Neolithic times have been sown.

Bicycles may be hired for exploring the megalithic sites in the area *(the trail is indicated by arrows).*

Leave St-Hilaire NE via the D 19.

Avrillé

In the municipal park behind the town hall stands the **Caesar's Camp Menhir**. This, the tallest menhir in Vendée (rising 7m/23ft above ground), is the sole survivor of what was once a group of stones.

Leave Avrillé Wvia the D 949.

Château de la Guignardière

Open daily 5 Apr–14 Jun and 1–27 Sept 11am–8pm; 15 Jun–Aug 10am–9pm. 11€. 02 51 22 33 06. www.chateau-aventuriers.com.

Building on the château began c.1555 for Jean Girard, the *panetier* (officer charged with the safeguard and distribution of bread) of Henri II, but was never finished because Girard was assassinated in 1563. The original garden façade is in the Renaissance style with 18C alterations.

Themed trails in the château and grounds allow visitors to explore at their own pace. Of particular note inside are the granite chimney-pieces and stairway; the attics with their magnificent three-stage rafter-work in oak; and vaulted cellars. Outside, there are ponds fringed by bald cypress trees with unique projecting features called "knees" (conical outgrowths of lateral roots); menhirs; and one trail suitable for youngsters.

Return to Avrillé and take the D 105 SE, then turn left along the D 91A. At Bernard, turn left along the D 91, then left again at the calvary.

The three **Savatole dolmens** can be seen on the right-hand side of the road *(explanatory panel).*

Dolmen de la Frébouchère

This granite monument, of the so-called Angevin type, consists of a stone portico leading to a rectangular chamber.

Continue S along the D 91.
At Longeville-sur-Mer, take the D 105 for 1km/0.6mi towards La Tranche-sur-Mer, then turn right.

The road along the north side of the Longeville Forest leads back to St-Vincent-sur-Jard.

ADDRESSES

STAY

Chambre d'hôte La Pinière – *3 km/1.8mi SW of Talmont-St-Hilaire towards the exit of Les Sables-d'Olonne and on the left, av. des Sports in front of the supermarket Super U. 02 51 22 25 66 or 06 70 30 55 16. 4 rooms.* The guest rooms are in the outbuildings, and the breakfast room in the old barn. There is also a *gîte* available to rent.

EAT

Le Chalet St-Hubert – *20 rte de Jard. 02 51 33 40 33.* Bright, modern dining-room. Traditional food served at reasonable prices. Best rooms are on the ground floor.

Marais Poitevin Maritime★

An artificial landscape of an almost supernatural horizontal panorama, the marshland is a vast polder intersected by dykes and canals. Here and there, former islands and tips of cliffs rise above this vast flat expanse of land covered with fields of cereal for as far as the eye can see.

- **Michelin Map:** 316: H–L-6–7 and 324: D–9-2
- **Info:** 62 r. Aligre, 17230 Marans. 05 46 01 12 87.
- **Location:** The Marais Poitevin covers a large triangular area covering the Vendée, Charente-Maritime and Deux-Sèvres. Divided into two parts, this one is located near the ocean.

MARAIS DESSÉCHÉ★

The **Dry Marsh** presents a very different aspect. A territory of wide open spaces crossed by canals and dykes, it produces wheat, barley and various types of bean despite the fact that the black earth of the *bri* (rock enclosing fossilised sea shells) needs constant fertilising. The pastureland has been given over to the rearing of salt-pasture sheep and cattle. Around Aiguillon Bay, which is slowly silting up, there are mussel beds *(bouchots)* particularly near Esnandes and Charron.

DRIVING TOURS

6 MARAIS DU PETIT POITOU

60km/37mi round tour. Allow 3hrs.

Marans

This is the market town of the Dry Marsh, and noted for its grain storage (silos). The small port, linked to the ocean by a canal, harbours a boatyard. Lock gates maintain the level of the tidal basin, where a number of coasters and pleasure craft are moored. There is a panoramic view of the marsh from the aluminium tower of the Notre-Dame Church *(05 46 01 12 87)*, which was built in 1988.

Drive N out of Marans along the N 137 towards Luçon. In Sableau, turn right onto the D 25A then left in Vouillé onto the D 25.

Shortly after La Groie *(2km/1.2mi farther on)*, note on the left a dyke, known as a *bot*, on the edge of the marsh. The road then skirts the cliffs of the Village de l'An VII (a former limestone island).

Chaillé-les-Marais

Built on what is now just a limestone bluff, the town commands the plain which was once under water. It is the centre of the Dry Marsh sector known as Petit Poitou, the first in the province to be drained and dried. From the viewpoint *(pl. de l'Église)*, there is a fine view of the marsh and of the former islands of Aisne and Sableau to the left.

Return to the N 137 and turn right (r. de l'An VII) towards Luçon, then left 900m/0.5mi beyond the tourist office.

Maison du Petit Poitou

7 r. de la Coupe du Rocher. Open Apr, Jun and Sept Sun–Fri 2–6pm; May public holidays 2–6pm; Jul–Aug Mon–Fri 10am–1pm, 2–7pm, Sun 2–7pm. 4€. 02 51 56 77 30. www.maisons.parc-marais-poitevin.fr. The former house of the dyke master offers information on the drying out of marshes, their flora and fauna, and the activities of their inhabitants. Outside, animals whose traditional habitat is the Marais roam about.

Continue along the N 137 towards Luçon; 700m/0.4mi farther on, cross Pont de la Coube and turn immediately left onto the D 10.

The road skirts the picturesque **Canal du Clain** offering an interesting view of the Chaillé cliffs. The canal is lined with sparse farmhouses, damp meadows on the left and cereal crops on the right.

Turn right onto the D 25 at Ste-Radegonde-des-Noyers crossroads. As you leave Champagné-les-Marais, turn left before the bridge onto the chemin Sud du canal.

The **Canal de Champagné**, one of the favourite haunts of anglers, crosses cultivated fields.

Turn left at the end of the long straight section of road, then continue straight ahead at the next crossroads (3km/1.8mi).

The road skirts round the **Marais Fou**. A belfry and a water tower emerge from a vast expanse of fields on the right. Farther on, the view embraces the small **Port de l'Épine** and, beyond, a farmhouse surrounded by umbrella pines (rare in this area).

Follow the D 10A on the right then, 1km/0.6mi farther on, turn left onto a minor road which crosses the Canal de Vienne; continue for another 100m/110yds and turn right.

At the crossroads, stop in front of the warehouse to look at the **bac à râteau**, once used to dredge the silted-up canals.

The road crosses several locks including the picturesque **Grands Greniers** lock. To the south, the Sèvre Niortaise supplies five canals, thus forming an important network of waterways.

Turn right at the end of the long straight road skirting the Mouillepied Canal, then left at Hutte de la Briand. At the lock-bridge, turn right onto the N 137 to return to Marans.

7 LE MARAIS MARITIME

70km/43mi round tour. Allow 3hrs.

St-Michel-en-l'Herm

This town is dedicated to the archangel St Michael. Notice the elevated placement of statues of this saint in local churches and sanctuaries.

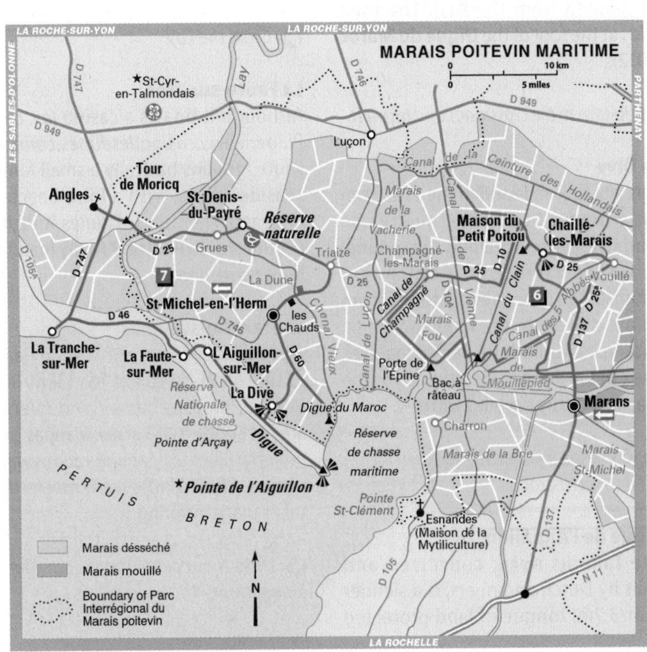

Benedictine Abbey – *9 pl. de l'Abbaye. Guided tour (45min) mid-Jun–mid-Sept Tue and Thu–Fri 10am, 11am, 3pm, 4pm, 5pm, 6pm, closed public holidays, 2.80€. 02 51 30 21 89.* Founded in the 7C by Ansoald, Bishop of Poitiers, the abbey prospered until the 9C when it was devastated by the Normans. Wars with the English during the 14C and 15C, the Wars of Religion in the 16C and the Revolution brought only more destruction. It was rebuilt each time, though only partly the last time, in the late 17C, when François Leduc was involved.

Musée André Deluol – *1 r. de l'Etendard. Open mid-Jun–Sept Tue–Sun 3–6.30pm; Oct–mid-Jun Sat–Mon and public holidays 3–5pm (with reservation). 3€. 02 51 30 25 15.* Paintings, drawings, pastels and sculptures by a local sculptor André Deluol (1909–2003).

Leave St-Michel S along the D 60.

La Dive mound comes into view on the right, past a silo. Shortly afterwards, the D 60 *(straight ahead at the crossroads)* crosses several dykes and polders (reclaimed from the sea). The road ends at the foot of the **Digue du Maroc** (1912).

Return to the crossroads and turn left.

La Dive

This was still an island in the 17C. From the entrance of a former quarry, the road rises and runs along the mound, above the marsh, over a distance of 700m/0.4mi. The view extends from Pointe d'Arçay to the Aiguillon creek, encompassing Île de Ré. Back at sea level, one can see the cliffside indented by the sea, now partly covered with ivy.

Continue towards the sea then turn left at the crossroads.

Digue de l'Aiguillon

The famous dyke, conceived and built by Dutch engineers, is a slender 6km/3.7mi tongue of land protected by a breakwater. To the left are former salt marshes turned into oyster beds; from Les Sablons, there is a succession of beaches bordered by sand dunes.

Go to the end of the dyke.

Pointe de l'Aiguillon★

The southeast extremity of the dyke where there is a wildfowl hunting reserve (Réserve de chasse maritime), projects into the grey waters of the silting-up bay. The wide **view** extends from the narrow estuary of the River Lay and Pointe d'Arçay *(NW)* to the Île de Ré *(SW)* and the port of La Pallice *(S)*. The famous mussel beds are visible only at low tide.

Follow the dyke in the other direction.

L'Aiguillon-sur-Mer

The low-built houses overlooking the estuary of the Lay face a denuded countryside, bleak beneath an immense sky. The local economy is based on nursery gardening, coastal fishing and the cultivation of oysters and mussels.

Cross the Lay.

La Faute-sur-Mer

Although it boasts a casino *(av. de la Plage; www.casinodesdunes.com)*, La Faute remains basically a small family seaside resort, with a long beach of fine sand. The string of dunes stretches southwards to **Pointe d'Arçay** (national hunting reserve).

La Tranche-sur-Mer

This seaside resort, with a wide beach of fine sand, stretches for 13km/8mi. Behind, pine woods extend over an area of 600ha/1 483 acres. Maupas Lake offers facilities for learning various water sports *(02 51 27 45 89)*. A flower festival takes place in spring.

Drive N out of La Tranche-sur-Mer along the D 747.

Angles
One of the gables on the old abbe church here is adorned with the representation of a large bear which, according to legend, was changed into stone by a hermit named Martin. Inside the church, the chancel and transept are Romanesque whereas the nave is in the Plantagenet style.

Return to the crossroads and continue straight ahead.

Tour de Moricq
rte du Pont Bertin.
This large 15C square tower standing in the middle of a field once guarded a small harbour on the River Lay.

Follow the D 25 towards Grues. Continue for 2km/1.2mi beyond St-Denis-du-Payré.

Réserve Naturelle de St-Denis-du-Payré
The nature reserve *(2km/1.2mi E)* encompasses 207ha/512 acres of marshland frequented by large numbers of birds, both nesting and migratory. A diorama with slides which can be viewed at the **Maison de la Réserve** *(9 bis r. de Gaulle; open daily, call for exact hours; closed public holidays; 5.35€ (includes observatory); 02 51 27 23 92)*, situated at the heart of the village, illustrates the various species which can be identified through telescopes from the nearby **observatory**.

Continue along the D 25. In Triaize, turn right onto the D 746.

Just before crossing the Chenal Vieux, note the former limestone islet on the right, at La Dune; 500m/550yds further on, a farmhouse stands on a mound made up of a curious pile of shells, once crushed to powder to feed poultry.

Continue along the D 746 to return to St-Michel-en-l'Herm.

ADDRESSES

STAY

Chambre d'hôte La Closeraie – *21 r. de la Paix, 85450 Champagné-les-Marais. 02 51 56 54 54. www.closeraie.fr. 5 rooms. Meals.* This charming 19C building, with all guest rooms on the ground floor, is furnished with antiques. Regional breakfast with home-made preserves and Vendée brioche. Special theme weekends; a cottage is also available.

Chambre d'hôte M and Mme Ardouin – *Basse-Brenée, 85580 St-Michel-en-l'Herm. 02 51 30 24 09. www.basse-brenee.fr. 3 rooms.* Isolated 1766 farm in the heart of the marshlands. Its no-nonsense rooms all open onto the countryside. The ground-level room with kitchenette and terrace is particularly pleasant.

Hôtel Les Chouans – *1 av. de la Plage, 85460 La Faute-sur-Mer. 02 51 56 45 56. www.les-chouans.com. Open all year. 10 apartments or 10 rooms. 6€.* This hotel, situated at 300m/330yds from the beach, has simple, but comfortable rooms. There are also apartments to rent.

Domaine Romaric – *2 chemin des Combes, 85520 Jard-sur-Mer. 02 51 20 35 19. www.residence-romaric.com. 2 rooms and 5 apartments.* The owners of this typical Vendée villa, with its white tower, have created two *chambres d'hôtes* and five well-equipped apartments.

EAT

Theddy-Moules – *72 r. du 14-Juillet, 17230 Charron (10km/6.2mi W of Marans on the D 105). 05 46 01 51 29. Reservation advised. Closed Mon (May–Jun and Sept) and Oct–Apr.* Frequented by the locals who come here to enjoy the seafood platters, or the famous mussels *à la Theddy* cooked in cream and Pineau. Relaxed, convivial atmosphere.

La Porte Verte – *20 quai Foch, 17230 Marans. 05 46 01 09 45. laporteverte@aol.com. Closed Wed and Nov–Feb. 5 rooms.* A charming, ivy-clad 19C restaurant by the banks of a canal with a garden terrace. Regional cuisine; well-kept rooms.

Charente-Maritime presents a coastline of rocks, dunes and sandy beaches, with a rural interior of forests, swampy marshlands and valleys. It extends from the port of La Rochelle with its medieval towers guarding the mouth of the harbour, to the Gironde estuary – whose Cordouan Lighthouse stands as sentinel – beyond to the low-lying islands of Oléron and Ré, scattered with pretty white houses. In addition to the countryside and coastal areas, there is the historic town of Rochefort, La Rochelle and the seaside resort of Royan.

Highlights

1. Walk around the picturesque Old Port of **La Rochelle** (p411)
2. Elegant **Rochefort** and its excellent museums (p430)
3. Enjoy a plate of fresh oysters on the **Île d'Oléron** (p441)
4. Feeding time at **Palmyre Zoo** (p447)
5. A boat trip to the "Versailles of the Sea" – **Cordouan Lighthouse** (p449)

Pierre Loti

The author Pierre Loti, whose real name was Julien Viaud, was born in **Rochefort**, the son of a municipal official. A much travelled naval officer, accomplished sportsman and something of a dandy with a distinguished bearing, he was also a novelist of great sensitivity and an exceptional storyteller. Inspired by his voyages to exotic destinations, he wrote *Pêcheur d'Islande* (*An Iceland Fisherman*; 1886), *Aziyadé* (1879), *Ramuntcho* (1897) and *Madame Chrysanthème* (1887), books that were instrumental in his acceptance as a member of the elite Académie Française at the unusually young age of 41. He is buried on the Île d'Oléron.

Gironde Estuary Legends

The Matata caves are named after the strange legend of Charlotte de Trémoille, the young wife of Duke de Condé, and her page who would have accompanied her several times during her visits to Meschers, before the duke died – he was poisoned. Charlotte was accused, then pardoned, but her page. out of either fear or guilt, fled. Years later, a miserable vagabond whom people had nicknamed "Matuta" ("The Dawn") and suspected of witchcraft, was stoned and walled up alive by a number of fanatics, in the caves where he used to shelter. This turned out to be Charlotte's page.

One of the **beaches** on the Charentais coastline, Meschers, is named after the man who once thwarted ships on stormy nights. Cadet, they say, hung lanterns to the horns of his goat Belin and walked

Vieux Port, La Rochelle

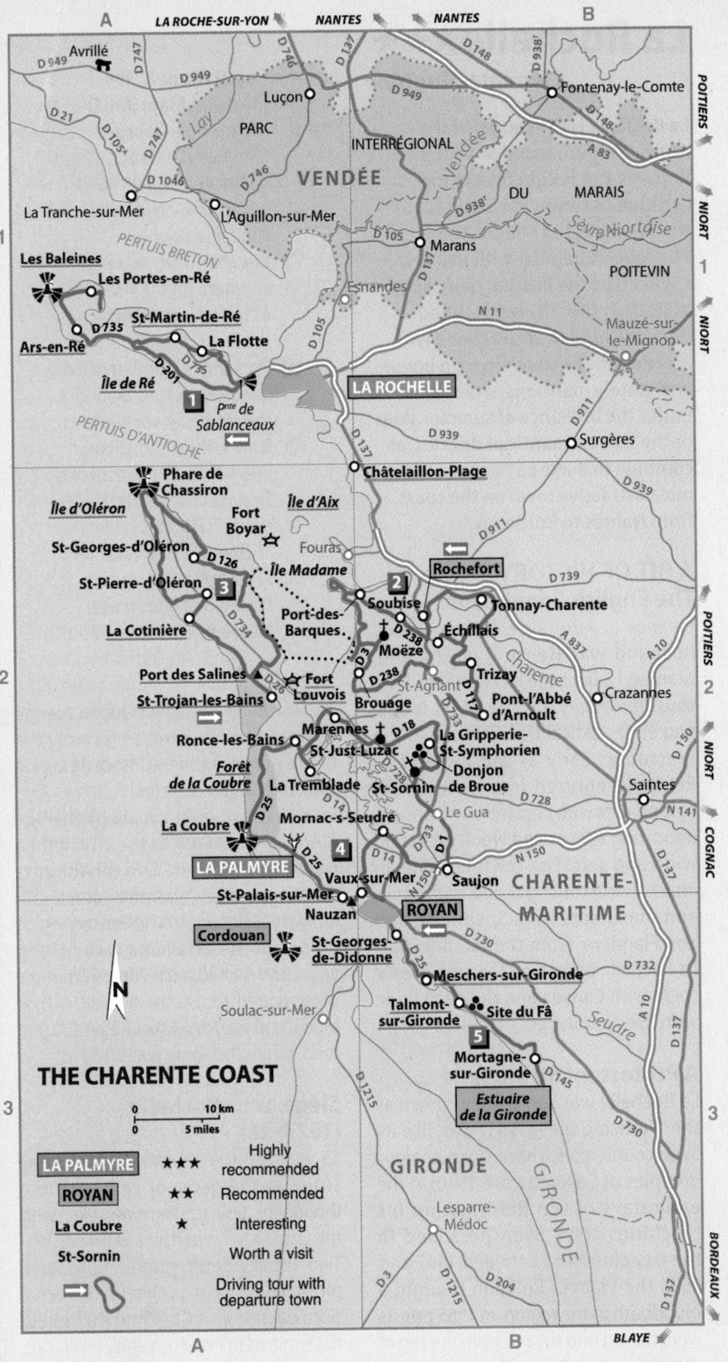

the animal along the cliffs tricking the sailors into following the light which led them straight onto the rocks. This young man would have also picked up many treasures from the wrecked boats.

La Rochelle★★★

Charente-Maritime

La Rochelle is the capital of the Aunis, a region founded by the Romans and fought over in the attrition between the English and the French in the Middle Ages. The town is popular with painters, seduced by the bustling atmosphere of its daily life. The old fortified port, the hidden streets lined with arcades, the ancient wooden houses and stately mansions, whether under the brilliance of summer skies or the most romantic of drizzles, all combine to make La Rochelle the most attractive town on the coast from Nantes to Bordeaux.

- **Population:** 77 196
- **Michelin Map:** 324: D-3
- **Info:** 2 quai Georges Simenon, Le Gabut, La Rochelle. 05 46 41 14 68. www.larochelle-tourisme.com.
- **Location:** The town is situated 38km/24mi NW of Rochefort, along the D137.
- **Parking:** A number of car parks are dotted around the centre (*see map*).
- **Don't Miss:** Old Town; Vieux Port; Tour St-Nicolas; Tour de la Lanterne; Maison Henri II; Hôtel de Ville; Musée d'Histoire Naturelle.
- **Kids:** Aquarium; Musée des Automates; Musée des Modèles Réduits.

A BIT OF HISTORY

The English Connection

Eleanor of Aquitaine, whose second husband was Henry II of England, granted La Rochelle its charter in 1199, thus liberating the city of its feudal and ecclesiastical ties. Ramparts were erected as early as the 13C and La Rochelle entered into commercial agreements with England and Flanders, importing canvas and wool, exporting wine and salt. The town became an international trading centre, with banks and merchants from Spain, England and Flanders. From the 15C onwards, La Rochelle prospered through the fur trade with Canada and the slave trade with the West Indies.

A Protestant Stronghold

La Rochelle was sometimes known as the "French Geneva" as it was, like its Swiss counterpart, a haven for numerous disciples of Calvin before 1540; in the early days of the Reformation his teachings were even preached in the city churches. Between 1562 and 1598 the Wars of Religion brought a bloodbath to the region. In 1565 priests were hurled into the sea from the top of the tall Lantern Tower. Three years later a National Synod was held here under the presidency of Calvin's follower, the writer and theologian Théodore de Bèze. The staunchly Calvinist Queen Jeanne d'Albret, her son Henri de Navarre (the future Henri IV) and the Prince de Condé took part in the debates.

In 1573 the royal army, led by the Duc d'Anjou, laid siege to the city. But La Rochelle held out. The inhabitants made use of a machine, derisively known as *L'Encensoir* (The Censer), which drenched the assailants with boiling water and melted pitch. After six months of continued attacks the city still had not fallen, and the Royalists had lost 20 000 men, when the siege was lifted.

Siege of La Rochelle (1627–28)

55 years later a second Royalist Army stood at the gates of La Rochelle – though this time the town was allied with the English, who had invaded Île de Ré. Two equally determined figures were pitted against each other on this occasion: outside was **Cardinal Richelieu**, determined to impose a unity on France, whatever the cost; inside was **Jean Guiton** (1585–1654), a small, abrupt man, uncultivated yet fanatic in temperament, who had been an admiral

in the navy and was now Mayor of La Rochelle.

Unfortunately for Guiton the blockade was organised by a masterly hand, both on land and at sea, from where help for the besieged from the English was expected: Richelieu himself took charge of the siege.

What was in effect a gigantic dyke was erected across the bay to block the entrance to the harbour. Both infantry and artillery were posted on top of the dyke with the result that the English fleet was unable to sail through and relieve the beleaguered garrison.

At first the people of La Rochelle were not overly concerned at the building of the dyke: storms, they were convinced, would sweep it away. In fact it held, though it took the besiegers 15 months to starve the town into submission. Richelieu made his victorious entry on 30 October 1628, followed two days later by Louis XIII.

From Rabelais to Fromentin

La Rochelle has always been a popular town with writers. **Rabelais**, one of the first, broke his journey here and described the light from the Lantern Tower in Pantagruel. **Pierre Choderlos de Laclos**, the author of *Les Liaisons dangereuses*, was garrisoned here c.786 as an engineer officer overseeing the construction of the arsenal. He lived in a house linked, via a concealed stairway and an underground passage, with the mansion owned by Admiral Duperré. It can only be guessed at whether De Laclos' marriage to Solange, the admiral's sister, was in any way connected to this ease of access.

The writer associated more than anyone with La Rochelle is **Eugène Fromentin** (1820–76), who was a painter and an art critic as well as a novelist. He was influenced by the artists Corot and Delacroix, and his painter's eye is obvious everywhere in his beautiful romance, *Dominique*, published in 1862 and dedicated to George Sand. In this novel he describes with the precision of a naturalist the life in 19C La Rochelle; the landscapes, the skies and the light of the Aunis are suggested with an incomparable lightness of touch.

Fromentin was a native Rochelais but many other eminent men from other parts of France were also associated with the town. They include Voltaire and Laclos, Corot, the Impressionist painters Signac and Marquet, Joseph Vernet who painted the port, and distinguished naturalists and scientists like Lafaille, D'Orbigny and Bonpland. Jean-Paul Sartre was at school in La Rochelle; Georges Simenon lived here for a while: his novel *Le Voyageur de la Toussaint (The All Saints Day Traveller)* is set in the town. An annual convention, held since 1732, brought together some of these eminent figures in sailing.

Cafés on Quai Duperré

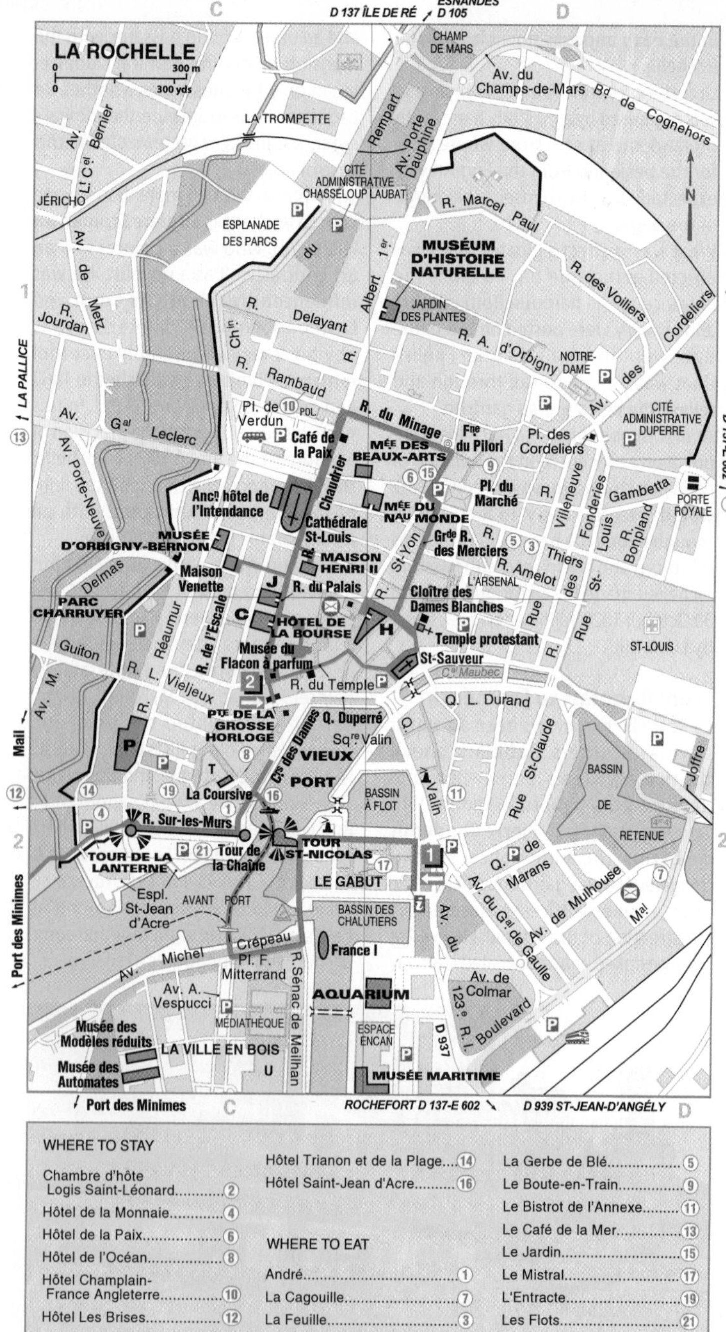

WHERE TO STAY

Chambre d'hôte Logis Saint-Léonard	2
Hôtel de la Monnaie	4
Hôtel de la Paix	6
Hôtel de l'Océan	8
Hôtel Champlain-France Angleterre	10
Hôtel Les Brises	12
Hôtel Trianon et de la Plage	14
Hôtel Saint-Jean d'Acre	16

WHERE TO EAT

André	1
La Cagouille	7
La Feuille	3
La Gerbe de Blé	5
Le Boute-en-Train	9
Le Bistrot de l'Annexe	11
Le Café de la Mer	13
Le Jardin	15
Le Mistral	17
L'Entracte	19
Les Flots	21

The port of La Rochelle is regularly on the route of several sailing races (La Solitaire du Figaro, Global Challenge yacht race and others).

The port's main asset is the presence of shipyards, renowned sail-makers and specialists in outfitting of ships' superstructure. It is therefore not surprising that several famous sailers should have chosen La Rochelle as their base including Philippe Poupon and Isabelle Autissier.

WALKING TOURS

1 OLD PORT★★

From the tourist office. Allow 1hr30min.

The old harbour (the modern harbour has been transferred to La Palice) is located deep inside a narrow bay. You can see the forward harbour, the old harbour, the small dock used by yachts, the outside dock used by trawlers and the reservoir supplied by a canal with water from the River Sèvre.

Gabut District

A picturesque residential and shopping development has been built on the site *(E of Tour St-Nicolas)* of an old bastion which was once part of the town's ring of fortifications (demolished in 1858). The façades with their wood cladding recall the fish-lofts and sheds of old-time sailors, while vivid colours and wide windows lend the place a Nordic air.

Tour St-Nicolas★

r. de l'Armide. Open daily Apr–Sept 10am–6.30pm; Oct–Mar 10am–1pm, 2.15–5.30pm. Closed 1 Jan, 1 May, 25 Dec. 6€ (combined ticket for the three towers 8€). 05 46 41 74 13. http://la-rochelle.monuments-nationaux.fr.

This slightly leaning tower, 42m/138ft high, and dedicated to the patron saint of sailors, is a fortress in itself. It was built in the 14C on a pentagonal plan, its five corners reinforced by three engaged circular turrets, a rectangular turret and a higher square tower forming a keep. An outside staircase forming a buttress leads to the main room, octagonal beneath elegant ribbed vaulting. From here, other staircases built in the thickness of the walls lead to a second chamber, which branches off into several rooms including a chapel, and out onto the lower parapet, surrounded by merlons.

Scale models, dioramas and watercolour maps from the **Musée Maritime** trace the development of the port from the 12C to the present day.

The upper parapet, surrounded by high machicolated walls with arrow-slits, affords views of the entrance to the harbour, the bay and Île d'Aix.

Turn S, cross a small bridge and turn right onto the alleyway running alongside av. Marillac.

Walk along the quayside past the multimedia library inaugurated in 1998 and admire the view of the towers and Vieux Port. Take the small boat which ferries passengers to the foot of Tour de la Chaîne.

Cours des Dames

Once the haunt of sardine mongers and fishermen repairing their nets, this esplanade, which is one of the most animated parts of the old port, now features a cinema and terrace restaurants.

La Coursive

4 r. St-Jean-du-Pérot. 05 46 51 54 00. www.la-coursive.com.

Now a theatre, formerly the Ancienne Chapelle des Carmes (chapel), it has an imposing 17C doorway surmounted with a scallop shell. Inside, there is a fine arcaded courtyard.

Tour de la Chaîne

Vieux Port. Same opening times and charges as the Tour St-Nicolas. 05 46 34 11 81. http://la-rochelle.monuments-nationaux.fr.

The tower owes its name to a huge and heavy chain which used to be stretched across the harbour mouth between this tower and Tour St-Nicolas at night, closing the port to ships. According to Rabelais the chain – still visible at the foot of

the tower – was used to keep the giant Pantagruel in his cradle.

Tour de la Chaîne, built in the 14C, was for a long time used as a powder magazine. Originally there was a turret attached to it but this was demolished in the 17C to widen the narrow channel. Inside, a superb vaulted chamber houses an exhibition devoted to the siege of La Rochelle.

Rue Sur-les-Murs

The tower is linked with Tour de la Lanterne by this narrow street which follows the top of the old medieval rampart – the only section not demolished by Richelieu, to defend against the English (at that time the foot of the wall was at the water's edge).

Tour de la Lanterne★

r. sur-les-Murs. Same opening times and charges as the Tour St-Nicolas. 05 46 41 56 04. http://la-rochelle.monuments-nationaux.fr.

The Lantern Tower is not as old as the other two (it dates from the 15C), and was built with strictly functional concerns in mind, eschewing aesthetic considerations in favour of military imperatives. The great mass of the building, its walls 6m/20ft thick at the base, contrasts starkly with the elegant octagonal spire and the fine lantern – originally used as a beacon – which surmount it. At ground level is the old guardroom in which the history of La Rochelle is now recounted through illustrated panels.

Within the spire are four rooms one above the other, the walls of which bear **graffiti**★ scrawled by soldiers as well as prisoners, mostly dating from the 17C and 18C. The best are glass protected.

At the second level of the spire, a projecting balcony affords a **panorama**★★ that embraces the old town, the port, the ocean and the off-shore islands. At low tide it is possible to make out the foundations of Richelieu's dyke, level with Fort-Louis, beyond the promenade.

Continue along the seafront then through the gardens.

Parc Charruyer★

Chemin des Remparts.

This park, built on the mounds and ditches of the old fortifications, encircles the town (2km/1.2mi long and 200m/656ft wide); alongside runs a river – home for swans and herons – and winding avenues.

To the west, the park becomes the **Mall** – a favourite with strollers – finishing up at the monument to the dead, one of Joachim Costa's major works. Between this majestic avenue of elms and the sea stretch the gardens and terrace of the casino and Parc d'Orbigny, followed by Parc Delmas.

Préfecture

38 r. Réaumur.

The *préfecture* (administrative headquarters of the *département*) is housed in the former Hôtel Poupet. The Louis XVI style of architecture is typical of local private buildings; the magnificent doorway crowned with balustrades faces onto the square.

From the préfecture, walk to porte de la Grosse-Horloge; here you have the choice of starting on the second walk or returning to the Gabut district via quai Duperré.

Quai Duperré

The cafés lining this quay offer a view of the waterfront activity. Beyond the masts and the rigging, and the manoeuvring of small boats, the perspective is closed by the two towers guarding the harbour mouth – Tour St-Nicolas on the left, Tour de la Chaîne on the right. On the extreme right, the conical roof of the Lantern Tower is visible.

The picturesque rue du Port and Petite-Rue du Port, inhabited mainly by fishermen and sailors, lead to the quay. On the western side, facing the clock, stands a statue of **Admiral Duperré**, who was born in La Rochelle in 1775 and commanded the French fleet at the time of the taking of Algiers in 1830.

2 OLD TOWN★★

Allow 1hr30min.

The oldest district of La Rochelle, which was built to a regular plan and protected, until 1913, by Vauban's fine ramparts, exudes an atmosphere part mercantile and part military. The busy, lively **shopping centre** is based around the town hall, its principal axes Grande-Rue des Merciers and rue du Palais. The streets are still paved with ancient stone slabs, secret passages, arcades and darkened "porches" where passers-by can stroll sheltered from bad weather.

Many of the houses are designed on a plan particular to La Rochelle. Almost all of them have two entrances, one on the main street, the other on a lane parallel to it. At ground-floor level, these buildings have one huge room, often converted into a shop, an interior courtyard with a staircase leading to a balconied gallery, and a rear courtyard surrounded by outhouses. On the upper floor is a room looking out on the street, a kitchen overlooking the courtyard, and a "dark room" with no direct light from outside. **Half-timbering** on the oldest houses is overhung with slates to protect the wood from the rain.

The **beaux quartiers**, the fashionable areas, are west of rue du Palais. The most stately are rue Réaumur and rue de l'Escale. Here, behind high walls pierced with gateways and sometimes (rue Réaumur) topped with balustrades, the old families live in their 18C mansions.

Follow the itinerary marked in green on the map.

Porte de la Grosse-Horloge★

quai Duperré, Vieux Port.

This gateway to the town is famous for its outsize clock. The original Gothic tower was modified in the 18C with a belfry surmounted by a dome and lantern. The turrets on either side are decorated with nautical emblems.

On the far side of the gateway is place des Petits-Bancs, a small square with a statue of Fromentin in the middle. On the corner of rue du Temple stands a charming house (1654) with a Renaissance façade.

Rue du Palais★

This street links the shopping centre with the residential district.

On the right, lines of shops extend beneath galleries varying in style. Public buildings alternate with galleries on the left-hand side, and there are some fine old houses – the fourth one along, for example, has windows adorned with miniature arches and carved masks.

Hôtel de la Bourse★ – This 18C Stock Exchange building, the seat of the local Chamber of Commerce since its founding, is an example of the early Louis XVI style. The attractive courtyard has an unusual layout with peripheral galleries. The inner façade is adorned with maritime emblems. In a corner on the left is a wrought-iron staircase.

A passageway across the road from the Stock Exchange (by no 29 rue du Palais) leads via Cour de la Commanderie to Cour du Temple (old half-timbered houses).

Palais de Justice – *No 10.*

The law-courts façade, majestic with its Corinthian columns, was completed in 1789. The inscription on the pediment reads "Temple of Justice", flanked by the two traditional symbols of justice, the sword and the scales.

At the intersection of rue Chaudrier and rue Eugène Fromentin stands a fine 17C house with a corner turret and staircase on carved corbels. Opposite, at the entrance to rue Dupaty, is an old half-timbered house protected by slates.

Turn left onto r. Eugène Fromentin.

Maison Venette

1 r. Nicolas Venette.

The picturesque **rue de l'Escale★** is paved with pebbles which were once used as ballast by ships from Canada, and is bordered partly by arcades and partly by the porches behind which the homes of 18C nobles were concealed. Maison Venette was built in the 17C for a doctor of that name. The façade of the house is sculpted with motifs representing celebrated doctors such as Hippocrates and Galen.

Return to r. du Palais.

Rue Chaudrier★

At no **6** stands an old half-timbered house with slate cladding. A plaque in front of the building is dedicated to Jean Chaudrier, a heroic defender of La Rochelle.

Turn right into r. des Augustins and continue to no 11 bis.

Maison Henri II★

11 bis r. des Augustins. The garden is freely accessible. 05 46 34 88 59.

This grand house, built in 1555 for Hugues de Pontard, the Seigneur de Champdeniers, rises at the far end of a garden. The façade, with its twin pavilions, gallery and loggia, is in the Henri II style. It includes a frieze sectioned by triglyphs (tablets with vertical grooves), medallions and bucranes (carved oxen masks). At ground-floor level two buttresses supporting the left-hand pavilion are decorated with *(right)* a satyr playing a guitar and *(left)* a winged woman grappling with a serpent.

Return to r. Chaudrier.

Cathédrale Saint-Louis

pl. de Verdun. Treasury open Jul–Aug Mon–Sat 2–6pm. No charge. 05 46 41 16 70.

The cathedral, sober and severe in aspect, was built in part on the site of a church dedicated to St Bartholomew. The plans were drawn up by the architects Gabriel, father and son. The west front is surmounted by a scrolled pediment in the Louis XVI manner.

In the third chapel of the north aisle simple votive paintings by sailors contrast with the "literary" and academic compositions by **William-Adolphe Bouguereau** (1825–1905), a native of La Rochelle, which cover the dome above the axial chapel. The **treasury** contains 18C and 19C liturgical items.

Café de la Paix

54 r. Chaudrier. 05 46 41 39 79.

This is the sole remaining example in La Rochelle of those flamboyant cafés of the last century, gleaming with gilt and glass, where the local burghers read their newspapers or played billiards. Glass panels in the form of arcades, decorated with frosted glass, adorn the façade. The interior is decked out with

Francofolies: When Music Takes the Town by Storm

Every year, around 14 July, a musical storm hits La Rochelle. For six days, the Old Port resonates with music and applause. The idea of the festival originated in Quebec where Jean-Louis Foulquier, a radio broadcaster, was captivated by the lively success of a "Francofête" of French songs. In 1985 he chose his home town to host the Francofolies, hanging a bright banner between the towers of the Old Port. The first year, 25 000 people attended the outdoor celebration. Over the years, a wide variety of entertainers, including Jacques Higelin, Charles Aznavour, Francis Cabrel, Johnny Halliday, Larra, M C Solar, Rita Mitsouko, Samson, Sapho and Alain Souchon, have enchanted the eclectic audience.

The festival is open to every style of music from hard rock to jazz and rap. At the foot of Lantern Tower, on esplanade Jean-d'Acre, a huge stage welcomes big names in the entertainment business (decibels and lighting effects guaranteed). A few yards away, La Coursive, Le Grand Théâtre and La Salle Bleue are better suited to more intimate performances and new talent. Le Carré Amelot (regional venue), l'Encan (the hip-hop spot) and Magic Mirrors (improvisation and jam sessions until the wee hours) complete the official Francofolies. An autograph session is held in cours des Dames every afternoon, so be sure to take your camera! *05 46 50 55 77. www.francofolies.fr.*

carved wood and gilded designs, arched mirrors, chandeliers and ceiling medallions painted in *trompe-l'œil*.

Rue du Minage

Arcades★ on each side of the street are irregular in shape – which brings an eccentric element into the perspective down the street. Some of the old houses are adorned with friezes and sculptures, others with windows beneath a triangular pediment (nos **43**, **22**, **4** and **2**). At the end of the street stands the **Fontaine du Pilori**, which dates from the 16C but was rebuilt in the 18C.

Continue, via r. Pas-du-Minage, towards the market.

Place du Marché

At the entrance to the Tout-y-Faut cul-de-sac two well-preserved old houses face one another. The half-timbered one, with mullion windows and a high-up dormer, dates from the 15C; the other (16C) is stone built with narrow, pedimented window bays.

Grande-Rue des Merciers★

This shopping street is one of the most characteristic arteries of La Rochelle, bordered by numerous galleries and houses built in the 16C and 17C. The medieval buildings, half-timbered under the familiar slate covering, alternate with Renaissance homes built of stone and distinguished by fantastic gargoyles.

The house on the corner of rue du Beurre and those at nos **33**, **31**, **29** and, at the far end, no **17** are all 17C buildings with pedimented windows. No **8** is late 16C, with narrow windows and heavy pediments; no **5** is early 17C with carved figures. No **3** dates from 1628. Mayor Jean Guiton lived in the last two.

Take r. de la Grille on the right, then turn left onto r. de l'Hôtel-de-Ville.

Hôtel de Ville★

pl. de l'Hôtel de Ville. Visit by guided tour (1hr) Jun, Sept and school holidays daily 3pm; Jul–Aug daily 3pm, 4pm; Oct–May Sat–Sun 3pm. Closed 1 Jan, 25 Dec. 4€. 05 46 51 51 51.

The town hall, a late 15C–early 16C composite building, is notable for its rich decoration. The rectangular central courtyard is protected by a walled Gothic enclosure surmounted by a machicolated watchpath reinforced by a belfry-tower.

The **main façade★**, built in the reign of Henri IV in the Italian style, overlooks the courtyard. Behind its fluted columns the ground-floor gallery of the façade hides a fine coffered ceiling. The decoration includes trophies, medallions and monograms entwining the initials of Henri IV and Marie de' Medici.

Finer still is the upper level, reached via a balustraded stairway. Here there are pillars and niches in the Tuscan manner, the niches housing effigies representing the four cardinal virtues: *(left to right)* Prudence, Justice, Fortitude and Temperance.

The **interior** contains Jean Guiton's study, complete with his armchair in Córdoba leather and the desk he struck forcefully with his dagger to emphasise his famous pronouncement before the siege; the walls are hung with Aubusson tapestries.

Henri Motte's 19C painting of the siege can be found in another room, along with a Jacques Callot engraving and a 1628 canvas by Van der Kabel depicting the same tragic event in the town's history.

The rear **façade** looks out over rue des Gentilshommes and also dates from the time of Henri IV; it includes a door studded with bosses which is known as the "Porte des Gentilshommes" because it was through here that the city aldermen filed on the day that the mandate granting them each "the style and title of Gentleman" expired.

Follow r. de la Ferté on the left. The Protestant Church is on your left, on the corner of r. St-Michel.

Protestant Church

2 r. St-Michel.

This church has a charming façade, with sculpted palm leaves and drapery. It is

the former Récollets Chapel, constructed in 1708. It houses a museum.

Musée Protestant

2 r. St-Michel. ♿ Open Jul–mid-Sept Mon–Sat 2.30–6pm; mid-Sept–Jun by prior arrangement. 2€. 05 46 50 88 03. www.museeprotestant.org.

The museum relates the history of Protestantism, particularly around La Rochelle. Among documents and objects on display: copy of the Confession of Faith of La Rochelle (1571) with ministers' signatures; a Bible from 1606 printed in La Rochelle; a collapsible altar and pulpit and a collection of *méreaux* (medals worn by Protestants for mutual recognition), reminders of the period of clandestine meetings, known as the *désert*.

Cloître des Dames Blanches

6 r. St-Michel. 05 46 51 51 51.

These cloisters, located next to the Protestant Church, are part of the former Récollets Convent. It has now become a cultural centre, and beneath the 32 arches exhibits and concerts are held *(in season)*.

Église St-Sauveur

r. St-Sauveur.

This 17C and 18C church is crowned by a lofty 15C bell tower.

The r. St-Sauveur leads to the r. du Temple.

Musée du Flacon à Parfum

33 r. du Temple. Open Jul–Aug 1–7pm; rest of year Tue–Sat 2–7pm. Closed public holidays. 5€ (under 10 years no charge). 05 46 41 32 40.

Charming collection of perfume bottles (some signed by Lalique, Dalí, Cocteau), powder boxes and labels, from 1920 to the present day.

Continue along the r. du Temple. Return to porte de la Grosse-Horloge.

ADDITIONAL SIGHTS

OLD TOWN★★

Musée d'Histoire Naturelle★★

28 r. Albert 1er. Open Jul–Sept Tue–Fri 10am–7pm, Sat–Sun 2–7pm; Oct–June Tue–Fri 10am–6pm and Sat–Sun 2–6pm. Closed 1 Jan, 1 May, 14 Jul, 1 Nov, 11 Nov, 25 Dec. 4€ (1st Sun of month no charge). 05 46 41 18 25. www.museum-larochelle.fr.

The museum stands by the entrance to a park, the Jardin des Plantes, and was renovated in 2007 to span five levels, including a fossil collection on the ground floor, a zoology gallery on the first floor and ethnographic exhibits on the second and third floors.

Musée du Nouveau-Monde★

10 r. Fleuriau. Open Jul–Sept Mon and Wed–Fri 10.am–12.30pm, 1.45–6pm, Sat–Sun 2–6pm, public holidays 2–6pm; Oct–June Mon and Wed–Fri 9.30am–12.30pm, 1.30–5pm, Sat–Sun 2–6pm. 4€ (under 18 years no charge. 05 46 41 46 50. www.ville-larochelle.fr.

The Hôtel Fleuriau, acquired by a shipowner of that name in 1772, houses within panelled Louis XV and Louis XVI salons a number of collections tracing the relationship between La Rochelle and the Americas. Shipowners and merchants grew rich trading with North America and the Caribbean, where they possessed huge plantations producing sugar, coffee, cocoa and vanilla. They prospered enormously too in "triangular commerce": the sale of cloth and purchase of slaves on the African coast.

Among the displays, ancient maps, coloured engravings, allegories of America, wallpapers (*The Incas* by Dufour and Leroy) and everyday objects used by the Indians are of particular interest. Note also the section on slavery, the fall of Quebec, West Indian engraving and relevant literary themes, including Chateaubriand's novel *Atala*, about the impossible love between an Indian and a Christian girl.

D. Mar/MICHELIN

Musée des Beaux-Arts★

28 r. Gargoulleau. Same opening hours as the Musée du Nouveau-Monde (see above). 4€ (1st Sun of month no charge). 05 46 41 64 65. www.ville-larochelle.fr.

The Fine-Arts Museum occupies the second floor of the old bishop's palace, which was built during the reign of Louis XVI; following local custom the courtyard is separated from the gardens by a high balustraded wall. A wrought-iron staircase with ovoli leads to the alcoved gallery and rooms in which the paintings hang. The most interesting work among the older paintings is an *Adoration of the Magi*, the last known painting by Eustache Le Sueur (17C French school). Portraits by local artists dating from the 18C include works by Brossard de Beaulieu and Duvivier. The 19C is represented by Bouguereau, Corot, Chassériau and Eugène Fromentin – including several evocative studies of Algeria.

A separate department is devoted to 20C work (glass by Maurice Marinot, Georges Rouault's **Miserere**), some of which is displayed in rotation.

Musée d'Orbigny-Bernon★

2 r. St-Côme. Same opening hours as the Musée du Nouveau-Monde. 4€ (1st Sun of month no charge). 05 46 41 18 83. www.ville-larochelle.fr.

This museum specialises in local history and ceramics from Europe and the Far East. Mementos of the siege of La Rochelle include liturgical items used by Cardinal Richelieu when he celebrated the first Mass after the fall of the town. A number of documents relate to the economic prosperity and intellectual life in the Aunis capital during the 18C.

On the first floor an exceptional collection of ceramics centres on the faïence (glazed earthenware) of La Rochelle but there are fine pieces also from Marseille, Nevers, Strasbourg and Moustiers. An interesting series of pharmacy flasks and bowls from Aufredi hospital is displayed in a number of 18C medicine cabinets.

The second floor is devoted to the Far East (precious Chinese porcelain from the Sung to the Ch'ing dynasties and musical instruments), while the basement houses an archaeology collection which includes a celebrated 12C tomb, attributed to Laleu, but is probably the work of a simple monk.

LA VILLE-EN-BOIS

The "wooden town" lies to the west of the larger tidal basin; it is an area of low wooden houses mainly used in the past as workshops for ships' repairs or chandlers and spare-part shops. Reorganised after a fire, this district has added cultural activities (university, museums) which sit side by side with traditional handicraft centres.

Aquarium★★

Allow 1hr30min. Quai Louis Prunier. Open daily Oct–Mar 10am–8pm; Jul–Aug 9am–11pm; Apr–Jun and Sept 9am–8pm. 14€ (children 11€). 05 46 34 00 00. www.aquarium-larochelle.com.

This large, modern aquarium founded by René Coutant presents a vast panorama of underwater fauna and flora from around the world in 65 tanks. Several rooms are devoted either to a particular ocean or to a specific marine area (such as the Atlantic, the Mediterranean and various tropical seas), their species displayed in superbly arranged tanks. A tunnel with transparent walls allows visitors to wander freely through a tropical marine environment, while an immense basin containing 2 500hl/ 54 992 gallons of water accommodates turtles and sharks. There is a large tropical house, a shop and a café with a terrace.

Musée Maritime★

pl. Bernard Moitessier. Open daily Apr–Jun and Sept 10am–6.30pm; Jul–Aug 10am–7pm. 8€. 05 46 28 03 00. www.museemaritimelarochelle.fr.

Spreading along the eastern quays of the Chalutiers docks, the entrance to this complex is distinguished by a slipway. Two separate museums tell the tale of maritime history in La Rochelle.

In the **Musée à Flot** is an armada of boats of all shapes and sizes are anchored along the quays (rowing boats, trawlers, open-sea tugs and yachts), including **Joshua**, the elegant red ketch manned by Bernard Moitessier in the Golden Globe Challenge, the first round-the-world solo race (1967–68). Formerly a meteorological frigate, the 76m/249ft-long **France 1** is the fleet's most impressive ship; visitors are free to wander up and down its five decks and take a closer look at interesting exhibits on life onboard and meteorology.

Musée des Automates

r. de la Désirée, La Ville-en-Bois. Open daily Jul–Aug 9.30am–7pm; Sept–Jun 10am–noon, 2–6pm. 7.50€ (children 5€); 11€/6.50€ combined with Musée des Modèles Réduits. 05 46 41 68 08. www.museeslarochelle.com.

Three hundred figures move to the sound of music against a sumptuous backdrop, ingeniously vying with each other for the attention of visitors. The astonishingly lifelike figures are animated by a cam system, demonstrated on a Harlequin figure cut in cross-section. Note, in particular, some more recent works, one of which evokes the inventor de Vaucanson and his famous duck, as well as animated shop windows, exhibits for children and historical reconstructions.

An imitation Paris metro entrance leads to **Place de Montmartre**★★, where the cosmopolitan atmosphere is faithfully re-created. Children will marvel at the mechanical billboards decorating the shops while adults can stroll in the cobbled streets and be taken by surprise as an overhead metro rattles by.

Musée des Modèles Réduits

r. de la Désirée, La Ville-en-Bois. Open daily Jul–Aug 9.30am–7pm; Sept–Jun 10am–noon, 2–6pm. 7.50€ (children 5€); 11€/6.50€ combined with Musée des Automates. 05 46 41 68 08. www.museeslarochelle.com.

A miniature train takes children through the museum. The tour starts with a collection of superb model cars and lorries, some remote controlled. The inside of a galleon tells the story of the great sea-going expeditions while a fabulous water setting provides the backdrop for a **naval battle**. An underwater world plunges the visitor into the ocean depths while trainspotters can admire model trains circuits, one of which includes a model of La Rochelle railway station, and gleaming locomotives of every shape and size, some of which are steam operated.

PORT DES MINIMES

Three thousand two hundred craft of all types can be accommodated at Minimes marina, on the southern side of the bay sheltering La Rochelle, which makes it

the largest pleasure port in Europe on the Atlantic side.
Three deep-water tidal basins – Bout-Blanc, Marillac and Lazaret – have been developed. Around the port is a zone of artisans: ship-fitters, sail-makers, painters and experts in repair work provide every service needed by the owners of yachts and cruisers. A sailing school of repute is based here, and there is also a residential area.

A regular waterbus service operates between Les Minimes and Vieux Port (20min; 1.30€; www.rtcr.fr).

EXCURSION

Châtelaillon-Plage★

12km/7.4mi S on the D 137.
5 av. de Strasbourg. 05 46 56 26 97. www.chatelaillon-plage.fr.
Châtelaillon stands on the former site of a fortified town, the capital of Aunis, that was gradually, from the 13C, swallowed up by the sea. Pleasant seafront, without any apartment blocks, dotted with pretty renovated villas overlooking a meticulously maintained beach which is regularly renewed with fresh sand. The beach is also patrolled and there are numerous activities offered, some free of charge: swimming lessons, trampoline, aquagym, beach-ball, croquet, minigolf. On Easter Sunday and Monday, a kite-flying competition takes place on the beach. All summer, many free events are held here (open-air cinema, music, children's shows).
From the promenade at the seafront, there is a semicircular view, from left to right, stretching over the Pointe de la Fumée, the Fort Enet, the Île d'Aix, Île d'Oléron in the background, and Pointe du Chay. Behind stands the casino, housed in a restored Belle Époque (1890) building.
From the Pointe des Boucholeurs *(3km/1.8mi S on the D 202)*, where there are oyster and mussel farms, there is a panoramic view over the Pertuis d'Antioche. Guided tours of oyster beds in a horse-drawn cart (*open Apr–Sept, contact for times; 7.50€ (3–18 years 4€); 05 46 56 26 97).*

ADDRESSES

STAY

Chambre d'hôte Logis Saint-Léonard – *6 r. des Chaumes-l'Abbaye, 17139 Dompierre-sur-Mer. 05 46 35 14 65. 5 rooms.* This renovated mansion, sitting in beautiful grounds, has five rooms in which the décor reflects the travels made by the owners to Polynesia and Africa. Delicious breakfast with home-made jams and cakes. Ping-pong, jacuzzi and pool. Friendly owners.

Hôtel de l'Océan – *36 cours des Dames. 05 46 41 31 97. www.hotel-ocean-larochelle.com. Closed 2 wks late Dec–early Jan. 15 rooms. 6€.* Located at the Vieux Port, this hotel has renovated rooms, bright, comfortable and with air-conditioning. The rooms overlooking the quay are soundproofed, and have a view out to sea. Breakfast room opens out onto a terrace Wi-Fi no charge.

Hôtel de la Paix – *14 r. Gargoulleau. 05 46 41 33 44. www.hoteldelarochelle.com. 19 rooms. 8.50€. Meals.* Situated between the old market and the place de Verdun, the Hôtel de la Paix is steeped in history. The guest rooms in this former 18C shipowner's home are spacious and regularly refreshed. Cosy dining room. Evening meal or half-board on request; Laurent's cuisine won't leave you indifferent.

Hôtel Les Brises – *1 chemin de la digue Richelieu (off r. Philippe Vincent). 05 46 43 89 37. www.hotellesbrises.com. 46 rooms. 13€.* How delightful to open the windows of your room and contemplate the ocean and breathe the sea air! This 1960s hotel is well situated between earth and water. Lovely view from the panoramic terrace, where breakfast can be taken in summer, and most of the rooms.

Saint-Jean d'Acre – *4 pl. de la Chaîne. 05 46 41 73 33. www.hotel-la-rochelle.com. 60 rooms. 12€.* Two 18C houses with soundproofed guest rooms, that are little by little being renovated. There is one suite with a lovely terrace overlooking the Old Port.

Trianon et de la Plage – *6 r. Monnaie. 05 46 41 21 35. www.hoteltrianon.com. Closed 18 Dec–1 Feb. 25 rooms. 9€. Meals.* This 19C *hôtel particulier* of standing has been in the same family since 1920. Breakfast room decorated in a winter garden theme. The rooms are quieter at the rear of the building. Cosy atmosphere in the restaurant; traditional cuisine.

⊜⊜⊜⊜ **Hôtel Champlain France-Angleterre** – *30 r. Rambaud. ℘05 46 41 23 99. www.hotelchamplain.com. 36 rooms.* On a busy street near the historic district, this old 16C convent has a discreet, pleasant garden. A marvellous place to unwind after a busy day sightseeing. The rooms, some quite spacious, are decorated with period pieces.

⊜⊜⊜⊜ **Hôtel de la Monnaie** – *3 r. de la Monnaie. ℘05 46 50 65 65. www.hotel-monnaie.com. 31 rooms. ⊒11.50€.* Right behind the Tour de la Lanterne, this splendid 17C mansion where coins used to be made is an agreeable address. You'll appreciate the serenity of the rooms between courtyard and garden, as well as their modern furnishings and spaciousness.

EAT

⊜ **La Feuille** – *26 r. Thiers. ℘05 46 34 31 81. www.la-feuille.fr. Closed Mon–Thu evening and Sun.* Adjacent to the old covered market, this is an appealing, small restaurant. In the refined décor of the dining room the chef offers a range of gourmet salads. Reservation strongly advised.

⊜ **La Gerbe de Blé** – *r. Thiers. ℘05 46 41 05 94. Closed evenings.* This very friendly bistro has a limited choice on the menu, but the quality is excellent, especially the snack of the day, delicious sandwiches, Charentais terrine or a plate of oysters.

⊜ **Le Café de la Mer** – *Port du Plomb, Lauzières, 17137 Nieul-sur-Mer (take the D 106E1 4km/2.5mi W of Nieul-sur-Mer). ℘05 46 37 39 37. Closed Oct–Mar. Mouclades* (mussels in a spicy cream sauce), oysters and crêpes in the summer, hearty dishes in the winter, all served in generous portions. This little restaurant has a view of the Île de Ré bridge.

⊜ **Le Jardin** – *5 bis r. Gargoulleau. ℘05 46 41 06 42. Closed Sun.* ♿. Near to the covered market, this restaurant-tea room is frequented by the locals. Pretty décor based on the theme of the "garden". On the menu every day, there is a gourmet breakfast, and at lunchtime giant mixed salads, open sandwiches and home-made desserts. Pleasant indoor terrace.

⊜ **Le Mistral** – *10 pl. des Coureauleurs (in the Le Gabut district). ℘05 46 41 24 42. Closed Sun–Thu evening (winter).* This wood-clad house is located at the heart of the Le Gabut district. The maritime-style dining room is on the first floor; a terrace overlooks the old fishing port.

⊜⊜ **La Cagouille** – *bd Joffre. ℘05 46 27 19 18.* ♿ 🅿. The kitchen is open plan, so from the restaurant you can see the chef preparing your meal. The menu has Charentais specialities. Lovely view of the woodland from the veranda.

⊜⊜ **L'Entracte** – *35 r. St-Jean-du-Pérot. ℘05 46 52 26 69. www.gregorycoutanceau.com.* ♿. Contemporary bistrot decorated nevertheless with a sense of nostalgia (woodwork, brass sconces, old posters). Modern dishes.

⊜⊜⊜ **André** – *7 r. St Jean. ℘05 46 41 28 24. www.restaurant-andre.abcsalles.com.* On the old docks, facing the Tour de la Chaîne, this enormous restaurant comprises a dozen bistro-style dining rooms where customers sit elbow to elbow to feast on seafood. Nautical ambience, marine paintings and objects de rigueur.

⊜⊜⊜ **Le Bistrot de l'Annexe** – *45 r. St-Nicolas. ℘05 46 50 67 71. Closed Sun.* In this bistro situated at the corner of rue St-Nicolas and rue de la Sardinerie the menu, frequently renewed, reveals creative recipes created using local produce. Attractive contemporary décor.

⊜⊜⊜ **Le Boute-en-Train** – *7 r. des Bonnes-Femmes. ℘05 46 41 73 74. Closed Sun.* Near the markets, this charming restaurant serves a variety of quiches and food fresh from the marketplace. Children's drawings adorn the walls of the bistro dining room; grab a crayon and add to their collection.

⊜⊜⊜ **Les Flots** – *1 r. de la Chaîne. ℘05 46 41 32 51. www.gregorycoutanceau.com.* An 18C tavern at the foot of the Tour de la Chaîne. Décor combines rustic, modern and nautical styles. Seafood dishes prepared with individuality and good wine list (900 wines).

Île de Ré★

Charente-Maritime

The surface of this unspoiled island is broken only by vineyards and an occasional pine wood. It has become a favourite retreat for summer holidaymakers in search of sunshine, sea air and wide open spaces. Although a bridge now links it to the mainland it retains most of its insular character and its famous salt marshes. Numerous marked and peaceful cycle tracks criss-cross the island.

- **Population:** 17 640
- **Michelin Map:** 324: C-3
- **Info:** 3 r. du Père Ignace, St Martin-de-Ré. ℘05 46 09 00 55. www.holidays-iledere.co.uk.
- **Location:** The Île de Ré is situated just off the port of La Rochelle.
- **Don't Miss:** St-Martin-de-Ré, Phare des Baleines.
- **Kids:** Réserve Naturelle de Lilleau des Niges; Ecomusée du Marais Salant.

GEOGRAPHICAL NOTES

L'Île de Ré, sometimes known as "L'Île Blanche", extends in a northwesterly direction for almost 30km/18mi. It largely comprises a series of Jurassic limestone outliers forming islets – principally Loix, Ars and Ré proper – which have become linked together.

In the north the deeply indented bay of Fier d'Ars, and the marshes surrounding it, constitute the **Réserve Naturelle de Lilleau des Niges**, the home of thousands of different species of birds including grey curlews, widgeon, teal, silver plovers and geese. In the south a line of sand dunes has formed on a rocky plateau, which stretches far away beneath the sea; the jagged cliffs eaten away by the encroaching tides have given rise to the name of this area: La Côte sauvage (The Wild Coast).

The southeastern part of the Île de Ré, the widest and most fertile, is broken up into tiny smallholdings producing early fruit and vegetables, asparagus and, above all, vines (the wine, red, white and rosé, is full favoured, with a hint of algae in the aftertaste). The fortified apéritif-wine made here on the island is as good as the better-known Pineau des Charentes.

To the north and west the vines share the land with pines, as far as La Couarde. Beyond that, Ars-en-Ré is salt marsh country – although the marshes are fast disappearing.

The people of Ré – the Rétais – are landlubbers rather than seafaring folk. Of the riches of the ocean they deal only in *sart* (seaweed and other wrack), harvested with huge rakes, shellfish and

Ile de Ré

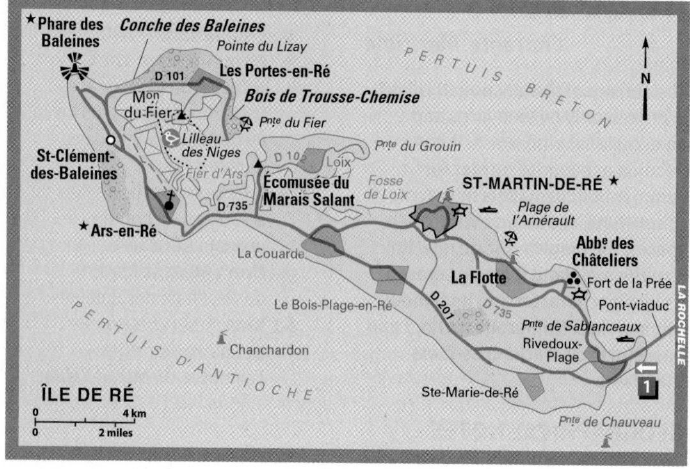

the prawns which teem on the rocky *platin* exposed at low tide. In addition, oyster farming has been introduced to the Fosse de Loix and Fier d'Ars inlets.

In the past the women of the island wore a long, narrow headdress to protect them against the fierceness of the sun; its name, the **quichenotte**, is said to derive from "kiss not", as its function was also, allegedly, to discourage the advances of amorous invading Englishmen. Today this tradition, like many others, has all but vanished – the island donkeys, for instance, which have disappeared entirely, were bedecked with straw hats and picturesque striped or plaid "trousers" to keep away flies and mosquitoes in the salt marshes. Such things can now be seen only on postcards in the village shops.

The villages are scattered all over the island; their single-storey houses, dazzling white, with typically green shutters, are brightened with hollyhocks, delphiniums and scarlet salvia, or a wisteria on a trellis.

ST-MARTIN-DE-RÉ★

The island capital, formerly an active port and a military stronghold, has turned into a charming tourist centre. The narrow streets, quiet, spotlessly clean, still bumpy with cobblestones, have largely managed to retain the atmosphere of the Grand Siècle (the 17C in France).

Fortifications★

quai Nicolas Baudin. Guided tours (1hr15min) available from tourist office. 5€. 05 46 09 20 06.

These date back to the early 17C but were entirely refashioned by Vauban after the siege of 1627. Vauban came to inspect the Île de Ré in 1674; the fortifications he designed for St-Martin were completed in 1692.

The **citadel**, built in 1681, was used as a prison under the Ancien Régime (19C) and later became a religious penitentiary.

The citadel is not open to the public, but a walk around the bastions on the seaward side reveals pleasing **views** of the Breton Straits and the mainland; note also the interesting watch-turrets and the cannon embrasures.

Parc de la Barbette

This sheltered park is a pleasant place for a shady stroll, looking down on the sea and the distant southern coast of the Vendée.

Hôtel de Clerjotte

13 av. Victor Bouthillier.

Tall slate roofs crown this fine building constructed in a style midway between

Flamboyant Gothic and Renaissance. It was originally the headquarters of an organisation owing allegiance to the local ruler, the Officiers des Seigneurs de Ré, and was at one time used as the town arsenal. Today the building houses a museum and the Tourist Information Centre. In the courtyard, bordered with Renaissance galleries, stands a staircase-tower at the foot of which is an elegant Flamboyant doorway.

Musée Ernest Cognacq

Open Apr–Jun and Sept Mon and Wed–Fri 10am–1pm, 2–6pm, Sat–Sun and public holidays 2–6pm; Jul–Aug Wed–Mon 10am–7pm; Oct–Mar Mon and Wed–Fri 10am–noon, 2–5pm, Sat–Sun and public holidays 2–5pm. Closed 1 Jan, 1 Nov, 11 Nov, 25 Dec. 4€. 05 46 09 21 22.

The maritime history of St-Martin and the island as a whole is presented through models, ships' figureheads, ancient weapons and tableaux (combat scenes, portraits of mariners and Napoleon's return from the Isle of Elba aboard the brig). These seafaring displays are supplemented with a collection of pottery from Delft and porcelain from China, a reminder of the island's former maritime trade with the rest of the world.

Port

Trade with Canada and the West Indies brought the port of St-Martin great prosperity during the 17C. Port and harbour between them girdle the old sailors' district, now busy with shops, forming a picturesque islet. The quays are paved with the ballast of long-gone merchant ships.

Église St-Martin

pl. Eude d'Aquitaine. 05 46 09 58 25.

The church dates from the 15C and was nicknamed the "big fort" because of the fortifications (still visible from the transept) which protected it. Ruined by the Anglo-Dutch naval bombardment of 1696, it was restored in the early 18C.

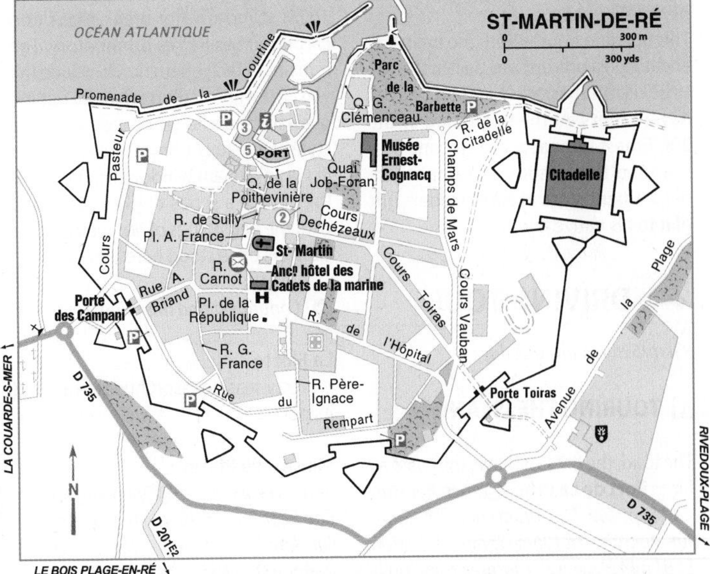

WHERE TO STAY

Chambres d'hôte Domaine de la Baronnie........②

WHERE TO EAT

La Baleine Bleue..............................③
Le Martin's Pub...............................⑤

Anglo-French Rivalry

From the Hundred Years' War to the fall of Napoleon, the Île de Ré was closely involved in the conflict between the English and the French, during which the the English made many attempts to storm its shores. The isle also suffered during the Wars of Religion, which brought misery and deprivation to the inhabitants.

In 1627 the brave **Marquis de Toiras** (1585–1636), a deeply spiritual and fiercely warlike man, was governor of the island, which he had wrested from the Protestants and then reinforced by building the St-Martin citadel and the fort of La Prée. An English fleet commanded by the Duke of Buckingham anchored off Les Sablanceaux and columns of infantry poured ashore to lay siege to the town of St-Martin, and the fort of La Prée. In no time there was an acute shortage of provisions. Just as rations were running out, a squadron of 30 ships from the French fleet sailed into the harbour at St-Martin.

The siege, nevertheless, continued. On 6 November 1627, 6 000 Englishmen hurled themselves at the town walls. After a bloody hand-to-hand battle they were driven back.

It was then that Louis XIII, arriving at La Rochelle, despatched a contingent of reinforcements to the island, under the leadership of Marshal de Schomberg. The English, caught between two fires, were massacred. Toiras was created Marshal of France in 1630.

A chapel dedicated to sailors contains 18C and 19C votive offerings.

Ancien Hôtel des Cadets de la Marine

pl. de la République.

This building houses both the town hall and the post office. It was built in the 18C to be used as barracks for a company of naval cadets. At the beginning of the 20C Ernest Cognacq, a merchant who founded the famous La Samaritaine department store in Paris, made a gift of it to his native town.

DRIVING TOUR

83km/52mi. Allow one day.

1 TOURING THE ISLAND

The road, the D 735, follows the coast as far as **Fort de La Prée** (*open Apr–Jun and Sept Tue–Sun 10am–noon, 2–6pm, Jul–Aug Sun–Fri 10am–7pm; 4€; 06 81 91 64 15; www.fort-la-pree.com*), built as part of the ring of defences around La Rochelle.

Take the first road to the right.

Ancienne Abbaye des Châteliers

Guided tours are organised through the Maison du Platin. 05 46 09 61 39.

The ruins of this Cistercian abbey, founded in the 12C and destroyed in 1623, stand on the bleak moorland carpeting Les Barres promontory. The remains of the abbey church include the west front and walls tracing the outline of a nave and a flattened east end in the style of Citeaux Abbey. The chancel was lit via an elegant window. On the left of the church a series of pillars crowned with the beginnings of ribs indicate that cloisters once stood here.

Continue along this minor road.

La Flotte

A pretty seaside resort huddled around its port.

Maison du Platin

4 cours Félix-Faure. Open Apr, Jun and Sept Tue–Fri 10am–1pm, 2–6pm; Jul–Aug Tue–Fri 10am–7pm, Sat–Sun 2–6pm; Oct–Nov Tue–Fri 10am–12.30pm, 2–5.30pm. 4.80€ (child 2.30€ and 4.20€). 05 46 09 61 39.

In Charentais, *platin* means the portion of the shoreline exposed at low tide. This

small museum on the seafront details some aspects of the islander's life. On the ground floor, models of boats are displayed alongside objects excavated from the Abbaye des Châteliers site. A small collection is dedicated to the island's shellfish and winegrowing industries. On the floor above, documents recall the era when the island was only accessible by the sea. The second floor has a reconstruction of a typical interior, as well as headdresses and clothes, and some remarkable photographs of the islanders taken c1920s. The top floor houses temporary exhibitions.

St-Martin-de-Ré★

See above.

Leave St-Martin and drive W along the D 735, then turn right onto the D 102 in the direction of Loix.

Écomusée du Marais Salant

About 1km/0.6mi before Loix village, on the left; follow the signs. Open mid-Jun–mid-Sept 10am–12.30pm, 2–7pm; rest of year 2.30–5.30pm. Closed Sun and Mon except school holidays and mid-Nov–mid-Feb. 4.60€ (8–18 years 2.30€ and 3.90€). 05 46 29 06 77. www.marais-salant.com.

Inside this information centre a guide explains, with the use of a model, the techniques involved in sea salt production. The visit continues outside with a tour of the Ré salt marshes and its vast evaporation circuit. Follow the seawater channels to the drying-out areas where the water becomes saturated and the salt crystallises. The shop sells a range of salt marsh products.

Take the D 102 in the opposite direction, and continue on the D 735 to Ars-en-Ré.

Ars-en-Ré★

This small port with a network of lanes and alleys so narrow that the corners of houses had to be shaved off to allow carriages to turn into them was once frequented by Dutch and Scandinavian vessels loading cargoes of salt.

In the main square stands **Église St-Étienne**, its needle-sharp belfry spire painted black and white as a landmark to sailors.

A fine Romanesque entrance leads to a nave of the same period reinforced with ribs. The Gothic chancel, longer than the nave, is flanked by wide side aisles. The domed vaulting here is in the Angevin style.

Just south of the church is the Renaissance period Seneschal's (Steward's) House, embellished with two corner turrets.

St-Clément-des-Baleines

The village is known for its beaches, which provided some of the filming locations for *The Longest Day* (1962), produced by Darryl F Zanuck.

Phare des Baleines★

155 rte du Phare, St-Clément des Baleines. Open daily Apr–Jun 10am–7pm; Jul–Aug 9.30am–9pm; Sept 10am–6.30pm; Oct–Mar 10.30am–5.30pm. 2.80€ (museum 3.50€). 05 46 29 18 23. www.lepharedesbaleines.fr.

The lighthouse, rising 55m/180ft above the headland, was built in 1854 to replace a 17C beacon-tower.

A staircase of 257 steps leads to the top gallery. From here there is a splendid **panorama★** over the Breton Straits, the Vendée Coast and Pointe de l'Aiguillon to the north and east and the Île d'Oléron to the south. At low tide it is possible to see the **fish-locks** around the cape.

Conche des Baleines

A forest track leads to this wide bay backed by dunes. The use of the word *baleine* (whale) in names in this area derives from the fact that, in Roman times, hundreds of whales were washed up on these shores.

Return to the D 101 and continue along it to Portes-en-Ré.

Les Portes-en-Ré

This former salt marsh workers' village is known as the "tip end of the island". Note the Chapelle de la Redoute *(rte Du Fier)*, a former powder magazine.

Réserve Naturelle de Lilleau des Niges
Maison du Fier, rte du vieux port. The Maison du Fier info centre is open daily 4 Apr–Jun 10am–12.30pm, 2.30–6pm; Jul–30 Aug 10am–12.30pm, 2.30–7pm; 31 Aug–27 Sept 2.30–6pm; 24 Oct–8 Nov 2.30–6pm. 4€ (children 2€). 05 46 29 50 74. www.lilleau.niges.reserves-naturelles.org.
This nature reserve is inhabited by thousands of birds, including curlews, grey plovers, teals and barnacle geese, which you can observe from the cycle track which skirts the southern part of the reserve.

Bois de Trousse-Chemise
This pleasant pine wood surrounds the vast beach of **Pointe du Fier**.

Take the D 101 in the opposite direction, then the D 735 to La Couarde. Rejoin the D 201, which leads to the Pointe de Sablanceaux via Ste-Marie-de-Ré.

ADDRESSES

STAY

Hôtel L'Hippocampe – *16 r. du château des Mauléons, La Flotte-en-Ré. 05 46 09 60 68. www.hotel-hippocampe.com. 12 rooms. 6€.* This modestly furnished 1927 house is located in a peaceful street in the village. Breakfast served outside in the summer.

Chambres d'hôte Le Clos Bel Ébat – *17 r. de la Grainetière, La Flotte. 05 46 09 61 49. Closed Jan–Mar. 3 rooms.* This old spirit storehouse has pretty little rooms. A breakfast basket is set in front of the bedroom door each morning.

Hôtel Le Sénéchal – *6 r. Gambetta, Ars-en-Ré. 05 46 29 40 42. www.hotel-le-senechal.com. Closed 3 Jan–14 Feb and 13 Nov. 26 rooms. 12€. 19 Dec.* This old island hotel has just received a facelift. White stones, blond wood and colourful textiles in the renovated rooms. Pleasant patio.

Chambre d'hôte Domaine de la Baronnie – *21 r. Baron de Chantal, St-Martin-de-Ré. 05 46 09 21 29. www.domainedelabaronnie.com. Closed 2 Nov–Easter. 6 rooms.* A unique address on the island. This superb listed mansion, tastefully restored, offers calm rooms of refined comfort. Breakfast served in a charming room.

EAT

Le Martin's Pub – *quai de la Poithevinière, 17410 St-Martin-de-Ré. 05 46 09 15 87. Closed Mon (Sept–Jul) and mid-Nov–early Feb.* This pub decorated in an authentic British style serves traditional cuisine at reasonable prices.

Les Embruns – *6 r. Chay-Morin, Îlot, St-Martin-de-Ré. 05 46 09 63 23. Closed Sun eveningand Wed (Sept–Jun).* Behind its green shutters, this little restaurant serves food fresh from the marketplace (often fish).

La Baleine Bleue – *L'Îlot, 17410 St-Martin-de-Ré. 05 46 09 03 30. www.baleinebleue.com. Closed Mon (Sept–Jun), Tue (Oct and Mar), 5 Jan–5 Feb and mid-Nov–mid-Dec).* Welcoming interior with a 1930s zinc counter and seafood based cuisine.

La Bouvette – *Raise Flottaise, Le Morinand, Le Bois-Plage-en-Ré (2km/1.2mi SE of St-Martin-de-Ré via the D 201E2). 05 46 09 29 87. www.labouvette.com. Closed 20 Nov–20 Dec.* Next to the Morinand mill, this former wine storehouse is now a restaurant. The slate menu changes with the seasons. Very relaxed atmosphere.

Le Bistrot de Bernard – *port d'Ars, 1 quai de la Criée, Ars-en-Ré. 05 46 29 40 26. www.bistrotdebernard.com. Closed Mon and Tue (Oct–Mar) and Dec–Jan.* On the wharf, this old, typical house has charm to spare. Marine décor in keeping with the fish on the menu.

Restaurant Le Chat Botté – *r. de la Mairie, St-Clément-des-Baleines. 05 46 29 42 09. www.restaurant-lechatbotte.com. Closed Mon off-season and1 Dec–1 Feb.* Through the piano bar to enter this regional-style house near the church. Fixed-price menus with traditional dishes.

Île d'Aix★

Charente-Maritime

Île d'Aix (the final x is not pronounced) is a small island in the Atlantic, only 133ha/329 acres in area. It has a mild climate and clear skies, which, combined with its impressive fortifications, make it an interesting place to visit. As the boat approaches Île d'Aix, sandy beaches and magnificent cliffs appear along the coast. Inland, pine trees, ilex and tamarisk give the landscape an almost Mediterranean air.

- **Population:** 199
- **Michelin Map:** 324: C–D-3
- **Info:** www.iledaix.fr/The-Island-of-Aix.
- **Location:** The island is accessible by boat, from **Pointe de la Fumée** and, during the high season, from La Rochelle, Île d'Oléron and Île de Ré. The direct route *(30min)* offers interesting views northwards along the coast up to La Rochelle and out towards Île de Ré; westwards to the offshore forts of Enet and Boyard and to Île d'Oléron. Boats land at the jetty at Pointe Ste-Catherine, below Fort de la Rade citadel.

THE VILLAGE

Wide streets intersecting at right angles, and a double line of fortifications separated by deep dykes, give the impression of a large town. However, the small church and single-storey whitewashed cottages reveal it as a small village. From here, visitors can tour the island on foot *(2hrs30min)* or enjoy a horse-drawn carriage ride *(see Leisure Activities, p428)*.

Place d'Austerlitz

At the mainland end of Pointe Ste-Catherine, a gate with a drawbridge leads to this pleasant open space, once the parade ground, with its shady walks between rows of fine cypress trees. Just beyond the drawbridge, on the right, stands the arcaded harbour office.

Fort de la Rade

This citadel overlooking the harbour was originally designed in 1699 by Vauban. Work on the five bastions and ring of fortifications was completed in 1702 but

Napoleon Bonaparte's Final Voyage

It was on Île d'Aix that Napoleon last stood on French soil. In July 1815 the frigate, which was supposed to take the exiled Emperor to America, was anchored off Fort Enet. Meanwhile, a potentially threatening British naval force was cruising in the Antioche Straits, blocking the frigate's exit to the open sea.

The following day, Napoleon landed on Île d'Aix and visited the fortifications. On his return to the ship, he learned what options lay open to his guards.

Negotiations lasted three days, during which time the Emperor's envoys were assured (falsely) that he would be permitted to seek asylum in England. Finally, escape appearing impossible, Napoleon accepted the advice of his officers and decided to surrender himself to his adversaries. On 12 July, Napoleon had gone ashore, and on 14 July he wrote his now-famous letter *(see Musée Napoléonien, p428)* to the Prince Regent in London. The next day he donned the green uniform of a colonel in the Imperial Guard and embarked on a brig, which was met by an admiral's barge. The barge then took him to the warship *Bellerophon*, where he was taken aboard. This was to be his last voyage, carrying him to St Helena in the South Atlantic Ocean, where he was to end his days.

55 years later, most of it was destroyed by the British. It was not until 1810 that Napoleon gave the order for rebuilding to start. Work was completed in 1837. The fort is completely surrounded by a water-filled moat and a circle of anti-siege defences. There are two lighthouses on the fort. The jetty below provides a view of Fort Boyard.

Église St-Martin

This was once the church of a Benedictine priory. All that remains today are the transept, apse and apsidal chapel. Note the foliate capitals in the 11C crypt.

Musée Napoléonien

r. Napoléon. Open Apr–Sept daily 9am–noon, 2–6pm; Oct–Mar Wed–Mon 9.30am–noon, 2–5pm (until 6pm Oct) (last admission 45min before closing). 4.50€ (includes Musée Africain) (1st Sun of month no charge). 05 46 84 66 40. www.musees-nationaux-napoleoniens.org.

The museum is housed in the building which was constructed on Napoleon's orders in 1808, and where he took refuge in July 1815. It is one of the few buildings on the island with an upper storey, surmounted by the imperial eagle. Baron Gourgaud, great-grandson of the Emperor's *aide-de-camp*, bought the building in 1925 and left it to the nation.

The 10 rooms contain memorabilia of Bonaparte, his family and his entourage. In the garden stands a Classical-style bust of the Emperor, which once served as a ship's figurehead.

Napoleon's room on the first floor is particularly evocative, as nothing in it has been changed since the days when he stood outside on the balcony, watching the manoeuvres of the British fleet through his telescope. It was in this room that he composed the famous letter to the Prince Regent in London:

"Faced with the factions dividing my country and with the enmity of the great powers of Europe, I have ended my political career and I come, like Themistocles, to seat myself at the table of the British people. I place myself under the protection of their laws and the indulgence which I crave from your Royal Highness as the most powerful, the most steadfast and the most generous of my enemies."

General Gourgaud was entrusted with delivering the letter to London, but he was refused permission to land at Plymouth. Napoleon made the general a gift of the document, and a facsimile of the Emperor's rough draft of the letter is on view in the museum.

GETTING THERE

Regular Service (20min) leaving from Fouras (Pointe de la Fumée). Oct–May 8.60€; Apr–Sept 13.20€; 08 20 16 00 17.

Driving Motor traffic is restricted to service vehicles, which means that the island can only be explored on foot, by bike or ***barouche***. P A car park is available 200m/220yds from the embarkation point at Fouras (1.20€ per hour; 05 46 84 57 44).

LEISURE ACTIVITIES

Bicycle Hire – It is easy to find bikes for hire at the port or in the village. Trailers available for small children.

Horse-Drawn Carriage Rides – *Apr–Sept. 05 46 82 76 72.* Look for the carriages on place d'Austerlitz, where the horses wait patiently in the shade for customers. Tour with commentary lasts for 50min. Maximum 50 passengers per tour.

Swimming – Beaches on the island (most pleasant at high tide) do not have lifeguards. On the western side, there are long sandy beaches (from Anse de la Croix to La Batterie de Jamblet). There is a small beach on the eastern shore (Anse du Saillant), and attractive little coves to the NE (Les Sables Jaunes, Baby Plage), where holm oak trees provide shade.

Coast of Île d'Aix

©ARCO/B. Boensch/age fotostock

Musée Africain

r. Napoléon. Open Apr–Sept daily 9am–noon, 2–6pm; Oct–Mar Wed–Mon 9.30am–noon, 2–5pm (until 6pm Oct) (last admission 45min before closing). 4.50€ (includes Musée Napoléonien) (1st Sun of month no charge). 05 46 84 66 40. www.musees-nationaux-napoleoniens.org.
This museum displays ethnographic and zoological items collected by Baron Gourgaud in Africa in 1913–31. Slides illustrate interesting examples of African fauna. The white Arabian camel ridden by Napoleon during the Egyptian campaign was later taken to the Jardin des Plantes in Paris, stuffed after its death, then transferred to Île d'Aix in 1933.

FORT LIÉDOT

Guided tours (1hr) Apr–Jun, Sept Wed 3pm; Jul–Aug daily 11am–5pm. 5€. 05 46 83 01 82.
During the 19C, Île d'Aix became a prison, and a variety of lodgers were imprisoned within Fort Liédot, on the northern coast. In the 20, Ben Bella, one of the leaders of Algeria's National Liberation Front, was detained here from 1956 to 1962.

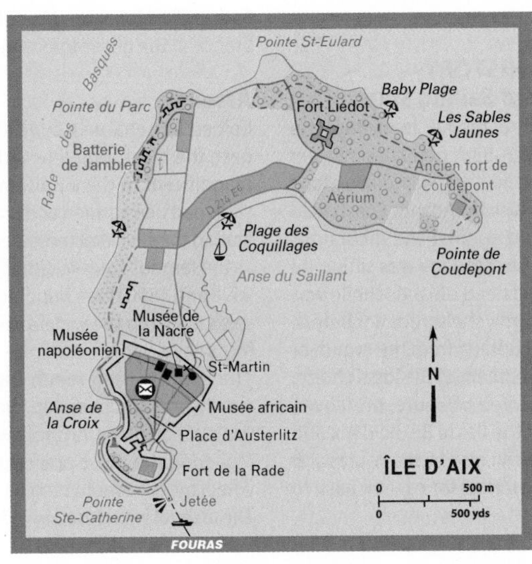

Rochefort★★

Charente-Maritime

Rochefort, known as the "town of Pierre Loti", is on the border of the Aunis and Saintonge regions, between the Right Bank of River Charente and the marshes, not far from the Atlantic Coast. The town takes great pride in its illustrious maritime history. There is still something exotic in the air around the arsenal, in which the great expeditions of the time were masterminded. Despite its air of severity, due to the grid pattern of its rectilinear roads set at right angles to each other (some of which still have their original blue Quebec cobblestones), Rochefort, created by Colbert in the 17C, is famous for the dignity and harmony of its architecture: one- and two-storey buildings, private mansions (highly decorated façades, wrought-iron balconies) and Royal Rope Factory, built of fine pale-coloured dressed stone. Its excellent museums, such as La Maison de Pierre Loti, Le Centre International de la Mer, which is laid out in the Rope Factory, Le Musée de la Marine and many others, add interest to the town. Rochefort's thermal springs were reopened in 1953.

- **Population:** 26 299
- **Michelin Map:** 324: E-4
- **Info:** av. Sadi Carnot, Rochefort. ℘05 46 99 08 60. www.paysrochefortais-tourisme.com.
- **Location:** Rochefort is situated 38km/24mi SE of La Rochelle.
- **Parking:** A number of car parks are dotted around the centre (*see map*).
- **Don't Miss:** Corderie Royale; Arsenal district; Maison de Pierre Loti; Musée d'Art et d'Histoire.

A BIT OF HISTORY

The Days of Sailing Ships

In the middle of the 17C **Jean-Baptiste Colbert** (1619–83), Louis XIV's minister in charge of the navy, was looking for a base from which the Atlantic Coast could be defended against the incursions of the English. Brouage was silting up and the roadstead of La Rochelle was not sufficiently sheltered. Rochefort, 15km/9.3mi upriver from the mouth of the Charente, seemed the ideal choice. It was protected offshore, moreover, not only by the Île de Ré, Île d'Aix and Île d'Oléron, but also by the Fouras and Le Chapus promontories – all easy to fortify.

It was decided, therefore, starting from scratch, to turn Rochefort into a military port with an arsenal as powerful as the one in Toulon, and from 1666 onwards work started on the docks and fortifications. By 1671 Rochefort could boast a population of 20 000; 13 men-of-war, a galley and several brigantines had been launched.

The town, originally constructed of wood, was rebuilt in stone in 1688 on the orders of the naval governor Michel Bégon – the man who gave his name to the begonia family: these exotic plants discovered in the West Indies by a priest, Father Plumier, were brought back to France at the governor's request.

Arsenal

Colbert's arsenal was, by 1690, "the biggest, the most complete and the most magnificent in the kingdom": 47 warships had been armed and provisioned, among them several three-deckers such as the famous *Louis-le-Grand*. Between 1690 and 1800 three hundred new vessels sailed into the waters from Rochefort's naval yards.

The *Sphinx*, the French Navy's first steam-powered warship, was built in the first half of the 19C, followed by the *Mogador*, the most powerful paddle-wheel frigate ever to be built in France. The arsenal was closed in 1926.

Between 5 000 and 10 000 workmen were employed in the arsenal. Everyday the flagship fired a cannon shot to signal the opening or closing of the gates.
It was from Rochefort, on 21 March 1780, that General La Fayette set sail for the second time to reinforce the "Insurgent" troops in America onboard a brand new frigate, *L'Hermione*, built at the arsenal. In 1816 the frigate *La Méduse* sailed from Rochefort for Senegal in West Africa, only to be wrecked off the coast of what is now Mauritania. The loss of the ship inspired Géricault to paint his celebrated dramatic work *The Raft of the Medusa*.

ARSENAL DISTRICT★

The arsenal was built on the banks of the River Charente in two sectors which still exist, interspersed with launching slipways and entrances to dry docks. From 1830 the entrance was via the famous Porte du Soleil. The arsenal contained 11 shipbuilding yards and four refitting basins, including **La Vieille Forme**, the oldest masonry dry dock (1669) in the world. The complex also housed a foundry that specialised in copper-plated nails, a boilermaking shop, forges, sawmills, rope-makers and a cooperage works that produced barrels for gunpowder as well as enormous warehouses for quartermasters' stores. Huge mast pits could contain up to 50 000cu m/ 65 400cu yd of wood rendered rot-proof by the briny water. A workshop of "naval sculptors" carved figureheads and embellished poops and prows.

Porte du Soleil

This entrance to the arsenal, dating from 1830, is in the form of a triumphal arch.

Chantier de Reconstruction de l'Hermione★★

pl. Amiral Dupont. Open Apr–June and Sept 10am–7pm; July–Aug 9am–7pm; Oct–Dec and Feb–Mar 10am–12.30pm, 2–6pm. Guided tours (1hr30min) daily Sept–Jun 11.30am, 3.30pm, 4.30pm. Closed 1 Jan, 25 Dec. 6€, guided tours 8€ (10€/14€ combined with the Corderie Royale). 05 46 82 07 07. www.hermione.com.
The double dock (1728) was specially restored and equipped for the construction of a replica of the *Hermione*, the frigate (fitted with guns using 12lb cannonballs) in which La Fayette sailed to America. Work began on 4 July 1997 using the same techniques as in 1779, when the *Hermione* was first built. The *Hermione* is due to set sail again in July 2012.

Hôtel de Cheusses

1 pl. de la Galissonnière.
A magnificent gateway leads to the courtyard of this 17C mansion which was once the local Admiralty headquarters. Today the building is a naval museum.

The Hulks of Rochefort

In 1792 the Republican "cleansing" of the clergy began. Hundreds of priests who had refused to swear that they accepted the "civil" status of the Church under the new Constitution were sent to Rochefort, where they were destined to be sent to the Guyana penal colony in South America. The prisoners were transferred to two dilapidated slave traders. The "villains" were crammed between decks in batches of 400. A communal tub of broth was all they had for food.
One day, after a short voyage, the hulks weighed anchor. Instead of deportation to Guyana, the priests found they were kept aboard ship off the Île d'Aix.
On deck shots were fired and cries of "Long live the Republic! Long live Robespierre!" rang out over the water. By now the deportees had only one aim: to survive. In January 1794, however, typhus made its grim appearance.
A dozen priests died every day; at each death there was a noisy celebration by the crew. Transferred at last to Île Madame, all those still living were freed in 1795.

Musée de la Marine★
Open daily May–Jun 10am–6.30pm; July–Sept 10am–8pm; Oct–Dec and Feb–Apr 1.30–6.30pm. Guided tours daily Jun and Sept 2.30pm, 4.30pm; Jul–Aug 10.30am, 2.30pm, 4.30pm; Oct–Dec and Feb–May 2.30pm. Closed 1 May, 25 Dec. 8€ (combined ticket with the Ancienne École de Médecine Navale). 05 46 99 86 57. www.musee-marine.fr.
Model ships, ships' figureheads, navigational equipment, paintings, charts, weapons and flags evoke the history of the French Navy from the 17C to the 20C. Maps, documents and explanatory models illustrate the story of Rochefort's old naval dockyard. Particularly impressive are the very large ship models (and those of windmills) in the outer hall. Of particular note is the enormous capstan from the privateer commanded by René Duguay-Trouin (1673–1736), whose great exploit was the capture of Rio de Janeiro in 1711 with "a feeble fleet".

Hôtel de la Marine

r. Toufaire.
Napoleon Bonaparte once stayed here, and the oldest part of the building dates back to the time of Louis XIV. In front of it is a monumental 18C gateway. A tall, square-sectioned tower at one side was formerly used for the exchange of visual signals with ships.

Jardin de la Marine

r. Toufaire.
The tree-lined riverside walks and terraced lime trees of this quiet, sheltered garden date back to the 18C. A handsome staircase terminating in a doorway with three arches leads down to the former Royal Rope Factory.

Corderie Royale★★

This Rope Factory below the garden and overlooking the Charente was founded by Colbert in 1666 and completed four years later; it stands on a kind of "raft", a grid of heavy oak beams, because of the nature of the soil. The factory supplied all the rigging for the entire French fleet from the time the factory was opened until the Revolution; once steam took over from sail, however, its activity declined and it was closed at the same time as the arsenal.

The Corderie Royale was severely damaged during World War II but has been the subject of an extensive restoration programme which has replaced the original lengthy and very harmonious façade (374m/1 227ft long). This is surmounted by a blue slate mansard roof with pediment dormers. The rear façade is reinforced by elegant scrolled buttresses. The building as a whole is a classic – and rare – example of 17C industrial architecture.

The **Centre International de la Mer** (*open daily Apr–Sept 9am–7pm, 1 Oct–3 Jan and 30 Jan–31 Mar 10am–12.30pm, 2–6pm; guided tours 1 Sept–3 Jan, 30 Jan–30 Jun daily 11.30am, 3.30pm, 4.30pm; closed 1 Jan, 25 Dec; 5€, guided tours 8€ (10€/14€ combined with l'Hermione); 05 46 87 81 40; www.corderie-royale.com)* houses a permanent exhibit on ropes and rigging: once the hemp had arrived from the Auvergne it was spun, assembled in strands and then twisted into its final form before being tarred – the length of the building both limiting and conditioning that of the rigging. Among the exhibits is an imposing 19C machine corder (twisting machine) which runs on rails. Temporary exhibits on maritime themes are also held here.

Surrounding the Corderie is the **Jardin des Retours**. Its rare and exotic species make it easy to imagine great expeditions returning to the port, laden with unknown plants such as begonias and magnolias. The riverside **Jardin des Amériques** includes the **Aire des Gréements** (Rigging Zone), evoking the vessels of the past; while the **Labyrinthe des Batailles Navales** is a maze of clipped yew hedges.

Magasin aux Vivres

quai aux Vivres.
This late 17C naval storehouse, next to the provisioning dock and facing the marina, was the site of a bakery able

to produce 20 000kg/44 100lb of bread each day.

Ancienne École de Médecine Navale

25 r. Amiral Meyer. Same as Musée de la Marine. 3€ (8€ combined with Musée de la Marine). 05 46 99 59 57. www.musee-marine.fr.

This 18C building stands at the heart of a park. The chapel, crowned with a pinnacle, lies behind a façade with a carved pediment. The École de médecine navale et tropicale was established in 1722. The library and various collections of anatomy, surgery and natural history can be visited.

Thermal Springs

Esplanade Pierre Soumet. 05 46 87 15 30.

Nearby is a small centre for thermal cures: the springs were first tapped after Napoleon I's visit in 1808 and rehabilitated once again in 1953, when the virtues of thermal treatment regained their popularity. The naturally hot waters (42°C/108°F) gush forth from the depths of the marshes. **La Source de l'Empereur** (Emperor's Spring) is especially effective in the treatment of rheumatism, osteoarthritis and dermatitis.

Opposite stands the old **water tower**, a fine quadrangular structure in stone, dating from 1900, which at one time supplied the whole town.

ADDITIONAL SIGHTS

Église St-Louis

r. Audry de Puyravault.

The church, built on the site of a chapel belonging to an old Capuchin monastery (1672), is imbued with the majesty of the Classical style.

Place Colbert

This fine square, huge and rectangular in shape and bordered by elegant façades, is the true centre of Rochefort. On the western side, the town hall is installed in the Hôtel d'Amblimont. The 18C monumental fountain on the other side of the square represents the Ocean and the River Charente mingling their waters.

Musée d'Art et d'Histoire★

63 av. Charles de Gaulle. Open mid-Jun–Sept Tue–Fri 10.30am–12.30pm, 2–7pm, Sat–Sun 2–7pm; Oct–mid-Jun Tue–Fri 10.30am–12.30pm, 2–6pm, Sat–Sun 2–6pm. No charge. 05 46 82 91 60.

The museum is housed in the former Hôtel Hèbre-de-Saint-Clément. A large picture gallery and an adjoining exhibit room contain a sketch by Rubens *(Lycaon Changed into a Wolf by Jupiter)*, a number of 17C flower paintings, portraits from the 16C Italian school, and others by Roques (Ingres' teacher) and a series from the Empire and Romantic epochs. More recent paintings hang nearby.

Fine collections of ethnographic interest from Africa and the South Pacific, including superb Polynesian masks, may be found in the Lesson Gallery.

In the following room hang seascapes and a copy of Géricault's dramatic work inspired by the Medusa tragedy. The Local History department has an extraordinary plan of Rochefort, in relief, from 1835, and Vernet's painting, *The Port of Rochefort*. The Camille Mériot Room has a shell collection.

Maison de Pierre Loti★

141 r. Pierre Loti. Guided tour (50min) Jun and Sept Mon and Wed–Sat 10.15am–12.45pm, 1.45–6.15pm, Sun 1.45–6.15pm; Jul–Aug Mon and Wed–Sat 9.45am–12.45pm, 1.45–7.15pm, Sun 1.45–7.15pm; Oct–Dec and Feb–Mar Mon and Wed–Sat 10.15am–12.45pm, 1.45–5.15pm, Sun 1.45–5.15pm. Closed 1 May, 25 Dec. 8.30€ (Jul–Aug), 7.90€ (Sept–Dec and Feb–Jun). 05 46 99 16 88.

Loti's house is two connected buildings, his birthplace and the house next door, concealing a remarkable interior behind a plain façade. There are two salons on the ground floor. Loti's piano stands in the first, which is hung with family paintings, some by his sister; the second houses Louis XVI furniture and a number of mementos and *objets*

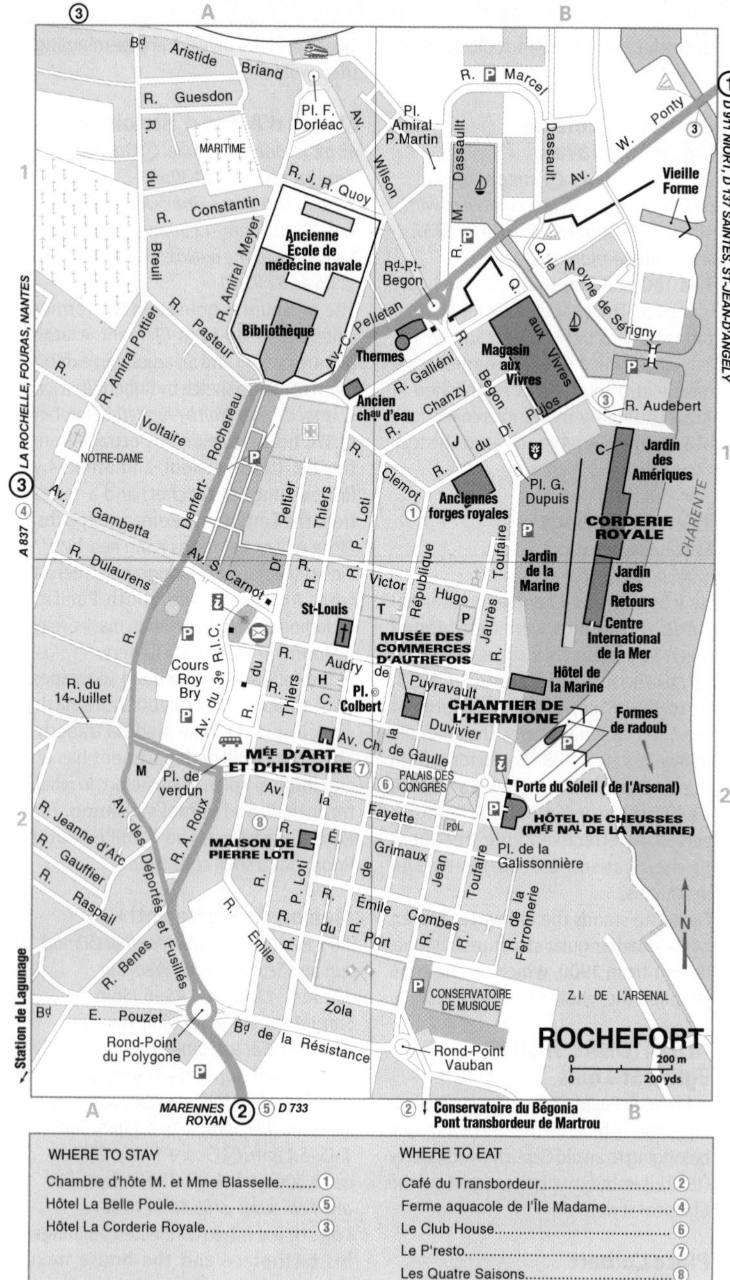

WHERE TO STAY

- Chambre d'hôte M. et Mme Blasselle......... ①
- Hôtel La Belle Poule.................................. ⑤
- Hôtel La Corderie Royale.......................... ③

WHERE TO EAT

- Café du Transbordeur.................................. ②
- Ferme aquacole de l'Île Madame................ ④
- Le Club House... ⑥
- Le P'resto.. ⑦
- Les Quatre Saisons...................................... ⑧

d'art. The **"Renaissance" Dining Room** includes a huge chimney-piece and a dais for musicians. On the mezzanine floor, the former studio used by the author's painter sister, transformed into a "15C salon", was the site of a famous "Louis XI dinner" in April 1888.

The spartan furnishings of the first-floor master bedroom are in striking contrast to the three apartments around it: the

Mosque, with décor largely from a mosque in Damascus; the **Turkish Salon** with its sofas, cushions, exotic wall hangings and a stucco ceiling inspired by the Alhambra in Granada; the **Arab Room**, glittering with enamelwork and adorned with a *moucharabieh*.

Musée des Commerces d'Autrefois★

12 r. Lesson. Open Apr–Jun, Sept–Oct Mon–Sat 10am–noon, 2–7pm, Sun 2–7pm; Jul–Aug daily 10am–8pm; Nov–Dec and Feb–Mar Mon–Sat 10am–noon, 2–6pm, Sun 2–6pm. 6.50€. 05 46 83 91 50. www.museedescommerces.com.

Here a series of workshops and stores dating from 1900 to 1940 have been re-created in meticulous detail within an old warehouse dating from the turn of the century. The picturesque evocation of life in days gone by includes a Rochefort bar with its Belle Époque façade, a pharmacy, a hatter's, a grocery store, a forge and a dyer's workshop.

Conservatoire du Bégonia

1 r. Charles Plumier. Guided tours (1hr) May–Sept Tue–Fri 2.30–4.30pm, Sat 3.30–4.30pm; Oct–Nov and Feb–Apr Tue–Fri 3.30pm, 4.30pm. Closed public holidays. 4€. 05 46 99 08 26. www.begonia.rochefort.fr.

Plumier was the botanist priest who first brought begonias back from the West Indies in the 17C. The plant was not, however, commercially available in France until the end of the 18C. Here, in a huge hothouse, over 850 species, natural and hybrid, are grown.

Pont Transbordeur de Martrou

av. Jacques-Demy (2.5km/1.5mi S). Call to confirm hours. 2€ (return). 05 46 83 30 86.

This iron transporter bridge, a splendid example of industrial art dating from 1900, is 176m/577ft long and stands more than 50m/164ft above the surface of the Charente. Five of these bridges were built in France by the engineer Ferdinand Arnodin. Transporter bridges enabled both pedestrians and vehicles to cross from one side of the river to the other, without sea-going ships being hindered by the structures of a fixed bridge. Martrou is the only one to have been reinstated (1994). It can be used by cyclists and pedestrians. A new toll bridge for vehicles was opened in 1991.

EXCURSION

Cabane de Moins

Le Liron, 4km/2.5mi N of Rochefort on the D 5 (signposted from Breuil-Magné). Open Jun–Aug 2–7pm; Sept–Jan 1.30–5.30pm; Feb–May 1.30–6.30pm. Closed Wed and Nov–Jan Sat–Sun. No charge. 05 46 84 48 60.

This 150ha/371-acre nature centre comprises freshwater marshes, meadows and lakes. Nearly 214 species of birds have been spotted, including the ciconia stork which has decided to take up residence here. Two trails lead to four observation huts, one of which is a former hunting hut at the edge of a vast lake. The cabin houses a small exhibition of stuffed animals, as well as information on the preservation of the ecosystem.

DRIVING TOUR

2 FROM MARAIS DE BROUAGE TO CANAL DE PONT-L'ABBÉ★

75km/47mi. Allow one day.

Leave Rochefort heading S on the D 733 in the direction of Royan.

You cross the impressive Charente viaduct. In service since 1991, it replaced a vertical lift span bridge built in 1967.

Leave at the first intersection, and turn right onto the D 238E1.

Soubise

Former barony and stronghold of the Rohans. The façade of the St-Pierre church, dating from the 16C has four

Ionic pilasters. Inside, the seigneurial frieze bears the arms of Rohan-Soubise. Opposite the church stands an elegant 17C *hôtel particulier.*

Leave Soubise heading W on D 125.

Port-des-Barques

This village of oyster farmers and fishermen has become a seaside resort with a marina.

Île Madame

Île Madame is connected to the mainland by the Passe aux Bœufs, exposed at low tide. The island, 1km/0.6mi long and 600m/2 000ft wide, has few dwellings. From the north coast, there are fine views of Fouras, the Île d'Aix, and the Île d'Oléron; in the south extend the abandoned salt marshes, now pastureland. There are oyster farms all around the island. At the southeast tip of the island, a large pebble cross marks the burial place of 254 priests who died, in 1794, of disease or exhaustion aboard the decks of slave trading boats. In August, each year, there is a pilgrimage in honour of these priests.

Back on the mainland, follow the road going S along the oyster beds.

Shortly, at a clearing, there is a pleasant view of the sea with a row of traditional fishing huts on stilts.

At St-Froult, head SW along the small road that follows the coast.

Réserve Naturelle des Marais de Moëze

Sentier des polders footpath open Feb–Aug 8am–6.30pm; Sept–Jan noon–6.30pm. Guided tours depending on the tides. 6€ (children no charge). 05 46 82 12 44.

The nature reserve, of around 6 700ha/16 556 acres, extends from the mainland to the east coast of Oléron. The area includes 200ha/495 acres of marshland with five zones from where migratory birds can be observed. The Maison de la Nature (*open Jul–Sept daily; Easter–Sept Sat–Sun)* organises guided tours of the reserve.

At the entrance to the reserve, turn right.

Moëze

A high Gothic belfry, which served as a landmark for ships, towers above the church. In the cemetery stands an early 16C Corinthian-style Hosanna cross or "Temple de Moëze".

Leave Moëze SW on the D 3.

Brouage★ *See BROUAGE.*

Continue on the D 3. At Hiers, turn E onto the D 238.

The road crosses the east section of the former salt marshes.

After Beaugeay, take the D 125, on the right, to St-Agnant. Before the church turn left onto the D 239. At Champagne, go E on the D 18.

Pont-l'Abbé-d'Arnoult

This formerly fortified city is on the canalised Arnoult river, developed around a Benedictine priory built in the 11C, on the behest of **Geoffroy Martel**, Comte d'Anjou. The explorer **René Caillé**, born in Mauzé-sur-le-Mignon in 1799, was buried in the graveyard of Pont-l'Abbé in 1838.

Leave Pont-l'Abbé N on the D 117.

Trizay

This village, situated in the Vallée de l'Arnoult, has an abbey and a leisure centre.

Prieuré St-Jean-l'Évangéliste – The construction of this imposing building remains a mystery, but it seems that monks from the Chaise-Dieu (*see The Green Guide Auvergne Rhône Valley)* settled here in the late 11C (*open mid-Jun–mid-Sept 10am–noon, 2–6pm, Sun 3–7pm, Feb–mid-Jun and mid-Sept–Nov 2–7pm; closed Mon; 05 46 82 34 25).*

Le Bois Fleuri – A wooded area in an old quarry surrounding a 5ha/12.3-acre lake.

From the leisure centre, follow the D 123. After the railway line, turn left onto the D 238.

Échillais

Église Notre-Dame – Admire the Romanesque Saintonge-style façade. To the left of the portal, a capital has one of those monsters that in Saintongeais is called **"Grand'Goule"**.

Maison du Transbordeur – At the foot of the bridge, this information centre has a permanent exhibition about the main bridges in the Rochefort and Charente-Maritime regions *(r. de Martrou; open Apr–Jun and Sept 10am–noon, 2–6pm; Jul–Aug 10am–noon, 2–7pm, closed Nov–Jan and Mon; no charge; 05 46 83 30 86).*

Return to the D 238 at the NE of Échillais, then return to the D 123. At St-Hippolyte, turn left onto the N 137.

Pont Suspendu de Tonnay-Charente

Access permitted only to pedestrians and cyclists. 204m/670ft long, it was constructed in 1842 by the engineer Louis Dor, then modified several times.

The road follows the railway line, then the N 137 leads back to Rochefort.

ADDRESSES

STAY

Chambre d'hôte M et Mme Blasselle – *55 r. de la République. 05 46 99 55 54. www.palmiersurcour.com. Closed mid-Dec–mid-Feb. 3 rooms.* This 18C *hôtel particulier*, standing in the historic quarter, has beautiful individually decorated rooms. Pleasant patio for breakfast.

Hôtel La Belle Poule – *102 av du 11 Novembre 1918 (3km/1.8mi S of Rochefort on the Royan road). 05 46 99 71 87. www.hotelrochefort.com. Closed Sun evening, Fri (off-season), 1 wk in Jan and Nov. 20 rooms. 8.50€. Restaurant.* Just next to the Martrou bridge, this hotel offers big rooms and a pleasant dining room with a fireplace.

Hôtel Corderie Royale – *r. Audebert (near the Corderie Royale). 05 46 99 35 35. www.corderieroyale-hotel.com. Closed Sun evening, Mon (Nov–Easter) and mid-Dec–mid-Jan. 53 rooms. Restaurant.* This hotel, across from the port, has been constructed out of the magnificent 17C buildings of the Royal Artillery. Superb view of the Charente river from the restaurant. Swimming pool.

EAT

Café du Transbordeur – *r. Jacques-Demy, at the base of the Transbordeur, bord by the Charente. 05 46 87 56 30. Closed late Sept–Easter.* A tiny café, with a large terrace overlooking the port. The choice includes sandwiches, salads, and plates of fresh oysters.

Le Club House – *21 av. Lafayette. 05 46 87 35 59. Closed Sun.* This pub, whose interior is successfully decorated using both modern and ancient styles, offers copious dishes.

Le P'resto – *55 av. Charles de Gaulle. 05 46 83 95 85. Closed during the Christmas holidays.* Located in the city centre, the restaurant serves generous portions. For those in a hurry, pizzas are made to order.

Les Quatre Saisons – *76 r. Grimaux. 05 46 83 95 12. Closed Sun–Mon and1st wk in Jan.* Friendly welcome from Madame, while Monsieur cooks in the kitchen: loves stuffed pigs trotters, veal sweetbreads, and good fish dishes as well. Reserve in advance because it only seats 20 people.

Ferme Aquacole de l'Île Madame – *17730 Port-des-Barques. 05 46 84 12 67. www.ilemadame.com. Reservations recommended. Closed Wed and 17 Nov–5 Dec.* This farm on an island is only accessible at low tide. You can savour seafood and *congers* raised here.

Brouage★

Charente-Maritime

The ramparts and turrets of Brouage, well preserved despite constant assault from the sea winds, soar above the desolate marshland around them. Memories of lost love and lost wars haunt the old walled town, now sunk into silence. Brouage still stands today as a memorial to the friendship between France and Quebec.

- **Population:** 627
- **Michelin Map:** 324: D-4
- **Info:** 2 r.de Québec, Brouage. ℘05 46 85 19 16. www.hiers-brouage-tourisme.fr.
- **Location:** In the middle of the marshes, 8km/5mi NW of Marennes.
- **Don't Miss:** The 17C ramparts.
- **Kids:** Walk around the ramparts, and look for the soldiers' graffiti.
- **Timing:** Brouage deserves at least 2hrs.

A BIT OF HISTORY

In medieval times Brouage played an important commercial role. The town, sheltered by Île d'Oléron at the inner end of "the finest haven in France", was the salt capital of Europe. Some 8 000ha/ 19 768 acres of salt marshes provided the precious mineral which was to be refined and sent abroad – particularly to Flanders and Germany.

At some time between 1567 and 1580, **Samuel de Champlain** was born into a Protestant family living in Brouage. The boy became an expert navigator and, on the orders of King Henri IV, sailed to Canada. In 1608 he left Honfleur in Normandy and discovered Quebec, opening up the fur trade in beaver and mink. A monument marks the place in Brouage where he was born.

During the siege of La Rochelle in 1628, Brouage became the royal arsenal and Cardinal Richelieu instructed the Picardy engineer, Pierre d'Argencourt, to rebuild the fortifications. With a garrison of 6 000 men, Brouage was the most impregnable stronghold on the Atlantic Coast.

At the end of the 17C, Brouage entered a period of decline. The founding of Rochefort and the revival of La Rochelle as a military base removed most of the military reasons for its existence. Vauban, nevertheless, undertook to reinforce the ramparts once more. However, the haven silted up, the salterns degenerated into rot marshes which bred fever, and the garrison was reduced.

Aerial view of Brouage

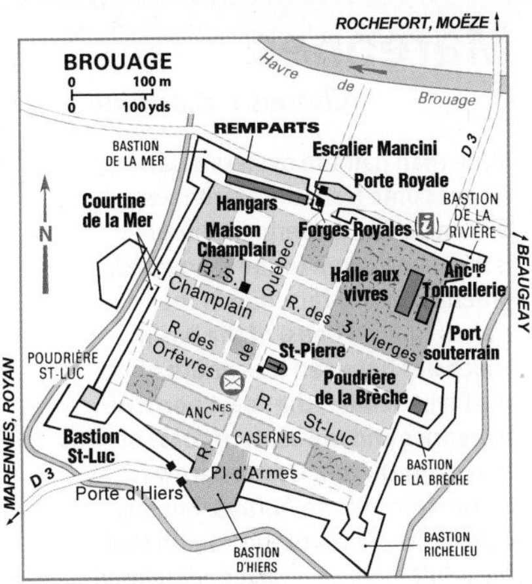

RAMPARTS★★

Guided tours available by reservation from tourist office.

Constructed in 1630–40, the ramparts exemplify the art of fortification before the Vauban era. They describe an exact square measuring four times 400m/440yds, and are protected by seven bastions, each equipped with corbelled turrets. The walls, 13m/43ft high, are topped by a brick parapet pierced with apertures for cannon fire. Two gateways, porte Royale and porte de Hiers, allow access to the enclave. The western rampart is protected by a ravelin detached from the curtain wall. Though most of the houses in Brouage, including the governor's mansion, have disappeared, the military dependencies have better resisted the erosions of time.

Watch-Path

It is possible to walk almost entirely around the town's circumference along the top of the old ramparts, now carpeted with grass. From here the neat rectilinear layout of the plan is apparent, and there is a good view across the marshes to Île d'Aix and Île d'Oléron.

Porte Royale

Located in the northern **Bastion Royal**, this gateway once opened onto the quays. On the right-hand wall of the vaulted passage, leading out, note ancient graffiti of various ships. The outside of the gateway is surmounted by a pediment with the armorial bearings of France and Navarre.

Forges Royales

The old blacksmiths' forges back onto Bastion Royal. In the middle of the one occupied today by the tourist office, a chimney furnace can still be seen. Left of the forge, **Escalier Mancini** is the stone stairway that was used by the King's beloved each time she climbed to the ramparts to dream her solitary dreams. Parallel to the steps is a ramp that was used to hoist cannons. To the left are the **Hangars de la Porte Royale**, a row of shops. The governor's mansion was just to the south.

Halle aux Vivres

1 r. du Port. Open daily Jun and Sept 10am–6.30pm; Jul–Aug 10am–7pm; Oct–Nov and Feb–May 10.30am–6pm; Dec–Jan 2–6pm. 05 46 85 77 77.

This is a restored food market located next to the old cooper's workshop *(Ancienne Tonnellerie)*. To the south is the underground harbour *(Port-souterrain)* and the old powder magazine *(Poudrière de la Brèche)*, which were enclosed by the Bastion de la Bréche. At the centre of the fort stands the 17C **Église St-Pierre**, with stained-glass windows commemorating Champlain installed in 1982.

Maison Champlain

Open Jun and Sept 10am–121.30pm, 2–6.30pm; Jul–Aug 10am–12.30pm, 2–7pm; Oct–May 10.30am–12.30pm, 2–6pm. Closed 25 Dec, 31 Dec. 3€ (10–18 years 2.50€). 05 46 85 80 60

The exhibition Champlain, traces the Saintongeais in the Americas. Follow in the footsteps of Samuel de Champlain, navigator under the orders of Henri IV, born at Brouage c.1569. He founded Quebec and colonised part of Canada. Brouage celebrates the friendship between France and Quebec.

Marennes

Charente-Maritime

More than half the oysters eaten in France come from the Marennes-Oléron basin. "Marennes-Oléron" is the name given to the renowned, greenish oyster fattened in the *claires* (special beds) of the basin, which lies between the mouth of the River Seudre, the coast north of Marennes and the eastern coast of the Isle of Oléron. Oysters grow to maturity in *parcs à huîtres*, but it is only in the *claires* of this region that the adult mollusc is fattened, refined and subjected to the effects of algae known here as *Navicules Bleues*, which give the seafood its delicate perfume and subtle hue.

- **Population:** 5 237
- **Michelin Map:** 324: D-5
- **Info:** pl. Chasseloup-Laubat, Marennes. 05 46 85 04 36. www.marennes.fr.
- **Location:** Marennes is situated 22km/13.7mi SW of Rochefort.
- **Don't Miss:** The tower of Église St-Pierre-de-Sales.
- **Kids:** Château de la Gataudière.

SIGHTS

Église St-Pierre-de-Sales

28 r. François Fresneau. 05 46 85 25 55.

This 15C church is built in a style known, in France, as English, with a tall square tower, buttressed at the corners, crowned by a spire decorated with crockets. The spire, rising to a height of 85m/279ft, is visible from miles away. The interior is noteworthy for its wide nave flanked by chapels beneath balustraded galleries. Eight-branched rib vaulting arches above the bays.

Terrasse de la Tour

28 r. François Fresneau. Open Jul–Aug daily 10am–12.30pm, 2–7pm; Sept–Jun with appointment. 2€. 05 46 85 03 86.

Accessible up 291 steps, this tower platform offers an impressive **panorama**★ – 55m/180ft high – over the oyster farms, the islands, the Avert peninsula and a stretch of the marshes.

Cité de l'Huître★

Access is from the car park by free shuttle. Open Apr–Jun, Sept and All Saints Holiday daily 11am–6pm; Jul–Aug daily 10.30am–7pm; Oct–Mar Sat–Sun 11am–6pm. 9€. 05 46 36 78 98. www.cite-huitre.com.

This interpretation centre in a series of five old cabins built on stilts over the **Chenal de la Cayenne** houses an interactive exhibition about oysters. In one hut the life cycle of the oyster and the secrets of the breeders are revealed. Details of the ecosystem and how it affects the oyster are detailed in another hut, while in another hut the history of the oyster is retraced using the latest in multimedia techniques.

One cabin is devoted to the life of several generations of oyster farmers. In addition, there is a restaurant and activities for children.

EXCURSIONS

Château de la Gataudière★

19 r. de la Gataudière (1.5km/0.9mi N). Open Apr–Jun Sat–Sun and Sept–Oct Tue–Sun 2–5pm; Jul–Aug daily 10am–noon, 2–6pm. 7€ (children 5€). 05 46 85 01 07. www.gataudiere.com.

The château was built c.1749, in the Louis XIV style, by François Fresneau (1703–70), an engineer who studied the production of rubber from the hevea tree in French Guyana and returned to France to lay the base for its industrial use. The château stands on the site of a medieval house in the heart of an old marsh village known as Les Gataudières. On the garden front, a terrace with a wrought-iron balustrade runs the length of the façade. A Classical pediment embellished with a Triumph of Flora surmounts a central block decorated with trophies symbolising the resources of the region.

Inside, the main reception floor is notable for the Grand Salon with its stone walls set with fluted Corinthian pilasters representing the arts, the sciences and the four seasons. Fine Louis XV furniture can be seen in the dining hall and the Blue Salon. The château now hosts a paintballing and an adventure park.

Bourcefranc-le-Chapus

4 km/2.5mi NE on the D 26.
You will see, all along the channels of this famous oyster farm, all sorts of vessels, shops and the shipping basins or *dégorgeoirs*.

Brouage★ *See BROUAGE.*

6.5km/4mi NE.

Fort Louvois★

7km/4.3mi N. Open May–Jun, Sept and school holidays at low tide; Jul–Aug daily 10.30am–6.30pm. 5.50€; no charge at high tide (Jul–Aug). 05 46 85 07 00. www.fort-louvois.com.
Access to the fort (also known as Fort Chapus) is by foot at low tide, and by boat when the tide is in.

ADDRESSES

STAY

Le Grand Chalet – *2 av. La Cèpe, Ronce-les-Bains (9km/5.6mi SW of Marennes via the D 728E). 05 46 36 06 41. http://pagesperso-orange.fr/le.grand.chalet-le.brise.lames. Closed 2 Nov–6 Feb. 26 rooms. 9€. Restaurant.*
This 1850s hotel with an unusual chalet-style façade sits at the water's edge. The guest rooms either overlook the garden or offer attractive sea views.

Île d'Oléron★

Charente-Maritime

The Isle of Oléron is just off the coast between Royan and La Rochelle. The island is a popular holiday resort famed for the scent of pines and the wonderful oysters.
Since 1966, Oléron has been linked to the mainland by a curving road bridge, the longest in France at 3 027m/1.8mi. The viaduct is built of prestressed concrete in simple, modern lines and rests on 45 rectangular piles; the central spans, 79m/259ft wide, rise 23m/75ft above the highest of high tides. A 7m/23ft carriageway, two cycle lanes and two walkways for pedestrians are incorporated in the viaduct's total width of 10.6m/35ft. From the mainland, the best view of the bridge is from the old ferry landing-stage at Le Chapus.

- **Population:** 20 991
- **Michelin Map:** 324: B-3–C-5
- **Info:** rte du Viaduc, Bourcefranc. 05 46 85 65 23. www.ile-oleron-marennes.com.
- **Kids:** Le Marais aux Oiseaux; St Trojan tourist train
- **Timing:** Allow a full day to explore the island..

GEOGRAPHICAL NOTES

Oléron, a prolongation seawards of the old province of Saintonge, is, except for Corsica, the biggest of all the French islands (30km/18.6mi long and 6km/3.7mi wide). The Pertuis (Straits) of Antioche and those of Maumusson, ravaged by dangerous currents, separate it from the Charente Coast.
The limestone foundation of the low-lying isle is streaked with areas of sand forming long strings of dunes, wooded in the north (Saumonards Dune) and west (on the Côte sauvage). The white houses and windmills of Oléron are surrounded by mimosa, oleander,

tamarisk, fig trees and the grey-green spines of agave.

Natural Resources – To the east, the coastline and the lowlands between Boyardville and St-Trojan are exclusively reserved for oyster farming, along with early fruit and vegetables and the cultivation of vines. The vineyards, mainly grouped around St-Pierre and St-Georges, produce white or rosé wines. The salt marshes, once numerous near Ors, St-Pierre and La Brée, have largely been transformed into oyster *claires*.

A more recent development on the island is the establishment of several fish farms raising eels, trout and clams.

The most important fishing port on Oléron is La Cotinière on the west coast, but an unusual form of coastal fishing also survives around the Chassiron headland to the north. Here, visitors may see the local catch caught in **fish-locks** – walled enclosures fitted with grilled apertures at the seaward end, through which the water filters as the tide goes out. At low tide the fishermen wade out to collect their prey with the aid of *fouënes* (a kind of harpoon) or *espiottes* (a type of sabre).

On the Côte sauvage (Wild Coast) locals go spear fishing – especially in June and September – for bass and Salmon-Basse.

ST-PIERRE D'OLÉRON

St-Pierre is situated in the centre of the island, on the edge of the marshes, and is both the commercial and the administrative capital of the island. In the summer months the town, with its attractive pedestrian precincts, becomes extremely busy.

Church

r. de la République. Open 15 Jun–15 Sept Mon–Fri 9.30am–1pm, 2.45–6.30pm. 2€. 05 46 47 11 44.

A pale, octagonal belfry dating from the 18C serves as a landmark for sailors at sea. On each side of the chancel, a chapel is preceded by clover-leaf arching supported by black marble pillars.

From the platform at the top of the tower (32m/105ft high), the whole of the island is visible in the foreground of a **panorama**★ embracing the Île d'Aix, the Île de Ré and the estuary of the River Charente.

Lanterne des Morts

pl. Camille Mémain. No charge. 05 46 47 02 83.

This Lantern of the Dead, rising to a height of 30m/98ft, stands on the site of a former cemetery. The monument was built during the English occupation in the 13C and its slender lines are typical of the early Gothic style.

Inside, a staircase still leads to the beacon at the top where the priest used to light the flame symbolising the immortality of the soul. An altar stands against one of the walls.

Maison des Aïeules

r. Pierre Loti. Closed to the public.

It was in this ancestors' house, home of his maternal grandparents at no **13** in the street now bearing his name,

Les Rôles d'Oléron

In 1199 the 76-year-old Eleanor of Aquitaine returned to her château here before retiring to Fontevraud Abbey, where she died in 1204.

Aged but not resigned, she set about restoring law and order to the island she ruled. The dangerous Côte Sauvage, for instance, had long been at the mercy of wreckers who looted and pillaged ships driven ashore. Eleanor decreed that henceforth such brigands must be punished.

Subsequently the dowager drew up a maritime code, known as *Les Rôles d'Oléron*, which served as a base for all subsequent charters regulating conduct on the high seas.

After the reign of Eleanor Oléron was coveted by both the French and the English. In 1372 the English abandoned the isle.

that the novelist Pierre Loti, member of the French Academy, spent many of his school holidays. In 1923 Loti was buried – like his Huguenot ancestors – in the family garden. In front of the town hall a bust of Loti, who was born in Rochefort, commemorates the writer's link with St-Pierre.

ST-TROJAN-LES-BAINS★

St-Trojan is a pretty seaside resort with Mediterranean-like vegetation. Warm water from the Gulf Stream laps its four sandy bathing beaches; the attractive villas scattered on the edge of a magnificent pine forest are fragrant with the scent of mimosa flower from January to March.

A thalassotherapy centre treats rheumatism and other complaints *(www.st-trojan-les-bains.fr)*.

Forêt de St-Trojan

This huge stretch of woodland, thickly carpeted with parasol pines, covers an area of 2 000ha/4 942 acres. Much of the forest, commercially harvested, grows on dunes, cresting as high as 36m/118ft.

Grande Plage

3km/1.8mi W of St-Trojan via the D 126E1.

This fine sand beach, rising to a line of dunes, exposed to the west wind and the Atlantic rollers of the Côte sauvage, stretches as far as the eye can see.

Pointe de Manson

2.5km/1.5mi SE of St-Trojan.

The road to the point ends by an *estacade* (dyke). From the top of this point there are **views** of the viaduct, the headlands of Ors and Le Chapus, the Seudre estuary and La Tremblade peninsula.

Plage de Gatseau

4km/2.5mi S of St-Trojan.

The road leads to a delightful beach of fine sand. On the way there are fine **views** of the Arvert headland, Ronce-les-Bains and the landmark tower of the church at Marennes on the mainland.

Pointe de Gatseau

This isolated promontory at the southern extremity of Grande Plage is one of the most evocative spots on the Côte sauvage (Wild Coast). Access is by a small **tourist train**, which runs between St-Trojan and the Côte sauvage. *(av. du Débarquement, St-Trojan-les-Bains; Open Jul–Aug 10am–6.15pm (every 45min), Sept and early Feb–Jun, please consult website; 11.50€; 05 46 76 01 26; www.le-ptit-train.com).*

DRIVING TOUR

3 ISLAND ROUND TRIP FROM ST-TROJAN-LES-BAINS

85km/53mi. Allow one day.

St-Trojan-les-Bains★

See above.

Le Grand-Village-Plage

This seaside resort combines leisure, sport and cultural activities.

La Maison Paysanne – *bd de la Plage. Open 15 Jun–19 Sept Mon 2.30–6pm, Tue–Sat 10am–12.30pm, 2.30–6pm. 4€. 05 46 47 43 44.*

This local costume museum re-creates the atmosphere of island life in the past. The farmhouse is fully furnished in the local style. The outbuildings contain exhibits of traditional activities relating to the sea and vine-growing.

The adjacent **Maison de la Coiffe et du Costume Oléronais★** includes an attractive display of traditional costumes worn on the island during the 19C.

Port des Salines★ – *r. des Anciennes Salines. Open Apr–Jun Tue–Sat 9.30am–12.30pm, 2.30–6pm, Sun–Mon 2.30–6pm; Jul–Sept Mon–Sat 9.30am–1pm, 2.30–7pm, Sun 2.30–7pm. Guided tours (1hr) available. Écomusée 4€, guided tour 3.50€. 05 46 75 82 28.* Set in an enclave formed by the road to the viaduct, oyster beds and a forest, this port is a revival of the old salt marshes. Two well-marked trails allow visitors to discover the site. At the entrance, brightly coloured **oyster huts** contain

exhibits retracing the island's recent history.

Visitors can explore the former salt works of **Cabane à Sau**, which was designed to store up to 200t of salt (the last salt maker retired in 1990).

Fine examples of trawlers and oyster boats are anchored in the waters of a small port which provides access to a channel encircling the tidal reservoir. **Boat trips** *(6€ for 1 or 2 people for 1hr)* provide the opportunity to discover the flora and fauna of the salt marshes. Quai des Hôtes offers visitors a selection of regional food products.

Return to the road bridge. In Ors, follow the D 275.

Le Château-d'Oléron

Guided tours Jul–Aug with pre-booking; nocturnal visits Jul–Aug Wed 8.15pm. 4€, nocturnal visit 6.50€. 05 46 85 65 23.

The remains of a 17C fortress, a citadel originally built on Richelieu's orders, stand here. In 1666 the construction of the port at Rochefort led Louis XIV to order the establishment of a *ceinture de feu* (girdle of fire) to protect the Charente estuary leading to this new port. Fouras and the Île d'Aix were therefore heavily fortified and the Oléron citadel redesigned and reinforced. Numerous deportees, both lay and religious, were imprisoned here during the Revolution.

The town is arranged geometrically around a huge central square containing a pretty Renaissance fountain. The port penetrates the built-up area: a picturesque local sight is the arrival and departure of boats bound for the oyster farms.

The coast road heading north towards Les Allards is known locally as the **Route des huîtres** (the "Oyster Road"). This narrow road permits the servicing of the many canals, sheds and ports strung out opposite the east-coast oyster farms.

Continue N along the rte côtière des Allards, also known as "Route des huîtres" (the "Oyster Road").

Le Marais aux Oiseaux

Les Grissotières, Dolus d'Oléron. Open Apr–Jun and Sept Mon–Fri 10am–1pm, 2–6pm, Sat–Sun 2–6pm; Jul–Aug daily 10am–7pm; Oct–Mar Wed and Sun 2–6pm; school holidays (Oct–Mar) Sun–Fri 2–6pm. Closed 1 Jan, 25 Dec. 4.50€ (children 2.80€). 05 46 75 37 54. www.centre-sauvegarde-oleron.com.

This area of former salt marshes surrounded by oak trees is now a **bird sanctuary** and nature reserve, providing a winter retreat for some species of migratory birds and a nesting site for others.

Return to Les Allards and continue along the D 126.

Boyardville

The name of the resort derives from a hutted camp established here for the army of workmen building **Fort Boyard**. Boyardville, once a training centre for the crews of torpedo boats, is today enlivened with a small marina. The 8km/5mi beach is in fact the seaward side of the Dune des Saumonards. A forest track leads to the old Saumonards Fort (military territory).

Fort Boyard

Closed to the public.

This is a curious stone structure rising, offshore, from the shallow sea in the middle of the Straits of Antioche, between the Île d'Oléron and the Île d'Aix. The fort, another project designed to protect the mouth of the Charente, was started in 1804 and completed in 1859 under Napoleon III; however, it was militarily out of date before it was even finished. In 1871 it was used as a prison: a large number of Communards (members of a Parisian workers' rebellion) were incarcerated there before their trial and deportation to New Caledonia.

In 1990 astute television producers turned the abandoned fort into the striking setting of a televised gameshow (called Fort Boyard), which brought international fame and still runs today. In

high season, boats take visitors to within a short distance of the fort.

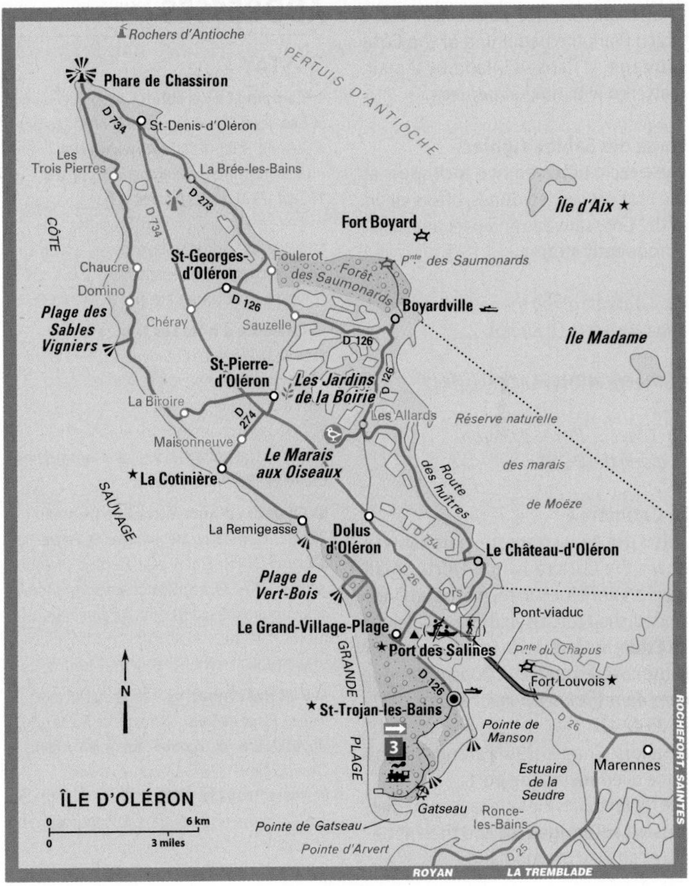

Continue along the D 126.

St-Georges-d'Oléron

The façade of the 11C–12C Romanesque church *(r. des Dames)* in this small town is attractively decorated with geometric motifs. The crowned arch of the central doorway and the Gothic vaulting over the nave were rebuilt in the 13C. The church was restored in 1618 and again in 1968. There is a fine covered market in the town square.

Drive NE to join the coast road and turn left towards St-Denis-d'Oléron.

Phare de Chassiron

Open daily Apr–Jun and Sept 10am–12.15pm, 2–7pm; Jul–Aug 10am–8pm; Oct–Mar 10am–12.15pm, 2–5pm. Closed 1 Jan in the morning, 25 Dec. 2.50€, guided tour 4€. 05 46 75 18 62. www.chassiron.net.

This black-and-white lighthouse built in 1836 is 50m/164ft high. The 224-step climb to the top is worthwhile for the huge **panorama**★, which encompasses the Île d'Aix, the Île de Ré, the port of La Rochelle, La Pallice and, offshore, the Rocher d'Antioche. Below the lighthouse, at low tide, the fish-locks around the cape are visible.

Follow the coast road S towards Chaucre via Les Trois Pierres.

The road, running above low cliffs which mark the beginning of the **Côte sauvage**, is flanked inland by a plain scattered with market gardens.

Plage des Sables Vigniers

The beach, between two rock spurs at the foot of wooded dunes, offers views of the Côte sauvage and over a sea that is frequently stormy.

Continue along the coast road and turn left in La Biroire.

St-Pierre-d'Oléron *See p442.*

Leave St-Pierre-d'Oléron SE along the D 734.

La Cotinière★

This is a busy, picturesque port halfway down the Côte sauvage. Thirty small trawlers are based in the harbour. Once landed, their catch is sold immediately at **La Criée**, the local term for a fish auction in the covered market *(open Mon–Sat 6am, 4pm; closed public holidays; 05 46 76 42 42).*

A Sailors' Chapel (1967) stands on the dune overlooking the port.

The route crosses the Côte sauvage dunes, passes **La Remigeasse** and then penetrates an area of woodland.

Plage de Vert-Bois

The road loops through a patch of duneland fringed with reeds before arriving at this beach; from here is an impressive **view★** of the ocean.

Continue along the same road via Grand-Village-Plage and follow the D 126 back to St-Trojan-les-Bains.

ADDRESSES

STAY

Camping Le Verébleu – *La Jousselinière, St-Georges-d'Oléron (2km/1mi SE of St-Georges-d'Oléron). 05 46 76 57 70. www.verebleu.tm.fr. Reservations recommended. Closed 14 Sept–29 May. 333 pitches.* A big aquatic theme park based on Fort-Boyard, a minigolf, a children's playground, a tennis court, archery, bike rentals. Mobile homes, chalets and cottages are also available.

Chambre d'hôte Les Trémières – *5 rte de St-Pierre, La Cotinière. 05 46 47 44 25. www.althaea-oleron.fr. 5 rooms.* Near to the La Cotinière port and its shops, this early 20C house is charming indeed. The small garden is the perfect place for a summertime breakfast. Bedrooms and suites.

Chambre d'hôte Micheline Denieau – *20 r. de la Legère, La Menounière, St-Pierre-d'Oléron (3km/1.8mi W of St-Pierre-d'Oléron). 05 46 47 14 34. http://pagesperso-orange.fr/denieau-gites. 5 rooms.* Simple, well-cared-for rooms have been built in the outbuildings of this typical regional-style house.

Hôtel L'Albatros – *11 bd du Docteur Pineau, Plage du Soleil, St-Trojan-les-Bains. 05 46 76 00 08. www.albatros-hotel-oleron.com. Closed 5 Nov–13 Feb. 12 rooms. 10€. Restaurant.* This old oyster breeder's house on the edge of the public forest has its toes in the water. The terrace is the ideal place to savour a seafood meal.

EAT

Le Relais des Salines – *Salines harbour, Petit Village, Grand-Village-Plage. 05 46 75 82 42. www.lerelaisdessalines.com. Closed late Nov–early Mar.* On the harbour, this wooden oyster breeder's cabin has a colourful interior. Simple à la carte seafood menu.

Les Alizés – *4 r. Dubois-Aubry, St-Pierre-d'Oléron. 05 46 47 20 20. Closed Tue–Wed and 12 Dec–14 Mar, .* The two brightly coloured dining rooms serve local dishes including *chaudrée charentaise*, sole, eel, etc.

Les Bains – *1 r. des Quais, Boyardville. 05 46 47 01 02. www.hoteldesbains-oleron.com. Closed late Sept–May.* You can enjoy the liveliness of the Boyardville harbour from the terrace of this restaurant. Rustic dining rooms and appetising menu. Spotless bedrooms.

Zoo de la Palmyre★★★

Charente-Maritime

This attractive 14ha/33-acre zoo is one of the most visited in France. Every year 250t of fodder, 180t of fruit and vegetables, 70t of straw, 50t of meat, 20t of fish, 30t of mixed food and 10t of grain support the animals. The zoo breeds species threatened with extinction.

- **Michelin Map:** 324: D-5
- **Info:** Zoo de la Palmyre, Les Mathes. ℘08 92 68 18 48. www.zoo-palmyre.com.
- **Location:** The zoo is situated in the middle of the Forêt de La Palmyre, 15km/9.3mi NW of Royan.
- **Kids:** A paradise for children, but the nursery, and lions feeding time are especially appreciated.
- **Timing:** Allow half a day.

THE ZOO

Open daily Apr–Sept 9am–7pm; Oct–Mar 9am–6pm; sea-lion and parrot shows Apr–Oct. 14€ (child 10€). ℘08 92 68 18 48. www.zoo-palmyre.fr.

Pink flamingos at the foot of a waterfall welcome visitors to La Palmyre.

It is advisable to follow the marked 4km/2.5mi trail, which has explanatory panels along the way.

More than 1 600 animals from every corner of the globe are scattered throughout the pine forest, in areas similar to their natural habitat.

Carnivorous species – The most dangerous predators (cheetahs, lions, wolves, Siberian tigers) live next to smaller mammals (small pandas, suricates).

Birds – A great variety of species are represented here including exotic birds with magnificent plumage like the parrots, cockatoos and midnight blue macaws.

Hoofed animals – The large species (elephant, hippopotamus, rhinoceros) offer a striking contrast with the more agile species (blesbok, impala and zebra).

Polar bears – The polar-bear enclosure is a huge pool (1 000cu m/1 308cu yds) set up as an ice floe. Below, a glass panel enables visitors to see the agility and ease with which these 450kg/990lb giants swim.

Reptiles – A vivarium houses crocodiles from the Nile, royal pythons from Africa and tortoises from the Seychelles.

Monkeys – Wide variety of monkeys such as the golden lion marmoset from Brazil or the male emperor marmoset with its white moustache. Only a sheet of plate glass separates visitors from the African gorillas, the most imposing of all the apes.

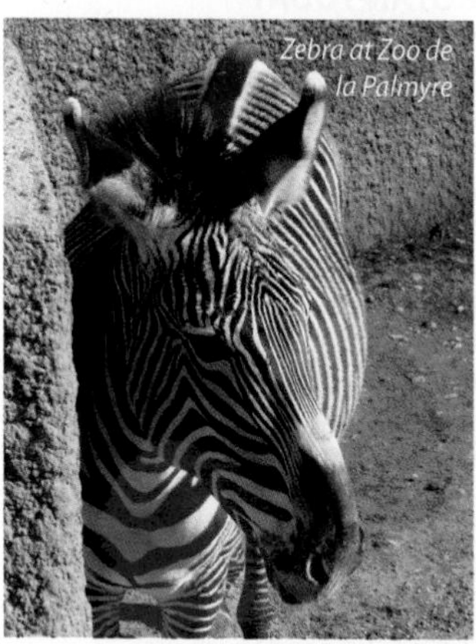

Zebra at Zoo de la Palmyre

©yannpro/Fotolia.com

Shows – Additional attractions are the lions' feeding time, a sea-lion show, and performing wild birds.

ADDRESSES

STAY

Palmyrotel – *2 allée des Passereaux, 17570 La Palmyre, Les Mathes. ℘05 46 23 65 65 www.monalisahotels.com. Closed early Nov–Mar. 46 rooms. Restaurant*. A big hotel complex in a pine forest a short distance from the zoo. It offers functional rooms, some duplexes, and Le Flamand Rose restaurant.

Royan★★

Charente-Maritime

Known as the "Perle de l'Océan" (the "Ocean's Pearl") by the painter Corot, Royan was at the height of its popularity in the Belle Époque era. Capital of the Côte de Beauté (Coast of Beauty), it was rebuilt after the bombardments that flattened it in 1945. Today, this modern town has regained the popularity and charm that characterised it at the end of the 19C.

- **Population:** 18 202
- **Michelin Map:** 324: D-6
- **Info:** Rd-pt de la Poste, Royan. ℘05 46 05 04 71. www.royan-tourisme.com.
- **Location:** Royan is located on the Atlantic Coast, 35km/22mi SW of Saintes.
- **Parking:** There are a number of car parks along the seafront, as well as in the town centre *(see map)*.
- **Don't Miss:** The seafront; Église Notre-Dame.
- **Kids:** Les Jardins du Monde.

ROYAN TODAY

Before World War II, Royan was noted for its ornate villas and chalets half-hidden among the palms, its great Victorian hotels, the casinos like Baroque temples or palaces from the Renaissance. Only the Pontaillac area today can evoke such memories; Royan town centre has been rebuilt following the norms of late 20C town planning. Huge perspectives have been opened up, bordered by apartment blocks with wide balconies and red-tiled roofs in the Charentais manner.

TRANSPORT

Buses – Several bus companies run services in Royan and from Royan to nearby towns, including Meschers, St-Palais, St-Georges-de-Didonne, Vaux-sur-Mer, La Tremblade, Ronce-les-Bains, Médis, Saujon and Saintes. *℘08 10 81 09 77. www.carabus-transport.com.*

SIGHTS

Église Notre-Dame★

1 r. de Foncillon. ℘05 46 23 99 77. www.notre-dame-royan.com.

The church was built between 1955 and 1958 to plans by the architects Guillaume Gillet and Hébrard. It is a structure of reinforced concrete coated with resin to protect it from wind erosion.

From place Notre-Dame, at a slightly lower level, the ascending perspective of the east end, forming a kind of prow, is accentuated by the belfry, which soars to a height of 65m/213ft.

On the left, detached from the nave, is a pyramidal baptistery.

Inside the church, visitors are at once struck by the spacious and light single nave. The great organ is the work of the Poitou master Robert Boisseau.

Front de Mer★

Royan's seafront curves around the northern end of the **Grande Conche** – an imposing crescent of buildings, commercial as well as residential. Off to the right the silhouette of Cordouan lighthouse can be recognised.

At the western end of the seafront is the port. This comprises a dock for trawlers and the sardine boats, a marina for yachts and cruisers, and a tidal basin with the jetty from which the ferry to Pointe de Grave leaves.

Boat trips are organised in summer.

Corniche de Pontaillac★

This walk should be taken at high tide for the best views. Follow boulevard Carnot and boulevard de la Côte-d'Argent. Having skirted the tennis courts and the old Fort du Chay, the route runs above a number of small coves from which there are fine views of the Gironde and the Côte de Beauté. The walk ends at the **Conche de Pontaillac**★, a sheltered inlet surrounded with smart villas scattered among the subtropical foliage. This small beach is the most popular in Royan.

The **Marché Central** – *(pl. du Marché central)* is a market with an original fine-concrete dome; the **Palais des Congrès** *(av. des Congrès)* is a glass-walled building.

Les Jardins du Monde★

5 av. des Fleurs-de-la-Paix. Open daily Jul–Aug 10am–8pm; Sept–Dec and Feb–Jun 10am–6pm (last admission 1hr before closing). 9€ (children 6€). 05 46 38 89 11. www.jardins-du-monde.com.

On the banks of the Marais de Pousseau (Pousseau Marsh), in an area which has been drained since the war, this 7.5ha/18-acre floral garden, open since 2002, is enshrined within a high metallic structure and three large steel sails. The vast semicircular entrance is followed by a large tropical greenhouse which shelters a beautiful **collection of orchids**★. The atmosphere changes completely as you reach the bonsai pavilion where you can admire rare specimens, which are sometimes more than centuries old. Then, in the open air, the gardens offer various styles: the Japanese zen garden, the Louisiana forest, the marsh house, the labyrinth of mist (bamboo forest).

The park can partly be visited by electrical boat: a 20min tour will enable you to cross the marsh canals and give you access to the swamp and the bamboo forest. You will also find a shop, a restaurant and activities for children.

EXCURSION

Phare de Cordouan★★

Crossings from the port of Royan (Royan Croisières 05 46 06 42 36 or Croisières la Sirène 05 46 05 30 93) or from Verdon-sur-Mer (05 56 09 62 93); reservation obligatory early Apr–mid-Oct. Operates according to the tide and weather conditions, wade to shore; wear boots or waterproof shoes. Allow 3hr30min round trip. 33€ (under 12 years 23€).

On a rocky island at the gateway to the Garonne, in the midst of extremely dangerous currents the so-called "King of lighthouses", "lighthouse of kings" or even "Versailles of the sea", is worthy of these titles. This Renaissance 68m/223ft tower with seven floors is one of the oldest lighthouses in France.

A postern gate leads to a circular bastion which protects the building from the fury of the ocean; this housed the keeper's quarters. On the ground floor, a monumental doorway opens onto the staircase of 311 steps that climb up to the lantern. On the first floor are the King's apartments. The second floor houses the most majestic room in the lighthouse: the chapel, surmounted by a beautiful cupola. The third, fourth and fifth floors are landings. The sixth floor houses the lantern, which has a balcony affording splendid views.

At the Pointe de Grave, stop off to visit the Musée du Phare de Cordouan.

The Royan Pocket

At the time of the Liberation of France, in the autumn of 1944, Nazi troops stationed in the southwest withdrew to a number of coastal enclaves – St-Nazaire, Verdon, Royan – and dug themselves in with the intention of holding out as long as possible. Royan was besieged by the French forces of General de Larminat when, on 5 January and 14–15 April 1945, two violent aerial bombardments almost totally destroyed the town.

The Germans surrendered on 17 April, only three weeks before the armistice on 8 May.

DRIVING TOURS

4 PRESQU'ÎLE D'ARVERT AND ESTUAIRE DE LA SEUDRE★

120km/75mi. Allow one day.

Drive NW out of Royan along the D 25.

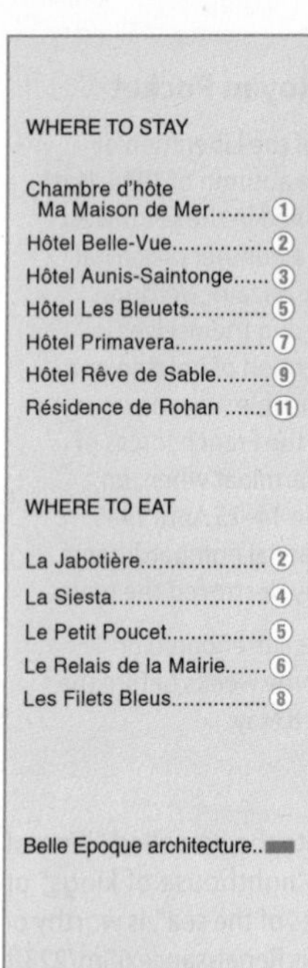

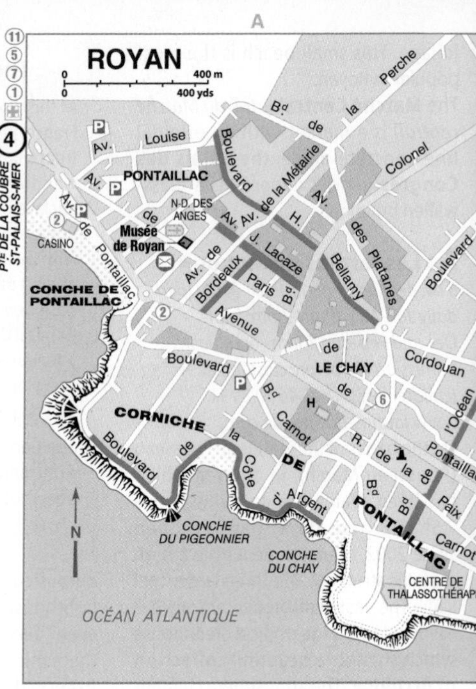

Vaux-sur-Mer

On one side of the valley stands a charming Romanesque church *(pl. de l'Église).*

 *Continue S to Nauzan.*

Nauzan

A cove with a beach of fine sand, sheltered from the wind by cliffs on either side.

St-Palais-sur-Mer★

This small, popular resort with its stylish elegance is surrounded by smart villas scattered among the pines and ilex trees. In 1935 Leon Trotsky resided in a villa close to the beach after his exile from the Soviet Union. The **Parc du Marais du Rhâ** (behind the covered market), laid out around a lake, is equipped for leisure activities. From the cove there is a view of the Cordouan lighthouse.

At the far end of the beach *(on the right, looking at the cove)*, take rue de l'Océan and then **Sentier de la Corniche**★ *(signposted, 45min round trip on foot).*

The path, also known as the Sentier des Perrières (Path of the Slate Quarries), twists through the woods and then crosses a gash in the cliff into which, at high tide, the ocean rollers hurl themselves. The path ends at a promontory where the jagged rocks have been smashed into bizarre shapes.

La Grande Côte★★

Park in the car park, on the left, where the D 25 turns away from the coast and plunges into the woods. Walk to the rock platform. Telescope available.

From left to right, the **view** embraces the Gironde, Pointe de Grave and the lighthouse of La Coubre.

A few yards away, on the right, there is a view sideways down onto the beaches and dunes of La Grande Côte, where long lines of breakers roll shorewards and bathing is very dangerous. Fishing with cast weights is practised along the strand, especially for bass.

Zoo de la Palmyre★★★

See ZOO DE LA PALMYRE.

The route passes the resort of **La Palmyre** then skirts **La Bonne Anse** – a refuge for boats during bad weather.

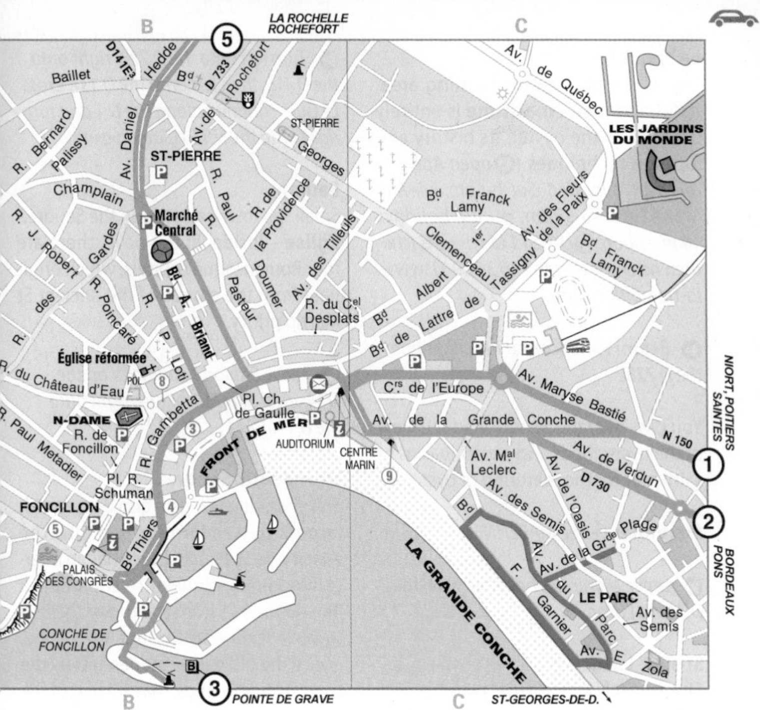

Phare de La Coubre★

Open 15 Apr–June Wed –Sun 10am–12.30pm, 1.30–6pm; Jul–15 Sept daily 10am–1pm, 2–6.30pm. 3€. 05 46 06 26 42. www.la-tremblade.com.

La Coubre Lighthouse has had to be rebuilt several times because the dune on which it stands is "mobile".

The present version dates from 1905 and rises to a height of 60m/197ft. Its two-tone tower overlooks the point from a position near the semaphore station. The beam from this lighthouse carries 53km/33mi, signalling the approaches to the Gironde.

From the top there is an extensive **panorama**★ over La Coubre Forest and the Isle of Oléron *(north and east)*; the extremity of the point and its coastal spit, La Bonne Anse, and Cordouan Lighthouse *(S)*. In the distance Pointe de Grave and the Côte de Beauté as far as the cliffs of Meschers-sur-Gironde are visible.

Forêt de la Coubre★

Most of this 8 000ha/19 768-acre forest is composed of maritime pines and ilex trees; there are still a few deer to be seen. A fire ravaged the area in 1976.

The forest serves to stabilise the dunes along the Arvert Coast, better known as the **Côte sauvage** (Wild Coast). Bike paths wind through the woodlands and lead to the beaches.

Half a mile north of La Coubre lighthouse *(car park)* a sandy track twists through the dunes to the strand, from which there is an impressive view of the Atlantic.

About 8km/5mi farther north, there is a wooded knoll on the right of route D 25. Crowning this rise, at the end of the chemin des Fontaines is the wooden **Tour des Quatre Fontaines**. From it ther are wide-ranging views over the forest and the ocean beyond.

Ronce-les-Bains

At the mouth of the Seudre estuary. Peaceful holiday resort, charming villas in the shade of the pine trees. The view encompasses the Pointe du Chapus, the Pertuis de Maumusson, and the south of Oléron.

La Tremblade
This is a major oyster farming area. Its small **Musée maritime** is entirely devoted to the oyster, its history and farming techniques (*open Apr–Jun and Sept Mon, Wed–Sat 3–6pm; Jul–Aug Mon–Sat 2–6.30pm, public holidays 10am–noon; closed 1 May; 3€ (children no charge); 05 46 36 30 11; www.la-tremblade.com).*

Return to Ronce and turn right onto the D 728E.

You pass over the Seudre viaduct: view of the oyster beds and *claires* (basins of saltwater for the maturing of oysters).

Marennes *See MARENNES.*

Leave Marennes heading SE on the D 241 to Luzac.

St-Just-Luzac
The church has a fine Flamboyant Gothic façade.
The museum collection at **Alantrain** includes 2 500 locomotives, trams, carriages and toys from 1875 *(16 r. du Musée; open mid-Jun–mid-Sept Tue–Sun 3–6pm; guided tour available; 4€ (3–10 years 2€); 05 46 85 33 35).*

Continue on the D 18, towards St-Jean-d'Angle.

La Gripperie-St-Symphorien
A tall round tower looks down on the Romanesque St-Symphorien church. The portal has finely sculptured archivolts.

Follow the road, and turn right onto the D 118.

Donjon de Broue
This is one of the three square keeps of Saintonge; the others stand at Pons and Islot.

Église de St-Sornin
Romanesque style, its octogonal cupola stands above the transept crossing. Admire the sculptured capitals, and in the choir, the naïve frescoes.

Turn left onto the D 728, right onto the D 118, then left onto the D 131. Cross Le Gua, continue along the D 1 and turn right onto the N 150 (Saujon exit).

Saujon
Small spa town situated on the Seudre.
Église – Inside, in the nave, there are four Romanesque capitals, which originate from the church of the ancient St Martin priory.

Leave Saujon heading W on the D 14; after 5km/3.1mi turn right onto the D 140E2.

Mornac-sur-Seudre
This charming village is also the second-largest oyster farming port on the estuary. Its St-Pierre church has an interesting Romanesque apse and offers a fine panorama from the top of the bell tower. As you walk through the village, notice the old ballast stones, left by the coastal trading ships, that are part of the limestone walls.
To visit the Seudre marshes take the marked footpaths or *taillées*, dykes that criss-cross the *claires (details from tourist office; 05 46 22 61 68).*

Leave Mornac heading SW on the D 140E2, cross the D 14, continue along the D 25, which leads to Royan.

5 ESTUAIRE DE LA GIRONDE★★

71km/44mi de St-Georges-de-Didonne à St-Sorlin-de-Conac. Allow one day.

St-Georges-de-Didonne★
Pointe de Vallières★ – At the west, via the rue du Port and the boulevard de la Corniche. it's worth going for the view, to Pointe de Grave opposite, Royan to the right, and to the left, the pine-clad Pointe de Suzac.
Phare de St-Georges – This 1900 lighthouse, today decommissioned, once signalled the entrance to the estuary. Since 2007 it houses a small museum dedicated to the maritime pilots on the Gironde. Near the lighthouse, the coastal path leads to the jetty *(open 15–30 Jun*

and Sept 3–7pm, Jul–Aug 10am–noon, 3–7pm; €1.60€ (6–14 years 0.80€); 05 46 05 28 32).

Pointe de Suzac★ – South of the St-Georges beach, continue in the direction of Meschers and take the first road on the right (a dead end).

The path that runs along the top of the cliff leads to fine sandy beaches. As you are walking along you will see some of the remains of the Atlantic Wall.

Parc de l'Estuaire – Nature centre accessible from either the chemin Fort de Suzac or 47 av Paul-Roullet *(towards Meschers; P; open May–Jun 2.30–6.30pm; Jul–Aug Mon–Sat 10am–7pm, Sun 2–7pm, Sept 10am–noon, 2.30–6.30pm except Sun am; rest of year, phone for details; 5€ (child 3€); 05 46 23 77 77; www.leparcdelestuaire.com).*

Hidden in the Suzac forest (350ha/865 acres) is the Estuary's Villa, a former private home today housing an information centre on the Gironde estuary. Designed like a submarine, the interactive museum traces the history of the estuary.

From the Villa's terrace, there is a splendid view over the estuary and the ocean, the Médoc shore, the Pointe de Grave, the Cordouan Lighthouse, the Conche de St-Georges and the coast to La Palmyre. From the Villa, follow the discovery trail which leads into the forest. Head to the watchtower; from its platform there is a 360° panorama.

Take the D 730 heading E.

Logis du Château de Didonne

Semussac. *Open Easter–late Sept. 1€. 05 46 05 18 10.*

This 18C château is a *chambres d'hôtes*. Its 5ha/12-acre arboretum is open to visitors.

Continue S along the D 117.

Meschers-sur-Gironde★

The white cliffs of Meschers, riddled with troglodyte dwellings, are bathed by the Gironde estuary.

Les Grottes – Hollowed out by erosion 75 million years ago, these caves were inhabited in prehistoric times. Gradually enlarged by man, they have sheltered an interesting variety of peoples: pirates and smugglers, Protestants persecuted after the revocation of the Edict of Nantes, and fishermen. Some have been converted into private homes, which are only visible from the river, except for two caves open to the public, one of which houses a hotel.

Grottes de Regulus et des Fontaines – 81 bd de la Falaise – signposted from the village church. *Open early Apr–mid-Jun and Sept 2.30–5.30pm; Jul–Aug 10.30am–6.30pm; rest of year, contact for details. Closed mid-Nov–mid-Mar. 4.70€ (children 3.10€). 05 46 02 55 36.*

The tour of the troglodyte site takes you through a series of caves each covering a different theme.

At the foot of the neighbouring cliffs there are carrelets, picturesque fishing huts perched on stilts.

Beaches – Nonnes, the principal beach at Meschers, has fine sand. To the north, in the direction of the Pointe de Suzac, there are three other beaches: Vergnes, Arnèche and Suzac.

Take the D 145.

Talmont-sur-Gironde★ –The charming "walled town" of Talmont, modelled on the *bastides* of Aquitaine, was built in 1284 by Edward I of England. Talmont is famous for its Romanesque church dedicated to St Radegund and streets lined with hollyhocks.

Église Ste-Radegonde★ – *Les Remparts. 05 46 74 23 82.* St Radegund's Church, a fine example of the Saintonge Romanesque style, stands on an impressive **site★** at the tip of the promontory.

From its small cemetery there is a fine **view** of the estuary and, off to the right, the white chalk cliffs of Meschers.

Musée d'Histoire Locale et de la Pêche dans l'Estuaire – *r. de l'Église. Open daily Apr–May and Sept 2–6pm; Jun–Aug 10.30am–12.30pm, 1.30–6pm. . Guided tours by request Apr–Dec, 05 46 90 16 25. 2.50€. 05 46 90 43 87.* Near the seamen's cemetery, the old

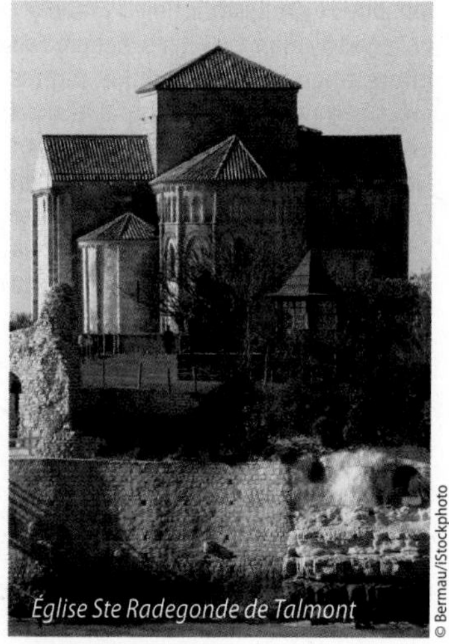
Église Ste Radegonde de Talmont
© Bermau/iStockphoto

school houses a museum with information of the town and the traditional fishing activities. Includes palaeontology, and Gallo-Roman history.

Leaving Talmont on the D 14 towards Barzan; follow Moulin du Fâ.

Site Gallo-Romain du Fâ★

At Barzan, 2km/1.2mi E of Talmont. Open Apr–Sept 10am–7pm; Oct–Dec and Feb–Mar Fri–Sun and school holidays 2–5.30pm. Closed 25 Dec. 4€ (child 2€). 05 46 90 43 66. http://fa-barzan.fr.

A major archaeological discovery extending over 40ha/99 acres believed to be the Gallo-Roman port of Novioregum. A clearing has been made to expose the ruins of a circular temple.

You can visit the thermal baths and surrounding residences. The tour takes you through the different rooms in the baths: the *frigidarium*, the *caldarium* and the *tepidarium*.

The excavations are still underway and in the adjacent fields there are traces of warehouses, and an amphithea stre. The information centre displays a model of the site, restored to its former splendour. A film tells the story of the discovery of the site, from the first aerial sightings to the excavation techniques in use.

Continue along the D 145.

Mortagne-sur-Gironde

Situated high on a cliff, Mortagne towers over port La Rive below. The former medieval fortress once protected the Ermitage St-Martial and chapel carved into the rock.

1km/0.6mi southwest along the D 6 is the port of **La Rive**. A type of canal-port, it has a wet dock. It was once the third-largest port of the Gironde.

1.5km/0.9mi southeast along the D 245 is the monolithic **Ermitage St-Martial** (*open May–Sept Tue–Sun 1.30–6.30pm*), founded in the 2C by St Martial. Further alterations were made between the 4C and the 10C. In the Middle Ages, the hermit fishermen helped pilgrims across the estuary on their way to Santiago de Compostella. The caves consist of four rooms, plus two cells and a **chapel**★, entirely carved into the rock.

Continue on the D 145.

St-Dizant-du-Gua

At the entrance to the village, on the right, a 13ha/32-acre park provides the perfect setting for this château.

Château de Beaulon – Ancient summer residence of the bishops of Bordeaux, this 15C Gothic manor house has beautiful gardens, the highlight of which is the Fontaines bleues. The outstanding blue colour of the water is due to microscopic algae (*open daily 10am–6pm; closed Oct–Apr Sat–Sun, 1 Jan, 25 Dec; 4€ (children no charge); 05 46 49 96 13; www.chateau-de-beaulon.com).*

Return to the D 145.

Pôle-Nature de Vitrezay

At St-Sorlin-de-Conac.

This large site (60ha/150 acres) aims to make the visitor aware of the natural environment of the Gironde estuary. Numerous activities on offer (*phone for details; 05 46 49 89 89).*

ADDRESSES

STAY

Hôtel Aunis-Saintonge – *14 r. Gambetta. 05 46 05 78 24. www.hotel-aunis-saintonge.fr. 14 rooms. 7€.* This hotel is situated only a few steps from the beach, the town centre, the marina and the shops. The rooms, including two family rooms and an apartment, are plain but well kept. Friendly atmosphere.

Belle-Vue – *122 av. de Pontaillac. 05 46 39 06 75. www.bellevue-pontaillac.com. Closed Nov–Mar. 18 rooms. 7€.* This modernised 1950s villa is situated on a wide avenue. The well-soundproofed rooms on the ground floor overlook a small garden. Mini-golf nearby.

Chambre d'hôtes Ma Maison de Mer – *21 av. du Platin, 17420 St-Palais-sur-Mer. 05 46 23 64 86. www.mamaisondemer.com. 5 rooms. Meals.* In the middle of a garden, and a pine forest, and 300m/325yds from the beach. An English family run this mansion decorated beautifully in a nautical theme – among others. At breakfast expect to find fresh market produce.

Les Bleuets – *21 façade de Foncillon. 05 46 38 51 79. www.hotel-les-bleuets.com. Closed late Dec–early Jan. 16 rooms. 8€.* Discrete nautical décor, pleasant renovated rooms, view of the sea (balconies) or the garden: an agreeable hotel situated between the port and town centre.

Rêve de Sable – *10 pl. Foch. 05 46 06 52 25. www.revedesable.com. Closed 1st 3 w ks Oct. 11 rooms. 7€.* Family hotel near to the beach and town centre. Bright rooms, well equipped, some have a sea view. Nautical touches to the décor (fishing nets). Patio (breakfast).

Hôtel Primavera – *12 r. du Brick (via av. de la Grande Côte), St-Palais-sur-Mer. 05 46 23 20 35. www.hotel-primavera.com. Closed 23 Nov–17 Dec.41 rooms. 14€. Restaurant.* Built in the late 19C, this elegant seaside villa is enhanced by a peaceful park. Whether in the old building or the new wing, the décor is bourgeois and most of the rooms have a view of the sea. Two simpler annexes, a covered swimming pool and a tennis court. Traditional cuisine with an emphasis on seafood.

Résidence de Rohan – *Conche de Nauzan. 05 46 39 00 75. www.residence-rohan.com. Closed early Nov–late Mar. 44 rooms. 11€.* Former literary meeting place of the Duchesse de Rohan, a pretty residence including a villa set in a park overlooking the beach. Romantic rooms, period furniture.

EAT

La Siesta – *140 r. Gambetta. 05 46 38 36 53. www.lasiesta-royan.fr. Closed mid-Dec–mid-Jan.* This restaurant, rebuilt on the exact site of the Brasserie des Bains where Pablo Picasso once stayed, faces a sailing harbour. Try the bruschetta, a slice of good Italian toast with a choice of toppings, before moving on to fish, Italian pasta or a Tex-Mex dish.

La Jabotière – *4 espl. de Pontaillac. 05 46 39 91 29. Closed Jan.* White-and-blue parasols, a wooden terrace and big bay windows overlooking the Conche de Pontaillac – this shoreside restaurant, a stone's throw from the casino, is a very enjoyable place for a meal. Less expensive fixed-price menu at lunchtime.

Le Petit Poucet – *La Grande Côte, St-Palais-sur-Mer. 05 46 23 20 48. www.restaurantlepetitpoucet.com. Closed Tue (Sept–Jun).* A magnificent view of the sea, especially from the terrace! This is the best feature of this unusual 1950s edifice built overlooking the beach. Cosy atmosphere in the dining room and simple cuisine at affordable prices.

Le Relais de la Mairie – *1 r. du Chay. 05 46 39 03 15. Closed Thu and Sun evenings, Mon and mid-Nov–mid-Dec.* Appearances can be deceiving! Behind the rather gloomy exterior, this restaurant's narrow dining room is colourful and pleasant. Interesting fixed-price menu offered daily. À la carte menu a bit pricey.

Les Filets Bleus – *14 r. Notre-Dame. 05 46 05 74 00. Closed Mon lunch, Sun, late Jun–mid-Jul, late Oct–early Nov and early Jan.* Restaurant specialising in seafood dishes, and decorated like a boat: blue-and-white tones, wood, portholes, hurricane lamps, etc. Special lobster menu, in season.

LE SAINTONGE

Saintonge, a former province of western France, is a small region west and south of the Charente, covering most of the present Charente-Maritime *département*. It derives its name from the Santones, an ancient Gallic tribe that lived in this area. Saintes, the main town, has a magnificent architectural heritage; the Église St-Eutrope has been named a UNESCO World Heritage Site. The surrounding Charente landscape is fascinating, with lush meadows and river valleys dotted with pretty towns, castles and churches.

Highlights

1. Roman and religious architecture of **Saintes** (p458)
2. Little-known churches on the drive around the **Saintonge** (p463)
3. The fascinating **Paléosite** centre (p467)
4. Fall under the spell of "Sleeping Beauty's Castle" – **Château de Roche Courbon** (p469)
5. Delicate Romanesque carvings of **Église St-Pierre d'Aulnay** (p473)

Crazannes, a Region of Stone

The famous white stone of Crazannes has been extracted by man for more than 2 000 years. But more recently is has been used to build Fort Boyard, La Rochelle port at Nantes, Tonnay-Charente suspension bridge, Pont Neuf in Paris, Cordouan Lighthouse and the town hall at Bilbao. Not forgetting the cathedrals of Bayonne, Cologne and Brussels. And it is even said to have been used for the pedestal of the Statue of Liberty. At Crazannes, stonemasons have crafted it to decorate the façade of the **château**. The stone industry here was at its peak in the late 18C, but the advent of new construction materials and the high cost of extraction of the stone led to the closure of the quarries in 1955.

There are two qualities of this fine-grained stone: Angeles stone, at the surface, which is tinged yellow and more brittle; and, separated by a bed of flint (the quarryman's nightmare), Anthéor stone – denser, whiter and of a superior quality, but more difficult to extract.

Château de Crazannes

Natura 2000

With a network of 25 000 sites, the Natura 2000 project, created in 1992, is an ambitious programme of nature conservation throughout the EU. With more than 1 700 sites in France, the country plays an important role in the formation of a network that aims to successfully combine nature conservation with sustainable human activities.

Boutonne Valley stretches from the south of the Deux-Sèvres, where it rises, to the north of the Charente-Maritime. With its small streams and rivers, it is an ecological site notable for the presence of endangered species: otter, large copper butterfly, stag beetle, Rosalia longicorn, great and lesser horseshoe bat, sculpin, brook lamprey, and so on. This peaceful valley is part of the European ecological network Natura 2000. Discover Natura 2000 sites in the Poitou-Charentes and the Vendée at www.developpement-durable.gouv.fr/-Natura-2000,2414-.html.

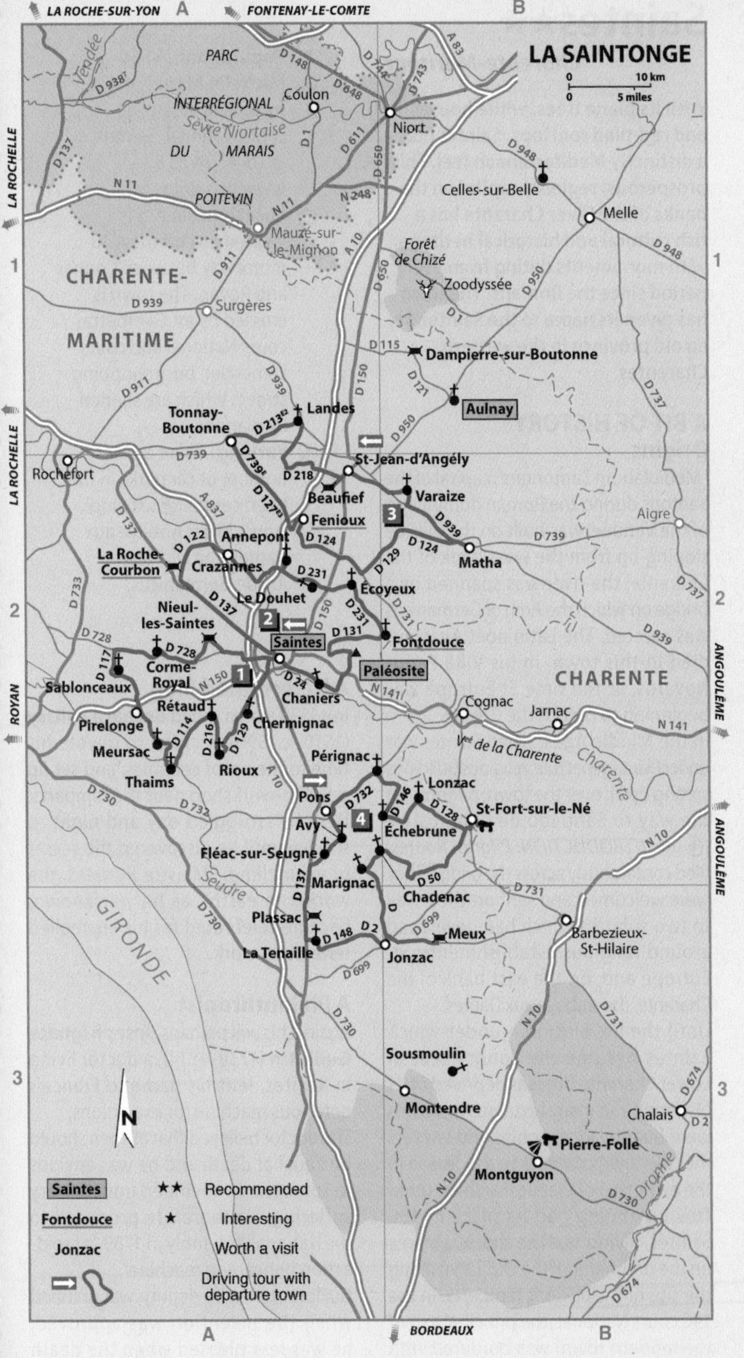
LA SAINTONGE
LA ROCHE-SUR-YON
FONTENAY-LE-COMTE
LA ROCHELLE
ROYAN
ANGOULÊME
BORDEAUX
PARC INTERRÉGIONAL DU MARAIS POITEVIN
CHARENTE-MARITIME
CHARENTE
GIRONDE
Coulon
Niort
Celles-sur-Belle
Melle
Mauzé-sur-le-Mignon
Forêt de Chizé
Zoodyssée
Surgères
Dampierre-sur-Boutonne
Aulnay
Tonnay-Boutonne
Landes
St-Jean-d'Angély
Rochefort
Beaufief
Varaize
Fenioux
Aigre
Annepont
Matha
La Roche-Courbon
Crazannes
Le Douhet
Écoyeux
Nieul-les-Saintes
Saintes
Fontdouce
Paléosite
Sablonceaux
Corme-Royal
Chaniers
Rétaud
Pirelonge
Chermignac
Cognac
Jarnac
Meursac
Thaims
Rioux
Pérignac
Lonzac
Pons
Avy
Échebrune
St-Fort-sur-le-Né
Fléac-sur-Seugne
Marignac
Chadenac
Plassac
Meux
La Tenaille
Jonzac
Barbezieux-St-Hilaire
Sousmoulin
Montendre
Chalais
Pierre-Folle
Montguyon
Vée de la Charente
Charente
Seudre
Sèvre Niortaise
Vendée
Dronne
Saintes ★★ Recommended
Fontdouce ★ Interesting
Jonzac Worth a visit
Driving tour with departure town
0 10 km
0 5 miles

Saintes★★

Charente-Maritime

With its plane trees, white houses and red-tiled rooftops, Saintes has a distinctly Mediterranean feel. This prosperous, regional capital on the banks of the River Charente has a rich cultural and historical heritage, with monuments dating from every period since the Romans. The town has given its name to the Saintonge, an old province in the western Charentes.

- **Population:** 26 531
- **Michelin Map:** 324: G-5
- **Info:** Villa Musso, 62 cours National, Saintes. 05 46 74 23 82. www.ot-saintes.fr.
- **Location:** Saintes is located just off the A 10 motorway between Cognac and Royan. The town is crossed by av. Gambetta, cours National and cours Lemercier, busy shopping streets which are shaded by plane trees.
- **Parking:** There are a number of car parks in the town centre (*see map*).
- **Don't Miss:** Abbaye aux Dames; the Old Town; Arc de Germanicus.

A BIT OF HISTORY

Origins

"Mediolanum Santonum", capital of the Santons during the Roman domination of the Vendée, was built on the hillside sloping up from the west bank of the Charente; the river was spanned by a bridge on which the Arch of Germanicus was erected. The Latin poet Ausonius died in this town, in his Villa Pagus Noverus, at the time St Eutrope was beginning to preach the Gospel.

In the Middle Ages, when Saintes was under Plantagenet rule, religious buildings sprang up all over the town; pilgrims on the way to Santiago de Compostela (*see INTRODUCTION: Pilgrim Routes*) filed continuously across the bridge. They were welcomed and sent on their way to two suburbs which had developed around religious establishments: St-Eutrope and, on the east bank of the Charente, the Abbaye aux Dames.

Until the Revolution – under which Saintes became the county seat of Lower Charente but was deprived of its bishopric – so many luxurious mansions were built by local nobles and lawyers that the town could serve as a lesson in the evolution of Classical architecture.

Town planning had its place in 18C Saintes, laying out the thoroughfares on the perimeter of the Old Town along the site of the ancient ramparts. In the 19C cours National (the principal axis of the modern town) was bordered with Neoclassical public buildings; among them, on opposite sides of the avenue, are the law courts and the theatre.

A Determined Man

In c.1539 a man called **Bernard Palissy** (1510–c.1590) decided to devote his time to the art of ceramics, and set up a studio-workshop near the ramparts. Here he struggled day and night to survive until he discovered the secret of enamelling. "Maistre Bernard, the worker in earth", as he was known, became celebrated for his enamelled terra-cotta work.

A Philanthropist

Against his will perhaps, **Joseph Ignace Guillotin** (1738–1814), a doctor living in Saintes, lent his name to France's notorious machine for executions.

The doctor believed that all men should be equal at death and he was anxious to spare the condemned unnecessary suffering. He therefore proposed to the National Assembly in 1789 "a rapid-action beheading machine".

Guillotin, himself a deputy, was gratified when the invention was approved; he was less pleased when the death machine was not unnaturally christened, in 1792 when it was first used, La Guillotine.

WALKING TOUR
OLD TOWN★

Park the car on the market square where the walking tour begins.

The Old Town district around the cathedral on the west bank of the river is characteristic of Saintes, proud of its distinctive image.

Cathédrale St-Pierre

r. St-Pierre. Open daily 9am–7pm. Guided tours (1hr) early Jul–late Aug Sat 11am. Guided tours 4€.

St Peter's Cathedral was built on the site of a Romanesque church; all that remains of the early building is a dome above the south transept.

Its construction, under the direction of three successive bishops of Saintes, all members of the Rochechouart family, dates in the main from the 15C. It was severely damaged by the Calvinists in 1568. The massive bell tower, made heavier still by enormous buttresses with projecting features, was never completed: a dome with lead panels replaced the spire proposed in the original plans. Angels, saints and prophets adorn the Flamboyant doorway within the porch at the foot of the tower.

Unity and simplicity characterise the architecture of the interior. Stripped of ornamentation, the large round columns of the nave, like the Gothic pillars in the chancel, support a bare upper wall roofed with visible timbers. Only the side aisles are vaulted in stone.

Both nave and aisles date almost in their entirety from the 16C, the great organ from the 16C and 17C. A door in the south transept opens onto the former canons' cloisters (13C), of which two galleries and the ruins of the chapter house remain.

The axial chapel, with its niches surmounted by elaborately carved canopies, exemplifies the final effervescence of the Flamboyant Gothic style; the credences were already Renaissance. The **treasury**, in an annex chapel, displays a collection of sacred vessels and vestments.

Leave pl. du Marché, which is beside the cathedral, and follow the whole length of r. St-Michel then turn left onto r. Victor-Hugo.

A succession of pretty stone houses in the characteristic Saintonge style can be seen in rue Victor-Hugo, once known as Grande-Rue, which follows

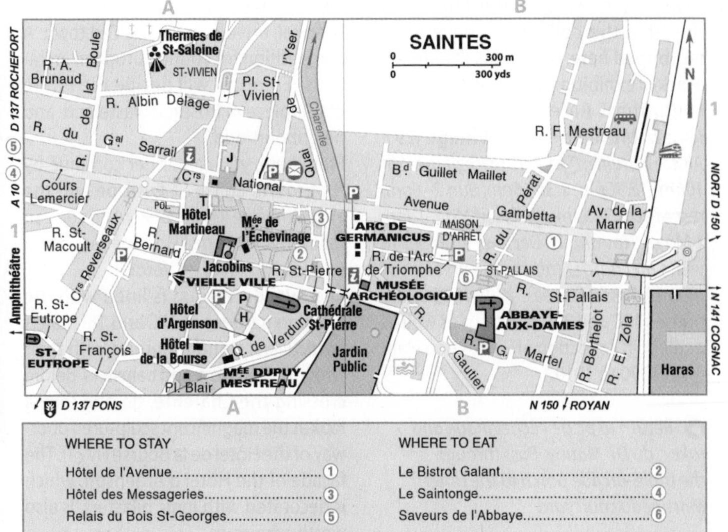

Arc de Germanicus

©JONATHAN/Fotolia.com

the course of the old road which led via the Germanicus arch to the bridge across the river.

At r. Victor-Hugo, walk past the Présidial (a fine example of 17C architecture), then turn left onto the r. Alsace-Lorraine.

Ancien Échevinage

Beyond the Classical gateway, an 18C façade is attached to a turret dating from the 16C. The spiral staircase of this former belfry provides access to two floors of the fine arts museum. After the closure of the Musée du Présidial the collections have been regrouped here, which has resulted in a lack of exhibition space, and cramped conditions. An expansion is under review. **Musée de l'Échevinage** *(29 r. Alsace Lorraine; open Apr–Sept Tue–Sat 10am–12.30pm, 1.30–6pm, Sun 2–6pm, rest of year 2–5pm; closed Mon, 1 Jan, 1 May, 1 Nov and 25 Dec; 2€ (under 18 years no charge) (no charge first Sun of month); Pass 3 Musées. 05 46 93 52 39)* houses 19C and 20C paintings as well as a splendid collection of Sèvres porcelain from 1890 to 1910.

Return to pl. de l'Échevinage and take r. du Dr-Mauny. Pass through the triple-arcade porch to the Hôtel Martineau courtyard.

Hôtel Martineau

r. du Dr-Mauny.

This mansion is now the home of the municipal library.

Chapelle des Jacobins

r. des Jacobins.

This chapel has an elegantly designed bay in the Flamboyant style.

From r. des Jacobins, turn right and take the steps up to the belvédère.

Belvédère du Logis du Gouverneur

This 16C pavilion, next to the former hospital, towers above the Old town. A competition for young European architects (Europan) will decide the future of this piece of hospital wasteland, and neighbourhood.

From here, you can either continue by foot to the Église St-Eutrope and the amphithéâtre (see below) or, you can follow the ruelle de l'Hospice back down to rejoin the quai de Verdun.

The quai de Verdun is lined with the hanging gardens of 17C and 18C *hôtels particuliers*, standing proud with their wrought-iron work and balusters. Before crossing the Charente, go and take a look at the magnificent sculptured doorway of the Hôtel de la Bourse (1771). The façade of the Hôtel d'Argenson, which is decorated with Ionic pilasters, is also worth admiring.

Musée Dupuy-Mestreau★

4 r. Monconseil. Open Apr–Sept Tue–Sat 10am–12.30pm, 1.30–6pm; Sun 2–6pm; rest of year 2–5pm. Closed Mon, 1 Jan., 1 May, 1 Nov, 25 Dec. 2€ (under 18 years no charge) (no charge first Sun of month); Pass 3 Musées. 05 46 93 36 71. www.ville-saintes.fr.

Housed in the former private home of the Marquis de Monconseil (18C), this regional art museum has an astonishing eclectic collection covering three floors. There are thousands of rare, precious and strange objects, assembled together at the turn of the 20C by the relentless collector Abel Mestreau, cognac merchant; it is so vast that it would be impossible to make an inventory. The guided tour is lively, punctuated with comments and fascinating anecdotes. This surprising place is home to a jumble of signs, pottery, nautical souvenirs, Santonge headdresses, peasant clothes, sumptuous costumes, medieval weapons, engravings, paintings, rare pearls, objects made by the convicts of Rochefort, jewellery, musical instruments etc.

The building also has interesting decorative elements, like the beautiful painted woodwork in the dining room, Louis XIV style (attributed to Bérain), originating from the Château de Tonnay-Charente where Mme de Montespan spent her childhood. There are reconstructions of an 18C bedroom, and the interior of a 19C Charente peasant's home.

Take the footbridge across the River Charente.

Jardin Public

These public gardens, laid over the town's former parade ground, are decorated with Roman ruins. One end is closed off by a façade built in 18C style and an orangery.

Musée Archéologique★

espl. André Malraux. Oct–Mar Tue–Sun 2–5pm; Apr–Sept Tue–Sat 10am–12.30, 1.30–6pm, Sun 1.30–6pm. Closed 1 May, 1 Nov, 25 Dec, 1 Jan. 2€ (1st Sun of month no charge). 05 46 74 20 97.

The museum houses an interesting stoneware collection, deriving mainly from discoveries made when the wall of the ancient Gallo-Roman *castrum* (fort) was demolished. It includes columns, capitals, architraves and remarkable bas-reliefs. Further traces of Roman remains can be seen nearby.

Arc de Germanicus★

pl. Bassompierre.

This fine Roman arch with its twin arcades stood until 1843 on the bridge that carried the main thoroughfare in Saintes across the River Charente. Threatened with destruction when the bridge, itself Roman, was about to be demolished, the arch was saved by the intervention of the writer Prosper Merimée, who held the post of Inspector of Historic Monuments. It was dismantled and rebuilt on the east bank of the river.

The structure, built of local limestone and erected in the year AD 19, was a votive, not a triumphal, arch. Inscriptions still visible dedicate it to Germanicus, to the Emperor Tiberius, and to his son Drusus. The name of the donor, Caius Julius Rufus, also appears. In the centre of the arch the groins of the three pillars supporting the double arcade are emphasised by fluted columns with Corinthian capitals.

From here it is possible to make a detour to Abbaye aux Dames and to come back to the market square via the footbridge.

ABBAYE AUX DAMES★

r. St-Pallais. Open Apr–Sept daily, 10am–12.30pm, 2–7pm; Oct–Dec and Jan–Mar Mon–Fri 9.30am–12.30pm, 2–6pm, Sat–Sun 2–6pm. Closed 24 Dec–1 Jan. 2€. 05 46 97 48 48. www.abbayeauxdames.org.

This "Ladies' Abbey", which stands on the east bank of the Charente, was consecrated in 1047. The abbey was dedicated to St Mary, and owed its prosperity to Agnès de Bourgogne, whose second husband was Geoffroy

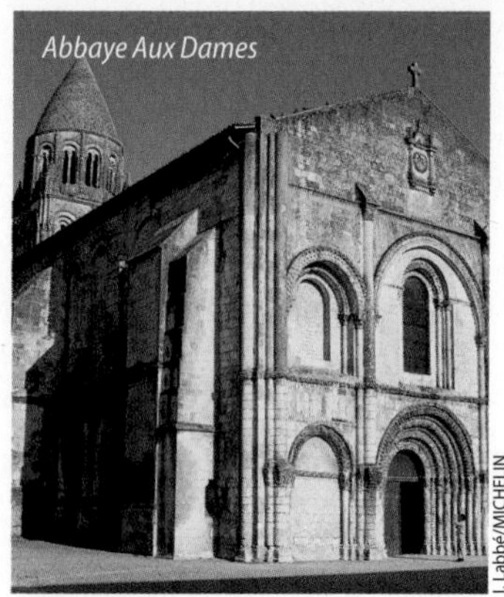
Abbaye Aux Dames

I. Labbé/MICHELIN

Martel, Comte d'Anjou and Seigneur of the Saintonge. The abbey, placed in the hands of Benedictine nuns, was directed by an abbess – customarily chosen from among the most illustrious families in France – who then bore the title "Madame de Saintes". Charged with the education of young daughters of the nobility, the convent counted among its boarders at one time Athenaos de Rochechouart, the future Marquise de Montespan and mistress to Louis XIV. After the Revolution and during the Empire period the abbey fell into decline. It was transformed into a barracks, freed after World War I, but required a great deal of restoration before it could be returned to the Church for religious use.

Abbey Church★

The Abbey Church is in the local Saintonge Romanesque style; it is reached via an 18C porch leading to the abbey's first courtyard, where it is surrounded by the usual convent buildings. The most remarkable features of the church are the façade and the bell tower. The **façade**★ presents a richly ornamented **doorway** at the centre, flanked by blind arcades. The carved coving in the doorway shows, from bottom to top: six angels adoring the Hand of God; the symbols of the Evangelists around the Lamb; the suffering of the martyrs, menaced by a whip, an axe or the Sword of Justice; 54 old men wearing crowns, facing each other two by two as they play music. The coving of the right arcade portrays the Last Supper; that on the left, the presence of a divine Christ facing five other figures suffused with light whose significance is uncertain. Note also the historiated capitals (a knight, monsters) and, on the gable, arms of Françoise I de La Rochefoucauld, abbess from 1559 to 1605.

The lower level of the **bell tower**, situated above the transept crossing, is square in section and pierced with three arcades on each face. Above this is a shallow octagonal level flanked by pinnacles which is in turn surmounted by a dome pierced by 12 twinned bays separated by small columns. The whole tower is topped by a scaled conical roof, the slopes of which are slightly convex.

Interior – In the first half of the 12C the interior was the subject of alterations, generally thought to have been made by the architect Béranger (an inscription carved into the outside of the north wall dates the work as pre-1150). The quadripartite vaulting in the transept arms – and the Gothic chapel in the northern arm – are later (15C) additions. The two-bay nave, lined with six heavy 12C pillars erected in front of the 11C walls, is covered with a timber ceiling which replaced the two original domes on pendentives, destroyed by fire in 1648. On the southern side of the transept entrance, a console supports a 12C head of Christ.

At the intersection of the nave and the transept, before the transept crossing and the belfry above it, four more heavy pillars support a dome on squinches. Half-barrel vaulting over the Romanesque chancel is prolonged by a slightly recessed, terminal oven vault.

Convent Buildings

The façade of the long 17C central block has been restored to its original purity of line: two storeys pierced by narrow windows and surmounted by an upper level punctuated by dormers with pediments. On the left, adjoining three renovated bays of the old 14C cloisters, is a fine 17C doorway, the pilasters of which are adorned with exuberant sculptures that contrast strikingly with the severity of the façade.

ADDITIONAL SIGHTS

Haras National

Guided tours Jun Sat–Sun 4.30pm; Jul–Aug daily 2.30pm; rest of year Mon –Fri 2–5pm. Closed public holidays (except 14 Jul, 15 Aug). Guided tour 5€ (4–17 years 2€ and 3€). 05 46 74 80 13.

In the heart of a 10 ha/25-acre park, discover the secrets of English and Anglo-Arab thoroughbreds, French trotters and riding horses, Breton draft horses, Percherons, Traits mulassiers and the famous Baudet du Poitou donkeys.

Amphithéâtre Gallo-Romain★

r. Lacurie. Open Apr–May Mon–Sat 10am–6pm, Sun 1.30–6pm; Jun–Sept daily 10am–8pm; Oct–Mar Mon–Sat 10am–12.30pm, 1.30–5pm, Sun 1.30–5pm. Closed public holidays. 2€. 05 46 97 73 85.

A short distance from the centre, the Roman amphitheatre owes part of its sylvan attraction and evocative atmosphere to the fact that grass covers a large proportion of the stepped terracing. This is one of the oldest amphitheatres of the Roman world – it was built in the 1C AD – but is relatively small.

Overall dimensions of the ellipse are 125m long x 102m wide (410ft x 335ft), while the actual arena, where performances took place, measures 64m x 39m (210ft x 128ft). The terraces could accommodate 20 000 spectators.

Halfway up the terraced slope, on the southern side, there is a gap in which a small fountain plays. This is dedicated to St Eustelle, a young female disciple of St Eutrope who was beheaded here.

Église St-Eutrope★

The reconstruction of the building in its current form was undertaken by the Cluny monks in the late 11C. The church was made a shrine to St Eutrope, Bishop fo the Santons in the 2C, and also became a major stop on The Way of St James. This dual function explains the original architecture of the interior consisting originally of a single nave and two superimposed choirs. This arrangement allowed the pilgrims to be welcomed while monastic services continued.

Mutilated in 1803 by the destruction of the nave, the transept and the Romanesque choir with magnificent illuminated capitals remain. The belfry, built in the 15C with funds given by Louis XI who had a special reverence for Saint Eutrope, has a slender appearance due to its spire of 65m/213ft.

Crypt★★ – It is a striking contrast to the upper church. Dimly lit by the aisles, this half-buried church is built to exactly the same plan as the upper church. It is entirely vaulted with groins, with thick transverse arches separating the bays of the nave.

In the apse of the south transept there is an impressive monolithic baptismal font. In the choir there is the reliquary sarcophagus of St Eutrope (4C), discovered in 1843 in the place where it had been hidden during the Wars of Religion.

Thermes de St-Saloine

The best-preserved part of the 1C thermal spa is the *caldarium* (hot plunge bath room). There is a lovely view of the town from here.

DRIVING TOURS

1 ROMANESQUE CHURCHES IN THE SAINTONGE★

80km/50mi round tour. Allow 5hrs.

Leave Saintes heading W (N 150 then the D 728). Then turn right onto the D 125.

Nieul-les-Saintes

Château fort – *Guided tour by reservation mid-Jul–late Aug Wed and Sat 2–6.30pm. 3€ (under 16 years 1€). 05 46 93 71 48.* Built in the late 14C by

Jean Chaudrier, Mayor of La Rochelle. At the entrance to the castle there is a gateway flanked by two towers, and two drawbridges. The fortifications, encircled by dry moats is reinforced by two angular towers. Of the living quarters you can still see interesting underground rooms, an ice house and a large furnished room.

Église – It has an interesting portal which, besides the usual sculptures, has figures of dancers and musicians.

Head SW on the D 127, then turn right onto the D 728.

Église de Corme-Royal

pl. de l'Église.

The church, a dependency of Abbaye aux Dames in Saintes, is noted for its two-storey west front decorated with a profusion of delicate carvings. The interior, which has regained its original vaulting, is lit by modern stained-glass windows.

Return via the D 728. At Nancras go left along the D 117.

Abbaye de Sablonceaux

Open Jul–Aug daily 3–6pm. No charge. 05 46 94 41 62.

This abbey was founded in 1136 by Guillaume X, the father of Eleanor of Aquitaine. Partially destroyed five times since the 14C, the abbey church with its Romanesque nave and tall Gothic tower has been restored to something like its original splendour. The convent buildings are being restored.

Take the D 243E1 to St-Romain-de-Benet.

Hameau de Pirelonge

The hamlet, which has a number of historic houses renovated using traditional methods, boasts a series of small museums which together preserve the local heritage.

Musée des Alambics – *Distellerie Brillouet, r. chez Pureay. Guided tours on reservation. 05 46 02 00 14).* Housed in a distillery, this museum displays a collection of alambics (stills) from the Charente region, of the type still in use for the refinement of Cognac. The museum also shows a series of "mobile" stills used by home distillers to make alcohol from wine or fruit. A collection of alcoholmeters is interesting.

Musée Charentais de l'Imprimerie – *Same as the Musée des Alambics.* An immense workshop containing about 30 machines (linotype machines and old printing presses) used to demonstrate the printing methods of the past. Young visitors will discover the amazing history of the printing industry before the age of the computer, when lead still reigned supreme. Some of the houses have displays of **church vestments** (albs, copes and chasubles), paper money (from promissory notes issued during the French Revolution to modern bills) and reconstructions of **craftsman's workshops** (blacksmith's, weaver's, barrel-maker's, etc.).

In the autumn, the ***Alambic and Harvest fairs*** *held in the hamlet revive local traditions.*

About 200m/220yds from the hamlet *(behind the railway line)* the **Tour de Pirelonge**, a Roman tower, is still partially roofed with carved stones. Between vineyards and woods, the tower stands on the edge of an old Roman road but its function remains a mystery.

Return via the N 150 towards Saintes. After 500m/550yds turn right onto the D 243E1.

Église de Meursac

r. de l'Église.

The Gothic church, shored up by powerful buttresses, ends in a Romanesque chancel with half-barrel-vaulting. Romanesque capitals in the chancel depict birds pecking lions and a human figure strangling two lions.

The altarpiece and tabernacle are of carved and gilded wood. A 5C crypt was discovered beneath the church in 1972; the large chamber was hollowed from the bedrock and has a domed roof.

Follow the D 243E1 SE.

Église de Thaims

5km/3.1mi SE of Meursac.

The modest church was built on the site of a Gallo-Roman villa (remains of the villa walls, up to a height of 2.5m/8ft, can be seen at the foot of the octagonal church tower). In the garden on the southern side of the church are a number of Merovingian sarcophagi. The cornices of the transept crossing inside are Merovingian too, with Carolingian engravings.

Leave Thaims NE via the D 114.

Église de Rétaud

9km/5.6mi NE of Thaims.

The 12C church is worth seeing for the decorative frieze of its west front, the octagonal belfry above the transept crossing, and for the carved, faceted walls of the apse. The consoles are fashioned into grotesques. Noteworthy features inside include the two capitals at the entrance to the apse, the small columns framing its bays, and part of a funerary litre (a black band on the church wall decorated with the armorial bearings of the dead).

Leave Rétaud heading S via the D 216.

Église de Rioux

6km/3.7mi SE of Rétaud.

This simple rural church, with a low nave and belfry-porch, is known to art enthusiasts for its brilliant sculptured décor; the **east end★** is of note.

Leave Rioux NE via the D 129.

On the way to Chermignac the road passes within view of the Château de Rioux *(now a chambre d'hôte; www.chateaudesrioux.com)*, which belonged in the Middle Ages to the family of the Seigneurs of Didonne, vassals of the Comtes de Poitou.

Église de Chermignac

7km/4.3mi NE of Rioux.

Frightening animals and different types of human characters adorn the covings above the church entrance. Near the church is a fine example of a **hosanna cross** (a 10–15C funerary monument).

Return to the D 129, which leads back to Saintes.

2 BASSE VALLÉE DE LA CHARENTE AND BOIS SAINTONGEAIS

97km/60mi round tour. Allow one day.

Leave Saintes NW on the D 137, towards Rochefort. At St-Porchaire, continue right on the D 122.

Château de Roche-Courbon★

See p469.

Continue along the D 122, then turn right onto the D 18 and right again onto the D 128.

Crazannes

Stone has played an important role in the village's history: the famous white stone of Crazannes, used for the construction of buildings not only in France, but farther afield, from Bilbao to Cologne and Brussels.

Trace the village's past by exploring the **anciennes carrières** now disused and overgrown *(Pôle-nature; guided tours Jun–Sept; 05 46 91 48 92)*, and by visiting the Maison des Pierreux, a museum where the process for extracting stone is explained.

Pôle-Nature La Pierre de Crazannes – *r. de la Mairie.*

Open Apr–May Tue–Sun 10am–noon, 2–5.30pm; Jun–Sept 10.30am–noon, 2–7pm; Oct–Mar Wed and Sat–Sun 10am–noon, 2–5pm. 05 46 91 48 92.

Learn about the traditional activity practised in the region for nearly 2 000 years.

Le Chemin de la Pierre –

10km/6.2mi round trip. Bikes available, at no charge, from the Maison des Pierreux. On hire from Garnier garage, rte de Saintes à St-Savinien (8km/5mi), Mon–Fri 8am–6pm.

Starting at Crazannes, a marked path goes in a loop linking all the sites relating to the local history of stone. From the Port de la Touche, then crossing the Lapidiales quarries, and rejoining the ancient quarries, and the Pôle-nature before finally returning to Crazannes.

Château de Crazannes– *Guided tours Apr–Jun and Sept–Oct Sat–Sun and public holidays; July–Aug daily 2–7pm. 8€ (7–14 yeards 4€). 06 80 65 40 96. www.crazannes.com.* The so-called "Puss in Boots château" owes its nickname to one of its former owners, the Marquis de Carabas, who inspired Charles Perrault, in the 18C, to create the character in his famous tale. This magnificent building was built at the end of the 14C on the site of an 11C fortress. The north façade, with Renaissance windows, has a Flamboyant Gothic **door**★ with delicate decorative carving.

An ancient stage on The Way of St James, the château was used as a summer residence, in the 18C, by the bishops of Saintes. The château also has *chambres d'hôtes* accommodation.

Continue along the D 128.

Château de Panloy

Guided tours May–Sept 11am, 5pm and 6pm. 7€ (under 12 years 4€), park 5€. 05 46 91 73 23. panloy@wanadoo.fr.

Built on the foundations of a former château, between 1770 and 1773, it has preserved the two original Renaissance pavilion houses. The harmonious façade overlooks a large courtyard. At the rear of the château stand the stables and dovecote (1620), which still has its spiral staircase. Inside, the visit starts with the dining room with Louis XV woodwork, the lounge, then a hunting gallery, added in the 19C, decorated with trophies. After the gallery, a small hallway, hung with 17C pictures, leads to the other pavilion furnished in the Renaissance style. Turn back to admire the decoration on the walls. In the Louis XV salon: wall panels hung with five Beauvais tapestries, designed by J-B Huet, representing 18C pastoral scenes.

Port-d'Envaux

A peaceful village that was once a busy port, from where cargos of stone, wine and spirits, salt and paper were shipped. The Charente riverbank provides the perfect setting for the white stone homes of wealthy shipowners. If you make a small detour on the D 119E2 going in the direction of Plassay, you will see a series of monumental sculptures, carved on the working faces of the ancient quarries, in a pleasant glade *(Les Lapidiales; 06 76 82 11 02)*.

Return to the D 128, then turn left and cross the Charente heading to Taillebourg.

Between St-James and the bridge over the Charente, overlooking the road, runs a Roman road rebuilt in 1220.

Taillebourg

Taillebourg gave its name to the first episode of a famous battle which ended at Saintes, where in July 1242, Saint Louis confronted Henri III Plantagenet. It ended in defeat for the English.

Château – Leave your car on the square by the Monument aux Morts (rte d'Annepont).

The path between two 18C pavilions leads you to the public park which is laid out in the ruins; there still stands a high corner tower with machicolations. From the park terrace admire the view of the Charente Valley, carpeted with meadows.

Leave Taillebourg heading E on the D 127.

Église d'Annepont

Small Romanesque building; to the right of the portal is a 15C alcove.

Return to Taillebourg. Before the D 127 crosses the A 10, turn left onto the D 231.

Église du Douhet

The church has a beautiful Romanesque portal, with archivolts decorated with sculptures of the Passover lamb sur-

rounded by angels and plant motifs and above, a Christ in Glory. Note the lateral arches decorated with geometric motifs and acanthus leaves, and the pillars of the nave, with their capitals sculpted with wrestlers, lions and eagles.

Follow the D 231, which shortly crosses the D 150.

Église de Écoyeux

The church *(05 46 97 48 48)* here is an imposing 12C building, fortified in the 15C – witness the two turreted watchtowers framing the west front.

Leave Écoyeux SE via the D 231.

Abbaye de Fontdouce★

St Bris-des-Bois. Open Apr Mon–Sat 2.30–6.30pm, Sun and public holidays 10.30am–6.30pm; Jul–Aug daily 10am–7pm; May–Jun and Sept–Oct daily 10.30am–6.30pm. 4.50€. 05 46 74 77 08. www.fontdouce.com.
This prosperous Benedictine abbey, half hidden in a steep, wooded valley, was sacked by the Huguenots. All that remains today is a small collection of monastic dependencies: a 12C cellar, a heating house with a 15C campanile, the main block dating from the 12C and 13C, and a Charente-style residential hall added to it in the 19C.
Visitors can tour the parlour, the two Romanesque chapels one above the other, and especially the magnificent **chapter house**★, with its 12 bays in which the ribbed vaulting rests on a forest of pillars. Notable here are the finely carved keystones, among them a curious three-faced head with four eyes, probably symbolising the Holy Trinity. The abbey church is now only a few ruined columns and a huge pillar base which would have been at the transept crossing.

Take the D 131 towards Saintes.

La Chapelle-des-Pots

Locally fashioned ceramics, in a tradition dating back to the 13C, are still made in this village today.

St-Césaire

Maison de pays Panier de Pierrette, pl. de la Mairie. 05 46 90 49 00. www.saintbris-saintcesaire.com.
In 1979 a major archaeological discovery was made at this small village in the Vallée du Coran. At La **Roche-à-Pierrot**, underneath a pile of tools previously believed to belong to Cro-Magnon man, a fragmented skeleton of a Neanderthal man, of around 20 years, was uncovered. It was given the name Pierrette and was unmistakable proof that the Neanderthals survived in the early Upper Paleolithic, contrary to what was believed, and that he coexisted for some time with Cro-Magnon man.
A small museum housed in the Maison de la Mérine, the **Musée des Bujoliers** recalls the life of the Saintonge people in the 19C in this former vigneron's house. Other rooms are dedicated to the local ceramic industry, geology and prehistory *(6 r. de la Mérine; 5.50€; 05 46 91 98 11; www.saintbris-saint cesaire.com)*.
Paléosite★★ – *Call for opening times and prices; 0 810 130 134 - www.paleosite.fr.* A real adventure that is both fun and educational, the tour at this interactive centre follows the traces of Neanderthal, man, 35 000 years ago. You follow a path that leads to the **archaeological site** where Pierrette was discovered.
In the **information centre**, the latest technology and special effects are used to try to explain the mystery of the death of the last Neanderthal known in France. In the **first room** the history of the universe is explained, and in the **amphitheatre** the evolution of man. In the **decrypting room**, the analysis of Pierrette's skeleton, using the most up-to-date scientific methods, reveals the cause of death. The investigation continues in the **projection room** where a film covers three possible scenarios. **The Morpho room**★ holds different interactive workshops that enable you to compare yourself with Neanderthal man (using morphing techniques) and to test your strength in an arm wrestling match with him!

The trail continues **outside**. Try your hand at spear throwing and take a path to see scenes from the life of prehistoric man re-created. The tour ends in the **laboratory** where the findings are analysed and interpreted, the highlight being the reconstruction of the face of Pierrette from the skull.

Follow the D 134 S.

St-Sauvant

Pretty village perched on a rocky cliff overlooking the valley of Coran.

Église – The fortified appearance of St-Sylvain church is accentuated by the steep slope that leads up to it. Massive buttresses support the façade and the Romanesque naves. The medieval tower, probably the remains of a castle, seems to confirm its role as sentinel.

Take the D 134 heading S, then turn right onto the D 24.

Chaniers

Église – Romanesque style, it has a fortified apse in a trefoil form and a bell tower above a cupola on squinches; 15C chapel.

La Baine –Lovely spot on the banks of the Charente river that divides here forming two islands connected by footbridges. Poplar grove and boats.

Leave Chaniers on the D 24, which leads back to Saintes.

ADDRESSES

STAY

Hôtel de l'Avenue – *114 av. de Gambetta. 05 46 74 05 91. www.hoteldelavenue.com. 15 rooms. 8.90€.* The rooms of this 1970s hotel in the centre of town are relatively calm because they all face away from the street. Attractive breakfast room.

Les Messageries – *r. des Messageries. 05 46 93 64 99. www.hotel-des-messageries.com. 33 rooms. 8€.* Near the historic district, this old stagecoach inn built around a courtyard dates from 1792.

Relais du Bois St-Georges – *r. de Royan. 05 46 93 50 99. www.relaisdubois.com. 31 rooms. 19€. Restaurant .* Built on the site of an old wine cellar, this hotel has individually decorated rooms, some very original: Capitain Némo, Tombouctou, Monte Cristo. Park with a lake. The rustic dining room overlooks the surrounding countryside. Cosy atmosphere and bistrot menu at La Table du Bois.

ST-SAUVANT

Design Hôtel des Francs Garçons – *1 r. des Francs-Garçons, 17610 St-Sauvant (13km/8mi E). 05 46 90 33 93. www.francsgarcons.com. 5 rooms, 2 suites. 12€. Restaurant (residents only).* Situated in a medieval village, renovated by architects. Décor modern, stone walls, design furniture, lighting effects. Pool facing the church.

EAT

Le Bistrot Galant – *28 r. St-Michel. 05 46 93 08 51. www.lebistrotgalant.com. Closed Sun except noon on public holidays, and Mon.* This little restaurant in a calm pedestrian street in the centre of Saintes is highly recommended. Interesting fixed-price menus, contemporary cuisine and two small, colourful dining rooms.

Le Saintonge – *Complexe Saintes-Végas. 05 46 97 00 00. www.saintes-vegas.com. Closed Sun and Mon evenings.* P. Part of the "Saintes-Vegas" complex, bright rotunda-shaped dining room in an elegant setting. Classic cuisine.

Saveurs de l'Abbaye – *1 pl. du Palais. 05 46 94 17 91. www.saveurs-abbaye.com. Closed Sun–Mon, late Sept–early Oct and Feb holidays.* Family restaurant, near to the Abbaye-aux-Dames, with a modern, yet cosy, dining room (wood, chocolate tones). Cuisine marrying regional dishes, herbs and spices. Modern rooms with a touch of individuality..

Château de Roche Courbon★

Charente-Maritime

This château overlooks a series of balustraded terraces and formal gardens. The building stands isolated at the heart of the oakwoods that inspired novelist Pierre Loti.

- **Michelin Map:** 324: F-4
- **Info:** 05 46 95 60 10. www.t3a.com/LaRoche Courbon.
- **Location:** 15km/9.3mi NW of Saintes and 19km/11.8mi SE of Rochefort.
- **Don't Miss:** The gardens.

A BIT OF HISTORY

"Sleeping Beauty's Castle"

This was the title of an article written by Loti in 1908, which appeared in *Le Figaro*, to stimulate interest in his campaign to save the woods around the long-abandoned old château. Loti recalled the memories of his youth, when his holidays were spent with a friend, later to be his brother-in-law, who became the tax collector in nearby St-Porchaire. Often as an adolescent, he wrote years later, he would stray "into the density of these oaken groves" sliced by a ravine buried beneath the foliage and pitted with small grottoes where "the greenish half-light filtered through leafy branches". The campaign, harnessed to another run by fellow writer André Hallays, was a success: not only was the forest saved from the woodsman's axe; from 1920 onwards the château was restored and its gardens brought back to life.

VISIT

The estate is entered via porte des Lions (Lions' Gate), a monumental 17C structure with three arches, adorned with caryatids on the inside. Having crossed a moat, which was bordered with balustrades in the 17C, visitors pass below the "keep", an ancient machicolated tower.

Château

Gardens, park, caves: *Open summer daily 10am–7pm; winter Mon–Sat 10am–noon, 2–6pm; Jan Sat–Sun 10am–noon, 2–7pm, Sun 2–7pm. Guided tour of the château (45min), contact for details. Closed 1 Jan, 25 Dec. Castle and gardens 9€, gardens 6€. 05 46 95 60 10.*

The château, like the keep, dates from the 15C but was substantially altered by Jean-Louis de Courbon in the 17C when windows, dormers and skylights were refashioned and arcades added at the

Château de Roche Courbon

foot of the garden façade to support a balcony. This façade is remarkable for the balance of its elements and its balustraded stairway.

Inside, the tour of the château starts with a **library** furnished in Louis XIII style, which serves as a gallery for the paintings, most of them from the old chapel: they include biblical episodes, allegories, landscapes and a series of painted panels illustrating *The Labours of Hercules*, from the time of Louis IV.

The 18C **Grand Salon**, with panelling and furniture from the same period, contains a bust of Hubert Robert after Pajou, and a painting by the Dutch artist Hackaert, which shows the château as it was in the 17C. Visitors then pass through a **Louis XVI vestibule** hung with rare, early 19C illustrated panoramic wallpaper, and landscapes painted by Casanova, the brother of the notorious libertine. The tour finishes with two 17C rooms with Louis XIII ceilings: in the first of these is an enormous stone fireplace bearing the Latin inscription: *Fide, Fidelitate, Fortitudine* ("By Faith, Fidelity and Courage"); the second room is a kitchen-banqueting hall.

Gardens★

Beyond the château formal parterres and basins, separated by clipped yew hedges and graced with statues, form a magnificent and colourful perspective focusing on a double stairway flanking an ornamental waterway. Partially laid over marshland, these gardens were preserved from flooding by having their supporting piles regularly rebuilt (works lasting 17 years).

Skirting these waters and the nymph at their far end, visitors reach a terrace offering a stunning **view**★★ of the château, reflected in the smooth surface of the pool beneath. The wide tree-lined walk leads to a column surmounted by a sphere; from here, by turning suddenly around, it is possible to experience that same sense of magic and surprise that so stimulated Pierre Loti.

Salle des Fêtes

The "festival hall" contains a superb late 16C stone stairway with balustrades.

Grottoes

30min round trip on foot.

The woodland walk ends in an avenue of holm oaks which leads to the narrow valley carved out by the Bruant. It is this stream which feeds the pools and waterways in the castle gardens.

The caves in the steep wall of the ravine, which intrigued the young Loti, were inhabited by prehistoric man.

St-Jean-d'Angély

Charente-Maritime

The town of St-Jean-d'Angély sits on a hill, in the peaceful Charente countryside, bordering the Boutonne river. Encircled by boulevards, the town centre is a maze of twisting streets and small triangular squares, lined with pretty half-timbered houses, and elegant *hôtels particuliers*. The Gothic apse and Classic monumental façade of the town's prestigious abbey never fail to impress.

- **Population:** 7 424
- **Michelin Map:** 324: G-4.
- **Info:** 8 r. Grosse Horloge, St Jean-d'Angély. ✆05 46 32 04 72. http://ot.angely.net.
- **Location:** 30km/18.6mi NE of Saintes.
- **Don't Miss:** The abbey ruins; the church and Lanterne des Morts at Fenioux.
- **Kids:** Trésors de Lisette.
- **Timing:** Allow 2hrs for the town, and a day for the Boutonne Valley.

THE TOWN

Ancienne Abbaye

Guided tours Jul–Aug daily 3pm, 4pm, 5pm. 3.50€ (under 12 years no charge). Access to towers Jul–Aug, Mon–Fri 11am–12.30pm, 2.30-6pm, Sat–Sun 3–6pm. 2.50€. 05 46 32 04 72. www.angely.net.

The abbey was built in the 9C to house the relic of St Jean-Baptiste's skull. After the destruction of the monastery by the Protestants in 1562 during the Wars of Religion, the monks undertook two rebuilding campaigns (17C and 18C). The latter, a very ambitious project, was left unfinished because of the Revolution.

Les Tours – Work on the abbey began in 1741, but only the beginnings of the arches for the nave, and a part of the monumental façade, known as the Tours, were completed. Appreciate the splendour of the majestic and powerful façade framed by tall domed towers, one of which served as a prison during the Revolution (**panorama**). The capitals and the keystones arejust sketched out. The doorway is framed by Doric columns.

Only a section of the apse remains from the ruined 1562 Gothic abbey. Inside the modern church, built in the late 19C, is a 17C Virgin and Child carved in wood and, in the choir, two large paintings: *Jesus in the Olive Grove* by Chassériau, and the *Presentation at the Temple of Sotta*.

Abbey Buildings – Home to the École municipale de musique. Classic buildings arranged around a courtyard.

Fontaine du Pilori

At the centre of the Old Town of St-Jean, it was moved, in 1819, from the neighbouring Brizambourg castle and brought to the Pilori district, where the condemned were exposed to the public. The fountain bears the inscription "In 1546 I was built and placed here".

Tour de l'Horloge

Open Jul–Aug Tue–Sat 10.30am–6.30pm, Sun 2.30–6.30pm; rest of year 2–6pm. Closed Mon, 1 Jan, 25 Dec. 2.50€(under 18 years no charge). 05 46 59 56 67. www.angely.net.

This tower spans the rue de la Grosse-Horloge where there are splendid half-timbered houses overhanging the street. The tower is a former Gothic machicolated belfry: its bell, the "Sin" (from the Latin *signum*, signal) formerly rang to announce the closing of the town gates. Today, it still rings on special occasions.

Hôtel de l'Échevinage – A 15C building, with an ogee-shaped doorway, housed the Municipal Court from the Middle Ages to the Revolution. Meetings of the town notables and the Royal Court of Assizes were held here.

DRIVING TOUR

3 VALLÉE DE LA BOUTONNE

100km/62mi. Allow one day.

Leave St-Jean-d'Angély heading SW on the D 127.

Château de Beaufief

Open Jul–Aug daily 3–7pm. 3.50€ (under 12 years 2€). 05 46 32 35 93.

An alley bordered by lawns unfolds at Beaufief. This country seat of Louis XV comprises a central building with two wings. Note the roof tiled in different materials, the colour of the stone, and the stylish windows. The staircase, with wrought-iron handrail, leads to a room where, above the fireplace, there is a fine sculpture representing summer. The wooden plinth of the staircase is painted to imitate marble. The small chapel has a sombre gypsum décor.

Return to St-Jean-d'Angély. After 2km/1.2mi, turn left onto the D 739E. After crossing the A 10, turn right; at Ternant, follow the D 218 on the left. Cross over the Boutonne near Torxé, then turn right onto the D 119.

Église de Landes

Romanesque, inside there are late 13C murals representing biblical scenes (the Baptism of Christ, the Annunciation, the Visitation).

Leave Landes going W on the D 213, then left on the D 213E2.

Tonnay-Boutonne

6 Grand-rue. 05 46 33 22 35.

The town still has some of its fortifications, particularly the moats and the magnificent 14C St-Pierre gateway. The museum **Les Trésors de Lisette** at Archingeay, 4.5km/2.8mi south of Tonnay-Boutonne on the D 114, traces the daily life of a Belle Époque family, composed of a widowed baron, his two chidren and his servant Lisette. There's an impressive collection of objects from 1900 exhibited in 12 display cases, each one representing a room in the house. Utensils, tools, period clothes and furniture are just a few of the thousands of items. Not forgetting, in Lisette's own room, a wonderful exhibition of 19C lithographed tin boxes *(open Jun–Aug daily 3–7pm, rest of year, phone for details; 6€ (5–18 years €4) ; 05 46 97 81 46; http://lestresorsdelisette.monsite.orange.fr).*

Leave Tonnay-Boutonne going S on the D 739E, then the D 127E3. After crossing the A 10, turn left.

Fenioux★

Église – The walls of the nave date back to the Carolingian era (9C): there are various characteristics that indicate that it dates from this time, few bays, and thin slabs of perforated stones, designed to form a Celtic knot pattern, called *fenestrelles*. The façade is Romanesque Saintonge in style. The clusters of small columns frame an immense portal which has 10 jambs (vertical uprights), and archivolts sculpted with scenes of the signs of the zodiac and the Labours of the Month, the Wise and Foolish Virgins, the angels worshipping the Lamb of God, the Virtues slaying the Vices. Notice on the left, a charming portal, with graceful plant décor. The bell tower is famous in the history of Romanesque art for the lightness of its architecture and audacity. It has often inspired the pastiche architects of the late 19C.

Lanterne des Morts★ – A curious edifice that stands, side-by-side with a vaulted cellar, in the middle of the ancient cemetery. It consists of a cluster of 11 columns supporting a lantern which itself is encircled by 13 columns. It is surmounted by a pyramid and finally a cross.

Leave Fenioux heading S on the ID 127. After 2.5 km/1.5mi, turn left onto the D 124 (St-Hilaire). Pass through St-Hilaire on the D 731, turn left onto the D 129, then right onto the D 124.

Matha

Église – Dedicated to St Hérie, the church has a Romanesque façade where you can see, in the right-hand archway, a charming statue said to be Ste Blandine.

Donjon – The huge gatehouse and corner turret are all that remains of a Renaissance castle. The buildings are topped by high slate roofs.

Leave Matha W on the D 939.

Église de Varaize

Romanesque style, it has a semicircular apse, a nave and aisles without arches, a transept crossing covered by a cupola on squinches. The south side entrance is remarkable for the finesse of the sculptured archivolts. Admire the angels worshipping the Lamb of God, The Vertues triumphing over the Vices, Christ in Glory accompanied by his apostles and elders of the Apocalypse.

Leave Varaize on the D 130, then the D 939 which leads back to St-Jean-d'Angély.

Dampierre-sur-Boutonne

Charente-Maritime

Dampierre-sur-Boutonne is known for its Renaissance château, built in an attractive setting on a tiny island in the river. Since 1981, Dampierre has also become famous as a breeding centre for the celebrated *baudets* (donkeys) of Poitou.

- **Population:** 297
- **Michelin Map:** 324: H-3
- **Info:** 290 av. de l'Église, Aulney. ℘05 46 33 14 44. www.aulnaytourisme.com.
- **Location:** The village is situated 8km/5mi NW of Aulnay.
- **Kids:** Asinerie du Baudet de Poitou.

CHATEAU★

Open Easter–Jun and Sept daily 2–6pm; Jul–Aug daily 10.30am–7pm; Oct–mid-Nov Sat–Sun and public holidays 2–6pm. 8€. ℘05 46 24 02 24. http://membres.lycos.fr/chateaudedampierre.

Of the four wings originally framing the inner courtyard, only the living quarters remain. The building is flanked by two massive towers designed to defend the building from attack. The most impressive feature is a two-tiered Renaissance **gallery**★ of basket-handle arches, with its two levels separated by a frieze of carved foliage. The upper gallery features a coffered ceiling whose 93 sections are carved with crests (a swan pierced by an arrow, the emblem of Claude of France, wife of François I), insignia (Catherine de' Medici and Henri II), and allegorical scenes and symbols (a labyrinth and a cherub astride a chimera, etc.). These are often bordered by scrolls bearing Latin mottoes. An interpretation and explanation of these decorations was proposed by Fulcanelli in his alchemical work, *Les Demeures Philosophales*, in 1931.

Among the furnishings on view in the apartments are fine Flemish tapestries and a superb Italian ebony cabinet (16C). In the guardroom, above the chimney-piece, reads the inscription *Estre, se cognestre et non parestre* ("To be is to know oneself rather than be known"). There are two exhibitions in the castle reception area – "Art and Alchemy" (which analyses details of the coffered ceiling) and "Dalí's Horses" (paintings inspired by the ceiling).

Château de Dampierre-sur-Boutonne

EXCURSIONS

Église St-Pierre d'Aulnay★★

The church of St-Pierre stands alone in its old cemetery amid the melancholic landscape of cypress trees. A UNESCO World Heritage Site, this masterpiece of Poitevin Romanesque art, built in warm-hued stone near to the village of Aulnay-de-Saintonge, boasts harmonious lines and a sumptuous sculptured décor. For the best overall panorama of the site, stand at the bottom of the cemetery at an angle bearing slightly left of the façade.

West Façade

This comprises, in the centre, a slightly pointed arched portal, formerly surmounted by an equestrian statue of Constantin. On each side of this portal, there are two blind pointed archways which form recessed bays (tombs). On the tympanum of the left-hand arch is sculptured the Crucifixion of St Peter; and on the right, Christ in Glory surrounded by two characters that are most likely to be Peter and Paul.

Transept

It is very complete. The square bell tower over the transept crossing served as a landmark to pilgrims and travellers.

The Right-Hand Transept★★ – This architectural gem has archivolts decorated with intricate sculptures. The 1st archivolt is ornamented with animals and foliage in low relief, inspired by the Orient. On the 2nd archivolt, supported on the underside by seated Atlantes figures, appear the apostles and disciples of Christ. On the 3rd archivolt, the Elders of the Apocalypse, each one holds a vial of perfume and a musical instrument; on the underside of the arch, more Atlantes figures, this time kneeling.

Finally, among the figures and fictional animals of the 4th archivolt, notice the donkey musician, the goat, the deer, the owl and the siren. Above this portal there is a large bay whose middle archivolt is decorated with statues of the Virtues slaying the Vices.

Apse

At each side of the central window of the apse, enigmatic figures are encircled by Oriental-style foliage.

Inside

The nave has a pointed vault and side aisles. Notice the depth of the openings, which are narrower in the north than the south, the massive pillars with two rows of capitals. The transept crossing is surmounted by a cupola, resting on pendatives, which has ribs radiating around a circular opening through which the bells were hoisted. The capitals are remarkable, especially those in the transept: elephants with tiny ears *(right-hand transept)*; a sleeping Samson held down by Delilah, while a Philistine cuts off his hair *(pillar northwest of the transept crossing)*; small devils pull the beard of a man *(left-hand transept)*, etc.

Cemetery

Littered with sarcophagus-shaped tombstones, it still has a 15C Hosanna cross, a pulpit from where the priest read the Gospel message, and statues of Sts Peter, Paul, James and John.

Asinerie du Baudet du Poitou★

At La Tillauderie, 5km/3.1mi NE on the D 127 towards Chizé. Open Apr–May Tue–Sun 10.30am–noon, 2–5.30pm; Jun–Sept daily 10am–noon, 2–6pm; Oct–Nov and Jan–Mar Wed and Sat–Sun 10.30am–noon, 2–4.30pm. 3€ (children no charge). 05 46 24 68 94.
The **baudet du Poitou** has been bred in this region for centuries. The museum traces the donkey's history and efforts being made to preserve the breed.

ADDRESSES

EAT

De la Place – *pl. de l'Hôtel de Ville, St-Jean-d'Angely (18km/11.2mi SW via rte de Dampierre). 05 45 32 69 11. www.hoteldelaplace.net. Closed 3 wks in Jan and Aug school holidays.* Moder, bistro-style dining. Hotel rooms available.

Pons

Charente-Maritime

The attractive little town of Pons (pronounced "Pon") is built on a hillside, its keep and ramparts overlooking the languid waters of the Seugne, a tributary of the Charente, as it branches out into a myriad of streams flowing through meadows, poplars and willows. A staging post on the road to Santiago de Compostela in the Middle Ages, Pons became a stronghold of military radicalism and anticlericalism at the turn of the 20C, in the person of its mayor, Émile Combes (1835–1921).

- **Population:** 4 454
- **Michelin Map:** 324: G-6
- **Info:** Donjon, pl. de la République, Pons. 05 46 96 13 31. www.pons-tourisme.fr.
- **Location:** Pons lies 20km/12.4mi S of Saintes and 23km/14mi SW of Cognac.
- **Don't Miss:** The Donjon of the château.
- **Kids:** The treasure trail at Château des Énigmes.

SIGHTS

Castle

The castle once covered the area now occupied by the square and public gardens. Its owners, the lords of Pons, answered to no one but the King of France; they commanded more than 60 towns and villages and more than 600 parishes and domains, giving rise to the motto, "What the King of France cannot be, the lord of Pons will."

Donjon★

Open May–Sept daily 10am–1pm, 2.30–6.30pm; Oct–May please contact tourist office. Closed public holidays. 2.50€ (12–18 years 1€). 05 46 96 13 31.

The 12C **keep**★ is 30m/98.4ft high; it was reached by ladders which could be withdrawn if there was a threat. Although the roof ridge, renovated in 1904, is rather fanciful, the rest of the building, supported by narrow buttresses, gives a powerful impression. From the top there is a **panorama** of the town and valley.

The old seigneurial abode includes a main 17C building flanked by an older staircase turret. It now houses the town hall.Farther on, the charming public gardens forming a terrace along the ramparts offer attractive views overlooking the streams branching out from the Seugne.

EXCURSION

Château des Énigmes

1km/0.6mi S on the D 249.

Open daily early Apr–Jun and Sept–early Nov 10am–7pm; Jul–Aug 10am–8pm. 12€ (children 7€). 05 46 91 09 19. www.chateau-enigmes.com.

A fine example of Renaissance architecture, the château was built by the Rabaine family near Lonzac, 9km/6mi east of Pons. Threatened with destruction at the end of 20C, it was transported and rebuilt, stone by stone, on its present site.

The courtyard is interesting for the variety of its ornamentation: at the back, the gallery with its basket-handle arches is remarkable for its medallions (the 12 Caesars), statues of marmosets and engraved maxims. At the end of one of the wings, a tower with its original roof is carved with coats of arms and emblems (shells and crescents from the Rabaine arms) and, just under the edge of the roof, a frieze divided into panels by short, hollow columns.

Inside, note the drawing room decorated with fine Regency **wood panelling**★, white with gold borders, from the château in Choisy-le-Roi and, in the main hall, the door of the former chapel, sculpted by Nicolas Bachelier, a pupil of Michelangelo. There is also a fun treasure trail organised for children, to uncover the mystery of the Templars!

DRIVING TOUR

4 THE PONTOISE REGION

95km/59mi. Allow 4hrs.

This region of Haute-Saintonge has wonderful castles and churches.

Leave Pons heading NE on the D 732.

Église de Pérignac

Admire the magnificent Romanesque Saintonge façade. The church is decorated with two rows of sculptured archways: in the lower part, the apostles encircle the Virgin contemplating the Ascension of Christ, and higher up the Vices confront the Virtues. The archivolt of the central window, ornamented with horses' heads, is characteristic of the region.

Leave Pérignac heading SE on the D 128. At Coulonges, turn right onto the D 146.

Église d'Échebrune

The portal of the Romanesque building stands out from the small side arcades, but its decoration is very simple, limited to capitals sculpted with acanthus leaves. Above the cornice there is a row of arches all along the front.

Leave Échebrune E on the D 700 towards Archiac. After 2.5km/1.5mi, turn left onto the D 148.

Église de Lonzac

Harmonious building combining Gothic architecture with Renaissance décor. **Exterior** – A 40m/131ft-high belfry towers above the church. The corners are reinforced with massive buttresses. A frieze around the walls bears the initials K and I (Katherine and Iacques or Jacques), alternating with symbols and the Galiot de Genouillac's motto: *J'aime fortune ou J'aime fort une*. The **portal★** has twin doors surmounted by three recesses. Above the doors, two low-reliefs relate the Labours of Hercules.

Interior – The nave has Gothic vaults resting on Renaissance pillars. On the keystones are the arms of Archiac and Genouillac and on other capitals, the arms of Galiot de Genouillac. Left of the choir, the seigneurial chapel, covered with a coffered ceiling, was designed to house the tomb of Lady Catherine. Above the altar hangs an *Adoration of the Magi*, painted by P Vincent in 1787.

Leave Lonzac SE on the D 128. At Cierzac, turn left onto the D 731 going to St-Fort-sur-le-Né.

Dolmen de St-Fort-sur-le-Né

See p499.

1.5km/0.9mi SE of the village on the D 151. Leave St-Fort-sur-le-Né heading S and return to Cierzac. Just after the church, turn left onto the D 150 and continue to Neuillac. At the crossroads, turn right onto the D 148.

You are following the ancient Roman road that linked Saintes to Périgueux. A path through the wood allows you to view part of the Roman road that was uncovered during an archaeological dig in 1996. There is an information panel nearby.

Continue along the D 148, then turn left onto the D 250.

Église de Chadenac

This Romanesque church has an elaborate façade decorated with sculptures on the theme of Good and Bad. The centre of the portal features the Ascension; the archivolts have saints, monsters and allegorical figures: Wise and Foolish Virgins *(middle archivolt)*, Virtues and Vices *(bottom)*. The side arches are lined with statues, mutilated in 1840 and surmounted by a hound attacking a fleeing lamb and an ox standing his ground; in the spandrels stand St George and the Princess de Trébizonde, St Michael and his dragon. The corner capitals of the façade represent holy women at the tomb, on the right, and on the left,

Constantine on his horse, near to a palm tree crushing Heresy.

Leave Chadenac SW on the D 146E2.

Marignac

Église St-Sulpice – This 12C building has an original trefoil Romanesque apse, the apsidal chapels blend with the curved arms of the transept. Admire the richly carved frieze decorated with motifs, characters and imaginary animals. The transept crossing has an interesting arrangement: double arches, corbels support the bases of the squinches of the cupola. The capitals *(hunting scene on the SW pillar, two lovers on the SE pillar)* are decorated with a frieze that corresponds with that on the outside; the Moorish influence is evident.

Leave Marignac SE on the D 142.

Jonzac

25 pl. du Château. ℘05 46 48 49 29. www.jonzac.fr.

The town of Jonzac has long been associated with cognac and Pineau des Charentes. More recently, it discovered a new asset: waters rich in mineral salts that are used as part of the treatment of illnesses in a rare troglodyte spa.

The stone bridge that crosses the Seugne, upstream, is an ideal place from where to enjoy the view over Jonzac. On the Right Bank, two hills: on one sits the church and its district, on the other the *cité*, where the fortifications formerly stood. On the Left Bank, the streets of Carmes, once busy with craftsmen, fellmongers, tanners and coopers.

Château – *Open (except the theatre). Guided tours only Jul–Aug Mon–Tue and Thu–Sat 4pm, Wed 11am; Sept–Nov and Mar–Jun Tue 3pm. No charge. ℘05 46 48 49 29. www.ville-jonzac.fr.*

Built on a rocky spur overlooking the Seugne Valley, the original 11C castle, which was badly damaged during the Hundred Years' War, was rebuilt in the 15C. It has seen many distinguished guests: Henri IV in 1609, and 50 years later Louis XIV, on his way to sign the Treaty of the Pyrénées and to marry the Spanish Infanta Maria Teresa at St-Jean-de-Luz. Today, it houses the Hôtel de Ville and the Sous-préfecture. A vast esplanade is reached by passing through a 15C fortified gateway. The west façade of the château is grandiose, with a sturdy 15C gatehouse, and towers, one of which is the belfry. During the visit, admire the ancient walkway, the wedding hall, also used by the town council, and a lovely little Napoléon III-style theatre. From the terrace, there is a view over the Vallée de la Seugne.

Opposite the château's esplanade, note the medieval rue de Champagnac, with its succession of arches and small cobbled courtyards.

Ancien Couvent des Carmes – *Phone for opening times and charges. ℘05 46 48 49 29. www.ville-jonzac.fr.*

Founded in 1505, the convent, destroyed by the Wars of Religion, was rebuilt in the 17., then confiscated as public property during the Revolution. It has been extensively renovated, and today houses a museum of local archaeology, as well as conference rooms and temporary exhibitions. Of particular interest are the cloisters, which still have part of their gallery.

Thermes – *Domaine d'Heurtebise. Open on request only in spring and autumn. ℘05 46 48 59 59.*

The troglodyte spa has been installed in the middle of the ancient quarries which were already in operation in the Middle Ages. Later in the 16C the Protestants sought refuge here, and then they were used for mushroom farming. During some hole drilling being carried out in 1980 a deep water table (65–68°C/149–154°F) was uncovered; its water was found to have therapeutic properties. A spa offers specialised treatments (rheumatology, osteo-articular injuries, respiratory problems and phlebology) as well as health and fitness programmes.

If you have the time, visit Château de Meux, 7.5km/4.7mi E on the D 2.

Château de Meux

Open May–Sept Wed–Mon 2–6.30pm. 5€ (6–16 years 3€). 05 46 48 16 61.

Built in 1453 upon the ruins of a 13C fortress, the château belonged, for four centuries, to the Chesnel family, two members of whom were Knights of the Order of Malta. Flanked by a tower, the façade, which has windows with mouldings, is preceded by a polygonal stair turret. The building has been reinforced with 18C buttresses. Inside, a spiral staircase leads up to the different floors, where there are noteworthy white carved stone fireplaces. In the outbuildings, notice the tanks or *buroirs* which were used for washing clothes.

Return to Jonzac in order to continue NW on the D 2. Around 1km/0.6mi after St-Germain-de-Lusignan, turn left onto the D 148.

Abbaye de la Tenaille

This Benedictine monastery is now a farm. The Saintonge façade of this Romanesque abbey has suffered the collapse of two of its three splendid cupolas on penditives. The château (1830) possesses a pure Louis XVI-style façade decorated with garlands and balustrades.

Return to the D 137 and turn right in the direction of St-Genis-de-Saintonge.

Château de Plassac

It was built around 1772, for the Bishop of Autun, by the architect Victor Louis. In 1832 the Duchess of Berry stayed at the château before she attempted to stir up the Vendée. Entering by the main alley, you can see in the farmyard, the Pilgrims tower, ruins of a 15C château.

Continue on the D 137. Before Belluire, turn right onto the D 144.

Église de Fléac-sur-Seugne

Admire the original design of the bell tower of this Renaissance building. A square base is topped by an octagonal dome, which is surmounted by a lantern. At each side of the doorway stand two twisted columns supporting two lions.

Continue along the D 144.

Avy

The façade of this Romanesque church has a portal where the archivolt represents a burlesque concert. Inside, on the left, stands a chapel decorated with a 14C mural: two donors presented by their patron saints worship the Virgin and Child, dressed as the perfect pilgrim: hat, bell, pouch, etc. The chapel has an ossuary which gives access to the exterior.

The D 142 leads back to Pons

ADDRESSES

STAY/ EAT

Auberge Pontoise – *23 av. Gambetta. 05 46 94 00 99. www.logis-de-france.fr. Closed Sun evening and Mon lunch (15 Sept–1 Jun).20 rooms. 8€. Restaurant.* Set right in the village, this cosy *auberge*, a former biscuit factory, has a busy restaurant which is popular with locals. Traditional cuisine, with an emphasis on local produce, is served in the comfortable dining room. The *auberge* also has some simple rooms.

Hôtel Bordeaux – *1 av. Gambetta. 05 46 91 31 12. www.hotel-de-bordeaux.com 16 rooms. 10€. Restaurant.* Housed in an old building, the interior décor of this hotel is fairly modern. Its small rooms are simple and functional. Don't miss the restaurant – the innovative cuisine is excellent and the prices reasonable. Terrace in the summer and a great choice of Cognacs.

Montendre

Charente-Maritime

The town of Montendre, with its narrow streets, nestles in the heart of the pine forest that extends to the borders of the Charente-Maritime and the Gironde. It has taken its name from the ancient site of a Roman settlement, the Mons Andronis, upon which it was built. From the square tower, dating from Middle Ages, enjoy the view of the town and surrounding countryside.

- **Population:** 3 140
- **Michelin Map:** 324: H-8
- **Info:** 1 pl. de l'Église, or pl. des Halles, Montendre. 05 46 49 46 45. www.montendre-tourisme.com.
- **Location:** 19km/11.8mi S of Jonzac.
- **Don't Miss:**A walk in the magical forest of Haute-Saintonge.
- **Kids:** Picnic in the forest.
- **Timing:** Allow around 1hr to visit the town, and take whatever time you need for a walk in the countryside.

THE TOWN

Tour carrée

Guided tours early Jul–mid-Sept Mon–Sat 10am–12.30pm, 3–7pm. Closed public holidays. 5€ (under 15 years 2€). 05 46 49 46 45.

All that stands of the château today are the ruins of ramparts, a razed round tower and the famous square tower, built in the 12C, then altered in the 15C and 20C. This reminds us that Montendre held a strategic postion, which was fought over by the French and the English in the Middle Ages. It now houses a small museum.

EXCURSIONS

Église de Sousmoulins

8km/5mi NE via the D 155.

Inside this Romanesque building dating from the 12C and 15C, there are four beautiful 18C painted panels, Classical style , representing the Assumption, the Visitation and the Nativity *(E transept)* and, above the door, God the Father.

Maison de la Forêt de Haute-Saintonge

12km/7.4mi SE via the D 730, at Montlieu-la-Garde.

Open Apr–Oct Mon–Fri 9am–noon, 2–6.30pm, Sat–Sun and public holidays 3–6.30pm; Nov–Mar Mon–Fri 9am–noon, 2–6pm. 2.50€(under 12 years no charge), 4€ ticket combined with the ludic trail. 05 46 04 43 67.

Situated at the heart of the Double Saintongeaise Forest, which extends into the districts of Montendre, Montguyon and Montlieu-la-Garde, this Charente-Maritime nature centre explains forest life. Appreciate its temporary exhibitions on the theme of wood, its ludic footpath (around 2km/1.2mi) among the maritime pines, ferns and alders, and its entertainment programme (sculpture competitions, etc.).

From the top of the watchtower, there is a panorama of the large 40 000ha/ 98 842-acre forest and the *bocage* that borders it to the north.

Montguyon

20km/12.5mi SE via D 730.

Saintonge village overlooked by the ruins of a medieval castle with an imposing keep. Formerly this castle belonged to an illustrious Poitou family: La Rochefoucauld *(see p504)*. Henri IV and Louis XIII have stayed here.

Allée Couverte de la Pierre-Folle

2km/1.2mi NE.

An avenue of elms leads to this megalith that has a colossal roof slab, 3.90m/12.8ft from the ground at its highest point. Lovely **panorama** over the countryside and its castles.

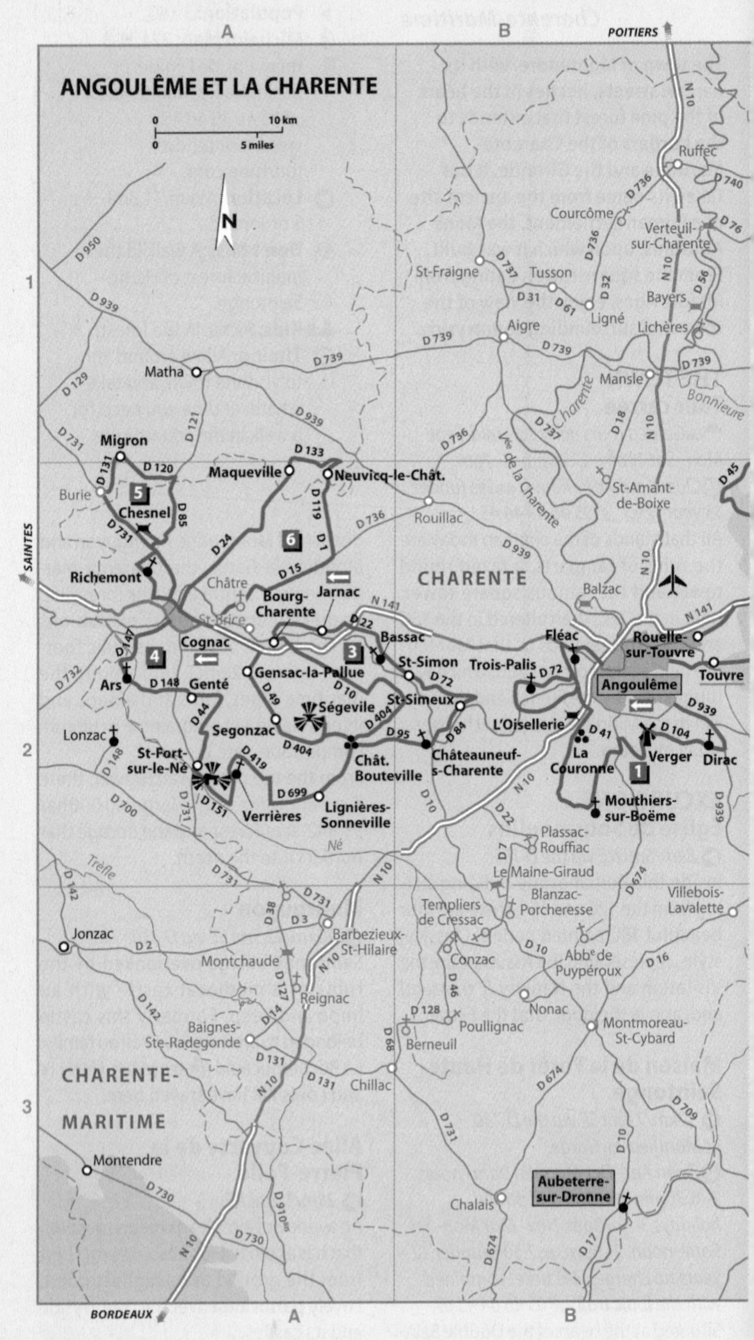
ANGOULÊME ET LA CHARENTE
POITIERS
BORDEAUX
SAINTES
CHARENTE
CHARENTE-MARITIME
Angoulême
Cognac
Jarnac
Ruffec
Verteuil-sur-Charente
Mansle
Aigre
Matha
Migron
Chesnel
Burie
Richemont
Maqueville
Neuvicq-le-Chât.
Rouillac
Bourg-Charente
Bassac
St-Simon
St-Simeux
Châteauneuf-s-Charente
Gensac-la-Pallue
Ségevile
Segonzac
Genté
Ars
Lonzac
St-Fort-sur-le-Né
Verrières
Lignières-Sonneville
Chât. Bouteville
Fléac
Trois-Palis
L'Oisellerie
La Couronne
Mouthiers-sur-Boëme
Verger
Dirac
Touvre
Rouelle-sur-Touvre
Balzac
St-Amant-de-Boixe
Courcôme
Tusson
Ligné
St-Fraigne
Bayers
Lichères
Plassac-Rouffiac
Le Maine-Giraud
Blanzac-Porcheresse
Templiers de Cressac
Villebois-Lavalette
Abbe de Puypéroux
Conzac
Nonac
Montmoreau-St-Cybard
Poullignac
Berneuil
Barbezieux-St-Hilaire
Reignac
Montchaude
Jonzac
Baignes-Ste-Radegonde
Chillac
Montendre
Chalais
Aubeterre-sur-Dronne

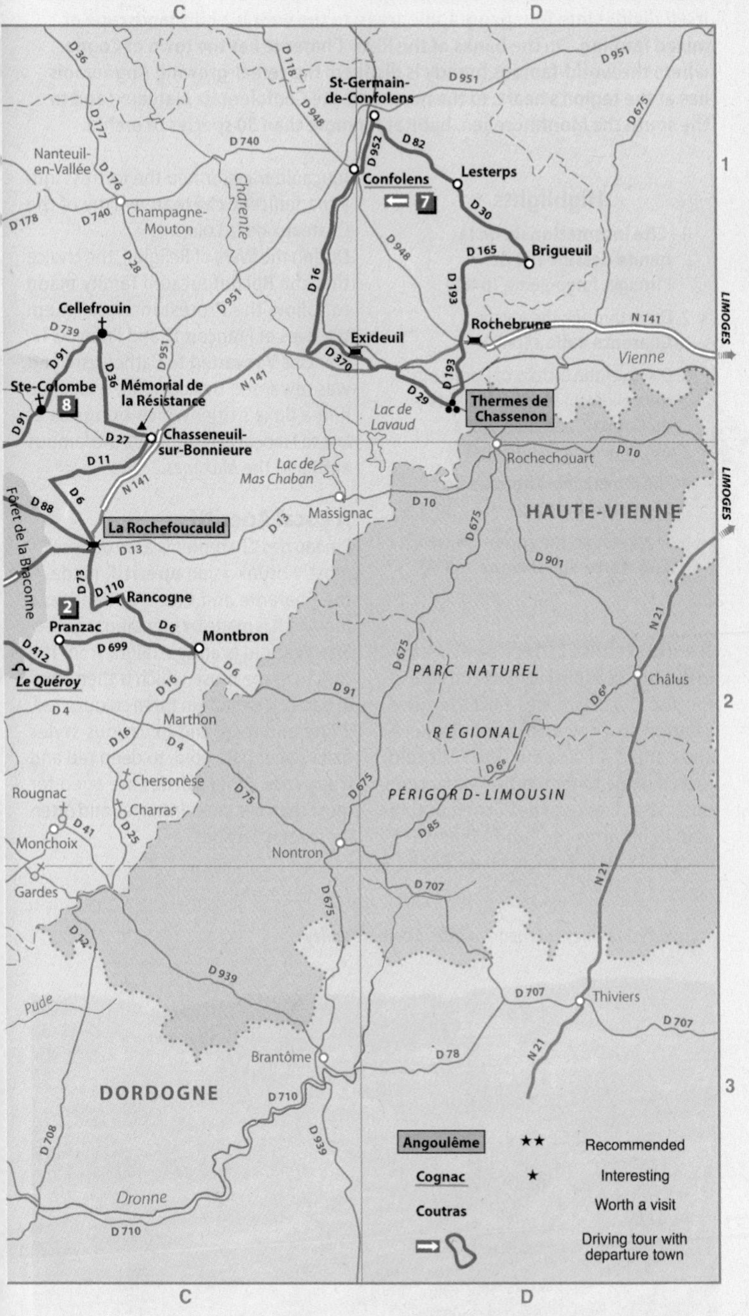
St-Germain-de-Confolens
Confolens
Lesterps
Brigueuil
Rochebrune
Exideuil
Thermes de Chassenon
Rochechouart
HAUTE-VIENNE
LIMOGES
Vienne
Lac de Lavaud
Lac de Mas Chaban
Massignac
Nanteuil-en-Vallée
Champagne-Mouton
Charente
Cellefrouin
Ste-Colombe
Mémorial de la Résistance
Chasseneuil-sur-Bonnieure
La Rochefoucauld
Forêt de la Braconne
Rancogne
Pranzac
Montbron
Le Quéroy
Marthon
Chersonèse
Charras
Rougnac
Monchoix
Gardes
Nontron
PARC NATUREL RÉGIONAL PÉRIGORD-LIMOUSIN
Châlus
Thiviers
Brantôme
DORDOGNE
Pude
Dronne
Angoulême
Recommended
Cognac
Interesting
Coutras
Worth a visit
Driving tour with departure town

The region known as the Charentes comprises the two *départements* of Charente and Charente-Maritime, separated by the River Charente. Charente itself divides into four geographic areas: to the west is a hilly landscape of mixed farming. On the banks of the River Charente lies the town of Cognac, where the world-famous brandy is distilled; the cereal-growing Angoumois lies at the region's heart; to the northeast the Confolentais plateaux; and to the south the Montmorélien, habitat for more than 30 species of orchid.

Highlights

1. **Cité internationale de la bande dessinée et de l'image**, Angoulême (p488)
2. Drive through the lovely **Charente Valley** (p492)
3. Discover the history of Cognac in the delightful **Musée des Arts du Cognac**, and then visit a distillery for a tasting (p495)
4. The remarkable **Thermes de Chassenon** (p501)
5. Stroll around the ancient town of **Aubeterre-sur-Dronne** (p504)

An Illustrious Line

In the 10C a certain Fucaldus, brother of the Viscount of Limoges, built a fortified camp on a rock overlooking the Tardoire and named it Fulcaldus, the Foucauld rock, a name to remember. A few centuries later, François I de Rochefoucauld held in his arms the future François I, King of France. François II de Rochefoucauld transformed the fortress into a magnificent **château** worthy of the Chateaux de la Loire.

During the Wars of Religion, the choice that the Rochefoucauld family made to follow the Protestants cost them the lives of François III and François IV. François V reverted to Catholicism and was rewarded by Louis XIII, who gave him a duke's title. Which brings us at last to François VI (1613–80), the famous author of the *Maximes*.

A Local Aperitif

Pineau des Charentes is a *vin de liqueur*, mostly drunk as an **apéritif**, made in the Charente and Charente-Maritime regions. It is made by blending together one-year-old brandy straight from the cask to grape must, which is then aged in barrel. It is made in three colours: red, white and rosé, and in various styles from sweet pale gold, to deep red and fruity rosé. Finer bottles are aged for more than five years in barrel, and often for several decades.

Countryside vineyards near Cognac, Charente Valley

Angoulême★★

Charente

Angoulême is best explored on foot, with its labyrinth of narrow streets, attractive old buildings and the fine views from its ramparts. Every year in January, a festival, created in 1974, crowns Angoulême as the world capital of the comic strip *(bande dessinée)*, a form of graphic art celebrated in the Cité Internationale de la bande dessinée et de l'image, which includes a museum and a multimedia library.

- **Population:** 42 096
- **Michelin Map:** 324: K-6
- **Info:** 7bis r. du Chat, pl. des Halles, Angoulême. 05 45 95 16 84. www.angouleme-tourisme.com.
- **Location:** From the N 141, to the NW of the town, there is a fine view of Angoulême and the River Charente. The town is divided into an upper town known as Le Plateau, built on a promontory and ringed by ramparts, and a lower town, which includes the outlying areas.
- **Parking:** There are car parks around the ramparts, the town hall and the tourist office *(see map)*.
- **Don't Miss:** The façade of Cathédrale St-Pierre; the attractive narrow streets of the Old Town.
- **Kids:** The Cité Internationale de la Bande Dessinée; Musée d'Angoulême.

A BIT OF HISTORY

Marguerite d'Angoulême

Marguerite de Valois, François I's sister, also known as **Marguerite des Marguerites** ("the Pearl of Pearls"), was born in the town in 1492 and spent much of her youth here. She was a woman of great culture and learning – her *Heptameron*, a collection of stories in the style of Boccaccio, won her a permanent place in French literature. She was also famous for her *fêtes* and parties, and was very influential in Court life. Her name lives on in two kinds of local confectionery: *marguerites* and *duchesses*.

The Two Balzacs

The local *lycée* (high/secondary school) is named after the author **Guez de Balzac** (1597–1654), who was born in Angoulême. A rigorous stylist, he was dubbed "the man who restored the French language". The other writer, **Honoré de Balzac** (1799–1850), the famous French author of *La Comédie Humaine (The Human Comedy)*, was adopted by Angoulême and described the town in his famous work *Les Illusions Perdues (Lost Illusions)*.

WALKING TOUR

UPPER TOWN TOUR★★

It is possible to walk around the fortifications in an anti-clockwise direction.

From the St-Martin calvary (*follow the r. de Bordeaux, then continue in the direction of the golf course*), enjoy a splendid view over the upper town, almost unchanged since the 19C.

The Ramparts★

You can drive around the entire ramparts in an anti-clockwise direction, but they are be best explored on foot *(1hr)*. Angoulême still has a large section of its fortifications. In the 18C, most of the towers and the medieval walls were taken down to make room for promenades. The following century, the gates disappeared. It is during this period that the vast aristicratic houses and opulent buildings appeared on the ramparts. The walk includes glimpses of the vestiges of the past, as well as the bourgeois way of living in the 19C.

Start from pl. des Halles and aim for the northern section of the ramparts to admire the view.

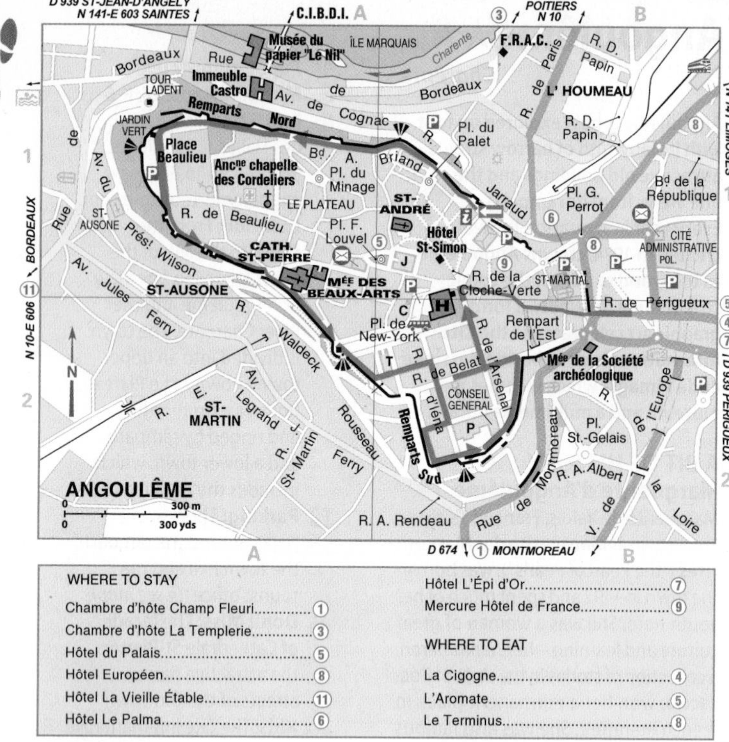

North Ramparts

Here there are impressive views over the river bridge, the suburb of St-Cybard, the valley of the River Charente and the industries dotted along it. In 1806 General Resnier (1729–1811), born in Angoulême, launched himself from the top of the Ladent Tower in a flying machine, which he invented himself, and thereby became the first man to achieve a non-powered flight.

However, since he broke his leg on landing, the general abandoned plans to exploit his invention which, it is said, was intended for a future airborne invasion of England by the Imperial Army. A plaque commemorates General Resnier and his attempt.

Retrace your steps along r. du Chat and follow r. de Genève on the left.

South Ramparts and 19C District★

Retrace your steps and leave the Jardin Vert. Walk back to the promenade which is level with pl. Beaulieu.

Place Beaulieu

This esplanade is at the end of the promontory, where a school has replaced the old Benedictine abbey. It offers views of the St-Ausone district and the church of the same name, built in the 19C by Paul Abadie (1812–84), one of the architects responsible for the Sacré-Cœur Basilica in Paris. Beyond, the confluence of the River Charente and River Anguienne can be seen. Immediately below is a small park, the *Jardin Vert*, filled with contemporary sculptures. A wooden cross is a reminder of the former hermitage of St-Cybard, one of the main evangelists in Aquitaine in the 5C.

The **rempart Desaix** overlooks the floral glazes that line the streets below, or border the large aristocratic houses, all 19C with the exception of the **hôtel Montalembert** (no 30), which dates from the 18C. After the statue erected in homage to Sadi Carnot, you will see three round 15C towers; one of them is called the tower of Clovis, where the Frankish king broke his leg during the siege of Angoulême.

Below, the rue Louis-Desbrandes, slightly curved, has tall houses where the tiled roofs are masked by balustrades.

Quartier de la Préfecture – Return to the place de New-York, lined with trees, and along to the hôtel de ville. This set of perpendicular streets, which are lined by plain, sometimes imposing, façades of the former private homes of the local aristocracy of the 18C and 19C, was built on the site of the ancient grounds of the castle in 1770.

Typical of the Second Empire, the theatre was built between 1867 and 1870. The interior was totally restored in 2000. As for the façade, it has a remarkable sculptured decoration representing allegories of the theatre, dance and music.

Go back up the r. d'Iéna, turn right onto the r. de la Préfecture and continue along the bd émile-Roux.

Before turning left onto the boulevard Émile Roux, turn around to look at the strange perspective formed by the road, with the spire of the Chapelle Notre-Dame d'Obézines.

From the bend in the ramparts, the view over the roofs and gardens, with the cathedral in the background, is especially beautiful at sunset.

Return to the r. d'Iéna, and then the r. de la Préfecture, lined with beautiful Neoclassical buildings built by Paul Abadie in 1834. Continue to the East Rampart.

In front of you, looming up from the roofs, stands the **Chapelle Notre-Dame-d'Obézines,** imposing and ethereal, built on the model of the Ste-Chapelle de Paris in the 19C. Its spire was added in 1953. Inside there are magnificent contemporary stained-glass windows in the upper chapel.

MURALS CIRCUIT

As befitting its status as a hub for the graphic arts, artists in the town have painted over twenty wall murals, which are dotted around the town. Additionally, you may notice that many of the street signs have been designed in a speech bubble format.

Maps of the murals are available from the tourist office. 05 45 95 16 84.

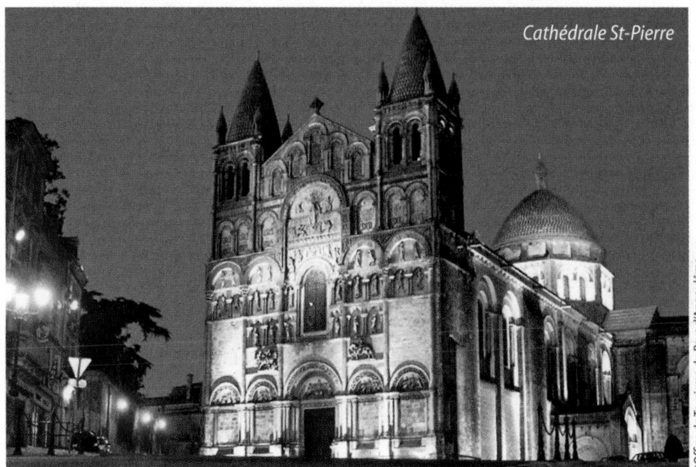

Cathédrale St-Pierre

Continue on the rue de Bélat. Admire the watchtower and 17C stronghold, remains of the fortified wall built by the Duke of Épernon around the castle.

Go back the way you came and take the r. de l'Arsenal to the hôtel de ville.

Hôtel de Ville

pl. de l'Hôtel de Ville. Guided tours (1hr) by reservation. 4.50€. 05 45 38 70 79. www.via-patrimoine.com.

Abadie built this Gothic-Renaissance town hall on the site of the old castle which was the seat of the Comtes d'Angoulême. All that remains of the castle today is the polygonal tower – a 13C and 14C keep from which a fine **panorama★** can be enjoyed – and the 15C round tower where Marguerite d'Angoulême was born. The staircase and the Second Empire-style sitting rooms can also be visited.

After passing through the gardens, take the **r. Hergé**, the busiest in Angoulême, to reach the shopping district of St-Martial. Continue to the place du Champ-de-Mars and its ultra-modern shopping centre, designed by the architect Alexandre Chemetoff. At the **place St-Martial** is the Romanesque gate tower of the church of the same name, built by Paul Abadie in 1852.

OLD TOWN

The district around the cathedral is fairly quiet, but around the Palais de Justice, there are lively bars, restaurants and shops, punctuated by old houses that line the picturesque streets and small squares.

Cathédrale St-Pierre★★

pl. St Pierre. Guided tours Jun–Sept daily 4pm; Oct–Nov and Mar–May Sat–Sun 3.30pm. No charge. 05 45 95 20 38.

Built in the 12C, the cathedral was partially destroyed by the Calvinists in 1562, and restored in 1634, followed by a more complete restoration started by Abadie in 1866.

Façade★★ – The impressive façade, decorated in the Poitiers style, is an enormous sculpted tableau in which 70 characters, statues and bas-relief sculptures portray the Last Judgement. The ensemble is presided over by a glorious *Christ in Majesty* surrounded by angels, saints set in medallions and symbols of the Evangelists. Both the archivolts and friezes above and around the side doors are decorated with intricately carved foliage, animals and figures. On the lintel of the first blind doorway, on the right, are strange scenes of combat from *La Chanson de Roland (Song of Roland).*

The tall tower with six diminishing storeys was partly restored by Abadie.

Interior – The inside has several striking features. Domes rest on pendentives, and in the north transept, a huge chapel sits beneath the Abadie tower.

Also of note is the Romanesque bas-relief in the nave depicting a Madonna and Child, and the 18C organ loft.

In the chancel, the capitals with floral decoration come from the 9C cathedral built by Grimoald de Mussidan.

Musée d'Angoulême★

1 r. de Friedland. Open Tue–Sun 10am–6pm. Closed 1 Jan, 1 May, 1 Nov, 25 Dec. 5€. 05 45 95 79 88. www.angouleme.fr/museeba.

Newly refurbished and opened in 2008, this museum is housed in the 12C former Bishops' Palace rebuilt in the 15C and 16C, best known for the quality and wealth of its exhibits from the South Pacific region and Africa and for the famous **Casque d'Agris★** (Agris' Helmet) on the upper floor, a masterpiece of 4C BC Celtic goldsmith's work. There are collections of medieval treasures, ceramics and 18C and 19C French paintings, as well as a wide selection of 17C and 18C Italian and Flemish paintings, and French works and sculptures by local artists.

A second section of the museum is devoted to local archaeology, including prehistoric finds in the neighbourhood, along with Gallo-Roman mosaics, lapidary collections from Roman times to the 18C, and various regional antiquities

(weapons, pottery, trinkets and enamels from the Limousin area).
On the third floor, the section dedicated to the Beaux-Arts counts among its treasures European works from the 16C to the 20C, beautiful ceramics and ancient weapons. A magnificent room with 18C woodwork has two Venetian paintings from the Canaletto School.

Leave the musem and continue along the r. du Minage.

No **61**, at the end of a cul-de-sac, has two old doors, one of which is a beautiful 17C example. Nearby **place du Minage** is charming, with a typical Second Empire fountain.

Take the r. Turenne.

No **15** has a Louis XIII doorway; opposite is the doorway of the former Carmelite convent (1739).

Take the r. J-Guérin.

On the corner of rue de Beaulieu and rue Guérin stands the Chapelle des Cordeliers. Notice the large gothic bay in the flat apse (14C).

Ancienne Chapelle des Cordeliers

r. de Beaulieu. Open daily 7am–8pm.
This chapel was once a convent church belonging to the Franciscan friars.
In 1556 one of the monks, André Thevet, brought the first samples of tobacco back from Brazil.
Now the hospital chapel, the building has a Gothic belfry with a projecting side supported on two squinches. In the nave is the tomb of Guez de Balzac *(see p483)*, buried here in 1654.

Walk along r. de Beaulieu.

No **79** boasts an imposing façade flanked with three square turrets and decorated with an Ionic colonnade (1783).

Return the way you came, r. de Beaulieu.

The trees and fountain of the place Francis-Louvel, known as Mûrier, lend a Mediterranean atmosphere which highlights the whiteness of the imposing Neoclassical façade of the Palais de Justice (1826).

Take the r. des Postes, then the r. Ludovic-Trarieux, lined with elegant shops and 19C façades. Turn left onto the r. St-André.

In **square St-André**, note the mural entitled Souvenir of the 20C, after an original drawing by Yslaire. Farther on, the imposing Neoclassical façade of the law courts dominates the tree lined place du Murier, giving the square a southern French feel.

Turn right onto r. Taillefer.

Step inside **St-André Church** to admire the carved wooden pulpit and Baroque altarpieces.

Continue along the r. des Trois-Fours, r. Henri-IV, then r. des Acacias, all lined with houses dating from the 16C to the 19C, to the pl. du Palet. Then take the r. Raymond-Audour.

At the bottom of a dead end, notice the lovely Hôtel de la Marbrerie; its rusticated façade dates from the 17C.

Turn left onto the r. des Trois-Notre-Dame and continue to the busy crossroads at the r. Massillon. From here, take the r. de Genève.

The reformer Calvin lived in 1534 at no **34** with his friend Canon Tillet.

Turn right onto the r. Massillon, then take the r. de la Cloche-Verte.

Hôtel St-Simon

At no 15, Hôtel St-Simon has a pretty Renaissance courtyard. The façade has pilasters decorated with lozenges and circles. The high dormer windows, decorated with shells and candelabras, typical of the French Renaissance, are similar to those found at the nearby château La Rochefoucauld (see p502).

ADDITIONAL SIGHTS

Musée de la Société Archéologique

44 r. de Montmoreau. Open by appointment, contact Via Patrimoine, 05 45 94 90 75 or 05 45 38 71 79. www.sahc.fr

In the exhibition rooms are prehistory collections and all types of regional antiquities. In the garden, Gallo-Roman mosaics and lapidary collections from the Roman era to the 18C.

Also noteworthy are the Romanesque sculptures from Angoulême Cathedral and other religious buildings.

FRAC Poitou-Charentes

63 bd Besson-Bey. Open Tue–Sat 2–7pm. No charge. 05 45 92 87 01.

Housed in a new centre (2008) designed by Jean-Marie Mandon, this is the regional centre of the Poitou-Charentes Contemporary Art Collection, with a collection of recent artistic works from around the world. It also has a documentation centre.

Cité Internationale de la Bande Dessinée et de l'Image★★ (CIBDI)

121 r. de Bordeaux (from the upper town, take a bus or walk from Tour Ladent; alternative entrance to av. de Cognac). Open Jul–Aug Tue–Fri 10am–6pm, Sat–Sun 2–6pm; Sept–Jun Tue–Fri noon–6pm, Sat–Sun 2–6pm. Closed 1 Jan, 1 May, 25 Dec. 6€ (children no charge). 05 45 38 65 65. www.citebd.org.

The Comic Strip Centre is housed in a group of turn-of-the-20C industrial buildings remodelled by the architect Roland Castro.

Inside, the **Médiathèque** *(1st floor)* houses almost all of French comic strip production since 1946. Since 1982, all comic strips published in France have been legally registered here for reasons of copyright.

In the **museum**, collections of original drawings are displayed in rotation. Rooms on the ground floor pay tribute to the great masters of the comic strip. Among comic strip pioneers are the Swiss Töpffer (mid-19C), Christophe (*La Famille Fenouillard*, 1889), Pinchon (*Bécassine*, 1905), Forton (*Les Pieds Nickelés*, 1908) and Alain St Ogen (*Zig et Puce*, 1925). Innumerable later talents represented include the Belgians Hergé (*Tintin*, 1929) and Franquin (*Gaston Lagaffe*, 1957); the Americans Raymond (*Flash Gordon*, 1934) and Schulz (*Peanuts*, 1950); and the French artists Goscinny and Uderzo (*Astérix*, 1959). Contemporary creators include Gotlib, Claire Bretécher, Reiser, Bourgeon, Wolinski, Loustal, Bilal, Baudoin, Tardi and Teule.

Musée du Papier "Le Nil"

134 r. de Bordeaux. Open Jul–Aug Tue–Fri 10am–6.30pm, Sat–Sun 1–6.30pm; Sept–Jun Tue–Fri 10am–noon, 2–6pm, Sat–Sun 2–6pm. Closed public holidays. No charge. 05 45 92 73 43. www.angouleme.fr/museep.

The former Bardou-Le-Nil paper mill, which specialised in the production of cigarette papers, operated here on the banks of the River Charente until 1970. The building has since been converted into a museum devoted to the paper industry, which brought wealth and prosperity to the region.

One of the six metal-vaned waterwheels which powered the machinery until the end of the 19C is on view, together with an exhibition detailing the different stages in the industrial production of paper and cardboard.

There are two other exhibitions – one devoted to industry in Charente, the other following the history of the paper trade worldwide. The 3rd floor has displays of contemporary art.

DRIVING TOURS

1 L'ANGOUMOIS

30km/18.6mi. Allow 3hrs.

Leave Angoulême W on the N 141.

Église de Fléac

This 12C Romanesque building, without a transept, has three sucessive domes surmounting the nave and the choir. Pretty portal decorated with fantastic creatures.

From the town hall's terrace, there is a splendid view over the Charente Valley and Angoulême.

Taking the D 103 you drive down through the vineyards and orchards, and reach the bottom of the valley, carpeted with meadows.

Continue west along the D 72.

Trois-Palis Église – Romanesque building with a two-storey belfry. Its façade has a gable decorated with Christ surrounded by Evangelist symbols. Inside, the nave and the choir are separated by a cupola on pendatives.

Continue along the D 72, then turn right onto the D 41.

The Nersac road leads to the Meure bridge, from where there is a pretty view of the river.

Turn left onto the D 699.

St-Michel Église – This 12C octagonal church has a single cupola and eight apsidal chapels. It was a refuge-chapel for Compostela pigrims, who were probably responsible for the sculptures. Notice the St Michael on the **doorway**★ and the corbels which support the cornices. The decorative motifs of the archivolts and the lateral arches are similar to the sculptures at Córdoba's mosque in Spain.

Cross the N 10, then turn right onto the D 103.

Château de l'Oisellerie

Built in the 16C, today it houses an agricultural college. Its name is derived from the training birds of prey for hunting. François I would have hunted here.A gatehouse leads to a courtyard, at the bottom of which rises a galleried building flanked by a crenellated tower.

Continue along the D 103, then turn left onto the D 41.

Ancienne Abbaye de la Couronne

Consecrated in 1201, the abbey has been built in a Transitional Romanesque-Gothic style. The layout has Cistercian influences: flat apse and a transept almost as long as the nave. The elevation is more Angevin in style. Admire the majesty of the choir and the transept with high arches. Little remains of the 13C cloister. However, the adjacent abbey palace, built in the 18C, has survived.

Head south on the D35 and then right on the D12.

Mouthiers-sur-Boême

The village is overlooked by the belfry of the fine Romanesque church. Several wash-houses still stand along the Boême.

At the **Jardins du logis de Forge**, seven water gardens fan out around a 15C and 16C manor house (*guided tours early Jul–mid-Aug daily 10am–noon, 2–6pm; 5€; 05 45 67 84 22).*

Head north on the D12. At the intersection of the D41, take a right towards Voeuil before heading north (left) on the D674. Le Verger is reached by turning right on the D104.

Moulin du Verger

Guided tour by reservation.
4€ per person group rate.
Gallery-shop open Mon–Fri 9am–noon, 3.30–6pm. 05 45 61 10 38.
www.moulinduverger.com.

In this paper mill, which dates from 1539, Jacques Brejoux still makes paper in the traditional way. The tour includes a paper making demonstration.

Continue to Puymoyen and turn right onto the D 104.

Église de Dirac
Admire its elegant Romanesque façade with beautiful sculptures.

Continue along the D 104, then turn left onto the D 939, which leads to Angoulême.

2 LA VALLÉE DE LA TOUVRE

80km/50mi. Allow one day.

Leave Angoulême NE on the D 941. Shortly after L'Isle-d'Espagnac, go right.

Magnac-sur-Touvre
From the bridge over the Touvre, downstream from the paper mills, there is a view of the church and gardens bordering the river.
Église St-Cybard – Romanesque, it has a square tower supported by a cupola on pendentives. The building is shaped like a Greek cross.

Continue on the D 699.

Touvre★
Église – Small Romanesque building fortified by a brattice on the façade. From the lawn there is a view over the springs and the Touvre Valley.
Sources de la Touvre★ –Leave the car in the car park and take the path along the riverbank.
Situated at the foot of the cliffs, the springs, the Bouillant, the Dormant, the Lussac and the Lèche, are in reality, the resurgences of rivers. The Touvre springs provide drinking water for Angoulême and the surrounding districts.

Take the road on the left which goes through the Bois Blanc forest and rejoin the D 699 (on the right). At the exit of Quéroy, turn right onto the D 412 to Ronzac.

Grottes du Quéroy★
16km/10mi E via the D 699 and the D 412. Open Apr–Jun and Sept–Oct Sun and public holidays 2–6pm; Jul–Aug daily 11am–7pm. 7€. 05 45 65 47 09. Labyrinth of impressive caves.
From the road the crenellated towers of the Château de la Tranchade (14C–17C) can be seen.

Return to the D 412. At Chazelles, take the D 33 on the left after the church.

Pranzac
On the site of the ancient cemetery stands a 12C lantern of the dead.

Leave Pranzac E on the D 699.

Montbron
On the portal of the Romanesque church, there are three archivolts decorated with garlands; to the right, recessed tombs. Inside, a cupola stands above the transept crossing. Also note the Chapelle de la Maladrerie.

Leave Montbron NE on the D 6, then turn left onto the D 110.

Rancogne
From the bridge over the Tardoire, there is a fine view of the surrounding countryside. There are several prehistoric caves in the cliff on the right bank of the river, downstream from the bridge.

Continue on the D 110, then turn right onto the D 73.

Château de La Rochefoucauld★
See p502.

Leave La Rochefoucauld W on the N 141, towards Angoulême, then the D 941 (intersection).

Rouelle-sur-Touvre
In 1750 the Marquis de Montalembert established a Fonderie nationale here. Today, the company makes mainly missiles. The town also has a research centre.

Continue on the D 941, which leads back to Angoulême.

ADDRESSES

STAY

Chambre d'Hôte La Templerie – *Denat, 16430 Champniers (9.5km/6mi N of Angoulême. Take the N 10 towards Poitiers then the D 105 to Balzac). 05 45 68 73 89. http://latemplerie-richon.pagesperso-orange.fr. 5 rooms.* You will be lodged in the old utility rooms of this magnificent vineyard farm. Not to worry – every room is very pleasant and colourful. Two of the ground-floor bedrooms look out on the pool. Self-catering cottage for six.

Chambre d'hôte Champ Fleuri – *chemin de l'Hirondelle (2km/1.2mi S of the map). 06 85 34 47 68. www.champ-fleuri.com. 5 rooms.* Lovely old house surrounded by a private garden, near to the golf course. Pretty individually decorated rooms, splendid view of Angoulême, terrace and swimming pool: a peaceful haven.

Européen – *1 pl. G-Perot. 05 45 92 06 42. www.europeenhotel.com. Closed 19 Dec–3 Jan. 31rooms. 9€.* Near to the ramparts, family hotel with practical soundproofed rooms, which are being renovated gradually. The rooms on the third floor have more character.

L'Épi d'Or – *66 bd René-Chabasse. 05 45 95 67 64. www.hotel-epidor.fr. 33 rooms. 10€.* Centrally located near to the place Victor-Hugo where there is a lively market. The rooms are spacious, those at the rear are quieter.

Hôtel du Palais – *4 pl. Francis-Louvel. 05 45 92 54 11. www.hoteldupalais16.com. 45 rooms.* Situated in the centre of the Old Town, housed in a building dating from 1778 that once belonged to the Tiercelettes convent, the rooms (which are being gradually redecorated) are in a beautiful setting. The elegant façade, facing south, looks out over the place Francis-Louvel with its lovely buildings, fountain and chestnut tree, and several cafés.

Le Palma – *4 rampe d'Aguesseau. 05 45 95 22 89 . lepalma@aliceadsl.fr. Closed Sat noon, Sun and 19 Dec–5 Jan. 9 rooms. 8€.* Comfortable non-smoking rooms, decorated tastefully with solid wood furniture: natural or painted. The restaurant is simply decorated but bright (traditional menu) comprising a dining room serving daily specials, and a selection of Spanish dishes.

Vieille Etable – *Les Plantes, 16440 Roullet-St-Estèphe. 05 45 66 31 75. http://hotel-vieille-etable.com. 28 rooms. Restaurant.* Despite lying close to the N 10 road, this restored farmhouse offers quiet accommodation in small chalets dotted around its peaceful grounds. The open fireplace makes for cosy evenings in winter, while the attractive terrace is perfect in summer.

Mercure Hôtel de France – *1 pl. des Halles-Centrales. 05 45 95 47 95. h1213@accor.com. 89 rooms. 14€. Restaurant.* The hotel is housed in the birthplace of Guez de Balzac onto which a modern annex has been added. Pleasant modern rooms and pretty garden from where you can catch a glimpse of the Charente. Small contemporary-style dining room opening out onto a lovely summertime terrace.

EAT

L'Aromate – *41 bd René-Chabasse. 05 45 92 62 18. Closed Tue, Wed and Sun evenings, Mon, 1–11 May, 25 Jul, 25 Aug and 21 Dec–5 Jan.* Convivial atmosphere in this rustic restaurant without frills. Splendid traditional dishes with a touch of innovation: this small neighbourhood bistro is always busy.

Le Terminus – *3 pl. de la Gare. 05 45 95 27 13. www.le-terminus.com. Closed Sun.* Chic contemporary brasserie, decorated in black and white. The cuisine, also modern, is based on local produce enlivened with the catch of the day from the Atlantic Coast. Lovely terrace.

La Cigogne – *5 impasse Cabane Bambou. 16800 Soyaux at the town hall. Take r. A-Briand 1.5km/0.9 mi. 05 45 95 89 23. www.la-cigogne-angouleme.com. Closed Wed and Sun evenings, Mon, 14–21 Mar, 25 Oct–10 Nov and 22 Dec–3 Jan.* Adjacent to an ancient mushroom farm, the veranda-dining room is modern and bright, complemented by a terrace overlooking the surrounding countryside. The cuisine is a combination of traditional and modern dishes.

Jarnac

Charente

The town of Jarnac is now linked with the name of François Mitterrand (1916–96), former President of France who chose to be buried in his home town in Grands' Maisons cemetery to the west of the town. The local economy is based on the distillation and shipping of brandies.

- **Population:** 4 535
- **Michelin Map:** 324: I-5
- **Info:** pl. du Château, Jarnac. 05 45 81 09 30. www.jarnac-tourisme.com.
- **Location:** Jarnac stands on the north bank of the River Charente, 14km/8.7mi E of Cognac.
- **Don't Miss:** Donation François-Mitterrand; Maisons Courvoisier and Louis Royer.

SIGHTS

Donation François-Mitterrand

10 quai de l'Orangerie. Open Jul–Aug daily 10am–12.30pm, 2.30–6.30pm (last admission 30min before closing); Jan–Jun and Sept–Oct Wed–Sun 2–6pm (last admission 45min before closing time). Closed 1 Jan. 5€. 05 45 81 38 88. www.musee-francois-mitterrand.com.

The museum, known as the Orangerie Cultural Centre, is housed in a former brandy store on the banks of Charente river. The library contains the complete collection of speeches given by François Mitterrand during his 14 years as French president. The vast glass building contains some of the many works of art presented to François Mitterrand during his presidency.

Maison Courvoisier

2 pl. du Château (entrance near the bridge). Guided tour (45min) May– Jun and Sept Tue–Thu 10am–1pm, reservation required; Jul–Aug daily 10am–1pm, 2–6pm. 7€–30€, depending on the Cognac tasting. 05 45 35 56 16. www.courvoisier.com.

A small **museum** traces the history of spirit distillation and the different stages in the production and refinement of Cognac. The silhouette of Napoleon I on the bottles of the Courvoisier brand recalls that Emmanuel Courvoisier, the founder of the company, supplied the Emperor himself, and that in 1869 the firm was appointed purveyor to the Court of Napoleon III by royal decree.

Maison Louis Royer

quai de la Charmille. Open Jul–Aug Wed–Fri 11am–1pm, 3–7pm, Sat 11am –1pm, 3–8pm, Sun 2–6pm. No charge. 05 45 81 02 72. www.louis-royer.com.

An entrance hall with beautiful inlaid work leads into the *Espace Voyage*, an original exhibit on the various stages in the production of Cognac. The tour includes a visit to *Chais de Vieillissement*, redolent with the aroma of ageing brandy. A temporary exhibit and reconstructed workrooms bring to life the various trades associated with the production of brandy.

DRIVING TOUR

3 VALLÉE DE LA CHARENTE★

55km/34mi. Allow half a day.

Leave Jarnac E on the D 22 that passes along the Right Bank of the Charente.

Abbaye de Bassac

pl. des Bénédictins, Bassac (7km/4.3mi E). Guided tour (45min) July–Aug 9–6pm; rest of year by appointment. 3€. 05 45 81 94 22. www.abbayebassac.com.

Bassac Abbey, founded soon after the year 1000 by Benedictine monks, was abandoned at the time of the Revolution and returned to religious life in 1947 by the Missionary Brothers of St Theresa of the Infant Jesus. A number of important relics were preserved here.

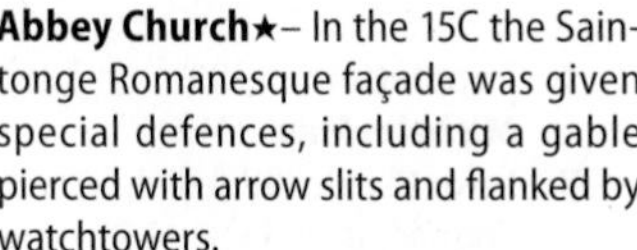

Abbey Church★ – In the 15C the Saintonge Romanesque façade was given special defences, including a gable pierced with arrow slits and flanked by watchtowers.

Inside, the single nave with its convex vaulting and flattened east end testifies to Angevin Gothic influences.

On the southern side, there is a 17C painted panel representing the Entombment. The monks' chancel was remodelled in the early 18C.

The **monastery buildings** were rebuilt in the 17C and 18C. A majestic doorway framed by Ionic columns leads to the old cloisters. The cloister galleries were demolished in 1820 but the monastic buildings still exist.

The ground floor contains the kitchens, the calefactory, a balustraded staircase in the south wing, and the old chapter house, nowadays used as a chapel. There is a small garden and terrace in front of the façade overlooking the River Charente.

St-Simon

Halfway between Angoulême and Cognac, is this village of gabarriers – the sailors of the *gabarre* – the flat-bottomed barges. Because of its situation, it was an important halt on the barge *(gabarre)* route, from the 16C. Over four centuries it provided the profession with construction sites, sailors, carpenters and other craftsmen, such as the caulkers who waterproofed the hulls with tar, pitch and resin.

Maison des gabarriers – *Open mid-Apr–mid-Oct daily 10am–noon, 2–6pm. 3€ (children 1.50€). 05 45 97 33 40.* This information centre traces golden age of navigation on the Charente with a few models and tools, but especially by offering a barge cruise on the waters of the Charente *(1hr30min boat trip; 6.25€, children 4€).*

Continue on the D 22. At Vibrac, follow the D 72.

St-Simeux

Flower-filled village on the banks of the Charente.

From the bridge on the D 422 to Mosnac, there is a charming viewa of the loop in the river bordered by a water mill, the village of St-Simeux and its church.

Continue on the D 84.

Châteauneuf-sur-Charente

Église St-Pierre – The Saintonge façade has a portal with archivolts richly sculptured with leaves, animals, and figures, that is flanked by two blind archways. The first level, separated by a cornice supported by carved corbels (amusing characters), has a bay framed by two statues of the apostles. To the left, note the equestrian statue of the Emperor Constantine (decapitated).

Leave Châteauneuf-sur-Charente W on the D 699, then right on the D 95.

Bouteville

See p497.

Leave Bouteville NE on the D 404 et rejoin the D 154. 3km/1.8mi after Graves, turn left onto the D 90. At St-Même, turn right onto the D 10.

Bourg-Charente

On the Left Bank of the Charente, Bourg-Charente watches over the river which divides several times, enclosing the low-lying islands,carpeted with meadows.

Église – Romanesque Saintonge style, the façade has three floors and is surmounted by a triangular tympanum. Notice its floor plan in the shape of a Christian cross, and the alignment of three cupolas on pendentives. On the left-hand wall of the nave, a 13C fresco represents the Adoration of the Magi.

Château – Built on a hill,on the opposite side of the Charente, it dates from Henri IV. Its pavilion, an imposing building with bays topped by gables, and high French-style roofs, is typical of the period.

Cross the Charente to rejoin the D 157, which leads back to Jarnac along the Right Bank.

Cognac★

Charente

Cognac is a peaceful little town, the birthplace of François I and cradle of the fine brandy that bears its name. The buildings around its famous cellars and stores have been darkened over the years by the microscopic fungi that thrive on the alcohol fumes.

- **Population:** 19 409
- **Michelin Map:** 324: I-5
- **Info:** 16 r. du XIV Juillet, Cognac. ℘05 45 82 10 71. www.tourism-cognac.com.
- **Location:** Cognac lies on the N 141 between Saintes and Angoulême, 28km/17.4mi SE of Saintes. Place François I, a busy square with an ornamental fountain, links the old part of Cognac, huddled on the slope above the River Charente, with the sprawling modern town.
- **Parking:** There are car parks in pl. Beaulieu and alongside the river near the Musée du Cognac.
- **Don't Miss:** The Old Town; a visit to one of the Cognac distilleries.

A BIT OF HISTORY

Royal Childhood

The literary and artistic House of Valois-Angoulême held court in the town from the late 14C until the accession of **François I** in 1515. It was here that François, the son of Charles of Angoulême and Louise of Savoy, was born "about ten hours after midday on the 12th day of September", in 1494. Part of his youth was spent in the Valois château near the River Charente.

OLD TOWN★

Porte St-Jacques and Rue Grande

The restored 15C gateway, flanked by two round towers with machicolations, leads to rue Grande, originally the main street in Cognac. The winding street is typically medieval, lined with 15C houses with their projecting, half-timbered upper floors.

Rue de l'Isle-d'Or

This street is lined with 17C town houses with fine façades *(restored)*.

Rue Saulnier

In contrast to rue Grande, rue Saulnier is bordered by aristocratic Renaissance buildings. Its name recalls one of the traditional activities of Cognac – the salt trade. The street has retained its cobblestone surface and its handsome 16C and 17C houses. At the far end is a Renaissance house with a shop.

The **rue du Palais, rue Henri Germain, rue Magdelaine** and the **Maison de la Salamandre** (also called l'Hôtel de Rabayne; *12 r. Magdelaine*) are also of interest.

Église St-Léger

r. Aristide Briand. ℘05 45 82 05 71.

This 12C church has been extensively remodelled. The most interesting part is the Romanesque west front with a 15C Flamboyant Gothic rose window. The archivolt of the doorway below has carvings representing the Signs of the Zodiac and the Labours of the Months. The vast nave dates from the 12C. In the south transept hangs a fine 17C *Assumption of the Virgin*.

On the right-hand side of the doorway, 18C cloisters lead to the library.

Couvent des Récollets

53 r. d'Angoulême. Open for temporary exhibitions. ℘05 45 82 07 73. www.maison-associations-cognac.fr.

This restored convent houses exhibitions and the headquarters of several charities.

Parc François-I

The park, bordered to the west by the River Charente, was part of the former castle grounds.

Musée d'Art et d'Histoire

48 bd Denfert-Rochereau. Open Wed–Mon May–Jun and Sept–Oct 11am–1pm, 2–6pm; Jul–Aug 10am–6.30pm; Oct–Apr 2–5.30pm. Closed 1 Jan, 1 Nov, 25 Dec. 4.50€ (combined ticket with Musée des Arts de Cognac). 05 45 32 07 25. www.musees-cognac.fr.

This municipal museum is housed in Hôtel Dupuy d'Angeac, in the grounds of the town hall. The displays on the **ground floor** cover the history and civilisation of the Cognac area from the earliest times to the present day. A section is devoted to archaeology.

There is also a reconstruction of the interior of a rural house, evoking the life of a local wine-grower c.1875.

The Cognac Ethnology Gallery in the **basement** displays a documentary illustration of the history of brandy. In the next six rooms, tools and machines re-create vine-growing and winemaking, distillation, the brandy and Pineau des Charentes trade, related crafts, cooperage and saddlery. Another room is devoted to traditional agriculture.

The fine arts section on the **first floor** houses paintings, sculpture, furniture and *objets d'art*, both French and foreign, from the 15C to the 19C.

On the landing are interesting works in molten glass by Émile Gallé (1846–1904), one of the main pioneers of Art Nouveau. The period paintings originate from countries which were clients of the Cognac brandy trade. One room on this floor has a display of contemporary paintings.

WINE CELLARS AND STORES

The cellars and wine stores *(chais)* are spread out along the riverside quays, near the port and in the suburbs.

Espace Découverte en Pays du Cognac

pl. de la Salle-Verte. Open Apr–Oct 10.30am–6.30pm (or 6pm); Nov and Mar 2–6pm Tue–Sun. Closed Nov–Feb (open by appointment), Mon (Sept–Jun). No charge. 05 45 36 03 65. www.espace-decouverte.fr.

Housed in the premises of a former *negoçiant* (1643), this centre is an instructive and entertaining way to discover the riches of Cognac and the surrounding region.

Musée des Arts du Cognac★★

pl. de la Salle-Verte. Open May–Jun and Sept 11am–6pm; Jul–Aug 10am–6.30pm; Oct–Apr 2–5.30pm. Closed 1 Jan, 1 Nov, 25 Dec. 4.50€ (children no charge), combined ticket with Musée d'Art et d'Histoire. 05 45 36 21 10. www.musees-cognac.fr.

Cognac cellar

Housed partly in the **Hôtel Perrin de Boussac** (1567) and partly in a modern building this remarkable museum is entirely dedicated to Cognac and its history. You will discover – through a collection of over a thousand objects – the different aspects of *terroir*, know-how and creativity of the Cognac industry.

Camus

21 r. de Cagouillet. Guided tours (1hr30min) Jun–Sept Mon 2–6pm, Tue–Sat 10.30am–12.30pm, 2–6pm. Reservations recommended. 7€. 05 45 32 72 96. www.camus.fr.

The tour offered by this Cognac trading company, founded in 1863, concentrates on the history of Cognac, its distillation, ageing and blending. Visitors are conducted through the cooper's shop and wine stores before watching the bottling process.

Hennessy

quai Hennessy. Guided tours every half-hour) daily 10–11.30am, 2–5pm; Mar and Oct–Dec Mon–Fri 10–11.30am, 2–5pm. Closed Jan –Feb, 1 May, 25 Dec. 9€. 05 45 35 72 68. www.hennessy.com.

After 12 years' service with Louis XV's Irish Brigade, Captain Richard Hennessy discovered the Charente region and settled in Cognac in 1760. Attracted by the taste of the delicious elixir distilled here, he sent several casks to his relatives in Ireland and, in 1765, founded a successful trading company. The captain's descendants still head the company today.

Quais Hennessy

The stores of this company are located on both banks of the River Charente. A modern white-stone building, standing on the Right Bank, was designed by Wilmotte. As an introduction to the world of Cognac, visitors are first taken across the river by boat and led into the wine stores where the various stages of brandy making are explained with the help of special effects involving sounds and smells. After watching a film and being shown round an exhibition, visitors can take part in a tasting.

Martell★

pl. Edouard Martell. Guided tours (1hr) Apr–Oct Mon–Fri 10am–5pm, Sat–Sun noon–5pm; Nov–Mar by appointment. 7€. 05 45 36 33 33. www.martell.com.

The oldest of all the Cognac distilleries owes its name to Jean Martell, native of Jersey, who settled in the town in 1715. The tour includes the semi-automated bottling process, and the stores and cellars where the brandy is left to age for six to eight years in oak barrels. In the blending room which follows, brandies of different origins are mixed to ensure consistently high quality. Three rooms have been restored in the house of this famous entrepreneur in order to re-create his life and work in the early 18C.

Before going back to the hall for a tasting session, visitors are invited to take a look at the most prestigious wine stores, known as *purgatoire* (purgatory) and *paradis* (heaven) in which some brandies have been ageing for over 100 years.

Otard★

127 bd Denfert-Rochereau. Guided tour (1hr) Apr–Jun and Sept–Oct daily 11am–noon, 2– 5pm; Jul–Aug daily 10–noon, 1.30–6pm (hourly); Nov–Dec Mon–Fri 11am, 2pm, 4pm. Closed public holidays (Nov–Dec). 7€. 05 45 36 88 86. www.otard.com.

The 15C–16C **château de Cognac** recalls the memory of the Valois family and François I, who was born here. It became the property of the Comte d'Artois (the future Charles X) under Louis XVI and was sequestrated by the Republicans during the Revolution. Since 1795 it has been used as a wine store by the firm **Otard**, which was originally founded by an old Scottish family.

The façade overlooking the Charente has a fine balcony, known as the King's Balcony.

Inside the old château, it is possible to visit Helmet Hall, where Richard the Lionheart married his son Philip to Amélie de Cognac. The huge rooms, with their ribbed vaulting are extremely elegant. The tour ends in the wine stores.

Rémy Martin

av. de Gimeux, Merpins (4km/2.5mi SW along the D 732. Drive towards Pons then turn left onto D 47 to Merpins). Open mid-Apr–mid-Oct Mon–Sat by reservation. 15€. 05 45 35 76 66. www.visitesremymartin.com.

This firm, founded in 1724, creates its Cognac exclusively from the elite Grande Champagne and Petite Champagne vintages. A **miniature train** takes visitors on a tour of the plant.

DRIVING TOURS

4 LA GRANDE CHAMPAGNE CHARENTAISE★

65km/40mi. Allow half a day.

The roads which wind through the Cognac vineyards reveal an elegant rural architecture, a string of Romanesque churches, and a host of wine-growers.

Leave Cognac SW via the D 732 heading to Pons. At Vieux-Bourg, turn left to La Frénade and follow the D 147.

Ars

St-Maclou church, late 12C, has a lovely portal with sculptured archivolts. The nave leads to a half-dome apse with a 17C altar.

Take the D 148, go through the place named "Treillis" and then the D 731 before continuing to Genté.

Genté

The village sits on a hillside, and has splendid views, especially from the church (12C) terrace.

Continue on the D 148 then turn right onto the D 44.

The road goes through Roissac, which has a strange fountain.

Follow the D 150 and go through Angeac-Champagne in the direction of Juiliac-le-Coq. Via La Vallade, return to St-Fort-sur-le-Né.

Dolmen de St-Fort-sur-le-Né

1.5km/0.9mi SE of the village on the D 151.

Megalithic monument in the middle of the vineyards.

Continue on the D 151 to the D 418; turn left onto this road heading to Verrières.

The Verrières church (12–17C) has Gothic vaulting with dropped keystones. Continue to Juillac-le-Coq, which has a lovely Romanesque church and the 18C Château de Beauregard *(open in summer).*

Via the D 419 and the D 49, return to Ambleville, then, on the D 699, Lignières.

Lignières

A pretty village typical of Grande Champagne with solid stone houses in the centre. There is also a charming river that runs past a 17C château, and a church, with a remarkable sculptured façade.

Continue along the D 699, which passes in front of a beautiful 16C Renaissance manor house (closed to public). At Bonneuil, turn left to Bouteville.

Bouteville

The village is overlooked by the ruins of its château, rebuilt in the 17C. From the outskirts of its grounds there is a magnificent panorama over the vineyards to Angoulême. Below the village, St-Paul church is all that remains of a 10C Benedictine priory.

Leave Bouteville N on the D 95 (extension of the road that goes through the village) and turn left onto the D 404.

Table d'Orientation

At the intersection of the D 404 with the D 90, turn right and follow the signs to the viewpoint, from where there are fine **views** of the vineyards, Cognac, Jarnac and the Charente Valley.

Return the way you came and take the D 90 to St-Preuil. At the intersection with the D 1, turn right to Segonzac.

Segonzac

The capital of Grande Champagne is home to the Université internationale des eaux-de-vie et boissons spiritueuses. The St-Pierre church has a 12C bell tower crowned by a pretty conical spire.

Follow the D 49.

Gensac-la-Pallue

Before arriving at Gensac, route D 49 skirts the *pallue* or marshland from which the small town derives its name. The interesting 12C **church** *(r. de l'Église; 05 45 35 90 08)* has a Romanesque west front decorated with haut-relief sculptures. The Romanesque nave, with its four domes supported by pendentives, leads to a Gothic chancel.

Return to Cognac.

5 LES BORDERIES

35km/22mi round tour. Allow 2hrs.

Drive W out of Cognac along the road to Saintes. At the roundabout, drive to Javrezac then follow the D 401.

Richemont

The church and the castle ruins rise, half-hidden, among the trees crowning a spur. The **church** *(pl. de l'Église; guided tours available Jul–Aug by reservation; 05 45 83 25 69)* is built on the site of an ancient stronghold and contains a delightful pre-Romanesque 10C crypt.

Continue N beyond Richemont towards l'Épine. Turn right onto the D 731 then, 1km/0.6mi farther on, turn right again onto the D 85 to Cherves.

Château Chesnel

Guided tours (1hr 30min) mid-Jun–mid-Sept Tue, Thu and Sat 10.30am, 2.30pm, Sun 3pm. 7€. www.roffignac.com.

This curious residence was built between 1610 and 1625 by Charles Roch-Chesnel. Architecturally, the château seems to hesitate between the Renaissance style and 17C Classicism while retaining a strong flavour of medieval military architecture.

Continue along the D 85. Shortly after Vignolles, turn left onto the D 120.

Écomusée du Cognac

Logis des Bessons, Migron (2km/1mi N; follow the signs). Open Apr–Sept daily 10am–12.30pm, 2.30–6.30pm. 4€. 05 46 94 91 16.

This little craft museum, located among vineyards, is dedicated to brandy making.

Drive S out of Migron along the D 131. In Burie, take the D 731 to return to Cognac.

6 VIGNOBLE DES FINS BOIS

40km/25mi round tour. Allow 2hrs.

Drive NE out of Cognac along the D 24. In Ste-Sévère, head for Les Buges and continue along the D 24.

Macqueville

This peaceful village, in the heart of the Fins Bois vineyards, has modern Cognac distilleries. The white houses, have Empire-style porches and closed courtyards. A façade and pepper-pot turret is all that remains of the 11C **Château de Bouchereau**. In the shady square, **Église St-Étienne** *(open Sat–Sun; no charge; 05 46 26 6 99)* is a charming Romanesque building.

Leave Macqueville eastwards along the D 227.

Neuvicq-le-Château

This is another picturesque village. The château incorporates a 15C main block with a staircase-turret, and a 17C pavilion.

Leave Neuvicq-le-Château southwards along the D 23. In Sigogne, take the D 15 to return to Cognac.

Confolens★

Charente

An attractive medieval town with a pleasant, relaxed atmosphere, Confolens lies at the confluence of the River Vienne and River Goire, hence its name. It was the home of a disciple of Louis Pasteur, Doctor Émile Roux (1853–1933), who discovered how to treat diphtheria in 1894. Confolens is also known for its International Folklore Festival, held every August *(www.festivaldeconfolens.org)*.

- **Population:** 2 808
- **Michelin Map:** 324: N–O-3
- **Info:** pl. 8 r. Fontaine-des-Jardins, Confolens. ℘05 45 84 22 22. www.mairieconfolens.com.
- **Location:** Confolens lies on the border between the regions of Limousin and Angoumois, 40km/25mi NE of La Rochefoucauld.
- **Don't Miss:** The Old Town.

WALKING TOUR

Allow 1hr30min.

OLD TOWN★

From pl. de l'Hôtel-de-Ville (parking) follow r. de la Ferrandie to the left.

Pont-Vieux★

The bridge was probably built in the 12C and modernised in the early 19C. For a long time it looked like a fortress, with its three towers – one in the centre and one on either bank. The tower on the west bank had a drawbridge, making it possible to cut off all access to the town, until it was replaced by an arch in the 18C.

It leads to the Fontorse district (named after an elegant ornamental fountain), the Old Town's busy suburb.

Turn right on r. Émile Roux, then, at pl. de la Liberté, turn left on r. des Buttes. Halfway up the street, a passageway leads to a fortified gatehouse.

Porte de Ville

On the other side of the gatehouse, once the obligatory passageway for those seeking to enter the town, is a façade pierced by two Romanesque clerestory windows, no doubt built in the late 11C. The wartime residence of the local overlord, it contained a courtroom and prison and was an integral part of the fortifications surrounding the town on the east bank of the River Vienne.

Go back through the gateway and take rue des Buttes to the 11C **keep**, which stands on what used to be the moat. In former times, travellers arriving from the southeast went through a doorway here, traces of which can still be seen at the base of the keep and on the lower tower opposite.

Plan d'Olivet nearby, a public garden, offers an attractive **view** of the rooftops of the town.

Go back towards the centre via r. du Vieux-Château, then take r. Pinaguet.

Rue Pinaguet

The street is lined with medieval houses (one of them, very tall, has a tower with a spiral staircase inside).

On the corner of rue Bournadour, another tower juts out, with a square half-timbered upper section.

Go back as far as the crossroads and turn left on r. Fontaine-de-Pommeau.

Église St-Maxime

r. de la Fontaine-de-Pommeau. ℘05 45 84 01 97.

Restored in the 19C, this church has an octagonal Gothic Troubadour tower surmounted by a spire with crockets. At its east end there is an attractive half-timbered house.

Take r. de la Côte.

Le Manoir

Rue de la Côte leads to a manor house with high gables and decorative carved finials. It was built in the 16C by the Comte de Confolens.

From the bridge over the River Goire, take r. du Soleil.

Rue du Soleil

This was the main street until the 19C. It is lined with tall houses backing onto hanging gardens and grounds which are not visible from the street. On the left is **rue des Francs-Maçons**, a staircase-street so narrow that the eaves of facing houses nearly cover it. Just beyond is the **Maison du Duc d'Épernon**★ *(r. du Soleil)*, used by the Duke of Épernon as a meeting point for the conspirators who helped Marie de' Medici to escape in 1619. The house dates from the 15C and 16C. It has three half-timbered upper storeys set back from the ground floor and sealed with cob (compressed loam, clay or chalk, reinforced with straw).

Return to pl. de l'Hôtel-de-Ville.

DRIVING TOUR

7 VALLÉE DE LA VIENNE

75km/47mi round tour. Allow 4hrs.

Leave Confolens by the N along the east bank of the Vienne (D 952).

St Germain-de-Confolens

St Germain-de-Confolens, once the site of an important feudal castle, is located in a picturesque setting at the junction of the River Vienne and River Issoire. Perched on a mound overlooking the valley of the River Issoire are the ivy-covered ruins of the huge towers of Château de St-Germain, at the foot of which is a tiny Romanesque chapel.

Drive SEout of St-Germain along the D 952, then turn left onto the D 82.

Lesterps

8km/5mi E along the D 30 (pronounced "Laytair").

Église St-Pierre – The remains of an abbey founded in the early 11C are preceded by an impressive grey granite **belfry-porch**★. Above the porch with its three bays, decorated with rather coarse capitals, is a massive belfry. Inside, the narrow side aisles contrast with the wide barrel-vaulted nave, which houses the remains of the old chancel and 12C capitals.

D 29 S, then the D 30.

Brigueuil

This historic burg perched on a hill still has many of its medieval fortifications ramparts with seven towers and two gatehouses. Near the Romanesque church (additions made in the 14C and 15C) are the remains of an old castle (11C truncated keep) and a manor house rebuilt in the 16C. There are also several other historic houses, a graveyard lantern, and in nearby Boulonie, a strange Romanesque mausoleum, said to be the tomb of St George.

Drive W along the D 165; in Saulgond, turn left onto the D 193.

Château de Rochebrune

Guided tours (45min) Jul–Aug Wed–Mon 2–6pm. 6€ (children 3€) . 05 45 65 26 69.

Built on a basalt rock, on the border of Poitou and Limousin, the castle is flanked with towers reflecting in the still water of the moat. In the 16C its owner, the governor of Guyenne, Marshall Blaise de Monluc, led a pitiless fight against the Protestant community.

One enters the main courtyard, past the outbuildings covered with curved tiles and across a small stone bridge spanning the moat. The four 11C–13C round towers are linked by three buildings. The arms of Marshall de Monluc are carved above the doors. The apartments are furnished in Renaissance and Empire style and contain numerous mementos of the Napoleonic period.

Continue along the D 193, cross the River Vienne; right onto the D 160.

Thermes de Chassenon★★

Guided tours (1hr, last departure 45min before closing) daily 15 Mar–May and 15 Sept–26 Oct 2–5pm; 1–29 Jun and 1–14 Sept 10am–noon, 2–7pm; 30 Jun–Aug 10am–7pm. 5€. 05 45 89 32 21. http://amis.chassenon.free.fr.

In 1958 a remarkable Gallo-Roman site was discovered in the Charente and Limousin area. It seems that Chassenon was a health resort in Roman times and was eventually abandoned in the 6C.

The building, whose walls are still 5m/16ft high, had three floors. The south wing was the mirror image of the north wing. Two aqueducts provided the building with a constant flow of water and a drainage system.

The tour starts with the north wing: follow the cart track (where the fuel was off-loaded) along the foot of the high walls, into the dark, vaulted underground chambers which seem to have been built to carry water. The zigzag passageways connecting the chambers were designed for decantation. Excavated items are displayed in one of the passageways.

The service or boiler rooms were located on the intermediate level. Note the ingenious underground heating system using a hypocaust, or hollow space under the floor. The coal-fired furnaces could be heated to more than 300°C/570°F. The resulting heat was routed to the hypocaust, a layer of tiles laid in a bed of clay mortar, and radiating flues distributed the heat into the room above. The temperature of about 20°C/68°F to 25°C/77°F was obtained in the rooms above.

The ground floor in the south wing has remained relatively intact, and the visitor can easily imagine what the rooms were like when they were full of bathers. The southern cold room and several other rooms lead into the largest room in the heart of the baths. Several hypotheses have been put forward concerning the function of this 232sq-m/2 500sq-ft room, with its six windows and six doors – a place of worship, a waiting hall, a physician's surgery or a room dedicated to the god of healing.

Continue W along the D 29. In Chabanais, take the N 141; then right onto the D 370 2km/1.2mi farther on.

Exideuil

The 16C Château de la Chétardie overlooks the town and the river. Built as a priory in 1200, **Église St-André** has a flattened chevet and ovolo mouldings over the porch. The broken-barrel-vaulted nave with its recessed pillars is invitingly simple. It houses three stone tombs and a 13C baptismal font in the middle of the baptistery.

Return to Confolens via the D 370 then the D 16.

The Thermal Baths

Traces of a high curtain wall and a few remnants of the temple and theatre can still be seen, but nothing of the forum. Only the thermal baths have survived intact. These baths were unusual, not only because they had two sets of everything, but also because they were used for healing. The people who came here were mainly pilgrims with health problems. When people came to the thermal baths, they entered through a doorway in the eastern façade. They then went into the changing room before going through to another heated room, where they may have paid or been checked. After that, they went through to the large central room, and into the *tepidarium* (warm room), where the skin was scraped with a curved metal instrument called a *strigile*; the *caldarium* (hot room) contained the steam room and boiling hot baths, and the *frigidarium* (cold room) was used for taking a cold plunge after leaving the *tepidarium*. The *palestra* next to the southern *frigidarium* was used for physical activities.

La Rochefoucauld

Charente

- **Population:** 3 111
- **Michelin Map:** 324: M-5
- **Info:** 1 r. des Tanneurs, La Rochefoucauld. 05 45 63 07 45. www.bandiat-tardoire.fr.

La Rochefoucauld is a small town with picturesque half-timbered houses, set on the banks of the River Tardoire. Near the old fairground (Champ de Foire) is a 17C bridge from where there are pleasant views of the river and the old château rising grandly above it. The prosperity of La Rochefoucauld depends on several small industries, among them the production of *charentaises* – a comfortable form of slipper. It was in the time of Louis XIV that this began as a cottage industry; they became so successful that they even found their way into the Court.

SIGHTS

Château★★

Open Apr–Dec daily 10am–7pm; Jan–Mar Sun 2–7pm. 8€. 05 45 62 07 42. www.chateau-la-rochefoucauld.com.

The Château de La Rochefoucauld was the home of an illustrious line whose chief has traditionally always had the Christian name of François; the best known is probably **François VI de La Rochefoucauld** (1613–80), the pessimistic author of the *Maximes*. The château, still owned by the same family, is constructed of soft white stone.

The remains of a square Romanesque keep are still visible, but the place as a whole, with its Renaissance façade and **main courtyard**★★, recalls the châteaux of the Loire more than any military stronghold. Note in particular the **spiral staircase**★ and its elegant vaulting, as well as Marguerite d'Angoulême's **boudoir**★, decorated with 17C painted panels.

The river front is framed by a medieval tower and the castle chapel.

Ancien Couvent des Carmes

r. des Halles. 05 45 63 12 26.

A restored chapter house and huge cloisters comprise the main points of interest in this former Carmelite monastery. Part of the building has been turned into a laboratory of palaeontology.

Église Notre-Dame-de-l'Assomption-et-St-Cybard

r. Liancourt. 05 45 62 02 61.

The church is built in a style rarely found in the Angoulême region: 13C Gothic.

Château de La Rochefoucauld

Ancienne Pharmacie de l'Hôpital

pl. du Champ-de-Foire. Guided tours reserve at tourist office, 2 days in advance, Mon–Sat. No charge. 05 45 63 07 45.

The old pharmacy of the hospital, which dates back to the 17C, houses an interesting collection of chemist's pots, flasks, mortars (16C and 17C) and a complete surgeon's instrument case from the Empire period. Also on display, a fine 17C Christ fashioned from ivory.

DRIVING TOUR

8 THE BELAIR AND BRACONNE FORESTS

55km/34mi round tour. Allow half a day.

Leave La Rochefoucauld NW on the D 6. At the Pont-d'Agris, turn right onto the D 11.

Chasseneuil-sur-Bonnieure, Memorial de la Résistance and Cimetière National

Open daily 9am–11.45am, 2–4.45pm. Guided tour of crypt (45min) Mon–Fri 9am–6pm. No charge. 05 49 39 65 21. www.cheminsdememoire.gouv.fr.

This monument occupies the centre of a cemetery laid out in terraces on the hillside – 2 026 soldiers and members of the Resistance, killed between 1940 and 1945, rest in peace beneath the lawns.

Cellefrouin

Église – Ancient abbey church of an Augustine monastery, flourishing in the Middle Ages, with a partly interred façade. The nave and aisles, resting on massive columns, have barrel-vaulting. An impressive cupola supports the bell tower. In the left- hand transept, there are recessed sculptures.

Lanterne des Morts – The lantern is made up of a cluster of eight columns surmounted by a conical roof.

Leave Cellefrouin W on the D 739. After 1.5km/0.9mi turn left onto the D 91.

Before going to Ste-Colombe, stop off at Coulgens, on the Right Bank of the Tardoire, to admire the St-Jean-Baptiste church (12C) and, nearby, a 15C house. Stop also at La Rochette, for its St-Sébastien church (11C–12C), and also the 16C château.

Rejoin the D 6 (on the left), then turn right onto the D 45. At Jauldes, turn left onto the D 11, then after 1km/0.6mi, turn right onto the D 88.

Église de Ste-Colombe

The church in this typical little Charente village has an interesting Romanesque façade adorned with statue-columns (St Colombe, St Peter) and bas-reliefs with symbols from the gospels.

Forêt de la Braconne

The Braconne massif (around 4 000ha/ 9 884 acres) is a limestone plateau extensively carved by underground waters which have produced dolines or sink-holes caused by subsidence of the surface. The best known – and the most spectacular – is **La Grande Fosse** (the Big Pit). Although it is smaller, **La Fosse Limousine** *(SE of the Grande Combe roundabout)*, hidden by tall beech trees, is also attractive. As for **La Fosse Mobile** *(closed to the public)*, legend has it that a wicked son who had murdered his father tried to dump the body in this sink-hole – but the nearer he got to the edge, the more it moved away.

Return to La Rochefoucauld via the D 88.

ADDRESSES

STAY

Château L'Âge Baston – *l'Âge Baston, St-Projet-St-Constant (3km/1.8mi S of La Rochefoucauld, towards Angoulême, then Pranzac on the D 33). 05 45 63 53 07. www.lagebaston.com. 4 rooms.* Authentic 16C and 17C building with spacious old-fashioned rooms.

Aubeterre-sur-Dronne★★

Charente

Aubeterre is a very old village huddled in a semicircle at the foot of its castle. One of the finest villages in France, it has steep, narrow streets, and stands out against the line of white chalk cliffs that give Aubeterre its name (*alba terra* in Latin, meaning "white land"). The writer Pierre Véry (1900–60) was born in Bellon, a few miles away from Aubeterre. One of his most famous books was *Les Disparus de St-Agil.*

- **Population:** 418
- **Michelin Map:** 324: L-8
- **Info:** 8 pl. du Château, Aubeterre-sur-Dronne. ℘05 45 98 57 18. www.aubeterresurdronne.com.
- **Location:** Aubeterre-sur-Dronne sits on the cliffs overlooking the Dronne Valley. The village is centred on pl. Trarieux, a quiet square home to a bust of Ludovic Trarieux, native of Aubeterre and founder of the League for the Defence of Human Rights. From here, visitors can climb up to Église St-Jacques, or walk down to the monolithic church.
- **Parking:** Park the car near the tourist office.
- **Don't Miss:** The rock-hewn monolithic church.

SIGHTS

Monolithic Church★★

r. St Jean. Open daily Jun–Sept 9.30am–12.30pm, 2–7pm; Oct–May 9.30am–12.30pm, 2–6pm. Closed 1 Jan, 25 Dec. 4.50€. ℘05 45 98 65 06.

The church, dedicated to St John, is one of a rare type which has been hewn from a single, solid block of rock. Another example of a monolithic church is to be found in St-Émilion near Bordeaux. A passageway lined with funerary recesses leads to a vast rocky cavern, whose crude materials and stark interior make it a captivating and impressive sight.

Monolithic church

J. Damase/MICHELIN

The 5C or 6C baptismal font, carved in the form of a Greek cross, indicates the existence of a previous church. The crypt may have originally been used by worshippers of Mithras, the ancient Persian deity, but was later taken over for Christian use some time in the 5C or 6C as a church.

Work on the church probably began in the 12C, to house the relics of the Holy Sepulchre from Jerusalem, brought back from the Crusades by Pierre II de Castillon, owner of the nearby castle. Used as a saltpetre works during the Revolution, it was the local cemetery until 1865.

The 12C nave, which runs parallel to the cliff, is 20m/66ft high.

A small spring still filters up through the single side-aisle. Its waters were no doubt considered beneficial and venerated by the early pilgrims. The apse houses a solid rock reliquary of monumental size set aside when the church was hewn. It used to enclose the shrine containing the relics of the Holy Sepulchre. At the opposite end of the nave is the original 6C chapel, turned into a necropolis in the 12C when the church was refurbished. A series of tombs has been hollowed out of the rock.

In the upper part of the nave, a gallery with a suspended ambulatory affords an interesting view of this once primitive place of worship. In former times, a castle stood above the church, linked by a hidden staircase still visible today, providing the lords of the castle with easy access to the gallery, from which they could spy on the congregation and attend religious services.

Église St-Jacques

r. St Jacques. ℘05 45 98 50 33.

This former Benedictine abbey church has a Romanesque west front enhanced by arcading delicately carved with geometric motifs in Moorish style. Note in particular the interesting frieze on the left of the central doorway, which depicts the various tasks to be performed throughout the year.

Below the church, a machicolated tower guards the residential quarters of the chapter.

EXCURSIONS

Chalais

2km/7.4mi W of Aubeterre-sur-Dronne.

Known for its fairs and markets, Chalais consists of a modern lower town, near the Tude, and an old quarter on the hill.

Église St-Martial – Access by the path branching off the D 674, north of Chalais. Interesting Romanesque façade. The portal archivolts are decorated with geometric designs and Moorish garlands.

Château – *Not open to public.* Imposing building, badly damaged by the Hundred Years' War, that belonged to Talleyrand-Périgord, princes of Chalais, for nearly 600 years. A late 16C gatehouse stands before the drawbridge which leads to the courtyard.

Montmoreau-Saint-Cybard

16km/10mi N of Chalais.

Église St-Denys – Ancient seat of an important Benedictine priory situated on The Way of St James, this 12C church has, on its façade, a portal decorated with Moorish trefoil garlands. The church has a harmonious style, except for its Chapelle de la Vierge, rebuilt in the 15C, and its bell, rebuilt around 1850 by Paul Abadie copying that of Courcôme.

Château – *Not open to public.* The château of the Marquis de Rochechouart dates from the 15C; on the side there is an unusual Romanesque 12C chapel. Circular, the chapel has a porch which also served as the entrance to the château. Admire its capitals sculpted with fantasy creatures, palms and acanthus.

Abbaye de Puypéroux

8km/5mi N of Montmoreau-St-Cybard on the D 674 and the D 54.

Ancient Benedictine monastery overlooking a crossroad of valleys. From a promonotory buffeted by winds, fine view below over to the borders of l'Angoumois and Périgord.

Église St-Gilles – Inside admire the beautiful finely sculptured Romanesque capitals at the transept crossing. The transept crossing, covered by an octagonal cupola, is surrounded by narrow passages, curved near the nave, straight by the choir, which allowed access to the apse from the nave without having to cross in front of the altar. The choir is surrounded by seven apsidal chapels.

Nonac

8km/5mi W of Montmoreau-St-Cybard on the D 10, then the D 74.

The Romanesque church of Nonac has pretty Gothic frescoes. Note on the vault of the apse, scenes from the life of Christ and in the crypt, a beautiful crucifixion.

From the D 74, returning towards Montmoreau, branches off a small path which leads to Château de la Léotardie (*not open to public*), ancient 12C fortified monastary. Admire its façade with two floors of Gothic arcades and tall tower, from the 15C and 16C.

INDEX

C

INDEX

E

F

G

S

Z

STAY

EAT

INDEX

THEMATIC MAPS

MAPS AND PLANS

MAP LEGEND

	Sight	Seaside resort	Winter sports resort	Spa
Highly recommended	★★★			
Recommended	★★			
Interesting	★			

Additional symbols

- Tourist information
- Motorway or other primary route
- Junction: complete, limited
- Pedestrian street
- Unsuitable for traffic, street subject to restrictions
- Steps – Footpath
- Train station – Auto-train station
- S.N.C.F. Coach (bus) station
- Tram
- Metro, underground
- Park-and-Ride
- Access for the disabled
- Post office
- Telephone
- Covered market
- Barracks
- Drawbridge
- Quarry
- Mine
- B F Car ferry (river or lake)
- Ferry service: cars and passengers
- Foot passengers only
- ③ Access route number common to Michelin maps and town plans
- Bert (R.)... Main shopping street
- **AZ B** Map co-ordinates

Selected monuments and sights

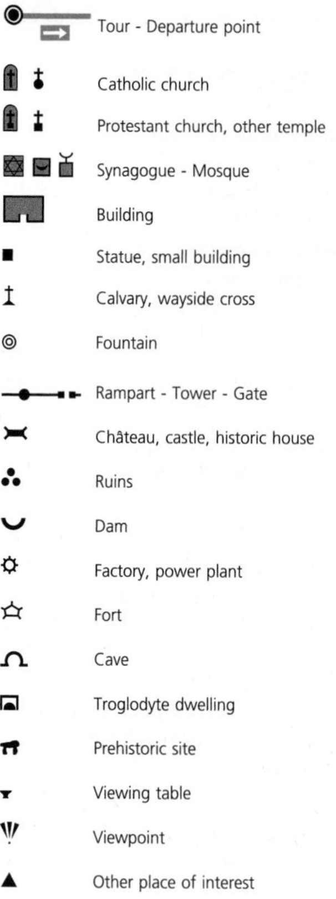

Sports and recreation

Racecourse

Skating rink

Outdoor, indoor swimming pool

Multiplex Cinema

Marina, sailing centre

Trail refuge hut

Cable cars, gondolas

Funicular, rack railway

Tourist train

Recreation area, park

Theme, amusement park

Wildlife park, zoo

Gardens, park, arboretum

Bird sanctuary, aviary

Walking tour, footpath

Of special interest
to children

Abbreviations

A	Agricultural office (Chambre d'agriculture)
C	Chamber of Commerce (Chambre de commerce)
H	Town hall (Hôtel de ville)
J	Law courts (Palais de justice)
M	Museum (Musée)
P	Local authority offices (Préfecture, sous-préfecture)
POL.	Police station (Police)
	Police station (Gendarmerie)
T	Theatre (Théâtre)
U	University (Université)

Special symbols

Water park

Beach

Boat trips
departure

Fortified town (bastide): in southwest France, a new town built in the 13-14C and typified by a geometrical layout.

COMPANION PUBLICATIONS

MICHELIN PRODUCTS ARE COMPLEMENTARY: for each of the sites listed in *The Green Guide*, map references are indicated which help you find your location on our range of maps.

To travel the roads in this region, you may use any of the following:

- the Regional maps at a scale of 1:200 000 **nos 518, 519, 521, 525** and **526**, which cover the main roads and secondary roads, and include useful indications for finding tourist attractions. These are good maps to choose for travelling in a wide area. In a quick glance, you can locate and identify the main sights to see. In addition to identifying the nature of the road ways, the maps show castles, churches and other religious edifices, scenic view points, megalithic monuments, swimming beaches on lakes and rivers, swimming pools, golf courses, race tracks, air fields, and more.
- the Local maps that cover all of France are illustrated on the map below.

And remember to travel with the latest edition of the **map of France no 721**, which gives an overall view of the region, and the main access roads which connect it to the rest of France.
The entire country is mapped at a 1:1 000 000 scale and clearly shows the main road network. Convenient Atlas formats (spiral, hard cover and "mini") are also available.

Michelin is pleased to offer a route-planning service on the Internet:
www.travel.viamichelin.com
www.viamichelin.com

Choose the shortest route, a route without tolls, or the Michelin recommended route to your destination; you can also access information about hotels and restaurants from the red cover *Michelin Guide*, and tourists sites from *The Green Guide*.

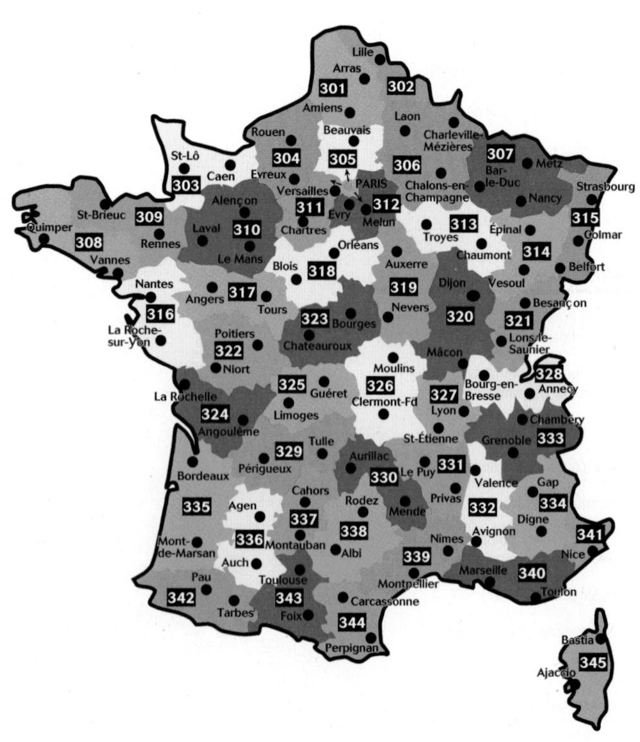

The Michelin Adventure

It all started with rubber balls! This was the product made by a small company based in Clermont-Ferrand that André and Edouard Michelin inherited, back in 1880. The brothers quickly saw the potential for a new means of transport and their first success was the invention of detachable pneumatic tires for bicycles. However, the automobile was to provide the greatest scope for their creative talents. Throughout the 20th century, Michelin never ceased developing and creating ever more reliable and high-performance tires, not only for vehicles ranging from trucks to F1 but also for underground transit systems and airplanes.

From early on, Michelin provided its customers with tools and services to facilitate mobility and make traveling a more pleasurable and more frequent experience. As early as 1900, the Michelin Guide supplied motorists with a host of useful information related to vehicle maintenance, accommodation and restaurants, and was to become a benchmark for good food. At the same time, the Travel Information Bureau offered travelers personalised tips and itineraries.

The publication of the first collection of roadmaps, in 1910, was an instant hit! In 1926, the first regional guide to France was published, devoted to the principal sites of Brittany, and before long each region of France had its own Green Guide. The collection was later extended to more far-flung destinations, including New York in 1968 and Taiwan in 2011.

In the 21st century, with the growth of digital technology, the challenge for Michelin maps and guides is to continue to develop alongside the company's tire activities. Now, as before, Michelin is committed to improving the mobility of travelers.

MICHELIN TODAY

WORLD NUMBER ONE TIRE MANUFACTURER

- 70 production sites in 18 countries
- 111,000 employees from all cultures and on every continent
- 6,000 people employed in research and development

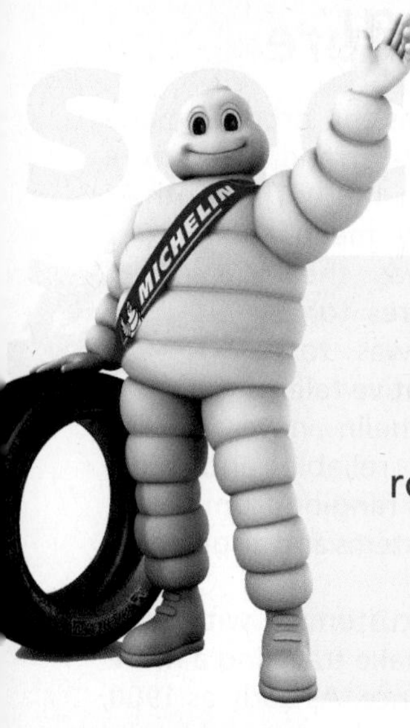

Moving for a world

Moving forward means developing tires with better road grip and shorter braking distances, whatever the state of the road.

CORRECT TIRE PRESSURE

- Safety
- Longevity
- Optimum fuel consumption

- Durability reduced by 20% (- 8,000 km)

- Risk of blowouts
- Increased fuel consumption
- Longer braking distances on wet surfaces

forward together
where mobility is safer

It also involves helping motorists take care of their safety and their tires. To do so, Michelin organises "Fill Up With Air" campaigns all over the world to remind us that correct tire pressure is vital.

WEAR

DETECTING TIRE WEAR

The legal minimum depth of tire tread is 1.6mm. Tire manufacturers equip their tires with tread wear indicators, which are small blocks of rubber moulded into the base of the main grooves at a depth of 1.6mm.

Tires are the only point of contact between the vehicle and road.

The photo below shows the actual contact zone.

NEW TIRE

WORN TIRE
(1,6 mm tread)

If the tread depth is less than 1.6mm, tires are considered to be worn and dangerous on wet surfaces.

Moving forward means sustainable mobility

INNOVATION AND THE ENVIRONMENT

By 2050, Michelin aims to cut the quantity of raw materials used in its tire manufacturing process by half and to have developed renewable energy in its facilities. The design of MICHELIN tires has already saved billions of litres of fuel and, by extension, billions of tons of CO2.

Similarly, Michelin prints its maps and guides on paper produced from sustainably managed forests and is diversifying its publishing media by offering digital solutions to make traveling easier, more fuel efficient and more enjoyable!

The group's whole-hearted commitment to eco-design on a daily basis is demonstrated by ISO 14001 certification.

Like you, Michelin is committed to preserving our planet.

Chat with Bibendum

Go to
www.michelin.com/corporate/en
Find out more about
Michelin's history and the
latest news.

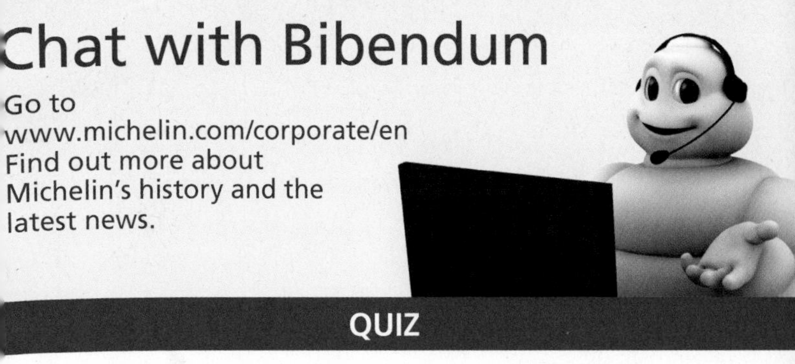

QUIZ

Michelin develops tires for all types of vehicles.
See if you can match the right tire with the right vehicle…

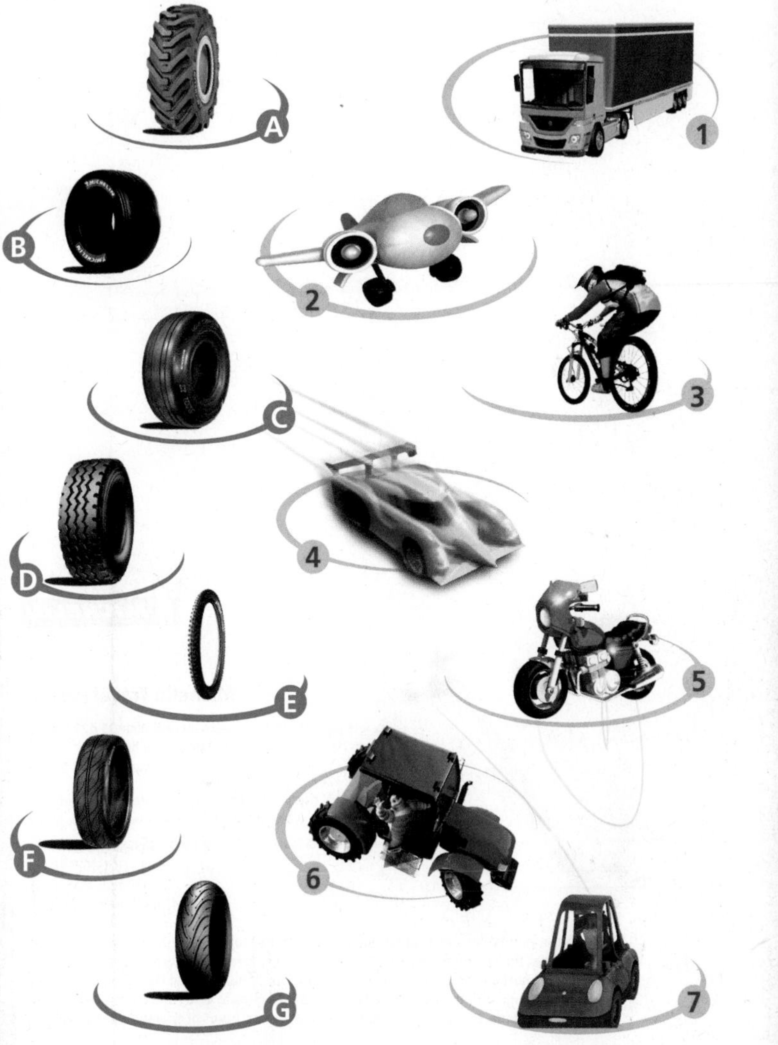

Solution : A-6 / B-4 / C-2 / D-1 / E-3 / F-7 / G-5

Michelin Travel Partner

Société par actions simplifiées au capital de 11 629 590 EUR
27 cours de l'Ile Seguin - 92100 Boulogne Billancourt (France)
R.C.S. Nanterre 433 677 721

ISBN 978-1-907099-54-0
Printed: March 2012
Printed and bound in Germany